Advanced Digital Architectures for Model–Driven Adaptive Enterprises

Vinay Kulkarni
TCS Research, Tata Consultancy Services, India

Sreedhar Reddy
TCS Research, Tata Consultancy Services, India

Tony Clark
Aston University, Birmingham, UK

Balbir S. Barn
Middlesex University, London, UK

A volume in the Advances in E-Business Research
(AEBR) Book Series

Published in the United States of America by
IGI Global
Business Science Reference (an imprint of IGI Global)
701 E. Chocolate Avenue
Hershey PA, USA 17033
Tel: 717-533-8845
Fax: 717-533-8661
E-mail: cust@igi-global.com
Web site: http://www.igi-global.com

Library of Congress Cataloging-in-Publication Data

Names: Kulkarni, Vinay, 1966- editor. | Reddy, Sreedhar, 1963- editor. |
  Clark, Tony (College teacher) editor. | Barn, Balbir S., editor.
Title: Advanced digital architectures for model-driven adaptive enterprises /
  Vinay Kulkarni, Sreedhar Reddy, Tony Clark, and Balbir S. Barn, editors.
Description: Hershey, PA : Business Science Reference, [2020]
Identifiers: LCCN 2019016863| ISBN 9781799801085 (hardcover) | ISBN
  9781799801092 (softcover) | ISBN 9781799801108 (ebook)
Subjects: LCSH: Business enterprises--Technological innovations. |
  Technological innovations--Management. | Information
  technology--Management.
Classification: LCC HD45 .A47 2019 | DDC 004.068--dc23 LC record available at https://lccn.loc.gov/2019016863

This book is published in the IGI Global book series Advances in E-Business Research (AEBR) (ISSN: 1935-2700; eISSN: 1935-2719)

British Cataloguing in Publication Data
A Cataloguing in Publication record for this book is available from the British Library.

For electronic access to this publication, please contact: eresources@igi-global.com.

Advances in E-Business Research (AEBR) Book Series

In Lee
Western Illinois University, USA

ISSN:1935-2700
EISSN:1935-2719

MISSION

Technology has played a vital role in the emergence of e-business and its applications incorporate strategies. These processes have aided in the use of electronic transactions via telecommunications networks for collaborating with business partners, buying and selling of goods and services, and customer service. Research in this field continues to develop into a wide range of topics, including marketing, psychology, information systems, accounting, economics, and computer science.

The **Advances in E-Business Research (AEBR) Book Series** provides multidisciplinary references for researchers and practitioners in this area. Instructors, researchers, and professionals interested in the most up-to-date research on the concepts, issues, applications, and trends in the e-business field will find this collection, or individual books, extremely useful. This collection contains the highest quality academic books that advance understanding of e-business and addresses the challenges faced by researchers and practitioners.

COVERAGE

- Electronic Supply Chain Management
- Telework and Telecommuting
- E-Business Management
- Mobile Business Models
- E-business standardizations
- Trends in e-business models and technologies
- Virtual organization
- E-business systems integration
- Web 2.0
- Semantic Web

IGI Global is currently accepting manuscripts for publication within this series. To submit a proposal for a volume in this series, please contact our Acquisition Editors at Acquisitions@igi-global.com or visit: http://www.igi-global.com/publish/.

Titles in this Series

For a list of additional titles in this series, please visit:
http://www.igi-global.com/book-series/advances-business-research/37144

Interdisciplinary Approaches to Digital Transformation and Innovation
Rocci Luppicini (University of Ottawa, Canada)
Business Science Reference • © 2020 • 368pp • H/C (ISBN: 9781799818793) • US $215.00

Implications and Impacts of eSports on Business and Society Emerging Research and Opportunities
David J. Finch (Mount Royal University, Canada) Norm O'Reilly (University of Guelph, Canada) Gashaw Abeza (Towson University, USA) Brad Clark (Mount Royal University, Canada) and David Legg (Mount Royal University, Canada)
Business Science Reference • © 2020 • 185pp • H/C (ISBN: 9781799815389) • US $165.00

Tools and Techniques for Implementing International E-Trading Tactics for Competitive Advantage
Yurdagül Meral (İstanbul Medipol University, Turkey)
Business Science Reference • © 2020 • 395pp • H/C (ISBN: 9781799800354) • US $225.00

Handbook of Research on Strategic Fit and Design in Business Ecosystems
Umit Hacioglu (Istanbul Medipol University, Turkey)
Business Science Reference • © 2020 • 775pp • H/C (ISBN: 9781799811251) • US $295.00

Business Transformations in the Era of Digitalization
Karim Mezghani (Al Imam Mohammad Ibn Saud Islamic University, Saudi Arabia & University of Sfax, Tunisia) and Wassim Aloulou (Al Imam Mohammad Ibn Saud Islamic University, Saudi Arabia & University of Sfax, Tunisia)
Business Science Reference • © 2019 • 360pp • H/C (ISBN: 9781522572626) • US $215.00

E-Manufacturing and E-Service Strategies in Contemporary Organizations
Norman Gwangwava (Botswana International University of Science and Technology, Botswana) and Michael Mutingi (Namibia University of Science and Technology, Namibia)
Business Science Reference • © 2018 • 366pp • H/C (ISBN: 9781522536284) • US $205.00

Multi-Sided Platforms (MSPs) and Sharing Strategies in the Digital Economy Emerging Research and Opportunities
Sergey Yablonsky (St. Petersburg University, Russia)
Business Science Reference • © 2018 • 192pp • H/C (ISBN: 9781522554578) • US $165.00

Crowdfunding and Sustainable Urban Development in Emerging Economies
Umar G. Benna (Ahmadu Bello University, Nigeria) and Abubakar U. Benna (Durham University, UK)
Business Science Reference • © 2018 • 343pp • H/C (ISBN: 9781522539520) • US $205.00

701 East Chocolate Avenue, Hershey, PA 17033, USA
Tel: 717-533-8845 x100 • Fax: 717-533-8661
E-Mail: cust@igi-global.com • www.igi-global.com

Table of Contents

Detailed Table of Contents

Section 1

Chapter 1

Vinay Kulkarni, TCS Research, Tata Consultancy Services, India
Sreedhar Reddy, TCS Research, Tata Consultancy Services, India
Tony Clark, Aston University, Birmingham, UK

Modern enterprises are large complex systems operating in dynamic environments and are therefore required to respond quickly to a variety of change drivers. Moreover, they are systems of systems wherein understanding is only available in localized contexts and is partial and uncertain. Given that the overall system behaviour is hard to know a-priori and that conventional techniques for systemwide analysis either lack rigour or are defeated by the scale of the problem, the current practice often exclusively relies on human expertise for adaptation. This chapter outlines the concept of model-driven adaptive enterprise that leverages principles from modeling, artificial intelligence, control theory, and information systems design leading to a knowledge-guided simulation-aided data-driven model-based evidence-backed approach to impart adaptability to enterprises. At the heart of a model-driven adaptive enterprise lies a digital twin (i.e., a simulatable digital replica of the enterprise). The authors discuss how the digital twin can be used to analyze, control, adapt, transform, and design enterprises.

Chapter 2

Ulrich Frank, University of Duisburg-Essen, Germany
Alexander C. Bock, University of Duisburg-Essen, Germany

This chapter presents a method for multi-perspective enterprise modeling (MEMO). Enterprise modeling fundamentally aims to support the conjoint analysis of business and IT to foster their integration. MEMO expands on this general aim with a specific concern for the professional perspectives of different stakeholder groups. MEMO is based on a language architecture that comprises an extensible set of domain-specific modeling languages, each addressing one or more professional perspectives. It is supplemented by an adaptable generic framework to support high-level 'ballpark' views of an enterprise and to serve as a common starting point for more elaborate analysis and design tasks. MEMO also supports the construction of corresponding process models to design customized modeling methods. The chapter motivates the use of MEMO and illustrates possible use cases. It also provides a description of the method's architecture, its DSMLs, and a tool environment that supports the development and analysis of enterprise models.

Chapter 3

Henderik A. Proper, Luxembourg Institute of Science and Technology, Luxembourg
Wided Guedria, Luxembourg Institute of Science and Technology, Luxembourg
Jean-Sebastien Sottet, Luxembourg Institute of Science and Technology, Luxembourg

Our society is transitioning from the industrial age to the digital age, thus also revolutionising the enterprise landscape. In addition, one can observe how the notion of economic exchange is shifting from goods-dominant logic to service-dominant logic, putting the focus on continuous value co-creation between providers and consumers. Combined, these trends drive enterprises to transform continuously. During enterprise transformations, coordination among the stakeholders involved is key. Enterprise models are traditionally regarded as an effective way to enable informed coordination. At the same time, the digital age also provides ample challenges and opportunities for enterprise modelling. The objective of this chapter is therefore threefold. The first aim is to reflect on the role of enterprise modelling for coordinated enterprise transformation. The second aim is to explore the challenges posed by digital transformations to enterprise modelling. The third aim is to reflect on how enterprise modelling itself may benefit from the new digital technologies.

Chapter 4

Souvik Barat, TCS Research, Tata Consultancy Services, India

Enterprises constantly aim to maximise their objectives while operating in a competitive and dynamic environment. This necessitates an enterprise to be efficient, adaptive, and amenable for transformation. However, understanding a complex enterprise and identifying effective control measure, adaptation choice, or transformation option to realise specific objective is not a trivial task. The digital twin that imitates the real enterprise provides an environment to conduct the necessary interrogative and predictive analyses to evaluate various control measures, adaptation choices, and transformation options in a safe and cost-effective manner without compromising the analysis precision. This chapter reflects on the core concept of the digital twin, evaluates the state-of-the-art modelling and analysis technologies, and presents a pragmatic approach to develop high-fidelity digital twin for large complex enterprises.

Chapter 5

Sagar Sunkle, TCS Research, Tata Consultancy Services, India
Suman Roychoudhury, TCS Research, Tata Consultancy Services, India
Deepali Kholkar, TCS Research, Tata Consultancy Services, India

Modern enterprises operate in an unprecedented regulatory environment with the possibility of heavy penalties for non-compliance. Previous research in the field of compliance has established that the manual specification/tagging of the regulations not only fails to ensure their proper coverage but also negatively affects the turnaround time both in proving and maintaining the compliance. The contribution in this chapter is a framework that aids the domain experts in the transformation of regulations present in legal natural language text (English) to a model form via authoring and validation of structured English rules.

This generated regulatory model is eventually translated to formal logic that enables formal compliance checking contrary to current industry practice, that provides content management-based, document-driven, and expert-dependent ways of managing regulatory compliance. The authors draw statistics from a real-world case study of money market statistical reporting (MMSR) regulations for a large European bank to demonstrate the benefits of aided authoring and validation.

Modern digital enterprises operate in a dynamic environment where the business objectives, underlying technologies, and expectations from the end-users change over the time. Therefore, developing agile and adaptive IT systems is a critical need for most of the large business-critical enterprises. However, it is observed that the traditional IT system development approaches are not capable of ensuring all desired characteristics. This chapter discusses a set of established concepts and techniques that collectively help to achieve the desired agility and adaptiveness. The chapter reflects on the core concept of model-driven engineering for agility, technology independence, and retargetability; focuses on component abstraction to introduce divide-and-concur and separation of concerns; and proposes the use of variability and the concept of productline for developing configurable and extensible IT system.

The key to a successful adaptive enterprise lies in techniques and algorithms that enable the enterprise to learn about its environment and use the learning to make decisions that maximize its objectives. The volatile nature of the contemporary business environment means that learning needs to be continuous and reliable, and the decision-making rapid and accurate. In this chapter, the authors investigate two promising families of tools that can be used to design such algorithms: adaptive control and reinforcement learning. Both methodologies have evolved over the years into mathematically rigorous and practically reliable solutions. They review the foundations, the state-of-the-art, and the limitations of these methodologies. They discuss possible ways to bring together these techniques in a way that brings out the best of their capabilities.

As we increasingly depend on technology, cyber threats and vulnerabilities are creating trust issues for businesses and enterprises, and cybersecurity is being considered as the number one threat to the global economy over the next 5-10 years. In this chapter, the authors explain this phenomenon by first describing the changing cyber ecosystem due to extreme digitalization and then its ramifications that are plainly visible in the latest trends in cyber-attacks. In the process, they arrive at five key implications that any modern enterprise needs to be cognizant of and discuss eight emerging measures that may help address consequences of those implications substantially. It is hoped that these measures will play a critical role in making enterprise security more proactive, cognitive, automated, connected, invisible, and risk aware.

Chapter 9

 Vivek Balaraman, TCS Research, Tata Consultancy Services, India
 Sachin Patel, TCS Research, Tata Consultancy Services, India
 Mayuri Duggirala, TCS Research, Tata Consultancy Services, India
 Jayasree Raveendran, TCS Research, Tata Consultancy Services, India
 Ravi Mahamuni, TCS Research, Tata Consultancy Services, India

The transformation of a conventional enterprise from a people-centric model to a technology-centric one has important implications for its human workforce. In this chapter, the authors look at three representative people-related focus areas for the digital enterprise, enhancing workplace wellbeing, enabling continuous learning and compliance to information security. They discuss each of these problems and then look at the technological infrastructure a digital enterprise would require to manage these areas.

Section 2

Chapter 10

 Sagar Sunkle, TCS Research, Tata Consultancy Services, India
 Deepak Jain, TCS Research, Tata Consultancy Services, India
 Krati Saxena, TCS Research, Tata Consultancy Services, India
 Ashwini Patil, TCS Research, Tata Consultancy Services, India
 Rinu Chacko, TCS Research, Tata Consultancy Services, India
 Beena Rai, TCS Research, Tata Consultancy Services, India

The chemical industry is expanding its focus from process-centered products to product-centered products. Of these, consumer chemical products and other similar formulated products are especially ubiquitous. State of the art in the formulated product design relies heavily on experts and their expertise, leading to extended time to market and increased costs. The authors show that it is possible to construct a graph database of various details of products from textual sources, both offline and online. Similar to the "generate and test" approach, they propose that it is possible to generate feasible design variants of a given type of formulated product using the database so constructed. If they restrict the set of products that are applied to the skin, they propose to test the generated design variants using an in-silico model. Even though this chapter is an account of the work in progress, the authors believe the gains they can obtain from a readily accessible database and its integration with an in-silico model are substantial.

Chapter 11

 B. P. Gautham, TCS Research, Tata Consultancy Services, India
 Sreedhar Reddy, TCS Research, Tata Consultancy Services, India

The materials and manufacturing industry is undergoing transformation through adoption of various digital technologies. Though the adoption of digital platforms for operational needs is significant, their adoption for core design and development of products and their manufacturing are limited. While the use of physics and data-driven modeling-and-simulation tools is increasing, these are not systematically leveraged for larger benefit. Besides these tools, product design and development requires deep contextual knowledge necessitating systematic capture of data and knowledge. To achieve this, we need flexible digital platforms that enable integration of diverse design domains and tools through a common semantic basis and construction of engineering decision workflows leveraging various simulation tools and knowledge. This chapter builds these requirements through presenting three case studies from the materials manufacturing industry and presents requirements for a digital platform. Finally, one such platform, TCS PREMAP, being developed by the authors is described in some detail.

Chapter 12

    Devadatta Madhukar Kulkarni, Tata Consultancy Services, USA
    Ramakrishnan S. Srinivasan, Tata Consultancy Services, USA
    Kyle S. Cooper, Tata Consultancy Services, USA
    Rajeev Shorey, Tata Consultancy Services, USA
    Jeffrey D. Tew, Tata Consultancy Services, USA

As businesses embrace digital technologies and drive business growth, this transformation demands a reimagination of their products, processes, and work beyond just "digitalization." The enterprise starts by capturing diverse sensor data and integrates just-in-time data to achieve "connected" stage. It further uses data along with contextual intelligence to drive integrated decisions in "collaborative" stage. It aspires to share decision making between machines and humans and evolves into "cognitive" stage. In this C3 journey—connected to collaborative, further to cognitive—enterprises need to take advantage of innovative technologies across machines, facilities, and operations in the ecosystem of products, processes, and partners. The authors highlight the nuances and opportunities across the C3 journey focusing on manufacturing value chains. Customers can orchestrate their C3 journey using innovative digital solutions outlined here for information sharing and interactive analytics that will deliver best business results with data-driven decisions.

Chapter 13

    Balbir S. Barn, Middlesex University, London, UK

This chapter presents a framing discussion around the notion of a digital enterprise in the context of higher education. The chapter makes the assumption that a university like a commercial enterprise can draw significant benefit from acting as a digital enterprise. The discussion indicates that some of a university's existing and historical activities are in line with notions of a digital enterprise. The chapter proposes a framework for assessing the readiness of a university with respect to its actions as a digital enterprise recognising the complexity of domains residing within the confines of a university environment. Critically, the chapter argues that such a future systems project should not only consider positive use cases but also recognise that a digital enterprise may have unplanned and unintentional consequences. Hence, this chapter argues that new forms of governance may also be required alongside the planned journey to a digital enterprise world.

Chapter 14
Harrick Vin, Tata Consultancy Services, India

Over the past decade or so, for most enterprises, information technology (IT) has shifted from being a support function to be a synonym for business wellness. During the same period, though, the scale and complexity of IT for running business has grown significantly; today, performing any business function requires complex interplay of many, often invisible and dynamically changing, technology components. This is making design resilient and interruption-free IT a significant challenge. This chapter discusses limitations of traditional approaches for managing enterprise IT operations; introduces the concept of cognitive automation, a novel approach that blends intelligence with automation to transform enterprise IT operations; and describes the design of ignio™, a cognitive automation platform for enterprises. The author concludes by highlighting the challenges in driving cognitive transformation of enterprise operations and providing some suggestions for embarking upon this journey.

Preface

Modern enterprises are large complex systems operating in highly dynamic environments thus requiring quick responses to a variety of change drivers. Due to the scale and nature of their operating environment, enterprises require continual monitoring and adaptation. Enterprises are systems of systems whose structure and behaviour is partially understood, contains stochastic features, and is limited to localized contexts. Conventional techniques for designing and controlling systems are not suitable for quality controlled enterprise-wide development since some approaches lack rigor and others are defeated by the scale of the problem. Therefore, current practice often exclusively relies on human expertise for monitoring and adaptation.

Modern enterprises have access to huge amounts of data in a variety of formats including: operational data, design documents, execution logs, customer information, product data. Furthermore, the different domains in which enterprises may operate create further heterogeneity in types of data. Such data is likely to increase significantly as systems and devices become interconnected through the Internet of Things (IoT). The availability of such rich data sets provides an opportunity to gain a better understanding of the system and derive insights as to its behavior thereby facilitating informed decision making. Ideas borrowed from fields such as Modeling and Simulation, Artificial Intelligence, and Control Theory can be combined and developed to reduce the current excessive dependence on human experts for enterprise-wide monitoring and adaptation.

The Software Engineering community has been using modeling and model driven techniques for well over two decades now. Their focus has largely been on *how to build systems right* wherein models are viewed as high-level specification from which system implementations can be automatically derived. By keeping the models free of implementation technology concerns, the same specification can be easily targeted to multiple technology platforms. Thus, model driven software development has led to increased productivity, uniform high quality, and platform independence. Going forward the focus needs to shift from *how to build systems right* to *how to build the right systems*.

More broadly, the Engineering Industry has been using modeling and simulation to help build the right systems. These models are hi-fidelity virtual representation of reality in a form that can be simulated i.e., a *Digital Twin*. Digital twins offer a variety of different use cases: Analysis (i.e. why a system is behaving the way it is, what would be the system response to a given perturbation etc), Control (i.e. what is the most appropriate intervention for a particular perturbation to bring the system back to the desired state), Adaptation (i.e. what is the right policy to keep delivering the stated goals in the face of a set of perturbations and changes in the environment), Transformation (i.e. how to identify the desired to-be state and a path towards it so as to deliver the stated goals in the face of disruptions), and Design (i.e. how to conceive the right system that delivers the desired goals).

Recent advances in Deep Learning and a significant reduction in the cost of processing power are making it possible to apply AI to large-scale real-life problems. Large data sets can now be processed to learn hi-fidelity models that can serve as purposive digital twins. Similarly, advances in natural language processing (NLP) can be exploited to author purposive digital twins from textual information in unstructured form. Recent advances in deep reinforcement learning (RL) make it possible to train a RL agent capable of making decisions for large scale complex systems.

Model Reference Adaptive Control (MRAC) is a control theory technique designed to enable a system to adapt its behavior by following a reference model. This has been used extensively in continuous control systems such as airplanes, chemical plants and automobiles. It can be suitably adapted to apply in the context of enterprises by integrating a Digital Twin with a RL agent where the digital twin serves as the reference model and RL agent is the controller.

This book aims to support Enterprise Architects to evolve the right enterprise architecture for the digital future and derive an effective implementation path. It will also be of interest to researchers, both industrial and academic, to identify appropriate problems to direct their research. We anticipate that this volume can also serve as supplementary reading material for a graduate level course on Enterprise Architecture, Enterprise Modeling, Enterprise Information Systems, and Systems Engineering.

This book explores how ideas from fields such as Modeling and Simulation, Artificial Intelligence, and Control Theory can be brought together to realize the vision of a *Model-Driven Adaptive Enterprise*. The book attempts to synergize industry practitioner's perspectives drawn from real world with theoretical rigour from academia. The book is divided into two sections: Section 1 develops the rationale for a Model-Driven Adaptive Enterprise and discusses the various aspects necessary for its realization, and Section 2 illustrates this vision in several real-life contexts.

In "Model-Driven Adaptive Enterprise: A Conceptual Outline," the editors discuss characteristics of modern enterprises and the need for dynamic adaptation. They argue that systems of systems nature of modern enterprises wherein understanding is only available in localized contexts and is typically partial and uncertain make it hard to achieve adaptation. The current practice often exclusively relies on human expertise for monitoring and adaptation which they argue is inadequate considering the scale, complexity and highly dynamic nature of modern enterprises. They propose a line of attack that leverages principles from modeling, artificial intelligence, control theory, and information systems design leading to a knowledge-guided simulation-aided data-driven model-based evidence-backed approach. At the heart of a Model Driven Adaptive Enterprise lies a Digital Twin i.e. a simulatable digital replica of the enterprise. They discuss how the digital twin can be used to meet the key needs such as analysis, control, adaptation, transformation and design.

In "Conjoint Analysis and Design of Business and IT: The Case for Multi-Perspective Enterprise Modelling," Ulrich Frank and Alexander Bock argue the need for joint analysis and design of business and IT. Towards this a method for multi-perspective enterprise modeling (MEMO) is proposed. It is based on a language architecture that comprises an extensible set of domain-specific modeling languages, each addressing one or more stakeholder perspectives. They also propose an adaptable generic framework to define high-level views of an enterprise that serve as a common starting point for more elaborate analysis and design. The chapter motivates the use of MEMO and illustrates possible use cases. It also provides a description of the method's architecture, its domain specific modeling languages (DSMLs), and a tool environment that supports the development and analysis of enterprise models.

In "Enterprise Modelling in the Digital Age," Henderik Proper, Wided Guédria and Jean-Sebastien Sottet discuss how the transition from the industrial age to the digital age is shifting the economic focus from a goods-dominant logic to a service-dominant logic which brings to the fore continuous value co-creation between providers and consumers. These trends drive enterprises to transform continuously where coordination among the stakeholders involved is key. The chapter reflects on the role of enterprise modelling towards coordination, explores the challenges posed by digital transformations on enterprise modelling, and also discusses how enterprise modelling itself may benefit in the process.

In "An Approach to Construct Digital Twin for Complex Enterprises," Souvik Barat makes the case for an enterprise digital twin that imitates a real enterprise by providing an environment to conduct the necessary interrogative and predictive analyses to evaluate various control measures, adaptation choices and transformation options in a safe and cost-effective manner without compromising the analysis precision. This chapter reflects on the core concept of the digital twin, evaluates the state-of-the-art modelling and analysis technologies, and presents a pragmatic approach to develop high-fidelity purposive digital twins for modern enterprises.

In "Authoring Models of Regulations: Providing Assistance and Validation," Sagar Sunkle, Suman Roychoudhury and Deepali Kholkar present the case for digital twins for regulatory compliance. Such a twin is a machine-processable model of the enterprise in terms of its processes, systems, controls and regulations. The chapter describes a framework that aids domain experts author these machine-processable models from natural language text. Formal machinery to validate the authored models is also presented. The chapter then discusses how a regulations model is translated to formal logic that enables automated compliance checking in contrast with current industry practice of document-driven and expert-dependent regulatory compliance. It also presents a real-world case study of Money Market Statistical Reporting (MMSR) regulations for a large European bank to demonstrate the benefits of the approach.

In "IT Systems for the Digital Enterprise," Souvik Barat and Asha Rajbhoj advance a case for agile and adaptive enterprise IT systems. They discuss a set of concepts and techniques that help achieve the desired agility and adaptiveness. The chapter reflects on how agility, technology independence and retargetability can be achieved using model driven engineering. It presents variability modeling and a software product line architecture for developing configurable and extensible IT systems.

In "Towards Adaptive Enterprise: Adaptation and Learning," Harshad Khadilkar and Aditya Paranjape argue that the key to a successful adaptive enterprise lies in techniques and algorithms that enable the enterprise to learn about its environment and use the learning to make decisions that maximize its objectives. The volatile nature of the business environment demands continuous and reliable learning, and rapid and accurate decision-making. In this chapter, authors investigate two promising techniques to design such algorithms: adaptive control and reinforcement learning. Authors review the foundations, the state-of-the-art and the limitations of these techniques. Possible ways to bring together these techniques, in a way which brings out the best of their capabilities, are also discussed.

In "Enterprise Security: Modern Challenges and Emerging Measures," Manish Shukla, Harshal Tupsamudre and Sachin Lodha discuss cyber threats and vulnerabilities that are creating trust issues for modern enterprises. The authors explain how cyber ecosystem is changing due to extreme digitalization, and discuss its ramifications visible in the latest trends in cyber-attacks. They arrive at key implications that any modern enterprise needs to be cognizant of, and discuss emerging measures that may help address their consequences. It is hoped that these measures will play a critical role in making enterprise security more proactive, cognitive, automated, connected, invisible, and risk aware.

In "People and the Digital Enterprise," Vivek Balaraman, Sachin Patel, Mayuri Duggirala, Ravi Mahamuni and Jayasree Raveendran discuss how the transformation of an enterprise from a people centric model to a technology centric model affects its human workforce. They look at three representative people related focus areas for the digital enterprise namely, enhancing workplace wellbeing, enabling continuous learning, and compliance to information security. They discuss technological infrastructure a digital enterprise would require for meeting these needs.

In "Generate and Test for Formulated Product Variants With Information Extraction and an In-Silico Model," Sagar Sunkle, Deepak Jain, Krati Saxena, Ashwini Patil, Rinu Chacko and Beena Rai discuss an application of digital twin in the Chemical Industry. The state of the art in formulated product design relies heavily on experts leading to an extended time to market and increased costs. The authors show how the textual information available in a variety of forms can be represented formally in a graph database using state of the art NLP technology. The database is processed to generate feasible design variants of desired formulated products that can be simulated on a digital replica of skin (digital twin) in an iterative process to arrive at the right formulation "in silico". Early results of this work in progress research are encouraging.

In "Materials Design, Development, and Deployment in Manufacturing Industry: A Digital Paradigm," BP Gautham and Sreedhar Reddy discuss application of digital twins in the Manufacturing Industry which is undergoing a transformation through the adoption of digital technologies. At present, digital twins in the form of physics and data driven models are being used in a localized manner to address specific problems. The authors argue that the next level of transformation requires the digital twins to be used in an integrated manner to support end-to-end engineering of materials, products and processes. Then they discuss a flexible digital platform that supports knowledge-guided model-driven simulation-aided decision making for integrated engineering of materials, products and processes.

In "Orchestrating the C3 Journey of the Digital Enterprise," Devadatta Kulkarni, Jeffrey Tew and Rajeev Shorey discuss the transformative journey of manufacturing value chain from Connected to Collaborative to Cognitive. This transformation demands a reimagination of products and processes beyond just "digitalization". The enterprise starts by capturing diverse sensor data and integrates just-in-time data to achieve a "Connected" stage. It uses data along with contextual intelligence to drive integrated decisions in a "Collaborative" stage. It aspires to share decision making between machines and humans and evolves into a "Cognitive" stage. The authors highlight the nuances and opportunities across the C3 journey focusing on manufacturing value chains. They outline how customers can orchestrate their C3 journey using innovative digital solutions for information sharing and interactive analytics that will deliver best business results with data driven decisions.

In "The Digital Enterprise as an Emerging Landscape for Universities and Their Operation," Balbir Barn presents a framing discussion around the notion of a digital enterprise in the context of higher education. The chapter discusses how a university can benefit from digital technologies and how a university's existing and historical activities are consistent with the notion of a digital enterprise. The chapter also proposes a framework for assessing the readiness of a university with respect to its actions as a digital enterprise. Critically, the chapter argues that such a future systems project should not only consider positive use cases but also recognize that a digital enterprise may have unplanned and unintentional consequences. Hence this chapter argues that new forms of governance may also be required alongside the journey to a digital enterprise world.

In "Enterprise IT Operations: Cognitive Automation and ignio™," Harrick Vin argues that information technology (IT) has shifted from being a support function, to be a synonym for business wellness. At the same time, the scale and complexity of IT for running business has grown significantly thus requiring complex interplay of many, often invisible and dynamically changing, technology components. As a result, making design resilient and interruption-free IT a significant challenge. This chapter discusses limitations of traditional approaches for managing enterprise IT operations; introduces the concept of cognitive automation, a novel approach that blends intelligence with automation to transform enterprise IT operations; and describes the design of ignio™, a cognitive automation platform for enterprises. The author concludes by highlighting the challenges in driving cognitive transformation of enterprise operations and provide some suggestions for embarking upon this journey.

The book argues that emerging digital forces are poised to revolutionise the enterprise landscape. This is an opportunity as well as a threat. All stakeholders need to understand how best to harness these forces to their advantage. This book identifies the distinguishing characteristics of a futuristic digital enterprise and discusses the digital forces that influence these characteristics together with approaches, mechanisms and technology required to realise them. It also discusses possible transformative paths from a current state to a desired future state with the help of a few real-life industrial use cases. The book is conceived with the enterprise architect as the principal audience and aims to help achieve the right enterprise architecture for the digital future and to derive an effective implementation path. It will also be of interest to researchers, both industrial and academic, to identify appropriate research challenges. The book can also serve as supplementary reading material for a graduate level course on Enterprise Architecture, Enterprise Modeling, and Enterprise Decision Making.

We would like to thank authors of the book chapters for their cooperation. Also, we would like to put on record the support provided by our organisations – Tata Consultancy Services, Aston University, and Middlesex University London – without which this book would not have been possible.

Section 1

Chapter 1
Model–Driven Adaptive Enterprise:
A Conceptual Outline

Vinay Kulkarni

https://orcid.org/0000-0003-1570-1339

TCS Research, Tata Consultancy Services, India

Sreedhar Reddy

TCS Research, Tata Consultancy Services, India

Tony Clark

https://orcid.org/0000-0003-3167-0739

Aston University, Birmingham, UK

ABSTRACT

Modern enterprises are large complex systems operating in dynamic environments and are therefore required to respond quickly to a variety of change drivers. Moreover, they are systems of systems wherein understanding is only available in localized contexts and is partial and uncertain. Given that the overall system behaviour is hard to know a-priori and that conventional techniques for systemwide analysis either lack rigour or are defeated by the scale of the problem, the current practice often exclusively relies on human expertise for adaptation. This chapter outlines the concept of model-driven adaptive enterprise that leverages principles from modeling, artificial intelligence, control theory, and information systems design leading to a knowledge-guided simulation-aided data-driven model-based evidence-backed approach to impart adaptability to enterprises. At the heart of a model-driven adaptive enterprise lies a digital twin (i.e., a simulatable digital replica of the enterprise). The authors discuss how the digital twin can be used to analyze, control, adapt, transform, and design enterprises.

DOI: 10.4018/978-1-7998-0108-5.ch001

INTRODUCTION

Modern enterprises are complex systems of systems operating in an increasingly dynamic environment. Due to their large size and scale of operation, understanding is usually limited to localized contexts. Even this localized understanding is typically partial and quickly gets outdated as some of the assumptions made of the operating environment no longer hold. In order to respond to a wide variety of change drivers, an enterprise must adapt by constantly changing its strategies, policies, business practices, and systems. However, such an adaptive enterprise cannot be realized without adequate understanding of its global behavior which is difficult to know a-priori as it emerges out of complex interactions among constituent systems.

Enterprise modeling practice views an enterprise on three related planes namely *Strategy plane*, *Process plane* and *Systems plane* as shown in Figure 1. The strategy plane focuses on goals, strategies, and policies that are expressed using modeling languages such as i* (Yu, Strohmaier, & Deng, 2006), KAOS (Dardenne, Lamsweerde, & Fickas, 1993), and TROPOS (Bresciani, Perini, Giorgini, Giunchiglia, & Mylopoulos, 2004). The process plane focuses on realizing these strategies and policies to achieve the stated goals using modeling languages such BPMN[1], System Dynamic models (Meadows & Wright, 2008), and Event-Driven Process Chains (Mendling, 2008). The systems plane focuses on implementing these processes through software systems using modeling languages such as UML[2] and SysML (Friedenthal, Moore, & Steiner, 2014). However, the links across these models whether in a plane or across the planes are informal and typically in document form. As a result, these models are not amenable to rigorous analysis and hence cannot establish whether a given implementation achieves the intended goal.

Figure 1. Three planes of enterprise

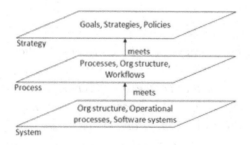

To meet the needs of an adaptive enterprise, the three plane view of Figure 1 needs to be refined as shown in Figure 2 where an enterprise is viewed in terms of three related planes namely: *Intent* plane addressing the *why* aspect in terms of goals, capabilities, and measures; *Design* plane addressing the *what* aspect in terms of models of organisational structure, processes, and information systems required to achieve the desired intent; *Implementation* plane addressing the *how* aspect in terms of organisation and its information systems; and interactions of the three planes with the environment as shown in Figure 2. An adaptive enterprise should be able to change its goals and capabilities in response to changes in its operational environment. It should then be able to effect appropriate modifications to its organizational

Figure 2. Adaptive enterprise

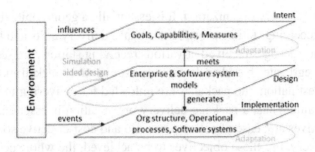

structure, operational processes, and software systems. Moreover, this needs to be achieved in the face of incomplete information and inherent uncertainty. This identifies several new needs:

- Analysis i.e., provide data-based justification for why the complex system of systems is behaving the way it is behaving,
- Control i.e., help arrive at suitable intervention so as to bring the system back to the original state in the presence of a perturbation,
- Adaptation i.e., help arrive at suitable policies (as a sequence of purposive interventions) so as to keep the system in the desired state in a continuously changing environment,
- Transformation i.e., help arrive at the desired to-be state and a plan of action that takes the system from the as-is state to the to-be state, and
- Design i.e., help define the desired system backed by data-based validation of the desired behavior.

A model driven adaptive enterprise is one that is capable of addressing these needs with the help of a set of suitable models. The design plane needs to provide the necessary machinery to arrive at the models of the right organisational structure, processes and information systems so as to meet the specified intent. To this end, a simulation-aided data-driven approach for design space exploration is required. The outcome of this human-in-the-loop process is a simulatable model of the enterprise *i.e.* an *enterprise digital twin*. Being a digital replica of the enterprise, the enterprise digital twin can be used to identify suitable response e.g. accentuate or attenuate goals, modify existing policies, arrive at new design strategies etc to the various changes in the environment. Simulatable nature of the enterprise digital twin enables validation of the response using real life data. In a model driven adaptive enterprise, these changes eventually manifest as modifications to the appropriate models. Model driven techniques can be used to transform business process and software system models into an efficient implementation of enterprise IT systems (Kulkarni & Reddy, 2003). The enterprise digital twin can also serve as the reference for adaptation of implementation plane systems.

We illustrate a complex system of systems and its adaptation needs in the following section.

ILLUSTARTION OF A COMPLEX SYSTEM OF SYSTEMS

Consider a large package delivery organization. It is essentially a geographically distributed ecosystem comprising of package receiving stations, sorting terminals, delivery units and transportation providers connecting all these. The packages received at various receiving stations are sent to the nearest sorting terminal where they are segregated based on destination to be suitably packed and loaded into appropriate vehicles. On reaching destination, the packages are unloaded for delivering to the appropriate address using suitable delivery unit. Thus, a package delivery organization is essentially a graph as shown in Figure 3. The key objectives are: ease of collection, rapid and cost-effective sorting, efficient transportation, and on-time delivery. For these objectives to be achieved, the whole ecosystem has to function in an optimal and coordinated manner. Any disruption in one system can have ripple effects on other systems. To simplify the discussion let's focus on sorting terminal that lies at the heart of this complex ecosystem and is itself a complex system.

Figure 3. System of systems - package delivery organization

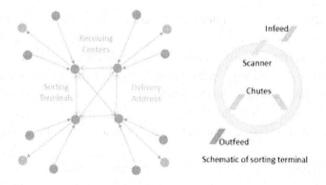

A sorting terminal comprises of:

- *Infeeds* where the transportation vehicles are docked for unloading onto the sorting belt through escalators.
- *Sorting belt* where the packages are scanned and pushed into appropriate chutes. After a predefined finite time, the unsorted packages get pushed into the reject chute.
- *Scanners* that determine the nature of the package (i.e. if it needs special handling) and destination.
- *Chutes* where packages meant for a specific destination are rolled off the sorting belt for collection.
- *Outfeeds* where the sorted packages are loaded into appropriate transportation vehicles for delivery.
- *Workforce* tasked to empty the chutes and also to perform manual sorting of packages from the reject chute.

Optimal operation of a sorting terminal hinges on: the package spending as little time as possible on the sorting belt, the chutes getting emptied as quickly as possible, and assigning as few packages as possible to the reject chute. The sorting terminal is a configurable system with parameters such as placement of scanners, activation of chutes, kind of chutes etc. A typical sorting shift is preceded by an estimation exercise wherein the likely workload in terms of number and nature of packages for each destination is predicted. Based on this workload, the sorting terminal is suitably configured and workforce allocated for each chute. In case the actual workload matches the predicted workload, operation of the sorting terminal is smooth. However, in reality, actual workload is rarely the same as predicted workload thus leading to several exception conditions which are typically handled manually relying on heuristics derived from past data. This puts serious cognitive burden on shift manager in order to meet the following needs:

- Analysis i.e., explain the current state of sorting terminal operation and explore means to improve the state by addressing questions such as: Are the current policies of managing the operation of sorting terminal effective? What are the right policies for optimal operation of the sorting terminal for a given workload? What is the right configuration of the sorting terminal for a given workload?
- Control i.e., help arrive at suitable interventions for exceptional condition such as: workforce allocated to a specific chute is turning out to be insufficient to empty the chute fast enough thus leading to chute overflow and eventual closure, how should the workforce be reallocated so as to address this exceptional condition with minimal disruption to the overall sorting terminal?
- Adaptation i.e., help arrive at suitable policies (as a sequence of purposive interventions to the observed exception conditions) so as to ensure optimal operation of the sorting terminal,
- Design i.e., help arrive at the most appropriate layout for the sorting terminal in the light of expected workload configurations.

To summarize, the key requirements of the shift manager of a sorting terminal are: (i) How to understand the emergent behavior of the sorting terminal (i.e. analysis), (ii) How to continue delivering the stated objectives in the presence of perturbations (i.e. adaptive control), (ii) How to learn to adapt to a-priori un-knowable situations as they arise, and (iv) How to provide a feel for the sorting terminal operation 'in silico' with a priori assurances (i.e. design).

SOLUTION APPROACH

A promising line of attack to impart dynamic adaptability to complex system of systems can be conceived drawing on principles from the fields of modeling, control theory and artificial intelligence.

Most Engineering fields use modelling as the means to address problems of the kind discussed above. Models are precise specifications of the essential aspects of a system. Where these specifications are amenable to quantitative analysis through what-if and if-what scenario playing, they are called a *Digital Twin* of the real system. The concept of a virtual, digital equivalent to a physical product or the Digital Twin was introduced in 2003 at University of Michigan Executive Course on Product Lifecycle Management (Grieves, 2014). Today the evolution of sensors and network technologies enables us to link physical assets to digital models. In this way, changes experienced by the physical object are reflected in the digital model, and insights derived from the model allow decisions to be made about the physical object, which can also be controlled with unprecedented precision[3].

Digital twins can also be applied to enterprise scale systems. An enterprise is a complex system of systems designed to deliver a set of stated goals while operating in a dynamic and uncertain environment. An enterprise digital twin is a virtual, high fidelity representation of the enterprise that is amenable to rigorous quantitative analysis through what-if and if-what scenario playing using real data to support justification-backed analysis, control and adaptation of the enterprise. Typically, digital twins of physical assets are used in an off-system mode and they themselves do not need to undergo adaptation during operation i.e., it is assumed that a digital twin forever remains a high fidelity representation of the physical system. However, the idea of an enterprise digital twin introduces a new use-case: dynamic adaptation, because of the scale, complexity and incompleteness of information. In other words, an enterprise digital twin needs to adapt / evolve as new information about the enterprise becomes available. Such dynamic adaptation can be realized in a number of ways, learning being one of them. Such an enterprise digital twin models the enterprise as a set of intentional autonomous adaptive learning agents that interact with each other and respond to the events of interest taking place in the environment. These agents can exist at different levels of granularity i.e. an agent can be seen as a composition of a set of next-level agents. An agent observes the environment, makes sense of the observations, and performs actions so as to achieve its objectives. The action could change the local state of agent or send a message to other agents (Clark, Kulkarni, Barat, & Barn, 2017). These actions are often stochastic due to uncertainty and incomplete domain knowledge (Kulkarni, Barat,

Clark, & Barn, 2017). An agent is capable of adapting its behavior in response to the changes in its environment. Essentially, an agent has a set of situation-specific behaviours and it is able to switch from one behavior to another depending on the situation it finds itself in. An agent needs to adapt and extend its behaviour not only to achieve its local objectives but also to ensure robustness of the overall system.

USING ENETERPRISE DIGITAL TWIN

Enterprise digital twin can help with analysis, control, transformation and design of an enterprise as a complex system of systems.

Analysis

An enterprise is a complex system of systems designed to deliver stated goals while operating in an uncertain and dynamic environment. The goals could either be quantitative or qualitative. The former are expressed as complex conditional expressions – possibly involving temporal logic operators – over observable parameters that are indicative of system execution. The latter typically constitute an experts interpretation of a set of quantitative and/or qualitative goals. Some of the key analysis questions are: can the current state be explained and/or justified? Can an accurate judgment of how far the current state is from the desired state be arrived at? Can a fair estimate of the impact of a perturbation – to system input or environment – be arrived at quickly enough? Can ripple effect of a response to such perturbations throughout the complex system of systems be arrived at quickly enough? For answers to these (and such) questions, current practice typically relies heavily on human experts who in turn rely on past data, knowledge and experience. The scale, complexity, partial and uncertain knowledge all contribute to make this approach quite unsatisfactory.

On the other hand, enterprise digital twin enables building of purposive automation aids to answer these questions in quantitative terms using real data thus significantly reducing the dependence on human expertise. Precise understanding in the localized contexts is modelled and also the interactions between these parts. Partial and uncertain knowledge imparts a stochastic nature to these models. Enterprise digital twin is subjected to real data and events in the environment to produce the required observable parameters as shown in Figure 4. Thus, it is possible to observe both local and emergent global virtual behaviours that

Figure 4. Digital twin enabled analysis of enterprise

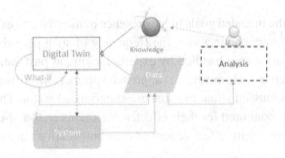

provide an accurate understanding of what is happening in the real system. Correlations between local behaviours and system goals can be arrived at through what-if scenario playing for a-priori known scenarios as well as new scenarios as they arise. The enterprise digital twin also enables if-what analysis, for instance, whether a desired global behavior can be achieved and how. Greater the fidelity of enterprise digital twin, more accurate the simulation results.

Figure 5. Digital twin enabled control of enterprise

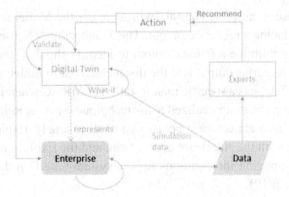

Figure 6. Model reference adaptive control

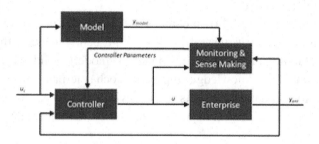

Adaptive Control

Enterprises need to deliver the intended goals in the presence of internal and external perturbations. With increased dynamism and system connectivity, the frequency of such perturbations will only increase. Traditionally, these perturbations are handled by experts looking at past data to come up with recommendations as shown in Figure 4. However, this approach suffers from a disadvantage that recommendations are arrived at based only on situations that are experienced so far. These recommendations are applied to real systems and monitored for their effectiveness. This trial-and-error approach can lead to long cycle times and high costs with effectiveness of recommendations depending largely on the level of human expertise.

In contrast, an enterprise digital twin improves effectiveness by enabling validation of recommendations in virtual space. Also, an enterprise digital twin can be subjected to a variety of scenarios a priori thus obtaining a more comprehensive data pertaining to situations that are possible though not seen so far.

An enterprise digital twin can be used for self-adaptation thus reducing dependence on human experts. Figure 6 depicts an adaptation architecture that draws its inspiration from a well-studied and widely used concept from control theory – Model Reference Adaptive Control (Butler, Hondred, & van Amerongen, 1992) – adapted for an enterprise context. The Model captures the desired reference behaviour of enterprise. The Enterprise is the complex system of systems to be controlled. The Monitoring & Sense Making constitutes the core technology infrastructure to observe and discern input and output of enterprise. The Controller constitutes the core technology infrastructure that, together with the Monitoring & Sense Making component, nudges the Enterprise as close to the Model as possible thus achieving a model-guided adaptive response.

For the digital enterprise, Enterprise Digital Twin serves as the Model which is fed the same input as the Enterprise thus producing a reference output. The Monitoring & Sense making component compares the Enterprise output with the reference output to identify the distance if any. The Controller is guided by the input, the Enterprise output and the distance signal to nudge the Enterprise behavior in the right direction. Figure 7 depicts a specific manifestation of MRAC wherein the Monitoring & Sense Making and Controller components are realized using techniques such as Reinforcement Learning (RL) (Sutton & Barto, 1998). This architecture supports two modes namely, Explore mode wherein the RL agent learns by interacting with the enterprise digital twin, and the Exploit mode wherein the RL agent comes up with suitable adaptation interventions for the system based on the knowledge gained from Explore mode (Barat et al, 2019).

Figure 7. Adaptation using reinforcement learning

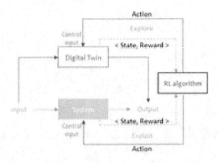

Design

Design is the process that is used to arrive at the right strategies, processes, organizational structure and supporting systems to achieve the intended goals and objectives as shown in Figure 8. Typically, enterprise goals form a complex decomposition structure wherein some goals may interfere with other goals as shown in Figure 9. Designing a system to deliver such goals in a static, fully known environment is a difficult task in itself. Large size, precise understanding being available only in localized contexts, and

Figure 8. A typical enterprise – operational view

Figure 9. Enterprise digital twin enabled design

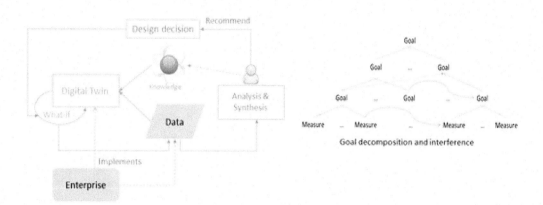

complex interactions between these contexts make the task even more difficult. Finally, partial knowledge and the uncertain and dynamic environment further exacerbate the problem. Traditionally, designing a system is a knowledge-intensive endeavor wherein experts analyze and synthesize available data to come up with design decisions. These decisions are typically implemented using a set of tried and tested templates. The resultant implementation may then be validated using controlled experimentation where the experts assess whether the design is meeting the intended goals. This process has long cycle times especially since each controlled experiment may involve setting up the necessary physical infrastructure, assigning resources, and conducting the experiments in realistic conditions. As a result, this approach is time-, effort-, cost- and intellect-expensive.

In contrast, an Enterprise Digital Twin can help explore the design space virtually as shown in Figure 9. Domain knowledge and past data help come up with first-cut definitions of goals, strategies, policies, processes, and organization structure, which are then modelled into the Enterprise Digital Twin. The simulatable nature of Enterprise Digital Twin enables what-if and if-what analysis of various scenarios of interest to arrive at the right design decisions virtually. These decisions can then be validated using the digital twin itself. This iterative process goes on until the desired objectives are met. Implementation of the real system is then a realization of the digital twin thus designed. As all the artefacts are models and solution space exploration is 'in silico', the design process is much faster and cheaper. Model-based analysis significantly reduces dependence on human expertise. Results of simulation can be mined to continuously augment the domain knowledge.

Transformation

Enterprises face disruptions due to emergence of new technologies, new business models, new regulatory frameworks, business events such as mergers and acquisitions etc. These disruptions necessitate large scale changes in enterprise strategies, organizational structure, processes, and systems. Due to the interconnected nature of complex systems, these changes ripple across. As the interactions are complex, it is difficult to predict the extent and exact nature of these ripple effects. Current practice of relying largely on human experts for effecting such transformations has clearly been found wanting. By some estimates, only 3% of enterprise transformation projects ever come to completion[4].

Figure 10. Digital twin guided enterprise transformation

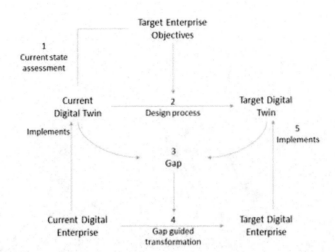

An Enterprise Digital Twin enables a transformation architecture that provides a tractable path to arrive at the desired target state as shown in Figure 10. The transformation process begins by specifying the target state. A digital twin can be used provide an accurate assessment whether target objectives can be achieved by the current enterprise. This can be supported through what-if and if-what analysis on the digital twin. In case the current enterprise cannot be made to achieve the desired target objectives through its existing controls, it needs to be structurally and behaviourally transformed. The transformation process constructs a digital twin for the desired target enterprise – this is essentially the design process described earlier starting with the current digital twin. It is followed by identifying the gap between current and target digital twins in terms of the various models. These gaps drive the transformation of current digital enterprise into the target digital enterprise. The final step of the transformation process checks whether the target digital enterprise correctly implements the target digital twin.

Model Driven Adaptive Enterprise Architecture

Digital enterprises are intentional, responsive, autonomous, modular, adaptive and continually learning systems of systems with complex interactions among the modular systems and with the environment. A digital enterprise operates in a manner to achieve its overall objectives while meeting the local goals of constituent modular systems. It monitors the events of interest taking place in its environment and responds suitably in order to achieve its stated goals. It has the necessary flexibility so as to adapt to the situation it finds itself in. It continually improves over time by learning from its own operations and their effects on the environment. Since aspects of a digital enterprise described above are inter-dependent, it is essential to have an architecture that addresses them in a holistic manner. Figure 11 presents a high-level view of architecture that facilitates knowledge-guided, data-driven, model-based, simulation-aided, justification-backed approach to analyze, control, adapt, design and transform enterprises.

Core to this architecture is the digital twin that is a virtual, simulatable replica of the real enterprise. It enables analysis, control, adaptation, transformation and design of enterprise through what-if and if-

Figure 11. Architecture to realize model driven adaptive enterprise

what scenario playing 'in silico'. This is an iterative process wherein the digital twin itself is modified as a result of analysis. The fixed point of this process is the digital twin that provides the specification of the desired enterprise for the intended purpose. Thus, a set of purposive digital twins together represent complete specification of enterprise for analysis purposes. This specification needs to be implemented to realize the desired enterprise. This is typically in terms of business processes, organizational structure, and IT systems. In a digital enterprise, these are in turn models that are amenable to analysis and simulation. In other words, we arrive at the specification of the right IT systems in an iterative process using what-if and if-what analysis. These specifications can be transformed into platform specific implementations using model-driven techniques (Kulkarni, 2016).

The implementations so generated are suitably instrumented to collect data at execution time. The collected data is then collated and further analyzed to derive insights that help in continual improvement of the enterprise. The digital twin itself can be used to perform this analysis thus completing the learning loop. These insights can be stored in a knowledge base for ready reference.

An enterprise digital twin is a set of models that are instances of a set of purposive meta models. Identifying the right set of meta models for the stated purpose is the key. These meta models then need to be instantiated suitably for the enterprise. This calls for examining the various information sources within enterprise such as documents, code, and data to populate the models suitably. The scale of the enterprise and the heterogeneity of information sources make this task very difficult to perform manually. Techniques such as Natural Language Processing, Machine Learning, and program analysis can be used to automate model population under human guidance. These models should be checked for internal consistency, completeness and correctness with respect to the real enterprise. Thus, the models need to be rigorous to support automated analysis. At the same time, they need to be usable by domain experts. To serve this need, suitable domain specific languages need to be developed. Also, it should be possible to use these models together to perform integrated analysis.

REALIZING THE CONCEPTUAL VIEW

This chapter presented a high level conceptual vision of an adaptive enterprise. It presented the idea of Enterprise Digital Twin and how it can be used to support the key needs of analysis, control, adaptation, transformation and design. Subsequent book chapters address how this conceptual view can be realized, along with detailing of the necessary technology infrastructure. The Natural Language Processing (NLP) and Machine Learning (ML) techniques required to construct digital twin from information available in the enterprise is discussed in detail. A detailed overview of how control theoretic and learning principles can provide support for dynamic adaptation using digital twin is presented. Architectures for realizing adaptive software systems in presence of uncertainty are discussed. A model-driven approach for automated realization of software systems from their high level specifications is presented. We discuss how the key principles from fields such as modeling, software engineering, artificial intelligence and control theory come together to realize the vision of adaptive enterprise in diverse domains such as materials engineering, chemical formulations, smart manufacturing, and smart services. Key issues of human behaviour, information security, and data privacy are also discussed.

REFERENCES

Barat, S., Khadilkar, H., Meisheri, H., Kulkarni, V., Baniwal, V., Kumar, P., & Gajrani, M. (2019, May). Actor Based Simulation for Closed Loop Control of Supply Chain using Reinforcement Learning. In *Proceedings of the 18th International Conference on Autonomous Agents and MultiAgent Systems* (pp. 1802-1804). International Foundation for Autonomous Agents and Multiagent Systems.

Bresciani, P., Perini, A., Giorgini, P., Giunchiglia, F., & Mylopoulos, J. (2004). Tropos: An agent-oriented software development methodology. *Autonomous Agents and Multi-Agent Systems*, 8(3), 203–236. doi:10.1023/B:AGNT.0000018806.20944.ef

Butler, H., Hondred, G., & van Amerongen, J. (1992). *Model Reference Adaptive Control: Bridging the gap from theory to practice*. Academic Press.

Clark, T., Kulkarni, V., Barat, S., & Barn, B. (2017, June). ESL: an actor-based platform for developing emergent behaviour organisation simulations. In *International Conference on Practical Applications of Agents and Multi-Agent Systems* (pp. 311-315). Springer. 10.1007/978-3-319-59930-4_27

Dardenne, A., Van Lamsweerde, A., & Fickas, S. (1993). Goal-directed requirements acquisition. *Science of Computer Programming*, 20(1-2), 3–50. doi:10.1016/0167-6423(93)90021-G

Friedenthal, S., Moore, A., & Steiner, R. (2014). *A practical guide to SysML: the systems modeling language*. Morgan Kaufmann.

Grieves, M. (2014). *Digital twin: Manufacturing excellence through virtual factory replication*. White paper, pages 1–7.

Kulkarni, V. (2016, May). Model driven development of business applications: a practitioner's perspective. In *Proceedings of the 38th International Conference on Software Engineering Companion* (pp. 260-269). ACM. 10.1145/2889160.2889251

Kulkarni, V., Barat, S., Clark, T., & Barn, B. (2017). Supporting Organisational Decision Making in Presence of Uncertainty. *The European Symposium on Modeling and Simulation (EMSS 2017)*, Barcelona, Spain.

Kulkarni, V., & Reddy, S. (2003). Separation of concerns in model-driven development. *IEEE Software*, *20*(5), 64–69. doi:10.1109/MS.2003.1231154

Meadows, D., & Wright, D. (2008). *Thinking in systems: A primer*. Chelsea Green Publishing.

Mendling, J. (2008). Event-driven process chains (epc). In *Metrics for process models* (pp. 17–57). Berlin: Springer. doi:10.1007/978-3-540-89224-3_2

Sutton, R. S., & Barto, A. G. (1998). Introduction to reinforcement learning: Vol. 2. *No. 4*. Cambridge: MIT Press.

Yu, E., Strohmaier, M., & Deng, X. (2006, October). Exploring intentional modeling and analysis for enterprise architecture. In *2006 10th IEEE International Enterprise Distributed Object Computing Conference Workshops (EDOCW'06)* (pp. 32-32). IEEE. 10.1109/EDOCW.2006.36

ENDNOTES

[1]   https://www.omg.org/spec/BPMN/2.0/

[2]   https://www.omg.org/spec/UML/2.0/About-UML/

[3]   https://www.logistics.dhl/content/dam/dhl/global/core/documents/pdf/glo-core-digital-twins-in-logistics.pdf

[4]   http://www.valueteam.biz/why-72-percent-of-all-business-transformation-projects-fail

Chapter 2
Conjoint Analysis and Design of Business and IT:
The Case for Multi–Perspective Enterprise Modeling

Ulrich Frank
University of Duisburg-Essen, Germany

Alexander C. Bock
University of Duisburg-Essen, Germany

ABSTRACT

This chapter presents a method for multi-perspective enterprise modeling (MEMO). Enterprise modeling fundamentally aims to support the conjoint analysis of business and IT to foster their integration. MEMO expands on this general aim with a specific concern for the professional perspectives of different stakeholder groups. MEMO is based on a language architecture that comprises an extensible set of domain-specific modeling languages, each addressing one or more professional perspectives. It is supplemented by an adaptable generic framework to support high-level 'ballpark' views of an enterprise and to serve as a common starting point for more elaborate analysis and design tasks. MEMO also supports the construction of corresponding process models to design customized modeling methods. The chapter motivates the use of MEMO and illustrates possible use cases. It also provides a description of the method's architecture, its DSMLs, and a tool environment that supports the development and analysis of enterprise models.

INTRODUCTION

The efficient use of information technology (IT) demands for the mutual adaptation of a company's action system and its information system. When designing an information system for a given action system, it is important to identify and pursue opportunities to organize the action system more efficiently through IT. Yet, it is usually not a good idea to adapt the action system to a given information system, such as an

DOI: 10.4018/978-1-7998-0108-5.ch002

'industry standard' ERP system, because that would threaten a company's specific profile and, hence, its competitiveness. Instead, a strategy of mutual adaptation of technology and organization is called for.

In times of the digital transformation, a company's ability to survive depends upon its ability to continuously adapt its operations, its information system, and even its business model. This ongoing need to change poses serious challenges. Information systems and corresponding IT infrastructures are of tremendous complexity. Often, they lack the desired level of integration, flexibility, and maintainability, since they have grown over time into heterogeneous collections of software systems and related data stores. From a technological perspective, it would often be preferable to replace old legacy systems. However, from an economic perspective that is often not regarded as an option, because the risks created by such fundamental interventions can be substantial. In addition, introducing new information systems requires changing the action system, for example, by re-designing organizational structures and business processes, which is likely to face resistance from employees. In summary, business and IT are mutually interdependent, and with the continuous penetration of action systems by IT, it will be more and more difficult to draw a clear borderline between them. Accordingly, means to support the conjoint analysis and (re-)design of business and IT are urgently needed.

The idea of enterprise modeling was introduced more than thirty years ago, arising out of the recognition that the alignment of business and IT needs to be improved in many firms. Zachman, who back then was a sales representative with IBM, was one of the early proponents of enterprise modelling. Zachman wanted to develop "some kind of framework for rationalizing the various architectural concepts and specifications … to establish credibility and confidence in the investment of system resources." (Zachman, 1987). Zachman's work was pioneering, but remained limited to a high-level framework. The purpose of this framework was to structure an enterprise together with its information system from various viewpoints and on different levels of detail. Many more elaborate approaches to enterprise modeling have been developed since then (ESPRIT Consortium AMICE, 1989), (Scheer, 1992), (Ferstl & Sinz, 1998), (Sandkuhl, Stirna, Persson, & Wißotzki, 2014). All these initiatives have in common that they seek to support the conjoint analysis and design of information systems through the construction and integration of specific models of an enterprise.

The evolution of the field resulted in a widely shared understanding of the term enterprise model: an enterprise model integrates at least one conceptual model of a company's action system, e.g., a business process model, with at least one model of its information system, e.g., a data model or an object model. Alongside the term 'enterprise model', the term 'enterprise architecture' has gained remarkable popularity in the last decade (The Open Group, 2009), (Aier et al., 2009). Like enterprise models, enterprise architectures are meant to aid the conjoint analysis and design of a company's action system and its information system, making extensive use of conceptual models. Two aspects, however, characterize enterprise architectures as a specific form of enterprise models. First, enterprise architectures typically aim at high-level representations suited for a management audience, rather than at more detailed representations suited for domain and IT experts. Second, enterprise architecture approaches are often associated with the claim to 'engineer' the enterprise, as is reflected in the related term 'enterprise engineering' (Dietz et al., 2013). While this claim promises an especially systematic and professional approach to information systems design, it is suspected by some to falsely equate social systems with formal or technical systems amenable to engineering. Despite these differences, the fundamental aim of enterprise modeling is endorsed in a wide range of instruments from academia and industry.

This chapter gives a comprehensive introduction to enterprise modeling. It is intended to provide a clear understanding of how to configure and use enterprise modeling for a wide range of problems related to transforming an enterprise and its information system. For this purpose, a specific method for enterprise modeling is presented in more detail. MEMO ('Multi-Perspective Enterprise Modeling') is to the best of our knowledge the most comprehensive method for enterprise modeling currently available. It features an extensible language architecture and is supplemented by an extensible modeling environment that enables the construction and integration of multiple diagram types. The chapter starts with a motivation, which is followed by a description of the components of MEMO. Subsequently, the use of MEMO is demonstrated in a case study. Finally, an integrated modeling tool is presented that implements the DSMLs specified with MEMO.

MOTIVATION

An enterprise is a complex action system permeated by software systems to an ever growing extent. Software systems are immaterial artefacts. The only way to understand and analyze them properly is through concepts. For example, without the notion of a compiler we would not be able to identify and to analyze one. Action systems cannot be perceived directly either. To interpret the actions in an enterprise, we need concepts, too. Without knowing what, for example, revenues, products, and customers are, we would have a hard time to make sense of what people are doing in a company.

The complexity of contemporary action systems and information systems calls for separation of concerns. Over time, this inevitably leads to the development of different technical languages and related perspectives. While specialized languages support the efficient analysis of specific problems, they are likely to be an obstacle to communication and collaboration of people with different perspectives. This situation recommends providing some kind of medium to foster communication between people entertaining different cognitive perspectives, e.g., between a manager in the sales department and an IT manager, or between a software developer and an accountant. In principle, communication implies the existence of a common language. If people speak different technical languages, the only way to build a bridge between the languages is to focus on concepts that both languages share, which amounts to an integration of the two languages. In addition, it is usually helpful to abstract from all those aspects of specific technical languages that are not pertinent to the given communication scenario.

Against this background, it is obvious that conceptual models are suited to support the communication about, and analysis of, different perspectives on the enterprise. For example, conceptual models may offer detailed representations of business processes or IT infrastructures. Furthermore, when integrating separate models describing different perspectives, a basis is provided for people with different backgrounds to detect, and talk about, the connections between their respective areas of concern. The interpretation and use of such integrated models can be further facilitated by visualizing the model with intuitive graphical symbols. The idea of multi-perspective enterprise modeling is a reflection of these considerations.

A multi-perspective enterprise model differentiates between various explicit perspectives, which will usually correspond to professional views. These perspectives are represented by models constructed with modeling languages.

The design of a method for enterprise modeling requires a reasonable conception of enterprises. In addition to what is considered in traditional theories of the firm, such a conception also needs to account for the specific features of information systems. 'Reasonable' is here taken to mean that the accepted conception of enterprises should apply to a suitably wide range of enterprises and that it is backed by convincing evidence and justification. Furthermore, the chosen conception should not be confined to characteristics of existing enterprises. It should also identify current problems and strategies to address them, thereby yielding conceptions of possible future enterprises. An enterprise is a managed social system. That is, it involves control mechanisms to structure and guide individual actions toward corporate goals. But being social systems, enterprises are also rife with contingencies. They often lack a clear and consistent goal system, and are characterized by individual, hidden agendas, which are often in conflict. As a consequence, enterprise models can help exerting control by providing a common reference in the sense of a common schema for coordinated action. It would, however, be naive to assume that enterprise models are a sufficient foundation to 'optimize' an enterprise. Instead, it is required to account for the contingencies of human action and social interaction – and for the crucial relevance of sense-making in the complex and fluctuating environments of the organizations of our time.

MEMO: Core Components

A modeling method consists of one or more modeling languages and at least one corresponding process model that guides the construction and use of models. Accordingly, MEMO comprises a range of DSMLs and various process models. Considering the variety of existing enterprises and problems residing in them, it is not realistic to assume that a given set of DSMLs and process models will be sufficient for all use cases. For this reason, MEMO includes a language architecture that allows to modify existing DSMLs and integrate further DSMLs. It also supports the construction of specific process models to create customized modeling methods. In addition MEMO includes an adaptable generic framework that offers a high-level view of an enterprise, which is especially useful at the beginning of a project. In what follows, the different components of MEMO will be explained more closely in turn.

Adaptable Generic Framework

The construction and analysis of an enterprise model will usually require the involvement of internal and external experts. Before starting to develop particular models, it is necessary to establish a common understanding of the company and the problems that are subject of the project. Since it would be too costly to develop such a common high-level model from scratch, it is advisable to make use of an existing, generic framework, which can be applied to a wide range of companies. Numerous generic frameworks to structure an enterprise on a high level of abstraction are found in the literature, e.g. (Scheer, 1992), (Zachman, 1987). The choice of a framework depends on the subject of a project, as well as on particular constraints and preferences. MEMO offers a generic framework that has proven useful in a number of projects. It consists of two dimensions. The first dimension distinguishes three perspectives. The strategic perspective focuses on strategic topics. The organizational perspective covers organizational or operational topics, while the information system perspective is dedicated to specific topics of managing corporate IT infrastructures. The second dimension distinguishes different generic aspects found in each perspective, such as structure, process, and resources. The representation of the framework in a two-dimensional table allows assigning specific topics to each focus (defined by the combination of a specific perspective and a specific aspect). This can be done interactively during a workshop at the beginning of a project to identify the issues regarded as most relevant. In a further step, it is possible to assign assessments and annotations to each focus. Figure 1 shows the basic framework with assessments attached to each focus, illustrating how it can help develop a common high-level understanding of an enterprise and to identify critical issues.

Figure 1. Basic two-dimensional MEMO Framework with symbols to indicate the assessment of the current state

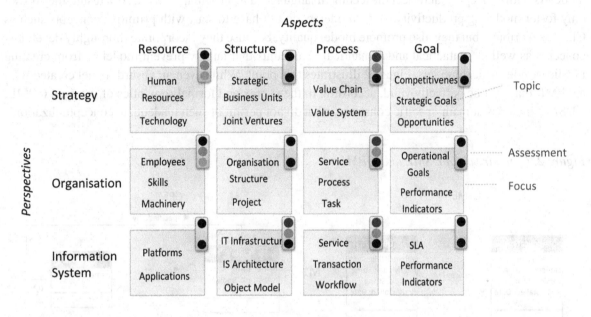

The basic framework provides a generic structure of the firm that should be applicable to most enterprises. However, it will not be satisfactory in all cases. First, the distinction between information system and the two other perspectives is not entirely convincing, since information system could also be seen as a specific aspect of organizational and strategic viewpoints. Second, it may be required to add further aspects, such as time or region. To meet these requirements, MEMO includes a meta model to construct frameworks with an arbitrary number of dimensions. In addition, the meta model allows to create frameworks based on different conceptions of the enterprise to support a larger variety of modeling and analysis purposes. Examples of such frameworks are Porter's value chain (Porter, 2001) or the business model canvas (Osterwalder & Pigneur, 2010). An example of a customized framework is shown in Figure 14. Frameworks can also be combined. For each focus within a framework, it is possible to define references to other frameworks. For example, the focus 'strategy/process' may include a reference to a corresponding value chain framework.

Generic frameworks are primarily used during the initial phase of a project, when it is most important to obtain a first overview of the enterprise and the current situation, and to identify areas in need of a more elaborate analysis. But the frameworks employed in MEMO also serve another important purpose. Each focus in the generic frameworks can be supplemented with references to more detailed models, such as business process models or goal models. For example, the focus 'Competitiveness, Strategic Goals, Opportunities' (top right in Figure 1) may be linked to a diagram showing an organizational goal system. In this way, the generic frameworks provides a high-level entry point to the overall enterprise model. This capacity of the generic MEMO frameworks will be exemplified again below in the section on the modeling tool MEMO4ADO.

Domain-Specific Languages

Domain-specific languages offer clear advantages over general-purpose modeling languages. They provide modelers with concepts that reflect the technical language of a particular domain. As a result, they do not only foster modeling productivity, since modelers do not have to start with primitive concepts such as Class or Attribute, but they also promote model quality, because they incorporate thoroughly developed concepts as well as syntactical and semantical constraints that largely prevent modelers from creating invalid or nonsensical models. Figure 2 illustrates this point. While even an absurd model created with a GPML may still be perfectly valid, according to the syntax and formal semantics of the used GPML, a DSML includes domain-specific constraints that do not permit of such inadequate conceptualizations.

Figure 2. Comparison of DSML and GPML

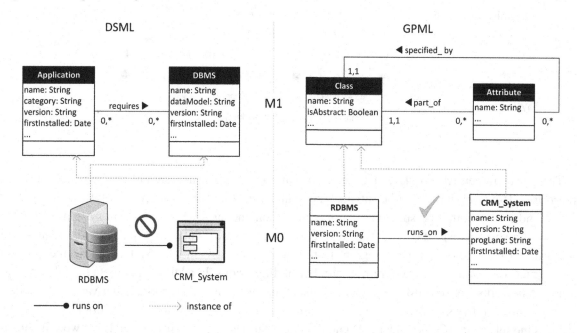

The development of a DSML is more challenging than that of a GPML. It does not only require a comprehensive analysis of the target domain. In addition, it needs to be decided whether a domain concept should be built into the language or rather be specified with the language. This decision relates to a principal conflict of system design, namely the trade-off between range of reuse and productivity of reuse. The more specifically a DSML is tuned to a particular domain, the more it will support the productivity of creating models in this domain. Conversely, the range of reuse of a highly specific DSML is likely to be low, which has a negative impact on economies of scale and, hence, on costs. The experience made with the development of the MEMO languages led to a method for the design of DSMLs, which can be used to guide modifications of existing languages or the construction of additional ones (Frank, 2013).

To provide an overview of the range of modeling areas addressed by MEMO, the remainder of this section is devoted to a structured exposition of four especially relevant MEMO DSMLs. For each language, a summary of its motivation, purpose, and core concepts will be given, and an example diagram will be presented. But it needs to be noted that the MEMO DSMLs allow to construct many more diagram types than are shown below. Also, since all MEMO DSMLs are integrated, a particular diagram is not restricted to models created with one language. Instead, diagrams can represent any combination of models constructed with the available MEMO DSMLs. Some examples of such integrative diagram types will be shown in the section on the MEMO modeling tool later on.

The GoalML

Motivation: A given situation can hardly be evaluated without knowing the relevant goals. Goals are even more important with respect to planning change. However, there is no common understanding of goals. Also, different actors may focus on different goals that are not coherent or even in conflict with each other. Modeling goal systems can be expected to promote more rational decision making and, as a consequence, more effective action.

Purpose: The main purpose of the GoalML (Overbeek, Frank, & Köhling, 2015), (Bock & Frank, 2016) is to enable the design of goal models. A goal model is meant to offer a way to build an elaborate representation of an organizational goal system. A goal system consists of goals and relationships between them. Goal models are used to guide the assessment of the current state of an enterprise and to develop an orientation for change.

Core Concepts: The GoalML is probably the most comprehensive language for modeling organizational goal systems. It offers a multitude of elaborate concepts to describe different kinds of goals and relationships between them. Core concepts comprise engagement and symbolic goals. An engagement goal aims at a result that is directly quantifiable. This means that for an engagement goal, it can be clearly decided whether an intended result was achieved or not. An example of an engagement goal would be 'Increase revenues by 10%'. In contrast, a symbolic goal resists against a straightforward quantification. An example of a symbolic goal may be, 'Create an excellent user experience'. A goal can be further specified, for example, with respect to its content (e.g. 'revenues in region A') and its temporal properties (e.g., the point in time until which it should be achieved, or the period in which it is valid). Each goal can be assigned a priority. There are various types of relationships between goals. A final relation between two goals G1 and G2 expresses that G1 was defined only to serve as a measure for achieving G2. Further relationship types permit to represent goal conflicts or the impact one goal has on another.

Example diagram: The concrete syntax of the language in illustrated in the diagram in Figure 3, depicting the goal model of a department store.

The OrgML

The organization modeling language MEMO OrgML consists of two parts. One part serves to represent static organization structures; the other serves to represent dynamic aspects, that is, business processes.

Motivation: To understand a company's action system, it is of pivotal relevance to develop models of its business processes and its organization structure.

Figure 3. MEMO GoalML: Example diagram

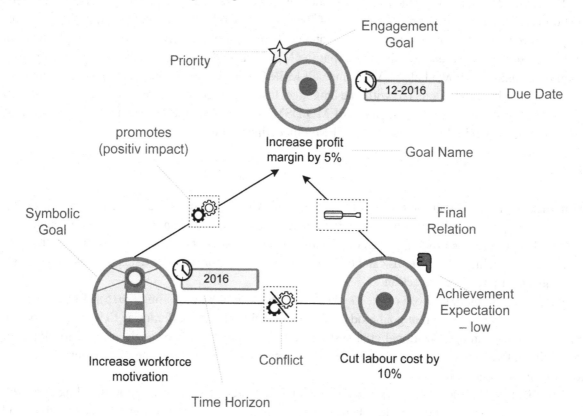

Purpose: The OrgML allows to model business processes and the organization structure of a firm and to integrate the resultant models. For example, a business process model may refer to elements of a corresponding organizational chart, such as the units executing a certain task. Thus, the language supports the analysis and design of a company's action system.

Core Concepts: To model organization structures, the language offers core concepts such as organizational unit, position, role, and various relationship types, such as aggregation and authority. Process modeling is supported with the core concepts activity and event, of which different more specific variants are offered, e.g., automated and partially automated activities, and machine detectable events and incoming phone call events. Furthermore, the OrgML includes various concepts to define the control flow of a process.

Example Diagram: The diagrams in Figure 4 and in Figure 5 illustrate the notation of the OrgML to describe organization structures and business processes. They also illustrate how a business process diagram can be integrated with a corresponding model of an organization structure by incorporating references to organizational units (shown in the text labels above the activities).

Figure 4. MEMO OrgML: Example diagram visualizing an organizational structure

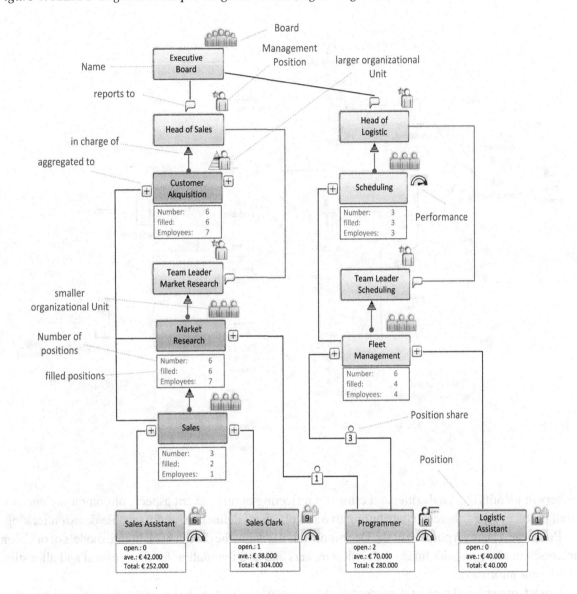

The DecisionML

Motivation: Decision making represents a pivotal aspect of a company's action system. In contrast to business processes, decision processes will usually not follow a certain schema. Instead, their structure depends on individual preferences, the relevant context, and the results obtained during problem analysis. But although decision processes cannot be structured rigidly ex ante, it is preferable for companies to follow a reflective and organized approach in making decisions. The Decision ML (Bock, 2015), (Bock, 2013) is based on the assumption that prototypical models of decision scenarios can support decision

Figure 5. MEMO OrgML: Business process model with references to organization structure

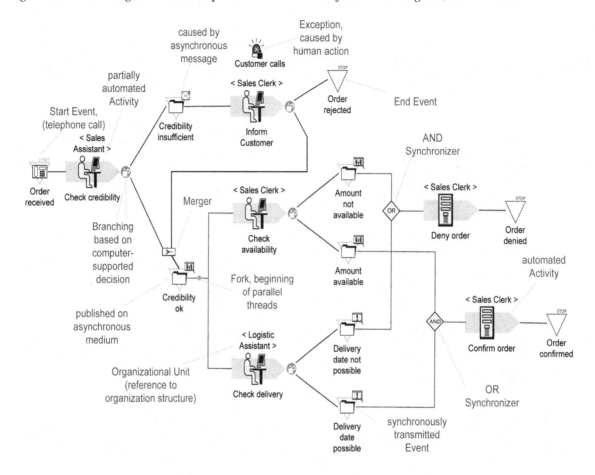

makers in identifying, analyzing, and critically reflecting upon relevant aspects of commonly encountered problem types, thereby contributing to more efficient, deliberate, and traceable decision making.

Purpose: The main purpose of the DecisionML is to enable the design of elaborate models of decision processes to serve as guidelines for decision makers and as a foundation for the retrieval and allocation of relevant information.

Core Concepts: The pivotal concept of the language is the decision process type. It can be further characterized by adding a specific focus like analysis, problem solving, search, evaluation or choice, or by specifying the required support (i.e., 'information need' or 'analysis need'). In addition, a decision process type can be associated with the stimulus by which it is triggered, as well as with action variables, environmental factors, and situational aspects.

Example Diagram: The diagram in Figure 6 illustrates how concepts of the Decision ML can be associated with concepts of other MEMO language, in this case the Goal ML.

Figure 6. MEMO Decision ML: Example of a decision process diagram, integrated with elements from a goal model

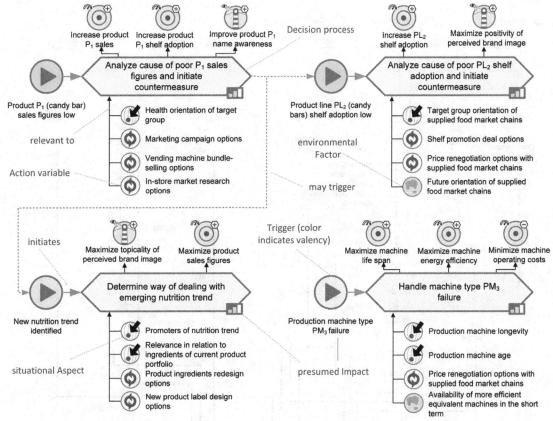

The ITML

Motivation: In many companies, IT infrastructures are the backbone of the operations. IT infrastructures are of remarkable complexity and hard to capture, because they largely consist of immaterial artefacts. At the same time, the ability to analyze, assess, and re-design its IT infrastructure is crucial for a company to survive in a changing environment.

Purpose: The ITML (Kirchner, 2005) serves the creation of models of IT infrastructures to enable various kinds of analysis, e.g., an analysis of integration or reuse potentials, and to support the systematic integration of IT and the business.

Core Concepts: The ITML includes concepts to represent various kinds of platforms and software systems, e.g., application system, middleware, and DBMS. In addition, it includes concepts to model networks and services, as well as various kinds of relationships between software. The concept of a data topic serves to analyze the integration level of an IT infrastructure. The example model in Figure 7 illustrates the use of that concept: associating an application system with a data topic indicates that the application system stores data of that kind (e.g., customer data). If two application systems share the same data topic, especially in write/access mode, this might indicate the need for integrating their data.

Figure 7. MEMO ITML: Example of an IT infrastructure diagram

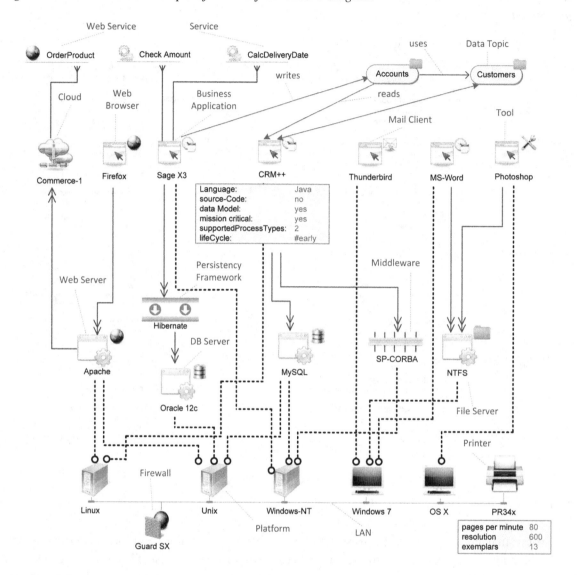

Example Diagram: The example diagram in Figure 7 shows an excerpt of an IT infrastructure model. The depicted concepts can be specified in more detail, as is demonstrated by two examples. Services can be introduced to add a further abstraction layer. In this case, business or decision processes can be linked to services rather than directly to software systems, providing a more abstract way to analyze the match between software functionalities and business needs

As noted earlier, MEMO enables to create many more diagram types than have been shown above. In particular, it is possible to create many further diagram types that integrate concepts from two or more MEMO languages. Examples of such integrative diagram types include 'IT-Business Process' diagrams, which integrate models of the IT infrastructure with models of business processes, and 'Goal Responsibilities' diagrams, which associate goal models with models of the organization structure.

Language Architecture and Semantics

The abstract syntax and semantics of the DSMLs of MEMO are specified with meta models. Two measures were taken to facilitate model integration. First, all DSMLs are specified with the same meta modeling language, the MEMO MML (Frank, 2011). Second, the meta models share common concepts. The resulting language architecture allows to successively add further DSMLs over time and to consistently integrate them with the existing languages. The meta models provide a straightforward foundation for the design of modeling tools, since they can be mapped to object models for the implementation of model editors. The MEMO language architecture is shown in Figure 8.

Figure 8. Illustration of MEMO language architecture

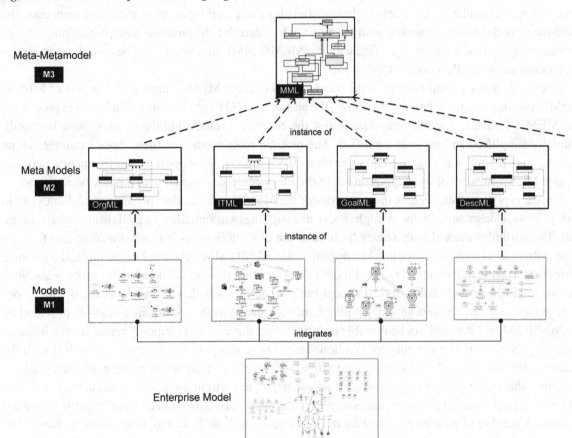

The DSMLs provided by MEMO support the analysis of models and promote their integrity. All languages were designed with the objective to enable the construction of elaborate and differentiated models of the target domains. This decision is based on the assumption that the analysis of a complex subject will usually require an appropriately sophisticated technical language. As a consequence, the meta models used to specify the abstract syntax and semantics of the DSMLs are so extensive that they cannot be reproduced in their entirety in this chapter. Nonetheless, to give an impression of how the meta models are defined and used, we will first present the relatively small meta-meta model that defines the MEMO MML. Subsequently, excerpts of selected meta models will be shown to illustrate how the DSMLs support the analysis of models and protect their integrity.

The concepts defined in the meta-meta model in Figure 9 largely correspond to those used in similar meta-meta models, e.g. the EMOF (OMG 2006). However, the MEMO MML also features several concepts not available in most other meta modelling languages. For example, the meta attributes derivable and derivableExtern serve to express that attribute values can be derived from other parts of the model or from external sources. Another, more significant example is the meta attribute isIntrinsic. This meta attribute allows to overcome a serious limitation of many traditional meta modelling languages. This limitation is that the concepts defined with these languages must invariably be instantiated on the type level M_1. In contrast, MEMO MML allows to mark concepts, attributes, and associations as intrinsic. In this case, the elements are to be instantiated not on the type level M_1, but on the instance level M_0 only. We will consider some examples below. Besides these and other meta modeling concepts, the meta-meta model is supplemented with various OCL constraints to promote meta model integrity. In the same way, the meta models specified with the MEMO MML themselves can be complemented with OCL constraints (see the concept Constraint).

Figure 10 shows a small excerpt of the meta models of three MEMO languages: the part of MEMO OrgML focusing on organizational structures, the part of MEMO OrgML focusing on business processes, and MEMO GoalML. For illustration purposes, the concepts presented in the excerpts have been substantially simplified and partially modified. The original meta models of these three languages alone include more than 90 meta entities and more than 80 constraints. To support a clear distinction between M_1 and M_2, the headers of meta types on M_2 in the meta model are shown with a black background.

The excerpt demonstrates how the semantics of the MEMO meta models promote model integrity in various ways. Constraint C53, for example, prevents assigning two contradicting goals to an organizational unit. The attributes marked with a black 'i', in turn, are those defined as intrinsic, meaning that they are to be instantiated on M_0 only (see the description of the MEMO MML above). For example, the intrinsic attribute startTime of the meta type AnyProcess describes the start time of a particular process instance, and the intrinsic attribute filled of the concept Position defines whether a position is filled with a concrete person at a certain point in time. Without such a concept as that of intrinsic features provided by the MEMO MML, it would not be possible to express that these model elements pertain to the instance level only. Next, consider the concept PositionShare. This concept offers an approach to deal with the challenge that often it will not be an option to model all positions in an organization explicitly. It allows assigning shares of a position type, that is, of its extension, to particular organizational units. Constraint C11 prevents the sum of position shares of a certain position type from becoming larger than the accumulated number of positions defined for the organizational units linked to those position shares. The definition of a feature as "obtainable" (notated by a white 'o') is achieved by setting the meta-attribute derivableExtern to true.

The MEMO meta models also enable many forms of model analysis and retrieval. Various metrics can be computed from a model, e.g., the average span of control of an organization structure, the average number of position types assigned to a process type, or the average labor costs per execution of business processes of a certain type. Also, it is possible to detect inconsistencies, like competing or contradicting goals. Furthermore, models enable the analysis of correlations, e.g., between the qualification specified for a certain position and the performance or costs of business processes managed by this position.

Figure 9. Meta-Meta Model that serves the specification of the MEMO MML

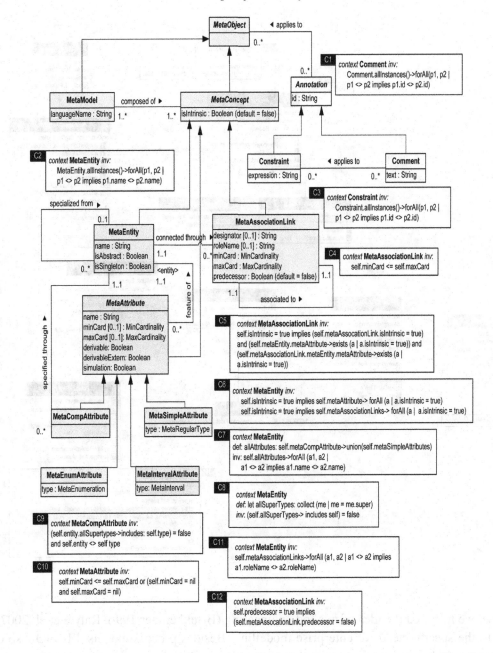

Method Construction

The professional design and use of an enterprise model requires a modelling method. A modelling method includes one or more modelling languages and a corresponding process model. Since enterprise models can be used for a wide range of projects, a limited number of modelling methods would not suffice to inform the use of MEMO in each of these cases. Therefore, MEMO does not only include a repository of pre-defined modelling methods, but also a DSML to define customized modelling methods. For

Figure 10. Excerpt of integrated meta models

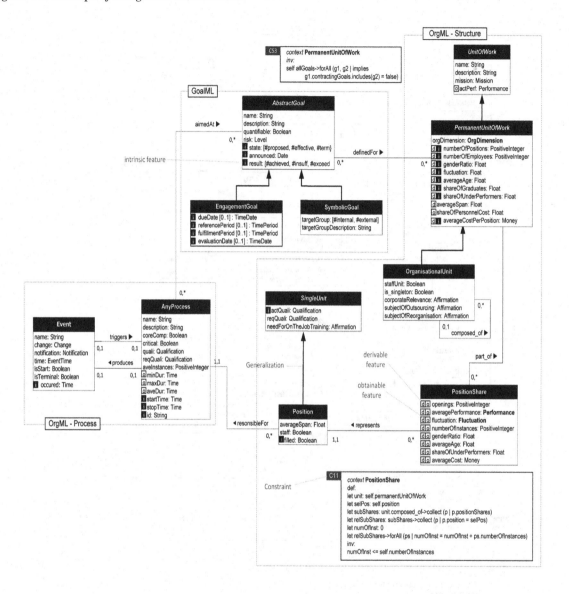

this purpose, we followed the idea of method engineering (Brinkkemper 1996, Ralyté et al. 2007) and adapted it to the specific needs of enterprise modelling. Besides process models, MEMO also offers domain-specific guidelines to support the proper use of its languages.

Configuration of Process Models

MEMO offers a meta model that can be instantiated into models to represent process types to guide the application of MEMO, as well as the relationships of these process types to the various MEMO DSMLs (see Figure 11). Hence, the meta model can be instantiated into (predefined or customized) MEMO modeling methods. When defining such a method, the meta type ModelingLanguage is instantiated into the representation of a particular MEMO DSML.

Figure 11. Meta model for the configuration of process models

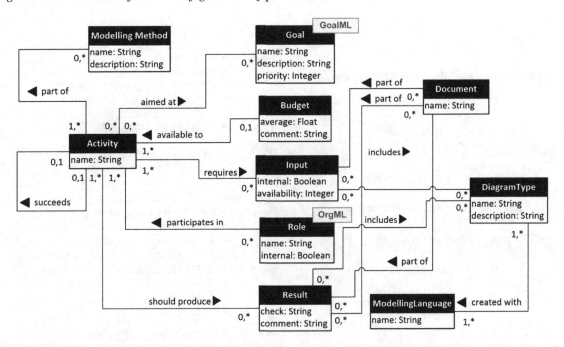

Just as the meta models of the various MEMO DSMLs considered above, this meta model for method construction, too, is specified with the MEMO MML. The meta model also includes concepts defined in other MEMO DSMLs. For example, the concept Role is originally specified in the MEMO OrgML. Here, this concept is reused to describe the roles involved in the application of a MEMO method. In a similar way, goals can be defined using the MEMO GoalML. Figure 12 illustrates the presentation of a method instantiated from the meta model. The links refer to diagram types and corresponding MEMO DSMLs.

Guidelines for the Construction of Models

Language specifications define the syntax and semantics of the DSMLs. Since a DSML includes domain-specific semantics, it provides more support for the construction of models than a GPML (see the previous section). Nevertheless, the application of a modeling language requires to make numerous non-trivial design decisions. To support users in making these decisions, MEMO offers an extensible repository of guidelines for its DSMLs. The following examples illustrate the support provided by these generic guidelines.

GoalML

- **Feasibility:** A goal should not be defined if it is obvious that it cannot be achieved.
- **Abstraction:** Especially strategic goals should be defined at a high level of abstraction in order to increase the range of options to accomplish them.
- **Sense Making:** Goals that demand for deviating from accustomed patterns of action should be supplemented with a rationale or a convincing story to ensure that they are perceived as meaningful.

Figure 12. Representation of a customized method

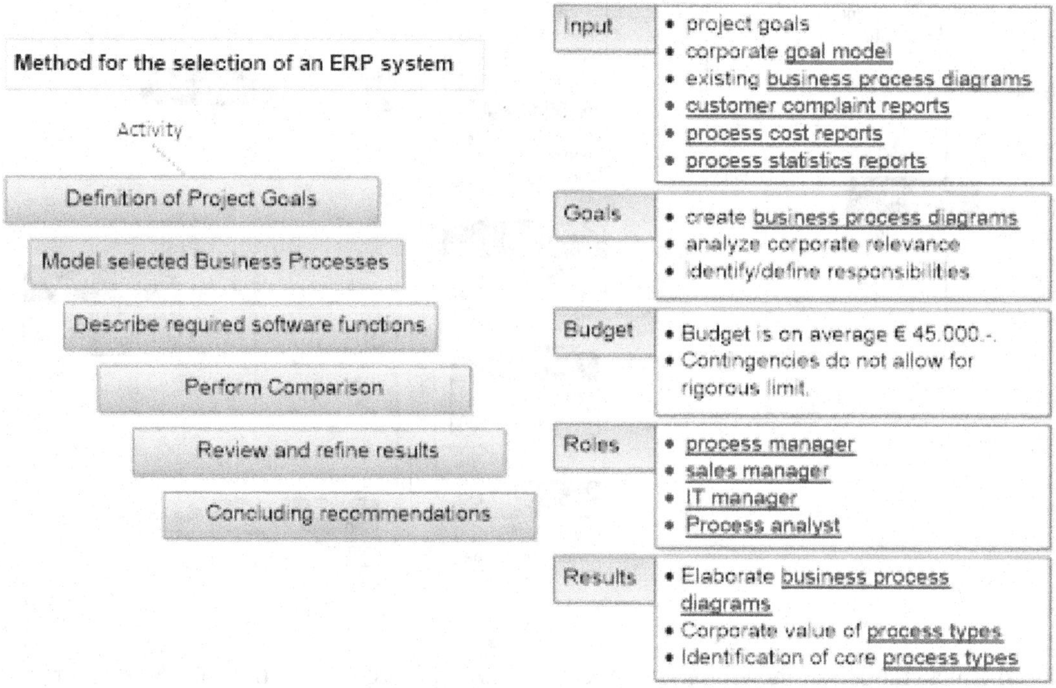

OrgML

- **Structure Follows Function:** Before designing the organization structure, one should focus on the functions an enterprise needs to fulfil. That will result in designing business and decision processes which form the foundation for developing an organization structure.
- **Contingency and Specialization:** The more contingent the environment in which a company operates is, the more problematic are highly specialized positions.
- **Automation and simplification:** The simplification of existing business processes is an established approach to prepare for. That, however, requires analyzing the possible tradeoff between the reduction of cost and service quality.
- **Unified Exception Handling:** Exceptions are a good option in those cases where certain events occur only very rarely. To promote reuse, exception handling should be standardized across the business process types of a company.

DecisionML

- **Balance Between Guidance and Creativity:** Models of decision processes should help approach organizational problems in a structured and deliberate fashion. They should not, however, dictate strict schemas that suppress open reflection and creativity. To pay heed to this trade-off, decision process models should be reviewed regularly as to whether their abstraction level is adequate. Especially for decisions that target a contingent subject, decision processes should not include too restrictive regulations.

- **Economics:** When defining decision process models, modelers should take into account the trade-off between effort and utility of an extended decision process. This means that the goals referenced by decision process models should give an indication of when a decision process can be terminated because it will lead to a sufficiently grounded decision.

ITML

- **Type or Instance:** The artefacts that form an IT infrastructure can usually be modelled on an instance or a type level. In cases with multiple instances such as PCs, it will usually promote the readability of a model to focus on types. In other situations, there might be the need to account for particular instances, too. In those cases where both type and instance level information is needed, a workaround can be applied. For example, a type whose instances serve to represent particular exemplars (such as PCs) could be associated via an 'instantiation' association with a corresponding 'meta' type whose instances represent types (see also the discussion in the conclusions).
- **Support for Analysis:** The model of an IT infrastructure serves to represent widely immaterial artefacts in order to make them amenable to study. However, that should not be the only purpose. Instead, many concepts provided by the ITML (such as data topics) also provide the ground for various kinds of more advanced analysis (such as IT integration potential analysis). Applying these concepts makes models of the IT infrastructure a versatile tool for IT management.

USE CASE

The following use case illustrates the application of MEMO. Its presentation is restricted to the most important aspects sufficient to give an idea of advanced enterprise modeling with MEMO.

'CycleMart' is a bicycle retailer that runs ten stores in four cities. The company offers bicycles in four categories: city bikes, racing bikes, mountain bike, and custom bikes. In addition, it offers repair services. During the last four years, there was only a marginal increase in revenues, while profits have considerably decreased to an alarming level. In this situation, the company's management decides to establish a project to develop options for re-arranging the business so that sustainable profits can be generated in the future. As a first step, a high level process model is designed (see Figure 13). The process model describes a general route for re-arranging a business, and it could be refined at a later stage.

The high-level assessment of the current situation mainly uses data from accounting and available market analyses. It results in the finding that the current business model is not suited to cope with the challenges of the future, such as increasing price competition and, simultaneously, increasing demands for customized products. To develop a first draft of a new corporate strategy, the corresponding MEMO meta model is used to create a high level framework (see Figure 14). Its emphasis is on the design and analysis of business models. For this purpose, it incorporates factors proposed by the Business Model Canvas (Osterwalder & Pigneur, 2010). Three further dimensions allow analyzing a business model from different perspectives. Each one of the topics assigned to a specific focus can be described in more detail using additional documents. The analysis can be performed for different years in order to outline possible paths of strategy implementation.

Figure 13. Initial process model and corresponding conceptual models and data

Method for Re-Arranging a Business

- data from accounting
- data from market analysis

Assessment of Current Situation

Outline future Strategy — customized framework

Design Goal Model — goal model

Outline future Products and Services — customized framework

Design Core Business Processes — business process models

Analyze IT Infrastructure
- IT infrastructure models
- business process models

(Re-) Design IT Infrastruture
- IT infrastructure models
- business process models

Outline Realisation Plan
- essential realization phases
- investment plan

Figure 14. Customized framework with focus on strategic aspects

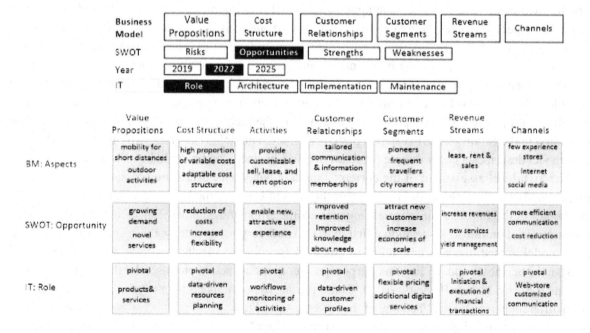

The management decides for a radical change. Cost reduction is to be achieved through automation. More and more, the traditional model of selling bicycles in a store is to be replaced by a powerful online store. Different from the current model, emphasis is placed not so much on selling bicycles anymore, but on providing customizable solutions for mobility and recreation needs. This includes various models of renting and leasing bicycles, the customization of bicycles, and additional services to improve customer experience. The design of a preliminary goal model (see Figure 15) serves to analyze the implementation of a particular business model. The example illustrates that goal models will usually become rather extensive. Although the model already contains a sizable number of goals, it is nowhere near exhaustive, missing, e.g., goals related to specific aspects of procurement, or the flexibility and quality of decision making. Furthermore, each element of a goal model can be described in more detail, which is done for the topmost goal in the example only.

The goal model provides a foundation for assessing investments, risks, and capital needs. Since it is obvious that the future strategy requires a modernized or new IT infrastructure, there is a need to develop an idea of core functions that have to be offered by the future IT infrastructure. To this end, the project team designs models of future business processes. Since it is too early to specify particular software systems required to run these processes, the models focus on a more abstract representation, that is, on services, which could later be linked to existing or new software systems. In addition, the process models are used to design patterns of the future organization structure. The diagram in Figure 16 shows an excerpt of a model that describes a customer order process. It also indicates how a business process model is integrated with other models. Links to services enable the integration of the business process model with a model of the IT infrastructure. The organizational units that are assigned to each activity in the process model serve as links to corresponding elements in a related model of the organization structure. Links to models of decision processes (top right in the figure) are useful at this stage to support planning for the required human resources.

The level of detail of models as well as the number of models designed at this time depends on the decisions to be supported. For purposes of analyzing investments into IT, it will often prove useful to create a high level model of the current IT infrastructure to assess its potential to realize future IT services. If it is required to obtain a more exact picture of the future IT strategy, a model of a revised IT infrastructure could be developed.

In summary, with its capacity to support the configuration of custom process models combined with its several detailed modeling languages, MEMO offers a basis to support all phases of different sorts of business and IT projects, including a complete redesign of the corporate strategy.

MEMO4ADO: AN INTEGRATED, EXTENSIBLE TOOL FOR ENTERPRISE MODELING

The practice of constructing, analyzing, and maintaining enterprise models requires modeling tools. The modeling tool MEMO4ADO implements large portions of MEMO, enabling to generate fully integrated enterprise models in a single environment. MEMO4ADO provides an implementation of six MEMO DSMLs, alongside a number of auxiliary languages and features, making it the most comprehensive enterprise modeling tool currently available. The tool has been in active use in our teaching since 2015,

Figure 15. Representation of preliminary goal model

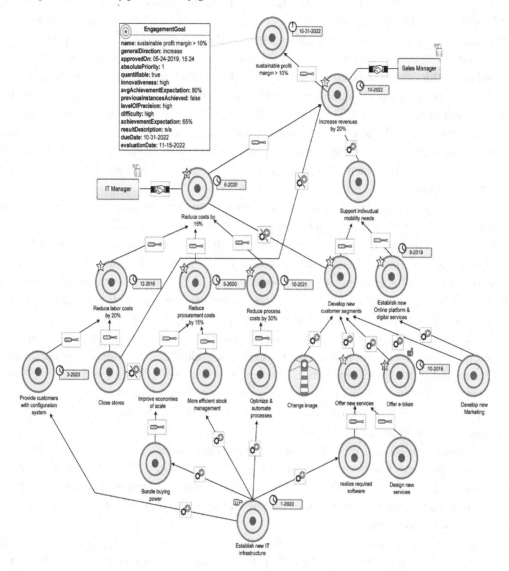

yet its capabilities reach far beyond teaching purposes, supporting a wide scope of multi-perspective enterprise design and analysis activities. The tool is freely available at https://austria.omilab.org/psm/content/memo4ado.

This section provides an overview of MEMO4ADO and its features. Attention will first be directed at the architecture of the tool. Following this, it will be shown how different MEMO modeling languages are incorporated in the tool, and some of the advanced features of the tool will be summarized. The section will close with the presentation of some basic guidelines concerning the use of the tool.

Figure 16. Excerpt of business process model integrated with other models

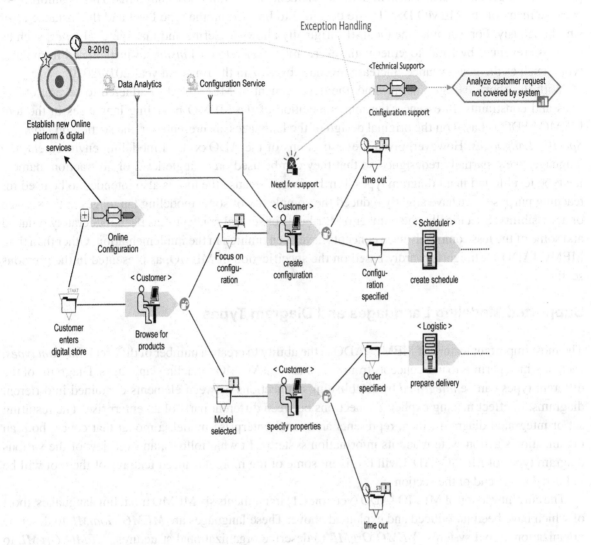

Architecture

MEMO4ADO is based on the meta modeling platform ADOxx (Fill & Karagiannis, 2013). ADOxx provides the capacity to develop modeling tools for user-supplied modeling languages. To implement a modeling language with ADOxx, the meta model of the language needs to be defined using the environment's meta modeling language called 'ADOxx MetaModel' (Fill & Karagiannis, 2013). Further, the notation of a language can be defined using static images and dynamic rules, and additional functionalities can be programmed using the proprietary script language 'ADOscript' (Fill & Karagiannis, 2013). On this basis, ADOxx permits to generate stable stand-alone modeling tools for the defined language, such as MEMO4ADO. Regrettably, the meta modeling environment of ADOxx is somewhat limited compared to the original meta modeling paradigm of the MEMO language architecture (Frank, 2011). The model editors generated by ADOxx are restricted to creating diagrams on the type level only, providing no possibility to generate further instances of the elements defined in these diagrams. This is unfortunate because many of the MEMO DSMLs are designed to be used on the type level and the instance level simultaneously. For example, the GoalML originally allows to define and manage goal *types*, such as 'Increase revenues by 10%', together with several more concrete goal *instances* instantiated from these types, such as the goal instance 'Increase revenues by 10% in the financial year 2019/2020'.

With the above background in mind, the development of MEMO4ADO adhered to several objectives and constraints. In essence, the implementation of the MEMO modeling languages in the tool MEMO4ADO is based on the original design of the languages, as presented in the section on *Domain-Specific Languages*. However, given the restrictions of the ADOxx meta modeling environment, the languages were partially redesigned so that they can be used on a single level of abstraction, namely the type level found in all diagram types. Furthermore, because the tool is also intended to be used for teaching purposes, we have slightly reduced the complexity of some modeling languages in the service of accessibility. Specifically, the number of attributes of several concepts has been moderately reduced and some of the less commonly used concepts have been omitted in the implementation. Other than that, MEMO4ADO is straightforwardly based on the specification of MEMO, as presented in the previous sections.

Supported Modeling Languages and Diagram Types

The most important feature of MEMO4ADO is the ability to create a number of different *diagram types*, each of which permits to use concepts from one or several MEMO modeling languages. Diagrams of the different types can be *integrated* by establishing connections between elements contained in different diagrams, in effect making explicit connections between different parts of an enterprise. The resulting set of integrated diagrams, then, represents an overall enterprise model, a model that covers both an organization's action system and its information systems. In what follows, an overview of the various diagram types of MEMO4ADO will be given; some of the more advanced features of the tool will be indicated at the end of the section.

The current version of MEMO4ADO (version 1.1) implements six MEMO modeling languages, most of which have been introduced and explained above. These languages are *MEMO GoalML* to describe organizational goal systems, *MEMO OrgML* to describe organizational structures, *MEMO OrgML* to describe business processes, *MEMO DecisionML* to describe organizational decision processes, *MEMO MetricML* to describe performance indicator systems, and *MEMO ITML* to describe IT infrastructures. Each of these languages can be used in one or several diagram types. Figure 17 shows an overview of the most important diagram types available in MEMO4ADO as well as some examples of integrative associations between them.

The following three features characterize the diagram types available in MEMO4ADO. First, for each incorporated MEMO language, there is a *core diagram type*, in which only or mostly concepts of a single language can be used. The most basic diagram type is the *Framework Diagram* (top left in the figure). This diagram type allows generating an instance of the basic MEMO framework, offering an entry point to explore the overall enterprise model (see the section *MEMO: Core Components*). Other examples of core diagram types are the *Goal System Diagram* (top middle in the figure) and the *IT Infrastructure Diagram* (bottom middle in the figure). In these diagram types, a modeler can focus solely on one area of an enterprise, such as its goal system or its corporate IT infrastructure, and describe this area in detail using the concepts from the relevant MEMO language, such as the GoalML or the ITML.

Figure 17. Overview MEMO4ADO diagram types and examples of integrative associations

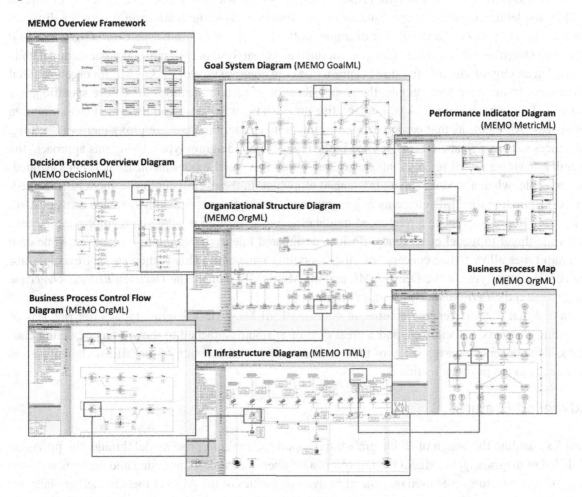

Second, an important feature of MEMO diagram types is that they can contain *references* to other diagrams. These references correspond to the integrative associations between common concepts of different MEMO languages, as explained in the section on *Language Architecture*. In the modeling environment, this means that diagram elements can hold links to model elements defined in other diagrams, or even other diagrams as a whole. Cross-diagram links can be defined simply by setting the values of special reference attributes of several modeling concepts. For example, the concept 'SubProcess' available in the *Business Process Control Flow Diagram* (bottom left in the figure) has the attribute 'Executing Unit or Software System'. When setting a value for this attribute, the tool allows to select appropriate elements from other existing diagrams, such as Organizational Structure Diagrams and IT Infrastructure Diagrams (center and bottom in the figure). As a result, the cross-diagram link will be recorded and, when studying or analyzing the diagram, it is possible to directly follow the reference to the target diagram by clicking on the reference attribute. The cross-diagram references of the MEMO4ADO diagram types are of immense significance because it is through them that the various diagrams become integrated and can thus be considered to form *one cohesive overall* enterprise model.

Third, there are *integrative diagram types*. These diagram types allow using the concepts of several MEMO modeling languages at once, making it possible to analyze the *relationships* between different domains of an enterprise in detail. For example, in the integrative diagram type *Goal–Organizational Structure Diagram* it is possible to link goals defined in a Goal System Diagram and organizational units defined in an Organizational Structure Diagram (the core diagram type of the OrgML for organizational structures). In this way, for example, the responsibilities of certain positions to achieve specific goals can be defined and examined. Again, integrative diagram types are based on the use of cross-diagram references. All elements that can be defined in integrative diagram types are proxy elements holding references to the original elements defined in the relevant core diagram types. Using this approach, the overall enterprise model remains integrated, and redundancy and model inconsistencies are avoided. For example, when a model element referenced elsewhere in the overall enterprise model is renamed, the corresponding surrogate elements in integrative diagrams are automatically renamed as well. Also, if the user attempts to delete a referenced model element, a warning will be given, informing the user about the threat to model consistency. Besides designated integrative diagram types, even some core diagram types allow to use concepts of other modeling languages. This is the case, for example, for the core diagram types of the DecisionML and the MetricML, namely the *Decision Process Overview Diagram* and the *Performance Indicator Diagram*.

In addition to these general features, of course, all MEMO4ADO diagram types offer rich sets of modeling concepts, associations, and a great deal of attributes attached to the various modeling concepts. The conceptual design of all of these elements follows the design of the MEMO languages, as introduced in the previous sections.

Advanced Features

Besides enabling the design of an integrated, multi-perspective enterprise model through the provision of different diagram types, MEMO4ADO offers a number of advanced modeling and analysis features. Some of these features are based on general analysis capacities of the ADOxx meta modeling platform, while others are specifically implemented in MEMO4ADO. Starting with the latter, MEMO4ADO offers a set of language-specific functionalities. In the modeling tool, these are found in the menu under 'Language-Specific Functionalities'. For example, it is possible to toggle between a 'High Details' view and a 'Low Details' view in Goal System Diagrams. Switching to the low details view can be helpful for modeling beginners or occasional users to avoid being overwhelmed by the many attributes and dynamic notation elements of the language. As another example, it is possible for most languages to display additional text box elements in the diagrams to show key attribute values at a glance. For example, the tool allows to display the implementation languages of application systems in IT Infrastructure Diagrams next to the systems, which may be useful when manually analyzing IT heterogeneity. Aside from language-specific functionalities, MEMO4ADO also incorporates the general model querying capacities offered by the ADOxx meta modeling platform (Fill & Karagiannis, 2013) These functionalities are available in the tool under the rubric 'Analysis'. For example, it is possible to query a large enterprise model for elements with a certain name, for elements with a certain attribute value, or for elements connected to specific elements defined in yet other diagram types. A paradigmatic use case concerns the analysis of IT integration demands. For instance, it is possible to search for all application and database systems that manage data related to a certain topic, helping to detect data redundancies. In sum, MEMO4ADO provides a range of advanced functionalities beyond the capacity to generate enterprise models in the first place.

Use of the Tool

As follows from the great number of perspectives addressed by the MEMO modeling languages, there is not a single way to use MEMO4ADO. Instead, models can be designed, analyzed, and maintained over time dependent on the needs of the enterprise. Still, two general use cases can be distinguished.

Starting from scratch. In case an enterprise does not yet have any enterprise models in place, and no suitable reference models are available, it is necessary to create all the diagrams that make up an overall enterprise models successively. Support for this process is found in the MEMO guidelines for model construction, as discussed in the section on *Method Construction*. It is generally preferable for modelers to begin by creating a *Framework Diagram* and reflect upon what they think are the areas of an enterprise most closely connected to present challenges. Basic estimations of performance can be recorded in the Framework Diagram using the attribute 'Performance' of the different foci. These estimations are visualized in the form of a traffic light metaphor. Following this, the most pressing problem areas may be modeled in sequence. In our experience, it is usually worthwhile to start with the more general modeling languages, namely the GoalML, the OrgML, and the ITML, and add diagrams concerning decision processes and business performance indicators when a closer analysis of strategic aspects is required.

Using a model repository. In an alternative case, a company can rely on existing models provided in a model repository pertinent to the present situation. In the best case, established reference models for the given industry are available. The main challenges here consist in adapting the predefined models so that they match the situation in enterprise, and in reflecting upon ways to still differentiate the strategic orientation of the firm from competitors. Often, it will be instructive to study existing enterprise models even in case only a few segments will be adopted for the own company, because the design of an enterprise model is a major project in its own right. An extensive MEMO example model, describing a case study from the beverages industry, is provided on the MEMO4ADO homepage under 'Tutorials'.

CONCLUSION AND FUTURE WORK

MEMO provides extensive support for developing comprehensive enterprise models. It has been used for several years in courses on enterprise models and in various industry projects. The corresponding modeling environment, MEMO4ADO covers most of the method's functionality, and it is still in active development.

It is fair to assess that the use of MEMO is not trivial. Above all, this is due to the complexity of the subject. The action systems and information systems of contemporary organizations are complex, ambiguous, and entangled systems permitting of no simplistic account. Second, it needs to be conceded that the MEMO languages are rather complex. But it is not required to make use of all concepts offered by a language in each and every case. Instead, a MEMO language can be reduced to a 'light version' that offers only essential concepts, reducing the required training costs. Furthermore, it is not always mandatory to model an entire enterprise, or to model it at a high level of detail. Instead, range and depth of a modeling project can be adapted to the purpose and the available budget. That said, the economics of enterprise modeling remains a critical issue. On the one hand, development costs are hard to judge in advance, and often high. On the other hand, the return on investment is also hard to calculate. But unless one is willing to abandon the aim of analyzing and (re-)organizing an enterprise and its information systems altogether, there is no other option than to use models. Wide parts of an enterprise, especially of its action system and its information system, are immaterial in nature. They cannot be perceived directly. Instead, it is mandatory to develop some kind of conceptual model of the present und possible future states of an enterprise. This insight is, of course, not new: "But besides intuition there is no other kind of cognition than through concepts. Thus the cognition of every, at least human, understanding is a cognition, not intuitive but discursive." (Kant, 1998, B93, A 68). Every manager, every employee depends on some kind of conceptual or mental model of the environment in which he or she operates. It seems plausible to assume that thoroughly designed DSMLs can contribute to the rationality of such inevitable model building. In addition, they enable the use of analysis and design tools that could not be deployed otherwise. It remains, however, a question for future research what level of detail and formalization of enterprise models is adequate under what circumstances.

Apart from the economic assessment of enterprise modeling, there is a further issue that deserves attention. During our long work on enterprise modeling, we realized that there are fundamental limitations in the dominant language paradigm as manifested, for example, in the MOF architecture. These limitations concern the design of DSMLs, the expressiveness of models, and the use of models during runtime. In the dominant paradigm, the specification of a DSML always starts from scratch by using a general-purpose meta language. That is dissatisfactory for two reasons. First, starting from scratch with generic concepts such as Class or Attribute is cumbersome and a threat to the quality of a DSML, because it allows for specifying almost any kind of absurd concepts. Second, it gives rise to the conflict between model productivity and range of reuse already mentioned above. A model should express the conceptualization intended by a modeler. In particular, it should allow for representing the modeler's knowledge about a domain at the highest possible level of abstraction to foster reuse and integrity. However, there are many cases where the traditional paradigm does not allow for that. If, for example, we know that a sales price is defined for all instances of a certain product model, it would be useful to be able to define this value for the class that represents the model. Since classes are not objects in the current paradigm, however, this would not be possible – leading to avoidable complexity of models and systems. The last version of the MEMO meta modeling language (Frank, 2011) relaxes this problem to a certain degree by allowing to mark properties as 'intrinsic', which means that they are not to be instantiated into immediate instances, but only into instances of instances. Unfortunately, the implementation of this feature with mainstream object-oriented programming languages is not possible without unsatisfactory workarounds. Finally, the transformation of models into code suffers from the notorious problem of synchronizing models and code. Therefore, using and modifying models at runtime and in consistency with the represented software is a serious challenge.

To cope with these challenges, our current research is focused on multi-level language architectures that allow for an arbitrary number of classification levels (Atkinson & Kühne, 2008), (Neumayr, Schrefl, & Thalheim, 2011), (Frank, 2014). These architectures allow for multi-level language hierarchies and the reuse of higher level DSMLs for the definition of more specific languages. Furthermore, the meta language we use, the FMML^x (Frank, 2014), (Frank, 2018), and the related development environment, the Xmodeler (Clark, Sammut, & Willans, 2008), afford a common representation of models and code. This enables an attractive perspective for future enterprise systems. Enterprise systems could integrate their code with a conceptual model of themselves and a conceptual model of their surroundings. In other words, an enterprise system of this kind would integrate enterprise software with a corresponding enterprise model. The architecture of such a self-referential enterprise system can be expected to contribute significantly to a company's agility and user empowerment, since it allows to explore a complex software system by navigating through its model and the model of its environment. At the same time, software can be adapted to changing requirements directly by changing the underlying conceptual (enterprise) model. Our future research aims at developing a multi-level enterprise modeling environment and a prototypical self-referential enterprise system. We currently work on a new version of the FMML^x, and we investigate the specification and implementation of complex change operations in multi-level models.

REFERENCES

Aier, S., Kurpjuweit, S., Saat, J., & Winter, R. (2009). Enterprise Architecture Design As An Engineering Discipline. *Ais Transactions On Enterprise Systems*, *1*(1), 36–43.

Atkinson, C., & Kühne, T. (2008). Reducing Accidental Complexity In Domain Models. *Software & Systems Modeling*, *7*(3), 345–359. doi:10.100710270-007-0061-0

Bock, A. (2013). *A Conceptual Modeling Method For Managing Decision Processes In Enterprises* (Master Thesis). University Of Duisburg-Essen.

Bock, A. (2015). Beyond Narrow Decision Models: Toward Integrative Models Of Organizational Decision Processes. In D. Aveiro, U. Frank, K. J. Lin, & J. Tribolet (Eds.), *Proceedings Of The 17th IEEE Conference On Business Informatics (Cbi 2015)*. Lisbon: IEEE.

Bock, A., & Frank, U. (2016). Memo Goalml: A Context-Enriched Modeling Language To Support Reflective Organizational Goal Planning And Decision Processes. In I. Comyn-Wattiau, K. Tanaka, I.-Y. Song, S. Yamamoto, & M. Saeki (Eds.), *Conceptual Modeling: 35th International Conference, Er 2016* (Pp. 515–529). Cham: Springer. 10.1007/978-3-319-46397-1_40

Brinkkemper, S. (1996). Method Engineering: Engineering Of Information Systems Development Methods And Tools. *Information and Software Technology*, *38*(4), 275–280. doi:10.1016/0950-5849(95)01059-9

Clark, T., Sammut, P., & Willans, J. (2008). *Applied Metamodelling: A Foundation For Language Driven Development* (2nd ed.). Ceteva. Retrieved From Http://Www.Eis.Mdx.Ac.Uk/Staffpages/Tonyclark/Papers/Applied%20metamodelling%20%28second%20edition%29.Pdf

Dietz, J., Hoogervorst, J., Albani, A., Aveiro, D., Babkin, E., Barjis, J., ... Winter, R. (2013). The Discipline Of Enterprise Engineering. *International Journal Of Organisational Design And Engineering*, *3*(1), 86–114. doi:10.1504/IJODE.2013.053669

Esprit Consortium Amice. (1989). *Open System Architecture For Cim*. Berlin: Springer.

Ferstl, O. K., & Sinz, E. J. (1998). Modeling Of Business Systems Using The Semantic Object Model (Som): A Methodological Framework. In P. Bernus, K. Mertins, & G. Schmidt (Eds.), International Handbooks On Information Systems: Vol. 1. Handbook On Architectures Of Information Systems (Pp. 339–358). Berlin: Springer.

Fill, H.-G., & Karagiannis, D. (2013). On The Conceptualisation Of Modelling Methods Using The Adoxx Meta Modelling Platform. *Enterprise Modelling and Information Systems Architectures*, *8*(1), 4–25. doi:10.1007/BF03345926

Frank, U. (2011). *The Memo Meta Modelling Language (Mml) And Language Architecture. 2nd Edition* (Icb Research Report No. 43). Retrieved From Icb University Of Duisburg-Essen, Campus Essen Website: Http://Www.Icb.Uni-Due.De/Fileadmin/Icb/Research/Research_Reports/Icb-Report_No43.Pdf

Frank, U. (2013). Domain-Specific Modeling Languages - Requirements Analysis And Design Guidelines. In I. Reinhartz-Berger, A. Sturm, T. Clark, Y. Wand, S. Cohen, & J. Bettin (Eds.), *Domain Engineering: Product Lines, Conceptual Models, And Languages* (pp. 133–157). Springer. doi:10.1007/978-3-642-36654-3_6

Frank, U. (2014). Multilevel Modeling: Toward A New Paradigm Of Conceptual Modeling And Information Systems Design. *Business & Information Systems Engineering*, *6*(6), 319–337. doi:10.100712599-014-0350-4

Frank, U. (2018). *The Flexible Modelling And Execution Language (Fmmlx) Version 2.0: Analysis Of Requirements And Technical Terminology*. ICB Research Report No. 66.

Guyer, P. (Ed.). (1998). Critique Of Pure Reason. Cambridge: Cambridge Univ. Press.

Kant, I. (1998). *Critique Of Pure Reason*. Cambridge: Cambridge Univ. Press. doi:10.1017/CBO9780511804649

Kirchner, L. (2005). Cost Oriented Modelling Of It-Landscapes: Generic Language Concepts Of A Domain Specific Language. In J. Desel & U. Frank (Eds.), *Lecture Notes In Informatics: P-75, Enterprise Modelling And Information Systems Architectures: Proceedings Of The Workshop In Klagenfurt, October 24-25, 2005* (Pp. 166–179). Bonn: Gesellschaft Für Informatik.

Neumayr, B., Schrefl, M., & Thalheim, B. (2011). Modeling Techniques For Multi-Level Abstraction. In R. Kaschek & L. Delcambre (Eds.), Lecture Notes In Computer Science: Vol. 6520. *The Evolution Of Conceptual Modeling* (pp. 68–92). Springer. doi:10.1007/978-3-642-17505-3_4

Object Management Group. (2006). *Meta Object Facility (Mof) Core Specification: Version 2.0*. Author.

Osterwalder, A., & Pigneur, Y. (2010). *Business Model Generation: A Handbook For Visionaries, Game Changers, And Challengers* [1 Sound Disc]. Willowbrook, IL: Audio-Tech Business Book Summaries.

Overbeek, S., Frank, U., & Köhling, C. A. (2015). A Language For Multi-Perspective Goal Modelling: Challenges, Requirements And Solutions. *Computer Standards & Interfaces*, *38*, 1–16. doi:10.1016/j.csi.2014.08.001

Porter, M. E. (2001). The Value Chain And Competitive Advantage. In D. Barnes (Ed.), *Understanding Business Behaviour. Understanding Business: Processes* (pp. 50–66). London: Routledge U.A.

Ralyté, J., Brinkkemper, S., & Henderson-Sellers, B. (2007). Situational Method Engineering: Fundamentals And Experiences. In *Proceedings Of The Ifip Wg 8.1 Working Conference, 12-14 September 2007, Geneva, Switzerland. Ifip - The International Federation For Information Processing* (Vol. 244). New York: Springer.

Sandkuhl, K., Stirna, J., Persson, A., & Wißotzki, M. (2014). Enterprise Modeling: Tackling Business Challenges With The 4em Method. The Enterprise Engineering Series. Berlin: Springer.

Scheer, A.-W. (1992). *Architecture Of Integrated Information Systems: Foundations Of Enterprise Modelling*. Berlin: Springer. doi:10.1007/978-3-642-97389-5

The Open Group. (2009). *The Open Group Architecture Framework (Togaf) - Version 9*. Retrieved From Http://Www.Opengroup.Org/Togaf/

Zachman, J. A. (1987). A Framework For Information Systems Architecture. *IBM Systems Journal*, *26*(3), 276–292. doi:10.1147j.263.0276

Chapter 3
Enterprise Modelling in the Digital Age

Henderik A. Proper
Luxembourg Institute of Science and Technology, Luxembourg

Wided Guedria
Luxembourg Institute of Science and Technology, Luxembourg

Jean-Sebastien Sottet
Luxembourg Institute of Science and Technology, Luxembourg

ABSTRACT

Our society is transitioning from the industrial age to the digital age, thus also revolutionising the enterprise landscape. In addition, one can observe how the notion of economic exchange is shifting from goods-dominant logic to service-dominant logic, putting the focus on continuous value co-creation between providers and consumers. Combined, these trends drive enterprises to transform continuously. During enterprise transformations, coordination among the stakeholders involved is key. Enterprise models are traditionally regarded as an effective way to enable informed coordination. At the same time, the digital age also provides ample challenges and opportunities for enterprise modelling. The objective of this chapter is therefore threefold. The first aim is to reflect on the role of enterprise modelling for coordinated enterprise transformation. The second aim is to explore the challenges posed by digital transformations to enterprise modelling. The third aim is to reflect on how enterprise modelling itself may benefit from the new digital technologies.

INTRODUCTION

Our society is transitioning from the industrial age to the digital age. The development and maturation of "digital technologies", such as mobile computing, pervasive computing, cloud computing, big data, artificial intelligence, robotics, social media, etc., further fuel the digital transformation, which now also revolutionises the enterprise landscape.

DOI: 10.4018/978-1-7998-0108-5.ch003

Where IT originally was a mere supportive tool for administrative purposes, it is safe to say that IT has now become an integral part of an organisation's primary processes, and has quite often become an integral part of the business model. As a result, only considering the *alignment* (Henderson and Venkatraman, 1993) of business and IT no longer suffices. The difference between business and IT is increasingly fading; they have been *fused* into one (Gils and Proper, 2018). Companies such as Amazon, AirBnB, Uber, Netflix, Spotify, N26, etcetera, illustrate how IT and business have indeed become fused. The CEO of a major bank can even be quoted as stating *"We want to be a tech company with a banking license"* (Hamers, 2017).

In addition, marketing sciences (Vargo and Lusch, 2008; Grönroos and Ravald, 2011; Lusch and Nambisan, 2015; Vargo and Lusch, 2016) suggests that the notion of economic exchange, core to the economy, has shifted from following a goods-dominant logic to a service-dominant logic. While the former focuses on tangible resources to produce goods and embeds value in the transactions of goods, the latter puts the focus on the continuous *value co-creation* between providers and consumers by way of resource integration. For instance, in the airline industry, jet turbine manufacturers used to follow a classical goods-dominant logic by selling turbines to airlines. However, since airlines are not interested in *owning* turbines, but rather in the realisation of *airtime*, manufacturers nowadays sell airtime to airlines instead of jet turbines. *Value co-creation* is shaping up as a key design concern for modern day enterprises (Gils and Proper, 2018).

These intertwined, and mutually amplifying, trends drive enterprises to transform continuously. As discussed in (Proper et al., 2018b), *coordination* among the stakeholders involved is key during such transformations. More specifically, a shared understanding, agreement, and commitment, is needed on (1) what the overall strategy of the enterprise is, (2) the current affairs of the enterprise, i.e. the current situation, as well as the relevant history leading up to it, and possible trends towards the future, (3) the current affairs of the context of the enterprise, and (4) what (given the latter) the ideal future affairs of the enterprise are.

Enterprise models, and ultimately enterprise (architecture) modelling languages and associated frameworks, are generally regarded as an effective way to *enable* such (informed) coordination. At the same time, however, the digital age also provides ample challenges, and opportunities, for enterprise modelling.

In line with this, the objective of this chapter is threefold. The first aim, addressed in section 2, is to reflect on the role of enterprise modelling towards the coordination of enterprise transformations in general. With this as a base, we then turn our focus to the transition to the digital age. In line with this, the second aim of this chapter, addressed in section 3, is to explore the challenges, which digital transformations pose to enterprise modelling. The third, aim of this chapter, covered in section 4, is to also reflect on how enterprise modelling itself may benefit from the new digital technologies.

THE ROLE OF ENTERPRISE MODELLING

In discussing the role of enterprise modelling in enterprise transformations in general, and digital transformations in particular, we will start by discussing the concepts of enterprise and model as such. Based on this understanding, we then address the important question of the *purpose* of enterprise modelling. As enterprise models are used in a coordinative context involving many different stakeholders, we will finish this section with a discussion on the collaborative dimension of enterprise modelling.

Enterprises

In defining the concept of enterprise, we start out from the concept of *organisation*. An organisation is a configuration of resources (social, digital and physical) and activities in pursued of a purpose (Magal-hães and Proper, 2017). As such, it is considered to be an invisible construct used to harness and direct the energy of the people who do the work. It exists when people interact with one another to perform essential functions that help to attain goals (Daft, 2007; Kates and Galbraith, 2007). This definition includes commercial businesses, government agencies, etc, but also includes *networks of organisations* (Friedman, 2005; Umar, 2005), such as joint ventures, entire product / service supply chains, etc.

The *purpose* of an organisation and the systematic way it endeavours to achieve this purpose can be regarded as its *enterprise*, in line with the definition provided by the dictionary: "*a systematic purposeful activity*" (Meriam-Webster, 2003). As such, an organisation can engage in multiple enterprises, and can even do so in collaboration with other organisations.

Models

Several scholars within the field of systems modelling (including information modelling, enterprise modelling, software modelling) have provided definitions of the concept of model (Stachowiak, 1973; Rothenberg, 1989; Frank, 1998; Falkenberg et al., 1998; Hoppenbrouwers et al., 2005; Bézivin, 2005; Mahr, 2011; Thalheim, 2011; Bjeković et al., 2013). Most of these definitions are based on the well-known *semiotic triangle* (Ogden and Richards, 1923), as depicted in Figure 1.

Figure 1. The semiotic triangle (Ogden and Richards, 1923)

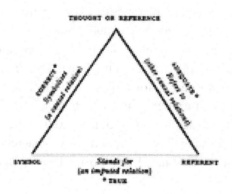

The semiotic triangle expresses how a person attributes meaning (*thought or reference*) to the *combination* of a *symbol* and a *referent*, where the former is some language utterance, and the latter is something that the person can refer to. The *referent* can be anything, e.g. something in the physical world (tree, car, bike, atom, document, picture, etc) or something in the social world (marriage, mortgage, trust, value, etc). Next to that, it can be something in an existing world, or in a desired / imagined world.

The semiotic triangle is often used as a base to theorise about meaning in the context of language (Morris, 1946; Ullmann, 1967; Searle, 1979; Cruse, 2000), and is essentially a continuation of the work by C.S. Peirce (Peirce, 1969). Based on this linguistic background, the semiotic triangle has also been used, directly or indirectly, by several authors to reason about the foundations of (information) systems modelling (Stamper, 1996; Krogstie, 2002; Kecheng et al., 2002; Lankhorst et al., 2017b; Guizzardi, 2006; Thalheim, 2011; Thalheim, 2013; Bjeković et al., 2012).

In line with the semiotic triangle, we define a model as (Bjeković et al., 2012): *"an artefact that is acknowledged by an observer as representing some domain for a particular purpose"*, where '*observer*' refers to the (group of) actor(s) involved in the creation and use of the model, and '*domain*' can be any '*part*' or '*aspect*' of the past / existing / desired / imagined world.

The Purpose(s) of Enterprise Modelling

During any enterprise transformation, *coordination* among the key stakeholders and the projects / activities that drive the transformations is key (Proper et al., 2018b). A shared understanding, agreement, and commitment, is needed on (1) what the overall strategy of the enterprise is, (2) the current affairs of the enterprise, i.e. the current situation, as well as the relevant history leading up to it, and possible trends towards the future, (3) the current affairs of the context of the enterprise, and (4) what (given the latter) the ideal future affairs of the enterprise are.

Models, and ultimately enterprise modelling languages, are generally considered as an effective way to support such coordination, in particular by enabling *informed decision making* (Op 't Land et al., 2008; Harmsen et al., 2009; Proper, 2014) and *informed sensemaking* (Proper and Lankhorst, 2014) (in the sense of Weick, 1995).

Enterprise models can zoom in on, or relate, different aspects of an enterprise, including its structures, purpose, value proposition, value propositions, business processes, stakeholder goals, information systems, underlying IT infrastructures, physical infrastructure, etc. Many languages and frameworks have indeed been suggested as a way to create and capture a different enterprise models. Examples include: BPMN (Freund and Rücker, 2012), UML (Object Management Group, 2010), ArchiMate (Lankhorst et al., 2017a; Band et al., 2016), 4EM (Sandkuhl et al., 2014), MEMO (Frank, 2002) and MERODE (Snoeck, 2014).

In general, enterprise models can be created for different overall purposes, including:

1. **Understand:** Understand the working of the current affairs of an enterprise and / or its environment.
2. **Assess:** Assess (a part / aspect of) the current affairs of an enterprise in relation to a e.g. benchmark or a reference model.
3. **Diagnose:** Diagnose the causes of an identified problem in the current affairs of an enterprise and / or its environment.
4. **Design:** Express different design alternatives, and analyse properties of the (desired) future affairs of the enterprise.
5. **Realise:** Guidance, specification, or explanation during the realisation of the desired affairs of an enterprise.
6. **Operate:** Guidance, specification, or explanation for the socio-cyber-physical actors involved in the day-to-day operations of an enterprise.
7. **Regulate:** Externally formulated regulation on the operational behaviour of (an) enterprise(s).

Depending on additional factors, such as the abilities of the actors involved in the creation and utilisation of the model, the intended usage of the model, the need for understanding / agreement / commitment to the model from different stakeholders, etc, these overall purposes can be refined further (Proper et al., 2018a).

As the creation of models involves effort, the level to which a model meets its purpose paves the way for its **R**eturn **o**n **M**odelling Effort (RoME, see Chapter 4 of Op 't Land et al., 2008)

Collaborative Enterprise Modelling

Enterprise models are quite often created and used in a collaborative context. For example, as discussed in (Proper et al., 2018b), *coordination* among the stakeholders involved is key during enterprise transformations. More specifically, it requires a shared understanding, agreement, and commitment, is needed on (1) what the overall strategy of the enterprise is, (2) the current affairs of the enterprise, i.e. the current situation, as well as the relevant history leading up to it, and possible trends towards the future, (3) the current affairs of the context of the enterprise, and (4) what (given the latter) the ideal future affairs of the enterprise are (Op 't Land et al., 2008; Proper et al., 2018b),.

As a consequence, the collaborative aspects of enterprise modelling are key. The, shared, *understanding* of a model is related to the notion of *model understanding*. Empirical studies have shown that diagrams can easily be misunderstood (Hitchman, 1995; Hitchman, 2002; Nordbotten and Crosby, 1999; Purchase et al., 2002; Masri et al., 2008; Caire et al., 2013), which is likely to lead to problems in practical use. Model understanding has also fuelled the work on e.g. the quality of models and modelling (see e.g. Krogstie et al., 1995; Krogstie, 2002; Bommel et al., 2007; Moody, 2009; van der Linden and Hadar, 2015).

On a more fundamental level, these challenges are also related to the concept of *boundary object* (Levina and Vaast, 2005), which originates from social sciences: "*They have different meanings in different social worlds but their structure is common enough to more than one world to make them recognizable, a means of translation. The creation and management of boundary objects is key in developing and maintaining coherence across intersecting social worlds.*" (Star and Griesemer, 1989). The applicability of this concept in the context of enterprise modelling has been explored in e.g. Abraham et al., 2013 and Abraham, 2013.

An early approximation of the concept of boundary object in the context of enterprise modelling can be found in terms of *views* and *viewpoints* (Lankhorst et al., 2017c) that enable the communication on the design of an organisation (and its different aspects) with different groups of stakeholders while respecting "*the language of the stakeholders*" (Proper et al., 2017). In addition, *natural modelling* (Bjeković et al., 2013; Zarwin et al., 2014), as also echoed more recently in the ideas on *grassroots modelling* (Sandkuhl et al., 2018), also aim to enable the involvement of a broader class of stakeholders in modelling activities.

The development of a shared agreement, and commitment, regarding models depends largely on the collaborative processes used in enterprise modelling. This has already triggered the development collaborative and / or participative modelling approaches (Stirna and Persson, 2007; Barjis, 2009; Ssebuggwawo et al., 2009; Sandkuhl et al., 2014). A complementary perspective is offered by the field of collaboration engineering (Briggs et al., 2006; Vreede et al., 2006), which aims to develop different strategies to structure collaborative processes by means of elementary building blocks called 'thinklets'. Results of applying collaboration engineering in the context of enterprise modelling have been reported in e.g. Nabukenya et al., 2009; Nakakawa et al., 2011; Nabukenya et al., 2011 and Nakakawa et al., 2018.

Enterprise Modelling for Digital Enterprises

The aim of this section is to explore some of the challenges which the transition to the digital age potentially poses to enterprise modelling. It will do so from five main angles:

1. **Dynamics of the Digital Age:** As the transition to the digital age revolutionises the enterprise landscape, the dynamics of enterprise transformations has also increased. Enterprises need to be more agile than ever.
2. **Beyond the Automation of Information Processing:** Traditionally, the role of IT in organisation has focussed on the "automation of information processing". The digital age requires a re-think of this. Business models have grown to be digital intensive, while autonomous vehicles and drones, and AI, will drastically change the way work is conducted.
3. **Modelling Frameworks for the Digital Age:** When modelling enterprises, one usually applies some framework to better structure different perspective / abstraction layers. The transition to the digital age makes it all the more important to ensure these frameworks are well structured.
4. **Modelling Concepts for the Digital Age:** The transition to the digital age results in changes of the types new ingredients (AI, sensors, drones, etc) that make up the resulting organisations, and the enterprises they engage in. New modelling concepts are needed to capture these new ingredients.
5. **Data Ecosystems:** Finally, as a result of the digitisation, data has become a primary resource. This leads to the need to more explicitly consider the data ecosystems, in which the data is gathered, stored, processed, etc.

THE DYNAMICS OF THE DIGITAL AGE

As the digital age revolutionises the enterprise landscape, enterprises are confronted with wave after wave of digital innovations. This results in a situation in which these enterprises need to work hard to keep their business models (Osterwalder and Pigneur, 2009), and their underlying operating models (Ross et al., 2006), up-to-date and viable. As a result, modern day enterprises needs to be agile (Lankhorst et al., 2012).

In the context of IT, the need for more agility has triggered the emergence of software development approaches, such as Agile, DevOps, etc. One of the key messages from these approaches is to avoid a big-design up front (BDUF), which may sound as a potential threat to enterprise modelling. Nevertheless, enterprise modelling as such is a mere means to an end. In line with the definition of models in general, and enterprise models in particular, as provided in the previous section, an enterprise model is seen as a means to an end (the model's purpose) with a clear (intended) return on modelling effort (see the discussion on RoME in section 2.3).

If the "sketch on the back of a napkin" of a new business process and its underlying IT support, suffices as a design document for an agile project, then this is fine. It would, indeed, imply that this "sketch" is a valid (albeit an ultra-light one) enterprise model fitting its purpose. At the same time, however, one might wonder if a pile of such "sketches" would suffice to conduct an enterprise-wide impact analysis, check compliance to e.g. the EU's GDPR[1] (General Data Protection Regulation), or conduct a well-founded security risk analysis. As such, while a "sketch" might suffice the project goals of an agile project, it might not meet the overall goals of the enterprise, and its ongoing transformations, as a whole (such as coherence management, risk management and compliance). Furthermore, when using a workflow engine to drive the business process, the sketch would still need to be elaborated in terms of a more detailed business process model (which is also an enterprise model) that can be "fed" into the workflow engine.

Whatever the outcome of such a debate, it leads to the need to define situational-factors that defines the purpose, the available resources for (enterprise) modelling efforts, and the potential return on modelling effort. The resulting challenge for the field of enterprise modelling is therefore to provide the means to identify what kind of enterprise modelling is needed in specific situations, including the ability to make a conscious trade-off between local project needs and more enterprise-wide needs to coordinate across enterprise transformations (Proper et al., 2018b).

The tension between the agile needs of development projects, and the need to manage a portfolio of projects as part of a larger enterprise transformation, does result in a need to reflect on the modelling concepts to be used in the different situations. For example, at an enterprise-wide level, it might be better to use so-called architecture principles (Greefhorst and Proper, 2011) to express the overall *direction of change*, rather than the more detailed boxes-and-lines diagrams such as ArchiMate (Band et al., 2016) models. At the same time, the latter type of models are indeed needed to conduct a detailed impact analysis, or a thorough GDPR compliance check. As such, the overall purposes as identified in section 2.3 will likely lead to the use of different modelling concepts. In other words, purpose specific modelling languages (PSML), as a refinement to domain specific modelling languages (DSML).

Beyond the Automation of Information Processing

Traditionally, the use of IT in organisation started out from the ambition to "automate information processing" (by means of data processing). One would typically (re)design an enterprise by first designing / growing the organisational structures and associated business processes, then consider what information processing would be needed to support these activities, and then finally turn to the question what part of this information processing could be automated. Later, Henderson and Venkatraman (Henderson and Venkatraman, 1993), as well as Tapscott and Caston (Tapscott and Caston, 1993) argued the case that Business and IT should essentially be co-designed, while Hammer (Hammer, 1990) already signalled that automation should not be used to fix structural problems in an organisation.

The digital age brings about the need to further mature this co-design in the sense that now even business models have become digital (Negroponte, 1996; Tapscott, 1996; Tapscott et al., 2000). The business models of companies such as Amazon, AirBnB, Uber, Netflix, Spotify, N26, etcetera, indeed illustrate this point, while, as also mentioned in the introduction, the CEO of a major (traditional) bank can even be quoted as stating *"We want to be a tech company with a banking license"* (Hamers, 2017).

An important aspect in the design of organisations is the division of labour. In other words: *who does what* and *who is responsible for it*? Traditionally, this question focussed on the role of human actors. With the increasing autonomicity of robots, drones, agents, autonomous vehicles, etc, the division of labour increasingly has to include the role of such "digital actors", as well as the collaboration between with the human actors and the digital actors.

Modelling Frameworks for the Digital Age

In moving beyond "automation of information processing", the transition to the digital age also results in new "ingredients" that make up the socio-technical fabric of modern-day organisations and their enterprises, including the digital actors as discussed above. In (Gils and Proper, 2018), we already explored some of the consequences this may have on enterprise modelling languages such as ArchiMate (Lankhorst et al., 2017a; Band et al., 2016). In this chapter, we take a broader view on this topic, whole not focusing on the possible impact of a specific modelling language.

Enterprise modelling languages usually involve some engineering / architecture framework (Proper and Op 't Land, 2010), defining different perspectives and layers in terms of which an enterprise can be modelled. Examples include ArchiMate (Lankhorst et al., 2017a), Enterprise Ontology (Dietz and Hoogervorst, 2007, TOGAF (The Open Group, 2011), IAF (Wout et al., 2010), and the Zachman framework (Zachman, 1987). These frameworks typically follow the aforementioned "Business-to-IT-stack" line of reasoning, identifying different abstraction layers. However, the abstraction layering(s) used quite often combines different dimensions, leading to confusion.

In (Gils and Proper, 2018) we posited that these frameworks generally use four key mechanisms in creating abstractions (in different dimensions, possibly combining these mechanisms):

1. **Function-Construction:** Making a distinction between, function referring to the way an enterprise / system is intended to function in light of what users, clients, and other stakeholders might deem useful, and construction pertaining to the way it is actually constructed to realise these functions.

2. **Infological Support:** Pertaining to the way in which needed "information processing" is realised, e.g. leading to a business level involving the activities conducted by an enterprise that have a direct impact in the socio-economical world, an infological level (Langefors, 1966) concerned with the information needed / created in the business activities and associated information processing, and a data level concerned with the way the latter is realised in terms of underlying data artefacts and associated processing. These levels provide the why, what, and how of (automated) data processing respectively.

3. **Infrastructure Usage:** This concerns the fact that one system (of systems), such as an enterprise, can use the functions of another system (of systems), where the actual construction of the latter is of no interest to the (designers) of the former (except to the extent of defining service-level agreements). In this case, the latter system (of systems) is considered to be an infrastructure to the former.

4. **Implementation Abstraction:** This concerns the gradual / stepwise introduction of details of the (socio-)technical implementation. For example, in IAF (Wout et al., 2010) this materialises in terms of a conceptual, logical, and physical level, while in TOGAF (The Open Group, 2011) this has resulted in the so-called architectural building blocks, and logical building blocks, and in an MDA context (OMG, 2003) in a platform independent model and a platform specific model.

Each of these abstraction mechanisms has a potential added value for enterprise modelling, in particular in the context of digital transformation. It is important to note that these abstraction mechanisms should not be thought of as a set of orthogonal dimensions. On the contrary. The *function-construction* mechanism and *informational support*, or *function-construction* and *infrastructural usage* can be combined easily within one dimension of an engineering / architecture framework. Nevertheless, as discussed in (Gils and Proper, 2018; Proper and Op 't Land, 2010), this should be done carefully and consistently. Even though we do not want to *prescribe* a specific set of dimensions for engineering / architecture frameworks, we do argue that one should ensure a consistent use of the chosen abstraction mechanisms within one dimension.

Consider, for instance, the traditional "Business-to-IT-stack". This stack tends to identify a "business layer", an "application layer" and "technology layer", where the three layers seem to follow the levels of the *infological support* mechanism. However, it seems that in parallel the *implementation abstraction* is partially mixed-in. For example, at ArchiMate's (Lankhorst et al., 2017a) *business layer* one is forced to mix a human-digital agnostic abstraction of business processes (i.e. still abstracting from the choice for human actors or digital actors to "do the work"), together with an elaboration of the human-actor-only parts of the implementation, while the digital-actor-only parts of the implementation are covered by the application layer and technology layer.

Finally, when using a specific engineering / architecture framework one should, of course, not mix the necessary free-flow of a creative design process, and the top-down structuring of the abstraction layers and dimensions contained in the framework (Proper and Op 't Land, 2010). Design choices at a lower level of abstraction, such as choices for technological platforms, may enable / inspire innovations at the higher levels of abstraction. For example, the choice to use "paper" to be "legal tender" representing an amount of gold as stored by a central bank, was an "implementation choice" that enabled a whole range of innovations in the way we deal with money. Similarly, the use of different "digital technologies" (e.g. AI, blockchains, sensors, drones, etc) in the implementation of existing business activities, is likely to trigger a ripple effect of further innovations.

Modelling Concepts for the Digital Age

In addition to an impact on the modelling frameworks as a whole, the transition to the digital age also results in a need to add new modelling concepts. Below we briefly highlight some of the areas in which we see a need for new modelling concepts. At the same time, we certainly do not claim to be complete.

Moving from the outside in, a first challenge is to include value co-creation considerations in the design of e.g. business models. Existing approaches such as the business model canvas (Osterwalder and Pigneur, 2009) and the complementary value proposition canvas (Osterwalder et al., 2015) focus on value exchange between economic actors in a traditional supplier and consumer role. Value network modelling techniques, such as e3Value (Gordijn and Akkermans, 2003), seem to be better positioned to deal with this shift. However, the shift to value co-creation, requires a re-think of the traditional producer and consumer roles (Chew, 2016), thus leading to a need for new / different modelling concepts (Razo-Zapata et al., 2018; Feltus et al., 2018). Value network modelling techniques, such as e3Value (Gordijn and Akkermans, 2003), seem to be better positioned to deal with this shift.

Moving inward, we arrive at the level of business processes. At this level, one can expect even more impact on the modelling concepts needed as a result of the transition to the digital age. For example, in (Mendling et al., 2018) the authors report on what the possible impact of blockchain on business process management can be, while (Paschek et al., 2017) reports on some of the possible effects of AI on business process management. More generally, as argued in (Gils and Proper, 2018) there is a need to more explicitly position the roles of human actors and digital actors, and their collaboration.

Finally, the transition to the digital age also introduces new risks, as well as the need for regulations (such as the GDPR). To analyse the possible exposure to these risks, and ensure compliance to new regulations, enterprise models can indeed be used (see section 2.3). However, this does require these enterprise models to capture the relevant aspects of an enterprise, thus requiring modelling concepts able to express this (see e.g. Mayer et al., 2015). For example, in the context of the GDPR, this may include aspects such as the location where data is stored, where it is processes, where / how it is gathered (e.g. sensors used), etc.

As argued in (Gils and Proper, 2018), the increase in the number of modelling concepts does require more modular modelling languages, where modelling standards should should focus primarily on providing a generic core of well-defined modelling concepts, in combination with refinement mechanisms that can be used to extend / tailor the core to the needs at hand. The latter may involve both specialisations of the core concepts, as well as e.g. the introduction of (purpose specific / user defined) layers.

The Emergence of Data Ecosystems

The shift to the digital age, also leads to a situation in which data has become a key resource. Data is gathered from sensors, consequently stored, processed, analysed and visualised, and is eventually consumed by (human and / or digital) actors to enable them to gain insight and / or make informed decisions (also see the *infological support* abstraction as discussed in section 3.3).

In the digital age, the systems involved in gathering, storing, processing, analysing, and visualising data have evolved to be complex systems themselves, involving different socio-technical actors with their own interests. Data may pertain to the behaviour of humans, thus making it subject to privacy considerations. Data has some correspondence to "something" in the social, economical, or physical world. As such, there is a need to consider the quality of this correspondence, while some actors may have an interest in maliciously changing the data. Data also comes with the question of ownership. Data may be of strategic value to some actors, leading them to want to control the access for others.

As such, these complex systems can be best thought of as data ecosystems involving a complex of human, organisational, and digital actors. Within a data ecosystem, we need to deal with technical concerns regarding reliability, performance, interoperability, semantics, etc, as well as social concerns, such as privacy, trust, ownership, etc.

A data ecosystem can also be regarded as a "data-management enterprise". In other words, a (networked) enterprise with "data-management" as its primary business. Such a "data-management enterprise" will typically be embedded in a larger enterprise, where the latter focuses on a "regular" products / services. The data handled in a data ecosystem can e.g. pertain to:

1. "Raw" observations from different sensors / informants,
2. "Processed" and / or "enriched" artefacts in terms of e.g. predictive models,
3. Digital replicas of real-world phenomenon, nowadays referred to as *digital twins* (Grieves, 2019),
4. Representations of "intentions" (e.g. plans, designs, etc), "specifications" (source code, work procedures, etc), or "norms" (regulations, principles, policies, etc).

The development of data ecosystems, as "data-management enterprises", can clearly benefit from the use of enterprise modelling approaches. As such, the above considerations directly apply, while at the same time suggesting the need to more specifically capture data ownership, data lineage, value of data (to specific stakeholders), access control, data regulations, etc.

ENTERPRISE MODELLING GOES DIGITAL

In this final section, we aim to explore how the transition to the digital age may impact enterprise modelling itself. As enterprise models are increasingly usually represented digitally, and as some of these models are based on digitally represented "evidence" (sensor data, log files, documents, etc), it makes sense to specialise the notion of a data ecosystem to an *enterprise-modelling* data-ecosystem, which manages the data that pertains to / is relevant for enterprise modelling activities.

Enterprise Cartography

In the past, it was already a challenge to keep enterprise models up-to-date. The dynamics of the digital age will only make this harder. Digital technologies can, indeed, be used to support this task. In particular, approaches that use different forms of sensor data (including log files) to infer up-to-date enterprise models, or at least (in)validate existing enterprise models in the light of new evidence. Existing approaches to deal with this challenge, such as software cartography (Krogmann et al., 2009), process mining (Aalst, 2011), and enterprise cartography (Tribolet et al., 2014), may indeed provide a good starting point.

Such approaches would benefit even more, when digital enterprises are actually designing with "mining in mind". In other words, include sensors in the design of the enterprise to enable future mining of process structures, application landscapes, (in)formal business communication, etc, as part of a broader enterprise-modelling data-ecosystem. The latter is, of course, an integral part the broader data ecosystem underlying an enterprise.

Models as Active Enterprise Knowledge

Increasingly, enterprise models are also used as artefacts in an operational sense. Business process models are used as a specification for business process engine to do its work, business rule specifications / models are similarly used to run rule engines. In the context of software engineering, this has resulted on concepts such as models at runtime (Blair et al., 2009; Vogel et al., 2011). A broader view on this was already provided by (Lillehagen and Krogstie, 2010), who suggest to treat models as ways to capture active knowledge that may support all operational activities in organisations / enterprises. Meanwhile, so-called Hybrid Wiki's (Buckl et al., 2010; Matthes et al., 2011) have also been suggested as a strategy to capture, and operationalise, enterprise knowledge in a semi-structured format.

Digital technologies, in particular in terms of an integrated enterprise-modelling data-ecosystem, will further enable the use of models to capture and utilise enterprise knowledge as part of the operational activities. A specific kind of enterprise models are, of course, models act as complete replicas of part of the enterprise, e.g. enabling detailed simulations. Such models are, nowadays, frequently referred to as *digital twins* (Grieves, 2019).

Interactive Models

As discussed in section 2.4, models quite often act as *boundary object* (Levina and Vaast, 2005) spanning between stakeholders with differing backgrounds. As a consequence, boundary objects a "form" that is engaging to its users, for instance in terms of tangible and / or interactive models. This is where digital technologies potentially have a key role to play.

Research using so-called tangible user interfaces, also indicates that it is possible to more effectively mix the social, digital, and physical actors, to better capture (and discuss) designs (Klemmer et al., 2001; Hornecker and Buur, 2006; Haller et al., 2006; Ras et al., 2012; Maquil et al., 2012). Interactive tabletops have already been shown to support modelling of concepts maps (Oppl and Stary, 2009) or business process models (Rangoni et al., 2014; Fleischmann et al., 2012).

The field of collaboration engineering (Briggs et al., 2006; Vreede et al., 2006) also relies on the use of digital technologies to support the collaborative process, e.g. allowing for anonymous collaborative brainstorming. Something that would be virtually impossible to do in real time using a pen-and-paper based approach.

What still seems to be missing, however, is a better integration of these techniques with traditional enterprise modelling tools. On might even go as far as stating that an integrating architecture is needed for enterprise-modelling data-ecosystem to bring such concepts to fruition.

Model Management

The primary artefact created and manipulated in enterprise modelling activities are, of course, the models themselves. This also implies a need to manage such models well. The need for managing different kind of models arises soon when dealing with complex systems (Barbero et al., 2008), such as, indeed, enterprises. Enterprise modelling, therefore, also involves many different stakeholders, with different cultures, concerns and probably. As a result, there is a crucial need to coordinate those viewpoints together as illustrated in the ISO42010 standard (ISO, 2013) .

Indeed, each viewpoint potentially involves its own modelling language. Anyway, dealing with such a landscape of different viewpoints requires a macroscopic (Barbero et al., 2008) approach to encompass, connect and manage the different viewpoints underlying the different models together. A megamodel (also referred to as a macromodel), as described in Hebig et al., 2012, helps in managing under a single unifying principle, but not necessarily centralized way any modelling elements: the models, supporting language structure (i.e. metamodels), the process (e.g. model transformation) applied to these models. Other relevant information should be added like, e.g., the purpose of the models (Bjeković et al., 2013).

Taking the use of a model into account is also a crucial point in model management. Similarly to the models themselves, the (domain / purpose specific) modelling languages are expected to evolve as well (Bjeković et al., 2014). Modern modelling languages, indeed, support, a certain level of the flexibility (Sottet and Biri, 2016) in order to cope with new situation, reuse in a different context, support uncertainty. History, and evolution traceability is then a necessary property for a proper management. It includes the evolution of the models but also meta-model, semantic annotation, etc. Being able to play past-scenario and ensure coherent update between metamodel and model then become crucial (Silva et al., 2019).

During enterprise modelling activities, new modelling languages / concepts may emerge naturally as well. At the end of the day, a modelling languages are the medium of exchange at the boundary of different proposes. They are collaboratively build by stakeholders for e.g., providing a common understanding of a given problem or sharing viewpoints (Bjeković et al., 2013; Zarwin et al., 2014). Moreover, enterprise stakeholders quite often still prefer the simple use of pen and paper (Malavolta et al., 2012). As a result, languages emerge from structured notation. By being reused and after reaching an agreement between the users, it becomes a purpose specific language (Wouters, 2013).

CONCLUSION

In this chapter, we explored the impact on the transition from the industrial age to the digital age, and the accompanying transition in the economy from a goods-dominant logic to a service-dominant logic, on enterprise modelling. In line with this, the objectives of the chapter were to first reflect on the role of enterprise modelling towards the coordination of enterprise transformations in general, to then explore the resulting challenges posed on enterprise modelling, and finally reflect on how enterprise modelling itself may benefit from the new digital technologies.

We identified the emergence of data ecosystems as a central element in impact on enterprise modelling. Both in terms of the data management of an enterprise in general, as well as the data management pertaining to enterprise modelling.

REFERENCES

Aalst, W. M. P. d. (2011). *Process Mining: Discovery, Conformance and Enhancement of Business Processes*. Heidelberg, Germany: Springer. doi:10.1007/978-3-642-19345-3

Abraham, R. (2013). Enterprise Architecture Artifacts As Boundary Objects - A Framework Of Properties. *Proceedings of the 21st European Conference on Information Systems (ECIS 2013)*.

Band, I., Ellefsen, T., Estrem, B., Iacob, M.-E., Jonkers, H., Lankhorst, M. M., ... Thorn, S. (2016). *ArchiMate 3.0 Specification*. The Open Group.

Barbero, M., Jouault, F., & Bézivin, J. (2008). Model driven management of complex systems: Implementing the macroscope's vision. In *15th Annual IEEE International Conference and Workshop on the Engineering of Computer Based Systems (ECBS 2008)*, (pp. 277-286). IEEE. 10.1109/ECBS.2008.42

Barjis, J. (2009). Collaborative, Participative and Interactive Enterprise Modeling. In *Enterprise Information Systems, 11th International Conference, ICEIS 2009, Milan, Italy, May 6-10, 2009. Proceedings*, volume 24 of *Lecture Notes in Business Information Processing*, (pp. 651-662). Springer.

Bézivin, J. (2005). On the Unification Power of Models. *Software & Systems Modeling*, *4*(2), 171–188. doi:10.100710270-005-0079-0

Bjeković, M., Proper, H. A., & Sottet, J.-S. (2012). Towards a coherent enterprise modelling landscape. In *Short Paper Proceedings of the 5th IFIP WG 8.1 Working Conference on the Practice of Enterprise Modeling, Rostock, Germany, November 7-8, 2012*, volume 933 of *CEUR Workshop Proceedings*. CEUR-WS.org.

Bjeković, M., Proper, H. A., & Sottet, J.-S. (2014). Embracing pragmatics. In Conceptual Modeling - *33rd International Conference, ER 2014, Atlanta, GA, USA*, October 27-29, 2014. *Proceedings*, volume 8824 *of* Lecture Notes in Computer Science, (pp. 431-444). Springer.

Bjeković, M., Sottet, J.-S., Favre, J.-M., & Proper, H. A. (2013). A framework for natural enterprise modelling. In *IEEE 15th Conference on Business Informatics, CBI 2013, Vienna, Austria, July 15-18, 2013*, (pp. 79-84). IEEE Computer Society Press. 10.1109/CBI.2013.20

Blair, G., Bencomo, N., & France, R. B. (2009). Models@ run.time. *Computer*, *42*(10), 22–27. doi:10.1109/MC.2009.326

Bommel, P. v., Hoppenbrouwers, S. J. B. A., Proper, H. A., & Weide, T. P. d. (2007). QoMo: A Modelling Process Quality Framework based on SEQUAL. Academic Press.

Briggs, R. O., Kolfschoten, G. L., Vreede, G. J. d., & Dean, D. L. (2006). Defining Key Concepts for Collaboration Engineering. *Proceedings of 12th Americas Conference on Information Systems (AMCIS 2006)*.

Buckl, S., Matthes, F., Neubert, C., & Schweda, C. M. (2010). A Lightweight Approach to Enterprise Architecture Modeling and Documentation. In *CAiSE Forum*, volume 72 of *Lecture Notes in Business Information Processing*, (pp. 136-149). Springer.

Caire, P., Genon, N., Heymans, P., & Moody, D. L. (2013). Visual notation design 2.0: Towards user comprehensible requirements engineering notations. *21st IEEE International Requirements Engineering Conference (RE2013)*, 115-124. 10.1109/RE.2013.6636711

Chesley, J. A., & Wenger, M. S. (1999). Transforming an Organization: Using models to foster a strategic conversation. *California Management Review*, *41*(3), 54–73. doi:10.2307/41165997

Chew, E. K. (2016). iSIM: An integrated design method for commercializing service innovation. *Information Systems Frontiers*, *18*(3), 457–478. doi:10.100710796-015-9605-y

Cruse, A. (2000). *Meaning in Language, an Introduction to Semantics and Pragmatics*. Oxford, UK: Oxford University Press.

Daft, R. (2007). *Understanding the Theory and Design of Organizations*. Mason, OH: Thomson South-Western.

Dietz, J. L. G. (2006). *Enterprise Ontology - Theory and Methodology*. Heidelberg, Germany: Springer. doi:10.1007/3-540-33149-2

Dietz, J. L. G. & Hoogervorst, J. A. P. (2007). Enterprise Ontology and Enterprise Architecture - how to let them evolve into effective complementary notions. *GEAO Journal of Enterprise Architecture*, 1.

Falkenberg, E. D., Verrijn-Stuart, A. A., Voss, K., Hesse, W., Lindgreen, P., Nilsson, B. E., . . . Stamper, R. K. (Eds.). (1998). A Framework of Information Systems Concepts. IFIP WG 8.1 Task Group FRISCO. IFIP.

Feltus, C., Proper, H. A., Metzger, A., Garcia Lopez, J. C., & Gonzalez Castineira, R. (2018). Value cocreation (VCC) language design in the frame of a smart airport network case study. In *32nd IEEE International Conference on Advanced Information Networking and Applications, AINA 2018, Krakow, Poland*, May 16-18, 2018, (pp. 858-865). IEEE Computer Society. 10.1109/AINA.2018.00127

Fleischmann, A., Schmidt, W., Stary, C., Obermeier, S., & Börger, E. (2012). *Subject-oriented Business Process Management*. Heidelberg, Germany: Springer. doi:10.1007/978-3-642-32392-8

Frank, U. (1998). *Evaluating Modelling Languages: Relevant Issues, Epistemological Challenges and a Preliminary Research Framework*. Technical Report 15. University of Koblenz-Landau.

Frank, U. (2002). Multi-perspective Enterprise Modeling (MEMO) - Conceptual Framework and Modeling Languages. In *HICSS '02: Proceedings of the 35th Annual Hawaii International Conference on System Sciences (HICSS'02)* (vol. 3, p. 72). Washington, DC: IEEE Computer Society Press. 10.1109/HICSS.2002.993989

Freund, J., & Rücker, B. (2012). *Real Life BPMN*. Camunda.

Friedman, T. L. (2005). *The World is Flat: A Brief History of the Twenty-first Century*. New York: Farrar, Straus and Giroux.

Gils, B. v., & Proper, H. A. (2018). Enterprise modelling in the age of digital transformation. In *The Practice of Enterprise Modeling - 11th IFIP WG 8.1. Working Conference, PoEM 2018, Vienna, Austria, October 31 - November 2, 2018, Proceedings, volume 335 of Lecture Notes in Business Information Processing*, (pp. 257-273). Springer.

Gordijn, J., & Akkermans, H. (2003). Value based requirements engineering: Exploring innovative e-commerce ideas. *Requirements Engineering Journal*, 8(2), 114–134. doi:10.100700766-003-0169-x

Greefhorst, D., & Proper, H. A. (2011). *Architecture Principles - The Cornerstones of Enterprise Architecture*. Heidelberg, Germany: Springer.

Grieves, M. (2019). Virtually Intelligent Product Systems: Digital and Physical Twins. In S. Flumerfelt, K. G. Schwartz, D. Mavris, & S. Briceno (Eds.), *Complex Systems Engineering: Theory and Practice* (pp. 175–200). American Institute of Aeronautics and Astronautics. doi:10.2514/5.9781624105654.0175.0200

Grönroos, C., & Ravald, A. (2011). Service as Business Logic: Implications for Value Creation and Marketing. *Journal of Service Management*, 22(1), 5–22. doi:10.1108/09564231111106893

Guizzardi, G. (2006). On Ontology, ontologies, Conceptualizations, Modeling Languages, and (Meta) Models. In *Databases and Information Systems IV - Selected Papers from the Seventh International Baltic Conference, DB&IS 2006, July 3-6, 2006, Vilnius, Lithuania, volume 155 of Frontiers in Artificial Intelligence and Applications*, (pp. 18-39). IOS Press.

Haller, M., Brandl, P., Leithinger, D., Leitner, J., Seifried, T., & Billinghurst, M. (2006). *Shared Design Space: Sketching ideas using digital pens and a large augmented tabletop setup*. Advances in Artificial Reality and Tele-Existence. doi:10.1145/1179133.1179163

Hamers, R. (2017). *We want to be a tech company with a banking license*. Academic Press.

Hammer, M. (1990). Re-engineering work: Don't automate, obliterate. *Harvard Business Review*, 68(4), 104–112.

Harmsen, A. F., Proper, H. A., & Kok, N. (2009). Informed governance of enterprise transformations. In *Advances in Enterprise Engineering II - First NAF Academy Working Conference on Practice-Driven Research on Enterprise Transformation, PRET 2009, held at CAiSE 2009, Amsterdam, The Netherlands, June 11, 2009. Proceedings, volume 28 of Lecture Notes in Business Information Processing*, (pp. 155-180). Amsterdam, The Netherlands: Springer. 10.1007/978-3-642-01859-6_9

Hebig, R., Seibel, A., & Giese, H. (2012). On the unification of megamodels. *Electronic Communications of the EASST*, 42.

Henderson, J. C., & Venkatraman, N. (1993). Strategic alignment: Leveraging information technology for transforming organizations. *IBM Systems Journal*, *32*(1), 4–16. doi:10.1147j.382.0472

Hitchman, S. (1995). Practitioner Perceptions On The Use Of Some Semantic Concepts In The Entity Relationship Model'. *European Journal of Information Systems*, *4*(1), 31–40. doi:10.1057/ejis.1995.4

Hitchman, S. (2002). The Details of Conceptual Modelling Notations are Important - A Comparison of Relationship Normative Language. *Communications of the AIS*, *9*(10).

Hoppenbrouwers, S. J. B. A., Proper, H. A., & Weide, T. P. d. (2005). A fundamental view on the process of conceptual modeling. In *Conceptual Modeling - ER 2005, 24th International Conference on Conceptual Modeling, Klagenfurt, Austria, October 24-28, 2005, Proceedings*, volume 3716 of Lecture Notes in Computer Science, (pp. 128-143). Springer. 10.1007/11568322_9

Hornecker, E., & Buur, J. (2006). Getting a grip on tangible interaction: a framework on physical space and social interaction. In *Proceedings of the SIGCHI conference on Human Factors in computing systems*, (pp. 437-446). ACM Press. 10.1145/1124772.1124838

ISO. (2013). *ISO/IEC/IEEE 42010:2011 - systems and software engineering - architecture description. Standard*. Geneva, Switzerland: International Organization for Standardization.

Jung, R., & Reichert, M. (Eds.)., R., Niemietz, H., de Kinderen, S., and Aier, S. (2013). Can boundary objects mitigate communication defects in enterprise transformation? Findings from expert interviews. In *Proceedings of the 5th International Workshop on Enterprise Modelling and Information Systems Architectures, EMISA 2013, St. Gallen, Switzerland, September 5-6, 2013*, volume 222 of *Lecture Notes in Informatics*, (pp. 27-40). Gesellschaft für Informatik.

Kates, A., & Galbraith, J. R. (2007). *Designing Your Organization: Using the STAR Model to Solve 5 Critical Design Challenges*. Jossey-Bass.

Kecheng, L., Clarke, R. J., Andersen, P. B., Stamper, R. K., & Abou-Zeid, E.-S. (Eds.). (2002). *IFIP TC8/WG8.1 Working Conference on Organizational Semiotics - Evolving a Science of Information Systems*. Kluwer.

Klemmer, S. R., Newman, M. W., Farrell, R., Bilezikjian, M., & Landay, J. A. (2001). The designers' outpost: a tangible interface for collaborative web site design. In *Proceedings of the 14th annual ACM symposium on User interface software and technology*, (pp. 1-10). ACM Press. 10.1145/502348.502350

Krogmann, K., Schweda, C. M., Buckl, S., Kuperberg, M., Martens, A., & Matthes, F. (2009). Improved Feedback for Architectural Performance Prediction Using Software Cartography Visualizations. In Architectures for Adaptive Software Systems, volume 5581 of Lecture Notes in Computer Science, (pp. 52-69). Springer. doi:10.1007/978-3-642-02351-4_4

Krogstie, J. (2002). A Semiotic Approach to Quality in Requirements Specifications. In *Proceedings of the IFIP TC8 / WG8.1 Working Conference on Organizational Semiotics: Evolving a Science of Information Systems*, (231-250). Deventer, The Netherlands: Kluwer. 10.1007/978-0-387-35611-2_14

Krogstie, J., Lindland, O. I., & Sindre, G. (1995). Defining Quality Aspects for Conceptual Models. In *Information System Concepts: Towards a consolidation of views - Proceedings of the third IFIP WG8.1 conference (ISCO-3)*, (pp. 216-231). Marburg, Germany: Chapman & Hall/IFIP WG8.1. 10.1007/978-0-387-34870-4_22

Langefors, B. (1966). *Theoretical Analysis of Information Systems*. Lund, Sweden: Studentlitteratur.

Lankhorst, M. M., Hoppenbrouwers, S. J. B. A., Jonkers, H., Proper, H. A., Torre, L. d., Arbab, F., ... Wieringa, R. J. (2017a). *Enterprise Architecture at Work - Modelling, Communication and Analysis* (4th ed.). Heidelberg, Germany: Springer.

Lankhorst, M. M., Janssen, W. P. M., Proper, H. A., Steen, M. W. A., Zoet, M. M., Molnar, W. A., ... Linden, D. J. T. d. (2012). *Agile Service Development: Combining Adaptive Methods and Flexible Solutions*. Heidelberg, Germany: Springer. doi:10.1007/978-3-642-28188-4

Lankhorst, M. M., Torre, L. d., Proper, H. A., Arbab, F., Boer, F. S. d., & Bonsangue, M. (2017b). Foundations. Academic Press.

Lankhorst, M. M., Torre, L. d., Proper, H. A., Arbab, F., & Steen, M. W. A. (2017c). *Viewpoints and visualisation*. doi:10.1007/978-3-662-53933-0_8

Levina, N., & Vaast, E. (2005). The Emergence of Boundary Spanning Competence in Practice: Implications for Implementation and Use of Information Systems. *Management Information Systems Quarterly*, *29*(2), 335–363. doi:10.2307/25148682

Lillehagen, F., & Krogstie, J. (2010). *Active Knowledge Modeling of Enterprises*. Heidelberg, Germany: Springer.

Lusch, R. F., & Nambisan, S. (2015). Service Innovation: A Service-Dominant Logic Perspective. *Management Information Systems Quarterly*, *39*(1), 155–175. doi:10.25300/MISQ/2015/39.1.07

Magalhães, R., & Proper, H. A. (2017). Model-enabled Design and Engineering of Organisations. *Organisational Design and Enterprise Engineeering*, *1*(1), 1–12. doi:10.100741251-016-0005-9

Mahr, B. (2011). On the epistemology of models. In G. Abel & J. Conant (Eds.), *Rethinking Epistemology* (pp. 1–301). De Gruyter. doi:10.1515/9783110253573.301

Malavolta, I., Lago, P., Muccini, H., Pelliccione, P., & Tang, A. (2012). What industry needs from architectural languages: A survey. *IEEE Transactions on Software Engineering*, *39*(6), 869–891. doi:10.1109/TSE.2012.74

Maquil, V., Zephir, O., & Ras, E. (2012). Creating Metaphors for Tangible User Interfaces in Collaborative Urban Planning: Questions for Designers and Developers. *Proceedings of COOP* 2012. 10.1007/978-1-4471-4093-1_10

Masri, K., Parker, D., & Gemino, A. (2008). Using Iconic Graphics in En-tity Relationship Diagrams: The Impact on Understanding. *Journal of Database Management*, *19*(3), 22–41. doi:10.4018/jdm.2008070102

Matthes, F., Neubert, C., & Steinhoff, A. (2011). Hybrid Wikis: Empowering Users to Collaboratively Structure Information. *6th International Conference on Software and Data Technologies (ICSOFT)*, 250-259.

Mayer, N., Barafort, B., Picard, M., & Cortina, S. (2015). An ISO Compliant and Integrated Model for IT GRC (Governance, Risk Management and Compliance). In Systems, Software and Services Process Improvement, volume 543 of Communications in Computer and Information Science, (pp. 87-99). Springer.

Mendling, J., Weber, I., Aalst, W. M. P., Brocke, J., Cabanillas, C., Daniel, F., ... Zhu, L. (2018). Blockchains for Business Process Management - Challenges and Opportunities. *ACM Transactions on Management Information Systems*, *9*(1), 1–16. doi:10.1145/3183367

Meriam-Webster. (2003). *Meriam-Webster Online*. Collegiate Dictionary.

Moody, D. L. (2009). The "Physics" of Notations: Toward a Scientific Basis for Constructing Visual Notations in Software Engineering. *IEEE Transactions on Software Engineering*, *35*(6), 756–779. doi:10.1109/TSE.2009.67

Morris, C. (1946). *Signs, Language and Behaviour*. Englewood Cliffs, NJ: Prentice Hall.

Nabukenya, J., Bommel, P. v., & Proper, H. A. (2009). A theory-driven design approach to collaborative policy making processes. In *42st Hawaii International International Conference on Systems Science (HICSS-42 2009), Proceedings (CD-ROM and online), 5-8 January 2009, Waikoloa, Big Island, HI, USA*, (pp. 1-10). IEEE Computer Society.

Nabukenya, J., Bommel, P., Proper, H. A., & Vreede, G. J. (2011). An Evaluation Instrument for Collaborative Processes: Application to Organizational Policy-Making. *Group Decision and Negotiation*, *20*(4), 465–488. doi:10.100710726-009-9177-7

Nakakawa, A., Bommel, P., & Proper, H. A. (2011). Definition and validation of requirements for collaborative decision-making in enterprise architecture creation. *International Journal of Cooperative Information Systems*, *20*(1), 83–136. doi:10.1142/S021884301100216X

Nakakawa, A., Bommel, P., Proper, H. A., & Mulder, J. B. F. (2018). A situational method for creating shared understanding on requirements for an enterprise architecture. *International Journal of Cooperative Information Systems*, *27*(4), 1850010. doi:10.1142/S0218843018500107

Negroponte, N. (1996). *Being Digital*. New York: Vintage Books.

Nordbotten, J. C., & Crosby, M. E. (1999). The effect of graphic style on data model interpretation. *Information Systems Journal*, *9*(2), 139–155. doi:10.1046/j.1365-2575.1999.00052.x

Object Management Group. (2010). *Unified Modeling Language - Superstructure. Technical Report version 2.4.1*. OMG.

Ogden, C. K., & Richards, I. A. (1923). *The Meaning of Meaning - A Study of the Influence of Language upon Thought and of the Science of Symbolism*. Oxford, UK: Magdalene College, University of Cambridge.

OMG. (2003). *MDA Guide v1.0.1. Technical Report omg/2003-06-01*. Needham, MA: Object Management Group.

Op 't Land, M., & Proper, H. A. (2007). Impact of principles on enterprise engineering. In *Proceedings of the Fifteenth European Conference on Information Systems, ECIS 2007, St. Gallen, Switzerland*, 2007, (pp. 1965-1976). University of St. Gallen.

Op 't Land, M., Proper, H. A., Waage, M., Cloo, J., & Steghuis, C. (2008). *Enterprise Architecture - Creating Value by Informed Governance*. Heidelberg, Germany: Springer.

Oppl, S., & Stary, C. (2009). Tabletop concept mapping. In *Proceedings of the 3rd International Conference on Tangible and Embedded Interaction*, (pp. 275-282). ACM.

Osterwalder, A., & Pigneur, Y. (2009). *Business Model Generation: A Handbook for Visionaries, Game Changers, and Challengers*. Amsterdam, The Netherlands: Self Published.

Osterwalder, A., Pigneur, Y., Bernarda, G., & Smith, A. (2015). *Value Proposition Design How to Create Products and Services Customers Want*. Hoboken, NJ: Wiley.

Paschek, D., Luminosu, C., & Draghici, A. (2017). Automated business process management - In times of digital transformation using machine learning or artificial intelligence. *MATEC Web of Conferences, 121*.

Peirce, C. S. (1969). *Volumes I and II - Principles of Philosophy and Elements of Logic. Collected Papers of C. S. Peirce*. Harvard University Press.

Proper, H. A. (2014). Enterprise architecture: Informed steering of enterprises in motion. In *Enterprise Information Systems - 15th International Conference, ICEIS 2013, Angers, France, July 4-7, 2013, Revised Selected Papers, volume 190 of Lecture Notes in Business Information Processing*, (pp. 16-34). Springer.

Proper, H. A., Bjeković, M., Gils, B. v., & de Kinderen, S. (2018a). Enterprise architecture modelling - purpose, requirements and language. In *Proceedings of the 13th Workshop on Trends in Enterprise Architecture (TEAR 2018)*. IEEE. 10.1109/EDOCW.2018.00031

Proper, H. A., Halpin, T. A., & Krogstie, J. (Eds.). (2007). *Proceedings of the 12th Workshop on Exploring Modeling Methods for Systems Analysis and Design (EMMSAD 2007), held in conjunction with the 19th Conference on Advanced Information Systems (CAiSE 2007), Trondheim, Norway*. CEUR-WS.org.

Proper, H. A., Hoppenbrouwers, S. J. B. A., & Veldhuijzen van Zanten, G. E. (2017). *Communication of enterprise architectures*. doi:10.1007/978-3-662-53933-0_4

Proper, H. A., & Lankhorst, M. M. (2014). Enterprise architecture - towards essential sensemaking. *Enterprise Modelling and Information Systems Architectures, 9*(1), 5–21. doi:10.100740786-014-0002-7

Proper, H. A., & Op 't Land, M. (2010). Lines in the Water - The Line of Reasoning in an Enterprise Engineering Case Study from the Public Sector. In *Practice-Driven Research on Enterprise Transformation - Second Working Conference, PRET 2010, Delft, The Netherlands, November 11, 2010. Proceedings, volume 69 of Lecture Notes in Business Information Processing*, (pp. 193-216). Delft, The Netherlands: Springer.

Proper, H. A., Winter, R., Aier, S., & de Kinderen, S. (Eds.). (2018b). *Architectural Coordination of Enterprise Transformation*. Heidelberg, Germany: Springer.

Purchase, H. C., Carrington, D., & Allder, J.-A. (2002). Empirical Evaluation of Aesthetics-based Graph Layout. *Empirical Software Engineering, 7*(3), 233–255. doi:10.1023/A:1016344215610

Rangoni, Y., Maquil, V., Tobias, E., & Ras, E. (2014). Implementing widgets using sifteo cubes for visual modelling on tangible user interfaces. In *Proceedings of the 2014 ACM SIGCHI symposium on Engineering interactive computing systems*, (pp. 205-210). ACM. 10.1145/2607023.2610271

Ras, E., Maquil, V., Foulonneau, M., & Latour, T. (2012). Using tangible user interfaces for technology-based assessment - Advantages and challenges. In CAA 2012 *International Conference*. University of Southampton.

Razo-Zapata, I. S., Chew, E., & Proper, H. A. (2018). VIVA: A visual language to design value co-creation. In *20th IEEE Conference on Business Informatics, CBI 2018, Vienna, Austria, July 11-14, 2018*, Volume 1 - *Research Papers*, (pp. 20-29). IEEE Computer Society. 10.1109/CBI.2018.00012

Ross, J. W., Weill, P., & Robertson, D. C. (2006). *Enterprise architecture as strategy: creating a foundation for business execution*. Boston: Harvard Business School Press.

Rothenberg, J. (1989). The Nature of Modeling. In *Artificial intelligence, simulation & modeling* (pp. 75–92). New York: John Wiley & Sons.

Sandkuhl, K., Fill, H.-G., Hoppenbrouwers, S. J. B. A., Krogstie, J., Matthes, F., Opdahl, A. L., ... Winter, R. (2018). From Expert Discipline to Common Practice: A Vision and Research Agenda for Extending the Reach of Enterprise Modeling. *Business & Information Systems Engineering, 60*(1), 69–80. doi:10.100712599-017-0516-y

Sandkuhl, K., Stirna, J., Persson, A., & Wißotzki, M. (2014). *Enterprise Modeling: Tackling Business Challenges with the 4EM Method*. Heidelberg, Germany: Springer.

Searle, J. R. (1979). A Taxonomy of Illocutionary Acts. In *Expression and Meaning: Studies in the Theory of Speech Acts*. Cambridge, UK: Cambridge University Press. doi:10.1017/CBO9780511609213.003

Silva, N., Gonçalves, P., Leite, I., Sousa, P., & da Silva, M. M. (2019). Lm2f: a life-cycle model maintenance framework for co-evolving enterprise architecture meta-models and models. *27th European Conference on Information Systems - Information Systems for a Sharing Society, ECIS 2019*.

Snoeck, M. (2014). *Enterprise Information Systems Engineering - The MERODE Approach*. Springer.

Sottet, J.-S. & Biri, N. (2016). Jsmf: a javascript flexible modelling framework. *FlexMDE@ MoDELS, 1694*, 42-51.

Ssebuggwawo, D., Hoppenbrouwers, S. J. B. A., & Proper, H. A. (2009). Interactions, goals and rules in a collaborative modelling session. In *The Practice of Enterprise Modeling, Second IFIP WG 8.1 Working Conference, PoEM 2009, Stockholm, Sweden, November 18-19, 2009. Proceedings, volume 39 of Lecture Notes in Business Information Processing*, (pp. 54-68). Springer. 10.1007/978-3-642-05352-8_6

Stachowiak, H. (1973). *Allgemeine Modelltheorie*. Heidelberg, Germany: Springer. doi:10.1007/978-3-7091-8327-4

Stamper, R. K. (1996). Signs, norms, and information systems. In Signs at Work, (pp. 349-397). Walter de Gruyter. doi:10.1515/9783110819014-013

Star, S. L., & Griesemer, J. R. (1989). Institutional Ecology, 'Translations' and Boundary Objects: Amateurs and Professionals in Berkeley's Museum of Vertebrate Zoology 1907-39. *Social Studies of Science, 19*(4), 387–420. doi:10.1177/030631289019003001

Stirna, J., & Persson, A. (2007). Ten Years Plus with EKD: Reflections from Using an Enterprise Modeling Method in Practice. Academic Press.

Tapscott, D. (1996). *Digital Economy - Promise and peril in the age of networked intelligence.* New York: McGraw-Hill.

Tapscott, D., & Caston, A. (1993). *Paradigm Shift - The New Promise of Information Technology.* New York: McGraw-Hill.

Tapscott, D., Ticoll, D., & A., L. (2000). *Digital Capital: Harnessing the Power of Business Webs.* Harvard Business Press.

Taylor, J. R., Cooren, F., Giroux, N., & Robichaud, D. (1996). The Communicational Basis of Organization: Between the Conversation and the Text. *Communication Theory, 6*(1), 1–39. doi:10.1111/j.1468-2885.1996.tb00118.x

Thalheim, B. (2011). The Theory of Conceptual Models, the Theory of Conceptual Modelling and Foundations of Conceptual Modelling. In *Handbook of Conceptual Modeling* (pp. 543–577). Heidelberg, Germany: Springer. doi:10.1007/978-3-642-15865-0_17

Thalheim, B. (2013). The Conception of the Model. In *Business Information Systems - 16th International Conference, BIS 2013, Poznań Poland, June 19-21, 2013. Proceedings, volume 157 of Lecture Notes in Business Information Processing*, (pp. 113-124). Springer. 10.1007/978-3-642-38366-3_10

The Open Group. (2011). *TOGAF Version 9.1* (10th ed.). Zaltbommel, The Netherlands: Van Haren Publishing.

Tribolet, J., Sousa, P., & Caetano, A. (2014). The Role of Enterprise Governance and Cartography in Enterprise Engineering. *Enterprise Modelling and Information Systems Architectures, 9*(1), 38–49. doi:10.100740786-014-0004-5

Ullmann, S. (1967). *Semantics: An Introduction to the Science of Meaning.* Oxford, UK: Basil Blackwell.

Umar, A. (2005). IT infrastructure to enable next generation enterprises. *Information Systems Frontiers, 7*(3), 217–256. doi:10.100710796-005-2768-1

van der Linden, D. J. T., & Hadar, I. (2015). Cognitive Effectiveness of Conceptual Modeling Languages: Examining Professional Modelers. *Proceedings of the 5th IEEE International Workshop on Empirical Requirements Engineering (EmpiRE).* 10.1109/EmpiRE.2015.7431300

Vargo, S. L., & Lusch, R. F. (2008). Service-dominant logic: Continuing the evolution. *Journal of the Academy of Marketing Science, 36*(1), 1–10. doi:10.100711747-007-0069-6

Vargo, S. L., & Lusch, R. F. (2016). Institutions and axioms: An extension and update of service-dominant logic. *Journal of the Academy of Marketing Science, 44*(1), 5–23. doi:10.100711747-015-0456-3

Vogel, T., Seibel, A., & Giese, H. (2011). The role of models and megamodels at runtime. In J. Dingel & A. Solberg (Eds.), *Models in Software Engineering* (pp. 224–238). Berlin: Springer Berlin Heidelberg. doi:10.1007/978-3-642-21210-9_22

Vreede, G. J., Kolfschoten, G. L., & Briggs, R. O. (2006). Thinklets: A collaboration engineering pattern language. *International Journal of Computer Applications in Technology, 25*(2/3), 140–154. doi:10.1504/IJCAT.2006.009064

Weick, K. E. (1995). *Sensemaking in Organizations*. Beverly Hills, CA: Sage.

Wout, J. v., Waage, M., Hartman, H., Stahlecker, M., & Hofman, A. (2010). *The Integrated Architecture Framework Explained*. Heidelberg, Germany: Springer. doi:10.1007/978-3-642-11518-9

Wouters, L. (2013). Towards the notation-driven development of dsmls. In *International Conference on Model Driven Engineering Languages and Systems*, (pp. 522-537). Springer. 10.1007/978-3-642-41533-3_32

Zachman, J. A. (1987). A framework for information systems architecture. *IBM Systems Journal, 26*(3), 276–292. doi:10.1147j.263.0276

Zarwin, Z., Bjeković, M., Favre, J.-M., Sottet, J.-S., & Proper, H. A. (2014). Natural modelling. *Journal of Object Technology, 13*(3), 1-36.

ENDNOTE

[1]   https://eur-lex.europa.eu/legal-content/EN/TXT/PDF/?uri=CELEX:32016R0679

Chapter 4
Enterprise Digital Twin:
An Approach to Construct Digital Twin for Complex Enterprises

Souvik Barat

TCS Research, Tata Consultancy Services, India

ABSTRACT

Enterprises constantly aim to maximise their objectives while operating in a competitive and dynamic environment. This necessitates an enterprise to be efficient, adaptive, and amenable for transformation. However, understanding a complex enterprise and identifying effective control measure, adaptation choice, or transformation option to realise specific objective is not a trivial task. The digital twin that imitates the real enterprise provides an environment to conduct the necessary interrogative and predictive analyses to evaluate various control measures, adaptation choices, and transformation options in a safe and cost-effective manner without compromising the analysis precision. This chapter reflects on the core concept of the digital twin, evaluates the state-of-the-art modelling and analysis technologies, and presents a pragmatic approach to develop high-fidelity digital twin for large complex enterprises.

INTRODUCTION

A digital twin is a comprehensive and machine-interpretable description of components, behaviours and operation of real systems, processes and products (henceforth they are referred as *systems*) for a range of interrogative and predictive analyses that lead to decision making (Grieves, 2012). Industry is now increasingly witnessing the economic significance of such *digital twins* for controlling, adapting and designing a wide range of complex systems (Grieves and Vickers, 2017). An effective digital twin helps to expedite the time to market and reduce the cost of system development by analysing the consequences of the prospective control, adaptation and design choices prior to their implementations in reality.

The core concept of digital twin is effectively adopted in engineering disciplines (Schleich et al., 2017) and mission critical systems (Glaessgen and Stargel, 2012). They develop high-fidelity physics and mathematical models to represent system behaviours to enable analytical simulation for understanding

DOI: 10.4018/978-1-7998-0108-5.ch004

system behaviour and evaluating the efficacy of various hypothetical changes with respect to specific system goals. The key objective for constructing such digital twins is to reduce or eliminate real-life experiments, which are often expensive and infeasible. While the benefits of a digital twin over controlled experiments are well established in engineering disciplines, its utilisation is not yet in mainstream practice for business enterprises, such as supply chain, telecom, business process outsourcing organisation and software service provisioning. State of the practice of interrogating and predicting business enterprises are still chiefly driven by the intuitions of human experts.

This chapter discusses the core concept of conventional digital twin, explicates the necessary aspects and characteristics that needs to be considered for conceptualising digital twins of modern business enterprises, and reviews the existing modelling and simulation techniques that are relevant for constructing digital twins for such business enterprises. It also discusses an *actor* (Agha, 1966a, Hewitt and Smith, 1975) based bottom-up approach along with relevant verification and validation techniques for constructing faithful digital twins to support evidence-driven informed decision making for business enterprises.

BACKGROUND

The core concept of digital twin of enterprises is traced back to *Information Mirroring Model* published in 2005 (Grieves, 2005). This primitive model is refined multiple times to support complex systems and termed as digital twin in *Virtually Perfect: Driving Innovative and Lean Products through Product Lifecycle Management* (Grieves 2011). Over the years, the efficacy of the digital twin are demonstrated using various state-of-the-art modelling paradigms, simulation technologies, Internet of Things (IoT), sensor technologies and a wide range of data analytics techniques. The utility of a digital twin is established in several engineering disciplines. For example, the concept has been widely adopted in several astronautics and aerospace researches since NASA has included it in their technology roadmap (Glaessgen and Stargel, 2012).

Conceptually such digital twin is formed using three core elements: (i) real environment, (ii) virtual environment and (iii) connection between two environments as shown in Figure 1. The real environment is an actual enterprise, system, product or process. The virtual environment is a faithful representation of the real environment. A virtual environment is typically formed for a range of in-silico interrogative and/or predictive analysis, where the key objectives are: (a) understand current system in precise form, (b) analyse the efficacy of hypothetical changes or adaptation strategies to realise specific goals of a real environment, and (c) explore design alternatives of a new environment.

The virtual environment in a digital twin is connected with a real environment using two-way connections as shown in Figure 1. The information link from real environment to virtual environment serves two purposes: (i) provides necessary information about the real environment, which help to construct a virtual environment and ensure its faithfulness, and (ii) supplies system data to set the state of a virtual environment same as a real environment. The information that helps to construct a model of a real environment and establish the model validity is necessary at the construction phase of a digital twin. The data flow that contains information about the state change of a real system is a periodic/continuous information flow that keeps a virtual environment up-to-date with respect to a real environment. This enables in-silico simulation driven analysis of enterprise. The reverse information link, *i.e.*, information link from virtual environment to real environment, communicates the effective control instructions and change recommendations that include the change in structure, behaviours and/or goal of a real environ-

Figure 1. Core concept of digital twin

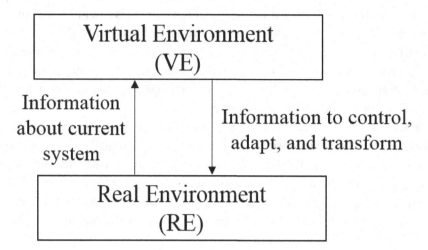

ment. Therefore, the efficacy of a digital twin as an analysis and decision-making aid chiefly rely on four factors: (i) construction of a virtual environment (ii) validity of constructed virtual environment, (iii) effective analysis techniques to quantitatively comprehend a virtual environment, and (iv) data sensing and transformation to make virtual environment up-to-date. The next section of this chapter discusses the complexities of modern enterprises that operates in a dynamic and uncertain context, and the remaining chapter reflects on the existing modelling, analysis and model validation approaches to effectively utilise digital twin in an enterprise context.

TENETS OF COMPLEX ENETERPRISE

An enterprise can be effectively comprehended by precisely knowing various aspects of interest and their characteristics. The questions are – *what* aspects of an enterprise are necessary to understand an enterprise? And *what* are the important characteristics that makes an enterprise complex? The Zachman Architecture (Zachman, et al. 1987) recommends a comprehensive list of integrative aspects to understand a complex system or an enterprise. The aspects are: *Why, What, How, Who, When,* and *Where.*

While there is a general consensus about relevant aspects of interest of an enterprise, the factors that make an enterprise complex are multifaceted. The classical model of enterprise as a closed and deterministic system has long been discredited in practice (Daft and Lewin, 1990, Simon 1991). An enterprise as a monolithic probabilistic entity, which can be specified and predicted using established mathematical and statistical techniques, is also turning out to be less relevant in the context of a dynamic business environment (Sipp and Elias, 2012). Recent management literature critically reflects on advanced system theories and organisation theory to understand the complexity of a large enterprises. In particular, an enterprise is chiefly visualized as a *complex open system* with multiple feedback loops. An enterprise is considered as a *system* as it consists of interconnected components that work together (Simon 1991). It is considered as *open* as it exchanges messages and resources with its environment. It contains multiple feedback loops with its environment for survival and success as described in General

Figure 2. System theoretic view of enterprise

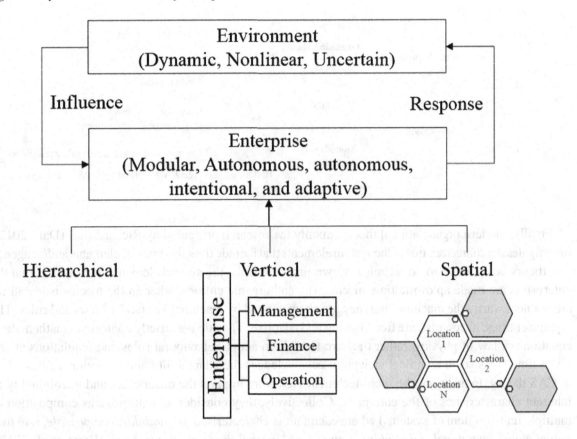

System Theory (GST) (Von Bertalanffy, 1968) and cybernetics (Ashby, 1981). The correlation with the complexity theory provides further insights, where an enterprise is considered as a complex entity as they compose a large number of interdependent subsystems or elements (Acnderson, 1999) in a nonlinear way (Casti, 1994). Daft and Lewin consider an enterprise as a complex entity due its formation – it is observed that enterprises often contains multiple loosely coupled autonomous elements (Daft and Lewin, 1990). Richard Daft emphasises the complex enterprise structure along three dimensions - vertical, horizontal and spatial (Daft, 2012). To that view, the organisational hierarchy forms the vertical structure, the functional units and departments form the horizontal structure, and the distributed geographical locations of an enterprise characterises the spatial structure of an enterprise as depicted in Figure 2. The reflection on Complex Adaptive System (Holland, 2006) further enriches the understanding of the enterprise complexity. In principle, a complex adaptive system is not deterministic automatons, rather their behaviours emerge from the interactions of the connected sub-systems, individuals or agents. A complex adaptive system evolves over time by changing linkages between the agents, shifting the pattern of interconnections, and changing the individual agent behaviours. Moreover, in an enterprise the individual sub-systems, elements or agents self-organise (Drazin and Sandelands, 1992) their structure and behaviour. These characteristics emphasise the emergent behaviour, adaptability and autonomy of an enterprise and their constituent units.

Figure 3. Spectrum of modeling and analysis approach

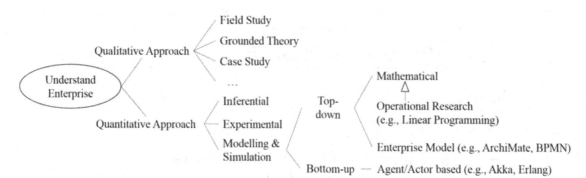

Finally, modern organisational theory, mainly the research presented by Richard Daft (Daft, 2012), investigates the characteristics of the system elements that include the sub-systems, elements and/or agents. The theory advocates a socio-technical viewpoint to describe the system elements. It considers that the enterprises are made up of multiple mechanistic and organic entities, wherein the mechanistic entities are not necessarily the machines but they are characterised by machinelike standard laws and rules. The organic entities, in contrast, are free-flowing and adaptive. They do not strictly conform to mathematical equations or law of physics, rather they are flexible to adopt behavioural rules and regulations at any given time. This socio-technical viewpoint acknowledges the adaptability and autonomy as described in CAS theory. In addition, the socio-technical viewpoint imparts the uncertainty and intentionality as inherent characteristics of the enterprise. Collectively, they consider an enterprise as composition of multiple units (system of systems) where each unit is characterised as: *modular, composable, reactive, autonomous, intentional, adaptable, temporal* and *probabilistic* as discussed in (Barat et al. 2018). Fundamentally, intentionality, reactiveness, autonomy, and adaptiveness characteristics are traced to *complexity theory*. The organisational theory imposes characteristics, such as modularity, composability, structural adaptiveness and behavioural uncertainties. Cybernetics and organisational theory highlight the existence of nonlinearity and temporal delays in the interactions within the enterprise units and between an enterprise and its environment.

A collective synthesis of these theories form an argument that an effective virtual representation of a real enterprise requires precise modelling and analysis support for all aspects of interest and the desired characteristics in an integrated form. The next section presents the state of the art of modelling and analysis techniques and their suitability with respect to these desired characteristics.

STATE OF THE ART OF MODELLING AND ANALYSIS TECHNIQUES

The analysis to understand a complex system or enterprise is typically approached using two broad categories: qualitative approach (Mcmillan, 1980) and quantitative approach (Currall and Towler, 2003). The qualitative approach is concerned with the subjective assessment of the underlying enterprise through a range of management techniques such as interviews, discussions, and field studies. The quantitative approach, in contrast, involves precise interpretation of system data, structure and behaviours.

The quantitative approach is further classified into three categories: (a) *inferential approach*, (b) *experimental approach* and (c) *modelling and simulation* approach (Kothari, 2004) as pictorially represented in Figure 3. The inferential approach (Michalski, 1993) analyses the existing system data (*i.e.*, trace or historical data) to infer the characteristics of an enterprise. The experimental approach comprehends an enterprise by manipulating the system variables and observing their effects in a controlled environment. The modelling and simulation approach, in contrast, relies on the philosophy of *science of the artificial* (Simon, 1996) where one or more aspect(s) of an enterprise is/are represented in an abstract form or a model. The modelling and simulation approach imitates a real enterprise using a (purposive) model, explores a range of scenarios by simulating the possible (forward looking) changes incorporated into the model, and develops a precise understanding about an enterprise by interpreting the simulation results. The modelling and simulation approach is classified into various classes and sub-classes as shown in Figure 3. In particular, the modelling and simulation approach visualises systems using two broad approaches: top-down approach and bottom-up approach (Thomas and McGarry, 1994). A top-down approach models an enterprise as a whole and adopts reductionist view to decompose it into smaller parts to understand the parts in isolation. This approach uses a range of models to represent and analyse enterprises. These models are: (i) mathematical model and (ii) enterprise model (EM). The mathematical models, such as linear programming (Candes and Tao, 2005) and integer programming (Schrijver, 1998), represent a system using mathematical formulae and use rigorous mathematical and statistical problem solving techniques for system analysis. Over the years, the Simulink and MATLAB (Klee and Allen, 2016) are extensively used for modelling, analysing and simulation complex systems. In contrast, the enterprise models (EMs), such as ArchiMate (Iacob, et al. 2012), i* (Yu et al. 2006) and BPMN (White, 2008), and System Dynamics (SD) (Meadows and Wright, 2008), are typically less rigorous than mathematical models. However they serve a wide range of modelling and analysis needs of the complex enterprises. A bottom-up approach starts from the parts or micro-behaviours and arrives at a holistic view of a system through composition. The bottom up approach uses the agent and actor based technologies, such as Erlang (Armstrong, 1996), Akka (Allen, 2013), and Scala Actor (Haller and Odersky, 2009), for modelling and analysing systems.

From the spectrum of modelling and analysis approaches presented in Figure 3, the efficacy of a qualitative approach is chiefly based on the human intuitions and the cognitive capabilities of involved stakeholders. With increasing enterprise complexity, significant non-linearity and inherent uncertainty, those qualitative approaches are becoming less effective for large complex enterprise. The inferential approach that relies on historical data works well for enterprises that are governed by mechanistic rules. The experimental approaches may not be an effective option in the current context for two reasons: (i) conducting experiments on a real environment is not always an economically viable option (Simon, 1996) and (ii) real life experiments are often restrictive and typically they are conducted in a localised context, which fail to understand the ramification of the localised changes in a global context. The modelling and simulation approach, in contrast, is less restrictive and free from historical biases as compared to the other two approaches. It helps to analyse the (hypothetical) changes and capable of observing the long term consequences under various anticipated/predicted environmental disruptions. Moreover, the simulation is considered as an effective epistemic engine to understand system when system data is not available, credibility of the existing data is questionable, conducting experiments on a real system is not a feasible option or other two options are not economically viable (Tolk et al. 2013). From modelling and simulation approaches, the mathematical model is useful consideration when relevant aspects of the system can be suitably modelled using algebraic equations, which is difficult proposition for an enterprise that

Table 1. Evaluation Summary of state of the art Enterprise modelling techniques

	Why	What	How	Who	When	Where	Modularity	Composability	Reactiveness	Autonomous	Intentional	Adaptable	Uncertainty	Temporal	Emergentism	Visualisation	Analysis	Simulation
Zachman	S	S	S	S	S	S	S	N	N	N	N	N	N	N	N	N	N	N
UML	I	S	S	S	I	I	S	S	N	N	N	N	N	N	N	S	S	N
ArchiMate	S	S	S	S	I	I	S	I	S	N	S	N	N	N	N	S	S	N
BPMN	N	I	S	S	I	I	S	S	S	N	N	N	N	N	N	S_{How}	S_{How}	S_{How}
ARIS	I	S	S	S	I	I	S	S	S	N	N	N	N	N	N	S_{How}	S_{How}	S_{How}
i*	S	N	N	S	N	N	S	S	N	N	N	N	N	N	N	S_{Why}	S_{Why}	S_{Why}
MEMO	S	S	S	S	N	N	S	S	I	I	N	N	N	I	N	S	S	I
DEVS	N	N	S	N	S	N	S	S	S	N	N	N	N	N	N	S_{How}	S_{How}	S_{How}
BMM	S	N	I	N	N	N	I	N	N	N	S	N	N	N	N	N	N	N
SD	N	I	S	N	I	N	I	N	I	S	N	N	I	S	N	I	S	S_{How}
EKD & 4EM	S	S	S	S	N	N	S	S	N	N	N	N	N	N	N	S	I	N
DEMO	N	I	S	I	N	N	I	I	S	N	N	N	N	N	N	S_{How}	S_{How}	N
EPC	N	I	S	N	I	S	S	S	S	N	N	N	I	S	N	S_{How}	S_{How}	S_{How}
Petri Net	N	I	S	N	S	S	S	S	S	N	N	I	S	N	N	S_{How}	S_{How}	S_{How}
KAOS	S	I	N	I	N	N	S	S	N	N	N	N	N	N	N	I	I	N
EEML	I	S	S	S	N	N	N	N	N	N	N	N	N	N	N	I	N	N
S=Suitable, Sx = Suitable for Aspect X, I=Inadequate, N=Not Suitable																		

exhibit socio-technical characteristics, significant uncertainty and emergent behaviours (Simon, 1991). It can be argued that their use is largely limited for deterministic and bounded systems or enterprises.

The EM techniques are used to comprehend large and complex business enterprises (Sandkuhl, 2016, Loucopoulos, 2015). From the spectrum of enterprise models (EMs), a class of enterprise models provide a well-defined structure to represent the enterprise aspects and offer a variety of visualisation techniques to help humans obtain the desired understanding of the enterprise. For instance, Zachman Framework and ArchiMate are such kind of specifications. The other class of enterprise models are machine interpretable and/or simulatable specifications. They are capable of precise analyses for one or limited aspects. For instance, BPMN analyses and simulates the behavioural aspect (*i.e.*, *how* and *who* aspects), i* analyses the high level goals and objectives (*i.e.*, *why* aspect), and System Dynamic model simulates dynamic behaviour of the system (i.e., *what* and *how* aspects). The multi-modelling and co-simulation environments, such as DEVS (Camus et al. 2015) and MEMO (Frank, 2002), demonstrate further advancements by supporting the analysis of multiple aspects. A comprehensive report high-lighting the suitability of EM techniques to specify and analyse necessary aspects and characteristics is presented in Table 1. Principally, the EM techniques adopt a top-down approach to model an enterprise as a whole and use a reductionist view for precise understanding. They are not suitable for specifying socio-technical characteristics such as intentionality, autonomy, adaptability and inherent uncertainty. Moreover, they are not congnisant of emergentism.

On the other hand, a wide range of actor and agent technologies exist as listed in Table 2. They help to understand emergentism through bottom-up modelling and simulation. Most of them fare better in analysing the systems with socio-technical characteristics, such as autonomy, reactiveness and adaptability.

However, they do not support the specification of complex goals (i.e., *why* aspect), complex hierarchies of an enterprise (*i.e.,* what aspect), and behavioural uncertainty. Their characteristics are largely generic with respect to the desired aspects and characteristics. A consolidated report on suitability analysis is presented in Table 3.

Table 2. State of the art actor and agent technologies

1. Erlang (Armstrong, 1996), 2. Akka (Allen, 2013), 3. BDI (Rao et al. 1995), 4. SALSA (Varela and Agha, 2001), 5. Act (Agha, 1986b), 6. E (Miller et al. 2005), 7. Rebeca (Sirjani et al. 2004), 8. Act 1, 2 and 3 (Lieberman, 1981), 9. ThAL (Kim, 1997), 10. Pony (Clebsch, 2015), 11. GAML (Grignard et al. 2013), 12. Scala Actor (Haller and Odersky, 2009),13. AnyLogic (Borshchev, 2013), 14. Kilim Srinivasan and Mycroft, 2008), 15. NetLogo (Tisue and Wilensky, 2004)), 16. JADE (Bellifemine et al. 1999)

As shown in Table 1 and Table 3, none of the existing modelling and analysis technique/technology is capable of supporting the desired modelling and analysis needs to represent and comprehend a complex enterprise. Therefore, developing a chain of non-interoperable tools supporting paradigmatically diverse modelling languages and analysis capabilities can be considered as an option for constructing a digital twin of an enterprise and enabling necessary analyses. One such tool-chain involving i*, BPMN and System Dynamic model is shown in Figure 4. As discussed in (Kulkarni et al. 2015a, 2015b), the efficacy of such an approach requires: (a) meaningful decomposition of an enterprise model into multiple models (*i.e.*, intrinsic complexity), and (b) correlation and synthesis of the analysis outcomes, which are produced from \various tools of a tool-chain (*i.e.*, accidental complexity). This chapter advocates an extended form of actor-based modelling and simulation approach to specify necessary aspects and characteristics

Table 3. Analysis summary of actor and agent technologies

Requirements	Support	Comments
Why	Supported only in BDI technology	No explicit construct to capture Why aspect in rest of the actor and agent technologies
What	Support simple structure	1. Most of the actor and agent technologies support simple actor structure, 2. Akka supports a hierarchical actor structure.
How	Supported	Constructs Behaviour, Turn and Message specify the *How* aspect
Who	Supported	*Who* aspect can be specified using the notion of *Actor* or *Agent*
When	Not supported	No guarantee in the order in which the Messages can be delivered makes the *When* computation difficult for an actor/agent system
Where	Supported	Where aspect can be represented using Actor/Agent
Modularity	Supported	Inherent characteristic of actor and agent technologies
Composability	Limited support	The actor and agent frameworks rely on the underlying languages for composition.
Reactive	Supported	Sending and receiving Messages help to specify the reactive nature
Autonomous	Supported	Inherent characteristic of all actor and agent technologies
Intentional	Supported only in BDI technology	No other actor and agent technology is capable of specifying the intention of an Actor/Agent
Adaptable	Supported	Constructs new and become help to specify the adaptability
Uncertainty	Not supported	No construct to capture uncertainty in an explicit manner
Temporality	Not supported	No construct to represent temporal behaviour in an explicit form
Emergentism	Supported	Actor and agent technologies are capable of producing emergent behaviour
Simulation	Partially Supported	Actor and agent technologies support bottom-up simulation
Visualisation	Not supported	Visualisation is not supported in most of the actor and agent technologies.

Figure 4. An illustration of ad-hoc and multi-modeling and co-simulation approach

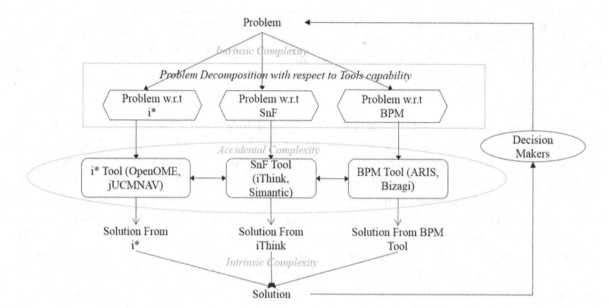

of the complex enterprises and enable required analysis needs, such that the intrinsic and accidental complexities are eliminated without compromising the expressibility, analytical rigour and intuitiveness.

AN ACTOR BASED APPROACH

A schematic overview of a digital twin to analyse, adapt, transform and design a complex enterprise is depicted in Figure 5. As shown in the figure, the approach adopts a model driven approach to represent an enterprise, relies on simulation techniques to produce quantitative evidences for various hypothetical courses of action (*i.e.*, possible control measures, adaptation choices, transformation alternatives and design choices), and a human-in-the-loop evaluation step to evaluate the produced evidences. The proposed approach considers an iterative loop where the courses of action can be introduced as model change and their consequence can be observed by simulating the changed model. Observation of multiple simulations of enterprise model with/without courses of action helps to understand the near-term and long-term consequences of the courses of action (without implementing them in reality). Presented approach uses an extended form of an actor abstraction to closely imitate an enterprise and its constituent elements in a bottom up manner. Fundamentally, the micro-behaviours of the constituent primitive units of an enterprise need to be specified using the notion of *actors* and the emergent macro behaviour of whole enterprise to be observed through actor-based simulation. A model-driven approach to replicate an enterprise in a synthetic form, ascertain the validity of the synthetic environment, and carry out various what-if analysis (*i.e.*, what will be consequence if a specific course of action is applied to the model) using a human-in-loop method are discussed next.

Figure 5. An approach to realize digital twin of complex enterprises

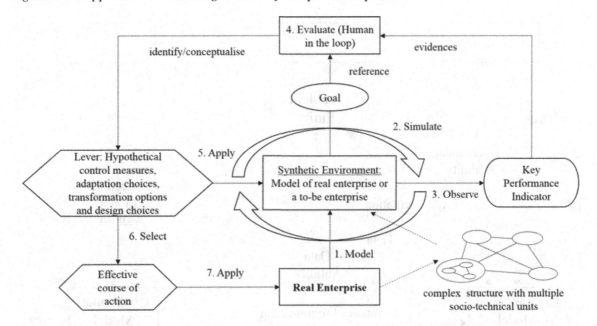

Overarching Method

An extended form of simulation method proposed by Robert Sargent in (Sargent, 2005) is considered as an integrated method for constructing and validating synthetic environment of a digital twin and supporting an iterative analysis to evaluate control, adaptation and transformation alternatives. The integrated method is shown in Figure 6, where extensions to the canonical method are shown using blue colored text and arrows. As shown in the figure, the canonical simulation method proposed by Robert Sargent in (Sargent, 2005) recommends three types representations: *problem entity*, *conceptual model* and *computerised model* (or simulation model). The problem entity is a real enterprise or the domain knowledge about a to-be enterprise. The conceptual model is a machine interpretable purpose specific view of a problem entity, and the computerised model is a simulatable representation of a captured conceptual model.

In this canonical method, a conceptual model is constructed for a problem entity during the *modeling* phase. It constructs conceptual model and ensures the fidelity or truthfulness of the constructed model from epistemological perspective as recommended by Stewart Robinson (Robinson, 2008) and Andreas Tolk *et al.* (Tolk et al. 2013). A computerised model is encoded or translated from conceptual model in *computer programming and implementation* phase. The synthesis on the problem entity is conducted by simulating/executing the computerised model (henceforth simulation model) in an *experimentation* phase.

This canonical method is extended along two dimensions – (a) establish a connection from problem entity to simulation model for initialising a simulation model with real data, and make simulation model up to date as shown in Figure 1, and (b) a human in the loop iterative what-if analyses. The second extensions adopts the decision-making process proposed by Richard Daft in (Daft, 2012) to evaluate the control, adaptation and transformation options through simulation, observation and application of courses of action loop as shown in Figure 6.

Figure 6. An overarching method to construct, validate and analyze digital twin

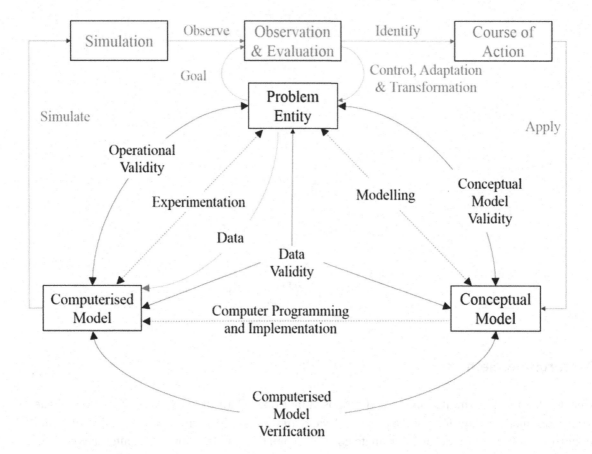

A Conceptual Model

The theoretical foundations of system theories and the management viewpoints advocate a set of constructs to sufficiently describe a broad class of enterprises as well as their environments. The key constructs and their relationships are depicted in a meta-model form as shown in the upper part of the Figure 7.

Modern organisation theory and general system theory (GST) consider that an enterprise comprises *Structure* (*i.e., what* aspect), *Behaviour* (*i.e., How, Who,* and *Where* aspects) and *State*. The perception of an open system imparts that an enterprise interacts with its *Environment*. Organisational theory considers a notion of an organisational memory (Levitt and March, 1988), i.e., a *Trace* describing the *What* and *When* aspects. The management literature further advocates that an enterprise has its own *Goal* (i.e., *Why* aspect).

The adaptation and transformation of an enterprise introduce two core concepts: *course of action* and *key performance indicator* (KPI) as shown in Figure 7. The course of action represents the changes in Structure, Behaviour, and Goal that need to be considered as part of adaptation and/or transformation. The *key performance indicator* describes the observable state of an enterprise that can be compared with respect to its *Goal*. Therefore, it is argued that the constructs highlighted in the upper part of the meta-

Figure 7. A meta-model to represent complex enterprises using actors

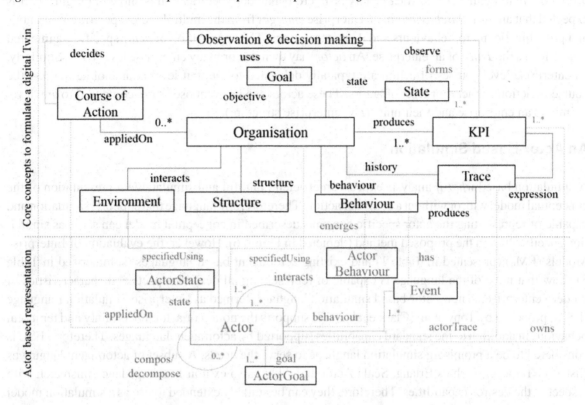

model depicted in Figure 7 are necessary aspects to represent an enterprise. However, these constructs are not capable of describing the desired characteristics in an explicit manner.

An actor-based representation of above constructs as depicted in the bottom part of Figure 7 is proposed to capture the desired characteristics of a complex enterprise. As shown in the figure, an enterprise can be represented using a set of *Actors* where these actors are *modular* and *reactive* units. They have their own *State*, *Goals*, (micro) *Behaviour* and *Trace*. They interact with other actors through *Events*. The collection of *ActorStates* form an enterprise *State*. The micro *Behaviours* of all actors collectively define the enterprise *Behaviour*. These micro behaviours can be *autonomous*, *adaptive*, *temporal* and

Figure 8. Abstract syntax of behavioral specification

```
behaviour    ::= event_spec                          Set of event definitions
event_spec   ::= on event when condition do action   On an event if condition is true then perform an action
condition    ::= exp                                 Expression on state variables
action       ::= update_state                        Update state variable
             |   send actor_event (message) to actor Send message to other actor
             |   new actor(initial_state)            Create new actor
             |   probably (int) do action            Probabilistic behaviour

event        ::= time_event                          Raised by the simulator
             |   actor event                         Raised by an actor
```

probabilistic in nature. An abstract syntax of micro behaviour specification is shown in Figure 8. It is expected that an overall *Behaviour* of an enterprise *emerges* from the multiple actor specific autonomous and probabilistic micro-behaviours and their interactions. The aggregation of *actor* specific fragmented *Traces* forms the *Trace* of an enterprise. An *actor* may own one or many enterprise level KPIs. Similarly, an enterprise level courses of action are typically delegated to the unit level course of action, *i.e.* the course of action for actor or a set of actors. These actors can be composed or decomposed to any level to imitate an enterprise and their units (*i.e.*, enterprise structure).

An Actor-Based Simulation

A simulation based *what-if* analysis expects an efficient, faithful and simulatable representation of the conceptual model with or without a course of action. Therefore, any language that supports simulation and capable of representing the actor specific concepts described in conceptual model can serve as simulation specification in the proposed method (depicted in Figure 6). However, the evaluation of Enterprise Models (EMs) (presented in Table 1) and existing actor/agent based languages (summerised in Table 3) show that none of the language is capable of representing all desired aspects and characteristics of modern enterprise. A new actor-based simulation language, termed as Enterprise Simulation Language (ESL), proposed by Tony et al. (Clark et al. 2017) supports the notion of actor, uncertainty and temporal behaviour in addition to the standard capabilities supported by actor/agent languages. Therefore, ESL is considered to be a promising simulation language to serve the needs. A subset of actor/agent languages (listed in Table 2), such as Erlang, Scala Actor and Akka, also exhibit less impedance mismatch with respect to the desired capabilities. Therefore, they can be suitably extended to use as a simulation model in the proposed approach.

Model and Simulation Validation

The canonical form of simulation method (Sargent, 2005) recommends four kinds of validity - conceptual model validity, computerised model validity, data validity and operation validity as shown in Figure 6. The *conceptual model validity* ensures the *assumptions* and *simplifications* for constructing a conceptual model of real system are reasonable and valid, *i.e.*, the intended purpose is sufficiently captured in constructed conceptual model and the underlying assumptions of the conceptual model are correct. The key consideration of this validity is to capture complete and accurate information of a problem entity in the form of a conceptual model as discussed by Nelson *et al.* in (Nelson et al. 2012), Krogstie in (Krogstie, 2008), and Moody *et al.* in (Moody et al. 2003). The *computerised model verification* ensures the faithful translation of a conceptual model into a simulation model. The *operational validity* ascertains that the simulation results are sufficiently accurate, whereas the *data validity* ensures the data necessary for model construction, model validation, and model simulation are adequate, correct and possibly taken from real system.

The simulation research extensively relies on operational validity as the data validity and conceptual validity are effort and time intensive. Moreover, they are infeasible for transformation initiatives. The commonly used operation validation techniques are:

- **Operational Graphics and Animation**: This technique verifies a model by observing simulation results through graphs and animations.

- **Data Comparison**: Establish validity of a model by comparing simulation results with respect to the simulation results of an established model. For example, comparison of a simulation model with an analytical model, comparison of a simulation model that is constructed using Stock-and-Flow with a valid simulation model that is constructed using linear programming, *etc*.
- **Historical Data Validation**: Compare simulation results with the historical data of the real system.
- **Traces**: Capture behaviour of the model entities in the form of traces and analyse them through appropriate visualisation or analytical techniques.

Data Sensing Mechanism

The constructed model (virtual environment) needs to be populated with the real data from enterprise (real environment) to faithfully imitate the current state such that the virtual enterprise can produce similar analysis results as a real environment. In the proposed model architecture (presented in Figure 7), a state of an enterprise can be replicated by two types of data: (a) data to populate initial *ActorStates* of all actors of an enterprise model, and (b) history/trace of an enterprise to form actor *Traces*. Both the data flows require a sense and transform architecture, where the necessary data to be sensed from real enterprise, and then transformed to mitigate the impedance mismatch between physical world and virtual world. Principally, the fragmented information about the *State* of an enterprise to be transformed into multiple *ActorStates*, and existing information about enterprise *Trace* to be transformed into actor *Traces* (*see*, Figure 7). The IoT technologies (Lee, 2017) are effective means to sense that data from real systems, and a model driven enterprise data integration approach (Reddy, 2010) is an effective technique for desired data transformation.

ILLUSTRATION

Presented approach is illustrated using a scenario of a grocery retailer network (Barat et. al, 2019) with multiple warehouses and stores that are served by a fleet of trucks for transporting products as shown in Figure 9. The warehouses stock a range of products and supply them to the stores. It involves packing the products (using trolleys), loading packed products to the trucks/carriers and delivering them to respective stores on predefined routes. These packaging, loading and delivering processes are typically governed by multiple spatio-temporal constraints, such as: (i) available stocks in the warehouses, (ii) labour capacity for picking and packaging products in the warehouses, (iii) the volume and weight carrying capacity of the trucks, (iv) the transportation times between warehouses and stores, (v) the product receiving capacity of each store, and (vi) available shelf space for each product in each store. They also exhibit several uncertainties that emerge due to the probabilistic behaviours of the individual elements, such as: unavailability and varying productivity of the labours, unavailability and unaccounted delays of the trucks, the propensity of damage of specific product when they are packed with other product types, transported in specific carrier/truck, and stochasticity of the customer arrival. The constraints and uncertainties significantly influence the state of the stores (*e.g.*, availability, non-availability and wastage of products at stores at specific moment), and subsequently the replenishment order process.

A typical retail chain that contains tens of warehouses, thousands of stores, thousands of trucks, and a hundred thousand unique product types often control, adapt and transform its operation to improve the

Figure 9. Pictorial representation of supply chain networks

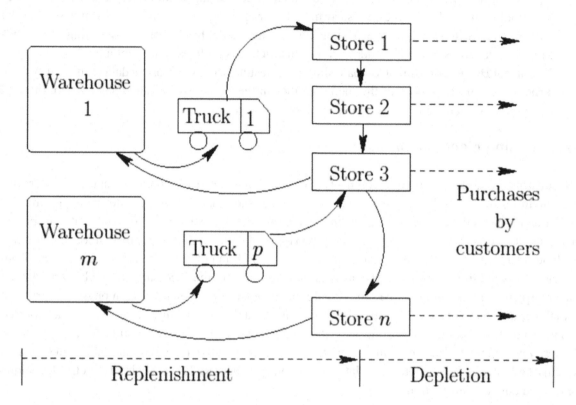

profit margin and customer base. The control, adaptation and transformation options that are frequently considered are:

• **Control options**: (a) optimum order at each ordering moment such that the product availability is high and wastage is minimum between two delivery moments, (b) optimum packaging of products such that the trolleys and trucks are appropriately utilised and damage due to product packaging is minimum, and (c) optimum labour strength.

• **Adaptation options**: (a) define appropriate ordering moment (OM) and delivery moment (DM) cycles (*i.e.*, elapse time between two DMs, OMs and OM-to-DM) such that product can be replenished effectively, (b) use of different types of carrier for different products (with appropriate volume, weight capacities, propensity of breakdown), and (c) define new route for product delivery.

• **Transformation options**: (a) introduce new product type with different life-span and characteristics, (b) introduce new stores, and (c) replace human labour with robots.

A representation of the retail network using presented actor based approach is shown in Figure 10. As shown in the figure, it comprises multiple interconnected subsystems, such as warehouses, stores, trucks, and store shelves, and several individualistic elements, such as products, labours and customers. These subsystems and individual elements are represented using *actors*, which have their own (hierarchical) composition structure, behaviour and state. For example, a warehouse actor contains multiple product

Figure 10. An actor based representation of supply chain network

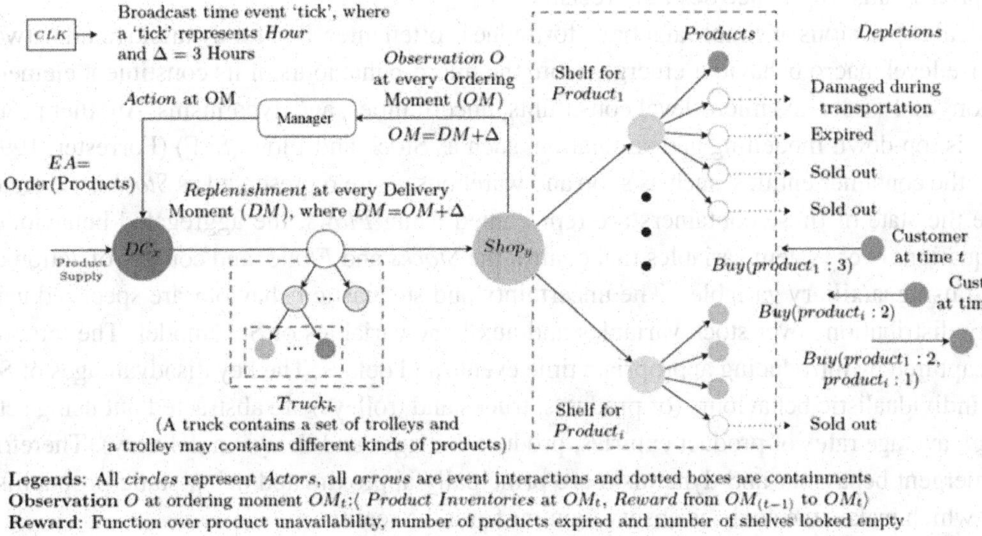

Legends: All *circles* represent *Actors*, all *arrows* are event interactions and dotted boxes are containments
Observation O at ordering moment OM_t:⟨ *Product Inventories* at OM_t, *Reward* from $OM_{(t-1)}$ to OM_t⟩
Reward: Function over product unavailability, number of products expired and number of shelves looked empty

actors, trolley actor, truck actors and labour actors. From behavioural perspective, a warehouse actor receives orders from multiple store actors at every ordering moments (OM). Internally, the warehouse actor utilise labour actor to pack the product actors into the trolley actors (try to use labours optimally to pack and load all ordered products before delivery moment), and uses truck actors to send trolley actors to the respective store actors at every delivery moment (DM). Similarly, a truck actor can accommodate a fixed number of trolleys based on its capacity (hence all ordered products are not guaranteed to deliver by next DM), follows a designated route and dispatches trolleys at stores (with or without any delay). On arrival of a truck, a store unloads products from trolleys and places them in designated shelves. Each store places

replenishment order based on the stocks of all products and other factors, such as wastage due product expiry, packaging, unavailability of products at ordering moments (OM). Each product has its own state (*e.g.*, damaged, expired, in store, sold, *etc.*), which is largely dependent on spatio-temporal conditions (*i.e.*, how it is packed while transportation, time taken to deliver, shelf life-span), customer arrival rate, availability of other related products, *etc.*

DISCUSSION

Deciding an effective control, adaptation or transformation option for a specific goal requires precise understanding of the whole network. It is argued that a representation and analysis of such complex and dynamic network using inferential approach is ineffective due to insufficient data. For example, the packaging of products in a trolley and truck is specific for an order, hence every delivery may have a new configuration of products, which may lead to unforeseen damage quantities. The combination of product order and customer footfall in a store also can be unique between two delivery moments.

Moreover, introduction of new product in an existing network leads to an unforeseen situation where an inferential approach fails to produce desired precision.

The analytical expressions or simple algebraic formulae is often infeasible for dynamic retail network as the enterprise level macro behaviour emerges from the micro-behaviours of its constituent elements, their interactions and associated micro-level constraints, uncertainties, and dynamisms. Another prominent approach is top-down modelling and simulation, such as Stock-and-Flow (SnF) (Forrester, 1994). In SnF model, the container entities, such as shop and warehouses, are represented as *Stocks*, the factors that influence the state of those containers are represented using *Flows*, the aggregated behaviour is encoded as equations over system variables that control the *Stocks* and *Flows*, and courses of action can be represented using auxiliary variables. The uncertainty and stochastic behaviour are specified using the probability distributions over stock variables and auxiliary variables of SnF model. The temporal behaviour is captured by introducing appropriate time events and delays. The key disadvantages of SnF model is: the individualistic behaviours (of products, trucks and trolleys) are abstracted out using set of equations (*e.g.*, average rates of product expiries, product damages and delays in delivery). Therefore, the overall emergent behaviour and dynamism are principally approximated using static probabilistic distributions, which makes the analysis observation far from the reality.

This chapter advocates an extended form of actor-based model and bottom-up simulation to represent complex and dynamic enterprise using digital twin and support necessary *what-if* analysis to evaluate control, adaptation, and transformation choices prior to their implementation. The actor-based modelling abstraction supports individualistic behaviour and socio-technical characteristics that include *modularity*, *composability*, *reactiveness*, *autonomy*, *intentional* and *adaptive* behaviours. The extensions in the form of probabilistic behaviour and notion of *time* event (as shown in abstract syntax in Figure 8) help in representing and analysing associated *uncertainty* and *temporal behaviour*. The bottom up simulation help to understand the emergentism and dynamic characteristics.

TECHNOLOGY SUPPORT

As discussed earlier that an effective ulilisation of a digital twin involves four activities: (i) constructing a virtual environment (ii) establishing faithfulness of the constructed virtual environment, (iii) instantiating virtual environment with real data, and (iv) performing what-if analysis on virtual environment. An actor based language, ESL, is proposed to specify virtual environment. However, the proposed approach expects the domain to specify virtual environment using ESL. This construction process can be made intuitive by supporting a specification workbench with a domain specific visual language and suitable model transformation technique to generate ESL programs from high-level specification. Further, it can be automated to an extent by constructing models from the existing artifacts of real systems, such as data and process definitions. The current form of validation uses methodological rigour to establish the faithfulness. Further research is required to automate the validation of constructed virtual environment from existing real data. Instantiation of virtual model is a continuous process where sensing technologies (Lee, 2017) can be effectively leveraged for automation. The what-if analysis is currently guided by human experts. The exploration can be aided by reinforcement learning agent as highlighted in Barat et al. (2019).

CONCLUSION

The necessary modelling and analysis supports for developing digital twin for complex and dynamic business enterprises are discussed in this chapter. Precise modelling and analysis needs for constructing an effective digital twin are derived by reflecting on the established system theories, organisational theory, information system theory, and management viewpoints as ground truth. The proposed approach consider the needs for all six interrogative aspects: *why, what, how, when, where,* and *who* as recommended in Zachman framework. The in-depth analysis also demonstrated the importance of socio-technical characteristics, such as *modularity, compositional, reactive, autonomous, intentional, adaptive, uncertainty* and *temporal behaviour,* to comprehend modern enterprise. The state-of-the-art modelling and analysis techniques that include enterprise modelling and analysis techniques and actor/agent languages are argued to be inadequate for the quantitative analysis of the modern enterprises and a novel approach to construct digital twin of complex enterprises to support quantitative what-if analyses is presented. The proposed approach advocates an actor-based bottom-up simulation and adopts an established method for model creation and model validation, and uses management rigour for systematic *what-if* analyses for quantitative, evidence-driven, informed decision-making using a digital twin.

REFERENCES

Agha, G. (1986a). *Actors: A Model of Concurrent Computation in Distributed Systems.* Cambridge, MA: MIT Press.

Agha, G. (1986b). An Overview of Actor Languages. *SIGPLAN Notices, 21*(10), 58–67. doi:10.1145/323648.323743

Allen, J. (2013). *Effective Akka.* O'Reilly Media, Inc.

Anderson, P. (1999). Perspective: Complexity theory and organization science. *Organization Science, 10*(3), 216–232. doi:10.1287/orsc.10.3.216

Armstrong, J. (1996). Erlang - a Survey of the Language and its Industrial Applications. *Proceedings of the symposium on industrial applications of Prolog (INAP),* 8.

Ashby, W. R. (1981). *Mechanisms of Intelligence: Ashbys Writings on Cybernetics.* Eipiphiny Society.

Barat, S., Khadilkar, H., Meisheri, H., Kulkarni, V., Baniwal, V., Kumar, P., & Gajrani, M. (2019). Actor Based Simulation for Closed Loop Control of Supply Chain using Reinforcement Learning. In *Proceedings of the 18th International Conference on Autonomous Agents and MultiAgent Systems* (pp. 1802-1804). International Foundation for Autonomous Agents and Multiagent Systems.

Barat, S., Kulkarni, V., Clark, T., & Barn, B. (2018). A Model Based Approach for Complex Dynamic Decision-Making. [Springer.]. *Communications in Computer and Information Science, 880,* 94–118. doi:10.1007/978-3-319-94764-8_5

Bellifemine, F., Poggi, A., & Rimassa, G. (1999). JADE–A FIPA-compliant agent framework. *Proceedings of PAAM, 99,* 33.

Borshchev, A. (2013). *The big book of simulation modeling: multimethod modeling with AnyLogic 6.* AnyLogic North America.

Camus, B., Bourjot, C., & Chevrier, V. (2015). Combining DEVS with multi-agent concepts to design and simulate multi-models of complex systems (WIP). *Proceedings of the Symposium on Theory of Modeling & Simulation: DEVS Integrative M&S Symposium*, 85–90.

Candes, E. J., & Tao, T. (2005). Decoding by linear programming. *IEEE Transactions on Information Theory*, *51*(12), 4203–4215. doi:10.1109/TIT.2005.858979

Casti, J. L. (1994). *Complexification explaining a paradoxical world through the science of surprise.* HarperPerennial - A Division of Harper Collins Publishers.

Clark, T., Kulkarni, V., Barat, S., & Barn, B. (2017). ESL: An Actor-Based Platform for Developing Emergent Behaviour Organisation Simulations. In *International Conference on Practical Applications of Agents and Multi-Agent Systems*, (pp. 311–315). Springer. 10.1007/978-3-319-59930-4_27

Clebsch, S. (2015). The pony programming language. *The Pony Developers*. https://www.ponylang.org/

Currall, S. C., & Towler, A. J. (2003). *Research methods in management and organizational research: Toward integration of qualitative and quantitative techniques.* Sage Publications.

Daft, R. (2012). *Organization theory and design.* Nelson Education.

Daft, R. L., & Lewin, A. Y. (1990). Can organization studies begin to break out of thenormal science straitjacket? An editorial essay. *Organization Science*, *1*(1), 1–9. doi:10.1287/orsc.1.1.1

Drazin, R., & Sandelands, L. (1992). Autogenesis: A perspective on the process of organizing. *Organization Science*, *3*(2), 230–249. doi:10.1287/orsc.3.2.230

Forrester, J. W. (1994). System dynamics, systems thinking, and soft OR. *System Dynamics Review*, *10*(2-3), 245–256. doi:10.1002dr.4260100211

Frank, U. (2002). Multi-perspective Enterprise Modeling (MEMO) conceptual framework and modeling languages. In *System Sciences, 2002. HICSS. Proceedings of the 35th Annual Hawaii International Conference on*, (pp. 1258–1267). IEEE.

Glaessgen, E., & Stargel, D. (2012, April). The digital twin paradigm for future NASA and US Air Force vehicles. In *53rd AIAA/ASME/ASCE/AHS/ASC Structures, Structural Dynamics and Materials Conference 20th AIAA/ASME/AHS Adaptive Structures Conference 14th AIAA* (p. 1818). Academic Press.

Grieves, M. (2005). Product lifecycle management: The new paradigm for enterprises. *International Journal of Product Development*, *2*(1-2), 71–84. doi:10.1504/IJPD.2005.006669

Grieves, M. (2011). *Virtually perfect: Driving innovative and lean products through product lifecycle management.* Space Coast Press.

Grieves, M. (2012, July). Virtually Indistinguishable. In *IFIP International Conference on Product Lifecycle Management* (pp. 226-242). Springer.

Grieves, M., & Vickers, J. (2017). Digital twin: Mitigating unpredictable, undesirable emergent behavior in complex systems. In *Transdisciplinary perspectives on complex systems* (pp. 85–113). Cham: Springer. doi:10.1007/978-3-319-38756-7_4

Grignard, A., Taillandier, P., Gaudou, B., Vo, D. A., Huynh, N. Q., & Drogoul, A. (2013). GAMA 1.6: Advancing the art of complex agent-based modeling and simulation. *International Conference on Principles and Practice of Multi-Agent Systems*, 117–131. 10.1007/978-3-642-44927-7_9

Haller, P., & Odersky, M. (2009). Scala actors: Unifying thread-based and event-based programming. *Theoretical Computer Science*, 410(2), 202–220. doi:10.1016/j.tcs.2008.09.019

Hewitt, C., & Smith, B. (1975). *A plasma primer. Draft.* Cambridge, MA: MIT Artificial Intelligence Laboratory.

Holland, J. H. (2006). Studying complex adaptive systems. *Journal of Systems Science and Complexity*, 19(1), 1–8. doi:10.100711424-006-0001-z

Iacob, M., Jonkers, D. H., Lankhorst, M., Proper, E., & Quartel, D. D. (2012). *ArchiMate 2.0 Specification: The Open Group.* Van Haren Publishing.

Kim, W. (1997). *ThAL: An actor system for efficient and scalable concurrent computing* (PhD thesis). University of Illinois at Urbana-Champaign.

Klee, H., & Allen, R. (2016). *Simulation of dynamic systems with MATLAB and Simulink. Crc Press. Kothari, C. R. (2004). Research methodology: Methods and techniques.* New Age International.

Krogstie, J. (2008). Using EEML for combined goal and process oriented modeling: A case study. *CEUR Workshop Proceedings*, 337, 112–129.

Kulkarni, V., Barat, S., Clark, T., & Barn, B. (2015a). Toward overcoming accidental complexity in organisational decision-making. In *Model Driven Engineering Languages and Systems* (pp. 368–377). MODELS.

Kulkarni, V., Barat, S., Clark, T., & Barn, B. (2015b). Using simulation to address intrinsic complexity in multi-modelling of enterprises for decision making. In *Proceedings of the Conference on Summer Computer Simulation*, (pp. 1–11). Society for Computer Simulation International.

Lee, I. (Ed.). (2017). *The Internet of Things in the Modern Business Environment.* IGI Global. doi:10.4018/978-1-5225-2104-4

Levitt, B., & March, J. G. (1988). Organizational learning. *Annual Review of Sociology*, 14(1), 319–338. doi:10.1146/annurev.so.14.080188.001535

Lieberman, H. (1981). *A preview of ACT 1.* MIT Artificial Intelligence Laboratory, A.I. Memo No. 625.

Loucopoulos, P., Stratigaki, C., Danesh, M. H., Bravos, G., Anagnostopoulos, D., & Dimitrakopoulos, G. (2015). Enterprise capability modeling: concepts, method, and application. In *Enterprise Systems (ES), 2015 International Conference on*, (pp. 66–77). IEEE. 10.1109/ES.2015.14

Mcmillan, C. J. (1980). Qualitative models of organisational decision-making. *Journal of General Management*, 5(4), 22–39. doi:10.1177/030630708000500402

Meadows, D. H., & Wright, D. (2008). *Thinking in systems: A primer*. Chelsea Green Publishing.

Michalski, R. S. (1993). Inferential theory of learning as a conceptual basis for multi strategy learning. *Machine Learning, 11*(2-3), 111–151. doi:10.1007/BF00993074

Miller, M. S., Tribble, E. D., & Shapiro, J. (2005). Concurrency among strangers. In *International Symposium on Trustworthy Global Computing*, (pp. 195–229). Springer. 10.1007/11580850_12

Moody, D., Sindre, G., Brasethvik, T., & Solvberg, A. (2003). Evaluating the quality of information models: empirical testing of a conceptual model quality framework. In *Proceedings of the 25th international conference on software engineering*, (pp. 295–305). IEEE Computer Society. 10.1109/ICSE.2003.1201209

Nelson, H. J., Poels, G., Genero, M., & Piattini, M. (2012). A conceptual modeling quality framework. *Software Quality Journal, 20*(1), 201–228. doi:10.100711219-011-9136-9

Rao, A. S., & Georgeff, M. P. (1995). BDI agents: from theory to practice. ICMAS, 95, 312–319.

Reddy, S. (2010). A Model Driven Approach to Enterprise Data Integration. In COMAD (p. 202). Academic Press.

Robinson, S. (2008). Conceptual modelling for simulation Part I: Definition and requirements. *The Journal of the Operational Research Society, 59*(3), 278–290. doi:10.1057/palgrave.jors.2602368

Sandkuhl, K., Fill, H.-G., Hoppenbrouwers, S., Krogstie, J., Leue, A., Matthes, F., ... Winter, R. (2016). Enterprise modelling for the masses – from elitist discipline to common practice. In *IFIP Working Conference on The Practice of Enterprise Modeling*, (pp. 225–240). Springer. 10.1007/978-3-319-48393-1_16

Sargent, R. G. (2005). Verification and validation of simulation models. *Proceedings of the 37th conference on Winter simulation*, 130–143.

Schleich, B., Anwer, N., Mathieu, L., & Wartzack, S. (2017). Shaping the digital twin for design and production engineering. *CIRP Annals, 66*(1), 141–144. doi:10.1016/j.cirp.2017.04.040

Schrijver, A. (1998). *Theory of linear and integer programming*. John Wiley & Sons.

Simon, H. A. (1991). The architecture of complexity. In *Facets of systems science* (pp. 457–476). Springer. doi:10.1007/978-1-4899-0718-9_31

Simon, H. A. (1996). *The sciences of the artificial*. MIT Press.

Sipp, C. M., & Elias, C. (2012). *Real Options and Strategic Technology Venturing: A New Paradigm in Decision Making* (Vol. 31). Springer Science & Business Media.

Sirjani, M., Movaghar, A., Shali, A., & De Boer, F. S. (2004). Modeling and verification of reactive systems using Rebeca. *Fundamenta Informaticae, 63*(4), 385–410.

Srinivasan, S., & Mycroft, A. (2008). Kilim: Isolation-typed actors for java. In *European Conference on Object-Oriented Programming*, (pp. 104–128). Springer.

Thomas, M., & McGarry, F. (1994). Top-down vs. bottom-up process improvement. *IEEE Software, 11*(4), 12–13. doi:10.1109/52.300121

Tisue, S., & Wilensky, U. (2004). Netlogo: A simple environment for modeling complexity. *International conference on complex systems*, 21, 16–21.

Tolk, A., Heath, B. L., Ihrig, M., Padilla, J. J., Page, E. H., Suarez, E. D., ... Yilmaz, L. (2013). Epistemology of modeling and simulation. In *Proceedings of the 2013 Winter Simulation Conference: Simulation: Making Decisions in a Complex World*, (pp. 1152–1166). IEEE Press. 10.1109/WSC.2013.6721504

Varela, C., & Agha, G. (2001). Programming dynamically reconfigurable open systems with SALSA. *ACM SIGPLAN Notices*, *36*(12), 20–34. doi:10.1145/583960.583964

Von Bertalanffy, L. (1968). General system theory. New York: Academic Press.

White, S. A. (2008). *BPMN modeling and reference guide: understanding and using BPMN*. Future Strategies Inc.

Yu, E., Strohmaier, M., & Deng, X. (2006). Exploring intentional modeling and analysis for enterprise architecture. *Enterprise Distributed Object Computing Conference Workshops*. d. doi:10.1109/ED-OCW.2006.36

Zachman, J. (1987). A framework for information systems architecture. *IBM Systems Journal*, *26*(3), 276–292. doi:10.1147j.263.0276

Chapter 5
Authoring Models of Regulations:
Providing Assistance and Validation

Sagar Sunkle

TCS Research, Tata Consultancy Services, India

Suman Roychoudhury

TCS Research, Tata Consultancy Services, India

Deepali Kholkar

TCS Research, Tata Consultancy Services, India

ABSTRACT

Modern enterprises operate in an unprecedented regulatory environment with the possibility of heavy penalties for non-compliance. Previous research in the field of compliance has established that the manual specification/tagging of the regulations not only fails to ensure their proper coverage but also negatively affects the turnaround time both in proving and maintaining the compliance. The contribution in this chapter is a framework that aids the domain experts in the transformation of regulations present in legal natural language text (English) to a model form via authoring and validation of structured English rules. This generated regulatory model is eventually translated to formal logic that enables formal compliance checking contrary to current industry practice, that provides content management-based, document-driven, and expert-dependent ways of managing regulatory compliance. The authors draw statistics from a real-world case study of money market statistical reporting (MMSR) regulations for a large European bank to demonstrate the benefits of aided authoring and validation.

DOI: 10.4018/978-1-7998-0108-5.ch005

INTRODUCTION

Regulatory compliance is a major concern for modern enterprises. Heavy penalties may be imposed on them due to non-compliance to a battery of regulations. Regulatory compliance therefore has become a top priority for the modern enterprises. To avoid unnecessary penalties and remain compliant with respect to newer regulations, enterprises are increasingly looking towards technologies that may assist them in their overall compliance checking process. The cost of building compliance systems from scratch is both effort intensive and time consuming due to enormous and complex collection of legal/compliance documents (Sunkle et. al, 2015a).

Prevalent solutions to regulatory compliance do not offer intelligent aids through the process of authoring and validating regulations. Typical solutions like the governance, risk, and compliance (GRC) offerings, rely on taxonomies, which are collection of predefined tags that can be affixed to data pertinent to the regulations (Sunkle et. al, 2015b). Taxonomy tagging tools used separately or from within the GRC frameworks, enables auto-population of, and in some cases, user definition of taxonomies (Racz et al., 2011). However, GRC based offerings do not support either validation or formal compliance checking of regulatory rules. Towards the other end of the spectrum, academic solutions to the compliance problem rely on using a formal specification of the regulatory rules (Becker et al., 2012). Such formal representation and subsequent checking of legal rules offers significant merit over existing GRC based frameworks in which compliance checking is manual (Roychoudhury et. al, 2017). Instead, we approach automated regulatory compliance checking with a focus on using targeted processing of legal texts to aid rule authoring in formal languages that would make both validation and checking possible.

We think that a high-level representation of regulatory rules in a domain-specific language is more suitable for adoption by domain experts (Roychoudhury et. al, 2017), since formal languages may present steep learning curve for the legal or domain experts. The high-level controlled natural language (CNL) acts as an abstraction layer on top of the formal specifications to hide the underlying complexities and provide a business friendly English like notation to express regulations. This language is adapted from Structured English (SE) compliant to OMG's Semantic of Business Vocabulary and Rules (SBVR)[1]. To help domain experts in authoring regulatory rules using our CNL seamlessly, we provide a machine-learning / natural-language processing (ML-NLP) based front-end engine that aids in constructing what we refer to as a domain model and dictionary (i.e., core concepts, relations, and mentions) from the regulatory text (Sunkle et al., 2016). We use the domain model and the dictionary to provide suggestions to domain experts in their authoring process.

Figure 1 motivates the above hypothesis and describes our end-to-end semi-automated compliance framework that has specific human touchpoints (i.e., manual intervention) (M) with tool support (T). Using machine-learning / distributional semantics techniques, a domain model (refer to number 1 in Figure 1) is first obtained by processing the given text with active participation by the domain expert (Sunkle et al., 2016). The domain model primarily captures the key concepts, relations and their mentions (i.e., ontology) in the given domain and serves as a core artefact for model authoring. For model authoring, the domain expert expresses the desired regulations in a controlled natural language (refer to number 2 in Figure 1) using the domain model / dictionary and rule suggestions originating from the ML-NLP engine (Roychoudhury et al., 2018). In our case, this language was built from scratch using the XText language engineering workbench[2] and adapted from OMG's SBVR Structured English (SE) specification. Once regulatory rules are authored in SE, a model of the regulation in SBVR is automatically generated (refer to number 3 in Figure 1). This model can be used as an intermediate representa-

Figure 1. Overview of automated compliance framework (Roychoudhury et al., 2018)

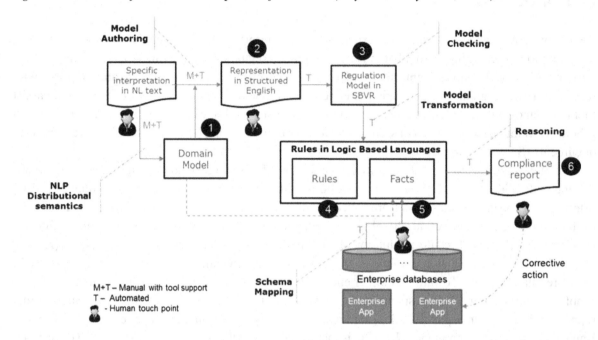

tion for translating to low-level logical specifications (e.g., DROOLs, refer to number 4 in Figure 1) (Roychoudhury et al., 2018).

The SBVR model is then also used for obtaining suitable data facts (refer to number 5 in Figure 1) from the enterprise databases (DBs), necessary for compliance checking. A DB expert maps the suitable data model obtained from SBVR with the database schema already available with the enterprise. Finally, rules are applied to the populated fact base to generate a compliance report (refer to number 6 in Figure 1) amenable for human understanding and suitable corrective action, if any.

Since the model forms the basis for all downstream artefact generation in the MDE framework, verification and validation (V&V) of the model is necessary to ensure correctness. SBVR has the advantage of its semantics being grounded in first-order logic (FOL), which makes it amenable to automated verification and validation. The SBVR models can be used to generate the formal specifications that can be solved using off-the-shelf solvers.

In the following, we present our approaches for legal text processing, regulatory rule authoring, and rule V&V along with the background. We do not present compliance checking, since once an SBVR model of regulations is obtained, we can obtain DR-Prolog or Drools rules that can be executed against enterprise data as explained in (Kholkar et al., 2018). In each of the following sections, we first describe the background/issues and then present our approach. We use regulations from Know Your Customer[3] and Markets in Financial Instruments Directive (MiFID II[4]) as examples to demonstrate the core ideas behind our approaches. Following the approaches, we present a case study of money market statistical reporting (MMSR[5]) regulations. We discuss the benefits of our approaches and conclude the chapter.

Figure 2. Domain model generation (Sunkle et al., 2016)

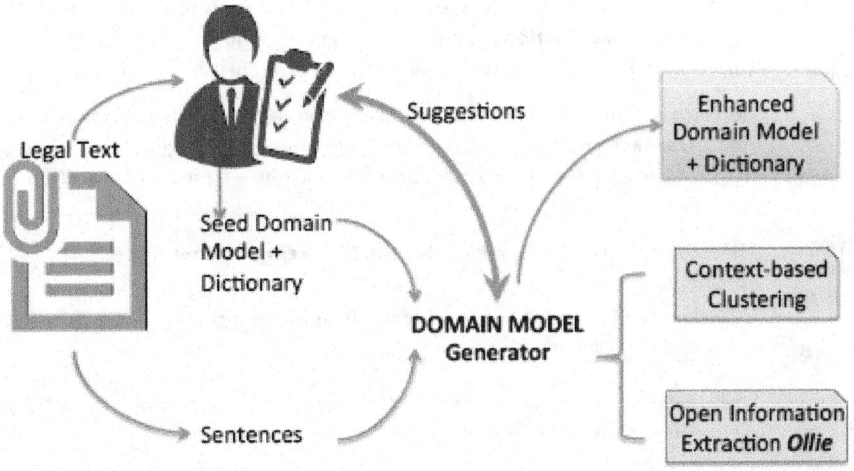

LEGAL TEXT PROCESSING USING NLP AND ML

Legal texts are unique to other natural language (NL) texts in terms of several complexities such as: a) legal texts are generally prescriptive in nature [9] meaning that they contain details of modalities like permissions, obligations, and prohibitions, b) legal texts often contain long sentences with complex clauses with several bulleted lists capturing norms and their applicability in specific conditions (Kiyavitskaya et al., 2008), and c) legal texts may contain cross references and amendments in terms of changes to the definitions of norms over time in terms of exceptions with supplementary annexes representing variety of repeals and amendments (Wyner et al., 2011).

Such complexity compels researchers to provide point solutions based on natural language processing (NLP) and machine learning (ML) techniques. This may include identifying structural units like chapters, sections, paragraphs, etc., specific to legal texts (van Engers et al., 2004), annotating legal texts to identify provisions, conditional and other expressions (Wyner et al., 2011), using regular expressions or other methods to simplify complex legal sentences (Breaux et al., 2005), (Kiyavitskaya et al., 2008), (Zeni et al., 2015). Being point solutions, applicability of such approaches becomes restricted in scope. These techniques process the legal NL text, but do not provide an explicit authoring aid. Moreover, these approaches require considerable participation of the domain experts, in some cases till the compliance checking stage. In contrast, we take different stance to modeling regulations. We use NLP-ML driven system to identify core concepts of the regulations with the premise that the regulations are likely going to specify conditions using the mentions of the core concepts.

Our Approach for Processing Legal Text

Our observation is that all regulations constrain the interactions of core concepts/domain entities within the domain of regulation in some manner. We therefore focus on helping the domain expert explicate core concepts underlying the regulations. Our approach to domain model generation is illustrated in Figure 2.

Figure 3. Clustering of contexts and mentions; examples from KYC (Sunkle et al., 2016)

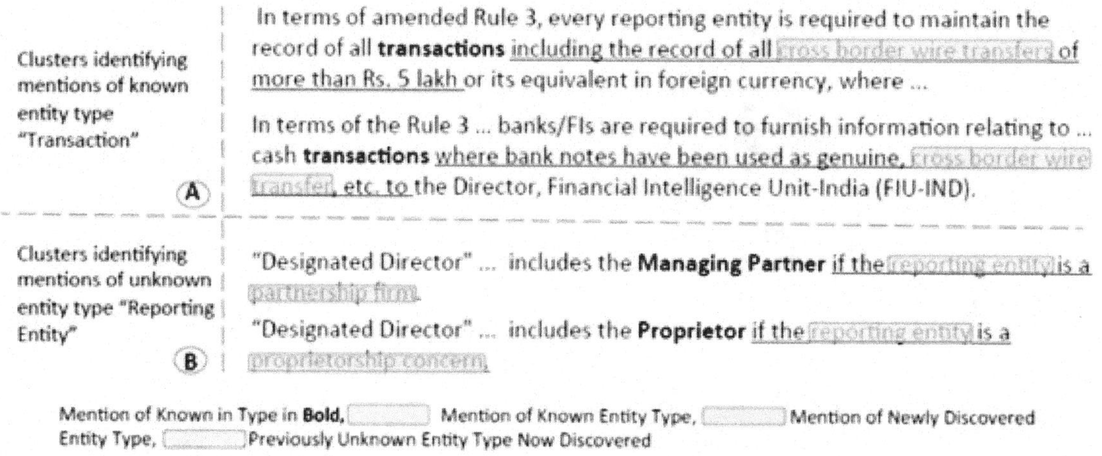

The domain expert provides seed domain model, i.e., entity types and relations immediately apparent. Most legal text tend to contain a definitions section. Even without a definitions section, the domain expert can start with a single core concept often present in the title of the regulation. For instance, 'Know Your Customers' regulations are about the core concept 'customer' and customer's identity, address, and risk profile, 'Markets in Financial Instruments Directive' are regulations about 'financial instruments' (more specifically, investment instruments), and 'Money Market Statistical Reporting' regulations are about transactions in 'money markets' focused on 'reporting'.

The domain model generator uses two techniques to retrieve mentions of seed concepts. The first technique that the generator uses is based on context-based clustering. The idea behind this technique is that the contexts, i.e., spans of texts, around the mentions of various domain entities are important and could be clustered to extract useful information, in our case, other entity types not covered in the definitions sections and mentions of all entity types so far known. The second technique that the generator uses is based on open information extraction to discover relations between the known entity types. The relations are used in modeling the rules.

Context-based Clustering for Concept/Entity Types and Mentions: To kick start clustering, we use as seeds, the entity types and mentions available in the definitions section. For instance, from the definitions section of KYC, we find the definitions of Customer, Designated Director, Document (that the customer has to submit to the reporting entity like a bank), and Transaction, which we take as seed entity types. This section in KYC also provides mentions, in terms of sub-type entities, instances, and synonyms, of these entity types. We find 12, 4, 33, and 15 mentions respectively of these entity types. These are generally very easy to spot. Interested readers are invited to look at the KYC definitions. It is not mandatory to start with several seed concepts. A single seed concept is sufficient to start the process of accumulating other concepts along with their mentions.

In most of financial services regulations that we have encountered apart from KYC, such as MiFID II, we have found that definitions of key concept types are provided clearly along with their sub-types and terms with which they are referred to in the text. In order to find entity types that could be part of the domain model but not yet known, i.e., not in the definitions section specifically, we use mentions of entities that we have so far found. We use a hypothesis known as distributional semantics (Harris,

Figure 4. Approximate mappings from English to Structured English

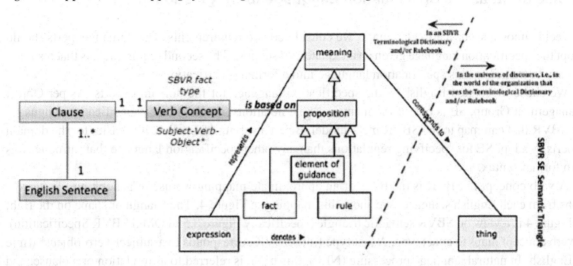

1968), which suggests that using the contexts that two words share improves the chance of correctly guessing whether they express the same meaning, in other words, semantically similar expressions occur in similar contexts. We cluster the contexts, i.e., n characters to the left and right of mentions of each entity type so far known and then cluster these to suggest to the domain expert, what looks like other possible mentions. This is illustrated in Figure 3.

The domain expert either adds to the dictionary a new mention of a known entity type as in the case of (A) in Figure 3 or as in the case of (B) has the option to add a new entity type along with the mention(s), if she recognizes that the mention(s) refers to different entity type not in the current set of known entity types. In (A), clustering the contexts of mentions of the entity type Transaction reveals a mention 'cross border wire transfer' which the domain expert deems to be of the same entity type Transaction. In (B), clustering the contexts of mentions of the entity type Designated Officer reveals the mentions partnership firm and proprietorship concern, which the domain expert adds along with previously unknown type Reporting Entity of which they are mentions (Sunkle et al., 2016).

Using Open Information Extraction Technique For Triples/Relations: In order to find relations between entity types identified in context-based clustering, we use open information extraction (IE). Open IE systems extract a diverse set of relational tuples without requiring any relation-specific human/ domain expert input. Open IE systems help when target relations are not known in advance. Open IE systems identify relation phrases, i.e., phrases that denote relations in English sentences, as triples of subject, verb, object components from sentences.

Once the domain expert is satisfied with a collection of concepts and mentions comprising the domain model and the dictionary, we use them to transform NL regulations to SE regulations. In the next sections, we first indicate why we chose SE as the specification language of regulations, followed by how we achieve an approximate transformation that enables the domain expert to edit and author rules.

Choice of SE as the Specification Language for Regulations

To decide upon a specification language, we considered two requirements. The domain experts should adopt the specification language given an adequate tool support. The second requirement is that it should be easy to transform this specification language into a formal specification.

We chose Structured English as the specification language for the domain experts. As per Object Management Group, SE is one of the many possible notations for SBVR, i.e., specification languages for SBVR that can map to the SBVR meta-model. Being a variant of English, it is easier for the domain experts to adopt SE for specifying regulations than any other specification language that introduces its own formal syntax.

A verb concept in SBVR is the basis of an approximate mapping we use in generating SE suggestions from each English sentence. We show this mapping in Figure 4. The triangular shape on the right of Figure 4 is a view on SBVR semantic triangle (specifically Figure 8.5 in OMG SBVR Specification). A verb concept maps to a fact type. A fact type from SBVR corresponds to a subject-verb-object* triple in English. In natural language processing (NLP), this triple is referred to as a relation or a clause, and the process of extracting relations is known as relation extraction.

Each English sentence is a set of one or more clauses (all of which may not be identifiable by a given relation extraction tool). The idea behind the approximate transformation is that if we used a relation extraction tool and extracted clauses and processed them to make them suitable for the syntax of SE, we get the material which the expert can use to author the correct SE. As we found out, this is not a farfetched assumption. Any SE sentence is made up of an optional element of guidance, a set of facts (which are instances of fact types or relations as described above), possibly leading to form a rule.

Transforming Legal Text in English to Structured English suggestions

Figure 5 illustrates our approach in generating the SE suggestions. We assume that the domain expert has already explicated the domain model and the dictionary from the legal NL text under consideration. In the following, we describe each step from Figure 5.

Figure 5. transforming legal text in english to structured English (Roychoudhury et al., 2017)

Figure 6. Structured English editor – multiple views (Roychoudhury et al., 2017)

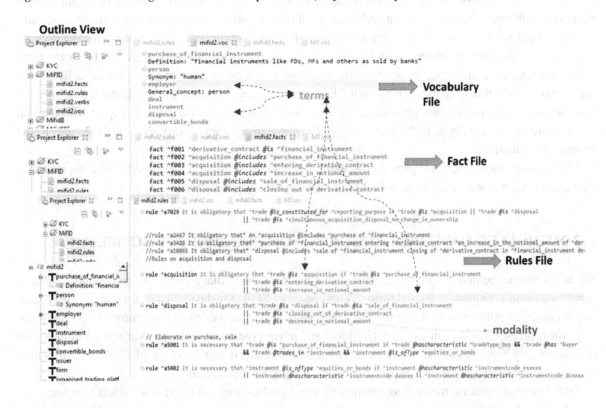

Detecting Sentences From Legal Text: In the first step of NL to SE transformation, the legal NL text is divided into a set of sentences. This step carries out pre-processing for cleaning the text, the removal of headers and footers, the removal of text encoding-related unidentifiable characters, the replacement of bullets with newline characters, or transforming a bulleted list into sentences equal to the number of bullets, etc.

Extracting Propositions/Relations from Sentences Using Open IE: We extract n-ary propositions i.e., triples of subject, verb, and one or more objects from each sentence obtained from the text. All of the propositions generated in this step are input to the next step.

Domain Model- and Dictionary-driven Chunking and Selection of Propositions: In this step, we use the domain model and the dictionary to identify chunks of text from each proposition that indicate a mention of one of the domain concepts. This step results in discarding the propositions from sentences that contain no mentions of domain concepts.

Modifying the Propositions for Target SE Syntax: In this step, we modify the propositions, specifically the relations and the mentions found in the subject and the arguments of a proposition for the target SE syntax.

Transforming Propositions with Modalities and Normalized Relations: In this step, we normalize relational phrases in the propositions, especially those that contain the modal verbs, i.e., can, could, may, might, must, shall, and should and their various forms. We transform these using four categories, which include past participles *be x* and *not be x* and third person singular present forms *x(e)*s and not *x*[7]. We include a modal operator as *"It is y that"*, where y is one of *obligatory*, *permitted*, or *necessary*, when one of the modal verbs above occur in a sentence. The verbs (and forms thereof) *must*, *shall*, and *should* map to the obligation operator and the verbs *can*, *could*, *may*, and *might* map to the permission operator.

We use the *necessary* operator to represent facts in the SE editor, i.e., it is available for the domain expert to state definitions, when it is indicated so in the legal text by the use of the verb *is*. For the third person singular present forms, we generate the requisite forms using a list of verbs, specifically for the "*es*" suffix. With this transformation, each SE suggestion now contains the modality indicator (if it was found), a normalized verb, and the target SE syntax as desired by the domain expert who uses an SE editor (discussed in detail in the following section) to edit the suggestions and bring the rules to the desired specification.

In the following section, we provide the main motivation behind SE and describe the approach by which the language was realized in XText language engineering workbench.

A CONTROLLED NATURAL LANGUAGE FOR REGULATORY COMPLIANCE

The main motive behind OMG SE is to provide a business vocabulary for capturing business rules in simplified natural English in textual format. Our choice of SE as the desired CNL for specifying regulatory compliance rules was based on the following facts – SE is capable of representing various regulatory constructs such as "count-as" or definitional and normative rules, including various modalities and is considerably more structured and less complex than NL. SE is just a variant of English, still, which makes it possible for the domain experts to use SE to specify regulations.

OMG provides general meaning of various SE concepts but does not provide a context-free language specification for it that would be necessary to create a parser. Prior attempts to provide a language implementation of SE approach this in an ad-hoc way without any details on the language grammar and which SE concepts they support. Some of these efforts never took off after initial basic implementation (De Tommasi et al., 2006, Šukys et al., 2016). We provide a formal implementation of SE that supports the core concepts that were intended in its original SBVR specification (Roychoudhury et al., 2017).

SE contains concepts like general terms, individual terms, facts, verbs, quantification, modality, quantifiers and rules. The English like semantics of SE makes it amenable for domain experts to specify rules at a level of abstraction appropriate to them (see Figure 6). Our DSL implementation of SE is developed in XText language builder and uses ANTLR 3 grammar specification with additional facilities like cross referencing, scoping etc. for minimalistic semantic validity. One should note that SE is not an executable language, rather a DSL for domain experts to specify regulatory rules in simple English, and final semantics is given by appropriate translation to logical forms like DR-Prolog. For details on how an SBVR model can be translated to DR-Prolog facts, refer our earlier work on this (Roychoudhury et al., 2017).

The SE editor is divided into 4 parts as shown in Figure 6 – vocabulary editor for capturing concepts, definitions, synonyms etc., the fact editor for relating terms or concepts in the underlying domain using verbs. We use two kinds of verbs - object verbs for relating binary terms and data verbs for relating unary terms (also known as characteristics). Finally, facts are expanded by adding implications, modality, quantification and qualification to form rules. Rules are the final product that domain experts author in the rules editor from their natural language representations. Rules can contain any number of valid facts that are checked and validated by the error handler. Figure 6 shows a snippet of the SE editor that is built as an eclipse plugin using XText. The top part of the figure shows how various terms, their definitions,

Figure 7. Automatic creation of regulatory model from SE Text using text-to-model transformation (Roychoudhury et al., 2017)

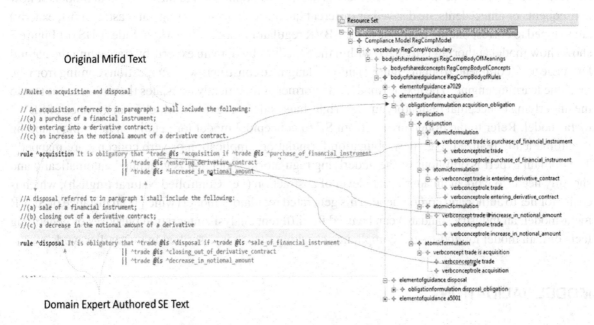

synonyms, concepts are captured in the .voc file (vocabulary editor). Facts (.facts file) relate terms using object or data verbs. Verbs are not shown in the figure (for brevity) but are captured in a separate verbs definition file. Finally, as mentioned before, rules expand facts and capture modalities, implications, quantifiers, qualifiers etc. and defined in a .rules file. Providing a formal SE language and editor is only a first step towards semi-automatic compliance checking, the next step is to create a conceptual regulatory model in an industry standard specification (i.e., SBVR) for further analysis and integration with other tools or languages. In the following section we describe the automatic conceptual model creation from the authored SE rules.

From Structured English to Regulatory Model Creation in SBVR

The very controlled English like nature of SE accounts for its easy acceptability by domain experts as there is nothing as easy to express regulations in natural language texts. However, to provide execution semantics to SE, an intermediate representation of SE in a conceptual regulatory model is needed. This intermediate regulatory model is language and platform independent and can be translated to any target formal language (i.e., not tied to a particular one), which provides the execution platform. Further, domain experts are completely oblivious of this conceptual model, which is generated automatically in the background.

Our text-to-model transformation engine is custom implemented using Xtend and uses both the eclipse modelling framework (EMF) APIs and the underlying SE parser APIs to collect information from the source text (i.e., its abstract syntax tree (AST)) as authored by domain or legal experts. The concrete syntax that gives position and other contextual information is derived from the SE parser (AST) whereas EMF gives handle to the target meta-model (SBVR) as well as extracting abstract syntax from the source

SE specification. Due to brevity, we do not show the complete mapping of SE®SBVR Model, but one can refer to Figure 7 to see how "if" statement is mapped to implication in the conceptual model, or how consequents or antecedents are derived or different quantifications in SE (e.g., at least, at most, exactly) are mapped to corresponding elements in the SBVR regulatory model. Left-Hand Side (LHS) of Figure 7 shows how model authoring is realized within the SE editor by domain experts by translating the natural language text (commented out in Figure 7) into SE language constructs with suggestions coming from the machine learning engine. The text-to-model transformer automatically translates the authored SE text to the underlying conceptual regulatory model (right-hand side of Figure 7), which is an instance of SBVR meta-model. Refer to the dotted arrows from SE to conceptual model for details on how this mapping is automatically realized (e.g., how obligation formulation, implication or verb concepts are mapped). The domain expert is oblivious of the underlying regulatory model that is generated automatically and she only needs to work at an appropriate level of abstraction (i.e., Controlled Natural English), which is easier for her to author and comprehend. This generated regulatory model (which is an instance of SBVR meta-model, an industry standard) can be used for different analysis/integration purposes or generating facts or data model for end-to-end compliance checking, which is described in our earlier work.

MODEL VALIDATION

Modeling languages need to be expressive enough to capture the complex requirements of business systems, and user-friendly in order to be usable by SMEs. In practice, most modeling languages that are high on usability are less formal and hard to verify e.g. Unified Modeling Language (UML), while formal modeling languages such as Alloy, Kodkod, CSP, and SAT specification languages are hard for SMEs to use.

SBVR is both expressive, being designed for modeling business vocabulary and rules of any domain as well as usable, with its CNL interface SBVR SE. Since the semantics of SBVR is based on first-order logic, an SBVR model can be translated into formal logic for verification and validation.

However, automated verification of models created using a flexible and expressive CNL notation such as SBVR SE poses several problems in translation to existing verification languages. SAT solvers used in existing model validation approaches (Gogolla & Doan, 2017; Anastasakis et al., 2007; Cabot et al., 2008; Fleurey et al., 2004; Feja & Fotsch, 2008) use specification languages that are far less expressive than SBVR and do not support aggregates, relations, or functions. The modeling languages Alloy, Kodkod, and Object Control Language (OCL) support encoding of aggregates, relations and constraints, but only alethic modalities i.e. necessity and impossibility in rules. Deontic modalities such as obligations and permissions are not supported in any of these languages, neither are default rules with exceptions. These constructs are frequently required in specifying real-world problem contexts.

SBVR supports modelling of deontic rules, defaults and exceptions, however validating such an SBVR model using any of the existing SAT solvers would require implementation of these features in the language of the solver, decidedly a non-trivial task. This chapter proposes validation of domain models built in SBVR using the expressive ASP logic programming paradigm that is specifically designed for finding solutions to complex search problems and also supports non-monotonic reasoning, needed for reasoning with defeasible deontic rules as well as defaults with exceptions. The subsequent sections briefly describe the SBVR language from a validation perspective, the ASP paradigm, and the

Figure 8. SBVR meta-model

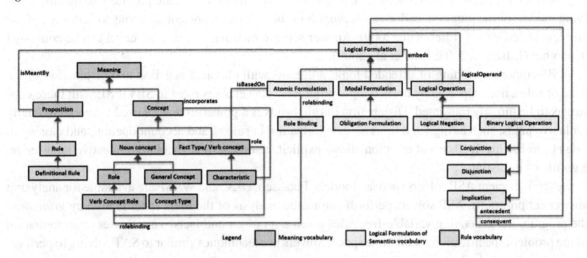

model verification and validation approach using ASP, with a case study example from the Know Your Customer (KYC) regulation for Indian banks.

SBVR

SBVR being a fact-oriented modeling language (Halpin, 2007; Nijssen, 2007), encodes *rules* as *logical formulations* over *fact types* that are relations between *concepts* ("OMG SBVR Specification V1.3", 2015).

The subset of the OMG SBVR meta-model ("OMG SBVR Specification V1.3", 2015) used in this approach for capturing regulation rules is shown in Figure 8. The meta-model comprises three sections, as shown in the figure.

- **Meaning Vocabulary**: Captures the body of *concepts* that includes *concepts, fact types* relating them, and *characteristics* of concepts. Concept hierarchies are captured using *general concepts*.
- **Logical Formulation of Semantics Vocabulary**: Logical formulations are defined over fact types that could be compound formulations e.g. *conjunctions, implications, negations* composed of *atomic formulations* based on *fact types*.
- **Rule Vocabulary**: *Rules* are based on logical formulations. *Rule* inherits from *Proposition* that *is meant by* a *logical formulation*.

Rules stated in SBVR SE are saved as an instantiation of this meta-model.

Answer Set Programming (ASP)

The validation approach described in this chapter selects ASP for automated verification since it a) is a powerful logic programming paradigm oriented towards difficult search problems (Lifschitz, 2009), b) is a highly expressive notation supporting aggregates, functions, and optimizations, c) provides non-monotonic reasoning, and d) maps directly onto SBVR's fact-oriented model and underlying first-order logic formalism.

The basic idea in ASP is to describe the problem in a non-monotonic logic program, so that the satisfying models of the program, called *stable models* or *answer sets* represent solutions to instances of the problem specification (Eiter et al., 2009). Answer sets are minimal, i.e. no answer set can be contained in another (Lifschitz, 2008; Eiter et al., 2009).

ASP supports encoding of extended logic programs with classical negation and disjunction in the head of rules, not supported by normal logic programs. This enables rules in SBVR SE with these constructs to be directly translated. Disjunction in rule heads is a powerful feature used to model mutually exclusive paths, such as high and low risk categorization in rule r1 and account opening and closing in rule r13 in Listing 1. Classical negation allows explicit statement or derivation of negative knowledge, e.g. rule r9 in Listing 1.

Several efficient ASP solvers such as smodels, Potassco, DLV, and WASP are available for analyzing answer set programs. ASP solvers perform automated analysis of the logic specification by *grounding* the program i.e. generating variable-free rules given a set of ground facts. This creates an instantiation of the problem specification, or the state space. Solvers use techniques similar to SAT solving to perform a state space search. The search finds inconsistencies if any exist, else finds solutions or answer sets satisfying the specification, from the instantiation. A major advantage of using ASP is its non-monotonic reasoning capability that is the ability to reason with conflicts by retracting earlier drawn conclusions when invalidated by another set of rules (Eiter et al., 2009), a situation often encountered in real-life applications. Examples of each of these cases are illustrated in subsequent sections.

KYC Case Study Example

KYC is an anti-money laundering regulation that lays down guidelines for banks to screen new customers and monitor their transactions on an ongoing basis in order to minimize risk of money-laundering and terrorist financing. It describes guidelines for acceptance of new customers approaching the bank for opening an account, including risk categorization and identification procedures based on their risk profile.

Listing 1 shows a few SBVR SE rules from the KYC example. Rules r1 to r7 define the three risk categories customers need to be classified into, based on their source of wealth being easily identifiable, which in turn depends on the customer type - whether salaried employee, person from lower income group, politically exposed person (PEP), government department, trust, etc. Rules r8, r9, and r13 define obligations on the bank to open an account for a customer if he submits all the right documentation, and refuse to open it if the customer is a banned or blacklisted entity, or submits false information.

Rule r8 is populated in the SBVR model as a *rule*, *meant by* an *obligationformulation* embedding an *implication logical formulation* over fact types *bank opensAccountFor customer* and *bank verifiesIdentityOf customer* that relate concepts *bank* and *customer*.

The next section describes verification and validation of the SBVR model of rules.

Listing 1. Section of SBVR SE Rules from the KYC Example

```
rule r1 It is necessary that customer @is lowRiskCustomer || customer @is highRiskCustomer
        || customer @is mediumRiskCustomer if customer @approaches bank
rule r2 It is necessary that customer @is lowRiskCustomer if
        customer @has sourceOfWealthEasilyIdentified
rule r4 It is necessary that customer @is highRiskCustomer if
        customer @has sourceOfWealthNotEasilyIdentified
rule r6 It is necessary that customer @has sourceOfWealthEasilyIdentified if
        customer @is salaried || customer @is lower_economic_strata || customer @is government_department ||
        customer @is regulator
rule r7 It is necessary that customer @has sourceOfWealthNotEasilyIdentified if
        customer @is PEP || customer @is non_residentCustomer || customer @is HNWI || customer @is trust ||
        customer @is charity || customer @is NGO
rule r8 It is obligatory that bank @opensAccountFor customer if
        bank @verifiesIdentityOf customer
rule r9 It is obligatory that bank not @opensAccountFor customer if
        customer @approaches bank && customer @is bannedEntity
rule r10 It is necessary that bank @verifiesIdentityOf customer if
        customer @approaches bank && customer @submitsReq document
rule r13 It is necessary that bank not @opensAccountFor customer || bank @closesAccountFor customer if
        customer @provides falseInformation
rule r14 It is necessary that bank not @harasses customer
rule r15 It is necessary that bank @harasses customer if
        bank @closesAccountFor customer &&  bank @failsTogiveDueNoticeTo customer
```

Verification and Validation Approach

Model verification seeks to check that the model does what it is expected to do, usually through an implementing program (Hillston, 2003) The approach described in this chapter proposes inconsistency checking and scenario generation from the model as verification techniques.

The objective of model validation is to ascertain that the model is a faithful representation of the problem space it represents (Hillston, 2003). This approach implements validation by generating scenarios from the model and having SMEs certify the scenarios for validity and coverage.

This approach uses the SBVR model to generate a formal logic specification in the ASP logic paradigm for verification and validation of the model, as shown in Figure 9.

The authors have developed a model-based generator that uses Eclipse Modeling Framework (EMF) generated model traversal functions to traverse the SBVR model and translate it to an answer set program comprising rules and constraints.

Rules in SBVR are translated to causal Prolog-style rules in ASP of the form

Head of rule:- Body of rule

where *Body of rule* is the rule antecedent that implies the rule consequent *Head of rule*.

Statement-type rules without antecedents are translated as constraints i.e. rules with empty head, as

:- Body of constraint.

Relations in SBVR become predicates in ASP. The concepts being related form the arguments to the predicate. Concepts are referred by their unique identifiers e.g. *bank @opensAccountFor customer* becomes *bankOpensAccountForCustomer(BankId, CustomerId)*. Listing 2 shows a fragment from the ASP program generated from the SE rules shown in Listing 1, for the KYC example.

Figure 9. Model validation in the MDE framework using ASP

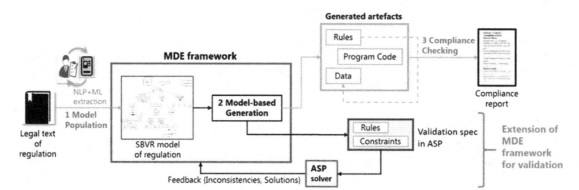

Listing 2. Section of ASP fragment for the KYC example

```
mediumRiskCustomer(Customerid) v highRiskCustomer(Customerid) v
lowRiskCustomer(Customerid) :- customerApproachesBank(Customerid,Bankid).
lowRiskCustomer(Customerid) :- sourceOfWealthEasilyIdentified(Customerid).
highRiskCustomer(Customerid):- sourceOfWealthNotEasilyIdentified(Customerid).
sourceOfWealthEasilyIdentified(Customerid) :- salaried(Customerid).
sourceOfWealthEasilyIdentified(Customerid) :- government_department (Custom-
erid).
sourceOfWealthEasilyIdentified(Customerid) :- regulator (Customerid).
bankOpensAccountForCustomer(Bankid,Customerid) :- bankVerifiesIdentityOfCustom
er(Bankid,Customerid).
bankVerifiesIdentityOfCustomer(Bankid,Customerid)) :-    customerApproachesBank
(Customerid,Bankid)), customerSubmitsReqDocument(Customerid,Documentid)).
customerSubmitsReqDocument(Customerid,Documentid) :- salaried(Customerid)),
documentType(Documentid,PAN).
customerSubmitsReqDocument(Customerid,Documentid) :- pep(Customerid), document
Type(Documentid,infofrompublicdomain).
-bankOpensAccountForCustomer(Bankid,Customerid)    :-    customerApproachesBank
(Customerid,Bankid), bannedEntity(Customerid).
:- bankHarassesCustomer(Bankid,Customerid).
bankHarassesCustomer(Bankid,Customerid)       :- bankClosesAccountForCustomer(Ba
nkid,Customerid)), bankFailsTogiveDueNoticeToCustomer(Bankid,Customerid).
bankClosesAccountForCustomer (Bankid,Customerid) v - bankOpensAccountForCus-
tomer (Bankid,Customerid) :- customerProvidesFalseInformation(Customerid).
```

The authors use the DLV system (Leone et al., 2006) as the solver for analyzing generated ASP programs.

Ground facts need to be provided to the solver for generating the grounded program or state space. The authors' framework provides assistance through automated generation of a set of ground facts by traversing the SBVR model. Fact types on which each rule depends are populated with valid values specified in the model to generate ground facts. Wherever specified as a value range, values are picked randomly from the range.

The solver grounds the ASP program using the given ground facts, instantiating the program and creating the state space for search. Since the set of ground facts is generated from the model, it is exhaustive, ensuring no required states are left out. The solver searches the state space for inconsistencies, pinpointing conflicting rules or constraints. It generates answer sets or solutions for paths where no conflicts exist. Since answer sets are minimal, these represent the minimal set of unique scenarios for the input model. Generated scenarios are presented to SMEs for review, to check for correctness and coverage of important scenarios. This helps check for completeness of the model, since missing scenarios could be identified by SMEs on reviewing the generated set, indicating missing or incorrect rules in the model. The next two subsections illustrate the validation process using the KYC example.

Inconsistency Checking

A subset of the generated set of ground facts input to the solver is shown in Listing 2. This results in two inconsistencies being displayed as shown in Listing 4.

Listing 3. Sample input ground facts

```
1.  customerApproachesBank(C01,B1).
2.  salaried(C01).
3.  document(101, PAN).
4.  document(121, infofrompublicdomain).
5.  bankClosesAccountForCustomer(B01,C01).
6.  bankFailsTogiveDueNoticeToCustomer(B01,C01).
7.  bannedEntity(C01).
8.  customerProvidesFalseInformation(C01).
```

Ground facts 5 and 6 indicate that bank closed the account for customer and failed to give due notice to them, amounting to harassment of the customer as per rule r15 from Listing 1. This results in the constraint of rule r14 being violated, as shown in inconsistency #1 in Listing 4.

Ground fact 7 stating customer C01 is a banned entity results in bank not being able to open account for customer, as per rule r9 of Listing 1. This conflicts with the conclusion reached by rule r8 that bank can open an account for the customer since its requisites are provided by ground facts 2 and 3, and is shown as inconsistency #2. This highlights a legitimate conflict between rules r8 and r9 where the customer fulfils the criteria for an account being opened for him in r8 while being a banned entity invalidates this conclusion in rule r9 and is an example of ASP's non-monotonic reasoning. The same inconsistency is found between rules r13 and r9, since fact 8 indicating that customer provided false information also results in bank not opening his account in one of the resultant scenarios of rule r13.

Listing 4. Inconsistencies shown by ASP solver

```
% Inconsistency #1: The following constraint will always be violated so this
program does not have any answer set.
```

```
:- bankHarassesCustomer(_0,_1).
% Inconsistency #2: Facts derived to be true in every answer set:
bankOpensAccountForCustomer(B1,C01).
% Inconsistencies:
:- bankOpensAccountForCustomer(B1,C01).
```

Inconsistencies need to be corrected in the model or data. Inconsistency #2 can be corrected by correcting the model to give rule r9 precedence over r8, as also rule r13 over r8. Inconsistency #1 needs to be corrected in the data, which means fixing the account closing process so that an account cannot be closed without notifying the customer. The next section illustrates model validation using scenarios.

Scenario Generation

In order to obtain scenarios, data facts 5,6,7 that caused inconsistencies are removed. On closer look, one sees that fact 2 from the complete fact set of Listing 2 will result in scenarios for only salaried customers. In order that SMEs can validate the exhaustive list of scenarios, here for all types of customers, one needs to omit ground facts that will result in only partial scenario generation. Removing fact 2 gives us the list of six possible scenarios, of which four are shown in Listing 4 due to space constraints.

Listing 5. Sample solution scenarios generated for the KYC example

```
#1 {customerApproachesBank(C01,B1), documentType(121,infofrompublicdo
main), documentType(101,PAN), customerProvidesFalseInformation(C01),
customerIsLowRiskCustomer(C01), bankClosesAccountForCustomer (B1,C01)}
#2 {customerApproachesBank(C01,B1), documentType(121,infofrompublicdo
main), documentType(101,PAN), customerProvidesFalseInformation(C01),
customerIsLowRiskCustomer(C01), -bankOpensAccountForCustomer(B1,C01)}
#3 { customerApproachesBank(C01,B1), documentType(121,infofrompublicdomain),
documentType(101,PAN), customerProvidesFalseInformation(C01), customerIsHighRi
skCustomer(C01), bankClosesAccountForCustomer(B1,C01)}
#4 { customerApproachesBank(C01,B1), documentType(121,infofrompublicd
omain), documentType(101,PAN), customerProvidesFalseInformation(C01),
customerIsHighRiskCustomer(C01) -bankOpensAccountForCustomer(B1,C01)}
```

Two solutions each are generated for the three risk categories, one with bank not opening account and the other with bank closing account as a result of fact 8. Reviewing solutions makes it easy for SMEs to validate whether expected scenarios appear correctly and important conditions have been covered.

Rule r10 is not reached, since fact 2 about customer being salaried was omitted. When we add fact 2, we get the complete scenario for salaried customer resulting in opening of account.

```
{customerIsLowRiskCustomer(C01), documentType(121,infofrompublicdomain),
documentType(101,PAN), customerHasSourceOfWealthEasilyIdentified(C01,132), cus
tomerSubmitsReqDocument(C01,101),bankVerifiesIdentityOfCustomer(B1,C01), bankO
pensAccountForCustomer(B1,C01)}
```

Since ground facts needed for all rules are generated, no rule remains unreachable during execution of the solver. Although an advantage from reachability perspective, it results in non-minimal answer sets since all cases become true in a single scenario – customer being salaried, PEP, trust, etc. Since this is incorrect, we need to add a constraint that states these customer types are mutually exclusive. This will force us to eliminate the extra incompatible ground facts such as *customer is PEP*, etc from the list of generated ground facts and keep only *customer is salaried*, since these will cause an inconsistency with the constraint. When all constraints are in place, the answer sets obtained are minimal.

Although minimal, number of answer sets can grow combinatorically with conditions and ground instances. To constrain number of scenarios, the following heuristics are used. Only critically important conditions are modeled as disjunctions that create independent scenarios for each condition. Non-critical conditions such as alternate types of id proof submitted by a customer e.g. PAN or Aadhar are modeled as disjunctions in the body of normal clauses. Ground facts are created with minimal number of instances of each entity, e.g. customer and bank, to prevent combinatorial explosion of states and scenarios.

CASE STUDY AND DISCUSSION

In this section we introduce Money Market Statistical Reporting (MMSR) and describe some of the key statistics that highlight the benefits of our approach. MMSR is a reporting regulation in the European Union involving the money markets and is regulated by the European Central Bank (ECB). All financial institutions, namely banks are mandated to report their daily transactions to ECB as prescribed by the MMSR regulatory document.

A MMSR regulation typically consists of four different sections pertinent to money market, namely, secured market, unsecured market, FX swaps and overnight index swaps. The structure and nature of regulations in all the four sections are similar, therefore modeling and validating one section will give a fairly good idea about validating other sections as well. For our case study, we chose secured market (Section 3) of MMSR, which captures the conceptual and field definitions of various variables that must be reported by individual banks to ECB. Overall, there are 24 such variables defined in Section 3 of MMSR, with each variable having their own conceptual definition and field definition. Conceptual definition pertains to the underlying semantics of the variable, while field definition pertains to how the variable should be constructed structurally.

Table 1. Metrics for MMSR secured market segment transactions reporting regulations

Avg. No. Suggestions in T2T	SE No. of Rules	Total No. of Instances of SBVR Elements					No. of Tables	No. of Columns	No. of Queries
		Terms	Atomic Formulations	Verb Concept Roles	(Con+Dis) junctions	Quantifications			
3	48	582	112	184	29	26	49	181	97
Avg. Time Ratios	X (2X-3X w/o T2T)				8X			*Additional 5X*	

The following statistics will highlight some of the benefits of our approach against pure manual or tagging based implementation. In Table 1, we summarize some of the specific contributions that the domain model generator and SE language along with editor support and its subsequent automated translation to SBVR model instance have enabled for domain experts. There are 24 variables for a transaction in the secured market, which need to be verified for their formation and formatting. For instance, a variable called trade date needs to be reported as: 1) a combination of date and time, 2) only date when time is not available, 3) time must be the execution time 4) trade date must be equal to or less than settlement date (another variable) except for novations. When reporting trade date, it must be formatted as YYYY-MMDDThh: mm:ss.sss+/-hh:mm. We cover 48 such rules (what should be reported in a variable (24) + with which formatting it should be reported (24)). Table 1 shows the metrics for each link in the chain of model transformation (i.e., from NL Text ®SE ®SBVR). For the generated SBVR model, we show the number of instances of some of the key SBVR elements. The counts for SBVR elements are obtained by traversing the SBVR model with element-wise counters.

We authored 48 rules in Structured English covering all the 24 variables with the help of the domain model that captured mentions and relationships pertaining to these variables. For MMSR Section 3, the domain model generator captured 55 core concepts, 201 mentions (i.e., 4 mention on an average for every concept) and 49 relations. Thus, the domain model serves as an ontology for the domain expert and aids her to author rules.

From here on, the next chain of transformations were fully automated. We generated the SBVR model from SE rules that consisted of 582 *Terms*, 112 *Atomic Formulations,* 184 *verb concept roles*, 43 *conjunctions/disjunctions* and 62 *characteristics*. Overall, the SVBR model consisted of more than 1000 model elements which would have taken a considerable amount of time and effort to create manually, yet difficult to comprehend by a domain (human) expert. Thus, abstracting SE over SBVR gave domain experts sufficient gain in comprehensibility, yet they remained oblivious to the underlying modelling details. For example, a typical SE rule, authored by the domain expert, has a *single implication* condition, *6 independent* concepts, *4 facts* and takes about *3 minutes* to author using the SE editor (see LHS of Figure 7). This gets automatically translated by our text-to-model transformation engine to a SBVR model (RHS of Figure 7), which has on average around *30 model elements, 3 nested* models with *maximum* depth of *nesting* as deep as *7, 5 atomic formulations* and *8 verbconceptrole*. Without a translation support as shown in (Roychoudhury et al., 2017), manually creating such model instances from SBVR meta-model having more than 1000+ model elements take considerable time and effort on behalf of the modeler and also subjected to human error.

On average, such a construction without SE editor and SE®SBVR translation support would take 20 minutes per SE rule as opposed to 3-4 minutes in case of SE authoring. Thus for a typical set of regulations, for example, KYC, which has nearly 187 rules, with SE support, one can author all of them in 600 minutes (approx. 10 hours). Whereas without SE®SBVR support, manual construction of SBVR model for 187 rules, will require nearly 56 hours or 7 person days[8]. This shows the distinct benefit of SE not just from abstraction point of view but also from automatic SBVR model construction perspective as opposed to manual model creation.

Since the model populated by SMEs is used to generate a logic specification, validating the specification automatically is successful in validating the model for consistency. Inconsistencies are pinpointed to the exact rules/ constraints/ ground data facts that are conflicting, so that they can be corrected in the model/ data/ process as the case may be.

Giving the right ground data facts to create the state space for searching for inconsistencies/ solutions to a logic specification is the key issue faced by model checking approaches. The approach described in this chapter is able to address this problem since it has a causal fact-oriented model representation of the logic specification available. The model can be traversed to find the exact conditions on which each rule depends, to try and generate the necessary and sufficient set of ground facts to ensure creation of the required state space so that all paths in the specification can be covered in the search and therefore all cases, in the scenarios and inconsistencies.

Although this is an intuitive way to assess semantic correctness and completeness of the input model, the number of scenarios generated could be very large for large models. The authors are working on evolving further heuristics to keep the number of scenarios compact. The guidelines for scenario generation are being further streamlined to get the most efficient way of validating all paths, and then focusing on specific parts of the model as described with the KYC example, in order to quickly get to the set of minimal, most interesting scenarios for validation.

CONCLUSION

This chapter describes a model-driven framework for semi-automatic compliance checking through a series of transformations involving interactive human touch points. Automated consistency checking and feedback in the form of scenarios is provided to experts for intuitive validation of the authored models. The novelty of the framework is the aided involvement and participation of domain-experts to author regulations in a Controlled Natural Language at an appropriate level of abstraction. In comparison to other industry practices, the described framework is built on the foundation of formal compliance checking and considerably reduced time and effort (via automation and as observed in the pilot case study) required by an enterprise to accomplish compliance checking without losing soundness, consistency or accuracy in terms of the desired result. As part of future work, the authors plan to explore how the framework can cater to rule changes and how to manage scalability issues with respect to validating high volume of regulatory data more effectively.

REFERENCES

Anastasakis, K., Bordbar, B., Georg, G., & Ray, I. (2007, September). UML2Alloy: A challenging model transformation. In *International Conference on Model Driven Engineering Languages and Systems* (pp. 436-450). Springer. 10.1007/978-3-540-75209-7_30

Becker, J., Delfmann, P., Eggert, M., & Schwittay, S. (2012). Generalizability and applicability of model-based business process compliance-checking approaches—A state-of-the-art analysis and research roadmap. *Business Research*, 5(2), 221–247. doi:10.1007/BF03342739

Breaux, T. D., & Anton, A. I. (2005, June). Deriving semantic models from privacy policies. In *Sixth IEEE International Workshop on Policies for Distributed Systems and Networks (POLICY'05)* (pp. 67-76). IEEE. 10.1109/POLICY.2005.12

Cabot, J., Claris, R., & Riera, D. (2008, April). Verification of UML/OCL class diagrams using constraint programming. In *2008 IEEE International Conference on Software Testing Verification and Validation Workshop* (pp. 73-80). IEEE. 10.1109/ICSTW.2008.54

De Tommasi, M., & Corallo, A. (2006, October). SBEAVER: a tool for modeling business vocabularies and business rules. In *International Conference on Knowledge-Based and Intelligent Information and Engineering Systems* (pp. 1083-1091). Springer. 10.1007/11893011_137

Eiter, T., Ianni, G., & Krennwallner, T. (2009, August). Answer set programming: A primer. In *Reasoning Web International Summer School* (pp. 40–110). Berlin: Springer.

Feja, S., & Fotsch, D. (2008). Model checking with graphical validation rules. In *Proceedings of 15th Annual IEEE International Conference and Workshop on the Engineering of Computer Based Systems ECBS 2008* (117-125). Belfast, UK: IEEE Computer Society.

Fleurey, F., Steel, J., & Baudry, B. (2004, November). Validation in model-driven engineering: testing model transformations. In *Proceedings. 2004 First International Workshop on Model, Design and Validation, 2004* (pp. 29-40). IEEE. 10.1109/MODEVA.2004.1425846

Gogolla, M., & Doan, K. H. (2017). Quality Improvement of Conceptual UML and OCL Schemata through Model Validation and Verification. In *Conceptual Modeling Perspectives* (pp. 155–168). Cham: Springer. doi:10.1007/978-3-319-67271-7_11

Halpin, T. (2007). Fact Oriented Modeling – Past, Present and Future. In J. Krogstie, A. L. Opdahl, & S. Brinkkemper (Eds.), *Conceptual Modelling in Information Systems Engineering* (pp. 19–38). Berlin: Springer-Verlag. doi:10.1007/978-3-540-72677-7_2

Harris, Z. (1968). *Mathematical structures of language. Interscience tracts in pure and applied mathematics*. Academic Press.

Hillston, J. (2003). *Model Validation and Verification*. Retrieved from http://www.inf.ed.ac.uk/teaching/courses/pm/Note16.pdf

Kholkar, D., Sunkle, S., & Kulkarni, V. (2017). Semi-automated creation of regulation rule bases using generic template-driven rule extraction. ASAIL@ ICAIL.

Kiyavitskaya, N., Zeni, N., Breaux, T. D., Antón, A. I., Cordy, J. R., Mich, L., & Mylopoulos, J. (2008, October). Automating the extraction of rights and obligations for regulatory compliance. In *International Conference on Conceptual Modeling* (pp. 154-168). Springer. 10.1007/978-3-540-87877-3_13

Leone, N., Pfeifer, G., Faber, W., Eiter, T., Gottlob, G., Perri, S., & Scarcello, F. (2006). The DLV system for knowledge representation and reasoning. *ACM Transactions on Computational Logic*, 7(3), 499–562. doi:10.1145/1149114.1149117

Lévy, F., & Nazarenko, A. (2013, July). Formalization of natural language regulations through SBVR structured english. In *International Workshop on Rules and Rule Markup Languages for the Semantic Web* (pp. 19-33). Springer. 10.1007/978-3-642-39617-5_5

Lifschitz, V. (2008). What is answer set programming? In *Proceedings of the Twenty-Third AAAI Conference on Artificial Intelligence, AAAI 2008* (pp. 1594-1597). Chicago, IL: AAAI Press.

Nijssen, S. (2007). *SBVR: Semantics for business. Business Rules Journal.*

Object Management Group. (2015). *SBVR Specification V1.3*. Retrieved from https://www.omg.org/spec/SBVR/1.3

Racz, N., Weippl, E., & Bonazzi, R. (2011, July). IT governance, risk & compliance (GRC) status quo and integration: an explorative industry case study. In *2011 IEEE World Congress on Services* (pp. 429-436). IEEE. 10.1109/SERVICES.2011.78

Roychoudhury, S., Sunkle, S., Choudhary, N., Kholkar, D., & Kulkarni, V. (2018). A Case Study on Modeling and Validating Financial Regulations Using (Semi-) *Automated Compliance Framework. In IFIP Working Conference on The Practice of Enterprise Modeling* (pp. 288-302). Springer.

Roychoudhury, S., Sunkle, S., Kholkar, D., & Kulkarni, V. (2017). A domain-specific controlled english language for automated regulatory compliance (Industrial Paper). In *Proceedings of the 10th ACM SIGPLAN International Conference on Software Language Engineering* (pp. 175-181). ACM. 10.1145/3136014.3136018

Šukys, A., Ablonskis, L., Nemuraitė, L., & Paradauskas, B. (2016). A Grammar for ADVANCED SBVR Editor. *Information Technology and Control, 45*(1), 27–41. doi:10.5755/j01.itc.45.1.9219

Sunkle, S., Kholkar, D., & Kulkarni, V. (2015a). Toward better mapping between regulations and operations of enterprises using vocabularies and semantic similarity. *Complex Systems Informatics and Modeling Quarterly,* (5), 39-60.

Sunkle, S., Kholkar, D., & Kulkarni, V. (2015b). Model-driven regulatory compliance: A case study of "Know Your Customer" regulations. In *2015 ACM/IEEE 18th International Conference on Model Driven Engineering Languages and Systems (MODELS)* (pp. 436-445). IEEE.

Sunkle, S., Kholkar, D., & Kulkarni, V. (2016). Comparison and synergy between fact-orientation and relation extraction for domain model generation in regulatory compliance. In *International Conference on Conceptual Modeling* (pp. 381-395). Springer. 10.1007/978-3-319-46397-1_29

van Engers, T. M., van Gog, R., & Sayah, K. (2004). A case study on automated norm extraction. Legal Knowledge and Information Systems. *Jurix,* 49-58.

Wyner, A. Z., & Peters, W. (2011, December). On Rule Extraction from Regulations. JURIX, 11, 113-122.

Zeni, N., Kiyavitskaya, N., Mich, L., Cordy, J. R., & Mylopoulos, J. (2015). GaiusT: Supporting the extraction of rights and obligations for regulatory compliance. *Requirements Engineering, 20*(1), 1–22. doi:10.100700766-013-0181-8

ENDNOTES

1   OMG SBVR: https://www.omg.org/spec/SBVR/About-SBVR/
2   XText: https://www.eclipse.org/Xtext/

[3] Know Your Customer: https://www.rbi.org.in/Scripts/BS_ViewMasterCirculars.aspx?Id=9914&Mode=0

[4] MiFID II: https://eur-lex.europa.eu/legal-content/EN/TXT/?uri=celex%3A32014L0065

[5] MMSR: https://www.ecb.europa.eu/stats/money/mmss/shared/files/MMSR-Reporting_instructions.pdf

[6] We use Spacy https://spacy.io/ for sentence detection as well as the rest of the NLP processes.

[7] x stands for the verb. The verb form is z, where z is not a verb, is transformed to itself.

[8] We assume 8 hours = 1 person-day.

Chapter 6
IT Systems for the Digital Enterprise

Souvik Barat
TCS Research, Tata Consultancy Services, India

Asha Rajbhoj
TCS Research, Tata Consultancy Services, India

ABSTRACT

Modern digital enterprises operate in a dynamic environment where the business objectives, underlying technologies, and expectations from the end-users change over the time. Therefore, developing agile and adaptive IT systems is a critical need for most of the large business-critical enterprises. However, it is observed that the traditional IT system development approaches are not capable of ensuring all desired characteristics. This chapter discusses a set of established concepts and techniques that collectively help to achieve the desired agility and adaptiveness. The chapter reflects on the core concept of model-driven engineering for agility, technology independence, and retargetability; focuses on component abstraction to introduce divide-and-concur and separation of concerns; and proposes the use of variability and the concept of productline for developing configurable and extensible IT system.

INTRODUCTION

Enterprises use IT systems as automatons for well-defined repetitive operational tasks. With past dynamics of business environment being low, the IT systems were expected to deliver a fixed set of capabilities for a static operating environment. But the business dynamics has changed significantly over the years. The modern enterprises need to be agile and adaptable to support new business capabilities, technology stacks, and operating environment in a cost effective manner to stay competitive (Kulkarni, 2019). However, most of the existing IT systems fall short of the agility and adaptability as they have been implemented by considering a fixed set of requirements along a layered architecture paradigm. The traditional IT systems can be seen to encòde specific choices along five dimensions, namely: Functionality (F), Business process (P), Design decisions (D), Architecture (A) and Technology platform (T) in a

DOI: 10.4018/978-1-7998-0108-5.ch006

scattered and tangled manner. These scattering and tangling are the principal obstacles to realise desired agility and adaptation. Large size further exacerbates the problem.

Component based IT system design and development (Heineman et al., 2001) that enables *separation of concerns* (Kulkarni et al., 2003) is a pragmatic step in the direction to achieve the desired agility and adaptation in IT systems. Business process management (BPM) (White, 2004) initiative that separates business process (P) dimension from functionality (F) dimension is the next step for solving the problem. The software product line concept (Pohl et al. 2005) and variability modelling (Berger et al., 2013) are further progress in software engineering (SE) to introduce agility and adaptableness along functionality (F) and business process (P) dimensions. The product line approaches and variability modelling collectively advocate systematic approach for configurability (*i.e.*, selecting one of the many available variants) and extensibility (*i.e.*, addition of a new variant) to achieve the desired characteristics. The Model Driven Development (MDD) (Selic, 2003) techniques detangle the functionality aspect (F) from design decision (D), architecture (A) and technology platform (T) by introducing the notion platform independent model (PIM), platform specific model (PSM), and model based code generation. They help to introduce new choice along design decision (D), architecture (A) and technology platform (T) dimensions without impacting the specification related to functionality and business processes. Introduction of product line concept to specify the code generator in an MDE technique as presented in (Kulkarni et al., 2012) is another advancements towards required agility and adaptation of IT systems. This chapter argues that an IT system with desired agility and adaptability can be developed by combining these existing concepts, techniques and approaches. The chapter first discusses the tenets of the modern IT systems that elaborate the problem space. The solution space that highlights the art of possibilities in the form concepts, techniques and approaches for agile and adaptable IT systems is discussed next. The chapter finally presents a pragmatic recommendation to use them in a systematic and coordinated manner using a conceptual framework. Essentially, an overarching meta-modelling framework that supports an advanced form of component abstraction, business process model, concept of productline architecture and variability modelling as an approach to realise the needs of modern enterprise in seamless manner is discussed.

PROBLEM SPACE: TENENTS OF MODERN IT SYSTEMS

The business-critical IT systems are often characterised by high business functionalities, low algorithmic complexity, significant database intensive operations, large size, and conforming to a distributed architecture (Kulkarni et al, 2004). Being business critical in nature, the system needs to be delivered quickly and is expected to be in use for a long time. The rich in functionality and large size expect suitable approach for functional decomposition, modularity and reusability so as to leverage large distributed development team. The choice of distributed architecture paradigm necessitates multiple technologies to be managed effectively and an interoperable manner. Moreover, a generic industrial experience is no two solutions, even for the same business intent, such as straight-through-processing of trade orders, back-office automation of a bank, automation of insurance policies administration, are identical. Though there exists a significant overlap across functional requirements for a given business intent, the variations are manifold too. Therefore, the developed IT systems are expected to be cognizant of commonality and variability. It is also expected a suitable approach to configure and extend the range of variants to support evolving requirements. In this chapter, we visualise an IT system along two broad dimensions:

- Business capabilities dimension which can be further divided into business functionality (F) and business processes (P).
- Solution architecture dimension which can be further divided into Design decisions (D), Technology platform (T), and Implementation architecture (A) sub-dimensions.

Both the dimensions and their sub-dimensions are independent in terms of their *evolution*, *i.e.*, the choices along each [sub-] dimension changes independently over time, but they are interdependent in terms of their *utility*, *i.e.*, collectively they offer a business functionality. From evolution perspective, new choices can be emerged in a [sub-] dimension and existing choices can be turned out to be inappropriate with the time. The frequency of these changes may vary significantly across [sub-] dimensions. For instance, changes along the technology platform sub-dimension are more rapid than changes along the functionality sub-dimension. In such situation, the interdependencies among various sub-dimensions make the effective utilisation complex. For instance, a change in solution architecture dimension may force an existing business functionality to be delivered using a different set of choices along solution architecture dimensions.

Therefore, development of an IT systems where a choice along a dimension can impact multiple program units (*i.e.*, scattering) and choices along a set of dimensions can impact the same program unit (*i.e.*, tangling) is no longer a feasible option for modern enterprises. It is expected that IT systems to be agile, adaptable and extensible in terms of all [sub-] dimensions and as a whole to address interdependencies. The core capabilities that are expected are suitable building blocks that are modular, adaptable configurable, portable, extensible, interoperable and seamlessly traceable. Rest of this chapter focuses on concepts, techniques and approaches in software engineering that help to develop IT systems with desired characteristics.

SOLUTION SPACE: EXISTING CONCEPTS, TECHNIQUES AND APPROACHES

The associated complexities of the current enterprises have led the software engineering community to explore a wide range of approaches and techniques to design, develop, and manage IT systems. Fundamentally, they conform to the concept of *separation of concerns* (Kulkarni et al., 2003) where an IT system can be visualised as the composition of building blocks from multiple [sub-] dimensions in a consistent whole. The software engineering community focuses on suitable abstractions to represent, configure and compose these building blocks in an effective manner. The *component* abstraction is an established concept to enable separation of concern along functionality sub-dimension. It help to capture logically coupled *functionalities* in an encapsulated form, enables horizontal decomposition. It also promotes modularity, composition and reuse.

The layered architecture that visualises an IT system along multiple layers, such as user interface (UI) layer, business process layer, application layer and database layer, is another form of separation of concerns. It enables vertical decomposition, support distributed architecture, and helps developers to focus on specific aspect involving a set of associated technology stacks.

The variability modelling and product line architecture are further extensions to introduce separation of concerns for developing a family of IT systems (Kulkarni, 2010). It helps to specify the common part of a family of IT systems and all variations that distinguishes the member of a family in a structured and modular form.

Figure 1. An illustration of advanced component abstraction and assemply

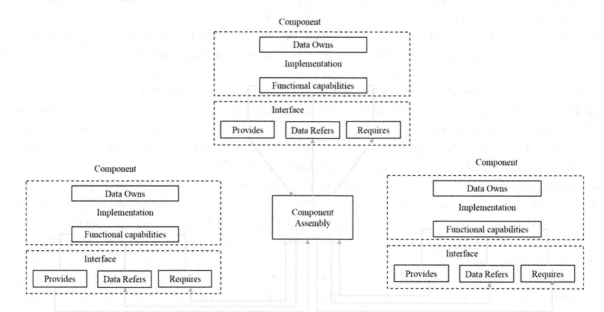

The use of model-driven development (MDD) approach opens up another dimension of the separation of concerns. It helps to separate functional capabilities, such as business functionalities and business processes, from solution architecture that includes design decisions, architectural choices and technology stacks. It helps developers to focus solely on specification of business capabilities in an intuitive manner that is closer to the problem domain (Kulkarni et al, 2004). In MDD approach, a set of code generators translate specifications of business functionalities and business processes into the desired technology platform. It delivers increased productivity, uniformly high code quality, platform independence and retargetability (Selic, 2003). This section presents overviews of concepts, techniques and approaches that are relevant for addressing the needs of an enterprise.

Component Abstraction

Component is an abstraction that enables modularity and helps in decomposing a large system in manageable units (Heineman et al., 2001) A traditional component exposes an interface that describes its capabilities (or services), and encapsulates data and business functionalities in a modular form. A schema representing an advanced form of component abstraction is depicted in Figure 1. As shown in the figure, the concept *component* is a building block that enables clear separation between its interface and implementation. The interface explicitly describes the services offered, and services required from external entities to realise its capabilities. It also describes the data that it owns and data that it refers from external entities. It is argued that such advanced form of component abstraction enables functional decomposition, composition, parallel development and testing process and reuse.

Layered Architecture

Most of the existing IT systems of enterprises conform to a layered architecture that typically includes four interacting layers as shown in Figure 2 (Kulkarni, 2016). The key capabilities of the conventional layers that include User Interface, Business Process layer, Application layer and Database later as described below:

Figure 2. Layered architecture

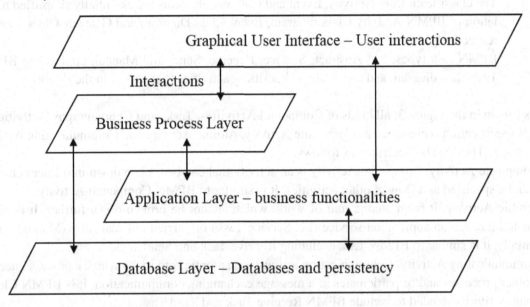

1. **User Interface:** User Interface is a part of an IT system that exposes the implemented system functionalities to the end users. Typical user interaction involves feeding in information using forms and/or browsing over available information using queries and reports. Forms, queries and reports are typically implemented in a target platform using standard graphical user interface primitives such as windows, controls and buttons. A window is a unit of interaction between the users and the system, and is composed of various controls and buttons invoking functionality. A control accepts or presents data in a specific format. The user can perform a specific activity by clicking on a button. The user interface is best specified in terms of windows, data to be shown in each window, controls to be used to represent data, possible navigation between windows and actions that can be performed.

2. **Business Process**: A business process is a control flow over a set of activities and events where an activity, *i.e.*, an operational task, is either an atomic unit or a composite activity. An atomic activity is either a manual task or well-defined business functionality that can be automated through a service. A composite activity can be decomposed into a set of fine-grained activities, *i.e.*, it is a control flow over a set of fine-grained activities. A meta-model that highlights the core concepts and their relationships for specifying business processes is depicted in Figure 3. Conceptually, a business process specification captures the flow relationship using the association between Flow

Object and Connecting Object. Meta-model supports Activity, Event, and Getaway as Flow Objects, and Sequence Flow and Message Flow as Connecting Objects. Essentially the depicted meta-model conforms to BPMN 2.0 specification (White, 2004) as follows:

a. Flow Objects classification conforms to BPMN Flow Element Class Diagram.
b. Connecting Object conforms to BPMN Sequence Flow Class Diagram and Message Flow Class Diagram.
c. Associations between Flow Object and Connecting Object conform to BPMN Sequence Flow Class Diagram.
d. The classifications of Activity, Event and Gateway elements are essentially simplified translation of BPMN Activity Class diagram, Event Class Diagram and Gateway Class diagram respectively.
e. BPMN task types, e.g. Abstract, Service, Receive, Send, and Manual, conform to BPMN Task class diagram and are used for describing activities (not shown in the figure).

As shown in the Figure 3, all kinds of Compound Activities, Tasks and Choreography Activities of BPMN specification is classified as Composite Activity, Atomic Activity and Communicating Activity respectively. They can be described as follows:

Composite Activity: Composite Activity is an activity that can be broken down into finer activities and can be specified as a flow of other activities. It is similar to BPMN Compound Activity.

Atomic Activity: It is an atomic unit of work, which cannot be broken down further. It is either automated through an application service (i.e. Service Task) or carried out manually (Manual Task). Essentially, it is similar to BPMN Task excluding Receive Task and Send Task.

Communicating Activity: Communicating activity is an atomic activity by which a process interacts with other processes and/or participates in a message exchanging communication. It is BPMN Choreography Activity extended to include BPMN Receive Task and Send Task.

3. **Application Layer**: The application layer implements the business functionality in terms of business logic, business rules. The functionality typically contains classes, attributes, methods and associations between classes. Some of the methods of classes are exposed as services. A business process contains set of activities and the order in which these activities are executed. These activities are implemented by services.

4. **DB Layer**: The database (DB) layer provides persistence for the application objects. An application may adopt a specific persistency strategy from a range of design choices, such as relational database or object database, RDBM or in-memory database, and time series database. In a relational database, the schema is made up of tables, columns and keys where a column has a name and a simple data type, and relations between tables are specified using foreign keys. An object model specifies similar information in terms of classes, attributes and associations.

Product Line Architecture

Software product line is an approach to develop purpose-specific software systems with lower development time, effort and cost (Pohl et al., 2005). Approach recognises a set of related software artifacts as one entity, termed as family, where each member of a family comprises a common part and a set of specialised functional extensions over common part. The specialised extension are modularised as units,

Figure 3. Business process meta model

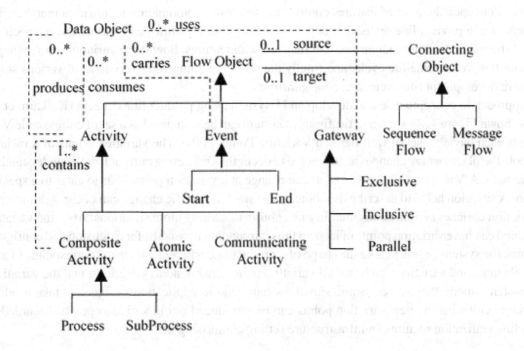

Figure 4. Architecting for configuration and extension

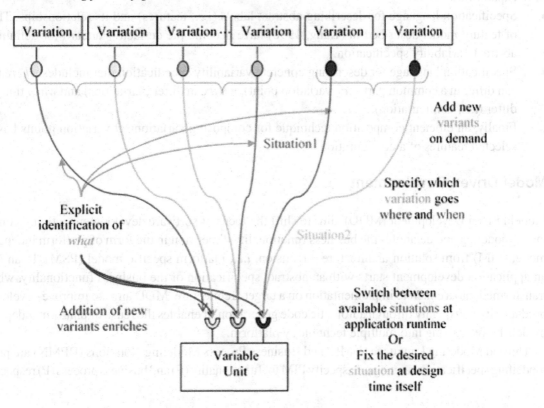

which is known as variations. Each variation is associated with a unique and abstract label, which is known as feature. Conceptually, a set of features conforming to a valid combination identifies a member. The effectiveness of a product line realisation depends on how commonalities and variations are specified, how well the variations are modularised and mapped with features, how these variations are managed throughout the product line life cycle, and finally the ability of composing variations at various stages of software development life-cycle, *i.e.*, *configuration*.

An approach to conceptualise and develop an IT system using product line concept (Kulkarni et al., 2012) is shown Figure 4. As shown in the figure, a system can be visualised as a set of composable Variable Units each having a set of well-defined Variation Points (VPs). The variation points of a variable unit denote the places *where* changes are expected to occur thus reflecting current level of understanding of the domain. A Variation (V) denotes *what* can change at a variation point so as to cater to a specific situation. A situation helps to describe the context, *i.e.*, *when* a specific change can occur. Addition of a new variation enriches system configurability i.e., ability to address more situations. Also, the variation being added can have variation points of its own thus introducing new paths for extension and configuration. Thus, the system begins to take the shape of a product line wherein a member corresponds to a set of variable units and variations such that all variation points are bound to variations, and the variations are consistent among themselves. Some situations may require application designer to take a relook at a variable unit whereby new variation points can be introduced or old variation points discarded. A product line realization requires an infrastructure setting comprising of:

- Specification language for describing common and feature-specific modules (*i.e.*, variations) of a product line. Variation specification language expects richer modularization and composition capabilities.
- Specification language for describing abstract labels (*i.e.*, features) and its relationships. The use of feature model described in (Kang, 1990) have become the de-facto standard for defining this abstract variability specification.
- Specification language for describing concrete variability specification that includes *where* things can differ in a common part (*i.e.,* variation point), *what* can differ (variations) and *when* things can differ (*i.e.,* configuration).
- Finally, an efficient composition technique for composing variations at variation points based on selected features of a configuration.

Model Driven Development

Model Driven Development (MDD) aims to shift the focus of software development activity from coding to modeling and detangles the business functionality dimension in the form of platform independent model (PIM) from solution architecture dimension, *i.e.*, platform specific model (PSM). In an MDD, an application development starts with an abstract specification of the business functionality, which is transformed into a concrete implementation on a target architecture. MDD aims to improve development productivity and quality through automatic code generation. It enables the reuse of platform independent models by retargeting into multiple technology platform.

Unified Modeling Language (UML) and Business Process Modeling Notations (BPMN) are popular modelling specification languages to specify PIM for functionality (F) and business process (P) respectively.

AN INTEGRATED APPROACH

With increasing business dynamics, the current IT systems are subjected to evolve along multiple dimensions. Those evolutions are often simultaneous and they follow their own pace and characteristics that ranges from sporadic to continuous, slow to rapid, and desirable to critical. The traditional code-centric software development techniques show unacceptable responsiveness to cope with such multi-dimensional dynamism. The software engineering (SE) community has been actively exploring effective and innovative means to manage with such complexities by applying the notion of *separation of concerns* along several dimensions as we have seen in the previous section. This section justifies a need for integrating multiple techniques for introducing the desired characteristics of current IT systems, and presents an integrated approach that has been effectively applied in software industry for more than a decade.

Rationale

In our approach, we consider component abstraction and layered architecture to introduce horizontal and vertical decomposition of functional capabilities, the MDE approaches to detangle functional capabilities from solution architecture, and the product line architecture to distinguish commonality and variability for a related set of systems. While these techniques are extremely important to realise agile and adaptable IT systems, none of them is sufficient to address the whole requirements. For instance, component abstraction can introduce the desired agility and adaptability for functional aspect by introducing a flexible plug-and-play component architecture - but they are not effective to address technology adoption and evolution. The layered architecture decomposes various aspects of an IT systems but it fundamentally provides an inadequate support to establish interoperability across layers. The MDE approaches help to introduce technology adoption using generative approaches (Czarnecki et al., 2002), and address interoperability though meta-model unification, but the traditional code generators are not inherently cognizant of modularity and componentization. Therefore, the code generators themselves are not agile and adaptable as expected. Moreover, the current needs make a strong case for bringing in the product line ideas *i.e.*, what can change where and when, to the code generators and model transformation techniques for desired agility (Barat and Kulkarni, 2010).

Based on these pragmatic observations, an integrated approach that adopts model-driven technique (Schmidt, 2006) as basis for seamlessly integrating an advanced component abstraction, layered architecture and product line concept is advocated. The key considerations of the proposed approach are:

C1: A model-driven specification-based IT system development whereby the system specification can be kept independent of solution architecture concerns, such as design decisions (D), solution architecture (A) and technologies (T). This enables system developers to focus solely on specifying the business capabilities in a manner that is intuitive and closer to the problem domain.

C2: A unified meta-modelling technique, which is cognizant of multi-layered architecture and enables seamless interoperability across layers. Essentially, the use of a unified meta-model to specify layers and their interoperability. This helps to manage the accidental complexity of using layer-specific technologies and their impedance mismatches in an effective manner.

C3: An affective utilisation of component abstraction to specify layers, *i.e.*, inherent support for component abstraction in meta-models that specify layers. This enables functional decomposition, reuse and plug-and-play architecture.

C4: Introduction of product line architecture across layers. This calls for an inherent support for suitable abstractions to specify commonality, variability, composition and resolution in a unified manner. Since IT systems are typically implemented conforming to a layered architecture wherein an architectural layer encapsulates a specific [set of] concern[s], the abstraction should be used consistently within all architectural layers, and also across them.

C5: A specification driven generation of code generators whereby technical architects can compose specification of the desired [set of] code generator[s] as a hierarchical composition of reusable artefacts. A generic code generator generator delivers the desired purpose-specific [set of] code generator[s] from this composite specification. This calls for an affective combination of meta-modelling technique, component abstraction, and the notion of product line architecture.

Solution Considerations

Model-Driven Multi-Layer Specification Approach

Model-driven development approach starts with definition of an abstract specification that is to be transformed into a concrete implementation on a given target architecture. The target architecture for modern enterprises usually conforms to a four-layered architecture that includes: user interface, business process, application functionality and database as discussed earlier. An approach to develop an IT system with four layered architecture is shown in Figure 5. As shown in the figure, there are four meta-models, namely GUI layer meta-model, Business Process meta-model, Application layer meta-model and DB layer meta-model, for the four aspect specifications. Each meta-model supports the necessary and sufficient concepts to specify aspect related requirements. All these meta-models are conceptualised as views of a single unified meta-model to specify integrity constraints that need to be satisfied by the instances of related model elements across different aspects.

Figure 5. Model based development approach

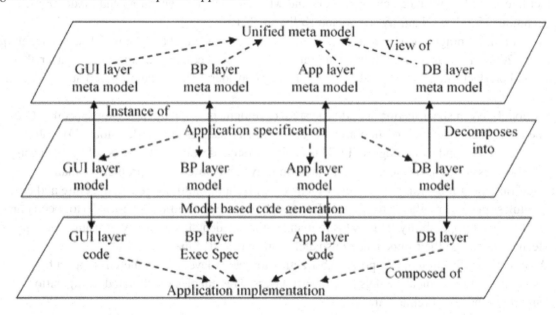

Addressing Inter Layers Interoperability

A single unified meta-model allows to specify integrity constraints to be satisfied by the instances of related model elements within and across different layers. A necessary and sufficient unified meta-model to capture the specification requirements of all the architectural layers is defined. Figure 6 shows a subset of such unified meta-model highlighting the associations spanning across the different architectural layer models. This enables independent transformation of layer specific models into their corresponding implementations namely GUI layer code, executable business process specification, Application layer code and DB layer code with assurance of integration of these fragments into a consistent whole. These transformations can be performed either manually or using code generators. Models can be kept independent of implementation technology, and the application specifications can be targeted to multiple

Figure 6. Unified meta-model

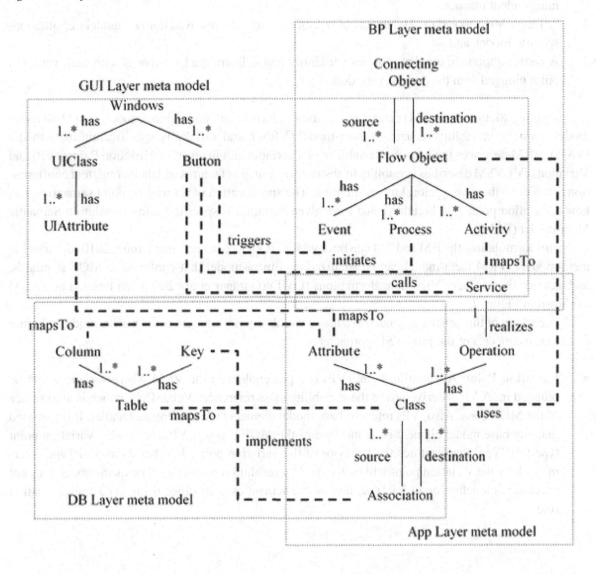

technology platforms through code generation. Construction of application specification in terms of independent models helps divide and conquer. Modeling helps in early detection of errors in application development cycle. Associated with every model are a set of rules and constraints that define validity of its instances. These rules and constraints could include rules for type checking and for consistency between specifications of different layers.

Approach to Introduce Model Driven Product Line

Figure 7 depicts a model-driven architecture for managing the concept variability and configuration, which are introduced in Figure 4. Key components of the architecture are:

1. A generic Base Meta-model (BM) that enables specification of a domain model. For example, the layer specific models or a unified meta-model as shown in Figure 6 can serve as a BM.
2. A generic Variability Meta-model that helps to specify variation points and variants in a domain-independent manner,
3. A Target Meta-model (TM) that enables specification of the resolved domain model i.e. situation-specific model, and
4. A configuration engine that resolves variability and delivers the base model with each variation point plugged with the desired variation.

Variability Meta-model (VM) describes variability of a domain model (base model) using two meta-models namely: variability realization meta-model (VRM), and variability specification meta-model (VSM). VRM describes the concrete variability of a variable unit in terms of Variation Points (VP) and Variations (V). VSM describes variability in abstract form such as features and their consistent configurations each describing an a priori known situation. The specification of a variation point semantics, *i.e.*, how a variation point is to be interpreted for a given variation is specified using Resolution Semantic Meta-model (RSM).

In this formulation, the BM and TM can be any MOF (Object Management Group, 2010) describable meta-models, VRM meta-model can be isualized as a meta-model that conforms to MOF standards, and an operational Query View Transformations (QVT) (Gardner et al., 2003) can be used as a RSM as shown in Figure 7.

A derivation of this generic approach to address variability is illustrated using a meta-model in Figure 8. The core concepts of the proposed approach are:

*   **Variation Point**: A Variation Point (VP) is a placeholder in the VRM where variations can be plugged in. A VP is derived from the variability class reference (VclassRef), which is an instance of the MOF class. Also, VPs refers to base model elements via a reference handler. It is assumed that any base model element is an instance of the MOF class. A VP must have a variation point type (VPType) that captures the behavior of the variation point. In other words, VPType determines how the variation point will be handled by resolution semantics. The meta-model does not make explicit definition of VPType, instead the semantics is specified using QVT transformation rules.

Figure 7. Overview of variability modeling and configuration approach

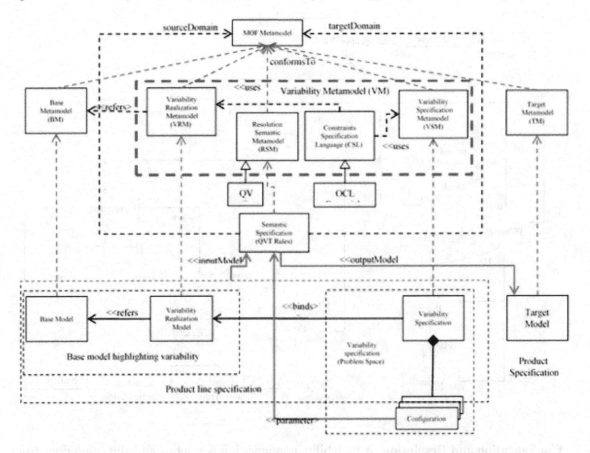

- **Variation**: Variations can be considered as individual parts that can be plugged into a variation point (with type safety). Variations are the second key component of VRM. Similar to VPs, variations are also derived from VclassRef and conform to MOF class. Constraint expressions on variation points and variations can be defined using OCL. Similar to VP, variations also refer to base model elements via a reference handler.
- **vXfm:** Variability transformation or vXfm signifies transformation applied on a variability class reference (i.e., variations points and variations). They capture the resolution semantics of VM and are expressed in QVT. The QVT rules are used to resolve a target model from unresolved product line input specification.
- **Feature**: A primary constituent of the VSM is a feature or vSpec tree. The top of the tree is denoted by a Root that facilitates in the composition of the tree. A feature tree can be composed of external references, i.e., external feature tree or external configurations (i.e., pre-configured). A feature is an abstract representation and is realized via bindings to concrete concepts like variation points and variations.

Figure 8. Variability meta model

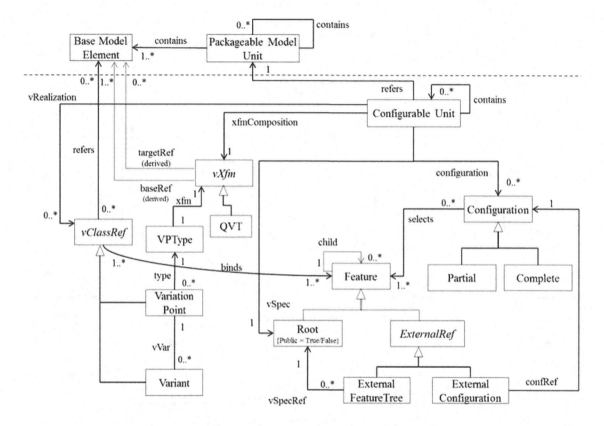

- **Configuration and Resolution**: A variability configuration is a set of all valid resolutions from a variability specification tree (i.e., feature tree) whereas variability resolution is the process of resolving a single feature (VP) to a distinct choice (variation) from a set of possible choices (variations). A configuration can be either partial (unresolved resolutions) or complete when all resolutions are resolved.

- **Configurable Unit:** A configurable unit is a reusable entity that can be composed of other configurable units. It refers to a composite Variable Unit (of Base Model) via a reference handler. A CU can be either preconfigured when it contains valid configurations (i.e. a CU without any feature tree) or a CU can be partially configured / unconfigured when it contains a set of valid configurations and a feature tree. A CU also guides in the composition of vXfms (resolution semantics). This is shown in Figure 7 by the xfmComposition association.

Specification Driven Code Generator

As discussed in the previous subsection, a product line groups together a set of products (or product variants) which share a set of features (i.e. common part) and have distinguishing features (i.e. variations). Producing a purpose specific product can be seen as selecting from the available variants at each variation point. A code generator operates on a base model and generate codes for a specific solution architecture.

Figure 9. Meta model of extensible and configurable code generator

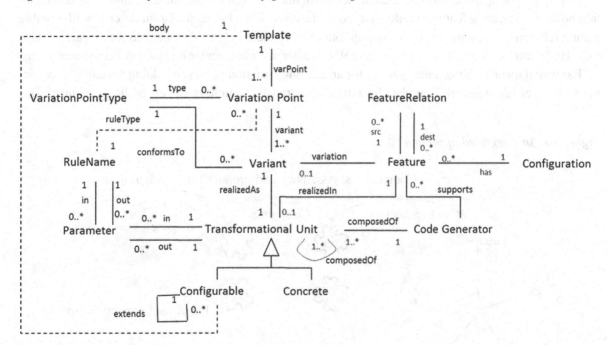

However, often there is a need to produce code for several solution architectures, such as the code for three-tier architecture on traditional Java technology stack, the code for a range of mobile platforms, or code for cloud-based architecture. Generating code for multiple solution architectures from a single base model can be visualised as code generator product line with a set of core and variable features. Figure 9 shows the proposed code generator product line meta-model describing commonality, variability and extensibility patterns. A brief description of the meta-model follows:

- A code generator is composed of several composable transformational units. Each transformation unit encodes model-to-text (MTT) transformation rules.
- Transformational unit can be of two types – concrete and configurable.
- Concrete transformational unit encodes simple MTT rules without any placeholder for extension and variation.
- Configurable transformation unit is a set of MTT rules with placeholder for extension and variation. Meta model is extended to specify the extensions and variations as follows:
  ○ Body of a configurable transformation unit is specified using Template.
  ○ Each template can have multiple variation points (placeholder for variations).
  ○ A set of variants, which are realized as transformational unit, can fit into each variation point.

The meta-model elements VariationPointType and RuleName (associated with parameters) is introduced to verify the semantic and syntactic correctness of the fitment between VariationPoint and Variant.

A code generator product line can be declaratively specified in terms of a set of features where each feature is associated with a transformational unit through realizedIn association.

Configuration operation is equivalent to selecting one amongst the available variants for each variation point, i.e. selecting features conforming to FeatureRelations. FeatureRelation describes all possible feature relations, i.e. exclusion, inclusion, optionality, dependency, etc. The selected set of features, also called as feature configuration, must be internally consistent – whatever the definition of consistency may.

Extension means adding a new variant for an existing variation point (i.e. adding variant of an existing feature) or adding a new Template by extending a transformational unit (i.e. adding new feature).

Figure 10. An integrated approach

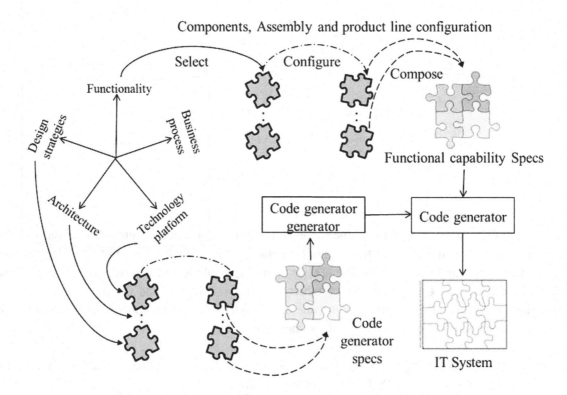

Integrating Solution Considerations

Figure 10 shows an integrated view of the techniques described in this section. As shown in the figure, an IT system can be visualised along five dimensions: Functionality (F), Business Processes (P), Decision Strategies (D), Architecture (A) and Technology platform (T). The specification of business capabilities that includes functionality (F) and business process (P) describe the platform independent (PIM) view of various layers, such as graphical interface layer, business process layer, application layer and database layer. The proposed approach supports component abstraction to decompose business capabilities as set of well-formed units, which can be composed for a consistent whole. Further, the proposed approach supports variability and the configuration by visualising some of the components as variable units with a set of variations. Therefore, the components can be configured (by selecting appropriate variation as variation points) and composed based on the desired business requirements.

The concerns such as design strategy (D), architecture (A) and technology (T) form the platform specific information. Similar to business capability specification, the information related to design strategy (D), architecture (A) and technology (T) can be captured in the form of high-level specification (i.e., application of MDE approach for developing code generators) with variation points and variations (i.e., application of product line). Therefore, the code generators can be generated through appropriate composition and configurations as shown in Figure 8. In the proposed approach, an IT system can be generated by applying generated code generator on configured and composed platform independent specification of business capabilities as shown in Figure 10.

VALIDATION AND EXPERIENCE

The concepts and proposed approach have been realised as a software development platform in a large software provisioning organisation, which has been effectively used for developing more than 100 large enterprise IT systems (several millions of lines of code) targeting on variety of technology platforms. The use of the proposed approach resulted in a significant productivity gain in terms of the lines of code. The encoding of design strategies, guidelines and best practices into the code generators resulted in uniformly high code quality. Generation of interface code between the various architectural layers ensured smooth integration of independently generated code artifacts. It also helped in retargeting business capabilities on multiple technology platforms with purpose-specific choice of architecture and design strategies. This was achieved using a relatively unskilled workforce as the technology and architecture concerns were largely taken care of by the code generators. The component-based development process helped in addressing complexity related to size and reuse.

Several IT systems were expected to be of a product-family nature wherein a product-variant needed to be quickly put together and customised to meet the specific requirements of a customer. An effective utilisation of product line concept in MDE, helped along two dimensions: addressing the product line characteristic of business capabilities and quickly develop/configure code generator to address evolving nature of solution considerations that include design decision, architecture and technology stacks.

Principally, the use of an advanced component abstraction, a model-based approach, elevating product line concept in MDE, a model-based code generator, infrastructure to realise a software factory for supporting variants of model-based code generators as a product line make the proposed approach effective to develop industry-scale IT systems. The overall experience of diffusion of a set of existing concepts and techniques is extremely encouraging for developing large IT systems.

However, all the project teams initially found it hard to switch over from the conventional code-centric development approach to model-centric approach. The difficulties were essentially due to the steep learning curve, perceived loss of control over development artifacts, and lack of debugging support for high-level specifications. The projects that were involved in developing small-to-medium sized IT systems found the proposed approach to be heavyweight and restrictive. Shorter project durations and additional overhead to resolve product line were the key bottlenecks for such engagement.

CONCLUSION

This chapter reflects on the characteristics of the modern enterprises, discusses the properties of interest, and proposes an effective industry-scale approach for conceptualizing and developing IT systems that address the needs of the modern enterprises. Chiefly, it presents an integrated approach that seamlessly augments the concept of component abstraction and product line with the MDE technique. Chapter argues that an effective utilisation of such an approach significantly improve the agility in terms of change management and adaptations that help to cope with the evolving business requirements and rapid technology advancements. It also brings significant productivity improvement, code quality, and retargetability, which are also critical factors for business success. Though the use of the proposed approach is found to be an involved approach for small to medium sized projects due to its steep learning curve, its effectiveness is undoubtedly significant for large development projects and enterprise product lines.

REFERENCES

Barat, S., & Kulkarni, V. (2010). Developing configurable extensible code generators for model-driven development approach. In SEKE (pp. 577-582). Academic Press.

Berger, T., Rublack, R., Nair, D., Atlee, J. M., Becker, M., Czarnecki, K., & Wąsowski, A. (2013, January). A survey of variability modeling in industrial practice. In *Proceedings of the Seventh International Workshop on Variability Modelling of Software-intensive Systems* (p. 7). ACM. 10.1145/2430502.2430513

Czarnecki, K., Østerbye, K., & Völter, M. (2002, June). Generative programming. In *European Conference on Object-Oriented Programming* (pp. 15-29). Springer.

Gardner, T., Griffin, C., Koehler, J., & Hauser, R. (2003, November). A review of OMG MOF 2.0 Query/Views/Transformations Submissions and Recommendations towards the final Standard. In *MetaModelling for MDA Workshop* (Vol. 13, p. 41). Academic Press.

Heineman, G. T., & Councill, W. T. (2001). *Component-based software engineering. Putting the pieces together*. Addison-Wesley.

Kang, K. C., Cohen, S. G., Hess, J. A., Novak, W. E., & Peterson, A. S. (1990). *Feature-oriented domain analysis (FODA) feasibility study (No. CMU/SEI-90-TR-21)*. Carnegie-Mellon Univ Pittsburgh Pa Software Engineering Inst. doi:10.21236/ADA235785

Kulkarni, V. (2010, October). Raising family is a good practice. In *Proceedings of the 2nd International Workshop on Feature-Oriented Software Development* (pp. 72-79). ACM. 10.1145/1868688.1868699

Kulkarni, V. (2016, May). Model driven development of business applications: a practitioner's perspective. In *Proceedings of the 38th International Conference on Software Engineering Companion* (pp. 260-269). ACM. 10.1145/2889160.2889251

Kulkarni, V. (2019). Towards an Adaptive Enterprise. In *Proceedings of the 12th Innovations on Software Engineering Conference* (p. 31). ACM.

Kulkarni, V., Barat, S., & Roychoudhury, S. (2012, September). Towards business application product lines. In *International Conference on Model Driven Engineering Languages and Systems* (pp. 285-301). Springer. 10.1007/978-3-642-33666-9_19

Kulkarni, V., & Reddy, S. (2003). Separation of concerns in model-driven development. *IEEE Software, 20*(5), 64–69. doi:10.1109/MS.2003.1231154

Kulkarni, V., & Reddy, S. (2004, October). Model-driven development of enterprise applications. In *International Conference on the Unified Modeling Language* (pp. 118-128). Springer.

Object Management Group. (2010). *Meta Object Facility 2.0.* Author.

Pohl, K., Böckle, G., & van Der Linden, F. J. (2005). *Software product line engineering: foundations, principles and techniques.* Springer Science & Business Media. doi:10.1007/3-540-28901-1

Schmidt, D. C. (2006). Model-driven engineering. *Computer-IEEE Computer Society, 39*(2), 25–31. doi:10.1109/MC.2006.58

Selic, B. (2003). The pragmatics of model-driven development. *IEEE Software, 20*(5), 19–25. doi:10.1109/MS.2003.1231146

White, S. A. (2004). Introduction to BPMN. *IBM Cooperation, 2*(0), 0.

Chapter 7
Towards Adaptive Enterprise:
Adaptation and Learning

Harshad Khadilkar
https://orcid.org/0000-0003-3601-778X
TCS Research, Tata Consultancy Services, India

Aditya Avinash Paranjape
TCS Research, Tata Consultancy Services, India

ABSTRACT

The key to a successful adaptive enterprise lies in techniques and algorithms that enable the enterprise to learn about its environment and use the learning to make decisions that maximize its objectives. The volatile nature of the contemporary business environment means that learning needs to be continuous and reliable, and the decision-making rapid and accurate. In this chapter, the authors investigate two promising families of tools that can be used to design such algorithms: adaptive control and reinforcement learning. Both methodologies have evolved over the years into mathematically rigorous and practically reliable solutions. They review the foundations, the state-of-the-art, and the limitations of these methodologies. They discuss possible ways to bring together these techniques in a way that brings out the best of their capabilities.

INTRODUCTION

A key objective of the digital enterprise is to improve the speed and quality of response of the enterprise to external inputs or context. IT infrastructure and its security are prerequisites for working towards this objective. In this chapter, we describe methodology to use the existing infrastructure and the idea of automated decision-making to make a digital enterprise *adaptive*. This is an overarching term that covers both the flexibility of the automated decision-making process when first deployed, and also its ability to respond to changing business environments.

DOI: 10.4018/978-1-7998-0108-5.ch007

As such, any methodology that leads to automated decision-making needs two common ingredients. First, it must be able to measure and suitably quantify its own performance vis-à-vis its objectives. Second, it must be able to build an internal model (either explicit or implicit) of its environment. The decision-making process solves the following problem: given the available information (model), maximise the performance metrics of the organization.

When the environment and/or the enterprise are volatile, or time-varying, it follows that the internal model used for decision-making (even if it is implicit) must be tweaked continuously. More often than not, the cues needed for tweaking come from an observation of the system's interaction with the environment rather than through any pre-defined prescription. We refer to this process as *learning* or *adaptation*, although the contexts in which these terms are employed are slightly different and this will become apparent in the chapter.

We cover two approaches, broadly divided into a model-based technique (Model Reference Adaptive Control, or MRAC) and a model-free technique (Reinforcement Learning, or RL). By model-free, we mean that the technique relies on an implicit model of the system rather than an explicit model. These notions will become clear later in the chapter. While RL can also accommodate model-based approaches, their implementation closely resembles existing model-driven control methods. MRAC and RL can be viewed as controllers for driving the state of a plant, which represents the enterprise. Figure 1 illustrates the conceptual similarities and differences between them. MRAC aims to track a reference signal r and uses a model M to update a control policy parameterised by $\hat{\theta}$. On the other hand, the form of RL shown in Figure 1, and known as advantage actor-critic [Konda and Tsitsiklis, 2000], replaces the model by a critic C, which evaluates the goodness of the current state of the plant. This estimate is fed to an actor, which computes the decisions or actions. The effect of the actions is quantified in the form of a reward signal R, which is used for the learning process.

Figure 1. High-level block diagrams of MRAC and a form of model-free RL known as A2C.

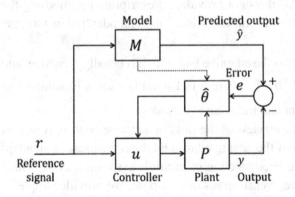

Model Reference Adaptive Control

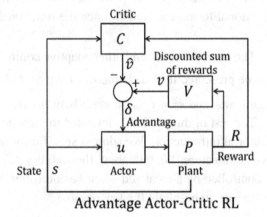

Advantage Actor-Critic RL

MODEL REFERENCE ADAPTIVE CONTROL

Adaptive control originated in the 1950s' race to develop high-performance combat aircraft. The aerodynamics of such aircraft were known to depend strongly on the flight parameters, and adaptive control emerged as a natural way to address these uncertainties. This legacy reflects in the typical (mathematical) structure of adaptive control problems, in the assumptions made while deriving the control laws, and also in some of the controversies that have shaped the development of adaptive control. It is not surprising that a large body of adaptive control has been developed for continuous (and, by extension, to discrete) time differential equations with predominantly parametric uncertainties. Even the notion of a *reference model* traces its roots to handling quality specifications, which map, in turn, to the eigenvalues of the controlled system. This approach to control design contrasts with model predictive control or reinforcement learning, where the objective is to *optimise* the behavior of the system in a suitable, long-term sense.

The abstraction of an adaptive architecture (specifically, a model reference architecture) has been shown in Fig. 1. When supported mathematically, such as by operator theory [Curtain and Zwart, 2012, Paranjape and Chung, 2018], adaptive control techniques are capable of embracing a far wider range of systems than those at its roots. We start by examining the key constituents of adaptive control.

Constituents of an Adaptive Controller

A typical MRAC architecture, shown in Fig. 1, is built upon four elements, which we introduce here.

The *system* to be controlled is referred to as the plant, the process or just the actual system. It is assumed to be in the form $Dx=f(x,u,\theta)$ where D is a (continuous/discrete) time difference operator while θ denotes a set of unknown parameters. It is customary to assume that θ is bounded with known bounds $\theta_{min} \leq \theta \leq \theta_{max}$. A *reference model* serves as a constant guide, and provides a reference output ym against which the system's output y is compared at every instant. The control input $u\left(x,\hat{\theta}\right)$ is sent to the plant, to ensure that the plant tracks the model reference system. The control law depends on the state x as well as the estimate $\hat{\theta}$. It is important to note that MRAC does not provide a prescription for choosing the functional form of u. Rather, once the functional form is chosen, MRAC uses an adaptive law to tune $\hat{\theta}$.

The core of MRAC and other adaptive controllers is the adaptive law, which is usually recursive, and can be presented in a mathematical form as $D\hat{\theta} = E\left(\hat{\theta},e\right)$, where E is a suitably chosen function of its arguments, and $e=y-y_m$ is the error between the plant and the reference model.

The rest of this section is intended to provide an overview of the field of adaptive control as well as a tutorial introduction. We address specific form(s) of the adaptive law, and the robustness of an adaptive architecture. We talk about the stability of an interconnection of multiple systems, each of which is controlled by a localized adaptive controller. Wherever it serves our purpose, we provide simple illustrations to highlight the key points.

Adaptive Laws

A key working principle of adaptive control is called the certainty equivalence principle, which we state somewhat informally as follows: if there exists θ^* such that $u(x, \theta^*)$ achieves the desired objectives, then the control law $u\left(x,\hat{\theta}\right)$ together with the adaptive law also ensures that the desired objective is met. The important point to note here is that the adaptive law only drives $\hat{\theta}$ towards $\theta*$. The certainty equivalence principle does not require that it actually ensure convergence. In fact, convergence is achieved under certain conditions, which we list later.

We consider a system given by $Dx=f(x,u)$, and with its output given by $y=h(x)$. The controller is chosen to be in the form $u = U\left(y, y_m, \hat{\theta}\right)$. Note that θ (more precisely, $\hat{\theta}$) may be purely intrinsic to the controller rather than being an explicit part of the plant.

One of the most fundamental ways to design an adaptive law is the MIT rule [Astrom and Wittenmark, 2013] which follows a gradient descent approach. In addition to being, historically, one of the first formal adaptive laws, it also has most of the essential elements of more advanced adaptive laws. Let us create a function $J\left(\hat{\theta}\right)=\frac{1}{2}e^2, e = y - y_m$, where we implicitly assume that the error arises on account of parameter mismatch. In order to drive $e\rightarrow0$, it suffices to ensure that $DJ<0$. We construct a recursive update law:

$$D\hat{\theta} = -\gamma\frac{\partial J}{\partial\hat{\theta}} = -\gamma e\frac{\partial e}{\partial\hat{\theta}}$$

The gain γ is called the adaptation rate, and its value needs to be chosen appropriately to stabilise the closed-loop system (see the next section). The MIT rule is fairly generic, but requires an explicit expression for the gradient $\partial e/\partial\theta$. The following example illustrates several fundamental features of adaptive control.

Example ([Astrom and Wittenmark, 2013], Example 5.2) Consider the scalar system $Dy=ay+bu$, where the exact value of b is unknown. It is known, however, that $b > 0$ (without loss of generality). The reference model is given by $Dy_m = -a_m y_m + b_m r$, where r is an exogenous signal and $a_m, b_m > 0$. We design the control law and the adaptive as follows:

We select the control law to be of the form $u = \hat{\theta}_1 r + \hat{\theta}_2 y$. The model tracking error can be written with a mild abuse of notation1 as

$$e = y_m - y = \left(\frac{b_m}{D+a_m} - \frac{b\hat{\theta}_1}{D-a-b\hat{\theta}_2}\right)r$$

so that

$$\frac{\partial e}{\partial\hat{\theta}_1} = \frac{-b}{D-a-b\hat{\theta}_2}r, \frac{\partial e}{\partial\hat{\theta}_2} = \frac{-by}{D-a-b\hat{\theta}_2}$$

Had we known a and b, we could choose the parameters to ensure that $a + b\hat{\theta}_2 = -a_m$ and $b\hat{\theta}_1 = b_m$. Although we cannot choose the parameter in this manner, for not knowing a and b, it does not stop us from writing the adaptive law as

$$D\hat{\theta}_1 = \gamma e \frac{a_m}{D+a_m} r, D\hat{\theta}_2 = \gamma e \frac{a_m}{D+a_m} y$$

Notice that we have conveniently ignored b in the adaptive laws: since $b > 0$, it can be thought of as being absorbed into $\gamma > 0$. This is why the sign of b must be known, even if its actual value is unknown. This is a standard assumption in adaptive control. More generally, we could replace γ with $\gamma sign(b)$. The alternative, where $sign(b)$ *is* unknown, is largely an open problem. The concept of universal stabilizers [Nussbaum, 1983] was proposed to solve such problems, but their robustness is highly questionable [Georgiou and Smith, 1997].

The parameter update laws can be simplified further using $y_m = b_m r/(D+a_m)$. Moreover, if the objective of the control design is to ensure that $y_m \to r$, we need $a_m = b_m$. This permits a further simplification to $D\hat{\theta}_1 = \gamma e y_m, D\hat{\theta}_2 = \gamma e z$, where z is the low-pass filtered form of y: $Dz = a_m(y-z)$. Notice that the low-pass filter has the same dynamics as the model system. This complies with the well-known internal model principle posits that a controller must contain a model of the reference signal in order to track it accurately. Finally, we note that since the reference model is decoupled from these three sub-systems, the stability of the closed-loop system is independent of its dynamics, but not necessarily the value of y_m due to the nonlinear nature of the adaptive laws. ■

The MIT rule has evolved into a series of adaptive laws based on Lyapunov functions, which can be viewed as a generalization of the function J defined above. A Lyapunov function, denoted by V, is a positive-definite function of the tracking error e and the parameter estimation error $\hat{\theta}$: typically as a weighted sum-of-squares, but not restricted to this form. The dynamics $D\hat{\theta}$ are chosen to ensure that DV is negative semi-definite. The most commonly used family of parameter update laws of this series is that of projection-based adaptive laws [Ioannou and Sun, 1996, Goodwin et al., 1980, Kreisselmeier and Anderson, 1986] which also enforce boundedness of $\hat{\theta}$. Incidentally, the boundedness of $\hat{\theta}$ cannot be guaranteed by the MIT rule directly. In fact, the earliest adaptive laws were flown on experimental aircraft by NASA in the 1960's, until one such flight ended in a fatal crash [Dydek et al., 2010]. The accident was traced back to a divergence in the parameter estimates.

At the same time, it is not necessary that $\hat{\theta}$ converge to the true value θ^* in order for the adaptive controller to work successfully: a projection-based adaptive law will ensure that $y \to y_m$ asymptotically, while $\hat{\theta}$ remains bounded.

The key points that we have seen in this section thus far are illustrated in Fig. 2 which shows the time histories of the system state, the model and the parameter estimate for a system similar to the Example above. We notice successful tracking, parameter convergence to non-ideal values, and a nonlinear response vis-a-vis the value of r. In order to ensure that $\hat{\theta} \to \theta^*$, the reference signal r (or the disturbances encountered by the system) must be sufficiently rich in frequencies. This can be achieved by artificially introducing probing signals satisfying this property, called *persistence of excitation* [Boyd and Sastry, 1986]. It is well-known that an adaptive control law equipped with persistent excitation is far more robust than its regular counterpart [Sastry, 1984].

Figure 2. Time histories for a system based on the Example above, with $a=a_m=b=b_m=1$. The ideal values of the parameters are $\theta_1^* = -1, \theta_2^* = -2$. The adaptive gain is chosen as $\gamma=0.2$

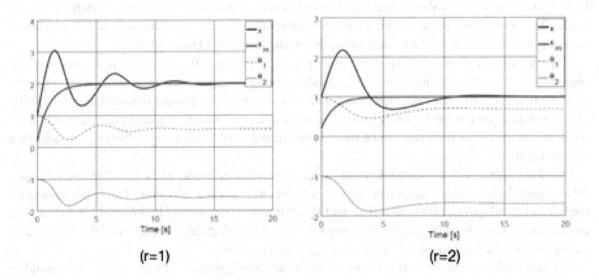

(r=1)   (r=2)

Robustness and Fast Adaptation

One of the first demonstrations of the inherent lack of robustness in adaptive algorithms was provided in [Rohrs et al., 1982], wherein it was argued that adaptive controllers could experience parameter drift (or bursting) when excited by reference signals or disturbances of specific frequencies. The lack of robustness was, in fact, shown to be far more general in nature [Georgiou and Smith, 1997] than just related to excitation at specific frequencies. It was shown in [Dobrokhodov et al., 2011] through flight testing that a control law based on [Cao and Hovakimyan, 2008], which uses a well-positioned low-pass filter together with the projection algorithm, can mitigate these problems.

The adaptive gain needs to be chosen to ensure that the closed-loop dynamics consisting of the plant, the controller and the adaptive laws are stable and sufficiently robust. At the same time, the general understanding, especially for continuous time systems, is that a larger adaptive gain implies faster adaptation. In principle, the value of the adaptive gain can be made arbitrarily large without compromising stability [Narendra and Lin, 1980]. However, it is apparent from the parameter update laws in the above Example that a large adaptive gain will saturate the parameter estimates (provided the estimates are bounded in a projection-like setting) leading to a bang-bang time history. While this may not necessarily jeopardize stability *per se*, it will prevent the system from learning the parameters correctly even if it is assisted by persistent excitation [Ioannou et al., 2014].

The second problem with choosing a large gain is that the resulting system may not be robust to external disturbances and time delays. The loss of robustness can be mitigated systematically by adding a low pass filter to the control signal using the small gain theorem [Cao and Hovakimyan, 2008], but it may compromise the system's ability to track arbitrary reference signals accurately [Ioannou et al., 2014].

Reference Models and Optimality

In designing MRAC, we make the implicit assumption that the plant can realistically track the reference model. This assumption is made from the point of view of performance and robustness, but may not be necessary for stability. It is worth considering the mechanism behind these plants.

For low order systems, a reference model is typically a low-pass filter with the necessary transient response characteristics. For instance, we may wish the transient response to subside within 1 s and within no more than 2 cycles. The reference model which fits these characteristics is a second order spring-mass-damper system. It can be safely prescribed as the reference model provided the time constants of the dominant modes of the plant can be made better than 1 s while retaining a damping of more than 0.7 (two cycles to converge).

An alternative to such arbitrary reference models is a controlled model of the actual plant itself. Such reference models can be of large orders, but have a better chance of being feasible. This hypothesis forms the basis of L_1 adaptive architectures [Cao and Hovakimyan, 2008, Dobrokhodov et al., 2011]. In fact, in such cases, the reference model effectively serves as a hypothetical reference model which is used purely for analytical purposes; i.e., proof of stability and robustness.

For practical applications, it is often necessary to achieve optimality in some sense. This could be in terms of tangible as well as intangible reward/penalty functions. An example of the former class of applications is reinforcement learning (RL), while linear quadratic regulators (LQR) are usually an example of the latter. We will discuss RL in the latter half of this chapter. We will presently review a recently-developed optimal adaptive architecture.

In several systems, the dynamics are of the form $Dx=Lx+f(x)+gu$, where L and g are known linear operators. All of the uncertainties are buried in the potentially nonlinear function $f()$. In such cases, we can decompose the parent system into two virtual sub-systems

$$Dx_h = Lx_h + gu, Dx_p = Lx_p + f(x)$$

together with an estimator for the virtual states. The adaptive laws are buried in the state estimator for x_p.

Notice that the first sub-system is linear and the only one which is amenable to control. The control u can thus be designed in a relatively simple setting to ensure that $\hat{y}_h \to y_m - \hat{y}_p$ optimally, using the LQR methodology. Here, $\hat{y}$ denotes the output of the corresponding state estimator.

This technique was demonstrated for an abstract class of systems in [Paranjape and Chung, 2016], subject to a conjecture about the approximation of adjoint states. This approximation is very similar to value function approximation in RL, and could serve conceptually as a bridge between the two sets of methodologies.

Interconnections of Systems

When designed using techniques from MRAC, the control law includes a reference mode and an adaptive law.

The central theme of this book is that of an adaptive enterprise, where the enterprise is modeled as a network of systems, or systems interconnected through a graph (see Fig. 3). The graph imposes a

Figure 3. Centralized versus decentralized control of a complex system of systems

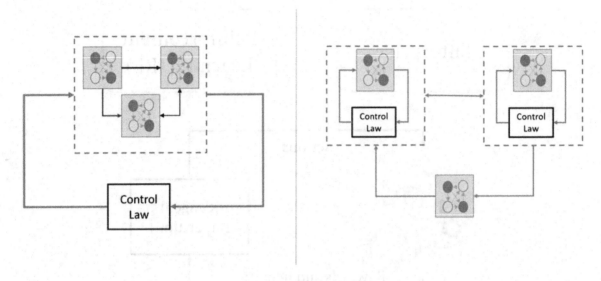

constraint on the immediate amount of information available to each system, as well as on any given system's ability to influence the complete enterprise.

A natural question for such systems concerns the number of individual systems we need to control in order to meet the objectives of the enterprise. A corollary to this question is this: if all of the individual systems are controlled, can the interconnection perform in a desirable manner?

These questions are fairly complex, but there exist several canonical results that shed light on these questions. The first question is that of controllability, and we refer the reader to [Liu et al., 2011, Subramanian et al., 2018] for insights in that direction. We consider the second question presently.

Figure 3 shows two broad approaches for controlling large systems. Centralized control involves a single bank of controllers, while decentralized architectures involve a multitude of controllers acting locally on individual sub-systems. Centralized architectures present a relatively simple control design problem, in that they deal with a single system. The large scale of the system is an obvious disadvantage, since exact models may be unavailable or intractable. However, if these models are available, it is possible at least in principle to design reliable, optimal control algorithms using the methods described earlier in this chapter.

The drawbacks of centralized architectures can be mitigated using distributed architectures. In the distributed scheme of Fig. 3, each controller would ideally need an accurate model of only its own sub-system. However, it is well-known [Ioannou, 1986] that the interconnections may destabilize the overall system, even if the individual sub-systems are adequately stable, when the local controllers do not compensate for the other sub-systems in some suitable manner. This is where some amount of global information is required. In the simplest setting, signals from the other sub-systems can be treated as disturbances and estimated using, say, a function approximator [Ioannou, 1986, Spooner and Passino, 1996]. Alternately, an adaptive law can be constructed using the reference models for all known sub-systems while using purely local state information [Mirkin and Gutman, 2003]. All of these control laws work under well-defined assumptions (e.g., known bounds or relative degrees). While we do not dwell on the exact assumptions here, we emphasize the necessity of verifying the assumptions before employing a particular control algorithm.

Figure 4. Vision of an adaptive enterprise achieved through reinforcement learning

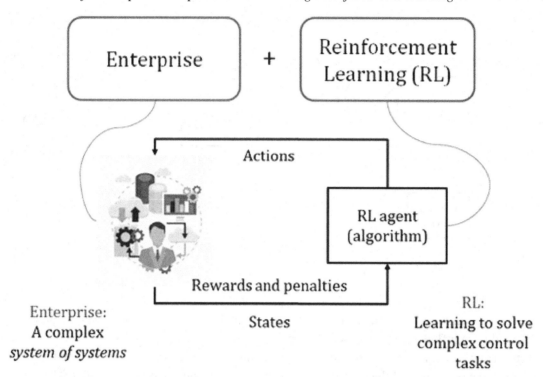

REINFORCEMENT LEARNING

Reinforcement learning (RL) is a class of machine learning algorithms used for closed-loop control of dynamic systems [Sutton and Barto, 2012]. Unlike supervised learning (which attempts to minimise the error with respect to ideal outputs) and unsupervised learning (which attempts to find patterns in the data), the goal of RL is to maximise some notion of long-term reward. The phrase long-term sets this class of algorithms apart from more greedy control approaches, and is discussed in greater detail later in this chapter. From the perspective of an adaptive enterprise, RL can be used in the form outlined in Figure 4. We encapsulate the enterprise in a single entity on the left, and the controller (called the RL agent) on the right. It is not necessary to have such a stark distinction as this, and we proceed with the caveat that the figure is illustrative rather than exact.

Consider the problem of computing optimal decisions (equivalently, actions) in an enterprise, so as to achieve some future goal state. Note that the time horizon of this goal state can be arbitrarily far away, and may not even be finite. At each time step in this exercise, the state of the enterprise is sensed and communicated to the RL agent. The agent computes a set of actions based on this state, and communicates these back to the enterprise, where they are implemented. The effect of these actions is evaluated quantitatively in the form of rewards or penalties, and returned to the RL agent (with a delay of one time step). This additional information is used to update the agent's beliefs and policies for the future. In the rest of this chapter, we describe the implementation of this concept in greater detail. A set of practical use cases where the authors have applied reinforcement learning are described towards the end of the chapter; but those descriptions will not be instructive without the following context.

Motivation for Using RL

The primary reason for using reinforcement learning as a control approach for adaptive enterprises, is its inherent ability to handle complex stochastic systems without extensive design effort. The characteristics that provide these advantages are highlighted below.

Figure 5. RL closes the decision loop, while the human moves to a supervisory role

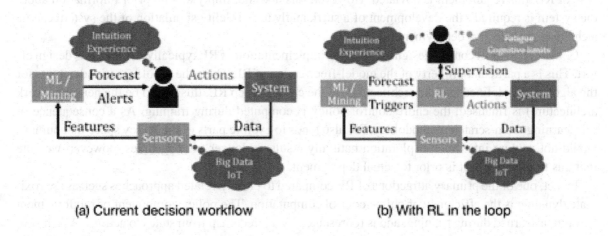

(a) Current decision workflow   (b) With RL in the loop

Reinforcement learning can work in scenarios where macro-level system behaviour cannot be defined analytically. In many real-world systems (such as enterprises), individual elements of the system have well known behaviour, but the overall behaviour is emergent and unpredictable. Analytical approaches may be insufficient for modelling such systems with sufficient fidelity to develop sensible control policies. This leaves us with a set of control approaches that include RL as well as approximate dynamic programming [Bertsekas, 2005], which are capable of handling systems with emergent behaviour.

Since RL improves by trying to improve its own observed rewards, it does not require knowledge of correct or optimal actions. This is an important departure from traditional control approaches [Utkin et al., 2009, Mayne et al., 2000] which either provide a reference signal to be tracked, as well as other machine learning approaches such as imitation learning [Ross and Bagnell, 2010, Harmer et al., 2018, Duan et al., 2017], which try to mimic an expert or optimal policy. Definition of the ideal state or control action can be tricky in complex systems, and the relaxation of this requirement leads to several positive effects.

The most powerful forms of RL are model-free. This means that the algorithm makes no advance assumptions whatsoever, about the system behaviour. Instead of including an expectation of system behaviour as part of the control computation, we build an external simulation of the system components. We assume that the components individually can be simulated and that they can interact with each other, allowing us to test the emergent effects of control actions. These effects are quantified as rewards/penalties, and used for training the algorithm. The model-free nature of the approach necessarily implies that the algorithm has more to 'learn' about the system, as compared to the model-based approaches discussed earlier in this chapter. As a result, the sample complexity of these approaches is greater than for adaptive control. On the other hand, once a simulator is developed for training the algorithm, one does not need additional data in the sense of supervised learning; one only needs to train the algorithm for more cycles (or 'episodes', in RL parlance). It so happens that this is an acceptable compromise for most applications.

Since reinforcement learning learns by interacting with the environment (a simulation of the system or the actual system), it does not require historical data for training. Instead, it generates data while training is in progress. Practical implementation of machine learning techniques in business enterprises are frequently hampered by the lack of high-quality historical data for training the algorithms. In the case of RL, this requirement is obviated. However, this does not imply that no prior information about the system is required - the development of a sufficiently high fidelity simulation of the system can be a challenge to effective deployment of RL.

Compared to most control design techniques, implementation of RL typically requires less design effort. This is a particular property of the model-free version of RL. Once the set of inputs and outputs for the algorithm is defined and the architecture (in the case of Deep RL, this would be the neural network architecture) is finalised, the entire control policy is computed during training. As a consequence of this learning-from-scratch methodology, RL also tends to explore parts of the policy space that humans would not venture into. Such exploration naturally results in longer training times; however, we note that this time investment is prior to actual deployment.

In fact, one of the primary attractions of RL compared to closely-related approaches such as approximate dynamic is the efficiency of online control computation. The policy component of reinforcement learning is learned during training, and is represented by a direct map from states to actions. As a result, the online computation of decisions does not require any roll-outs or tree-based exploration, and is a one-shot forward pass through (typically) a set of neural networks. This is achieved without losing the focus on long-term reward, as we shall explain subsequently.

How RL fits Into the Existing Flow

Business-critical systems need to continually make decisions to stay competitive and economically viable in a dynamic environment. The typical decision-making flow in a modern enterprise is shown in Figure 5 (a). In a heavily sensed system, a large amount of raw data points are generated at every time instant. State of the art enterprises employ intelligent Internet of Things (IoT) embedded systems and Big Data analysis techniques to convert the raw data into a set of curated features that represent the current state of the system. These features are fed to various machine learning and data mining systems (for example, time-series forecasting, clustering, and anomaly detection) in order to provide decision-support in the form of forecasts and alerts. The outputs of these algorithms are viewed by a human, who decides the actions to be taken.

The principal problem with the flow in Figure 5 (a) is the dependence on a human-in-the-loop for every action to be taken on the system. Repetitive tasks are likely to cause fatigue in humans, which can lead to mistakes. Further, the sheer volume of information generated by modern IoT/Big Data systems can cause cognitive overload for the human-in-the-loop, leading to suboptimal decision making. Therefore, the vision for RL (Figure 5 (b)) is to take over the regular decision making task, learning to optimise the system during nominal operation. The human moves up to a supervisory role, where his/her intuition and experience can be used to monitor system behaviour, identify developing problems, and to intervene when required. We note that unless specifically trained to do so, RL is not meant to handle large external disruptions. This is still the job of a human supervisor or fail-safe algorithm. Gradual system changes, of course, will be automatically adjusted for by the adaptive nature of RL.

Alternative Control Approaches

So far, we have made the case for using reinforcement learning to perform automated, adaptive decision making in an enterprise. However, we may ask whether it is possible to use an alternative algorithmic approach to achieve the same tasks. In the following description, we take a brief look at the available options, and weigh their applicability to the current context.

Most state-of-the-art automation systems use heuristic control algorithms for decision-making. The motivation for this can be found in the fact that immediately prior to this automation, there was an actual human being doing the same job. It therefore makes sense to encode the thumb rules used by the human in the automated system, resulting in the heuristic algorithm. However, such an approach has limitations because, (i) the quality of the solutions computed by the heuristic is dependent on the ability of the human who provided the rules, (ii) the heuristics are developed with some assumptions about the system behaviour, but this behaviour can change over time, (iii) typically no analysis is made as to the optimality or otherwise of the approximation, (iv) rules themselves are not easy to articulate and to write in computer code, and (v) every instance of the same task may require a separate implementation effort, depending on context. Instead, RL offers the opportunity to deploy a single pre-designed intelligent agent into many different (yet similar) situations, and letting this agent learn the specific rules by itself.

At a more formal level, one can imagine modelling enterprise operations as a dynamic system, with a set of states and a set of relationships driving the evolution of these states over time. The canonical version of a multivariable system with dynamics, is to represent the state by a vector of variables, and their evolution over time using matrix differential equations [Ogata and Yang, 2002]. Examples of multivariable problems are transportation networks [De Oliveira and Camponogara, 2010] and inventory management in supply chains [Van der Laan and Salomon, 1997]. The preferred control approach for multivariable problems is to use a linear time invariant (LTI) model of the system and to design a controller using classical methods in the frequency domain or using state feedback [Bouabdallah et al., 2004, Golnaraghi and Kuo, 2010]. Non-linear versions of the problem are solved using techniques such as sliding mode [Utkin et al., 2009] and model predictive control [Mayne et al., 2000]], while robust control under stochastic disturbances is handled using techniques such as H_∞ [Doyle et al., 1989]. The key takeaway from these techniques is that they address one complex aspect of the problem in isolation. There are almost no techniques in traditional control that can tackle the level of complexity and stochasticity of a modern enterprise.

As we have seen earlier in this chapter, there exists a large volume of existing literature on adaptive control for dynamic systems. However, adaptive control typically requires analytical models of the control and adaptation laws. Approximate Dynamic Programming (ADP) [Bertsekas, 2005, Powell, 2007] has a similar dependence on analytical forms. The closest form of ADP for problems of the current type is the literature on Adaptive Critics [Si et al. 2004], which has considerable overlap with reinforcement learning. ADP has been used in prior literature for relatively large task allocation problems in transportation networks [Godfrey and Powell, 2002, Topaloglu and Powell, 2006]. These studies use non-linear approximations of the value function, but the forms are still analytically described. Furthermore, they require at least a one-step rollout of the policy. This may not be feasible in the current context, since the number of possible actions can be very high. Imitation learning (IL) is a well-known approach for learning from expert behaviour, but it assumes that expert decisions have considered all the constraints of the system in order to accomplish the objective. IL has been used in variety of problems including games [Ross and Bagnell, 2010], 3D games [Harmer et al., 2018], and robotics [Duan et al., 2017]. The inherent problems of design complexity and performance limitations apply here as well; to the definition of the expert policy rather than to the IL algorithm. Additionally, the general form of the enterprise control problem may not admit an obvious expert policy to train with.

The review of alternate approaches tells us that the main lacunae in traditional control methodologies lie in (i) requiring analytical models of the system operation, which may not be available in an enterprise setting, (ii) requiring online exploration, search, or roll-out of alternative actions, which may not be computationally feasible, and (iii) requiring an expert or optimal action to imitate in any given state, which may not be available. On the other hand, RL works well when there is a long-term reward to be achieved, the reward is path-dependent, and there is uncertainty or noise in system behaviour. Reinforcement Learning (RL) has achieved a degree of success in control applications such as online gameplay and robotics, but has rarely been used to manage enterprise-wide operations or business-critical systems. A key aspect of using RL in the real world is to train the agent before deployment, and thereby minimise experimentation in live operation. While this is feasible for online gameplay (where the rules of the game are known) and robotics (where the dynamics are predictable), it is much more difficult for complex systems due to associated complexities, such as uncertainty, adaptability and emergent behaviour. In the rest of this chapter, we will review these challenges and ways to overcome them.

Defining an RL Problem

A reinforcement learning problem is described by a Markov Decision Process (MDP) [Sutton and Barto, 2012] represented by a tuple S,A,R,P,γ. In simple terms, the property of an MDP is that its future evolution is independent of its past, subject to whatever state it is presently in. Here, S is the set of states of the system, A is the set of available control actions, R is the set of possible rewards, P is the (possibly stochastic) transition function from $(S,A)\rightarrow S$, and γ is a discount factor for future rewards. In several cases, the agent is unable to observe the state space entirely, resulting in a partially-observable MDP or POMDP [Sutton and Barto, 2012]. Observations O are derived from S to represent what the agent can sense. The RL agent should compute a policy $O\rightarrow A$ that maximises the discounted long-term reward. We shall describe some concrete examples later in the chapter.

There are many approaches available for computing the mapping from $O\rightarrow A$ starting with simple look-up tables (each possible observation is associated with a corresponding action) to the use of deep learning or artificial neural networks (ANNs). The latter methodology is referred to as Deep RL, and is commonly divided into two sets of techniques. The first are called *value-based* methods, and involve the estimation of the long-term reward $Q(s,a)$ achievable by taking an action $a \in A$ in a given state $s \in S$. Given the current state, the action chosen is the one associated with the highest estimate of $Q(s,a)$ or 'Q-Value'. The estimates of $Q(s,a)$ are updated post-facto based on the actual evolution of the system. If the estimate is computed using a neural network with s and a as the inputs and $Q(s,a)$ as the scalar output, the method is called a Deep Q-Network (DQN). Deep Q-Network [Mnih et al., 2015] was used to achieve superhuman performance on Atari using raw pixel inputs. Subsequent modifications were proposed to stabilize the training and making it more sample efficient [Van Hasselt et al., 2016, Schaul et al., 2015].

The second set of techniques for mapping $O\rightarrow A$ are known as policy-based methods. Here, we do not attempt to explore the action space in search of the action with the highest expected long-term reward.

Instead, a neural network is typically used to output the action a directly, given the state s as the input. Recently, policy gradient methods have been shown to be capable of handling continuous action spaces [Islam et al., 2017]. However, the most promising area of current research is a hybrid between value-based and policy-based methods, and are broadly known as actor-critic methods [Konda and Tsitsiklis, 2000] (Figure 1). The 'actor' part of these methods is a neural network designed to output the action given the state as input. However, the actor is also fed information by the 'critic', which estimates the value (or goodness) of the current state of the system. Deep Deterministic Policy Gradients (DDPG) [Lillicrap et al. 2015] improves upon the basic advantage actor critic by using the actions as inputs to the critic, and using sampled gradients from the critic to update the actor policy. DDPG has been shown to work well on continuous action spaces, although results so far are limited to a few (less than 10) action outputs. Trust Region Policy Optimization [Schulman et al., 2015] and Proximal Policy Optimization [Schulman et al., 2017] have also proven effective for optimal control using RL.

While the majority of research in RL has focussed on online gameplay applications, there is recent interest in system dynamics problems as well. The computation of torque commands for robotic applications [Powell, 2012, Kober et al., 2013] including locomotion [Kohl and Stone, 2004] and manipulation [Theodorou et al., 2010] is a good example. A number of these methods are model-based [Nagabandi et al., 2018], because of the availability of accurate dynamic models of the robots. The action spaces are naturally continuous and are either discretised for tractability or are represented by function approximations. Alternatively, the policy is parameterised for simplicity [Theodorou et al., 2010]. The key point of complexity is the curse of dimensionality, which is much more acute in the enterprise context than in typical robotic applications with fewer than 10 degrees of freedom. Applying methods such as DDPG to problems with hundreds of degrees of freedom is difficult even with recent sample-efficient techniques [Gu et al., 2017]. A recent approach for exploration in large state-action spaces is learning by demonstration [Nair et al. 2018]. However, this requires the equivalent of an expert policy for imitation learning.

Intelligent transportation systems [Bazzan and Klugl, 2013] also require online decisions for managing transportation network operations for maximizing safety, throughput, and efficiency. Adaptive traffic signal control has been a major challenge in transportation systems. In literature, it has been solved by modeling it as a multiple player stochastic game, and solve it with the approach of multi-agent RL [Shoham et al., 2007, Busoniu et al., 2008, El-Tantawy et al., 2013]. However, these approaches are difficult to scale. Other approaches [Khadilkar, 2019] tackle the scalability issue by dividing the global decision-making problem into smaller pieces, with both local and global performance affecting the reward. This relates to the current context, since one may choose to decompose the action space for tractability while attempting to maximise global reward.

Applying RL to a Toy Problem: A number of textbooks on reinforcement learning, including [Sutton and Barto, 2012], describe the application of RL on smaller examples. Here, we do not go into the mathematics of the formulation or the computational steps, but provide an intuitive description of the approach. This should help the reader follow the remaining portion of the chapter, without necessarily having to read supplementary material.

Consider the problem of learning to play a standard 3x3 tic-tac-toe game. Without loss of generality, we assume that the RL agent is playing X, and the opponent is playing O. Our agent could be playing first or second, according to a randomly chosen order. The state S of the system can be represented by a 3x3 matrix, corresponding to the tiles of the board. Each tile can take one of three values: empty, filled by X, or filled by O. The number of possible states is thus $(3x3)^3$. The action A chosen by the agent is a choice of one out of the nine tiles, to place an X. Some of the action choices may be invalid if they are already occupied, but nine choices is the maximum that the agent has. The reward R reflects the result of the game. A common choice is to provide a terminal reward of +1 for winning, 0 for a tie, and –1 for a loss. Step rewards may be set to 0. The transition caused by the player itself is deterministic (placement of an X resulting in a new state), but the opponent's move is stochastic. The possible moves made by an opponent can be modelled using the transition matrix P. The discount factor may be set to any value in this case, since the game runs for a finite number of steps (at most 9). With the game now modelled as a standard MDP, we can use one of several applicable RL algorithms to compute the policy that maps states to actions. The agent will require several games to be simulated (typically numbering in the hundreds of thousands) against a variety of opponent strategies, in order to learn effectively.

The finite nature of the state and action spaces, and the closed nature of the game (operating according to a known and fixed set of rules) makes this a relatively simple task. As we shall see below, translating this into the real world is more challenging.

Applying RL in the Real World

A significant majority of academic research in reinforcement learning has focussed on problems such as single- or multi-player gameplay and autonomous driving. These problems differ significantly in terms of scale and stochasticity from the type of problems we are interested in. Enterprises operate in environments that are far more complex, large scaled, and noisy than the ones for which RL algorithms have been developed. The differences can be encapsulated in the form of two threads, as described below. The first pertains to the technical challenge of applying RL in a practical setting, while the second relates to acceptability of the proposed algorithms in a business-critical system.

The most critical challenge is that of **large scale,** especially in terms of the decision or action space. The typical gameplay situation involves choosing one out of a handful of discrete actions, while autonomous driving can have continuous actions in limited number. On the other hand, decisions in an enterprise setting can be high-dimensional (for example, managing inventory logistics in a supply chain) as well as highly constrained. A corollary of the scaling challenge is that each problem instance can be of **variable scale.** For example, while managing port operations, each ship can be of different size and layout. This implies that the input and output sizes of the problem instances need not be fixed. Finally, there is the **complexity and uncertainty** associated with simulating enterprise operations, which are required for training the algorithms effectively.

The flip side of the technical challenges are those of their perception as black box approaches. One of the primary obstacles to the implementation of machine learning methods in business-critical systems is not their solution quality, but their trustworthiness. The more **explainable** an algorithm is, the faster it is accepted by operational personnel. Secondly, the algorithms that are implemented should work with **limited computational resources.** At this moment in time, businesses are not willing to make multi-million-dollar hardware investments to run truly deep learning algorithms. Instead, the goal of an algorithm designer should be to use limited computational power. This can be achieved by interpreting (pre-processing) raw input using domain expertise, and providing the RL agent with key features. Not only does this reduce computational requirements and limit the scale of the problem, but it also increases the explainability of the algorithm. We illustrate these aspects with a few examples.

Scheduling of Railway Lines

Railway networks are composed of individual railway lines with junctions. Within each railway line is a sequence of stations, and trains run in both directions along this line. The timetable developed for scheduled services ensures that these trains do not compete for the same resources (railway tracks). However, whenever an external disturbance (in the form of a delay) is imposed on one or more trains, such competition may occur. Recovering from delays and disruptions can have non-linear knock-on effects on other trains on the same line, as well as other intersecting railway lines, leading to emergent behaviour.

In prior work [Khadilkar (2019)], we describe an algorithm for scheduling bidirectional railway lines (both single- and multi-track) using a reinforcement learning (RL) approach. The goal is to define the track allocations and arrival/departure times for all trains on the line, given their initial positions, priority, halt times, and traversal times, while minimising the total priority-weighted delay. The challenge of scale (there can be upwards of a thousand trains in a nationwide network, and each train can pass through a hundred or more stations) is solved by dividing the decision-making responsibility. A high-level heuristic decides the order in which trains are to be processed, while a lower-level reinforcement learning algorithm learns to move or halt each train depending on local resource congestion. This methodology is similar to the way human controllers take decisions, thus improving its acceptability to operators.

Container Loading in Ports

The shipping industry has seen steady growth in the first half of this decade, with the busiest ports handling more than 30 million containers per year, or over 80 thousand containers per day. Container loading and unloading operations in the storage yard are among the most complex in the industry, and reducing the time it takes to load a ship can have a significant effect on the yard efficiency. We consider the specific of loading an outbound ship with containers from the yard, with the goal of minimising the number of crane movements required. At any given time, there could be a hundred thousand containers in the yard, and over a thousand slots on the ship. Therefore, the basic assignment problem contains a very large number of variables.

We developed [Verma et al., (2019)] an RL framework for selecting and sequencing containers to load onto ships in ports. It can be viewed as a version of the assignment problem in which the sequence of assignment is of importance and the task rewards are order dependent. The proposed methodology is developed specifically to be usable on ship and yard layouts of arbitrary scale, by dividing the full problem into fixed future horizon segments and through a redefinition of the action space into a binary choice framework.

Replenishment in Supply Chains

We consider the scenario of a grocery retailer with a network of stores and warehouses served by a fleet of trucks for transporting products. The goal of replenishment is to regulate the availability of the entire product range in each store, subject to the spatio-temporal constraints imposed by (i) available stocks in the warehouses, (ii) labour capacity for picking and packaging products in the warehouses, (iii) the volume and weight carrying capacity of the trucks, (iv) the transportation times between warehouses and stores, (v) the product receiving capacity of each store, and (vi) available shelf space for each product

Figure 6. Schematic of the replenishment problem in supply chains

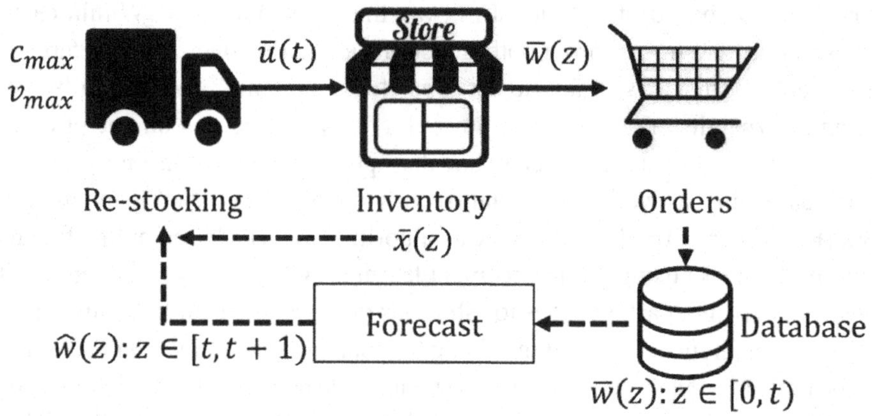

in each store. A typical retailer could have tens of warehouses, thousands of stores, thousands of trucks, and a hundred thousand unique product types within its network.

We will return to the larger problem in the last part of this chapter; at the moment, consider the simplified version shown in Figure 6. This illustrates the control problem with the example of a single store served by a single truck from a warehouse (not shown) with an inexhaustible supply of products. The replenishment of inventory is assumed to take place periodically (typically every 6 hours). The goal of the reduced replenishment problem is to maintain inventory of the entire product range in the store, while minimising wastage of perishable products. In prior work [Barat et al., (2019)], we define the state space as the inventory $\bar{x}$ of all products in the store at the time of decision-making, as well as the forecast $\hat{w}$ of sales over the next time period. The control vector $\bar{u}$ denotes the replenishment quantity of each product sent to the store, while adhering to volume and weight capacity constraints on the truck. As currently depicted, Figure 6 represents a microcosm of a more complex system, which is the entire supply chain. Similarly, the other two examples also considered decision-making in fairly compact and well-defined systems. To move to true *systems of systems* problems, we need one more string to our bow: that of multi-agent reinforcement learning, or MARL.

Multi-Agent Reinforcement Learning (MARL)

Among the challenges to implementation of RL in the real world as listed in the previous section, the first one - that of large scale - is the most important. In fact, the other challenges are corollaries of this problem. The training effort required because of the large problem size restrains us from training independent models for different problem instances. The difficulty of predicting the macro behaviour of large-scale systems limits our ability to model the environment accurately. Complex architectures required for large instances require proportionally more computational power for training as well as online operation, and their very size increases the opacity of logic underlying the decision-making process. Work on multi-agent reinforcement learning (MARL) [Littman, (1994)] has introduced the possibility of circumventing these challenges by dividing the decision-making process along functional or spatial lines.

The MARL problem is defined by the tuple (n,S,A,P,R) where n is the number of agents, S is the state space, A is the action space, P is a transition function from a state-action pair to the next state of the system, and R is the set of rewards. Note that the only addition to the canonical representation of RL is the existence of n agents. Other theoretical assumptions such as the Markov property remain the same. Each of the n agents interacts with a common environment (actual system or a simulation of the system). Rewards are generated for each agent, which tries to maximise its own long-term expected reward. The collection of agents is nudged towards system optimality through reward or state sharing, or communication of sub-goals. The approach is inherently scalable (because each agent operates semi-independently), explainable (because the number of inputs for each agent is limited), and robust (because some agents can fail while the rest are operational).

At this point, we inject a note of caution about some known pitfalls in the MARL approach. If the number n of agents becomes very large, we can run into a *credit assignment* problem. Intuitively, this is the challenge of identifying the source of reward or penalty in an environment where a very large number of decentralised decisions are being computed. A corollary to this problem is the *lazy agent* problem, where the correlation between the actions of an agent and the reward that it receives becomes so low that the learning is hampered. Finally, an extreme version of this problem can actually cause *policy destabilization*, where a negative correlation between actions and rewards actually leads to the agent unlearning good policies.

Several architectures, reward mechanisms, and communication protocols have been developed in literature for managing these problems while retaining the advantages of MARL. These include fully decentralised swarms [Foerster et al., (2016), Omidshafiei et al., (2017)] and hierarchical versions [Dietterich, (2000), Barto and Mahadevan, (2003)] of MARL. The latter is of special interest to us in the current context, because it closely mimics the structure of an enterprise. In what follows, we postulate an approach for decision-making in the original supply chain problem with all its inherent complexity.

Figure 7. Two architectures for supply chain control using reinforcement learning: [Left] Centralized approach, [Right] Decentralized approach

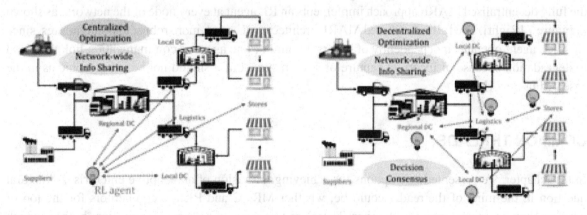

Using Multi-Agent Reinforcement Learning for Complex Systems

We illustrate the generic reinforcement learning problem in the context of supply chain replenishment, which presents well-known difficulties for effective control [Lee et al., (1997), Sabri and Beamon, (2000)]. Figure 7 illustrates a retail supply chain with brick & mortar stores as the final customer-facing nodes. These stores are periodically stocked by warehouses or local distribution centers (LDCs) using delivery trucks. The local DCs are themselves stocked at sparse intervals by regional distribution centers (RDCs), which receive products directly from suppliers. The DCs stock a large range of products, upwards of one hundred thousand unique varieties.

Moving the products through the supply chain involves packing the products (using trolleys), loading packed products to the trucks/carriers and delivering them to respective stores or downstream DCs on predefined routes. Each sub-process contains constraints such as the warehouse labour capacity, machine capacity, number of trucks, and the truck volume/weight capacities. The uncertainties that emerge due to the probabilistic behaviours of the individual elements include unavailability and varying productivity of labour, delays or breakdowns of the trucks. Trucks are constrained by the volume and weight capacities, and could be constrained to carry only a specific set of product types (fresh, frozen, etc.).

The first step in our solution approach is to ensure an accurate representation of the next state and reward, and consequently a better estimate of the long-term consequences of a series of actions for this complex system. In this case, we do not rely on macro level simulation, and instead use a bottom-up multi-agent simulation approach [Clark et al., (2017)]. This ensures that the emergent behaviour of the system is captured as accurately as possible during the training of the RL algorithm. Next, we enable the communication of system states, control actions, and rewards throughout the network using suitable IoT sensing architectures. With these basics in place, we turn to the problem of control design.

Every example that we have given so far (including the scheme in Figure 4) has utilised a single RL agent for decision making. Theoretically, this is possible for the supply chain scenario as well, and the centralised architecture is depicted in Figure 7 [Left]. However, such an architecture not only leads to higher complexity of the algorithm (in terms of scale and variety of input), but is also vulnerable to failures. A single point failure of the RL agent could lead to loss of control of the entire system. Instead, the fully decentralised MARL approach implements an RL agent at every node of the network, as shown in Figure 7 [Right]. The fully distributed MARL architecture is much more robust to point failures, since each RL agent operates independently of others. Failure of one agent or communication link may lead to degradation because of incorrect capture of system state, but it should not be catastrophic as in the case of Figure 7 [Left].

COMMON THREADS

In this chapter, we presented two options for achieving the vision of an adaptive enterprise. A natural question in the mind of the reader could be, whether MRAC and RL are competitors for the job or whether they can complement each other. There are two ways to answer this question, both of which invoke the notion of hierarchy. To the best of the authors' knowledge, both of these are open problems at the time of writing this chapter.

Figure 8. Conceptual layout of hierarchical MARL and MRAC

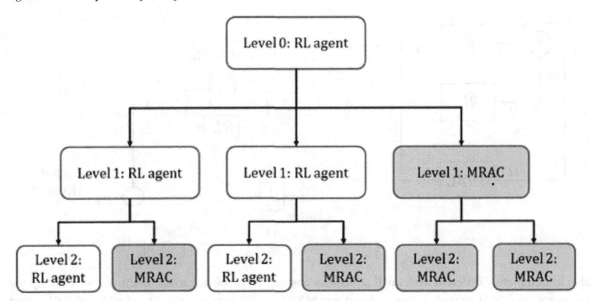

Hierarchical Control

We address the question by noting that MRAC can (and should) be used for parts of the system that can be modeled to a sufficient extent. MRAC is faster to train, it makes use of whatever domain knowledge already exists, and is also inherently explainable. RL should be used where the system behaviour is unknown. This is especially true if we consider a hierarchical multi-agent setting, where the high-level controllers work with really uncertain dynamics. As a final point, we note that RL and MRAC can work together, as illustrated in Figure 8. Neither MRAC nor RL restricts the source of the data that provides the state and reward information, or the eventual actuator for whatever decisions are computed. They can train and adapt in very flexible ways, and one can imagine the topology of Figure 8 without requiring extensive retraining for the agents or controllers already active in the system.

Transfer Learning

Suppose now that we have developed an RL-based agent for controlling a nominal model of the system. This training would involve real-world data as well as simulation of the system (e.g., using the digital twin concept developed elsewhere in this book). Once the RL agent is deployed on the field, its performance is likely to be sub-optimal, at least at the outset, as it adjusts itself to the real-world dynamics.

In such cases, MRAC can be used to augment the RL agent (see Figure 9). The reference model for MRAC would be the nominal model (or the digital twin) controlled by the RL agent itself. The assumption behind this choice of reference model is that the RL agent has tuned itself to deliver a satisfactory reward for the nominal model. Moreover, this reference model would come close to satisfying the model-matching conditions required by MRAC. MRAC would, essentially, ensure that the real-world reward is at least as good as that obtained under nominal conditions. This application is akin to transfer learning, wherein an RL-trained agent is employed with minimal tweaking not just in off-design scenarios but

Figure 9. RL agent forms an integral part of MRAC

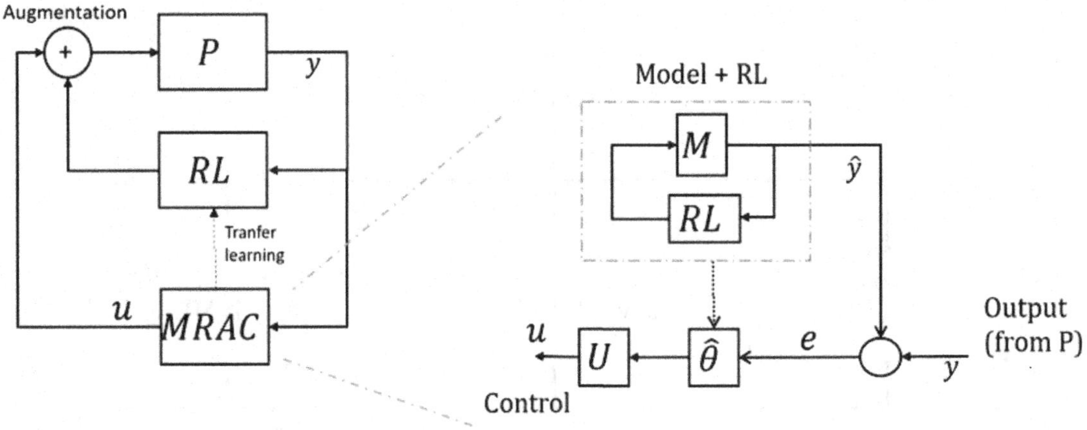

also in completely different systems that bear an abstract resemblance to the one used for training the RL agent. In MRAC-enabled transfer learning, MRAC could improve the rate at which the RL agent tunes itself to the new (real-world) system. One limitation of this approach is that MRAC would likely limit the exploration undertaken by the RL agent in the initial course of implementation. This restriction is a trade-off, in return for ensuring that the actual rewards do not deviate too far from the nominally expected rewards.

REFERENCES

Astrom, K. J., & Wittenmark, B. (2013). *Adaptive control*. Courier Corporation.

Barat, S., Kumar, P., Gajrani, M., Meisheri, H., Baniwal, V., Khadilkar, H., & Kulkarni, V. (2019). Reinforcement learning of supply chain control policy using closed loop multi-agent simulation. *Multi-Agent Based Systems Workshop (AAMAS)*.

Barto, A. G., & Mahadevan, S. (2003). Recent advances in hierarchical reinforcement learning. *Discrete Event Dynamic Systems*, *13*(1-2), 41–77. doi:10.1023/A:1022140919877

Bazzan, A. L., & Klugl, F. (2013). Introduction to intelligent systems in traffic and transportation. *Synthesis Lectures on Artificial Intelligence and Machine Learning*, *7*(3), 1–137. doi:10.2200/S00553ED-1V01Y201312AIM025

Bertsekas, D. P. (2005). Dynamic programming and optimal control. Athena Scientific.

Bouabdallah, S., Noth, A., & Siegwart, R. (2004). PID vs LQ control techniques applied to an indoor micro quadrotor. *Proc. of The IEEE International Conference on Intelligent Robots and Systems (IROS)*, 2451-2456. 10.1109/IROS.2004.1389776

Boyd, S., & Sastry, S. (1986). Necessary and suffcient conditions for parameter convergence in adaptive control. *Automatica*, *22*(6), 629–639. doi:10.1016/0005-1098(86)90002-6

Busoniu, L., Babuska, R., & De Schutter, B. (2008). A comprehensive survey of multiagent reinforcement learning. *IEEE Transactions on Systems, Man and Cybernetics. Part C, Applications and Reviews, 38*(2), 2008. doi:10.1109/TSMCC.2007.913919

Cao, C., & Hovakimyan, N. (2008). Design and analysis of a novel L_1 adaptive control architecture with guaranteed transient performance. *IEEE Transactions on Automatic Control, 53*(2), 586–591. doi:10.1109/TAC.2007.914282

Clark, T., Kulkarni, V., Barat, S., & Barn, B. (2017). ESL: an actor-based platform for developing emergent behaviour organisation simulations. In *International Conference on Practical Applications of Agents and Multi-Agent Systems*, (pp. 311-315). Springer. 10.1007/978-3-319-59930-4_27

Curtain, R. F., & Zwart, H. (2012). *An introduction to infinite-dimensional linear systems theory* (Vol. 21). Springer Science & Business Media.

De Oliveira, L. B., & Camponogara, E. (2010). Multi-agent model predictive control of signaling split in urban traffic networks. *Transportation Research Part C, Emerging Technologies, 18*(1), 120–139. doi:10.1016/j.trc.2009.04.022

Dietterich, T. G. (2000). Hierarchical reinforcement learning with the maxq value function decomposition. *Journal of Artificial Intelligence Research, 13*, 227–303. doi:10.1613/jair.639

Dobrokhodov, V., Kaminer, I., Kitsios, I., Xargay, E., Cao, C., Gregory, I., ... Valavani, L. (2011). Experimental validation of L1 adaptive control: The Rohrs counterexample in flight. *Journal of Guidance, Control, and Dynamics, 34*(5), 1311–1328. doi:10.2514/1.50683

Doyle, J. C., Glover, K., Khargonekar, P. P., & Francis, B. A. (1989). Statespace solutions to standard H_2/H_∞ control problems. *IEEE Transactions on Automatic Control, 34*(8), 831–847. doi:10.1109/9.29425

Duan, Y., Andrychowicz, M., Stadie, B., Ho, J., Schneider, J., Sutskever, I., ... Zaremba, W. (2017). *One-shot imitation learning* (Vol. 31). NIPS.

Dydek, Z., Annaswamy, A., & Lavretsky, E. (2010). Adaptive control and the NASA X-15-3 ight revisited. *IEEE Control Systems Magazine, 30*(3), 32-48.

El-Tantawy, S., Abdulhai, B., & Abdelgawad, H. (2013). Multiagent reinforcement learning for integrated network of adaptive traffic signal controllers (MARLINATSC). *IEEE Transactions on Intelligent Transportation Systems, 14*(3), 1140–1150. doi:10.1109/TITS.2013.2255286

Foerster, J., Assael, I. A., de Freitas, N., & Whiteson, S. (2016). Learning to communicate with deep multi-agent reinforcement learning. *Advances in Neural Information Processing Systems*, 2137-2145.

Georgiou, T., & Smith, M. (1997). Robustness analysis of nonlinear feedback systems: An input-output approach. *IEEE Transactions on Automatic Control, 42*(9), 1200–1221. doi:10.1109/9.623082

Godfrey, G. A., & Powell, W. B. (2002). An adaptive dynamic programming algorithm for dynamic eet management, i: Single period travel times. *Transportation Science, 36*(1), 21–39. doi:10.1287/trsc.36.1.21.570

Golnaraghi, F., & Kuo, B. (2010). Automatic control systems. *Complex Variables, 2*, 1–1.

Goodwin, G., Ramadge, P., & Caines, P. (1980). Discrete-time multivariable adaptive control. *IEEE Transactions on Automatic Control, 25*(3), 449–456. doi:10.1109/TAC.1980.1102363

Gu, S., Holly, E., Lillicrap, T., & Levine, S. (2017). Deep reinforcement learning for robotic manipulation with asynchronous o_-policy updates. *Robotics and Automation (ICRA), 2017 IEEE International Conference on*, 3389-3396.

Harmer, J., Gisslen, L., del Val, J., Holst, H., Bergdahl, J., Olsson, T., . . . Nordin, M. (2018). *Imitation learning with concurrent actions in 3D games.* arXiv preprint arXiv:1803.05402

Ioannou, P. (1986). Decentralized adaptive control of interconnected systems. *IEEE Transactions on Automatic Control, 31*(4), 291–298. doi:10.1109/TAC.1986.1104282

Ioannou, P., Annaswamy, A., Narendra, K., Jafari, S., Rudd, L., Ortega, R., & Boskovic, J. (2014). L_1-adaptive control: Stability, robustness, and interpretations. *IEEE Transactions on Automatic Control, 59*(11), 3075–3080. doi:10.1109/TAC.2014.2318871

Ioannou, P. A., & Sun, J. (1996). *Robust adaptive control* (Vol. 1). Prentice-Hall.

Islam, R., Henderson, P., Gomrokchi, M., & Precup, D. (2017). *Reproducibility of benchmarked deep reinforcement learning tasks for continuous control.* arXiv preprint arXiv:1708.04133.

Khadilkar, H. (2019). A scalable reinforcement learning algorithm for scheduling railway lines. *IEEE Transactions on Intelligent Transportation Systems, 20*(2), 727–736. doi:10.1109/TITS.2018.2829165

Kober, J., Bagnell, J. A., & Peters, J. (2013). Reinforcement learning in robotics: A survey. *The International Journal of Robotics Research, 32*(11), 1238-1274.

Kohl, N., & Stone, P. (2004). Policy gradient reinforcement learning for fast quadrupedal locomotion. *Robotics and Automation, 2004. Proceedings. ICRA'04. 2004 IEEE International Conference on, 3*, 2619-2624. 10.1109/ROBOT.2004.1307456

Konda, V. R., & Tsitsiklis, J. N. (2000). Actor-critic algorithms. Advances in neural information processing systems, 1008-1014.

Kreisselmeier, G., & Anderson, B. (1986). Robust model reference adaptive control. *IEEE Transactions on Automatic Control, 31*(2), 127–133. doi:10.1109/TAC.1986.1104217

Lee, H. L., Padmanabhan, V., & Whang, S. (1997). Information distortion in a supply chain: The bullwhip effect. *Management Science, 43*(4), 546-558.

Lillicrap, T. P., Hunt, J. J., Pritzel, A., Heess, N., Erez, T., Tassa, Y., Silver, D., and Wierstra, D. (2015). *Continuous control with deep reinforcement learning.* CoRR, abs/1509.02971.

Littman, M. L. (1994). Markov games as a framework for multi-agent reinforcement learning. In *Machine learning proceedings 1994* (pp. 157–163). Elsevier. doi:10.1016/B978-1-55860-335-6.50027-1

Liu, Y., Slotine, J., & Barabasi, A. (2011). Controllability of complex networks. *Nature, 473*(7346), 167–173. doi:10.1038/nature10011 PMID:21562557

Mayne, D. Q., Rawlings, J. B., Rao, C. V., & Scokaert, P. O. (2000). Constrained model predictive control: Stability and optimality. *Automatica, 36*(6), 789–814. doi:10.1016/S0005-1098(99)00214-9

Mirkin, B. M., & Gutman, P. (2003). Decentralized output-feedback MRAC of linear state delay systems. *IEEE Transactions on Automatic Control, 48*(9), 1613–1619. doi:10.1109/TAC.2003.817000

Mnih, V., Kavukcuoglu, K., Silver, D., Rusu, A. A., Veness, J., Bellemare, M. G., & ... . (2015). Human-level control through deep RL. *Nature, 518*(7540), 529. doi:10.1038/nature14236 PMID:25719670

Nagabandi, A., Kahn, G., Fearing, R. S., & Levine, S. (2018). Neural network dynamics for model-based deep RL with model-free fine-tuning. *Robotics and Automation (ICRA), 2018 International Conference on*, 7559-7566.

Nair, A., McGrew, B., Andrychowicz, M., Zaremba, W., & Abbeel, P. (2018). Overcoming exploration in reinforcement learning with demonstrations. *Robotics and Automation (ICRA), 2018 International Conference on*, 6292-6299. 10.1109/ICRA.2018.8463162

Narendra, K., & Lin, Y. (1980). Stable discrete adaptive control. *IEEE Transactions on Automatic Control, 25*(3), 456–461. doi:10.1109/TAC.1980.1102365

Nussbaum, R. (1983). Some remarks on a conjecture in parameter adaptive control. *Systems & Control Letters, 3*(5), 243–246. doi:10.1016/0167-6911(83)90021-X

Ogata, K., & Yang, Y. (2002). *Modern control engineering* (Vol. 4). Prentice Hall.

Omidshafiei, S., Pazis, J., Amato, C., How, J. P., & Vian, J. (2017). Deep decentralized multi-task multi-agent reinforcement learning under partial observability. *Proceedings of the 34th International Conference on Machine Learning, 70*, 2681-2690.

Paranjape, A., & Chung, S. (2016). Sub-optimal boundary control of semilinear PDEs using a dyadic perturbation observer. *Proc. 55th IEEE Conference on Decision and Control*, 1382-1387. 10.1109/CDC.2016.7798459

Paranjape, A. A., & Chung, S. (2018). Robust adaptive boundary control of semilinear PDE systems using a dyadic controller. *International Journal of Robust and Nonlinear Control, 28*(8), 3174–3188. doi:10.1002/rnc.4075

Powell, W. B. (2007). *Approximate Dynamic Programming: Solving the curses of dimensionality* (Vol. 703). John Wiley & Sons. doi:10.1002/9780470182963

Powell, W. B. (2012). *AI, or and control theory: A rosetta stone for stochastic optimization*. Princeton University.

Rohrs, C., Valavani, L., Athans, M., & Stein, G. (1982). Robustness of adaptive control algorithms in the presence of unmodeled dynamics. *Proc. IEEE Conference on Decision and Control*, 3-11. 10.1109/CDC.1982.268392

Ross, S., & Bagnell, J. A. (2010). Efficient reductions for imitation learning. *Proc. of The International Conference Artificial Intelligence and Statistics*.

Sabri, E. H., & Beamon, B. M. (2000). A multi-objective approach to simultaneous strategic and operational planning in supply chain design. *Omega, 28*(5), 581–598. doi:10.1016/S0305-0483(99)00080-8

Sastry, S. (1984). Model-Reference Adaptive Control: Stability, Parameter Convergence, and Robustness. *IMA Journal of Mathematical Control and Information, 1*(1), 27–66. doi:10.1093/imamci/1.1.27

Schaul, T., Quan, J., Antonoglou, I., & Silver, D. (2015). *Prioritized experience replay.* arXiv preprint arXiv:1511.05952.

Schulman, J., Levine, S., Abbeel, P., Jordan, M., & Moritz, P. (2015). Trust region policy optimization. *International Conference on Machine Learning*, 1889-1897.

Schulman, J., Wolski, F., Dhariwal, P., Radford, A., & Klimov, O. (2017). *Proximal policy optimization algorithms.* arXiv preprint arXiv:1707.06347.

Shoham, Y., Powers, R., & Grenager, T. (2007). If multi-agent learning is the answer, what is the question? *Artificial Intelligence, 171*(7), 365–377. doi:10.1016/j.artint.2006.02.006

Si, J., Barto, A. G., Powell, W. B., & Wunsch, D. (2004). *Handbook of learning and approximate dynamic programming* (Vol. 2). John Wiley & Sons. doi:10.1109/9780470544785

Spooner, J. T., & Passino, K. M. (1996). Adaptive control of a class of decentralized nonlinear systems. *IEEE Transactions on Automatic Control, 41*(2), 280–284. doi:10.1109/9.481548

Subramanian, J., Mahajan, A., & Paranjape, A. (2018). On controllability of leader-follower dynamics over a directed graph. *Proc. IEEE Conference on Decision and Control*, 2048-2055. 10.1109/CDC.2018.8619474

Sutton, R. & Barto, A. (2012). *Reinforcement learning: An introduction.* MIT Press.

Theodorou, E., Buchli, J., & Schaal, S. (2010). Reinforcement learning of motor skills in high dimensions: A path integral approach. *Robotics and Automation (ICRA), 2010 International Conference on*, 2397-2403.

Topaloglu, H., & Powell, W. (2006). Dynamic-programming approximations for stochastic time-staged integer multicommodity-ow problems. *INFORMS Journal on Computing, 18*(1), 31–42. doi:10.1287/ijoc.1040.0079

Utkin, V., Guldner, J., & Shi, J. (2009). *Sliding mode control in electromechanical systems.* CRC Press. doi:10.1201/9781420065619

Van der Laan, E., & Salomon, M. (1997). Production planning and inventory control with remanufacturing and disposal. *European Journal of Operational Research, 102*(2), 264–278. doi:10.1016/S0377-2217(97)00108-2

Verma, R., Saikia, S., Khadilkar, H., Agarwal, P., & Shroff, G. (2019). A reinforcement learning solution for the container selection and sequencing problem in ports. *Autonomous Agents and Multiagent Systems (AAMAS), 2019 International Conference on.*

ENDNOTE

[1]   The symbol '*D*' can be viewed, equivalently, as the argument of the Laplace/Z transform. We have ignored this technicality for simplicity, but note that the operator $1/(D+a)$ is defined via a convolution with $\exp(-at)$.

Chapter 8
Enterprise Security:
Modern Challenges and Emerging Measures

Manish Shukla

TCS Research, Tata Consultancy Services, India

Harshal Tupsamudre

TCS Research, Tata Consultancy Services, India

Sachin Lodha

TCS Research, Tata Consultancy Services, India

ABSTRACT

As we increasingly depend on technology, cyber threats and vulnerabilities are creating trust issues for businesses and enterprises, and cybersecurity is being considered as the number one threat to the global economy over the next 5-10 years. In this chapter, the authors explain this phenomenon by first describing the changing cyber ecosystem due to extreme digitalization and then its ramifications that are plainly visible in the latest trends in cyber-attacks. In the process, they arrive at five key implications that any modern enterprise needs to be cognizant of and discuss eight emerging measures that may help address consequences of those implications substantially. It is hoped that these measures will play a critical role in making enterprise security more proactive, cognitive, automated, connected, invisible, and risk aware.

INTRODUCTION

Due to the extensive digitalization in the last decade, the cost of entry into cyberspace has rapidly come down. Importantly, it has induced major changes in the enterprise and in its operating environment as manual and paper oriented processes are being replaced with software. Large scale digitalization has also made it possible for enterprises to better analyze their performance, cost drivers, customer behavior and associated risks. With the emergence of Internet of Things (IoT), there is now an explosion of interconnectivity that has led to the rapid blurring of the boundaries between virtual and physical worlds.

DOI: 10.4018/978-1-7998-0108-5.ch008

Information flows that originally were within the digital spaces are now flowing into physical spaces, leading to numerous benefits and several concerns, especially with regards to safety, security and privacy.

Indeed, a cyber threat is a possibility of an attack, via cyberspace, targeting the cyberspace of an organization for the purpose of disrupting, disabling, destroying, maliciously controlling a computing environment or stealing sensitive information (Kissel, 2011). According to 'The Global Risk Report 2019' by World Economic Forum, cyber threat is ranked 5th in terms of likelihood and ranked 7th with respect to overall impact (World Economic Forum, January 15, 2019). A large majority of respondents (82%) expect increased risk of data and money theft, and disruption in critical services (80%). The survey results clearly show the perception of new risks due to increased digitalization. This belief is substantiated by the fact that cyber threats can come from any direction, as shown by a massive distributed denial of service (DDoS) attack by IoT devices which were infected by Mirai botnet starting in 2016 (Antonakakis et al., 2017). Similarly, Meltdown (Lipp et al., 2018) and Spectre (Kocher et al., 2018) hardware vulnerabilities in modern processors allow malicious programs to steal data which is being processed on the vulnerable computer. Additionally, there are threats which are equally applicable to software and hardware, for example, ransomware attacks (Shukla, Mondal, & Lodha, 2016). The current generation of cyber threats are getting more sophisticated and have the ability to spread rapidly due to high interconnectivity between systems.

CHANGING CYBER ECOSYSTEM

To better understand the explosion of cyber-attacks, we have to look at the changes in the cyber ecosystem due to digitalization and hyper interconnectivity.

1. **Increase in Attack Surface:** Traditionally, attack surface of a system is defined as the exposure of an application, its interfaces and objects to an attacker (Heumann, Keller, & Turpe, 2010). However, from an enterprise perspective, a system consists of a combination of hardware and software assets and the humans using them.

   It has been demonstrated multiple times that even if the software is bug free, yet it is possible to steal personal and sensitive data by exploiting hardware vulnerabilities (Lipp et al., 2018; Kocher et al., 2018). In a recent paper, researchers have shown systematic degradation in deep-neural-networks (DNN) under bitwise errors that are induced by hardware fault attacks (S. Hong, Frigo, Kaya, Giuffrida, & Dumitras, 2019). According to (Ornes, 2016), only 5 million IoT devices went online in 2016 and it is estimated that 20-50 billion devices will be online by 2020. Thus, the hardware part of attack surface is growing at a rapid pace, and, that too, without security bedded into it.

   Typically, software creation process involves multiple people with varying level of skills in information security, which results in buggy software. Attacks on software can be broadly divided in two classes: a) exploitation of benign software, and b) threat from malicious software. Both of these classes are fairly prominent, for example, authors in (Evtyushkin, Ponomarev, & Abu-Ghazaleh, 2016) have shown an attack on branch predictors to bypass address space layout randomization (ASLR). Similarly, authors have demonstrated exploitation of web-applications for mounting cross-site scripting (XSS) attacks and performing parasitic computation on victim's system (Eskandari, Leoutsarakos, Mursch, & Clark, 2018; Steffens, Rossow, Johns, & Stock, 2019). The other class of attacks using software is well-known, for example, ransomware (a class of malware), which sabotages the system and extort money from the user (Shukla et al., 2016). In 2018 30% data breaches were due to vulnerability in the system (Verizon, 2019).

According to researchers, human behavior is not consistent, irrational at times, and is influenced by multiple factors (Evans, Maglaras, He, & Janicke, 2016). Further, people willingly perform risky activities even if the consequences are known. Due to this, humans are considered as the weakest link in any security chain. Therefore, there is a long history of attackers exploiting human behavior (Mann, 2017). The data breach report (Verizon, 2019) mentions that 34% of breaches in 2018 happened because of insiders and 15% users misused their privileges.

2. **Scalable Attack:** A process, software or system is said to be scalable if it adapts to increasing demands or change in operational environment. With that respect, cyber-attacks are inherently scalable as they just have to exploit the resources on a computational device. One of the major reasons for their scalability is the continuous growth in the attack surface. This situation is further augmented by the lack of proper patching of buggy software or the lack of knowledge about the benefits of the regular patching of system. Often enterprise does not know the worth of a system, and hence, the associated risk to it (Shukla, Manjunath, Saxena, Mondal, & Lodha, 2015). It leads to poor prioritization of the vulnerabilities that needs to be patched and how it will affect the stability of the overall network (Abraham & Nair, 2015).

   Cyber-attacks on IoT devices are more prominent as there are no good agreed upon security standards in the community (Ornes, 2016). Mirai botnet had shown that in IoT ecosystem even the basic cybersecurity hygiene of changing the default password is not followed, which enabled the botnets rapid spread (Antonakakis et al., 2017). According to a latest study (Abolhassan, 2017), the chances of finding a victim and the success of an attack improve steadily with time for a slight variation in the attack pattern. One variant of Mirai botnet caused crashing of 900 thousand routers and affected over 20 million users in Germany (Wang et al., 2017).

   There is an emergence of newer attacks where the attacker tries to directly monetize the victim's compute resources for mining cryptocurrency on each affected node (Eskandari et al., 2018). The JavaScript based mining attack is highly scalable as it is executed inside a browser. Spam is another classic example of highly scalable attack as real email addresses are cheaply available in the underground markets. In an even simpler scenario, a dictionary based spam attack is sufficient to target large number of individuals as people tend to have 'firstname.lastname' as their email id.

   Certain classes of attacks are usually harder to detect because they are indistinguishable from their benign lookalike, for example, ransomware is indistinguishable from a benign process (Shukla et al., 2016). Due to this, the detection of an ongoing attack takes some time, which is sufficient for the attack to spread.

3. **Accessible Attack:** Due to the extensive digitalization in the last decade, the cost of entry into cyberspace has rapidly come down. The underground economy related to cyber threats is seeing positive growth (Lusthaus, 2019). For example, attack vectors like malicious programs, also known as malwares, are easily available as a paid service. In this business model, also called Malware-as-a-Service, the malware is advertised and distributed like a normal commercial software (Gutmann, 2007). For example, Trojans like Locky can be purchased for as low as three-figure sum (Abolhassan, 2017). This has lowered the barrier for a naive attacker as extensive computer expertise is not al-

ways necessary, although it could help in generating strategic effect in and from cyberspace. The similar trend is observed for ransomware (Shukla et al., 2016) where it is offered as a service and for phishing campaigns where easy entry is possible through phishing kits (Ramzan, 2010). These underground shops either provide the malware as a service, where they take cut for each successful attack, or accept one-time payment for their exploit kits. In both the cases, they lower the expertise needed to mount a cyber-attack and make them easily accessible (Abolhassan, 2017).

Also, source-code of multiple malwares are openly and freely available on internet which can be used for creating new variants, for example, Mirai botnet and its variants (Wang et al., 2017). The availability of free SSL certificates from Certificate Authorities like 'Let's Encrypt' (Ma et al., 2019) makes the malware, phishing sites and malicious advertisements look more authentic and harder to detect. Additionally, certain hacker groups also release the unknown vulnerabilities in public for exploitation, for example, WannaCry ransomware utilized the vulnerability in the Server Message Block (SMB) protocol, which was initially discovered by a well-known security agency of the US government, and later disclosed by the 'Shadow Broker' group (Shao, Tunc, Satam, & Hariri, 2017).

4. **Desired Impact:** In cyberspace, the action and reactions can affect the entire global community by just a click of button, that is, cyber-threats have the potential to be far more widespread and in far less amount of time (Leon, 2015). As the cost of entry into cyberspace is also lowered due to digitalization, it is easier to have a desired impact by launching a cyber-attack. The main motivating factors for a threat actor to launch a cyber-attack are:

   a. **Personal Gains:** The attacker utilizes the confidential information of a victim for self-benefit, for example, credit card number of the victim for online shopping, or intellectual property of an enterprise for monetary gains (Homoliak, Toffalini, Guarnizo, Elovici, & Ochoa, 2019; Verizon, 2019).

   b. **Revenge:** The attacker is driven by a desire to harm the victim, for example, a disgruntled employee leaking customer information in public domain (Homoliak et al., 2019; Verizon, 2019).

   c. **Fame/Ego/Vanity:** The attacker tries to establish or show-off their intellectual capabilities. Mirai botnet is a typical example of this kind of attack (Antonakakis et al., 2017).

   d. **Sabotage:** The goal here is to bring down the operations of an enterprise or a state or an industrial internet of things (IIoT) by compromising their cyberspace, or physically damaging their infrastructure (Langner, 2011; Giles, 2019). Sabotage is different from the 'Revenge' motive as the latter has emotional motivations, whereas the same might not be the case with the former. These attacks are mostly sponsored by nation states for their own good and typically show high level of sophistication, for example, Stuxnet and WannaCry.

   e. **Extortion:** The attacker asks for favor in lieu of returning or restoring something important to the victim. It is similar to the 'Personal Gain' motive, but more direct and coercive in nature. For example, a ransomware which encrypts the user files on a system and then asks for ransom for decrypting it (Shukla et al., 2016).

   f. **Political and Social Justice:** The attacker tries to get vigilante justice against the unjust and powerful. A well cited example is 'Anonymous Collective', a hacktivist group which hacks websites or computer networks in order to convey social or political messages (George & Leidner, 2019).

g.   **Patriotism and Ideology:** The attacker's sole motivation is to help own country by crippling another country's cyberspace, or spy on someone, or install a backdoor (Vacca, 2019).

5.   **Attribution is Difficult:** In case of cyber-attack it is hard to determine who initiated the attack and who is responsible for it (Finlay & Payne, 2019). Attribution is difficult, as more than often attacks are complicated and they are not physically observable. Also, attackers use sophisticated tools to hide their digital traces. Detection and damage assessment of a cyber-attack usually takes time, which in turn delays the attribution of attack (Langner, 2011; Giles, 2019). Further, it requires coordination between multiple independent affected or unaffected entities, and might require analysis of classified information that participating entities would not prefer to reveal (Finlay & Payne, 2019). Thus, making attribution of a cyber-attack even harder task. The risk of misattribution is even greater as it can create diplomatic or military conflict between the victim and the falsely accused entity. Certain nations promote and follow 'hack back' as a possible countermeasure to cyber-attacks. It gives the victim of a cyber-attack a chance to hunt down the suspected attackers (Messerschmidt, 2013). This is, however, a problematic countermeasure when attack attribution is hard, and also quite drastic if a third party utilizes it for deteriorating relations between two entities. For example, in 2014 Microsoft obtained ex parte order for controlling 22 domains for stopping two botnet networks. However, this also reportedly blocked 5 million valid users of Vitalwerks (Hiller, 2014). Cyber-attacks flourish due to multi-dimensional, hard and time consuming nature of the attack attribution.

Latest Trends in Cyber-Attacks

The cyber-attacks are getting increasingly more sophisticated, and involve malware, artificial intelligence, cryptocurrency and social engineering. This has put the data, software, hardware and human assets of an enterprise, government and nation at a constant risk. According to a latest Data Breach Report (Verizon, 2019), 52% breaches were due to hacking, 33% involved social engineering and 28% involved malware. Following is the list of trending cyber-Attacks:

1.   **Attrition**: An attack which tries to degrade, destroy or disable the network based services of an enterprise by flooding it. For example, a botnet utilizes a number of internet connected devices for mounting a distributed denial-of-service (DDoS) attack. As mentioned earlier, Mirai botnet (Antonakakis et al., 2017) is one such instance wherein the attacker used the IoT devices for performing DDoS.

2.   **Social Engineering Attacks** - In this, the attacker first harvests the personal information of the user from social networking sites like Facebook and Linkedin. He either tries to get additional information from the user either through phone, or by spear-phishing campaign, or by defrauding the user. The following are two well-known examples of social engineering attack:

   a.   **Web Phishing:** It is one the most prevalent web based attack. The attacker tries to fool the user in clicking a link, embedded in an email or SMS, to a malicious website. The website in turn may have a form for capturing personal and sensitive information of the user, or try to launch a drive-by download attack (J. Hong, 2012). Here, drive-by-download is an exploitation technique which takes advantage of the browser vulnerabilities to automatically download a dropper (an application which in turn downloads the malware) or an actual malware.

However, to use this technique, the attacker needs to take control over the legitimate websites for automating downloads.

b. **Email Phishing:** The attacker sends a fake email to the victim and tricks her into sharing private and sensitive data or execution of malware (J. Hong, 2012). A more advanced form of phishing is known as 'spear phishing' which targets specific individuals and uses specific knowledge about them. That way, the attacker appears more legitimate and increases the success rate of the attack. If the 'spear phishing' attack is used against a high level target within an enterprise, then it is known as 'whaling' (J. Hong, 2012).

3. **Cryptojacking**: In this exploit, the user's browser downloads a JavaScript while visiting a website, which then uses the CPU cycles of the user's system for mining crypto-currency. Often this happens without the user's consent or knowledge, however, the owner of the website may or may not have the knowledge about this parasitic computing (Eskandari et al., 2018).

4. **Spam**: This is an attack in which the attacker abuses or manipulates the email ecosystem by injecting or producing undesired content for changing the behavior of the user or the system for long term self-gains (Ferrara, 2019). As per (Nahorney, 2017), it continues to represent the bulk of email traffic (more than 50%) in 2017. Without proper filtering at email gateway, an enterprise has to assign two employees for every hundred employees just for filtering the spam emails. Spam can be effectively utilized for unsolicited sales, political manipulation, dispersing incorrect information on public health, swaying stock markets and data leaks (Ferrara, 2019).

5. **Malware**: According to Data Breach Report (Verizon, 2019), 28% data breach happened due to malware. This involved losses due to usage of Trojans, ransomware, worms and viruses. Email is the most abused medium for malware delivery and quite a serious one for enterprises (Nahorney, 2017), wherein the attacker lures the user by carefully crafted subject and message into clicking on an embedded link or malicious attachment. The embedded link usually leads to a compromised website for drive-by-download attack. In case of an attachment, it could be a malicious binary or a benign downloader for downloading the malware in a separate process.

6. **Business Email Compromise (BEC)**: This attack is continuously growing and has huge impact on enterprises and small businesses in terms of monetary losses (Nahorney, 2017). In 2018 alone, Internet Crime Complaint Center (IC3) received 20,373 BEC complaints with total losses amounting to over 1.2 billion USD (FBI, 2018). In this attack, the victim receives a fake email purportedly from a person in authority requesting some urgent data, money transfer or validation of details on some embedded link in email. If the victim hastily follows to fulfil the request, then it could result in financial losses, data leakage or drive-by-download attack. IC3 further classifies the BEC attack based on the impersonation level and the requested data.

7. **Hacking the Human**: The attacker either manipulates the human emotion or is motivated by the emotions. Based on that, this attack can be further divided into two subcategories:

a. **As Targets:** Humans are the weakest link in any security chain, therefore there is a long history of attackers exploiting people (Mann, 2017). They are susceptible to social engineering attacks and render the most secure system useless, for example, Stuxnet was able to get into an air-gapped system due to an individual using an infected USB drive. Like any computer system, humans are hackable (Mann, 2017) who have their own vulnerabilities (unique at times), behavioral traits, and they are prone to fatigue. A large workforce translates into a larger attack surface for the attackers.

b.   **As Attacker:** Insider-threat is attributed as one of the key threats to the enterprises (Homoliak et al., 2019). This is particularly worrisome and hard to detect as insiders are the individuals associated with the enterprise who misuse their access rights and internal working of the enterprise, knowingly or unknowingly (mostly through social engineering).

8.   **Adversarial Machine Learning**: Cyber attackers are finding newer ways of exploiting artificial intelligence as more and more safety, security and privacy critical systems are starting to use it. For example, the authors in (Eykholt et al., 2017) demonstrated an attack on deep-neural-network (DNN) of an autonomous vehicle by perturbing the physical objects that reliably caused classification errors in DNN based classifiers. Further, researchers (Ferrara, 2019) describe a possible future scenario consisting of an AI fueled multimedia spam which uses real-time reenactment of a video sequence. This is an example of abusing AI based systems for generating fake content, also known as Deep Fake (Blitz, 2018). It is a worrying trend as the generated fake content seems indistinguishable from the real content. Fredrikson et al (Fredrikson, Jha, & Ristenpart, 2015) describe a model inversion attack wherein the attacker could extract the recognizable image of an individual's face from the model. Another kind of attack is presented by Biggio et al (Biggio, Nelson, & Laskov, 2012), wherein they poisoned the input data to machine learning algorithm and caused degradation in its predictive ability. Authors in (Yuan, He, Zhu, & Li, 2019) have shown multiple such security and privacy attacks on AI based systems.

Impact of Cyber-Attack

More than often, the impact of cyber-attack on a victim is multi-dimensional and has a temporal nature. The most common impact of a successful cyber-attack is economic. It is observed that post attack, the stock price of the victim organization suffers losses in the following days. The effect is even worse when the breach is not disclosed by the organization, but later discovered by the investors (Amir, Levi, & Livne, 2018). This is accompanied by a drop in daily excess return, increase in trading volume and deterioration of liquidity after the public disclosure (Bianchi & Tosun, 2019). As a side effect, there is also a negative impact on the organization's reputation and customer base (Cashell, Jackson, Jickling, & Webel, 2004; Bianchi & Tosun, 2019; Smith, Jones, Johnson, & Smith, 2019). Also, the estimated cost of downtime itself is between \$6.3 million and \$8.4 million a day (Leon, 2015).

The cyber-attack may also result in loss of intellectual property, critical business secrets, personal information and customer data. This is in addition to the decreased productivity, damage to physical infrastructure, regulatory fines and legal fees (Cashell et al., 2004; Leon, 2015; Ausherman, 2018).

In rare cases, a cyber-attack could prove fatal to the human life, for example, the Triton malware (Giles, 2019) attack on petrochemical plants could disable safety systems designed to prevent catastrophic industrial accidents. Authors in (Yan, Xu, & Liu, 2016) demonstrated a contactless attack on the sensor system of the autonomous vehicle and caused malfunction. Similarly, researchers (Gaukstern & Krishnan, 2018) have discussed the cyber-attacks targeting networked critical medical devices, for example, pacemakers and insulin pumps.

In general, cyber-attacks also increase the operating cost of a business as they either have to maintain some surplus for recovering from a cyber-attack or they have to get insurance as a financial protection against the inevitable threat (Watkins, 2014).

Implications

Cyber threats are continuously evolving and there exists no silver-bullet solution to address them all. Therefore, the enterprise should have at its disposal a repertoire of tools and techniques to guard data, software, hardware and human assets against the evolving cyber threats. In particular, enterprise should select and implement measures by taking into considerations the following things:

1. *Defend against the best attacker*, with sophisticated malicious programs such as malware and ransomware becoming easily accessible as a paid service, it is now easy even for a naive attacker to launch state-of-the-art attacks against any target of their choice.
2. *Compliance oversight is growing*, since enterprises rarely think about security and privacy first, governments across the globe are intervening and enforcing strict regulations (e.g., GDPR), failing to which the enterprise could incur hefty fines and reputation loss.
3. *Compliance is not substitute for security*, being compliant with regulations and policies do not shield enterprises from security breaches.
4. *Security is everyone's responsibility*, defending hardware and software assets is must, however there exists a possibility of attacks penetrating the enterprise network and reaching its employees and partners. Hence, it is equally important to strengthen the weakest link in the security chain, that is, humans.
5. *Security can never be 100%*, one can only increase the levels of deterrence, thereby making the existing cyber-attacks more costly.

MEASURES

Security is inherently an asymmetric game between an attacker and a defender, where the attacker has to find a *single* exploit in the defense and the defender has to guard against *all* types of attacks. Traditional security measures such as network firewalls and end-point protection are not enough to address modern security threats. The deluge of cyber-attacks sweeping across the world has enterprises and governments thinking about new ways to protect their digital assets, and the corporate and state secrets stored within. As malicious actors continue to push the boundaries and discover new frontiers to exploit, enterprises need to be on the cutting edge and ensure their critical assets are protected.

In this section, we describe various emerging measures to counter cyber threats, discuss their benefits and highlight their pitfalls.

Bug Bounty Programs

Bug bounty programs are a modern way for enterprises to identify security vulnerabilities in their systems by harvesting the efforts and knowledge of security researchers and ethical hackers across the globe in exchange for monetary rewards. These programs have become the new norm, with organizations big and small, private and government, offering lucrative incentives to encourage hacker community to disclose high value software bugs in their systems. The adoption of bug bounty programs by prominent government agencies such as the U.K.'s National Cyber Security Centre, Singapore's Ministry of Defense, and the U.S. Department of Defense may have set a new standard for the future of cybersecurity practice.

Bug bounty programs are also on the rise in risk-averse and highly regulated industries such as financial services, banking, insurance, healthcare and education (Hackerone, 2019). There even exists a bug-bounty program for improving the security of the internet (Internet Bug Bounty, 2019).

Benefits of bug bounty programs are two-fold. First, bug bounty programs offer a unique opportunity for organizations to employ a large and diverse population of security researchers and ethical hackers to examine their software products and hence offer protection against the best attacker. Secondly, the public nature of these programs indicates to their users that the organization is committed towards security improvements. As organizations benefit from the best security researchers around the globe, conversely, security researchers also benefit from searching for bugs in multiple bug bounty programs. Elite hackers can earn more than a million USD per year searching for security bugs as internet-scale companies e.g., Dropbox, GitHub, Google, Intel, and Twitter shell out thousands of dollars for high severity bugs (Hackerone, 2019). Fortunately, enterprises can use bug bounty programs to incentivize security researchers and ethical hackers to find security bugs or vulnerabilities before the public becomes aware of them.

The crowdsourcing platforms such as HackerOne and Bugcrowd enable organizations to launch bounty programs and connect with a global force of hundreds of thousands of hackers. The platforms are impressively effective as 77% of the public bug bounty programs receive their first valid vulnerability within the 24 hours of its launch (Hackerone, 2019). In 2018 alone, hackers had earned more than 19 million USD for valid results. However, the work is still in progress, as 93 percent of the Forbes Global 2000 companies still do not have known vulnerability disclosure policies. Google with its Project Zero has started an altogether different trend of finding vulnerabilities not only in their own products but also in the products of other vendors on which their own products rely. Interestingly, Project Zero has a policy of making the bug report public if the vendor fails to release the security patch within 90 days after bug disclosure.

Bug bounty programs also present a challenge since anyone can participate, and submit a low quality bug reports (Laszka, Zhao, & Grossklags, 2016). In fact, the key challenge many bug-bounty programs face is managing noise, or the proportion of low quality reports they receive. These low quality reports include spam (i.e., completely irrelevant reports), false positives (i.e., security issues that do not actually exist), and out-of-scope reports. Bug bounties are becoming a popular tool to mitigate software vulnerabilities; however, it is still unclear how to design mechanism and incentive structures to influence the long-term success of bounty programs. In a phenomenon known as front-loading effect, newly launched programs attract researchers at the expense of older programs since the probability of finding bugs decays after the launch of a program, even though bugs found later yield on average higher rewards (Thomas Maillart & Chuang, 2016). Further, current bounty programs lack rigorous techniques for setting bounty amounts and attract economically rational hackers. Rather than claim bounties for serious bugs, hackers often sell or exploit them. A majority of bug bounty programs are private, where a set of elite hackers is selected and invited to find bugs. One major challenge in the private bug bounties is to solve a matching problem involving bug bounty programs and specialized people based on various factors such as experience, reputation, skills, availability and rewards. The problem is computationally hard if the preference lists of both the parties is bounded and contain ties (Gharote, Phuke, Patil, & Lodha, 2019).

Cloud Computing

Cloud computing is an on-demand, cost-efficient and fault-tolerant delivery of compute, storage, databases, analytics, networking, mobile, developer tools, management tools, IoT (Internet of Things), security and enterprise applications. With the cloud, businesses no longer need to plan for infrastructure capacity needs; instead, they can instantly scale up and down as required in minutes and deliver results faster. Cloud computing allows enterprises, start-ups, small and medium-sized businesses, and companies in the public sector to access the resources they need to respond quickly to evolving business requirements.

The main benefit of cloud infrastructure is that it allows enterprises to scale and innovate, while maintaining a secure environment and paying only for the services that are required. Cloud is particularly beneficial for small and medium scale enterprises that cannot afford to keep up with a rapidly evolving regulatory landscape. Cloud providers typically have many compliance-enabling features that enterprises can use to achieve a higher level of security at scale (LMark Judd, Joerg Fritsch, 2018). Cloud providers engage globally with governments, regulators, standards bodies, and non-governmental organizations to ensure that they are compliant. Cloud environments are regularly audited, and cloud infrastructure and services are approved to operate under several compliance standards and industry certifications across geographies and industries, including PCI DSS, ISO 27001 and HIPAA. In most of the cases, cloud providers also allow enterprises to choose the country where their data can reside in order to be compliant with data residency regulations of different countries. Cloud vendors equip enterprises with tools that allow them to determine where their content will be stored, secure their content in transit or at rest, and manage access to services and resources. However, *being compliant with industry regulations and policies do not shield enterprises from security breaches.*

Cloud vendors also provide several security capabilities and services to increase privacy and control network access. These include DDoS mitigation, data encryption, monitoring and logging, identity and access control, and penetration testing. Therefore, enterprises can retain the control of the security to protect their content, platform, applications, systems, and networks. While security of the cloud is the responsibility of the cloud vendor, the security in the cloud is the responsibility of the enterprise. Much like an on-premises data center, the enterprise is responsible for managing the operating system (including installing updates and security patches), application software, and the configuration of the firewall. Enterprise should carefully consider the services they choose, as their responsibilities vary depending on the services they use, the integration of those services into their IT environments, and applicable laws and regulations. In addition, when using cloud services enterprises are responsible for managing the security of content, including:

- The cloud services that are used with the content,
- The country where their content is stored,
- The format and structure of their content whether it is masked, anonymized, or encrypted and
- The management of access rights.

As companies continue to adopt more cost efficient cloud-based solutions, attackers are adapting their tactics to locate and steal the data they find to be of most value. Consequently, there has been a corresponding increase in hacking cloud-based email servers via the use of phishing attacks and credential theft (Verizon, 2019). Further, the loss of information caused by misconfigurations is unprecedented. According to a research report by McAfee, 99% of misconfigurations in the public cloud go unreported, suggesting there are numerous companies around the world unwittingly leaking data (McAfee, 2019).

Although enterprises can encrypt sensitive data and store it securely on cloud, it is infeasible for many business organizations to adopt cloud if they need to perform operations on sensitive data. Historically, encrypted data has been impossible to operate on without first decrypting them. To address this gap, homomorphic cryptosystems were invented that could perform unlimited chaining of algebraic operations in the cipher space, which means that an arbitrary number of additions and multiplications can be performed on the encrypted data (Gentry, 2009). However, the technology in its current form is too slow for practical applications.

Privacy by Design

Almost every enterprise is now data driven, that is, they gather data about their customers for operational and analytical purposes. This data-driven approach helps them in better decision making, investments, improving information technology usage, and providing tailored services and other benefits to their customers. However, the customer data often includes sensitive and personally identifiable information, which can lead to significant exposure of sensitive information when used in the business processes of the enterprise. Further, enterprises are now adopting cloud for lowering their costs and product development life-cycle. In the last few years, the cloud computing ecosystem has changed significantly. There are more cloud providers offering more features and value added services (Varghese & Buyya, 2018). Enterprises leverage this heterogeneity in the cloud ecosystem by utilizing resources from different providers, however this also increases the attack surface for the enterprise.

In the last decade, users are getting more concerned about their privacy rights. This behavior is clearly reflected in the 2014 landmark decision of the top European court in favor of 'right to be forgotten' plea from Mario Costeja Gonzalez against Google. The court directed Google to delete 'inadequate, irrelevant or no longer relevant' data from its result on request from an individual (Travis & Arthur, 2014). In a more recent scandal, personal data of millions of Facebook users was harvested without their consent and then used for political advertising (Cadwalladr & Graham-Harrison, 2018). 'Cambridge Analytica' achieved this by exploiting Facebook's Open API for gathering friends' data of users who permitted it to access their profile (Isaak & Hanna, 2018). Incidents like this tarnish the reputation of the enterprises and has long lasting operational and financial impact on them. For example, post scandal Facebook's share prices went down, governments got suspicious of Facebook's operating procedure and there was a delete Facebook accounts movement (Gonzalez, Yu, Figueroa, Lopez, & Aragon, 2019).

Also, regulations like, General Data Protection Regulation (GDPR) empower consumers by obligating enterprises for anonymizing data, notification of breach, across border data transfer and consent requirement from the user for any data processing. Failure to comply may result in legal and monetary penalties. For example, for severe violations, GDPR penalty is maximum of 20 million euros or 4% of total global turnover of the enterprise in preceding fiscal year.

There is a statutory requirement in GDPR for 'Privacy by Design' (PbD), which means 'data protection through technology means'. In other words, privacy should not be considered after the product is developed, rather, privacy requirement and controls should be considered in the design and implementation phase (Bird, 2016). The 'California Consumer Privacy Act' also recommends that enterprise should consider PbD. It is a system engineering approach which prescribes that privacy must be considered during all phases of the engineering process. It was developed as a framework to assimilate privacy into information technology, networked infrastructure and actual designs (Cavoukian, 2010). However, PbD became a necessity in sectors where data privacy concerns persist. Further, PbD compliance is mandatory under newer regulations (Romanou, 2018). The seven core features of PbD are as follows (Cavoukian, 2010):

1. **Proactive not Reactive; Preventative not Remedial**: The privacy must be proactive rather than reactive, that is, instead of a post facto measure, PbD prevent them from occurring.
2. **Privacy as the Default**: The privacy of an individual should not be affected if she does nothing, that is, privacy rules should be embedded with default privacy rules.
3. **Privacy Embedded into Design**: Privacy should not be an add-on or patch up work after the product development, rather it should be considered during all phases of the engineering.
4. **Full Functionality**. Positive-Sum, not Zero-Sum. Unnecessary trade-offs should not be considered while embedding privacy, rather include all legitimate requirements in a 'win-win' manner.
5. **End-to-End Security**: Life Cycle Protection. Data should be securely acquired, retained and then destroyed in a timely fashion when it is no longer required.
6. **Visibility and Transparency**: Assure stakeholders that data is being used according to prior stated promises and objectives and could be audited later on.
7. **Respect for User Privacy**: Architect and data users must respect an individual's preferences by providing strong privacy defaults, suitable notifications and usable options.

However, the recommendations in PbD should be considered with a pinch of salt. Researchers and practitioners have pointed out that PbD is vague, it is difficult to adopt, difficult to apply in certain domains, values corporate interests over consumer's interests and does not stress on restriction on data collection (Gurses, Troncoso, & Diaz, 2011; van Rest, Boonstra, Everts, van Rijn, & van Paassen, 2012; Rubinstein & Good, 2013). For example, according to (van Rest et al., 2012), the original PbD guidelines fail to say anything about legacy systems, and there is a trust deficit with respect to consumers' adoption of PbD. Furthermore, researcher described the seven principles of PbD as more aspirational than practical since they do not offer any design guidance and appear impractical or repetitive in some scenarios (Rubinstein & Good, 2013).

DevSecOps

DevOps is a conceptual and operational blend of development and operations (Myrbakken & Colomo-Palacios, 2017). It suggests practices that help in streamlining of software delivery process, inclusion of feedback from production to development, and reducing the overall time from inception to delivery. DevOps promotes the four principals consisting of culture, automation, measurement and sharing (Myrbakken & Colomo-Palacios, 2017). DevSecOps is a natural extension to DevOps which prescribes bringing operations and development together with security functions (Bird, 2016). DevSecOps is a proactive approach to cybersecurity where secure practices are embedded into the entire lifecycle of software development. It is an improvement over the older security model for continuous integration and delivery models provided by the modern agile frameworks. Additionally, DevSecOps promote communication and collaboration within the team and ensures that everyone is responsible for security. Further, it is easier to plan and execute integration of security controls early in development life-cycle by involving security experts. Additionally, this also reduces delays and issues while incorporating security controls as compared to implementing security once the system is developed. This early inclusion of security experts in the design and development phase is known as 'Shift Security Left' (Bird, 2016). Figure 1, shows the comparison between a 'waterfall' cycle and 'DevOps' cycle. It can be seen that DevOps prescribes iterative, incremental and automated inclusion of security into the development cycle, which makes the process more efficient, repeatable, and easy to use (Bird, 2016).

Figure 1. The waterfall cycle versus the DevOps cycle, adapted from (Bird, 2016).

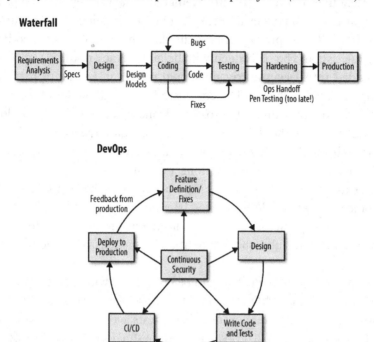

DevOps does not prescribe cloud as a requirement to run a system, although following DevOps practices on cloud may greatly help in continuous integration and delivery of the application. It also provides security and other important services, for example, account management, auditing, encryption, key management and monitoring. Even though a success enabler, the 'Cloud Security Alliance' lists down 12 major security and privacy threats to cloud and its users (Bird, 2016). Apart from this, the other major aspects of DevOps also increase the threat to enterprise and its assets. For example, microservices allow designing of self-contained isolated functions which can be tested, deployed and managed independently, however they also increase the attack surface, implementation complexity and other issues. Similarly, there are issues pertaining to separation of duties, change control and inherent issues in software container (LXC or Docker) (Bird, 2016). All of this makes the security as a vital component that must be included in agile methodology like DevOps.

Isolation

In cybersecurity, isolation is a conceptual solution in which a software operates within a very restrictive environment with no impact on the application providing the isolation, system or platform on which it is run. It guarantees about what a piece of code can or cannot do irrespective of the input parameters (Shu et al., 2016). There are different types and levels of isolation which are possible to restrict a software, for example, application sandboxing is one such technique for application isolation. Isolation is a useful method to evaluate software which are not trusted (security isolation) or expected to have some bug or vulnerability which might affect the rest of the system (fault isolation) (Shu et al., 2016). The idea of isolation is particularly important as most of the applications utilize one or more third party libraries which may have unknown vulnerability (Kula, German, Ouni, Ishio, & Inoue, 2018). Isolation limits the damage and, therefore, is a useful defense against the best attacker.

Network Isolation. Perfect cybersecurity is not possible due to multiple reasons and all enterprises experience a breach at some point in time. Network isolation is used for hardening the systems with large attack surface and running trusted programs, for example, web server, domain name server and email server (Shu et al., 2016). Isolating network components makes it difficult for the attacker to damage the entire network of the victim as we limit communication throughout the network, thereby reducing the attack options available to the attacker. However, moving from a flat network model to a segmented network has some side-effects, for example, it increases the complexity of the overall system and reduces the system performance. An extreme example of network isolation is an 'air gapped' network, wherein a secure network is physically isolated from an unsecured network or a network which connects to an unsecured network (Kim Zetter, 2014). However, an air-gapped does not offer any guarantees of being 100% secure (Guri, Zadov, & Elovici, 2019). Virtual Private Network (VPN) is another network isolation method, which enables a user to send and receive data on a shared or public network by extending a private network across a public network.

Network isolation or segmentation is a very useful concept and it is used for enabling other security architectures. For example, 'Zero Trust Architecture' is based on the principal of 'never trust, always verify' to protect network resources. It leverages network segmentation as one of the key enablers for separating a trusted 'protect surface' from the rest of the resources (Kindervag, 2010). Further, understanding the users, application and their access patterns with respect to the 'protect surface' helps in putting appropriate access controls as close to the 'protect surface' as possible. The 'Cloud Security Alliance' defines the Software Defined Perimeter (SDP) which enforces a need-to-know based access model that verifies the posture and the identity of the device before granting access to the application infrastructure.

OS Level Isolation: Here the operating system (OS) kernel allows multiple instances of the user-space. It decouples applications from the OS so that individual applications execute in their own virtualized environment commonly known as containers. An application running inside a container has access to devices and data which are assigned to the container. OS level virtualization is different from hardware level virtualization as the later virtualizes the hardware architecture by implementing a virtual machine monitor and decouples the OS from the hardware. Additionally, OS virtualization allows more control over individual processes, which is more beneficial than hardware virtualization, for example, OS level virtualization allows an easy migration of individual applications as compared to the complete OS migration. However, there are few security problems with OS level isolation that need to be considered before its adoption, for example, kernel exploits, denial of service attacks, container breakouts, poisoned images and compromising secrets (Bird, 2016).

Compute Isolation: Intel introduced a set of security related instructions for some of its new central processing units (CPU), called Software Guard Extension (SGX). These instructions allow the user and OS code to create private regions of memory called *enclaves*. The content in the enclave is encrypted and it is inaccessible for reading and writing by any process (irrespective of their privilege level) outside the enclave. As and when needed, the CPU decrypts the content only for the code which is running within the enclave. This way the enclave isolates the computation from rest of the system and avoids any data exfiltration attack by enabling secure computation. However, it is also possible to use the SGX in a cyber-attack, which makes their detection very hard, for example, botnet creation or malware operating in enclave (Davenport & Ford, 2014). Recently, researchers have shown an attack based on SGX and return-oriented-programming (ROP) which bypassed ASLR, stack canaries, and address sanitizer to mount a code-reuse attack (Schwarz, Weiser, & Gruss, 2019). The SGX-ROP attack in turn could invoke arbitrary system calls from the host process to gain arbitrary code execution. Similarly, SGX is also shown to conceal a malware attack (Schwarz, Weiser, Gruss, Maurice, & Mangard, 2017). Apart from this, there are well known side channel attacks on SGX, for example, cache attacks (Brasser et al., 2017).

Sandboxing: It is a technique of isolating one process from the rest of the system. The isolation can limit access to benign OS from a malicious process or access to an application from a malicious OS (Li et al., 2014). A sandbox is a heavily restricted environment with access to tightly controlled set of resources. A less restrictive sandbox is also known as process compartmentalization (Gudka et al., 2015). Sandbox environment is quite useful for evaluating an untrusted software or for fault isolation (Shu et al., 2016). For example, Chrome Web Browser uses a sandbox for rendering untrusted web-pages with JavaScript code (Barth, Jackson, Reis, Team, et al., 2008).

Security Operations Center

From an enterprise perspective, Security Operations Center (SOC) is a facility that is responsible for its information security issues like: a) securing its cyberspace, b) monitoring and analyzing incidents and events, c) proactively and appropriately handling incidents, and, d) assessing regulatory compliance (Kowtha, Nolan, & Daley, 2012). As the volume of data and attacks have gone up in the recent past (Verizon, 2019), it is imperative to have a specialized facility like SOC to handle cyber incidents and gather threat intelligence. This helps an enterprise in proactively taking more informed decisions in a short duration against their adversaries and reduce the number of possible breaches. It has been shown that SOC benefits from coordinated and collaborative handling of incidents. For a successful SOC the

Figure 2. The core building blocks of a SOC, adapted from (Torres, 2015).

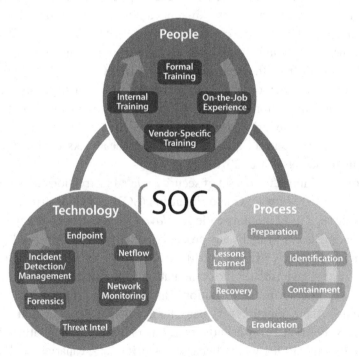

coordination and collaboration must exist between people, technology and processes (Torres, 2015), as shown in Figure 2. Technology aspect of SOC usually deals with data collection, aggregation, analytics, detection, reporting and mitigation. The processes aspect of SOC prescribes repeatable incident management workflows, clear responsibilities of team members and appropriate actions for each incident. This helps in proper resource allocation and investigation procedures. Finally, people aspect mandates suitable skill set for analyzing the incidents. Further, the team working in a SOC should consistently update their skills by attending the necessary training to deal with constantly changing cyber-attack ecosystem. As shown in Figure 3, for an effective SOC, the data gathered from the continues monitoring should be aggregated, processed and analyzed for investigating and reviewing suspicious activities that caused the incident (Torres, 2015).

Figure 3. Data aggregation and compatible technologies aid detection, adapted from (Torres, 2015).

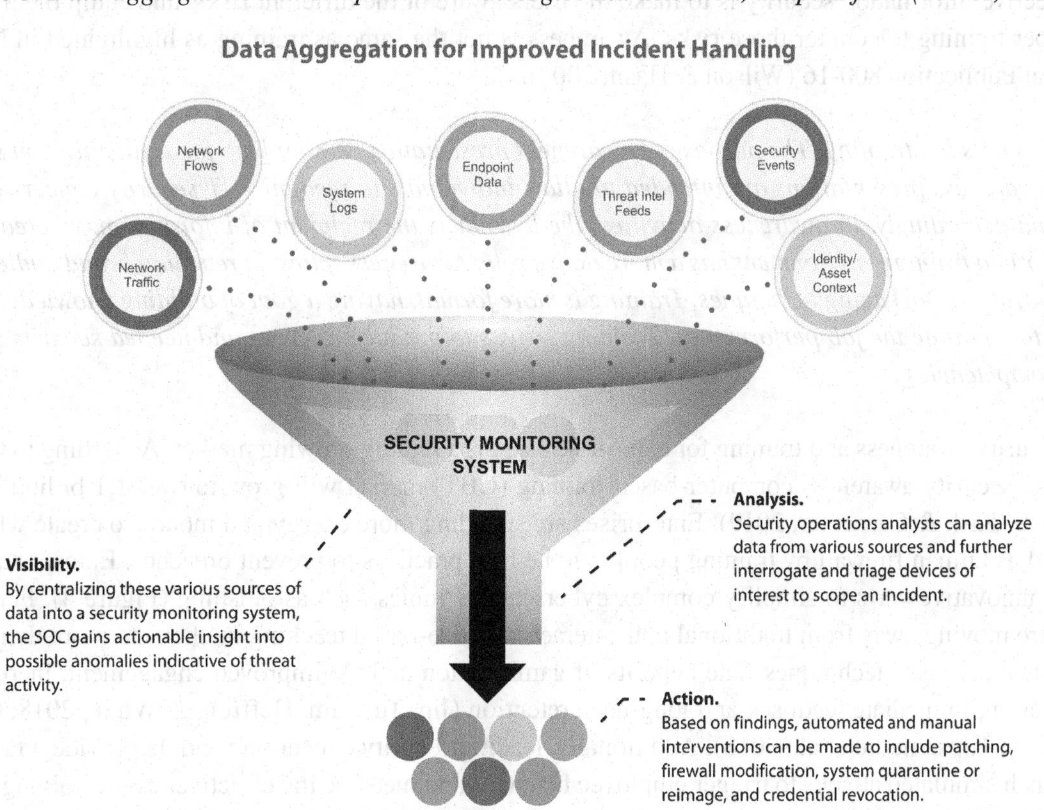

Data Aggregation for Improved Incident Handling

Network Flows

System Logs

Endpoint Data

Security Events

Network Traffic

Threat Intel Feeds

Identity/ Asset Context

SECURITY MONITORING SYSTEM

Visibility.
By centralizing these various sources of data into a security monitoring system, the SOC gains actionable insight into possible anomalies indicative of threat activity.

Analysis.
Security operations analysts can analyze data from various sources and further interrogate and triage devices of interest to scope an incident.

Action.
Based on findings, automated and manual interventions can be made to include patching, firewall modification, system quarantine or reimage, and credential revocation.

However, the SOC operations are often marred with too many false positives. This is either due to a stretched workforce, lack of additional contexts to help the analyst, large volume of events or incomplete analysis, which eventually leads to human 'alert fatigue' (Torres, 2015). It is an information overload problem in which true alerts are missed due to large number of false alarms. Another major problem is the lack of skilled information security professionals in enterprise. It is estimated that by 2019 there will be a shortage of over 1 million cybersecurity professionals. To counter the shortage, enterprises invest substantially in cybersecurity technologies (Nobles, 2018). To a certain extent, automation of SOC can help in alleviating fatigue related issues as it minimizes the human-in-the-loop and, hence, fatigue related issues (Hassan et al., 2019). Similarly, enterprise can leverage the large amount of data that is available to SOC for building an effective machine learning system for reducing the false positives and remediating the skilled workforce issue.

Awareness and Training

Humans are the weakest link in the security chain. More than 50% of data breaches in enterprises involve social attacks or human error (Verizon, 2019). While the majority of employees do not set out to cause harm, many of them do it inadvertently through bad password habits, visiting phishing websites or opening malicious attachments. Therefore, in addition to strengthening organizational defenses against cyber threats, it is equally important to provide security training to employees. The most important factor in effective information security is to make the users aware of the different risks, and equip them with a proper training to counter those risks. Awareness is not the same as training as highlighted in NIST Special Publication 800-16 (Wilson & Hash, 2003):

Awareness is not training. The purpose of awareness presentations is simply to focus attention on security. Awareness presentations are intended to allow individuals to recognize IT security concerns and respond accordingly. In awareness activities, the learner is the recipient of information, whereas the learner in a training environment has a more active role. Awareness relies on reaching broad audiences with attractive packaging techniques. Training is more formal, having a goal of building knowledge and skills to facilitate the job performance. Training strives to produce relevant and needed security skills and competencies.

Security awareness and training for enterprise users is a rapidly growing market. According to Gartner, the security awareness computer-based training (CBT) market will grow to over 1.1 billion USD by 2020 (Kish & Carpenter, 2019). Enterprises are spending more energy and money to create what is termed as human firewall by training people on the best practices to prevent breaches. Enterprises are using innovative ways to simplify complex cybersecurity topics such as phishing (Figure 4). Further, they are moving away from traditional non-interactive video-based teaching methods to more dynamic gamification based techniques. The benefits of gamification include improved engagement, increased motivation, immediate feedback and long-term retention (Jin, Tu, Kim, Heffron, & White, 2018; CJ et al., 2018; Tupsamudre et al., 2018). Additionally, leading security education vendors provide a facility to launch simulated attacks to trigger employee behavior and measure the effectiveness of training over time (Huisman, 2019). Enterprises that treat security education as an inherently unproductive investment are a diminishing group, and training companies are increasingly focusing on security education that is effective as well as efficient at driving enterprise security performance.

The world of cyber security is constantly evolving as attackers learn new information and sophisticated techniques to attack enterprise systems. Therefore, it is necessary to keep up with cyber criminals and rejuvenate the cybersecurity training program of an enterprise at regular intervals. It is equally important to keep employees in charge of enterprise security up-to-date with the constantly evolving security guidelines and practices. For instance, once an ardent supporter of password composition policy and password expiry, NIST now recommends organizations to banish password composition rules and password expiry in favor of long passwords (Grassi et al., 2019).

Figure 4. Enterprises are using graphical ways to teach employees about complex cybersecurity topics (Credit: Tata Consultancy Services Ltd. 2019).

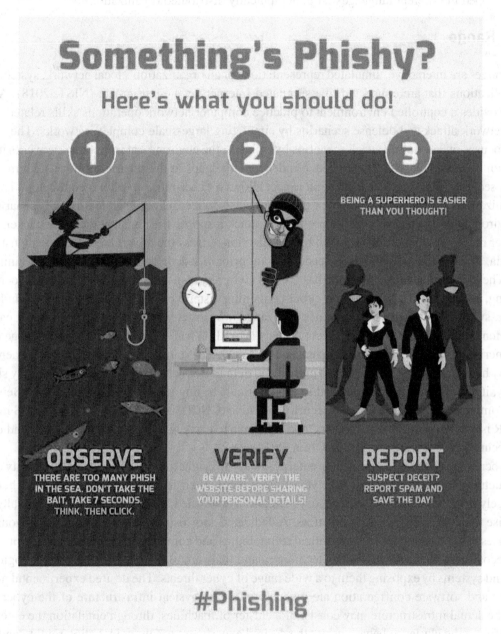

Another challenge is to design effective games that will resonate with diverse audience of an enterprise ranging from HR to technical personnel. Training should be relevant and continuous so that everybody understands that security is everyone's responsibility. It is also important to customize the content as per the needs of particular roles or responsibilities. For instance, training for sales team should be different from the training aimed at executives. Further, the interactive learning experience has to be delivered on computing devices of different shapes and sizes, such as laptop computers, tablets and smartphones, and developed in different languages for geographically distributed organizations.

Cyber Range

Cyber ranges are interactive, simulated representations of an organization's local network, system, tools, and applications that are connected to a simulated Internet level environment (NIST, 2018). A cyber range provides a controlled environment to practice computer network operations skills related to real-world network attack and defense scenarios by simulating large-scale complex networks. The training aspect focuses on evaluating attack scenarios by isolating the environment from other networks in order to contain live malicious activity, to better understand the gaps in the security posture, and implement the best security practices. The evaluation aspect allows a cyber-range to offer a commercial incentive as organizations evaluate the security of their products/services, experience real-attack scenarios in a safe environment, and measure and improve their attack response time against the best attacker.

Cyber ranges are in use and provided by organizations across the government, private industry, and academia. The cyber range efforts in academics are primarily dedicated for research and training purposes. The Lincoln Laboratory at MIT has created Cyber Systems Assessments Group that focuses on analyzing, understanding, and assessing cyber-containing systems by involving in activities including red teaming, system exploitation, building of cyber range infrastructure and evaluations of cyber capabilities. Defense Advanced Research Projects Agency (DARPA) has built a National Cyber Range (NCR) by partnering with Johns Hopkins University and Lockheed Martin (a global security and aerospace company headquartered in Maryland) to protect and defend US's critical information assets. By size and capacity, it has Global Information Grid or Internet scale testing (Davis & Magrath, 2013). Being part of the Comprehensive National Cyber security Initiative (CNCI), in addition to serving the US military, the NCR is open to government, industry, and academia to carry out tests on both classified and unclassified technologies (Ferguson, Tall, & Olsen, 2014).

A cyber range would immensely help enterprises with a critical ability to evaluate the security of their infrastructure in view of ever growing cyber threats before their live adoption at onsite. A cyber range can closely bring the reality of cyber ecosystem into a controlled lab environment and gradually helps enterprise to adopt strong security practices. A dedicated and custom-oriented cyber range would help enterprises test the resilience of their critical technologies and commercial infrastructures. It provides a secure ecosystem with the latest tools, techniques and malware to integrate and test technologies, networks and systems by exposing them to a wide range of cyber threats. The desired experimental network topology and software configuration are mapped onto the physical infrastructure of the cyber range. While the actual infrastructure may consist of a cluster of machines, through emulation the enterprises can configure the cluster to behave as per the desired experiment topology including routing and WAN links. The costs associated with the set up and on-going maintenance of dedicated computer and network resources can be partially compensated through virtualization which allows a smaller physical network to emulate a larger network. Using a cyber-range is indicative of extreme maturity for an organization's security stance.

However, there are several disadvantages to this approach as well (IXIA, 2016). In a purely virtualized environment, it is not possible to model certain attacks scenarios that are prevalent in the real world, purely because of physical performance constraints of virtual architectures. A great example of this is realistic distributed denial-of-service (DDoS) attacks. In many cyber range environments, DDoS analysis mitigation by a response team can work only at low-scale because of the limits of virtualization. Two more examples of why pure virtualization can cause issues are network throughput, which is always lower in a virtualized environment, and firewall IPS/IDS performance, which are greatly constrained in terms of performance when those elements are purely virtualized. Other challenge is that cyber ranges simulate large environments consisting of thousands of machines and network nodes. Therefore, creation, deployment, control and maintenance of these environments is a lot of work. These overheads add-up when the organization is deploying multiple diverse cyber range scenarios to train their workforce.

Cyber Insurance

There is no such thing as foolproof security. Cyber-attacks are likely to occur and can cause moderate to severe losses for enterprises large and small. As part of a risk management plan, organizations routinely must decide which risks to avoid, accept, control or transfer. Transferring risk is where cyber insurance comes into play. Cyber insurance is a risk management and mitigation strategy having a corollary benefit of improving the adoption of preventive measures (products, services, and best practices), thus, helping improve the cyber security posture of organizations as well as country (DSCI, 2019). Cyber Insurance is designed to guard businesses from the potential effects of cyber-attacks. It helps an organization mitigate risk exposure by offsetting costs, after a cyber-attack/breach has happened. To simplify, cyber insurance is designed to cover the fees, expenses and legal costs associated with cyber breaches that occur after an organization has been hacked or from theft or loss of client/employee information.

Digitization of businesses have increased threat surface and vulnerabilities. Further, attacks are becoming more complex, menacing, and stealthy causing heavy financial losses to the enterprises. Moreover, the danger of insider threat makes it extremely difficult for enterprises to ensure a foolproof protection from attacks. Apart from the monetary loses, the hidden costs of a data breach, which includes lost businesses, partnerships, and reputation could be even more damaging, necessitating a better risk management strategy. While most enterprises highlight the adequacy of their spending on cyber security products and solutions as a means to safeguard businesses, none can really assure complete security, as attacks are getting more sophisticated with each passing day. Further, newly enacted regulations such as EU GDPR impose hefty fines (up to 20 million Euros or 4% of global turnover whichever is higher) on enterprises for non-compliance. Cyber insurance cannot protect an enterprise from cyber-attacks, but it can keep its business on stable financial footing should a significant security event occur (Lindros & Tittel, 2016).

One major challenge that inhibits robust risk assessment and, hence, cyber insurance is the shortage of data on cyber-attacks. This problem is further aggravated by enterprises' reluctance on sharing data that can help insurance providers evaluate risks. It is difficult to quantify comprehensiveness and adequacy of cover damages owing to cyber extortion, reputational loss, and rapidly evolving data and privacy landscape. Some of the cyber-attacks seen in the wild are not just from random hackers, but from state actors or quasi-state actors operating directly or indirectly at the behest of governments. Further, there are hackers working for criminal enterprises financially connected to terror organizations. Many cyber insurance contracts state that the insurer does not have to pay for incidents caused by an act of war or act of terror. If insurers attempt to use this exception to avoid paying for damages caused by malware suspected of being tied to state actors or terrorist organizations, cyber insurance could become virtually worthless. Despite all these challenges, cyber insurance market is set to grow (Souter, 2019). The total value of premiums is forecasted to reach 7.5 billion USD by 2020. According to PwC, about one-third of U.S. companies currently purchase some type of cyber insurance (PWC, 2019).

Blockchain

A blockchain is an open, distributed ledger that can record transactions between two parties efficiently and in a verifiable and permanent way (Blockchain, 2019). Each block contains transaction data, time-stamp and a link (cryptographic hash) to its previous block. The linked blocks form a chain and, hence the name blockchain. Once recorded, the data in any given block cannot be altered without alteration of all subsequent blocks, which requires consensus of the network majority. Blockchain is becoming increasingly popular and is used in a wide range of applications including cybersecurity. There are three types of blockchains – public blockchain, private blockchain and hybrid blockchain. While a public blockchain has absolutely no access restrictions and anyone with an Internet connection can join the network, a private blockchain is permissioned; only a restricted set of users have the rights to decide what will be recorded in the blockchain. Permissioned blockchains have a number of advantages over public blockchains (Scherer, 2017). Most notable is the ability to split the network into segments where only a subset of nodes needs to validate transactions to a particular application, allowing the use of parallel computing and better scaling. Public blockchains can only process a couple of transaction per second and is therefore far from usable.

Blockchain is emerging as a viable technology when it comes to protecting businesses and other entities from cyber-attacks. Recently, NASA implemented permissioned blockchain technology in order to boost cybersecurity, and prevent denial of service and other attacks on air traffic services (Reisman, 2019). The traditional Domain Name System (DNS) that maps network node names into IP addresses depends on a centralized trust model, and it is highly regulated. Blockchain based DNS on the other hand is decentralized and cannot be controlled or manipulated by a single central authority (Barret, 2019). Decentralized DNS offers many benefits such as countering censorship by authorities, or preventing DNS spoofing, where attackers can corrupt DNS data so that the name server returns an incorrect IP address and redirects traffic to an attacker computer. However, decentralized DNS can also be abused by attackers for malicious purposes (Amado, 2018). Blockchain based solutions have also been proposed for IoT security and privacy (Dorri et al., 2017).

Blockchains allow entities who do not trust one another to share valuable data in a secure, tamperproof way. Blockchains employs cryptography and innovative software rules to store data that are extremely difficult for attackers to manipulate. However, implementing blockchain in practice is harder. Even when developers use tried-and-tested cryptographic tools, it is easy to accidentally put them together in ways that are not secure or make mistakes while setting them up (Orcutt, 2018). Creating blockchain-based bug bounty programs and incentivizing people to report flaws could be a way forward.

Quantum Computing

Quantum computing harnesses quantum mechanical phenomena, such as superposition and entanglement, to perform information processing in ways not possible or not practical by classical computing (Chiu, 2019). Classical computers operate on bits which can have one of two states - 0 or 1, whereas quantum computers operate on quantum bits (or *qubits*) which can be in both 0 and 1 states simultaneously. A qubit operation exploits this quantum superposition by allowing many computations to be performed in parallel - a two-qubit system performs the operation on 4 values, a three-qubit system on 8, and so on. Quantum computers have the potential to revolutionize computation by solving certain types of intractable problems that would take millions of years on classical computers. Therefore, the realization of quantum computers could achieve new breakthroughs in medicine, artificial intelligence, optimization and many others. John Preskill coined the term quantum supremacy (Preskill, 2018) to characterize computational tasks performable by quantum devices, which classical devices could not. Despite the reports of quantum supremacy (Tavares, 2019), a practical quantum computer may not emerge for another decade or more (Gwynne, 2018), nevertheless organizations must prepare for cybersecurity threats in the post-quantum era.

Quantum computer have capabilities to break existing asymmetric key cryptosystems, which protects internet and powers global e-commerce. Symmetric encryption and asymmetric encryption are two cornerstones of modern cryptography. While symmetric encryption employs a single key for encryption as well as decryption (e.g., AES), asymmetric encryption employs a key-pair, one (public key) for encryption and the other (private key) for decryption (e.g., RSA). The development of a quantum computer may affect symmetric key encryption and asymmetric key encryption differently. For instance, Grover's algorithm provides a quadratic speedup on a quantum computer, which has the effect of cutting the encryption strength of AES in half (Grover, 1996). Whereas, Shor's algorithm provides an exponential speedup on a quantum computer enabling one to crack RSA (Rivest-Shamir-Adleman) cryptosystem, which is based on the hard mathematical problem of large, prime number factorization (Shor, 1994). The quantum speedup also yields many other mainstream cryptographic algorithms such as Digital Signature Algorithm (DSA), Elliptic-curve Diffie–Hellman (ECDH), etc. vulnerable to attack. The implication is that, while AES can be made robust against a quantum computer by increasing the key size, asymmetric cryptosystems are vulnerable to quantum attack, and there is no alternative but to replace them by quantum-resistant ones. The potential negative consequences are severe given the ubiquity of asymmetric encryption schemes in securing internet, IoT and cloud computing.

In response to the emerging quantum threats, in 2016 NIST called upon cryptographers for submissions for quantum-resistant public-key algorithms as part of its Post-Quantum Cryptography project. NIST received sixty-plus cryptographic algorithms from around the world during the first round of submissions of which 26 algorithms were shortlisted for the second round for further analysis (NIST, 2019). Unlike the factorization of large prime numbers used by RSA - which is vulnerable to quantum attack - these algorithms are based on different mathematical classes (lattice, code, multivariate and hash schemes) not known to be susceptible to quantum attack. The standardization process is in progress and the draft standard is expected to be available between 2022 and 2024.

CONCLUSION

Trust is essential to cooperation as it produces positive-sum outcomes that strengthen society and benefit its individual members. However, as we increasingly depend on technology, cyber threats and vulnerabilities are creating trust issues for businesses and enterprises. As per the latest 2019 CEO Imperative study (Yonge, 2019), CEOs see cybersecurity as the number one threat to the global economy over the next five to ten years.

This should not be surprising to the reader based on the early discussion we had in this chapter on the changing cyber ecosystem, latest trends in cyber-attacks and their impact. We then delved into their five key implications that any modern enterprise need to be cognizant of and described eleven emerging measures that may help address consequences of those implications substantially. For each measure, we also highlighted some open issues and challenges that need attention from both researchers' and practitioners' communities. If anything, it simply confirmed 'no free lunch' nature of cybersecurity.

Decades ago, enterprise security was predominantly audit driven, based on static defenses with controls centered on passwords and perimeter security. It then evolved into more of reactive security that was rule and signature based, with focus on protection and detection. It now needs to be more proactive, risk aware, cognitive, automated and connected. It has to be baked into processes, systems, and new digital channels with the intent to manage risk across the entire business ecosystem of customers, suppliers, and other third parties. Moreover, it has to be largely invisible, that is, it should enable protection, governance and control without impacting usability or hindering operations and at the same time providing assurance of delivering on aspects of data protection and privacy.

Different measures that we brought up in this chapter can help in this mission, for example, Bug Bounties, Cyber Range, Privacy by Design can help enterprise with being more proactive, Cloud Computing, Cyber Insurance and Isolation can play their part in managing risks, Security Operations Center provides ample play ground to be cognitive, automated and leverage connectedness. These are not solved problems by any imagination, and offer a fertile ground for contributing to both theory and practice of cybersecurity and privacy research.

REFERENCES

Abolhassan, F. (2017). *Cyber security. Simply. Make it happen.* Springer. doi:10.1007/978-3-319-46529-6

Abraham, S., & Nair, S. (2015). *A predictive framework for cyber security analytics using attack graphs.* arXiv preprint arXiv:1502.01240

Amado, R. (2018). *How Cybercriminals are using Blockchain DNS: From the Market to the Bazar.* Retrieved December 5, 2019, from https://www.digitalshadows.com/blog-and-research/how-cybercriminals-are-using-blockchain-dns-from-the-market-to-the-bazar/

Amir, E., Levi, S., & Livne, T. (2018). Do firms underreport information on cyber-attacks? Evidence from capital markets. *Review of Accounting Studies, 23*(3), 1177–1206. doi:10.100711142-018-9452-4

Antonakakis, M., April, T., Bailey, M., Bernhard, M., Bursztein, E., Cochran, J., . . . Zhou, Y. (2017). Understanding the Mirai Botnet. In *26th USENIX Security Symposium (USENIX Security 17)* (pp. 1093-1110). USENIX.

Ausherman, N. (2018). *Dealing with Cyber Attacks - Steps You Need to Know.* NIST.

Barret, T. (2019). *Blockchain, IoT and DNS.* Retrieved December 5, 2019, from https://ccnso.icann.org/sites/default/files/field-attached/presentation-blockchain-iot-dns-11mar19-en.pdf

Barth, A., Jackson, C., Reis, C., Team, T., & Google Team. (2008). *The Security Architecture of the Chromium Browser.* Technical report. Stanford University.

Bianchi, D., & Tosun, O. K. (2019). *Cyber Attacks and Stock Market Activity.* Available at SSRN 3190454

Biggio, B., Nelson, B., & Laskov, P. (2012). *Poisoning Attacks Against Support Vector Machines.* arXiv preprint arXiv:1206.6389

Bird, J. (2016). *DevOpsSec: Securing Software Through Continuous Delivery*. Academic Press.

Blitz, M. J. (2018). Lies, Line Drawing, and Deep Fake News. *Oklahoma Law Review*, *71*, 59.

Blockchain. (2019). *Wikipedia - Blockchain*. Retrieved December 5, 2019, from https://en.wikipedia.org/wiki/Blockchain

Brasser, F., Müller, U., Dmitrienko, A., Kostiainen, K., Capkun, S., & Sadeghi, A. R. (2017). Software Grand Exposure: SGX Cache Attacks are Practical. In *11th USENIX Workshop on Offensive Technologies*. USENIX.

Cadwalladr, C., & Graham-Harrison, E. (2018). Revealed: 50 Million Facebook Profiles Harvested for Cambridge Analytica in Major Data Breach. *Sat*, *17*, 22–03.

Cashell, B., Jackson, W. D., Jickling, M., & Webel, B. (2004). The Economic Impact of Cyber-attacks. Congressional Research Service Documents, CRS RL32331.

Cavoukian, A. (2010). Privacy by Design: The Definitive Workshop. A Foreword by Ann Cavoukian, ph.d. *Identity in the Information Society*, *3*(2), 247–251. doi:10.100712394-010-0062-y

Chiu, E. (2019). *Preparing Enterprises for the Quantum Computing Cybersecurity Threats*. Retrieved December 5, 2019, from https://cloudsecurityalliance.org/artifacts/preparing-enterprises-for-the-quantum-computing-cybersecurity-threats/

CJ, G., Pandit, S., Vaddepalli, S., Tupsamudre, H., Banahatti, V., & Lodha, S. (2018). Phishy - A Serious Game to Train Enterprise Users on Phishing Awareness. In *Proceedings of the 2018 annual symposium on computer-human interaction in play companion extended abstracts* (pp. 169-181). New York: ACM.

Davenport, S., & Ford, R. (2014). SGX: the Good, the Bad and the Downright Ugly. *Virus Bulletin, 14*.

Davis, J., & Magrath, S. (2013). *A survey of cyber ranges and testbeds (Tech. Rep.). Defence Science And Technology Organisation Edinburgh*. Cyber And Electronic Warfare Div.

Dorri, A., Kanhere, S. S., Jurdak, R., & Gauravaram, P. (2017). *Blockchain for IoT security and privacy: The case study of a smart home. In 2017 IEEE international conference on pervasive computing and communications workshops (PerCom workshops)* (pp. 618–623). IEEE. doi:10.1109/PERCOMW.2017.7917634

DSCI. (2019). *Cyber Insurance in India*. Retrieved October 3, 2019, from https://www.dsci.in/sites/default/files/documents/resourcecentre/Cyber%20Insurance%20In%20India.pdf

Eskandari, S., Leoutsarakos, A., Mursch, T., & Clark, J. (2018). A First Look at Browser-Based Cryptojacking. In *2018 IEEE European Symposium on Security and Privacy Workshops (EuroS&PW)* (pp. 58-66). IEEE.

Evans, M., Maglaras, L. A., He, Y., & Janicke, H. (2016). Human Behaviour as an Aspect of Cybersecurity Assurance. *Security and Communication Networks*, *9*(17), 4667–4679. doi:10.1002ec.1657

Evtyushkin, D., Ponomarev, D., & Abu-Ghazaleh, N. (2016). Jump Over ASLR: Attacking Branch Predictors to Bypass ASLR. In *The 49th Annual IEEE/ACM International Symposium on Microarchitecture* (p. 40). IEEE.

Eykholt, K., Evtimov, I., Fernandes, E., Li, B., Rahmati, A., Xiao, C., . . . Song, D. (2017). *Robust Physical-World Attacks on Deep Learning Models*. arXiv preprint arXiv:1707.08945

FBI. (2018). *Internet crime report*. Retrieved September 20, 2019, from https://pdf.ic3.gov/2018IC3Report.pdf

Ferguson, B., Tall, A., & Olsen, D. (2014). National cyber range overview. In *Proceedings of the 2014 IEEE Military Communications Conference* (pp. 123-128). Washington, DC: IEEE. 10.1109/MIL-COM.2014.27

Ferrara, E. (2019). The History of Digital Spam. *Communications of the ACM, 62*(8), 82–91. doi:10.1145/3299768

Finlay, L., & Payne, C. (2019). The Attribution Problem and Cyber Armed Attacks. *AJIL Unbound, 113*, 202–206. doi:10.1017/aju.2019.35

Fredrikson, M., Jha, S., & Ristenpart, T. (2015). Model Inversion Attacks that Exploit Confidence Information and Basic Countermeasures. In *Proceedings of the 22nd ACM SIGSAC Conference on Computer and Communications Security* (pp. 1322-1333). ACM. 10.1145/2810103.2813677

Gaukstern, E., & Krishnan, S. (2018). Cybersecurity Threats Targeting Networked Critical. *Medical Devices (Auckland, N.Z.)*.

Gentry, C. (2009). *A Fully Homomorphic Encryption Scheme* (Unpublished Doctoral Dissertation). Stanford University. crypto.stanford.edu/craig

George, J. J., & Leidner, D. E. (2019). From Clicktivism to Hacktivism: Understanding Digital Activism. *Information and Organization, 29*(3), 100249. doi:10.1016/j.infoandorg.2019.04.001

Gharote, M., Phuke, N., Patil, R., & Lodha, S. (2019). Multi-objective Stable Matching and Distributional Constraints. *Soft Computing, 23*(9), 2995–3011. doi:10.100700500-019-03763-4

Giles, M. (2019). *Triton is the World's Most Murderous Malware, and it's Spreading. MIT Technology Review*.

González, F., Yu, Y., Figueroa, A., López, C., & Aragon, C. (2019). *Global Reactions to the Cambridge Analytica Scandal: An Inter-Language Social Media Study*. Academic Press.

Grassi, P. A., Fenton, J. L., Newton, E. M., Perlner, R. A., Regenscheid, A. R., Burr, W. E., & Richer, J. P. (2019). Digital Identity Guidelines. *NIST Special Publication, 800*, 63–3.

Grover, L. K. (1996). *A fast quantum mechanical algorithm for database search*. arXiv preprint quant-ph/9605043

Gudka, K., Watson, R. N., Anderson, J., Chisnall, D., Davis, B., Laurie, B., ... Richardson, A. (2015). Clean Application Compartmentalization with SOAAP. In *Proceedings of the 22nd ACM SIGSAC Conference on Computer and Communications Security* (pp. 1016-1031). ACM.

Guri, M., Zadov, B., & Elovici, Y. (2019). Odini: Escaping Sensitive Data from Faraday-Caged, Air-Gapped Computers via Magnetic Fields. *IEEE Transactions on Information Forensics and Security*.

Gürses, S., Troncoso, C., & Diaz, C. (2011). Engineering Privacy by Design. *Computers. Privacy & Data Protection, 14*(3), 25.

Gutmann, P. (2007). The Commercial Malware Industry. *DEFCON Conference.*

Gwynne, P. (2018). *Practical quantum computers remain at least a decade away.* Retrieved December 5, 2019, from https://physicsworld.com/a/practical-quantum-computers-remain-at-least-a-decade-away/

Hackerone. (2019). *The Hacker Powered Security Report 2010.* Retrieved October 3, 2019, from https://www.hackerone.com/sites/default/files/2019-08/hacker-powered-security-report-2019.pdf

Hassan, W. U., Guo, S., Li, D., Chen, Z., Jee, K., Li, Z., & Bates, A. (2019). Nodoze: Combatting Threat Alert Fatigue with Automated Provenance Triage. NDSS.

Heumann, T., Keller, J., & Türpe, S. (2010). *Quantifying the Attack Surface of a Web Application. Sicherheit 2010.* Sicherheit, Schutz und Zuverlassigkeit.

Hiller, J. S. (2014). Civil cyberconflict: Microsoft, Cybercrime, and Botnets. *Santa Clara Computer and High-Technology Law Journal, 31*, 163.

Homoliak, I., Toffalini, F., Guarnizo, J., Elovici, Y., & Ochoa, M. (2019). Insight into Insiders and it: A Survey of Insider Threat Taxonomies, Analysis, Modeling, and Countermeasures. *ACM Computing Surveys, 52*(2), 30. doi:10.1145/3303771

Hong, J. (2012). *The Current State of Phishing Attacks.* Academic Press.

Hong, S., Frigo, P., Kaya, Y., Giuffrida, C., & Dumitras, T. (2019). *Terminal Brain Damage: Exposing the Graceless Degradation in Deep Neural Networks under Hardware Fault Attacks.* arXiv preprint arXiv:1906.01017

Huisman, J. (2019). *Magic Quadrant for Security Awareness Computer-Based Training.* Retrieved October 3, 2019, from https://www.gartner.com/en/documents/3950454/magic-quadrant-for-security-awareness-computer-based-tra

Internet Bug Bounty. (2019). *The Internet Bug Bounty.* Retrieved October 3, 2019, from https://internetbugbounty.org/

Isaak, J., & Hanna, M. J. (2018). User Data Privacy: Facebook, Cambridge Analytica, and Privacy Protection. *Computer, 51*(8), 56–59. doi:10.1109/MC.2018.3191268

IXIA. (2016). *Cyber Range: Improving Network Defense and Security Readiness.* Retrieved October 3, 2019, from https://www.testforce.com/testforce files/newsletter/Aug 2016/ixia.pdf

Jin, G., Tu, M., Kim, T.-H., Heffron, J., & White, J. (2018). Game Based Cybersecurity Training for High School Students. In *Proceedings of the 49th ACM Technical Symposium on Computer Science Education* (pp. 68-73). New York, NY: ACM. 10.1145/3159450.3159591

Judd, M., & Fritsch, J. (2018). *Comparing Security Controls and Paradigms in AWS, Google Cloud Platform and Microsoft Azure.* Retrieved October 3, 2019, from https://www.gartner.com/en/documents/3877942/comparing-security-controls-and-paradigms-in-aws-google-

Kim Zetter. (2014). *Hacker Lexicon: What is an Air Gap?* Retrieved September 20, 2019, from https://www.wired.com/2014/12/hacker-lexicon-air-gap/

Kindervag, J. (2010). *Build Security Into Your Network's DNA: The Zero Trust Network Architecture.* Forrester Research Inc.

Kish, D., & Carpenter, P. (2017). *Forecast Snapshot: Security Awareness Computer-based Training, Worldwide, 2017.* Retrieved October 3, 2019, from https://www.gartner.com/en/documents/3629840/forecast-snapshot-security-awareness-computer-based-trai

Kissel, R. (2011). *Glossary of key information security terms.* Diane Publishing. doi:10.6028/NIST.IR.7298r1

Kocher, P., Genkin, D., Gruss, D., Haas, W., Hamburg, M., Lipp, M., . . . Yarom, Y. (2018). *Spectre Attacks: Exploiting Speculative Execution.* arXiv preprint arXiv:1801.01203

Kowtha, S., Nolan, L. A., & Daley, R. A. (2012). Cyber Security Operations Center Characterization Model and Analysis. *IEEE Conference on Technologies for Homeland Security*, 470-475. 10.1109/THS.2012.6459894

Kula, R. G., German, D. M., Ouni, A., Ishio, T., & Inoue, K. (2018). Do developers update their library dependencies? *Empirical Software Engineering*, 23(1), 384–417. doi:10.100710664-017-9521-5

Langner, R. (2011). Stuxnet: Dissecting a cyberwarfare weapon. *IEEE Security and Privacy*, 9(3), 49–51. doi:10.1109/MSP.2011.67

Laszka, A., Zhao, M., & Grossklags, J. (2016). *Banishing Misaligned Incentives for Validating Reports in Bugbounty Platforms.* Computer Security-ESORICS.

Leon, A. D. (2015). *Impacts of Malicious Cyber Activities* (Unpublished Doctoral Dissertation). Johns Hopkins University.

Li, Y., McCune, J., Newsome, J., Perrig, A., Baker, B., & Drewry, W. (2014). Minibox: A Two-way Sandbox for x86 Native Code. *USENIX Annual Technical Conference*, 409-420.

Lindros, K., & Tittel, E. (2016). *What is Cyber Insurance and Why You Need It.* Retrieved October 3, 2019, from https://www.cio.com/article/3065655/what-is-cyber-insurance-and-why-you-need-it.html

Lipp, M., Schwarz, M., Gruss, D., Prescher, T., Haas, W., Mangard, S., . . . Hamburg, M. (2018). *Meltdown.* arXiv preprint arXiv:1801.01207

Lusthaus, J. (2019). Beneath the Dark Web: Excavating the Layers of Cybercrime's Underground Economy. *IEEE European Symposium on Security and Privacy Workshops*, 474-480. 10.1109/EuroSPW.2019.00059

Ma, Z., Reynolds, J., Dickinson, J., Wang, K., Judd, T., Barnes, J. D., ... Bailey, M. (2019). The Impact of Secure Transport Protocols on Phishing Efficacy. *USENIX Workshop on Cyber Security Experimentation and Test.*

Maillart, T., Zhao, M., Grossklags, J., & Chuang, J. (2016). Given Enough Eyeballs, All Bugs are Shallow? Revisiting Eric Raymond with Bug Bounty Programs. *Journal of Cybersecurity*, 3(2), 81–90. doi:10.1093/cybsec/tyx008

Mann, I. (2017). *Hacking the Human: Social Engineering Techniques and Security Countermeasures.* Routledge. doi:10.4324/9781351156882

McAfee. (2019). *Cloud-native: The Infrastructure-as-a-service Adoption and Risk.* Retrieved October 3, 2019, from https://cloudsecurity.mcafee.com/cloud/en-us/forms/white-papers/wp-cloud-adoption-risk-report-iaas.html

Messerschmidt, J. E. (2013). Hackback: Permitting Retaliatory Hacking by Non-state Actors as Proportionate Countermeasures to Transboundary Cyberharm. *Colum. J. Transnat'l L., 52,* 275.

Myrbakken, H., & Colomo-Palacios, R. (2017). Devsecops: A Multivocal Literature Review. *International Conference on Software Process Improvement and Capability Determination,* 17-29. 10.1007/978-3-319-67383-7_2

Nahorney, B. (2017). *ISTR Email Threats 2017.* An ISTR Special Report.

NIST. (2018). *Cyber Ranges.* Retrieved October 3, 2019, from https://www.nist.gov/sites/default/files/documents/2018/02/13/cyber ranges.pdf

NIST. (2019). *Post-Quantum Cryptography – Project Overview.* Retrieved December 5, 2019, from https://csrc.nist.gov/projects/post-quantum-cryptography/

Nobles, C. (2018). Botching Human Factors in Cybersecurity in Business Organizations. *HOLISTICA-Journal of Business and Public Administration, 9*(3), 71–88. doi:10.2478/hjbpa-2018-0024

Orcutt, M. (2018). *How secure is blockchain really?* Retrieved December 5, 2019, from https://www.technologyreview.com/s/610836/how-secure-is-blockchain-really/

Ornes, S. (2016). Core Concept: The Internet of Things and the Explosion of Interconnectivity. *National Academy of Sciences, 113*(40), 11059-11060.

Preskill, J. (2018). Quantum Computing in the NISQ era and beyond. *Quantum, 2,* 79. doi:10.22331/q-2018-08-06-79

PWC. (2019). *Insurance 2020 & Beyond: Reaping the Dividends of Cyber Resilience.* Retrieved October 3, 2019, from https://www.pwc.com/gx/en/industries/financial-services/publications/insurance-2020-cyber.html

Ramzan, Z. (2010). Phishing Attacks and Countermeasures. In Handbook of Information and Communication Security (pp. 433-448). Academic Press.

Reisman, R. J. (2019). *Air Traffic Management Blockchain Infrastructure for Security.* Authentication, and Privacy.

Romanou, A. (2018). The Necessity of the Implementation of Privacy by Design in Sectors where Data Protection Concerns Arise. *Computer Law & Security Review, 34*(1), 99–110. doi:10.1016/j.clsr.2017.05.021

Rubinstein, I. S., & Good, N. (2013). Privacy by Design: A Counterfactual Analysis of Google and Facebook Privacy Incidents. *Berkeley Technology Law Journal, 28,* 1333.

Scherer, M. (2017). *Performance and Scalability of Blockchain Networks and Smart Contracts* (Dissertation). Retrieved from http://urn.kb.se/resolve?urn=urn:nbn:se:umu:diva-136470

Schwarz, M., Weiser, S., & Gruss, D. (2019). Practical Enclave Malware with Intel SGX. In *International Conference on Detection of Intrusions and Malware, and Vulnerability Assessment* (pp. 177-196). 10.1007/978-3-030-22038-9_9

Schwarz, M., Weiser, S., Gruss, D., Maurice, C., & Mangard, S. (2017). Malware Guard Extension: Using SGX to Conceal Cache Attacks. In *International Conference on Detection of Intrusions and Malware, and Vulnerability Assessment* (pp. 3-24). 10.1007/978-3-319-60876-1_1

Shao, S., Tunc, C., Satam, P., & Hariri, S. (2017). Real-time IRC Threat Detection Framework. In IEEE 2nd International Workshops on Foundations and Applications of Self Systems (pp. 318-323). IEEE.

Shor, P. W. (1994, November). Algorithms for quantum computation: Discrete logarithms and factoring. In *Proceedings 35th annual symposium on foundations of computer science* (pp. 124-134). IEEE. 10.1109/SFCS.1994.365700

Shu, R., Wang, P., Gorski, S. A. III, Andow, B., Nadkarni, A., Deshotels, L., ... Gu, X. (2016). A Study of Security Isolation Techniques. *ACM Computing Surveys*, *49*(3), 50. doi:10.1145/2988545

Shukla, M., Manjunath, S., Saxena, R., Mondal, S., & Lodha, S. (2015). Poster: Winover Enterprise Dark Data. In *Proceedings of the 22nd ACM SIGSAC Conference on Computer and Communications Security* (pp. 1674-1676). ACM.

Shukla, M., Mondal, S., & Lodha, S. (2016). Poster: Locally Virtualized Environment for Mitigating Ransomware Threat. In *Proceedings of the 2016 ACM SIGSAC Conference on Computer and Communications Security* (pp. 1784-1786). 10.1145/2976749.2989051

Smith, K. T., Jones, A., Johnson, L., & Smith, L. M. (2019). Examination of Cybercrime and its Effects on Corporate Stock Value. *Journal of Information. Communication and Ethics in Society*, *17*(1), 42–60.

Souter, G. (2019). *Cyber Insurance Market Set to Grow Despite Challenges: Panel*. Retrieved October 3, 2019, from https://www.businessinsurance.com/article/20190924/NEWS06/912330822/Cyber-insurance-market-set-to-grow-despite-challenges-Panel

Steffens, M., Rossow, C., Johns, M., & Stock, B. (2019). Don't Trust the Locals: Investigating the Prevalence of Persistent Client-side Cross-site Scripting in the Wild. *Network and Distributed System Security Symposium*. 10.14722/ndss.2019.23009

Tavares, F. (2019). *Google and NASA Achieve Quantum Supremacy*. Retrieved December 5, 2019, from https://www.nasa.gov/feature/ames/quantum-supremacy/

Torres, A. (2015). *Building a World-Class Security Operations Center: A Roadmap*. SANS Institute.

Travis, A., & Arthur, C. (2014). EU Court Backs 'Right to be Forgotten': Google Must Amend Results on Request. *The Guardian*. Retrieved October 3, 2019, from https://www.theguardian.com/technology/2014/may/13/right-to-be-forgotten-eu-court-google-search-results

Tupsamudre, H., Wasnik, R., Biswas, S., Pandit, S., Vaddepalli, S., Shinde, A., ... Lodha, S. (2018). GAP: A Game for Improving Awareness about Passwords. In *Joint Conference on Serious games* (pp. 66-78). 10.1007/978-3-030-02762-9_8

Vacca, J. R. (2019). *Online Terrorist Propaganda, Recruitment, and Radicalization*. CRC Press. doi:10.1201/9781315170251

van Rest, J., Boonstra, D., Everts, M., van Rijn, M., & van Paassen, R. (2012). Designing Privacy-by-design. In *Annual Privacy Forum* (pp. 55-72). Academic Press.

Varghese, B., & Buyya, R. (2018). Next Generation Cloud Computing: New Trends and Research Directions. *Future Generation Computer Systems, 79*, 849–861. doi:10.1016/j.future.2017.09.020

Verizon. (2019). *Data Breach Investigations Report*. Retrieved September 20, 2019, from https://enterprise.verizon.com/resources/reports/dbir/

Wang, A., Liang, R., Liu, X., Zhang, Y., Chen, K., & Li, J. (2017). An Inside Look at IOT Malware. In *International Conference on Industrial IOT Technologies and Applications* (pp. 176-186). 10.1007/978-3-319-60753-5_19

Watkins, B. (2014). *The Impact of Cyber Attacks on the Private Sector. Briefing Paper*. Association for International Affair.

Wilson, M., & Hash, J. (2003). Building an Information Technology Security Awareness and Training Program. *NIST Special Publication, 800*(50), 1–39. doi:10.6028/NIST.SP.800-50

World Economic Forum. (2019). *The Global Risks Report 2019*. Retrieved September 20, 2019, from https://www.weforum.org/reports/the-global-risks-report-2019

Yan, C., Xu, W., & Liu, J. (2016). *Can You Trust Autonomous Vehicles: Contactless Attacks against Sensors of Self-driving Vehicle*. DEFCON.

Yonge, J. d. (2019). *For CEOs, Are the Days of Sidelining Global Challenges Numbered?* Retrieved September 20, 2019, from https://www.ey.com/en gl/growth/ceo-imperative-global-challenges

Yuan, X., He, P., Zhu, Q., & Li, X. (2019). Adversarial Examples: Attacks and Defenses for Deep Learning. *IEEE Transactions on Neural Networks and Learning Systems, 30*(9), 2805–2824. doi:10.1109/TNNLS.2018.2886017 PMID:30640631

Chapter 9
People and the Digital Enterprise:
Challenges and Approaches

Vivek Balaraman

TCS Research, Tata Consultancy Services, India

Sachin Patel

TCS Research, Tata Consultancy Services, India

Mayuri Duggirala

TCS Research, Tata Consultancy Services, India

Jayasree Raveendran

TCS Research, Tata Consultancy Services, India

Ravi Mahamuni

TCS Research, Tata Consultancy Services, India

ABSTRACT

The transformation of a conventional enterprise from a people-centric model to a technology-centric one has important implications for its human workforce. In this chapter, the authors look at three representative people-related focus areas for the digital enterprise, enhancing workplace wellbeing, enabling continuous learning and compliance to information security. They discuss each of these problems and then look at the technological infrastructure a digital enterprise would require to manage these areas.

INTRODUCTION

A digital enterprise's core functions are technology driven (Araujo, 2016). Technology lies at the heart of things not at the periphery. While the movement towards this paradigm shift has been going on for a long time with early adopters like Dow Corning beginning this journey as early as 2002 (Rosencrance,

DOI: 10.4018/978-1-7998-0108-5.ch009

2002), this has been accelerated by recent technological advances such as the Internet of Things, mobile technology and AI. We can collect information continuously from a variety of environments, be informed about a situation wherever we may be and have continuous learning and evolution built into the very fabric of a system. Due to this, earlier boundaries between the organization's external functions such as marketing & sales and the internal such as production have blurred and sometimes disappeared (Cemex, 2019).

Now while a newly hatched startup may begin life from day 1 as a digital enterprise, most existent organizations have to go through a disruptive transformation process as they remake themselves from a people centric to a technology centric enterprise. At the extreme end of the transformation journey organizations may even be trying to go from a model where automation existed to assist people at work to one where the people help create and assist the automation at work (Wired Inc, 2018), (Meister, AI plus human intelligence is the future of work, 2018). That is not all. Part of the digital journey involves connecting the parts of the enterprise separated normally either by function or geography. Curiously this has also led to a phenomenon which Bailey (Bailey & A, 2017) calls workforce fragmentation where conventional models of what forms a 'team' (co-located, functionally similar, all team members are employees of the organization) are challenged and reinvented. Given all this, it is natural that the most profound impact of an organization's transformation into a digital enterprise is on its people, its workforce.

This chapter's focus is on the people, the workforce of the digital enterprise.

If this topic is already vast in scope, its scope could be further broadened by the realisation that while organizations are making the digital journey, people too have been making their own digital journeys. Thus, not only do we have a digital enterprise, we have a digital workforce. A study by Nokia referenced in (Colbert, Yee, & George, 2016) showed that the normal American smartphone user checked their phone upto a 150 times a day. The authors also note in the same paper how increased usage of technology has reduced the ability of people to understand another's points of view, something to be concerned about given that most people in an enterprise work in teams and have to factor in each other's views. All these signal that not only must the workforce adjust to the digital enterprise, the enterprise too must adjust to the digital workforce.

But while this two way adjustment of enterprise to people and vice versa is a fascinating topic, we decided that rather than cover every people aspect of a digital enterprise, leading to a shallow treatment of an important subject, we would restrict our focus to three topics that we expect will be important representative focus areas in a digital enterprise. These topics are not new and are prevalent too in non-digital enterprises. However, each of these acquires an increased gravitas in a digital enterprise and furthermore, the digital enterprise paradigm facilitates the creation of technological systems to address these problems in new and powerful ways. The three topics are, enhancing workforce well-being, creating a continually learning workforce and ensuring workforce compliance to organizational norms. Underlying all three is how enterprises manage change though we do not discuss separately but cover it in the context of each of the three sub-areas. We also touch upon a topic of increased importance, both within the organization and without, that of data privacy.

The rest of this chapter is divided into two sections.

Section 1 discusses and details three scenarios which represent some of the people related challenges in a digital enterprise.

Section 2 discusses how a digital enterprise would engage with people and behavioural issues of the sort discussed in Section 1. We present an integrated and multi-disciplinary architecture of methods, tools and techniques to study, analysis, understand behaviour as well as design and deliver interventions. We show how these can tackle the scenarios discussed in the previous sections as well as resultant challenges that remain to be solved. Since the technological movements discussed in this section are very current, we briefly discuss the potential evolution of these solutions in the concluding section.

WORKPLACE WELLBEING

Wellbeing is increasingly viewed as a critical aspect of how well we function, as individuals and as members of social groupings. Wellbeing is an umbrella term that covers a wide spectrum of conditions ranging from the extremely negative to negative, for example, psychotic illnesses, substance abuse, self-harm, burnout, anxiety, depression, etc., to the more positive experiences of gratitude, hope, optimism, resilience, contentment, flow, etc. (Dodge, Daly, Huyton, & Sanders, 2012) Wellbeing research has spanned several decades of research from domains as varied as psychology, sociology, economics, on the one hand to business and management, clinical medicine, public health and epidemiology on the other. These scientific disciplines have sought to unravel the experience of low and high wellbeing, at the physiological, contextual or environmental and psychological conditions.

In parallel, there is growing evidence showing how lack of wellbeing can have individual, business, economic as well as large scale social ramifications. The costs of negative wellbeing and the need to foster positive wellbeing have been recognized by enterprise management worldwide. A recent Deloitte report (Deloitte, 2018) indicates that over 50% of CXO survey respondents listed wellbeing as being "highly valuable" or "valuable".

A report (World Economic Forum, 2011) recently estimated the global economic burden of mental illness between 2011 and 2030 at $16.3 trillion. In the UK, recent evidence (Health and Safety Executive, 2018) has indicated that 1.4 million working people suffer from a work related illness with stress, depression and anxiety accounting for 44% of the total work-related illnesses. In India, 3 out of 4 mental wellbeing problems are due to workplace depression with 46% suffering some form of workplace stress (Bhattacharyya & Vijayaraghavan, 2016). The World Health Organization estimates that in India, the age-adjusted suicide rate per 100,000 population is 21.1 (World Health Organization, 2019). In addition, the same report suggests that the economic loss due to mental health conditions between 2012-2030, is estimated to be around 1.03 trillion of 2010 dollars. A recent study specifically around stress at work estimates that the largest excess healthcare costs were due to high job demands with a total of $46 billion, work-family conflict costs at $24 billion, long work hours at $13 billion and low job control at $11 billion (Denning, 2018).

Across the world, the challenges of wellbeing measurement and management have been termed wicked problems. A recent paper highlights the core dilemmas of wellbeing management at the policy level: reliability of measurement of wellbeing, responsibility of promoting wellbeing and trust in wellbeing data management (Bache, Reardon, & Anand, 2016). Thus in the measurement, intervention and management of wellbeing a multipronged, multidisciplinary approach is required.

Shift to Employee Experience and Integrated Learning Focus

As per Qualtrics (Qualtrics, 2019), only 62% of workers in the US are engaged at work, while the numbers for other countries are even worse, 48% in the UK, 56% in Australia, and Hong Kong – the lowest scoring country with just 42%. Forbes reports that $11 Billion is lost annually due to employee turnover (Forbes, 2013). Enterprises are now realizing such poor engagement may be related to what can be called the employee experience. The better the experience, better the engagement and better the performance. The experience gathering may even precede an employee's entry into the organization and begin from the moment a prospective employee decides to apply to an organization. This aspect covers a wide territory from employee engagement to role fitment to seamless and even pleasurable transition to different roles within organizations.

As technology based forces reshape the workplace, often the only certainty that exists is that the nature of the work done by people in the enterprise is changing and evolving. People have to be constantly on new learning curves as new technological systems and processes arrive. Old job roles are vanishing but new roles are coming into being (Meister, 2018). As many commentators have indicated, your co-worker tomorrow may not be a person but a bot or AI based system (Wired Inc, 2018). How enterprises enable their workforce to both buy into change and how they deliver learning to their employees will be key aspects of the Digital Enterprise.

Enhancing Information Security in Organizations

With the rise of digital enterprises, a significant challenge that organizations face is on the cybersecurity front. The fundamental tensions that arise between the business's need to digitize and cybersecurity's responsibility to protect the organization, its employees and its customers, within existing cyber operating models and practices is invariably noted in many studies and reports (Kaplan, Richter, & Ware, 2019). A significant trend witnessed is that organizations now own a shrinking percentage of the number of devices employees use to connect to corporate assets. Second, organizations control a diminishing percentage of the platforms that house the most critical information assets. The result of these two trends is that corporate IT security policies must shift from controlling how people utilize hard physical assets like computers and networks, to how employees interact with soft organizational assets such as data (Wittkop, 2017). This will also now mean that users have to become more responsible in information use, which requirements are generally laid out in information security policies in organizations

However, a key challenge here is that individuals generally tend to see the convenience or a sense of benefit that may trigger a compromise with information security, rather than think of potential harm from such a compromise. Apathy, ignorance, negligence, lack of awareness, mischievousness and resistance to information organisational policies are the roots of information security incidents in many cases (Safa, Solms, & Furnel, 2016). As per Alex Blau at the Harvard Business Review, (Blau, 2017) while it is not uncommon to think of cybersecurity as primarily a technological challenge, it is really more of a human one, in that most cyberattacks take advantage of human error.

Different forms of threat to information security have made businesses vulnerable to risks, consequently resulting in considerable damage in terms of reputation and money. For example, lost business was the biggest contributor to data breach costs. The average cost of lost business for organizations due to data breaches in a 2019 study was $1.42 million, and it found that breaches caused abnormal customer turnover of 3.9 percent in 2019. While malicious breaches were most common, inadvertent breaches from human error and system glitches were still the root cause for nearly half (49 percent) of the data breaches studied in the report (Ponemon Institute, IBM, 2019). Major security breakdowns have occurred because individuals misplace trust, organizations create perverse incentives, or adversaries discover and exploit design flaws. Increasingly, the approach to dealing with these security challenges which is getting attention is by integrating the social, behavioral and decision sciences with technology based approaches (National Academies of Sciences, 2017).

Thus, an important people related challenge that we focus on is the aspect of compliance to information security requirements by employees in an organization. Within this space, we specifically focus on the problem of insider threat in organizations, defined as the potential for an individual who has or had authorized access to an organization's assets to use that access, either maliciously or unintentionally, to act in a way that could negatively affect the organization (CERT National Insider Threat Center, 2018). Insider threat via a company's own employees (and contractors and vendors) is one of the largest unresolved issues in cybersecurity. It is present in 50% of breaches reported in a recent study (McKinsey, 2018). Organizations are certainly aware of the problem but have not been able to devise successful strategies to overcome them, by and large owing to the nature of the problem in itself which is considered a wicked problem.

SCENARIOS FROM THE DIGITAL ENTERPRISE

In this section we discuss the three problems discussed above in more detail.

Employee Wellbeing

With regard to wellbeing challenges in the workplace, research has highlighted how individual, team and organizational factors act as barriers as well as enablers to specific aspects of wellbeing, and in turn affect key individual and organizational outcomes. Some of the phenomena associated with workplace wellbeing include stress and burnout (Maslach, Schaufeli, & Leiter, 2001), person-job fit (Park, Monnot, Jacob, & Wagner, 2011), worklife balance (Kinman & Jones, 2008), presenteeism (Hemp, 2004), anxiety and depression in the workplace (Haslam, Atkinson, Brown, & Haslam, 2005), etc. These have been shown to have significant adverse impact on not only individual engagement and performance at work (Renee Baptiste, 2008) but also that of business outcomes of revenue and profitability (Huppert & Cooper, 2014).

We now discuss some of the specific forms of low wellbeing of interest to workplace or organizational wellbeing. One big focus area in the workplace wellbeing research is that of exploring workplace stress and productivity. Research has indicated how stress at work affects not only workplace engagement, productivity, absenteeism and other work-related outcomes but can also have adverse impacts on individual physical and mental health status. A range of factors have been associated with stress, ranging from job insecurity, balancing work and family demands and other personal and organizational factors. Workplace stress manifests itself in several ways ranging from anger episodes, verbal abuse even physical violence to other physical symptoms like sleeping difficulties, vision problems, neck and hand pain and an increase in sick leaves for the employee (The American Institute of Stress, n.d.).

In the digital enterprise context the proliferation of collaboration technologies has facilitated a distributed workforce and given rise to the emergence of virtual teams. The digital workplace has on one hand, led to a greater intersection of disciplinary and business boundaries, while on the other, has also led to its own set of challenges and opportunities, which merit deeper research (Riemer & Schellhammer, 2018) . In parallel, the rise of the digital enterprise has led to several challenges associated with wellbeing, most significantly the blurring of work and home boundaries, digital addiction or overload, lower work-life balance, lower attention and lower overall wellbeing (Barrett, 2019). To counter these challenges, there has been recent evidence suggesting the need for digitally enabled organizations and digital leadership to help improve employee wellbeing (Zeike, Bradbury, Lindert, & Pfaf, 2019).

Specific Challenges in Employee Wellbeing: Burnout

Burnout is described as a psychological syndrome involving emotional exhaustion, depersonalization, and a diminished sense of personal accomplishment that occurs in challenging situations (Maslach, 1982). While originally studied in the context of human service occupations, that is, occupations such as emergency medical personnel, fire fighters, physicians etc, burnout as a phenomenon has been now studied for several other contexts such as academia and organizations as well. In the US, medical professionals across the career spectrum, ranging from students and physicians in training to practicing physicians are at significant risk of burnout with the prevalence of burnout exceeding 50% (Rothenberger, 2017). According to some estimates, the physical and psychological costs of burnout result in approximately $125-190 billion annually in healthcare costs (Kraft, 2018) in the US while the cost to US employers is around $150-300 billion annually (Garton E., 2017) . In a 2016 study of HR leaders, 95% of respondents said burnout is influencing workforce retention (Azahar, 2017). Top factors associated with burnout include unfair compensation, unreasonable workload, too much overtime or after-hours work. Employee burnout has therefore emerged as one of the top challenges that HR and business leaders in most organizations must address to improve overall retention and employee engagement. A range of interventions such as improving work-life balance, improved compensation and rewards, better training and development, etc., among others have been suggested as ways in which employee burnout can be addressed in organizations today (CSP, 2018). In the digital enterprise context as mentioned above, the detrimental effects of multitasking, task switching and the 'always-on' culture has been shown to lead to poor time management practices and overloading of the most capable employees leading to employee burnout (Garton E., 2017).

The symptoms of burnout span the physical, psychological and the behavioral dimensions. On the physiological side, burnout is associated with chronic fatigue, lowered immunity, back pain, muscle ache, change in appetite, disturbed sleeping, dizziness and palpitations, etc. Among the psychological dimensions associated with burnout, evidence suggests symptoms such as irritability, inability to relax, feelings of helplessness, loss of motivation, pessimism, decreased satisfaction and sense of accomplishment. These factors lead to specific behaviors such as withdrawal from key responsibilities, delay, absenteeism, social and emotional isolation (Bianchi, Schonfeld, & Laurent, 2018) .

Specific Challenges in Employee Wellbeing: Workplace Depression

Among the growing areas of concern within the workplace is the phenomenon of workplace depression. In the US alone, workplace depression costs over $51 billion in absenteeism and lost productivity and $26 billion in direct treatment costs. It is especially challenging since depression tends to impact people in their prime working age and could potentially last a lifetime if left untreated (Mental Health America, 2019). Symptoms of depression include persistent sad, anxious or "empty" moods, sleep related problems, appetite and weight fluctuations, loss of interest in activities, restlessness, irritability, persistent physical symptoms, concentration problems, fatigue, guilt and thoughts of suicide or death. Its prevalence in the workplace is compounded by the fact that people often do not seek help due to fears that it might influence their job, resulting in job loss and related adverse consequences. Other concerns associated with workplace depression being unaddressed range from lack of awareness of depression as a manageable illness and stigma associated with depression as well as with other mental health conditions such as stress and anxiety (Mental Health America, 2019).

The areas above are a representative description of a wider landscape of research and practitioner challenges in the organizational behavior, HR and management landscape spanning a diversity of topics, methodological approaches and outcomes of interest. Taken together these insights highlight not only the prevalence of wellbeing challenges in the organizational context, but also suggest the need for a greater understanding of these challenges from a business standpoint with the ultimate goal of not only prevention of adverse events for the individual but also promotion of positive mental health outcomes for the employee at work.

The main challenges in managing mental health in the enterprise context range from issues such as stigma, lack of awareness of the importance of mental health as well as low awareness of the resources available for mental health. If detected early, many of the mental health issues at the workplace, whether they manifest as stress, anxiety, depression or burnout can be managed by therapy and / or medication. Early identification of these issues is therefore critical for preventive interventions and management. Another key facet of mental health issues in the workplace are that while symptoms can emerge over time, they can be also be triggered by specific events at work and/or life in general. These might impact both the physical as well as the mental health of the individual; and therefore while the symptoms of low or fluctuating mood or cognition occur, these are often coupled by other physiological symptoms such as fatigue, sleeplessness, loss of appetite, etc., or contextual demands of high work pressure, job complexity, personal issues, etc. Therefore, the need for individual as well as contextual or environmental sensing is needed for preventive strategies for mental health and their management.. These issues are also reflective of wellbeing measurement and management as wicked problems, in that wellbeing in organizations is multidimensional, difficult to measure using a single approach, has issues related to privacy, trust and data ownership. Each of these issues are to be negotiated by a set of approaches that are inherently human-centered but also scalable to reach a wider population facing a growing set of wellbeing related challenges.

The above challenges call for a technology-driven, well rounded approach to longitudinally measuring and enhancing mental health in the workplace, grounded in the context of the organization itself as well as anchored in the individual's own past experiences in the workplace and other contextual events. Another need is that of evidence from past research and practice to suggest the prevalence of mental health conditions as well as evidence of suitable measurement and interventions in mental health and wellbeing. Further, the individual's right to privacy and confidentiality is another key challenge in enabling better adoption to mental health services in the workplace. Reach and scalability of mental health solutions are other priority areas for workplace stress, depression and anxiety. Given the low prevalence of skilled doctors and therapists worldwide, the need for a technology-based approach becomes even more acute.

Associate Learning and Integrated Learning Environment

Emerging Expectations of Enterprises and Associates

With the emergence of what commentators are calling Industry 4.0, today's enterprises are embracing advanced digitalization, bringing smart connected systems, products, and services into the forefront of their customer offerings (Deloitte Insights, 2018) (PWC, 2016). This has resulted in enterprises looking both to hire a workforce who are in tune with these technological advancements as well as the means to train the existing workforce to accept, welcome and leverage these changes so as to bring new products and services to the market by leveraging disruptive innovative technologies. A new-age enterprise expects its associates to be agile in their behavior, be proactive in learning and collaborative activities, embrace calculated risks and harness the power of new-age technologies both for personal growth as well as locate develop new business opportunities for the enterprise (Tata Consultancy Services Limited, 2019). Now the mantra for new age associates is to be an agile and proactive learner on a continual basis. Associates, today, have easy access to information through the internet and social media. They are also well connected with their counterparts across the globe. Having said that, associates prefer enterprises that help them to maintain their personal interests and wellbeing while choosing the destination of work.

The paradigm shift of enterprises towards various versions of Industry 4.0 also compels existing working population to adapt and become capable and competitive given changing job demands and the job market. This requires them to be continually updated with the knowledge and experience of the latest technologies and global practices, and avail mentorship and decision making support for both professional work and personal wellbeing. An enterprise that facilitates career growth, that transparently provides role clarity, enables effective communication between leaders, associates, and clients, and provides recognition is always desirable by an associate. Associates are no more interested in transactional roles or jobs but looking for fulfilling rich experiences, which add meaning to their lives and heft to their resumes. In an arena filled with tough competition, these individual rich experiences are the differentiators. Work culture and how associates are treated by various stakeholders help build their experiences.

Associate Onboarding and Integration Challenges

Every large enterprise takes on board a constant stream of new associates joining its ranks either due to a need to bring vital new skills and experience in growth areas or as replacements to existent skilled associates. Each new associate brings distinct aspirations, prior experience, skills, expectations, life situation, culture as compared to other associates. However most enterprises tend to roll out a single non-individualised induction and integration service that is ruthlessly applied to all. This generic service often fails to understand and accommodate the problems, aspirations and needs of the large pool of associates who happen to be from various domains, expertise, experience and roles. Furthermore, one generic integration service often does not embrace the cultural and geographical diversity of its associate pool, which reflects back negatively on the associate's acculturation with the enterprise.

Enterprises have a daunting task of being desirable to digital native, new generation candidates, as well as be innovative to its competition. This requires the enterprise to innovate and enforce massive changes to its training and learning platforms, talent acquisition and resource management services, and offer a seamless journey experience to its associates. Some of the most prominent factors and dimensions for associate integration as shown in **Error! Reference source not found.** are organizational clarity (Lyons, 1971), cohesion (Chin, Salisbury, Pearson, & Stollak, 1999), acculturation, collaboration, and domain learning (Anderson, 2001). A large enterprise usually has multiple channels, stakeholders and access procedures to offer services to the associate so as to facilitate domain learning activities, acculturation and build organizational and role clarity. Hence, it is important that these services are coherently interlinked and provide an associate a seamless integration journey.

Figure 1. Dimensions of associate integration

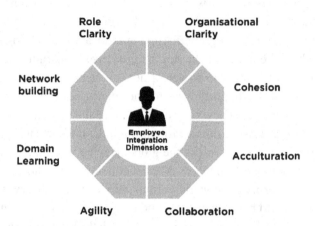

The journey of associate learning starts from the point they join the organization till they leave the organization. Learning is an essential part of getting an associate ready for a project or workspace requiring specific skills. However, associates are often required to move from that project or workspace to other projects requiring differing skills spanning other technology domains. It is essential therefore for an associate to continually update their learning with regard to competency in the newer domains where they have to operate as well as competency in interpersonal skills such as being able to communicate efficiently with teams and clients. However, allocating dedicated work-days for learning activities is often a large cost to the company with a loss in project time. To mitigate this, the enterprise needs to offer the associate opportunities, channels, time, and behavioural nudges for regular self-learning activity which an associate can undertake along with day-to-day work. This will not just reduce the time of an associate to be project ready but also facilitate the enterprise to leverage on individual competencies for building creative, innovative solutions. *Figure 1* shows some of the associate integration aspects need to look at while designing the interventions. The challenge within a digital enterprise is how this can be done using a variety of digital means.

Associate Experience Scenarios

It is being observed that the current associate onboarding and integration mainly focusses on information dissemination. Most times information is provided from the enterprise's perspective without considering the actual needs of individual associates. During a user research study we conducted, it was observed that associates are looking for fulfilling experiences, which are meaningful to them. Associate experiences are formed from all the interactions that one has with the enterprise they are employed in. This often becomes the main criteria of how one perceives their value in the enterprise, clarity of their role, and their relationship with the employer. By understanding associate goals, challenges, and perceptions, designing a positive associate experience is critical to building long-term relationships with associates and reduce attrition (Dukes, 2019). A good associate experience often etches a strong value perception in the minds of its associates, begetting work ownership, job loyalty, and proactivity towards business

Figure 2. Associate integration aspects

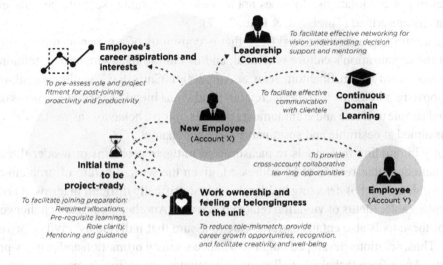

innovation and development. It is imperative to say that a good associate experience often reflects directly on the company culture and experiences of the clients and customers in their interactions with the company. Today the role of HR has evolved from maintenance and mitigation of compliance issues to facilitate the creation of an ecosystem that is associate centric (Branson, 2018). HR is now looked upon as a partner in the associate's career development and not as a mere transactional help provider.

In this era, digital technology is playing a crucial role in facilitating and inducing behaviour change as well as making employees ready to face tomorrow's challenges. Design thinking and service design methodologies also serve as a foundation for enterprises to conceive effective and experiential solutions to complex problems in the organizational sector. Training enterprise functions towards developing a holistic view of problems and engaging in systemic design of services will generate low rate of service failures, efficient recovery mechanisms and integrated use of advanced technologies to be constantly and appropriately informed. Thus, a well-designed continual learning environment both for the new employees as well as the existing employees who support enterprise functions is imperative for enterprises to generate higher revenue and share a symbiotic relationship with all the stakeholders in the ecosystem.

Compliance to Information Security

Enterprise Information Security: Problems and Challenges

Detrimental security-related behaviors have been identified in the information security literature from different perspectives. Researchers (Guo, Yuan, Archer, & Connelly, 2011) have consolidated the undesirable behaviors to include computer abuse (e.g. Data theft, unauthorized use), IS misuse (e.g. Use unlicensed software, access confidential information), security contravention (e.g. Software piracy, steal information, crack passwords), unethical use (e.g. Illegal software copying, hacking competitors' systems), IS security policy violation (e.g. Copy sensitive data to USB drives, disabling security configurations, revealing confidential information to outsiders), and security omissive behaviors (e.g. Not changing passwords, not back up, not update security patches. Although a security policy of organization may specify what end users should (or should not) do with organizational IS assets, and spell out the consequences of policy violations, this does not necessarily guarantee security because end users may not always act as prescribed (Turel, Xu, & Guo, 2017).

In aiming at building a resilient workforce that is conscious of a cyber-secure culture, it has been realized that the organization's culture is critical, and its culture must emphasize, reinforce, and drive behavior toward security (Lim, Shanton, Sean, & Atif, 2009) (Chris, n.d.). Building a cultural ecosystem to meet the above requirements will mean creating a judicious blend of various elements of technology, processes, and people to create and communicate policies, inform behaviors as well as design and deploy interventions aimed at desirable and sustainable behavior change.

Specifically in building these tools to measure and mitigate problems of insider threat, there are a number of challenges that remain to be addressed, given the wicked nature of problem as mentioned earlier. The problem intent of detecting insider threat is specifically difficult in terms of arriving at measures that explain antecedents of violation related behaviors. Another significant challenge in this space is that, use of these tools also entails extreme care to assure that individuals' civil or privacy rights are not violated. Thus, solutions developed ought to balance security promotion and privacy preservation at the same time. Apart from technical challenges of continuous unobtrusive measurements, there is also the challenge of communicating the purpose of data collection given the GDPR laws.

Specific Problems in Information Security

Specifically, when it comes to dealing with insider threat two important classes of problems are encountered. One is the prevalence of Non Malicious Security Violations (NMSV), which is defined as a violation which is intentional in nature, is a self-benefiting activity without malicious intent, involves voluntary rule breaking and has the possibility of causing damage or security risk (Guo, Yuan, Archer, & Connelly, 2011). An example of a security violation that is non malicious in nature is a case where employees transfer official content over personal mails or might be using pen drives to transfer data from laptops. The other is a violation that is malicious in nature, where an insider (current to former employee) has intentionally exceeded or intentionally used that access in a manner that negatively affected the confidentiality, integrity, availability, or physical well-being of the organization's information, information systems, or workforce (CERT National Insider Threat Center, 2018).

Information security research has looked at a number of end user security behaviors, presenting empirical evidence on the various behavioral influences that lead to compliant or non-compliant behaviors. Certain reasons as to why violations occur are attributed to factors such as perceived non-traceability of a violation (Chatterjee, Sarker, & Valacich, 2015) or to situations where there are goal conflicts – where it is found that performance goals always take precedence over compliance requirements, and thus violations can take place to address a performance goal (Peter, Nina, Ronja, Melanie, & Vogt, 2017). Biases are also found to play a role, which affect the way we think and act. For example, a bias can influence individuals to perceive benefits of violation more rather than the consequences of it, or can lead individuals to engage in excessive risk taking (Kahneman, Lovallo, & Sibony, 2011). Similarly there could also be malicious motives leading to more planned methods to commit a violation for personal benefits (Myyry, Siponen, Pahnila, Vartiainen, & Vance, 2009). On the other hand, aspects such as intrinsic motivation and moral standards that people set for themselves (Pahnila, Siponen, & Mahmood, 2007), Organizational Citizenship Behaviors, (which concerns a person's voluntary commitment to act on the organization's interest) (Ifinedo, 2015) and work group norms i.e. how information security practices are perceived to be followed in work groups (Bulgurcu, Cavusoglu, & Benbasat, 2010), (Guo, Yuan, Archer, & Connelly, 2011) are known to increase compliance in IS context.

Past studies (Beautement, Angela, & Mike, 2009), (Bulgurcu, Cavusoglu, & Benbasat, 2010), (Cram, Jeffrey, & D'Arcy, 2017) also suggest that the key factors in the compliance decision are the actual and anticipated cost and benefits of compliance to the individual employee, and perceived cost and benefits to the organization. Perceived costs of compliance include increased physical load, increased cognitive load, time consumed to meet requirements, missed opportunities and a perceived hassle factor. Perceived benefits of compliance include avoiding the consequences of a security breach and protection from sanctions. External factors that influence compliance include design, awareness, training, and education, the culture of the organization, monitoring and sanctions.

Understanding Information Security Behaviors

If information security violations were to be decoded from a behavioral standpoint, they can be attributed broadly to the following reasons:

- **Inadvertence:** Negligent behavior of employees due to lack of awareness, cognitive limitations including biases and mental models
- **Inability:** Lack of ability to comply due to reasons such as lack of self-efficacy, task ambiguity, or time pressure although there may be awareness and intent to comply
- **Intentional:** Non-compliance with malicious intentions of creating harm to individuals / organizations.

We can also see that information security threats can emanate from different classes of employees - a newly joined employee who is unaware of risks due to violations, or from a careless employee although experienced, or an employee who violate norms for a self -benefit without a malicious intent, or a privileged insider who has access to valuable information and can have a malicious intention for violation of norms. It would be interesting to find patterns in such violations among employee categories in the organizational context to map appropriate interventions, however such research evidence is currently sparse. Different sources of threats would need different detection mechanisms ranging from monitoring to using advanced analytics such as UEBA (User Entity Behavior Analytics) to advanced insider intelligence methods (Litan, 2018)

From a psychological standpoint, workplace disgruntlement and employee dissatisfaction are identified as two key underlying causes of deviance in the workplace and organizational crime (Willison & Warkentin, 2009). When an individual has unsatisfied expectations of the organization, they might be motivated to address the expectations through malicious action against the organization. The findings by (Keeney, et al., 2005) reveal that 85% of the insiders identified in their study experienced grievances before carrying out attacks and in 92% of the sabotage cases the grievance was related to employment. Personality traits such as Machiavellianism, excitement-seeking, and Narcissism were found to relate to insider threats and antisocial behaviour (Shaw & Stock, 2011) (E.T, Sticha, Brdiczka, & Shen, 2013)

Organizations are now are taking one further step to identify groups or individuals early in the threat life cycle: predictive insider-persona analytics (McKinsey, 2018). Organizations can identify the markers of these personas and actively monitor these markers for specific personas, rather than looking for divergence from normal. This analysis can identify a group or individual likely to represent a threat well before the event takes place; companies can then take steps to mitigate the threat.

That said another stream of literature looks at the role of positive incentives with regard to mitigation of insider threat. Instead of solely focusing on making sure employees do not misbehave, positive incentives create a work environment where employees are internally driven to contribute to the organization only in positive ways. There is evidence to suggest that positive incentives such as better job engagement, organizational support and connectedness at workplace can deter insider misbehavior in a constructive way from the outset of the employee-organization relationship (Moore, et al., 2016) . In combination with traditional practices, positive incentives offer the possibility of a more balanced and constructive organizational approach to reducing the insider threat with fewer negative consequences.

Thus, focusing on early-stage detection of at-risk behaviors and moreover, a focus on the prevention of employee alienation by fostering positive attitudes about the organization and the employee's work experience is also seen to add value, for which, necessary interventions that are technology driven are needed and discussed in the sections below.

TECHNOLOGY FOR THE PEOPLE ENTERPRISE

The digital enterprise from a people perspective would be a seamlessly integrated set of technologies that puts people in better control of their lives. A necessary change of perspective is that we need to see technology as a vehicle for people, rather than, for a business or an enterprise. The technologies should serve people by engaging them, providing desirable experiences, helping them work and play together while remaining well aligned to the business goals. This would serve to address the challenges articulated within wellbeing and norm compliance sections as being wicked problems. These problems are inherently unsolvable, however these need constant interventions that will help keep them under check. This necessitates creation of technologies and platforms that cater to different aspects of the problem. Towards this objective, we present the core elements of process and technology components to enable this to happen. To aid a better understanding of the technologies and their role in the enterprise, we classify them into three classes, viz. engage, sense and intervene. A discussion on these classes and the relationship between them follows.

The Engage-Sense-Intervene Cycle

The scenarios discussed in the previous sections have something in common, which is that, a certain behaviour change is expected of people. Whether it is associates wanting to improve their own wellbeing, or someone who is adjusting to a role change or a security officer seeking to improve compliance to policies, all require people to exhibit behaviour change.

Every behaviour change process requires a sense and intervene mechanism. The "sense" mechanism, as the names implies, senses or understands the current state of the behaviour. The "intervene" mechanism is expected to recommend an action that causes the behaviour to change to the target or desired state. It is evident that in order for the "sense" mechanism to get access to the individual and for the "intervene" mechanism to get delivered, it would be necessary to have systems that "engage" the people through the behaviour change process. This forms the third core element of the behaviour change process. The "engage" layer is essentially the front end of the digital enterprise. People interact with this layer.

Figure 3, is a visual depiction of the three elements. The items mentioned in each of the boxes are examples of the kind of technologies and designs that are being applied to solve problems in each area. We dwell upon the promises, state of the art and open challenges in some of these areas, in the following sub-sections.

Figure 3. The engage-sense-intervene cycle

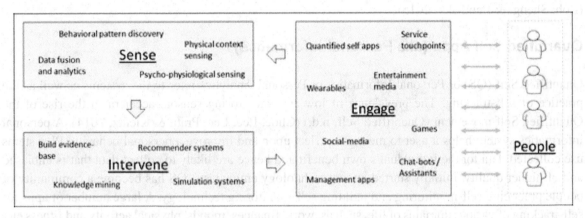

Technology Enablers for "Engage"

Human Computer Interaction designers and researchers have been continuously working on making these systems engaging and providing an immersive experience. While there exist newer ways of engaging people like augmented reality, virtual reality etc. this space is largely dominated by designers who create designs that connect with people.

Designing systems that are engaging, transparent and can gather meaningful information from people is critical for the success of the digital enterprise. We discuss two powerful designs viz. purposeful games and quantified self apps that are aimed at this very purpose. We also discuss the overarching space of service design and its role in achieving objectives of all stakeholders of the enterprise. This is followed by a discussion on privacy, its impact on user experience and its implications for design and technology.

Purposeful Games

Purposeful games (also called Serious Games) are designed to have an impact on the target audience, which is beyond pure entertainment. Serious games have seen widespread application particularly in learning. (Bellotti, Kapralos, Lee, Moreno-Ger, & Berta, 2013). For example, In the Dragon Box Elements game players have to defeat a dragon and save Euclid's island. In order to do this however, they have to learn basic geometry and Euclid's theorems. Since the game part of good serious games have a fun and sticky element, players keep returning to the game and through that process absorb whatever the serious part is trying to teach or instruct or get across. By exploiting multimodal interaction they can also provide immersive environments where advanced users can practice knowledge and skills. While several purposeful games have been developed, further research is necessary to investigate in greater detail the real effectiveness of the various types of purposeful games (Bellotti, Berta, & De Gloria,

2010). How would stakeholders know what play-learners have done in the game environment, and if the actions performance brings about learning? Could they be playing the game for fun, really learning with evidence of performance improvement, or simply gaming the system, i.e., finding loopholes to fake that they are making progress? (Loh, Sheng, & Ifenthaler, 2015) are all questions that need further user research. Another category of purposeful games are those used for behavioral data collection. In-game behavior may provide indicators of real world behaviors and mental states of players. In-game behavior has been of great interest and has given rise to a community and sub area of serious game analytics. (Loh, Sheng, & Ifenthaler, 2015)

Quantified Self Apps (aka Personal Informatics)

Quantified Self (QS) or Personal Informatics or Personal Analytics refer to the systems as well as the practice of self-tracking. The prevalence of low cost monitoring sensors accelerated the rise of the Quantified Self movement (Quantified Self, n.d.) (Choe, Lee, Lee, Pratt, & Kientz, 2014). A personal informatics system helps a user to measure, reflect upon and improve a personal behavior. PI systems use collected data for the individual's own benefit and hence are likely to collect data that is unbiased and of higher quality. Initially started among technology enthusiasts, QS has become a community of people practicing self-monitoring and building self-monitoring technology. A large number of apps for self-tracking of various domains of life, such as, work, finances, moods, physical activity and fitness etc. are available for free on the internet and have empowered people to take charge of their lives. Although the value of self-tracking technologies has been widely acknowledged, researchers have also discovered a long list of barriers toward the adoption of self-tracking technologies. These barriers included lack of time, insufficient motivation, unsuitable visualization and analytics tools, poor skills for analyzing data, and fragmented data scattered across multiple platforms (Li, Dey, & Forlizzi, 2010) (Choe, Lee, Lee, Pratt, & Kientz, 2014). Specific areas for future research include exploring ways to provide early feedback, to support designing rigorous self-experimentation, to leverage the benefits of—while easing the burden of—manual tracking, and to promote self-reflection. Once a motivated tracker meets a well-designed self-tracking tool, exciting possibilities will arise for gaining insights for health, wellness, and other aspects of life. (Choe, Lee, Lee, Pratt, & Kientz, 2014)

Service Touch Point Design for Enhanced User Experience

We need to design for experiences that reach people through different touch-points and where these points are human as well as technology, and which happen over time (Live Work Studio, 2013) Newer interfaces such as surfaces, augmented reality interfaces, smart devices not only provide immersive experiences but coupled with artificial intelligence based analytics allows us to deliver services with a personalized experience to employees. An example of how these technologies might transform learning is the newer breed of micro-learning platforms that are being developed. These not only make learning easy to consume but also makes it engaging and fun. For example, mLevel is a micro-learning and gamification solution that aims to boost corporate training efforts and offer employees a gamified, engaging and rewarding way of training (MLEVEL, 2019). This is in stark contrast with the traditional classroom model where the end user experience was not so much in focus. Artificial Intelligence technologies are enabling the creation of bots, assistants and self-service apps that eliminate the need for support staff and empower employees to get the help they need just-in-time and feel fully in charge of their life. An example of such a bot is Cara, a HR assistant that can answer queries about any policy in a leading IT organization. It is backed by an AI conversational agent platform that uses AI and NLP technologies (Tata Consultancy Services, 2016). Such a bot not only reduces the load on HR staff, but also improves the employee experience by providing them information in real-time. While using digital technology extensively, the human in the loop model is critical to maintain the human touch to provide a meaningful and fulfilling experience. Technology access points to collect and disseminate the information along with the personalized multi-channel interventions can play a crucial role in integrating the employees in the organizations (Kulkarni & Rajamani, 2017)It my however be an error to look at service experience as the only end goal. Behaviour change varies from micro in nature such as influencing buying behaviour to large-scale social changes like lifestyle changes. It is evident that usually there are many stakeholders involved in any situation and therefore the question arises as to whose preferences are to be addressed for design intervention. (Mahamuni, Khambete, & Mokashi-Punekar, 2019) have represented this as 'empathy square' (Figure 4) that combines the important dimensions such as perspectives from the service user, society and environment, human touchpoints such as service staff and service organization like governments or businesses. The empathy square comes handy to scrutinize the service designs from the perspective of four prime stakeholders. It also forms the basis of a Behaviour Progression Framework being developed by them.

Data Privacy

In the context of digitizing of an enterprise, a key concern of the engagement layer is that of data privacy. To create an engaging experience, the system needs to gather enough data about the individual so that a personalized experience may be delivered, however such a data collection might compromise the privacy of the user or the security of the user's personal data. Regulations such as the General Data Protection Regulation (GDPR) provide guidelines on building systems that safe guard the user's inherent right to control personal information, however these also add design elements to the system that affect the user experience. For example, users having to go through difficult to understand consent forms, not once but time and time again. Given the criticality of privacy in the digital era, there has been a drive towards the value-sensitive approach of "Privacy by design". (Langheinrich, 2001) develops six principles for guiding system design, based on a set of fair information practices common in most privacy legislation in use today: notice, choice and consent, proximity and locality, anonymity and pseudonymity, security, and access and recourse. Privacy by design calls for privacy to be taken into account throughout the whole engineering process. Apart from designing for user experience, privacy enhancing technologies (PETs) help engineer systems for privacy. PETs include encryption tools, data masking and obfuscation techniques, anonymizers, consent management systems, tools for enforcement of data handling conditions and infrastructure to allow users to inspect, correct or delete all their data.

Technology Enablers for "SENSE"

The "Sensing" element comprises of the whole process of capturing data, analyzing and interpreting it. This involves the very basic act of measuring the phenomena using sensors, to performing analytics on the data to attaching meaning to it. Data science techniques such as fusion of data from multiple sources, pattern discovery, data analytics are all necessities of this space. Artificial Intelligence (AI) techniques, such as machine/deep learning are used to develop algorithms that can learn and detect various human

Figure 4. Empathy square (Mahamuni, Khambete, & Mokashi-Punekar, 2019)

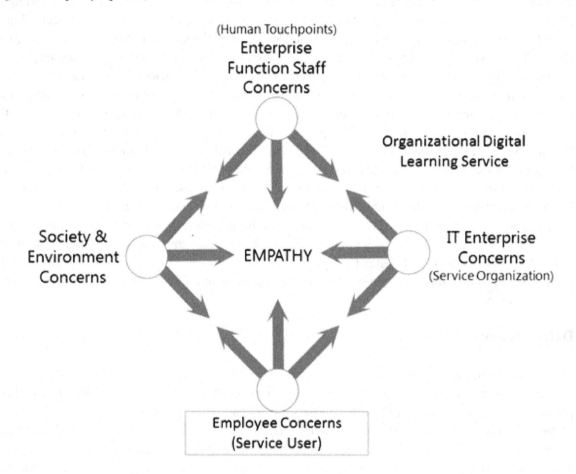

factors from sensor observations. AI techniques also help discover patterns in data and build predictive models for forecasting/intervention. In this section, we describe how psycho-physiological sensing and physical context discovery enable us to gain richer insights into human behavior.

Psychophysiological Sensing

New developments in the signal processing, physiological sensing and machine learning technologies have enabled the measurement of a wide range of behaviors. Wearables and mobile devices are now capable of measuring physical activity, sleep patterns, heart rates with a fair degree of accuracy. Newer techniques are being developed that will help measure a variety of factors such as stress, fatigue, cognitive load and so on. Traditionally self-reports have been used to measure subjective experiences. These involve participant introspection and self-ratings of internal psychological states or physiological sensations, and have the possibility of participants misunderstanding a scale or incorrect recall of the experience. Physiological responses also can be measured via instruments that read bodily events such as heart rate change, electrodermal activity (EDA), muscle tension, and cardiac output. Brain waves (electroencephalography, EEG), fMRI (functional magnetic resonance imaging) provide immense possibility to measure and understand brain activity. Electrodermal activity (skin conductance response or galvanic skin response) has been shown to accurately assess arousal and consequently stress levels. Cardiovascular measures (heart rate, HR; beats per minute, BPM; heart rate variability, HRV; vasomotor activity) also hold potential for measurement of affective states. Changes in pupil diameter with thought and emotion (pupillometry), eye movements have been used to measure phenomena such as attention. (Cacioppo, Tassinary, & Berntson, 2007) These measures are beneficial because they provide accurate and objective data about the mind and body. A survey on psycho-physiological analysis and measurement methods (Baig & Kavakli, 2019), presents a detailed list of studies that use these kind of measures. The survey concludes that the classification accuracy of >90% has been achieved in classifying emotions with EEG signals. A strong correlation between self-reported data, HCI experience, and psychophysiological data has been observed in a wide range of domains including games, human-robot interaction, mobile interaction, and simulations. The downsides, however, are that any physical activity or motion can alter responses, and basal levels of arousal and responsiveness can differ among individuals and even between situations. Many of these sensors are contact based, which means that they have electrodes connected to the body of the subject. This makes the measurement very inconvenient and prone to errors caused by movement. Further, sensor signals could easily be contaminated with uncertain noises or interferences and responses to these signals could also be different for different persons. In such cases, when analyzing sensor measurements, multiple sensors could provide more robust and reliable decisions. In recent years, sensor data fusion is becoming an emerging technology and researchers are applying new methods and techniques to introduce sensor fusion in various domains. (Begum, Barua, & & Ahmed). *Table 1* is a summary of some interesting phenomena that sensors are able to measure.

Table 1. Use of sensors for behavioral measurement

#	Sensor Name	Measures	Behaviours / States
1	Accelerometer	Movement	Physical activity, fitness behaviour, sleep patterns
2	Photoplethysmography (PPG)	Heart rate, breathing patterns	Stress, anxiety, palpitations, fluid retention
3	Galvanic skin response (GSR sensor)	Electro dermal activity	Stress, Restlessness, anxiety
4	Microphone	Speech/Voice	Emotional Valence, Stress,
5	Eye tracker	Pupil movement	Concentration, attention, emotion, cognitive load
6	Electrencephalogram (EEG)	Brain activity	Cognitive load,
7	Camera	Image/Video	Emotion, Activity,

Physical Context Sensing

While psycho-physiological sensing measures aspects of the individual, the context is to do with the situation, circumstances, environment, location the individual is situated in. The ubiquity of computing devices owing to use of mobiles, IOT have enabled a wide variety of contextual factors to be measured. Important sensors used are GPS (for location and speed), light and vision (to detect objects and activities), microphones (for information about noise, activities, and talking), accelerometers and gyroscopes (for movement, device orientation, and vibration), magnetic field sensors (as a compass to determine orientation), proximity and touch sensing (to detect explicit and implicit user interaction), sensors for temperature and humidity (to assess the environment), and air pressure/barometric pressure. (Nielsen, 2013). Fusion of data from multiple sensors holds the possibility of generating new contextual information. For example, an accelerometer in the user mobile may detect the movement caused by a travelling vehicle, while the GPS may provide information on location and speed. Together with the daily activity patterns detected from the devices used by the individual, we would be able to find out if the individual is on his daily commute to work. Authors of (Servia-Rodríguez, et al., 2017) presented an Android app that used physical and software sensors in smartphones to automatically and accurately identify routines. They measured location traces using GPS, amplitude/noise levels using microphone, social activity using messages and phone calls, and survey to measure psychological variables. They demonstrate the strong correlation between these routines and users' personality, well-being perception, and other psychological variables. They were able to use passive mobile sensing to predict users' mood with an accuracy of about 70%. While the promises of physical sensing are immense, there exist some issues with continuous context sensing — in particular that the energy required to sense continuously is high enough that the user notices. This problem becomes particularly difficult when multiple sensing tasks, such as activity recognition and indoor location, need to run concurrently. In this situation, it becomes hard to optimise the energy consumption of the sensing as the benefits gained in one task could be overridden by the higher rate sensing (for accuracy reasons) of another task. (Balan, Lee, Wee, & Misra, 2014)

Detection of Non-Compliance Threats

In cybersecurity domain, current methods and security tools available to help cybersecurity professionals detect and analyze insider attacks include Intrusion Detection and Prevention (IDS/IPS) Log Management and Security Information and Event Management (SIEM) tools. UEBA solutions look at patterns of human behavior, and then apply algorithms and statistical analysis to detect meaningful anomalies from those patterns—anomalies that indicate potential threats (Sandle, 2018). Approaches to detect insider threats also could look at data mining non-security related data in employee records, from enterprise social networks, or from fraud detection networks. That is, data obtained from violations of policy in one area of employment could relate to a propensity to commit violations in information security (Crossler, Johnston, Lowry, & Hud, 2013). Research in this domain categorizes the behaviors related to insider threats into four major classes: biometric behaviors, cyber behaviors, communication behaviors, and psychosocial behaviors (Ko, Divakaran, Liau, & Thing, 2017). A classification of detection mechanism is given below:

It may be noted that each behavior class is further composed of several behavior types and the authors allude to the fact that insider threat detection is not a single research field, but a conglomeration of disjoint ones.

Another lens that can be used to understand an insider's pathway is guided by the substantial body of research in counterproductive work behaviors (CWB) – employee behavior that goes against the legitimate interests of the workplace. Literature in this space points to the fact that the stress that results from negative life events on the job and in personal lives can lead, if unmitigated, to problematic behaviors in the workplace. Some of the emotional states that can be antecedents to CWB include the following: anger aggression, negative mood in general, emotional exhaustion and stress (Moore, et al., 2016). There can be many external events or internal perceptions of such events that can provoke general CWB as a

Table 2. Classification of detection mechanisms, Source: (Ko, Divakaran, Liau, & Thing, 2017)

Behavior class	Detected threat
Biometric behavior Cyber: Mouse & keyboard strokes, User Interface interaction, File search Physical traits: Eye-colour, Face recognition, Thumbprint, Gaze	Masquerading
Communication behavior: Email, Messaging, Telephone, File-sharing / transfers	Collusion
Psycho-social behavior: Friendliness, Attitude against authority, Social media behavior	Sabotage
Cyber behavior: Printing, Web-browsing, Device usage, Login behavior, File access, Download/Upload activities	Information theft

response. Examples of triggers also include the large bodies of literature on job satisfaction, frustration, and perceived stress as predictors of counterproductive behaviors (Marcus & Heinz, 2004) .

While CWB is observed as a predictable phenomenon through analysis of the aforesaid factors, this also suggests that it may be worthwhile to establish an "early warning system" based on a behavioral approach to insider threat with goals of improving early warning of vulnerability (Intelligence and National Security Alliance, 2017). Negative emotions create psychological, physical, and behavioral strains that can result in counterproductive work behaviors and ultimately a major insider act. Sensing of sustained negative emotions among employees in workplace and correlating the same with other metrics such as performance record, incident records etc. can help understand and profile potential insider threats. This entails not only defining behavioral models, but also seeking methodologies and tools that can assist in swift, continuous identification and assessment of risk from insider threat.

The 2017 INSA report also highlights three relevant tools to assess whether an individual may be moving toward a malicious act to include personality mapping, life-event detection, and emotion detection (Intelligence and National Security Alliance, 2017). Employers are seen to recognize the importance of leveraging innovative technology and data sources to monitor and evaluate individuals on a continuous basis towards this. However, it is also to be mentioned that such ongoing scrutiny does not substitute effective personnel security and counterintelligence processes; rather, it provides employers the opportunity to enhance their ability to detect and divert insiders on the critical pathway to dangerous acts.

Technology Enablers for "Intervene"

The most important component in this category is an intervention knowledge-base. Knowledge about interventions exists in a dispersed form in research publications. The infrastructure that enables the digitization of this knowledge and the recommender systems that deliver the interventions to matching profiles together make the intervention delivery possible. Relying on research evidence in one way to decide an intervention. The other way is to create computational models of people and simulate the effects of an intervention on computational agents. A discussion of these two intervention design approaches follows:

Fine Grained Behavior Modelling and Simulation

Simulation models help us get a sense of the dynamics of an environment, understand both current state as well as implications of changes, whether it be change in an environment or change in the behaviour of individuals. Simulation techniques such as agent based simulation (ABS) have been exensively used, to model the behaviour of human populations at varying scales. However, most of these models have trivial agent behaviour involving just a few behaviour rules and are used either by social scientists trying to understand social phenomena such as the formation of ghettos (Schelling, 1969), norm formation or collapse (Axelrod & Hamilton, 1981) or for policy formulation of various kinds (Hidas, 2002), (Nagel K. S., 1997). However these models are unsuited for environments where a multitude of behavioural factors are at play. For example to understand how various forms of stress impact the performance of a work team, we need to be able to factor in personality, positive and negative affect, forms of stress etc as well as the relationship between these factors.

This is challenging since these need to be grounded in behavioural science. The category of models in this space are called Fine Grained ABS (FG-ABS) and methods to build such models have to be precise in order that the constructed model can be justified (Duggirala, Malik, Kumar, & Balaraman, 2017) to how supportive team environments impact outcomes. Figure 5 alongside gives a pictorial view of such a model.

Figure 5. Fine grained behaviour model

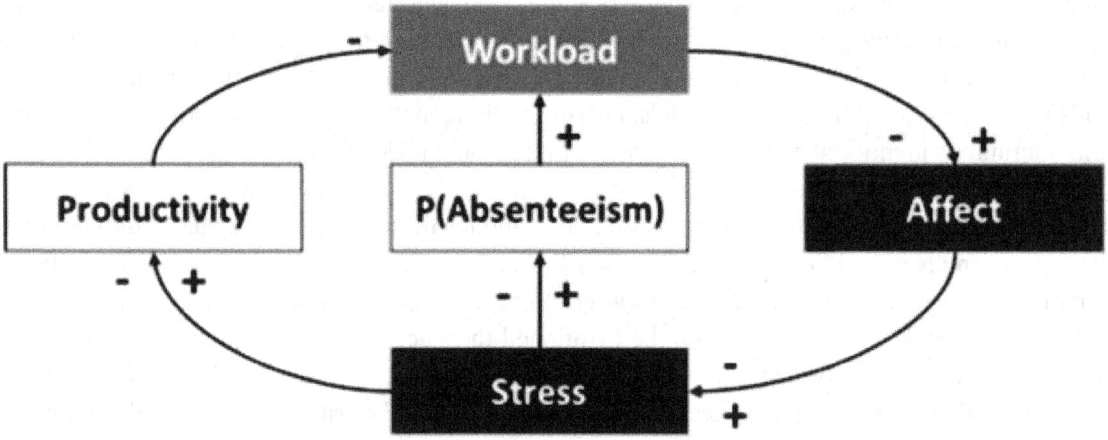

Digital Repositories and Knowledge Mining

The need for repositories as sources of information in a domain has been a critical requirement across scientific disciplines. In medicine for example, the Cochrane Collaboration is the preeminent resource for key stakeholders in healthcare, patients, doctors, nurses etc., to help them make key decisions in healthcare. Like in the physical, material and medical science domains, repositories pertinent to the behavioral and social sciences are also emerging and gaining wider acceptance by the researchers in the management field. The research evidences in the behavioural sciences remain dispersed in the form of research publications. Natural language processing, text mining, machine learning technologies and crowd sourcing platforms are being used to transform these publications into structured behavioural knowledge that can be used as evidences for designing interventions and composing behavioural models for simulation. While these possibilities exist, mining the literature is still a round-about way to generate

Figure 6. Platform for behavior modelling

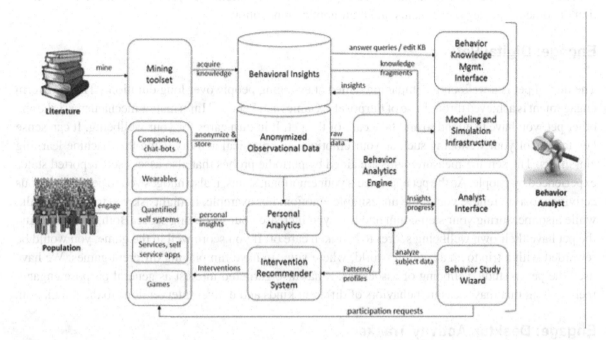

the knowledge-base. The move towards open science will be inevitable going forwards. Open science is the movement to make scientific research (including publications, data, physical samples, and software) and its dissemination accessible to all levels of an inquiring society, amateur or professional. (Woelfle, Olliaro, & Todd, 2011) This would mean that open and online platforms would exist for conducting research and the experiment progress, data collected, empirical evidence generated would all be accessible to the society and could benefit from the knowledge.

The Behavior Modelling Platform

While the technology enablers presented above have their own applications in the enterprise, we believe that a definition of how these will work together is necessary. In this section, we present the schematic of a Behavior Modelling platform. Various platforms for behavior change exist and are aligned to different needs of people. For example Life Dojo is a platform for behavior change and is targeted towards improving employee health. (LifeDojo: Behaviour Change Solution, n.d.). LifeDojo engages employees in a journey of motivation, planning and weekly action that is both scientific and engaging. This is expected to achieve meaningful engagement and lasting behavior change. Another platform on similar lines, is the Behaviour Change for Good Initiative of the University of Pennsylvania. (Behaviour Change for Good Initiative, n.d.). They are developing an interactive digital platform to improve daily decisions about health, education, and savings.

At our organization we have developed a behaviour modelling platform that aims at supporting the entire behavior change life cycle as envisaged in the engage-sense-intervene cycle. The figure below is a schematic that shows the key components in the platform.

The platform and its elements have been applied to study problems in a variety of contexts. A description of some of the key components and their applications follows:

Engage: Digital Pet

The digital pet is a wellbeing companion aimed at engaging people over long durations. The long term engagement is achieved through use of Purposeful Games and Personal Informatics mechanisms. Like any other pet, you have to attend to and take care of the pet. It in turn cares for your wellbeing. It can sense key factors of your wellbeing such as your emotions and physical activity using the machine learning classifiers. The sensing measurements are aided by periodic probes that also assess self-reported states experienced by people. As the pet app detects your emotional states, it also nudges you to perform various activities so as to relieve you of the undesirable emotion. For example, it might ask you to go for a walk, while also measuring your step-count and help you increase your wellbeing score. Both, the player and the pet have their own wellbeing scores to be taken care of. If you score well in the game, you would be rewarded with a trip to an adventure world, where you can have fun playing different games. We have used the pet to study wellbeing of associates. It has also garnered interest as general purpose engagement system that may measure behaviors of different kinds and deliver interventions to the population.

Engage: Desktop Activity Tracker

The desktop activity tracker is a personal monitoring system that tracks user initiated activities performed in the computer. We have used it to study routines of associates in the enterprise. The tracker generates a log of activities performed, which are then classified into various categories of work such as, technical, documentation, communication etc. An analysis of these categories revealed routines that people follow, differences in work patterns of associates in different roles and correlations with key metrics such as associate engagement and productivity. The tool protects privacy of associates by allowing only pattern and correlation level information to be accessed by the study administrators.

Engage: Survey System

The survey app is used to measure various psychological and subjective variables that are difficult to sense using external observations. This tool is a mobile app that has a server component that allows different kinds of surveys to be configured and administered to the associates. We have used the survey app in conjunction with other tools to study a variety of problems such as correlates of absenteeism and productivity in support projects, study of financial behavior in pink collar workers, compliance to information security practices etc.

Engage: Personal Wellbeing Portal

The portal serves as an aggregator of data collected by all the systems mentioned above. It presents personal dashboards to the user based on the data collected. These dashboards aid self-reflection and improvement. Various workflows that engage the user are also made accessible through this portal. The portal provides a self-assessment module that helps associates screen themselves for various mental health conditions and also get various personality tests over the platform. This helps build a richer profile of associates and is useful for studying problems in all contexts. The GDPR features such as ability to get a copy of all personal data, withdraw from the data collection, delete all data from the system etc. are made accessible through this portal. The platform enables researchers to design and publish field studies and recruit volunteers for research. The volunteering requests also appear on this portal and can be used to incentivize associates to participate in behavioral research.

Sense: Affect and Activity Sensing

The sensing library comprises of machine learning / deep learning classifiers that analyze observations made from microphones (voice), camera (images/videos) and text (spoken or typed). We have built algorithms to detect emotion from all three modalities mentioned above. There are integrated into the digital pet app and helps it recognize emotion. We have achieved accuracies in the range of 78 to 85% using these. Other algorithms we have built include detection of activities from daily journals of associates, classification of those activities into classes that represent various domains of life, detection of the expression of stress and sources of stress in the daily journal. Thee accuracies achieved in these ranges from 72% to 80% and these will improved as we get more real world data. The text analysis algorithms that are currently being used to analyze daily journals are also now being integrated in analyzing conversations with chatbots. Another set of algorithms we have developed help make the digital pet more fun to play with, for example, we have developed an algorithm that detects laughter from the microphone and is used to play a game with the pet, where the player has to laugh for certain period of time and intensity to gain certain points in the game. The voice based emotion detector has also been integrated with the desktop activity tracker to study emotion and its correlates with activity. This will help get richer insights from the studies in the norms compliance space. Another application currently being developed is a qualitative survey analysis tool where long interviews taken in the process of service design are analyzed using these algorithms.

Sense: Pattern Discovery

As the name indicates this module performs analytics on the measured behaviors to discover patterns of interest. We have implemented the capability of discovering sequential and repeating patterns in the behaviors measured by the digital pet. Some examples of these patterns being: persistently negative emotional states, lack of physical activity over a period of time, too much physical activity along with frequent negative emotional states and so on. The patterns comprise of both healthy and unhealthy patterns. We also have pattern discovery algorithms built on the desktop activity tracker data that help understand routines of associates. Currently work is in progress on discovering patterns in wellbeing data that can help predict chronic conditions such as burnout and depression. Such predictive modeling will help early detection of associates tending towards the chronic conditions and help arrest the condition in time. Sensing of sustained negative emotions among employees in workplace and correlating the same with other metrics such as performance record, incident records etc. is used to understand potential insider threats. For example, detecting emotional change is critical to understanding the individual's level of stress and can help in identification of an 'at-risk' employee.

Intervene: Knowledge Mining Toolkit

The platform contains a "Behavior Knowledge Base", semi-automatically mined from the behavioural sciences literature. It comprises of behavioral insights mined from the behavioral sciences literature. It also contains evidence for interventions that have been validated in the field. This is a set of software components that enable the creation of the behavioral knowledge base. It comprises of a crawler, a document classifier, section classifier, and NLP routines that mine the target knowledge fragments into the repository. We have mined about 6000 papers from the social sciences literature to build this knowledge base of interventions and behavioral relations.

Intervene: Intervention Recommender

This module is responsible for finding a matching intervention for a give pattern discovered in the data. It leverages the Behavior Knowledge base to choose the intervention. For example, if a user is being sensed to be in a "negative" emotional state for a long period of time, the pattern discovery module would discover this as an unhealthy pattern and would find a matching intervention for such a condition in the repository. If a match is found that intervention would be dispatched to the engagement layer (digital pet or the desktop tracker) and the user would be prompted to perform the suggested action, as recommended in the intervention. If no matching intervention is found, an expert such as a psychologist would be asked to enter an intervention for that condition. This features also has applications that will also potentially help to deliver mitigation strategies before a possible malicious / non-compliant activity can take place thus preempting behavior at the right time.

Intervene: Behavior Simulator

The knowledge repository as well as data collected from the field are used to compose behavioral models which help in understanding dynamics of a situation to predicting future behaviors. The behavior simulator module helps create models of stress and productivity at the workplace and enables a variety of what if analyses around the antecedents of workplace stress, work demands, individual needs etc. and their impact on outcomes of interest (Balaraman, Hayatnagarkar, Singh, & Duggirala, 2016). Such models are useful as a sandbox to test a certain intervention before it is deployed on a large scale.

CONCLUSION

In this chapter, we have attempted to discuss some of the people related challenges of a digital enterprise such as workplace wellbeing, improving associate experience and complying with information security norms as well as the multi-disciplinary set of tools and techniques a digital enterprise can use in addressing these challenges. We also discussed the Behavior Modelling Platform, a computational platform to tackle such people related challenges around the Engage-Sense-Intervene model and take the reader through representative components in each of the Engage, Sense and Intervene modules to give the reader a concrete feel for the function and use of the components and how these come together.

The people challenges mentioned in this chapter are of course only representative of the larger space of such challenges within a digital enterprise. Two other examples of such challenges are role fitment or finding the best fit between role and individuals and assisting employees in maintaining work life balance. Each of these challenges require us to engage with them and see how existing approaches can be used or extended to tackle them. Today as the nature of work is being continually reimagined we can imagine that the list of challenges too will change as well. In particular, the increasing capabilities of AI based automation will require digital enterprises to constantly evaluate the balance of work between human and machine. Old roles will perish and new ones come into being. Opportunities and challenges thus will continue to grow and evolve.

REFERENCES

Anderson, L. W. (2001). *A taxonomy for learning, teaching, and assessing: A revision of Bloom's taxonomy of educational objectives, abridged edition*. White Plains.

Araujo, C. (2016, March). The Digital Enterprise Hype Cycle. *Institute for Digital Transformation*. Retrieved from https://www.institutefordigitaltransformation.org/defining-digital-enterprise/

Aravind. (2017). *Technology providing a helping hand to those fighting with mental health issues*. Retrieved from Technology providing a helping hand to those fighting with mental health issues: https://economictimes.indiatimes.com/industry/healthcare/biotech/healthcare/technology-providing-a-helping-hand-to-those-fighting-with-mental-health-issues/articleshow/61083373.cms

Axelrod, R., & Hamilton, W. (1981). The evolution of cooperation. *Science*, *211*(4489), 1390–1396. doi:10.1126cience.7466396 PMID:7466396

Azahar, W. (2017). *Is employee burnout affecting your workforce turnover rate?* Retrieved from Is employee burnout affecting your workforce turnover rate?: https://www.humanresourcesonline.net/employee-burnout-affecting-workforce-turnover-rate/

Baig, M. Z., & Kavakli, M. (2019). A Survey on Psycho-Physiological Analysis & Measurement Methods in Multimodal Systems. In *Multimodal Technologies Interact* (pp. 3, 37). Academic Press.

Bailey, A. (2017, March 24). *Future workforce: Defining the digital enterprise leader*. Retrieved from Accenture Website: https://www.accenture.com/gb-en/blogs/blogs-defining-digital-enterprise-leader

Bailey, A. (2017, February 21). *Future Workforce: The network organization*. Retrieved from Accenture Website: https://www.accenture.com/gb-en/blogs/blogs-future-workforce-network-organisation

Bailey, A. (2017, March 10). *Future Workforce: Fragmentation*. Retrieved from Accenture Website: https://www.accenture.com/gb-en/blogs/blogs-future-workforce-fragmentation

Balan, R. K., Lee, Y., Wee, T. K., & Misra, A. (2014). The challenge of continuous mobile context sensing. *Sixth International Conference on Communication Systems and Networks (COMSNETS)*, 1-8. 10.1109/COMSNETS.2014.6734869

Balaraman, V., Hayatnagarkar, H., Singh, M., & Duggirala, M. (2016). *Towards better crisis management in support services organizations using fine grained agent based simulation*. Phuket, Thailand: PRIMA. doi:10.1007/978-3-319-44832-9_24

Banks, J. C. J. (1984). Discrete Event Simulation. Prentice Hall.

Barrett, P. (2019). *Digital wellbeing: caring for employees in an 'always on' culture.* Retrieved from https://www.hrzone.com/lead/future/digital-wellbeing-caring-for-employees-in-an-always-on-culture

Beautement, A., Angela, S., & Mike, W. (2009). The Compliance Budget: Managing Security Behaviour in Organisations. In *Proceedings of the 2008 Workshop on New Security Paradigms* (pp. 47–58). ACM.

Begum, S., Barua, S., & Ahmed, M. U. (2014, July 3). Physiological sensor signals classification for healthcare using sensor data fusion and case-based reasoning. *Sensors (Basel), 14*(7), 11770–11785. doi:10.3390140711770 PMID:24995374

Behaviour Change for Good Initiative. (n.d.). Retrieved from Wharton, University of Pennsylvania: https://bcfg.wharton.upenn.edu/

Bellotti, F., Berta, R., & De Gloria, A. (2010). Designing Effective Serious Games: Opportunities and Challenges for Research. *International Journal of Emerging Technologies in Learning*, 22-35.

Bellotti, F., Kapralos, B., Lee, K., Moreno-Ger, P., & Berta, R. (2013). Assessment in and of Serious Games: An Overview. *Advances in Human-Computer Interaction, 2013*, 1–11. doi:10.1155/2013/136864

Bhattacharyya, R., & Vijayaraghavan, K. (2016). *Retrieved from 46% of workforce in firms in India suffer from some or the other form of stress: Data.* https://economictimes.indiatimes.com/jobs/46-of-workforce-in-firms-in-india-suffer-from-some-or-the-other-form-of-stress-data/articleshow/52696795.cms

Bianchi, R., Schonfeld, I., & Laurent, E. (2018). Burnout syndrome and depression. In Y. Kim (Ed.), Understanding depression: Volume 2. Clinical manifestations, diagnosis and treatment (pp. 187-202). Singapore: Springer. doi:10.1007/978-981-10-6577-4_14

Blau, A. (2017, December). Better Cybersecurity Starts with Fixing Your Employees' Bad Habits. *Harvard Business Review*.

Bose, A. (2017). *The illness India doesn't recognise: Why we cannot afford to ignore mental health.* Retrieved from The illness India doesn't recognise: Why we cannot afford to ignore mental health: https://www.moneycontrol.com/news/trends/health-trends/the-illness-that-india-doesnt-recognise-why-we-cannot-afford-to-ignore-mental-health-2384243.html

Branson, C. (2018, Dec 20). *Employee Experience Designer: The New Role of HR.* Retrieved from HR Daily Advisor: https://hrdailyadvisor.blr.com/2018/03/22/new-role-hr-employee-experience-designer/

Bubna, R., Raveendran, J., Kumar, S., Duggirala, M., & Malik, M. (2018). A partially grounded agent based model on demonetization outcomes in India. *Summer Simulation Conference*.

Bulgurcu, B., Cavusoglu, H., & Benbasat, I. (2010). Information security policy compliance: An empirical study on rationality-based beliefs and information security awareness. *Management Information Systems Quarterly, 34*(3), 523–548. doi:10.2307/25750690

Cacioppo, J., Tassinary, L., & Berntson, G. (2007). *Handbook of Psychophysiology*. Cambridge University Press.

Cassenti, D. (2009). *Performance Moderated Functions Server's (PMFserv) Military Utility: A Model and Discussion*. Army Research Laboratory.

Casti, J. (2000). BizSim - Business in a box. *Artificial Life and Robotics*, *4*(3), 125–129. doi:10.1007/BF02481332

Cemex. (2019). *Smart Silo - How it works*. Retrieved from https://www.cemexusa.com/products-and-services/services/smart-silo

CERT National Insider Threat Center. (2018). *Common Sense Guide to Mitigating Insider Threats*. CERT, Carnegie Mellon University.

Chatterjee, S., Sarker, S., & Valacich, J. S. (2015). The Behavioral Roots of Information Systems Security: Exploring Key Factors Related to Unethical IT Use. *Journal of Management Information Systems*, *31*(4), 49–87. doi:10.1080/07421222.2014.1001257

Chin, W. W., Salisbury, W. D., Pearson, A. W., & Stollak, M. J. (1999). Perceived cohesion in small groups: Adapting and testing the perceived cohesion scale in a small-group setting. *Small Group Research*, *30*(6), 751–766. doi:10.1177/104649649903000605

Choe, E. K., Lee, N. B., Lee, B., Pratt, W., & Kientz, J. A. (2014). Understanding quantified-selfers' practices in collecting and exploring personal data. In *Proceedings of the 32nd annual ACM conference on Human factors in computing systems (CHI '14)* (pp. 1143-1152). New York: ACM. 10.1145/2556288.2557372

Chris, R. (n.d.). *6 ways to develop a security culture from top to bottom*. Retrieved from https://techbeacon.com/security/6-ways-develop-security-culture-top-bottom

Colbert, A., Yee, N., & George, G. (2016). The digital workforce and the workforce of the future. *Academy of Management Journal*, *59*(3), 731-739.

Cram, A., Jeffrey, P., & D'Arcy, J. (2017). Seeing the forest and the trees: A meta-analysis of information security policy compliance literature. *Proceedings of the 50th Hawaii International Conference on System Sciences*. 10.24251/HICSS.2017.489

Crossler, E., Johnston, A. C., Lowry, P. B., & Hud, Q. (2013). Future directions in information security resarch. *Computers & Security*, *32*, 90–101. doi:10.1016/j.cose.2012.09.010

CSP. (2018). *Employee Burnout: Tackling One of the Biggest HR IssuesPosted October 8, 2018 | By csponline*. Retrieved from https://online.csp.edu/blog/human-resources/employee-burnout

Deloitte. (2018). *The Rise of the Social Enterprise*. Deloitte Consulting.

Deloitte. (2018). *The rise of the social enterprise, 2018 Deloitte Human Capital Trends Report*. Deloitte. Retrieved from https://www2.deloitte.com/content/dam/insights/us/articles/HCTrends2018/2018-HCtrends_Rise-of-the-social-enterprise.pdf

Deloitte Insights. (2018). *Deloitte Insights, The Fourth Industrial Revolution is here—are you ready?* Deloitte Development LLC. Retrieved 2019 5, Feb, from https://www2.deloitte.com/content/dam/insights/us/articles/4364_Industry4-0_Are-you-ready/4364_Industry4-0_Are-you-ready_Report.pdf

Denning, S. (2018). *How Stress Is The Business World's Silent Killer*. Retrieved from How Stress Is The Business World's Silent Killer: https://www.forbes.com/sites/stephaniedenning/2018/05/04/what-is-the-cost-of-stress-how-stress-is-the-business-worlds-silent-killer/#6cc30bb46e06

Dery, K. (2019, May 29). *How to future proof your workforce for the digital era*. Retrieved from The Enterprisers Project: https://enterprisersproject.com/article/2019/5/digital-transformation-how-future-proof-workforce

Dodge, R., Daly, A. P., Huyton, J., & Sanders, L. D. (2012). The challenge of defining wellbeing. *International Journal of Wellbeing*, *2*(3), 222–235. doi:10.5502/ijw.v2i3.4

Duggirala, M., Malik, M., Kumar, H. H., & Balaraman, V. (2017). Evolving a grounded approach to behavior composition. *Winter Simulation Conference*.

Dukes, E. (2019, Jan 8). *The Employee Experience: What It Is and Why It Matters*. Retrieved from Inc.: https://www.inc.com/elizabeth-dukes/the-employee-experience-what-it-is-and-why-it-matt.html

Enterprisers Project. (2019). *What is digital transformation?* Retrieved from https://enterprisersproject.com/what-is-digital-transformation

E.T., A., Sticha, P. J., Brdiczka, O., & Shen, J. (2013). A Bayesian network model for predicting insider threats. *IEEE symposium on security and Privacy workshops*.

Etzioni, A. (1964). *Modern Organizations*. Prentice Hall.

Forbes. (2013). *Why Are So Many Employees Disengaged?* Retrieved from www.forbes.com: https://www.forbes.com/sites/victorlipman/2013/01/18/why-are-so-many-employees-disengaged/#2f5878ed1e22

Garton, E. (2017). Employee burnout is a problem with the company, not the person. *Harvard Business Review*.

Gibbons, S. (2017, July 9). *Service Design 101*. Nielsen Norman Group.

Gibson, I. (2007). An approach to hospital planning and design using discrete event simulation. *Proceedings of the Winter Simulation Conference 2007*. 10.1109/WSC.2007.4419763

Grint, K. (2010). Wicked problems and clumsy solutions: The role of leadership. In The New public leadership challenge (pp. 169-186). Academic Press.

Guo, H., Yuan, Y., Archer, N. P., & Connelly, C. E. (2011). Understanding Nonmalicious Security, Violations in the Workplace: A Composite Behavior Model. *Journal of Management Information Systems*, *28*(2), 203–236. doi:10.2753/MIS0742-1222280208

Haslam, C., Atkinson, S., Brown, S. S., & Haslam, R. A. (2005). Anxiety and depression in the workplace: Effects on the individual and organisation (a focus group investigation). *Journal of Affective Disorders*, *88*(2), 209–215. doi:10.1016/j.jad.2005.07.009 PMID:16122810

Hayatnagarkar, H., Singh, M., Kumar, S., Duggirala, M., & Balaraman, V. (2016). Can a buffering strategy reduce workload related stress? Autumn Simulation Multi-conference.

Health and Safety Executive. (2018). *Work-related ill health and occupational disease in Great Britain*. Retrieved from Work-related ill health and occupational disease in Great Britain: https://www.hse.gov.uk/statistics/causdis/index.htm

Hemp, P. (2004). Presenteeism: At work-but out of it. *Harvard Business Review*, 49–58. PMID:15559575

Hidas, P. (2002). Modelling lane changing and merging in microscopic traffic simulation. *Transportation Research Part C, Emerging Technologies*, *10*(5), 351–371. doi:10.1016/S0968-090X(02)00026-8

Horl, S. (2016). *Agent-based simulation of autonomous taxi services with dynamic demand responses*. Academic Press.

Huppert, F. A., & Cooper, C. L. (2014). *Wellbeing: A Complete Reference Guide, Interventions and Policies to Enhance Wellbeing* (Vol. 6). John Wiley & Sons.

Ifinedo, P. (2015). Effects of Organizational Citizenship Behavior and Social Cognitive Factors on Employees' NonMalicious Counterproductive Computer Security Behaviors: An Empirical Analysis. *International Conference on Information Resource Management, AIS2015*, 1-13.

Intelligence and National Security Alliance. (2017). *Assessing the mind of the malicious insider: Using behavioral model and data analytics to improve continuous evaluation*. Academic Press.

Jones, S., & Scott Evans, R. (2008). An Agent Based Simulation Tool for Scheduling Emergency Department Physicians. *AMIA Annual Symposium Proceedings*, 338-342.

Kahneman, D., Lovallo, D., & Sibony, O. (2011, June). The Big Idea: Before You Make That Big Decision. *Harvard Business Review*.

Kaplan, M. J., Richter, W., & Ware, D. (2019, August 1). Retrieved December 2019, from https://www.securitymagazine.com/articles/90637-how-cybersecurity-can-best-support-the-digital-enterprise

Keeney, M., Kowalski, E., Cappelli, D., Moore, A., Shimeall, T., & Rogers, S. (2005). Insider Threat Study:Computer System Sabotage in Critical Infrastructure Sectors. SEI, Carnegie Mellon University.

Kefalidou, G. (2015). *Overview of the state of the art (SoA) requirements: Personalised Airport Systems for Seamless Mobility & Experience*. University of Nottingham.

Khambete, P. (2011). *A pattern language for touch point ecosystem user experience: a proposal*. Bangalore: ACM. doi:10.1145/2407796.2407805

Kinman, G., & Jones, F. (2008). A life beyond work? Job demands, work-life balance, and wellbeing in UK academics. *Journal of Human Behavior in the Social Environment*, *17*(1-2), 41–60. doi:10.1080/10911350802165478

Ko, L. L., Divakaran, M. D., Liau, Y. S., & Thing, S. (2017). Insider threat detection and its future directions. *International Journal of Security and Networks*, 168-187.

Kolbjørnsrud, V., Amico, R., & Thomas, R. (2016, November 2). How Artificial Intelligence will Redefine Management. *Harvard Business Review*, 2–6.

Kraft, S. (2018). *Companies are facing an employee burnout crisis*. Retrieved from https://www.cnbc.com/2018/08/14/5-ways-workers-can-avoid-employee-burnout.html

Kulkarni, R., & Rajamani, A. (2017). *Here's how you should customize learning*. Retrieved from People matters: https://www.peoplematters.in/article/create-the-future/heres-how-you-should-customize-learning-16898

Kumar, S., Duggirala, M., Hayatnagarkar, H., & Balaraman, V. (2017). Understanding impact of supervisory support on work outcomes using agent based simulation. *Modelling Symposium, ISEC.*

Li, I., Dey, A., & Forlizzi, J. (2010). *A stage-based model of personal informatics systems*. CHI. doi:10.1145/1753326.1753409

LifeDojo: Behaviour Change Solution. (n.d.). Retrieved from LifeDojo: https://www.lifedojo.com/programs

Lim, S. J., Shanton, C., Sean, M., & Atif, A. (2009). *Exploring the Relationship between Organizational Culture and Information security culture. Australian Information Security Management.* Edith Cowan University.

Litan A. (2018, April 5). Retrieved from https://blogs.gartner.com/avivah-litan/2018/04/05/insider-threat-detection-replaces-dying-dlp/

Live Work Studio. (2013). *The Changing Nature of Service & Experience Design*. Retrieved from Live Work Studio: https://www.liveworkstudio.com/blog/the-changing-nature-of-service-experience-design/

Lobo, S., Sharma, S., Hirom, U., Mahamuni, R., & Khambete, P. (2019). *Extending Service Blueprint for New Age Services*. doi:10.1007/978-981-13-5977-4_68

Loh, C. S., Sheng, Y., & Ifenthaler, D. (2015). *Serious Games Analytics - Methodologies for Performance Measurement, Assessment, and Improvement*. doi:10.1007/978-3-319-05834-4

Lyons, T. F. (1971). Role clarity, need for clarity, satisfaction, tension, and withdrawal. *Organizational Behavior and Human Performance, 6*(1), 99–110. doi:10.1016/0030-5073(71)90007-9

Mahamuni, R. H., Khambete, P., & Mokashi-Punekar, R. (2019). *Behaviour Progression Framework for Designing Sustained Behaviour Change. In Research into Design for a Connected World* (pp. 39–50). Bangalore, India: Springer. doi:10.1007/978-981-13-5974-3_4

Marcus, B., & Heinz, S. (2004). Antecedents of Counterproductive Behavior at Work: A General Perspective. *The Journal of Applied Psychology, 89*(4), 647–660. doi:10.1037/0021-9010.89.4.647 PMID:15327351

Maslach, C., Schaufeli, W. B., & Leiter, M. P. (2001). ob burnout. *Annual Review of Psychology, 52*(1), 397–422. doi:10.1146/annurev.psych.52.1.397 PMID:11148311

Maslach. (1982). *Burnout: The Cost of Caring*. Englewood Cliffs, NJ: Prentice-Hall.

Mc Kinsey. (2018). *Insider threat: The human element of cyberrisk*. Retrieved December 2019, from https://www.mckinsey.com/business-functions/risk/our-insights/insider-threat-the-human-element-of-cyberrisk

Meister, J. (2016). Consumerization Of HR: 10 Trends Companies Will Follow In 2016. *Forbes*. Retrieved from https://www.forbes.com/sites/jeannemeister/2016/01/07/consumerization-of-hr-10-trends-innovative-companies-will-follow-in-2016/#272dd7d06b5a

Meister, J. (2018, Jan 11). AI plus human intelligence is the future of work. *Forbes.com*. Retrieved from https://www.forbes.com/sites/jeannemeister/2018/01/11/ai-plus-human-intelligence-is-the-future-of-work/#3ccb9db62bba

Mental Health America. (2019). *Depression In The Workplace*. Retrieved from Depression In The Workplace: http://www.mentalhealthamerica.net/conditions/depression-workplace#i

MLEVEL. (2019). *The training optimization platform*. Retrieved from MLEVEL: http://www.mlevel.com/platform/

Moore, A. P., Perl, S. J., Cowley, J., Collins, M. L., Cassidy, T. M., & VanHoudnos, N. (2016). *The Critical Role of Positive Incentives for Reducing Insider Threats*. Software Engineering Institute, Carnegie Mellon University.

Myyry, L., Siponen, M., Pahnila, S., Vartiainen, T., & Vance, A. (2009). What levels of moral reasoning and values explain adherence to information security rules? An empirical study. *European Journal of Information Systems*, *18*(2), 126–139. doi:10.1057/ejis.2009.10

Nagel, K., Stretz, P., Pieck, M., Donnelly, R., Leckey, S., & Barrett, C. (1998). Transim Report Series: Transims traffic flow characteristics. Academic Press.

Nagel, K. S. (1997). *TRANSIMS traffic flow characteristics*. arXiv preprint adap-org/9710003

National Academies of Sciences. (2017). Foundational Cybersecurity Research: Improving Science, Engineering, and Institutions. Washington, DC: The National Academies Press.

Nielsen, L. (2013). The Encyclopedia of Human-Computer Interaction (2nd ed.). Academic Press.

NIMHANS. (2016). *Summary-National Mental Health Survey-NIMHANS*. Retrieved from Summary-National Mental Health Survey-NIMHANS: http://indianmhs.nimhans.ac.in/Docs/Summary.pdf

North, J., Macal, C., Aubin, J., Thimmapuram, P., Bragen, M., Hahn, J., ... Hampton, D. (2010). Multiscale Agent Based Consumer Market Modeling. *Complexity*, *15*(5), 37–47.

Pahnila, S., Siponen, M., & Mahmood, A. (2007). Employees' Behavior Towards IS Security Policy Compliance. *40th Hawaii International Conference on System Sciences (HICSS07)*. 10.1109/HICSS.2007.206

Park, H. I., Monnot, M. J., Jacob, A. C., & Wagner, S. H. (2011). Moderators of the relationship between person-job fit and subjective well-being among Asian employees. *International Journal of Stress Management*, 67.

Passera, S., Kärkkäinen, H., & Maila, R. (2012). *When, how, why prototyping? A practical framework for service development*. Academic Press.

Peter, M., Nina, G., Ronja, M., Melanie, V., & Vogt, J. (2017). Productivity vs security: Mitigating conflicting goals in organizations. *Information & Computer Security*, *25*(2), 137–151. doi:10.1108/ICS-03-2017-0014

Ponemon Institute, IBM. (2019). *Cost of a data breach.* Ponemon Institute, IBM.

Price Waterhouse Coopers. (2018). Workforce of the future: The competing forces shaping 2030. *Price Waterhouse Coopers.* Retrieved from https://www.pwc.com/gx/en/services/people-organisation/publications/workforce-of-the-future.html

Prosser, W., P, J., Emanuelle, A., Brown, S., Matsinhe, G., Dekoun, M., & Lee, B. (2017). System redesign of the immunization supply chain: Experiences from Benin and Mozambique. *Vaccine, 35*(17), 2162-2166.

PWC. (2016). *Industry 4.0: Building the digital enterprise.* PWC. Retrieved Feb 04, 2019, from https://www.pwc.com/gx/en/industries/industries-4.0/landing-page/industry-4.0-building-your-digital-enterprise-april-2016.pdf

Qualtrics. (2019). *Employee Experience.* Retrieved from www.qualtrics.com: https://www.qualtrics.com/blog/employee-experience-stats/

Quantified Self. (n.d.). Retrieved from http://quantifiedself.com

Remis, N. (2016). *A Guide to Service Blueprinting.* San Francisco: Capital One.

Renee Baptiste, N. (2008). Tightening the link between employee wellbeing at work and performance: A new dimension for HRM. *Management Decision, 46*(2), 284–309. doi:10.1108/00251740810854168

Riemer, K., & Schellhammer, S. (2018). Collaboration in the Digital Age: Diverse, Relevant and Challenging. In Collaboration in the Digital Age (pp. 1-12). Springer Link.

Rosencrance, L. (2002, March 14). *Dow Corning launches business unit, Xiameter.* Retrieved from https://www.computerworld.com/article/2587477/dow-corning-launches-business-unit--xiameter.html

Rothenberger, D. (2017). Physician burnout and well-being: A systematic review and framework for action. *Diseases of the Colon and Rectum, 60*(6), 567–576. doi:10.1097/DCR.0000000000000844 PMID:28481850

Safa, N. S., Solms, R. V., & Furnel, S. (2016). Information security policy compliance model in organizations. *Computers & Security, 56*, 1–13.

Sandle T. (2018, January 27). http://www.digitaljournal.com/business/how-businesses-can-protect-their-organizations-from-within/article/513278

Schelling, T. (1969). Models of Segregation. *The American Economic Review*, 488–493.

Servia-Rodríguez, S., Rachuri, K. K., Mascolo, C., Rentfrow, P. J., Lathia, N., & Sandstrom, G. M. (2017). Mobile Sensing at the Service of Mental Well-being: a Large-scale Longitudinal Study. *International World Wide Web Conference Committee.*

Shaw, E. D., & Stock, H. V. (2011). *Behavioral risk indicators of malicious insider theft of intellectual property: Misreading the writing on the wall.* Symantec.

Shostack, G. L. (1984). Designing services that deliver. *Harvard Business Review*, 133–139.

Silverman, B. (2004). *Towards realism in human performance simulation.* University of Pennsylvania, ESE.

Singh, M. e. (2018). KNADIA: Enterprise KNowledge Assisted DIAlogue Systems using Deep Learning. *IEEE International Conference on Data Engineering.* 10.1109/ICDE.2018.00161

Singh, M., Duggirala, M., Hayatnagarkar, H., Patel, S., & Balaraman, V. (2016). Towards fine grained human behavior simulation models. *Winter Simulation Conference.*

Tata Consultancy Services. (2016). *A Personalized Humane Customer Experience – Delivered to you by Bots.* Retrieved from TCS: https://www.tcs.com/blogs/a-personalized-humane-customer-experience-delivered-to-you-by-bots

Tata Consultancy Services Limited. (2019, Feb 4). *Digital transformation to business 4.0.* Retrieved from https://sites.tcs.com/bts/digital-transformation-to-business-4-0-pov/

The American Institute of Stress. (n.d.). Retrieved from https://www.stress.org/workplace-stress

Turel, O., Xu, Z., & Guo, K. (2017). Organizational Citizenship Behavior Regarding Security: Leadership Approach Perspective. *Journal of Computer Information Systems,* 1–15. doi:10.1080/08874417.2017.1400928

Volini, E., Occean, P., Stephan, M., & Walsh, B. (2017). *Digital HR: Platforms, people, and work, 2017 Global Human Capital Trends.* Retrieved from https://www2.deloitte.com/insights/us/en/focus/human-capital-trends/2017/digital-transformation-in-hr.html

Willison, R., & Warkentin, M. (2009). Motivations for employee computer crime: Understanding and addressing. *IFIP TC 8 International Workshop on Information Systems Security Research,* 127 - 144.

Wired Inc. (2018, April). *AI and the future of work.* Retrieved from https://www.wired.com/wiredinsider/2018/04/ai-future-work/

WittkopJ. (2017, December 21). Retrieved from https://www.intelisecure.com/blog/future-information-security/

Woelfle, M., Olliaro, P., & Todd, M. H. (2011). Open science is a research accelerator. *Nature Chemistry, 3*(10), 745–748. doi:10.1038/nchem.1149 PMID:21941234

World Economic Forum. (2011). *The Global Economic Burden of Non-communicable diseases.* World Economic Forum, Harvard School of Public Health.

World Health Organization. (2019). *Mental health in India.* Retrieved from Mental health in India: http://www.searo.who.int/india/topics/mental_health/about_mentalhealth/en/

Yellowlees, P., & Chan, S. (2015). Mobile mental health care-An opportunity for India. *The Indian Journal of Medical Research, 142*(4), 359. doi:10.4103/0971-5916.169185 PMID:26609025

Zeike, S., Bradbury, K., Lindert, L., & Pfaf, H. (2019). Digital Leadership Skills and Associations with Psychological Well-Being. *International Journal of Environmental Research and Public Health, 16*(14), 2628–2640. doi:10.3390/ijerph16142628 PMID:31340579

Section 2

Chapter 10
Generate and Test for Formulated Product Variants With Information Extraction and an In-Silico Model

Sagar Sunkle
TCS Research, Tata Consultancy Services, India

Ashwini Patil
TCS Research, Tata Consultancy Services, India

Deepak Jain
https://orcid.org/0000-0001-5849-454X
TCS Research, Tata Consultancy Services, India

Rinu Chacko
TCS Research, Tata Consultancy Services, India

Krati Saxena
TCS Research, Tata Consultancy Services, India

Beena Rai
TCS Research, Tata Consultancy Services, India

ABSTRACT

The chemical industry is expanding its focus from process-centered products to product-centered products. Of these, consumer chemical products and other similar formulated products are especially ubiquitous. State of the art in the formulated product design relies heavily on experts and their expertise, leading to extended time to market and increased costs. The authors show that it is possible to construct a graph database of various details of products from textual sources, both offline and online. Similar to the "generate and test" approach, they propose that it is possible to generate feasible design variants of a given type of formulated product using the database so constructed. If they restrict the set of products that are applied to the skin, they propose to test the generated design variants using an in-silico model. Even though this chapter is an account of the work in progress, the authors believe the gains they can obtain from a readily accessible database and its integration with an in-silico model are substantial.

DOI: 10.4018/978-1-7998-0108-5.ch010

INTRODUCTION

The chemical industry is a diverse sector, with a vast range of processes and products. As per (Zhang et al., 2017), chemical engineering has been expanding its focus from process-centered products such as chlorine and ammonia to product-centered products such as mosquito repellent sprays. Gani and Ng (2015) classified chemical products into molecular products, formulated products, functional products, and devices. Such products include basic organic materials such as olefins, aromatics, biochemicals and plastics and basic inorganic materials such as engineered particles, inorganic chemicals, acids, gases produced from raw extracted materials and sustainable feedstocks. These basic chemicals, or ingredients, are used as the building blocks for the formulation of complex materials and substances such as speciality chemicals and consumer products known as formulated products.

Formulated products comprise a combination of raw materials engineered and designed to form powders, granules, tablets, creams, suspensions, foams, gels and emulsions, all displaying a set of targeted properties. Formulated products are ubiquitous in everyday applications such as lubricants, fuels, paints, inks, dyes, coatings, adhesives, detergents, cosmetics, personal care, household and professional care, medicines, foods, pesticides, construction materials, fuel additives and pharmaceutical products[1]. Individual ingredients used within a formulation may be incorporated to provide active functionality, enhanced delivery or as a protective or stabilizing agent (Chatterjee and Alvi, 2014).

Formulations of organic formulated products contain ingredients that undergo a step-by-step procedure such as heating, cooling, stirring, mixing, and so on to obtain specific target properties, both physical and chemical. A general understanding of the formulated products research area is that several types of data, methods and tools are necessary to tackle formulated product design problems to achieve an optimal design. Several approaches, conceptual models and frameworks have been proposed toward this goal (Bernardo and Saraiva, 2015; Conte et al., 2011; Gani and Ng, 2015; Hill, 2009; Lee et al., 2014; Martín and Martínez, 2013; Zhang et al., 2017; Zhang et al., 2018). Many approaches suggest using a database of relevant details for product design (Dionisio et al., 2018). The frameworks suggest using knowledge from experience, models or databases to choose a product form such as cream; then select types of ingredients such as solvent; generate candidates for each selected ingredient type and finally combine the ingredients (Zhang et al., 2017). Experts find similar formulations using standard file search and compilation. Lee et al. (2014) suggest a knowledge-based ingredient formulation system to support formulators in their attempt to select the most appropriate ingredients using past formulation cases. Lee et al. assert that without any knowledge support tools, chemical product development becomes iterative and time-consuming without a list of acceptable ingredients. In most of these approaches, the assumption is that either a relevant database/ knowledge-base is available or should be created manually.

We take the stance that it is possible to use the text of existing formulations to generate such a database. With a proper design of this database, it is also possible to make it highly searchable.

A vast amount of textual data is available occurring in sources such as textbooks, handbooks, journal articles, and specialized web sites. These texts are available in a form that makes at best a file search possible, but it is difficult to query the text flexibly. The information present in such texts contains a variety of domain-specific information such as the type of ingredients, mixtures of ingredients, functionalities and their compositions, and their physical attributes such as weights or weight fractions (Isaacs et al., 2016; Isaacs et al., 2018). In the search for a new formulation, an expert must refer to the already existing recipes to make rational judgments when choosing on the ingredients, their respective quantities and the procedure to follow to get a stable formulation that has the desired chemical function. This process

Figure 1. Extraction, storage, and retrieval of formulations

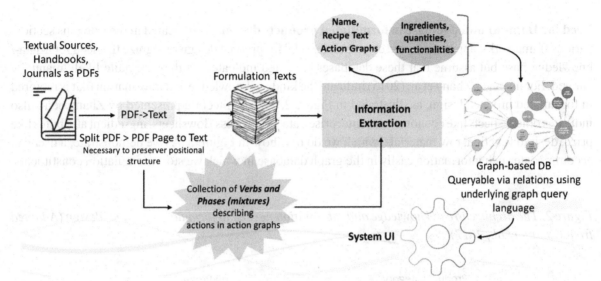

becomes easier if the existing data is available in a readily queryable form. Such queriability implies extracting information from textual sources (rather than humans providing inputs manually), designing a schema to store specifically organic chemical formulations, and enabling retrieval based on a query language. The chapter shows how we fill in each of the above-stated gaps.

Figure 1 illustrates our approach for the generation of a database from existing formulations using information extraction techniques. We demonstrate our approach using selective cream formulations obtained from Flick, E. W. (1989-2014) Volumes 1 to 8. Although initially developed in the scope of cream formulations, it is possible to apply the basic ideas, and the techniques of the methodology here proposed (Figure. 1) to any formulated product, whose specific functionalities result from the proper blend of ingredients and specific interactions between them. Our technology enables extraction, storage, and retrieval of details about chemical formulations using a) state of the art natural language processing and machine learning models to extract relevant details from textual sources b) store the details in a graph domain model and retrieve the details using SQL-like queries in the graph query language. Our approach is a work in progress. However, our approach yields a detailed formulation database that the user can grow subsequently. It also provides the ability to execute non-trivial queries along with additional facets of the database such as an ingredients dictionary (multiple names of an ingredient) (Michalun and DiNardo, 2014). A graph of ingredients with their functionality enables finding ingredients with specific functionality arriving at intended properties of the end product.

In the following, we briefly review state of the art in each section and then present our approaches for extraction, storage, and retrieval of formulation constituents along with our approaches for creating ingredient and ingredient-functionality dictionaries. We also describe how we plan to use this technology in combination with in-silico models toward testing the generated product design variants.

EXTRACTION OF FORMULATION CONSTITUENTS

Need for Data-/knowledge-base in formulated products design. As indicated in the previous section, various frameworks, approaches, and conceptual model for product design recognize the need for a data-/knowledge-base but assume that these databases exist and indicate that they are quite likely manually curated. For instance, Zhang et al. (2015) indicate the kinds of knowledge and information that is required in formulated product design, as illustrated in Figure 2. The architecture presented by Zhang et al. also indicates other aspects like economic and enterprise data and process flowsheets, ingredient attributes like price, desired function, raw materials, which we do not show in Figure 2. As we demonstrate, a user can accommodate such information easily in the graph database in which we store formulation constituents.

Figure 2. The architecture of knowledge and information needed in formulated product design (Adapted from (Zhang et al., 2017)

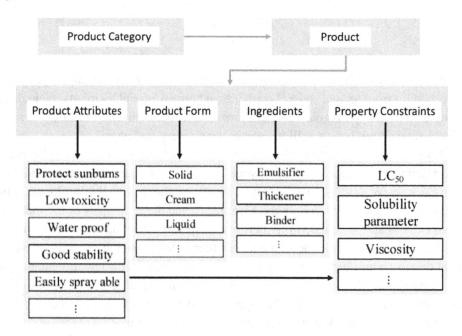

Product attributes describing functional requirements indicate the main reason why a consumer may want to buy a product, e.g., an insect repellent must repel mosquitoes and a sunscreen lotion must protect skin from UV and skin ageing. Product attributes that are sensorial requirements indicate aspects of colour, smell and taste. Zhang et al. (2017) indicate that knowledge and rule-based systems need to be used to find the relationship between product attributes and property constraints, but do not show how. Property constraints pave the way for possible candidate ingredients which need to be combined to obtain the desired product attributes. It is in the selection of candidate ingredients that the need for a database is most felt. As we demonstrate, the graph database provides a highly intuitive query mechanism. It enables the specification and execution of non-trivial queries that reveal additional information about formulation constituents based on an ontology we present in the next section.

Arrieta-Escobar et al. (2019) indicate that experts refer to several heuristics during the formulation stage regarding the qualitative function of ingredients, their incompatibilities, synergies and antagonisms, as well as their impact on sensorial attributes. Arrieta-Escobar et al. point out that an experiment-based trial-and-error approach seeking formulations that meet targeted performance is the practice followed particularly for emulsified cosmetic product design. Such trial-and-error procedures are very resource-consuming, especially during the early stages of product design or reformulation, also shown by Conte et al. (2011).

Wibowo and Ng (2001, 2002) proposed incorporating heuristic knowledge in the product design procedures for creams and pastes. Martín and Martínez (2013) showed the same for detergents. Arrieta-Escobar et al., (2019) also say that the cosmetic formulations domain has an extensive history with hundreds of different ingredients and richness in heuristic knowledge, namely regarding the qualitative function of ingredients, their incompatibilities and positive synergies, as well as their impact on sensorial attributes. Harper and Gani (2000) had proposed a multi-step and multi-level approach of the *generate and test* method for chemical product design that included incorporating a knowledge base for the identification and setup of the design criteria during the problem formulation step.

Martín and Martínez (2013) point out the first stage in formulated products is essentially identifying the main ingredients necessary for the kind of product under consideration and indicate that several books are available with a number of detailed formulation recipes such as "cosmetic and toiletry formulations" by Flick, E. W. (1989-2014) with 8 volumes of formulations for various cosmetics. In a way, Martín and Martínez indicate that this already existing knowledge should be utilized as a source during the product formulation process for similar formulations and other relevant information about ingredients.

To summarize, several researchers point out the use of data-/knowledge-base or models, especially to find candidate ingredients with requisite functionalities. We show that it is possible to extract and store various details about a formulated product, the recipe of which is available as text, including details of ingredients, their functionalities, their weights, and the actions performed on individual ingredients or as a part of a mixture. Once a user of the proposed approach constructs such a database, it is possible to query it in intuitive ways to obtain information that can be used to put together product variants (alternate formulations).

Preparing the text of formulations. An organic chemical formulation text usually contains the name of the formulation, ingredients, mixtures (if any), weights or proportions of ingredients, and actions to be performed on the ingredients and mixtures, with conditions such as specific temperatures or states. We refer to these details as constituents of a formulation. This is shown with a formulation in Figure 3.

In the following, we use the cream formulations from volumes 1 to 8 of "cosmetic and toiletry formulations" (Flick, 1989-2014). These texts are available as PDF files. We use Apache PDFBox[2] API to extract text from the PDF files while preserving the layout. As we will show, without preserving the layout of the formulations, it is difficult to process the constituents, especially the ingredients, which are arranged in a columnar vertical manner in the source.

We apply simple sentence (boundary) identification for the text of each text file to find out whether it contains sentences, indicating that the formulation under consideration is not devoid of recipe text. To showcase the extraction and storage of cream formulations, we choose those cream formulations which contain ingredient listing along with a recipe text (several formulations do not contain recipe text). In spite of the ability of PDFBox to recognize text, the transformation may also yield a garbled list of ingredients. We ignore formulations where the ingredients table is garbled with unidentifiable characters. In the end, we are left with 410 cream formulations from across the eight volumes.

Figure 3. Structure of a formulation from a textual source

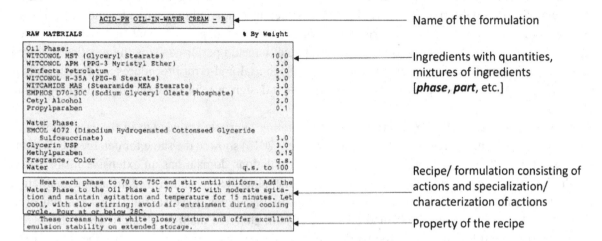

EXTRACTION OF INGREDIENTS, MIXTURES, AND INGREDIENT WEIGHTS

To extract ingredients and ingredients weights, it helps to preserve the layout while transforming the PDF to text. With a preserved layout, the ingredient and its weight occur in a single line of text. Additionally, the formulation may use the ingredients as a part of a mixture. To recognize the mixture indicators separately, we prepare a small list of mixture phrases. The list we use to process 410 cream formulations contains indicator phrases like 'phase a', 'phase b', 'phase c', 'oil phase', 'water phase', 'part a', 'part b', 'part c', and 'part d'. These indicator phrases appear in a line before the list of ingredients that are part of that mixture begins, as shown in Figure 3.

To recognize the ingredients and their weights, we use a regular expression. In Python, this regular expression is "\d+\s*\.\s*\d+|q.s|USP". The "\s*" flag takes care of multiple white spaces between the integer and the fraction part of an ingredient's weight represented by flag "\d". The + sign in front of the flag indicates more than one digits in the integer part of the weight. Words such as q.s. (indicating "the amount which is needed") can be added as more of such phrases are encountered.

To process the ingredients as part of the mixture, we first identify if there is a mixture and which of the dictionary entry it matches. Then till the next mixture is encountered in a line, all ingredients obtained till then are associated with the current mixture.

To ensure that we only consider the part of the text that contains the ingredients for the processing of ingredients, we apply the sentence (boundary) identification previously mentioned. As illustrated in Figure 3., the ingredients occur in the part of the text that is NOT a set of sentences (whereas the recipe text is).

EXTRACTION OF RECIPE TEXTS AND REPRESENTATION AS ACTION GRAPHS

The recipe text describes actions performed a) on the ingredients individually or b) ingredients as a part of a mixture and c) on the mixtures if present. For product design, we need to associate actions, along with conditions, to an ingredient or a mixture. Additionally, we need to store the functionalities of each ingredient extracted.

Mysore et al. (2017) presented an approach for automatically extracting structured representations, called as action graphs (originally termed so by Kiddon et al. (2015)), for capturing synthesis routes in inorganic materials. The nodes in such a graph represent operations or actions in the synthesis and the arguments associated with each operation represent ingredients or mixtures. The edges in the graph represent the association of an operation or an action with a) an argument or b) an ingredient or c) a mixture. The edges may also indicate an argument (resulting mixture or ingredient) as having originated from a given action.

Given synthesis procedure text, Mysore et al. first extract individual events in the synthesis using a neural network entity tagger and a set of dependency parse-based heuristics. They then induce edges to compute the sequence of synthesis steps. Computing the sequence of steps requires linking the ingredients/mixtures, which are the result of or an object of the previous action (necessarily, an object of the preceding verb) to the next action.

The critical problems faced in extracting action graphs are that- a) the recipes (whether formulations or even cooking recipes) contain instructions which are imperative sentences, and b) Objects may be alluded to but could be missing from the sentences (Kiddon et al., 2015). Since the sentences are instructions, they begin with an instructional verb and therefore often lack a subject (from the typical subject-verb-object structure of a sentence). Additionally, with the flow of instructions, the previous object acted upon is often implicitly considered without explicitly mentioning it in the next instruction.

For data availability, we consider recipes in material science rather than cooking recipes for which considerable open data exists on cooking sites. Mysore et al. (2017) treat this as a named entity recognition problem, create a dataset of recipes texts from 42 material science papers, and train various structured prediction machine learning models. Their models can predict about 56% of explicit ingredient/mixture mentions. They assert that identifying individual operations and their arguments is the challenge.

We take the stance that instead of creating annotated data and training structured prediction models it is perhaps better to use natural language processing in a manner that enables extracting and associating actions with the ingredients/mixture on which the actions are performed.

In doing so, we primarily use the subject-verb-object structure of a sentence. We evaluate two approaches to obtain verbs and objects, respectively, actions and ingredients/mixtures, from each sentence of the recipe.

The first approach is known as open information extraction or open IE. An open IE implementation returns a triple of subject-verb-object*[3]. Specific implementations may return individual triple, replicating the subject and verb for each if there are many objects. Open IE models are often trained by bootstrapping on other open IE models which could have been trained on manually extracted triples from sentences.

The second approach is using a dependency parser to identify action and ingredient/mixtures from within each sentence of a recipe.

In both the approaches, we make use of a dictionary of verbs that are representative of actions performed on ingredients and/or mixtures. We compile the list using the 410 files and applying sentence identification and open IE (which returns subject-verb-object* triples as explained below) to identify the verbs. Some of the example verbs are 'maintain', 'heat', 'add', 'stir', 'moisturize', 'cool', 'extract', 'demineralize', 'mix', 'disperse', 'blend', 'emulsify', 'select', 'distil', 'chelate', and so on. We use a total of 129 lemmatized verbs thus collected as indicators that signify that a given sentence represents a part of the recipe.

Figure 4. using open information extraction with stacks to preserve missing arguments

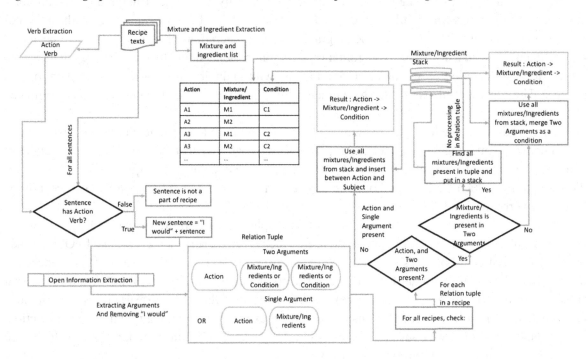

To address the issue of missing arguments, i.e., implicit reference to a previous set of ingredients/ mixtures, we use a novel mechanism of stacking. In the following we describe both the approaches.

Using Open IE[4] With Stacking for Creating Action Graphs

For all 410 formulations, we extract mixtures, ingredients, and actions in the form of objects and verb, respectively. Here, verbs are representative of actions in the recipe. Note that open IE model returns multiple (and possibly overlapping) relation tuples of up to 4 values; first value is the subject of the sentence, the second value is the verb of the sentence, the third value is the first object of the sentence, and the fourth value is the second object of the sentence. We illustrate the complete process of applying open IE to extract action graph in Figure 4.

We first check if one of the verbs in the dictionary is present in a sentence. We prefix such a sentence with "I would" to add a subject to the sentence for processing using open IE. The reason we add a subject to such sentence is that generally these are instructional or imperative sentences and lack a subject. Our observation is that open IE fails for imperative sentence returning an incorrect relation tuple. We, therefore, transform such sentences before further processing, e.g., 'Heat phase A and phase B to 70-75C.' becomes 'I would heat phase A and phase B to 70-75C.'.

After applying open IE to the transformed sentence, we process the relation tuple to separate actions and their arguments. We make another observation that open IE may return verb and objects that contain the action as well as condition. We differentiate the condition from an action such that condition often describes the action in more detail. For instance, in 'heat ... to 70-75C', 'heat' is the action and '70-75C' is the condition. We process the relation tuples to get Action -> Mixture/Ingredient -> Condition format (henceforth A-M-C).

Figure 5. Using dependency parsing with stacks to preserve missing arguments

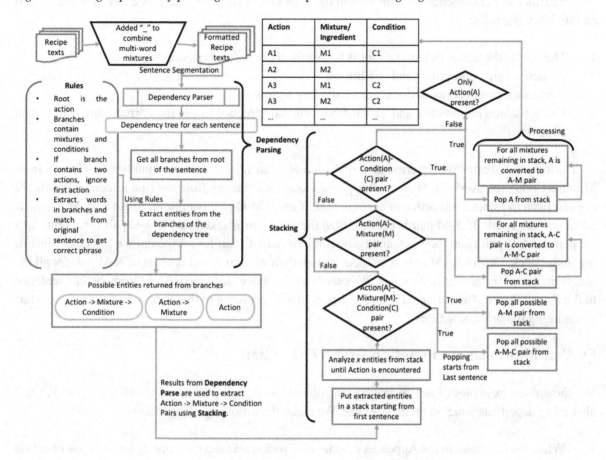

For all the recipe texts, we check each relation tuple to find the number of values returned. If action and two arguments are present, then we find all mixtures (from the mixtures dictionary) and ingredients (from earlier processing). If a mixture or an ingredient exists, we push it to a stack, and the action and the two arguments represent A-M-C. If a mixture or an ingredient does not exist, then the two arguments (values apart from the action verb) contain conditions. In this case, we use all mixtures from the stack and process output as Action, Mixture or Ingredient, and the two arguments as a single entry, which now represents A-M-C. If relation tuple only contains one argument, then we use all mixtures from the stack and process output as Action, Mixture or ingredient, and single argument to represent A-M-C.

Using Dependency Parser[5] With Stacking for Creating Action Graphs

As indicated earlier, recipe text contains instructions that are imperative sentences where an implicit actor performs some action on some object with a defined condition. To recognize the mixtures and conditions properly, we convert multi-word mixtures to a single word by adding an underscore between the words. We identify sentences and apply spacy dependency parser to each sentence. We illustrate the process of using the dependency parser with stacking in Figure 5.

We extract all the branches from the root in the dependency tree and then process each branch based on the following rules:

1. The root is the action (when the root is a verb from the verbs dictionary).
2. Branches contain mixtures and conditions.
3. If a branch contains two actions, ignore the root action.
4. Extract words in branches and match from original sentence to get the correct phrase to obtain condition

The Rule-based extraction returns tuples of Action-Mixture (A-M), Action-Condition (A-C) or Action-Mixture-Condition (A-M-C). This result is pushed to a stack starting from the first sentence. Words are popped from the stack until action is encountered. If an A-M-C pair is present, then the A-M-C pair is taken out as a result. If A-M pair is present, then the A-M pair is taken out. If A-C pair is present, then we pop the A-C pair from the stack and convert it into A-M-C pair for all the unique mixtures remaining in the stack. Otherwise, if only A is encountered, then we pop A and convert to A-M pair for all the unique mixtures remaining in the stack. We carry out the above steps recursively from the last sentence to the first sentence. The extracted results get rearranged according to their occurrence in the text, thus maintaining the order of actions.

Further Improvement in Action Graph Extraction

We show three examples of action graph extraction in the Appendix using open IE with stacking and also using dependency parsing with stacking. We make the following observations:

1. While the examples in the Appendix contain only recipe text and no property text, the use of action verbs helps in separating the recipe text from the property text like "These creams have a white glossy texture and offer excellent emulsion stability on extended storage". An alternative is to train a classifier to recognize recipe text as distinct from property text such as the one above using manual annotation.
2. Of the two outputs, i.e., one obtained by using open IE and the other by using dependency parsing (both with stacking), we observe that the action graph that contains more actions is usually the more exhaustive action graph, meaning that it captures the mixture/ingredients and actions on them separately and more correctly (not missing an action or combining it with a condition). When the number of actions is the same, the graph that contains more elaborate condition is more accurate, in the sense that it captures A-M-C structure without missing details or with less additional details in the C part (conditions) of the A-M-C structure. Empirically proving that open IE/dep parsing + stacking achieves better extraction of the A-M-C structure is part of our future work.

In the next section, we present the storage and retrieval of the formulation constituents that we have extracted.

STORAGE AND RETRIEVAL OF FORMULATIONS

In the previous section, we showed how we extract the constituents of a formulation. Our overall objective involves storing the constituents in a structure that leads to intuitive storage and retrieval. We also observe that instead of storing a) the name of the formulation, b) the ingredients and their weights, c) the mixtures and the ingredients that are part of it, and d) the actions on the ingredients and/or mixtures as tables in a relational database is not intuitive because of the needless maintenance of primary and foreign keys. Additionally, adding different formulation categories apart from creams would lead to maintaining another table. It is known that for this kind of connected data, relations databases end up causing delays in retrieval due to the joins involved.

Graph databases are the best way to represent and query such connected data. Connected data is data whose interpretation and value require us first to understand how its constituent elements are related. More often than not, to generate this understanding, we need to name and qualify the connections between the constituents (Robinson et al., 2013). Relationships are first-class citizens of the graph data model. By using the abstractions of nodes and relationships into connected structures, graph databases enable us to build arbitrarily sophisticated models that map closely to our problem domain (Angles and Gutierrez, 2008). The resulting models are intuitive and at the same time more expressive than those produced using traditional relational databases and the other NOSQL (Not Only SQL) stores.

In contrast to relational databases, where join-intensive query performance deteriorates as the dataset gets bigger, with a graph database performance tends to remain relatively constant, even as the dataset grows. Graphs are also naturally additive, implying that we can add new nodes to represent hierarchies or taxonomies, new kinds of relationships between nodes, new nodes, and new subgraphs to an existing structure without disturbing current queries and application functionality (Robinson et al., 2013).

Figure 6 shows the graph domain model for cosmetic and toiletry formulations. Notice that what we show here is a labeled property graph (Robinson et al., 2013). A labeled property graph has the following characteristics: a) it contains nodes and relationships, b) nodes contain properties that are key-value pairs and c) relationships are named and directed, and always have a start and end node.

Figure 6. Example of the graph domain model for creams as a category of cosmetics and toiletry formulations

Type of formulation	`FormulationType name: 'Cosmetic and Toiletry'`
Category within a type formulation	`FormulationCategory name: 'Creams'`
Name of the formulation	`Formulation name: 'acid ph. oil-in-water cream - b'`

Ingredients with quantities, mixtures of ingredients [*phase*, *part*, etc.]	`Ingredient name: 'witconol mst (glyceryl stearate)',`
	`quantity:'10.0'`
	`(:Mixture (name : 'oil phase'))`

Recipe/ formulation consisting of actions and specialization/ characterization of actions	`RecipeText RecipeActionGraph`
	`RecipeActionGraphStringRepr`
	
	`Action name : 'heat', node_id:'1')-[:Uses]->`
	`(:Constituent name : 'each phase')-[:UnderCondition]->`
	`(:Condition name : 'to 70 to 75c'),`

Figure 7. Example of a graph of an "all purpose cream" ingredients and weights

```
                              ALL  PURPOSE  CREAM

          RAW  MATERIALS                                    % By  Weight
            Phase  A:
          Methyl  Glucose  Sesquistearate     (Glucate SS)         1.5
          Coconut  Oil,  76                                        7.5
          Glyceryl  Monostearate,  Neut.                           7.5
          Phase  B:
          Methyl  Gluceth-20 Sesquistearate   (Glucamate SSE-20)   1.5
          Methyl  Gluceth-20  (Glucam E-20)                        5.0
          Water                                                   76.0
          GERMABEN   I1                                            1.0
```

```
MATCH (a:FormulationCategory) where a.name='Creams'
CREATE (a)-[:HasFormulation]->(f:Formulation {name:'all purpose cream'}),
(f)-[:Source]->(:Source {name:'Vol1-1004.txt'}),
(f)-[:HasIngredient]->(:Ingredient {name:'methyl glucose sesquistearate (glucate ss)', quantity:'1.5'})-[:PartOf]->(:Mixture (name:'phase a')),
(f)-[:HasIngredient]->(:Ingredient {name:'coconut oil, 76', quantity:'7.5'})-[:PartOf]->(:Mixture (name:'phase a')),
(f)-[:HasIngredient]->(:Ingredient {name:'glyceryl monostearate, neut.', quantity:'7.5'})-[:PartOf]->(:Mixture (name:'phase a')),
(f)-[:HasIngredient]->(:Ingredient {name:'methyl gluceth-20 sesquistearate (glucamate sse-20)', quantity:'1.5'})-[:PartOf]->(:Mixture (name:'phase b')),
(f)-[:HasIngredient]->(:Ingredient {name:'methyl gluceth-20 (glucam e-20)', quantity:'5.0'})-[:PartOf]->(:Mixture (name:'phase b')),
(f)-[:HasIngredient]->(:Ingredient {name:'water', quantity:'76.0'})-[:PartOf]->(:Mixture (name:'phase b')),
(f)-[:HasIngredient]->(:Ingredient {name:'germaben i1', quantity:'1.0'})-[:PartOf]->(:Mixture (name:'phase b')),
```

In Figure 6., the node *FormulationType* indicates the high-level formulation category. Since all our formulations are of creams which are of the type cosmetic and toiletry, for all 410 formulations under consideration, we set the label name of the *FormulationType* to cosmetic and toiletry. In case we were storing the details of a non-cosmetic and toiletry formulation, we would begin by adding a node of type *FormulationType* and setting the name property appropriately.

Next, the node *FormulationCategory* captures the specific type of cosmetic and toiletry formulation, in our case, creams (or cream). Typically, for other cosmetic and toiletry formulations like antiperspirants and deodorants, baby products, bath and shower products, beauty aids, fragrances and perfumes, we would set the name accordingly.

At this point, it is clear that this simple structure can already support all cosmetic and toiletry formulations as well as other top-level categories we may wish to store similarly.

The rest of the graph domain model captures ingredients, mixtures, and weights of the ingredients. A specific example is shown in Figure 7. We use the Cypher[6] query language. The *PartOf* relation represents if an ingredient is part of a mixture. For standalone ingredients that are not part of any mixture, this relation does not exist.

The recipe text can be stored as the literal text, as an action graph, or any other representation as shown in Figure 6. We show the graph representation of the action graph for the same formulation in Figure 8. Note the nodes *RecipeActionGraph*, *Action*, *Constituent*, and *Condition*. We call the node representing a mixture or an ingredient from the A-M-C structure as Constituent. In Figure 8. a1, a2, a3, and a4 are variables representing specific Action nodes. Note that we store the order between the nodes using *FollowedBy* relationship.

We generate and execute the combined MATCH and CREATE query parts in Figure 7. and 8. for each formulation, such that we process a formulation text, generate a query and execute it to add a specific formulation to the graph.

This graph structure lends itself to intuitive queries. We show some example queries in Figure 9. Note the query to find the weights of "Cetyl Alcohol". Compared to a relational version, the graph structure makes it straightforward to find all ingredients matching (using CONTAINS operator, since here we want to find all alternate ingredient names that contain the said phrase) and then retrieve their weights. This is an example of a query with which we can establish ranges of weight proportions for specific ingredients.

Figure 8. Example of a graph of an "all purpose cream" recipe action graph

```
Procedure:
        Heat  Phase  A  and  Phase  B  separately   to 75C.  Mix  Phase  A  until
uniform.  Add  Phase  A  to  Phase  B with   constant   stirring   and  cool
        to  room   temperature.

(f)-[:HasRecipe]->(g:RecipeActionGraph),
(g)-[:Contains]->(a1:Action {name:'heat', node_id:'1'})-[:Uses]->(:Constituent {name:'phase A and phase B'})-
[:UnderCondition]->(:Condition {name:'separately to 75C'}),
(g)-[:HasStartNode]->(a1),
(g)-[:Contains]->(a2:Action {name:'mix', node_id:'2'})-[:Uses]->(:Constituent {name:'phase A'})-
[:UnderCondition]->(:Condition {name:'until uniform'}),
(g)-[:Contains]->(a3:Action {name:'add', node_id:'3'})-[:Uses]->(:Constituent {name:'phase A + phase B'})-
[:UnderCondition]->(:Condition {name:'constant stirring'}),
(g)-[:Contains]->(a4:Action {name:'cool', node_id:'4'})-[:Uses]->(:Constituent {name:'phase A + phase B'})-
[:UnderCondition]->(:Condition {name:'to room temperature'}),
(a1)-[:FollowedBy]->(a2),
(a2)-[:FollowedBy]->(a3),
(a3)-[:FollowedBy]->(a4)
RETURN f.name
```

Figure 9. Example queries

Get action graph of all "all purpose" creams
```
MATCH (f:Formulation)-
[:HasRecipeStringRepr]-
>(r:RecipeActionGraphStringRepr)
WHERE f.name CONTAINS "all purpose"
RETURN f.name, r.repr
```

Get quantity of all ingredients of the name 'Cetyl Alcohol'
```
MATCH (f:Formulation)-
[:HasIngredient]->(ingd:Ingredient)
WHERE ingd.name CONTAINS 'Cetyl
Alcohol'
RETURN  f.name as Formulation,
ingd.name as IngredientName,
ingd.quantity as WeightQT
```

Get the formulations containing 'Cetyl Alcohol' as one of the ingredients
```
MATCH (f:Formulation)-
[:HasIngredient]->(ingd:Ingredient)
WHERE ingd.name CONTAINS 'Cetyl
Alcohol'
RETURN  COUNT(f.name) as
nnumFormulations, collect(f.name) as
Formulations
```

The query to retrieve ingredients of all cream of the specific kind such as "all purpose" or "skin whitening" would be similar to the one retrieving action graphs of all "all purpose" creams. In theory, having built a database of formulations of a specific type (with *FormulationType* nodes and the specific instances thereof), it is possible to query the details of similar *FormulationCategory* nodes and their constituents. This kind of query ability paves the way to the first step of intelligent design of formulated products as we show next.

Towards NLP-ML-Driven Formulation Design

Now that we have a database (and in effect a method to create such a database), it is possible to start planning the creation of a design variant. New design variant generation is an ongoing work, and much remains to explore, but we present an account of basic ideas around NLP-ML-driven design variant generation.

It is possible to query specific actions that are generally applied to an ingredient (either as a standalone ingredient or as a part of the mixture; see Figures 6, 7, and 8.) and then arrange them in order. While arranging the possible actions in a proper order remains a challenge, we show how we can realize the rest of the above-stated ideas.

One crucial observation we make is that an ingredient can appear in one of several possible names that it has (depending on the source of the formulation text).

Combining with the ingredient-functionality association, the naming of ingredient leads to the following tasks:

1.   Creating a dictionary of ingredients that captures other names of that ingredient
2.   Creating a mapping between ingredients and their functionalities
3.   Associating specific kind of *FormulationCategory* (such as "all purpose cream" or "skin whitening cream") to specific functionalities (of ingredients that it usually contains).

Once we complete these tasks, it is possible to design new variants as follows:

1.   First, given a specific kind of *FormulationCategory,* query the functionalities it usually contains
2.   Second, for each functionality, query all the ingredients associated with it
3.   Third, query the weight ranges of the ingredients
4.   Fourth, finalize the set of ingredients and/or mixtures
5.   Fifth, query the actions generally performed on each ingredient as a standalone or as a part of a mixture
6.   Sixth, order the actions suitably to arrive at a complete formulation variant.

Note that step 4 above requires the consideration of additional constraints, heuristics, and so on, which are out of the scope of this chapter and part of our ongoing work. Similarly, step 6 is where we establish the order of actions to be performed, i.e., generate a correctly ordered recipe. For both steps 4 and 6, we believe that the notion of a neighbourhood can be useful. We do not define neighbourhood formally in this chapter but explore what it could mean and how it can be useful.

In the following, we focus first on tasks 1 and 2, and later on the notion of a neighbourhood. Finally, we show how if we establish the "generate" capability, it is possible to "test" the variants with a skin model.

Figure 10. Ingredient details extraction utility steps

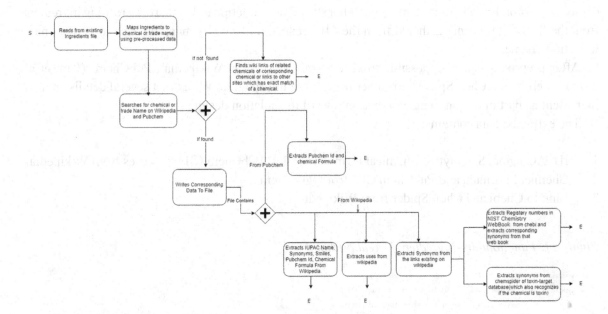

CONSTRUCTING INGREDIENT DICTIONARY FOR SYNONYMS AND FUNCTIONALITIES

We observe that there are scarce offline resources to collect synonyms or additional names of an ingredient. There are several online resources including ingredient entries at Wikipedia and specialized databases like the EU Cosmetic Ingredient Database7. We apply web scraping to several online resources to construct an ingredient synonyms dictionary.

Table 1. Number of formulations/constituents from offline and online resources

Formulations/Constituents	Number
Total Number of Ingredients in 410 Formulations	2633
Total number of Unique Ingredients	1086
Total number of Ingredients repeated more than once	333
Total number of Corresponding Chemical Names for Ingredient Names	447
Total number of entries, which has different name but same structure	599

Manually traversing a list of ingredients and searching synonyms for an ingredient is tedious. Web scraping automates the task of manually extracting the requisite data. The preparation/preprocessing step to scrape the data from the internet is to map the corresponding chemical name to an ingredient name, as chemical names are prominently available in public datasets. If the ingredient name is a trade name, it is less likely to occur on a given site as information about trade name is not always publically available.

Figure 10 shows the steps followed by our extraction utility. Table 1. shows the total number of ingredients, corresponding chemical names, and other stats. The extraction utility starts by reading ingredients from the list of ingredients gathered from the 410 creams, followed by mapping each ingredient name to its trade name.

After preprocessing, it is possible to search sources such as Wikipedia[8], PubChem[9] (Kim et al., 2015), Chebi[10], and ChemSpider[11] to gather the desired information. We extract several details about an ingredient as part of our ongoing exploration toward formulation design.

The extracted data contains:

1. IUPAC name, Synonyms, Chemical formula, Smiles, PubChem CID, and uses from Wikipedia.
2. Chemical Formula and PubChem CID from PubChem.
3. Link to Chebi and ChemSpider from Wikipedia.

Figure 11. Functionality-Ingredient Neighbourhood

antioxidant	{tocopherol oil clr}
antistatic	{triton x-400, glucam p-20 distearate, isopropyl palmitate}
binding	{isopropyl myristate, isopropyl stearate, isopropyl palmitate}
buffering	{triethanolamine, triethanolamine, potassium hydroxide 20%, potassium hydroxide 20%, magnesium sulphate, 12. triethanolamine, 15. triethanolamine, 16. sodium borate, anhydrous}
cleansing	{stearic acid, xxx, 12 hydroxystearic acid}
denaturant	{glycerin, glycerin 86%, glycerin 86%}
emollient	{glyceryl monostearate, s.e., cetyl alcohol, glyceryl monostearate, s.e., cetyl alcohol, methyl glucose sesquistearate (glucate ss), coconut oil, 76, glyceryl monostearate, neut., u.s.p. white mineral oil, cetyl alcohol, stearyl alcohol, cetyl alcohol, oil, isocetyl stearate, isopropyl myristate, …}
emulsifying	{cetyl alcohol, stearic acid, xxx, cetyl alcohol, methyl glucose sesquistearate (glucate ss), coconut oil, 76, cetyl alcohol, cetyl alcohol, armotan mo (sorbitan oleate), 12 hydroxystearic acid, armotan mo (sorbitan oleate), 7. arlacel 60, 9. tween 60, ethoxylated oleyl alcohol, 8. arlacel 60, 9.…}
emulsion stabilising	{stearic acid, xxx, stearyl alcohol}
foam boosting	{stearyl alcohol}
hair conditioning	{germaben ii}
hair dyeing	{solulan 16, cutina fs 25, 6. solulan 25}
humectant	{propylene glycol, propylene glycol, methyl gluceth-20 sesquistearate (glucamate sse-20), methyl gluceth-20 (glucam e-20), propylene glycol, sorbitol 70%, sorbitol 70%, glycerin, glycerin 86%, glycerin 86%, 8. sorbitol (70%), 11. sorbitol (7 0%), 9. sorbitol (70%)}
moisturising	{methyl gluceth-20 sesquistearate (glucamate sse-20), methyl gluceth-20 (glucam e-20), 3. dow fluid 556, 4. dow fluid 556, 5. dow fluid 200, 350 cs.}
opacifying	{cetyl alcohol, cetyl alcohol, cetyl alcohol, stearyl alcohol, cetyl alcohol, ethoxylated oleyl alcohol, triglycerin diisosteatrate}
plasticiser	{sorbitol 70%, sorbitol 70%, 8. sorbitol (70%), 11. sorbitol (7 0%), 9. sorbitol (70%)}
preservative	{methyl paraben, triton x-400, dowicil 200, dowicil 200}
refatting	{stearic acid, xxx, stearyl alcohol}
skin conditioning	{amerchol c, propylene glycol, amerchol c, propylene glycol, methyl glucose sesquistearate (glucate ss), germaben ii, propylene glycol, elfacos c 26, isocetyl stearate, isopropyl myristate, sorbitol 70%, isopropyl stearate, sorbitol 70%, beeswax, vegetable oil, isopropyl palmitate, tocopherol oil …}
solvent	{mineral oil, 70 vis., propylene glycol, mineral oil, 70 vis., propylene glycol, propylene glycol, mineral oil, 70 vis., isopropyl myristate, glycerin, glycerin 86%, glycerin 86%, mineral oil, 70 vis., isopropyl palmitate, 2. mineral oil, 70 vis., 4. mineral oil, 70 vis.}

If an entry exists at Wikipedia, then we extract the details mentioned above starting with the Wikipedia entry. Chebi often contains links to registry numbers from NIST Chemistry WebBook, which may contain additional synonyms. Using the retrieved link of ChemSpider, the utility selects the link to Toxin Target Database, and if the ingredient is a toxin, we extract additional synonyms.

Figure 11. shows a snapshot of functionalities and the corresponding ingredients from the 410 formulations. From the point of view of database storage, we save the ingredients and functionality as a separate graph rather than incorporating this information in the schema presented earlier[12]. All ingredients representative of a functionality, connect to a node representing that functionality. If an ingredient has several functionalities, it connects to individual nodes representative of those functionalities.

Note that certain pieces of text in various sites offer functionalities for which the ingredient is used. Consider the following paragraph from Wikipedia[13] about Triethanolamine, which we process to obtain functionalities for which Triethanolamine may be used- "Triethanolamine is used primarily in making surfactants, such as for emulsifier. It is a common ingredient in formulations used for both industrial and consumer products. The Triethanolamine neutralizes fatty acids, adjusts and buffers the pH, and solubilizes oils and other ingredients that are not completely soluble in water. Triethanolammonium salts in some *cases are more soluble than salts of alkali metals that might be used otherwise, and results in less alkaline products than would from using alkali metal hydroxides to form the salt. Some common products in which Triethanolamine is found are sunscreen lotions, liquid laundry detergents, dishwashing liquids, general cleaners, hand sanitizers, polishes, metalworking fluids, paints, shaving cream and printing inks.*"

Simple open IE applied to above text leads to facts such as below. The processing involves looking for "be", "consider", and "use" lemmatized verbs.

Used (in/for/as)?
-in making surfactants, such as for emulsifier
-a common ingredient in formulations
-for both industrial and consumer products
-completely soluble in water
-more soluble than salts of alkali metals
-alkali metal hydroxides to form the salt
-sunscreen lotions, liquid laundry detergents, dishwashing liquids, general cleaners, hand sanitizers, polishes, metalworking fluids, paints, shaving cream and printing inks

A more sophisticated scheme is also possible wherein we look for preselected verbs in the triples extracted by open IE. It turns out that the verbs list we obtained for identifying actions in action graphs of formulations can be quite useful for this purpose. We are currently further exploring this thread.

Figure 12. Ingredient-ingredient neighbourhood

	Mineral Oil	Glycerol	Isopropyl Stearate	ABIL Wax 9801	Isopropyl Myristate	OCtyl Palmitate
Mineral Oil	0	-8	0	0	0	4
Glycerol	-8	0	0	0	0	0
Isopropyl Stearate	0	0	0	1	0	0
ABIL Wax 9801	0	0	1	0	3	0
Isopropyl Myristate	0	0	0	3	0	0
OCtyl Palmitate	4	0	0	0	0	0

0 = Never occur together
>0 = Occur together in same phase
<0 = Occur together in same formulation but different phases

Constructing Various Neighbourhoods

Figure 12. shows ingredients that never occur together[14], as well as those that occur together, esp. in the same phase. Such neighbourhoods or clusters of ingredients are useful because using the membership within a specific ingredient-ingredient neighbourhood, the choice of other ingredients can be informed.

We can extend the notion of a neighbourhood to functionality-ingredient and ingredient-actions in both directions. This arrangement brings about natural clustering to the ingredients and functionalities as evident in Figure 13.

As shown in Figure 13., it becomes possible to further cluster or rank the neighbourhoods of a) ingredients for functionalities, b) ingredients for actions performed on them, and c) actions for ingredients to which they apply. Note that all the statistics are from the 410 formulations, but already explicate useful insights that tend to be implicit knowledge even if well understood. Functionalities such as "emollients" "viscosity controlling" dominate due to formulations being creams of various kinds. "Water", "Propylene Glycol", "Fragrance", "Triethanolamine", and "Cetyl Alcohol" are the most common ingredients and "Heat", "Add", and "Cool" are some of the frequently occurring actions.

On top of such neighbourhoods, we can also relate functionalities of ingredients to specific kinds of formulations ("massage creams" or "chamomile creams") and thereby to formulation categories ("creams" and types ("cosmetic and toiletry formulations") represented respectively as Formulation, *Formulation-Category*, and *FormulationType* nodes in the graph schema in Figure 6. For instance, "massage cream" instances tend to contain ingredients with antistatic, binding, buffering, and denaturant functionalities, among others. Similarly, "chamomile cream" instances tend to contain functionalities such as bulking, humectant, plasticizer among others.

Figure 13. Functionality-ingredient, ingredient-actions and actions-ingredients neighbourhoods

Top 10 Functionalities with Max Ingredients		Top 10 Ingredients with Max Actions		Top 10 Actions applied to Max Ingredients	
emollient	387	water	89	heat	678
emulsifying	254	propylene glycol	65	add	553
viscosity controlling	242	fragrance	57	cool	453
skin conditioning	234	triethanolamine	49	stir	357
solvent	233	cetyl alcohol	48	continue	342
humectant	151	mineral oil	46	mix	279
opacifying	139	deionized water	46	stirring	276
antistatic	105	preservative	45	melt	266
binding	98	glycerin	43	mixing	241
emulsion stabilising	95	isopropyl myristate	42	cooled	163

Although the correlations in the neighbourhood are induced by the underlying set of formulations (410 cream formulations in our case) and will likely differ to various degrees as more formulations are added to the database, this approach shows that it is possible to establish the neighbourhoods in the first place. The steps proposed earlier in this section can be executed on the *Formulation, FormulationCategory,* and *FormulationType* nodes via the additional information now available in terms of neighbourhoods. For instance, it is possible to query the functionalities usually associated with a specific kind of *FormulationCategory,* query all the ingredients associated with it for each functionality, and then query the weight ranges of the ingredients, completing the first 3 steps. With sufficient heuristics enabling the choice of ingredients within the suggested set, it is possible to query the actions generally performed on each ingredient as a standalone or as a part of a mixture. Finally, these actions should be ordered. In theory, it is possible to inform this last step as well by storing the processing order in the ingredient-ingredient neighbourhood. We are currently working to further elaborate on this possibility.

This chapter intends to describe how we have enabled this kind of automated design of a formulation. Several challenges still need to be addressed including how to expand the database of formulations and to what extent, how to incorporate heuristics on combinations of ingredients, allowing economic and other constraints in the choice of constraints, and how to come up with a correctly ordered recipe of the chosen ingredients.

If on the other hand, we were able to address these challenges practically, we can match this "generate" step with a "test" step for which we already have specialized models such as a skin model. In the following, we first elaborate on the structure of human skin, describe a skin model, and then show how the generated design variants may be tested.

TOWARD TESTING THE FORMULATION VARIANTS WITH SKIN MODEL

Skin is the largest external organ of the human body, covering approximately 1.5 – 2 m2 of surface area. It's been more often referred to as the body's armour because of the protective role it plays. It prevents our body from excessive loss of water, attack of foreign pathogens, irritation from harmful chemicals and much more. Moreover, it is the most pampered organ of the human body due to its direct impact on one's external appearance. Anatomically, human skin is composed of three primary layers – epidermis, dermis and hypodermis. The epidermis forms the topmost layer and is responsible for skin's health apart from providing the skin with its glow, youthfulness and texture. The epidermis is further divided into 5 sub-layers of which stratum corneum (SC) is the first and the one which we see as our skin. Dermis forms the second layer beneath the epidermis and is primarily made up of collagen and elastin. Collagen fibers help provide a structural framework, while elastin supplies elastic properties to the skin. The hypodermis is mostly composed of adipose tissues and provide the heat resistance (controls the temperature).

Humans often tend to use many formulated products which are in direct contact with the skin. These products can be broadly categorized depending upon their intended use; pharmaceutics (topical creams, oils, ointments for pain-relieving), cosmetics (antiaging creams, moisturizers) and toiletries (shampoos, face wash). Each of these products is a combination of multiple ingredients, commonly grouped as active ingredients and inactive/supporting ingredients. Active ingredients refer to the chemicals (either synthetic or natural, lone or mixtures) which provide the product with its primary functionality, for example, pharmaceutics (diclofenac – a typical Nonsteroidal anti-inflammatory drug or NSAID for pain relief), cosmetics (acetyl hexapeptide-8, an anti-wrinkle peptide) and toiletries (ammonium glycolate

– cleanser). On the contrary, inactive/supporting ingredients are necessarily added, either to confer an enhancing effect on the active ingredient - better absorption, enhanced solubility or to provide additional functionality to the product – such as reduced viscosity, soothing smell, improved stability.

Ironically, each of these products and in effect, their ingredients interact with the skin at various level of granularity[15]. For example, diclofenac- the pain-relieving drug used in topical creams is required to pass through all the layers of skin and reach to its site of action, whereas active ingredients such as alpha hydroxy acids (AHAs) used in cosmetics need not even cross the SC. From this perspective, it is vital that all skincare professionals, estheticians or physicians have a good understanding of the interaction of products and/or their ingredients with the skin's anatomy and physiology.

The Need for Digital Disruption

The current best practices in cosmetic and pharma industry are to conduct numerous in-vitro/in-vivo tests on animals, followed by clinical trials for any new/improved formulations/ingredients. These tests are incredibly time-consuming, incur enormous expenses, kill more than 100 million animals, and yet, 9 out of 10 experimental drugs fail in clinical studies[16]. The one reason could be – animal models do not translate well with humans, due to noticeable anatomical and physiological differences between the two. With the recent ban on animal testing across various global geographies[17] and considering the time and costs involved in the development and testing of new drug/cosmetics formulations (Bagajewicz, 2007), it is imperative to supplement/replace some of these elaborate in-vivo/in-vitro tests with in-silico tests.

There exists an in-silico skin model based on the multiscale modelling framework linking atomistic-molecular-mesoscale to macroscale to study molecular transport across the stratum corneum (Gupta and Rai, 2017), (Gupta et al., 2018). The model thus developed has provided a base to develop an IT-enabled platform for the simulation-based design and development of pharma/cosmetics products. We are also currently looking at developing a multiscale model to characterize the viscoelastic nature of the skin. The multiscale model should capture the skin's mechanical behaviour at various length scales from the molecular level to the macro level.

In order to gauge the practical ability of the *in-silico* skin model to aid in designing of formulated products, it is essential to understand its performance as described by following use cases:

1. Permeation of molecules through skin lipid bilayer Gupta et al. (2016) performed physics based simulations (molecular dynamics (MD)) to study permeation of 12 molecules, including ingredients like ethanol and DMSO, which are widely studied for their permeation enhancing capabilities in various formulations. It was observed that diffusion and permeation coefficients calculated from MD simulations agree well with experimental data, thus validating the applicability of the in-silico model to be used as a screening tool

2. Penetration of proteins with gold nanoparticles Gupta et al. (2017) demonstrate the usefulness of the in-silico skin model to design drug delivery mechanisms for transdermal applications. Simulations reveal that horseradish peroxidase protein (HRP) on its own is unable to breach the skin barrier, while in presence of the gold nanoparticle (approx. 3 nm in size) it first binds to the particle and then breaches the barrier. These findings were also in concurrence with a separate experimental study performed on rat skin by Huang et al.

3. Testing of permeation enhancers Gupta et al. (2019) developed a multilayer in-silico skin model to study the partition and diffusion coefficients of chemical permeation enhancers from a variety

of chemical functionalities (fatty acids, esters and alcohols) at different concentrations. The results showed a good correlation between the experimental enhancement ratio and calculated overall lipid order parameter.

4. *Multiscale simulation of drug transport* Gajula et al. (2017) demonstrate the development of a multiscale framework to predict the drug release profile for caffeine, fentanyl and naphthol when delivered via transdermal route. The diffusion coefficients of the drug calculated using molecular simulations were used as input for macroscale models to obtain the release profile. The simulated results thus obtained are in good agreement with those from experiments.

5. *Skin mechanical model* Jayabal et al. (2019) studied the change in the mechanical properties of human skin with age by developing a 1D linear viscoelastic phenomenological model. The authors show that the presence of a thin layer of cosmetic polymer on the skin enhances its mechanical properties, thus giving it an antiaging effect.

It is evident from above and many more use cases (Gupta and Rai, 2017; Gupta and Rai, 2018; Badhe et al., 2019) that such a skin model can be used as a detailed testing paradigm to screen pharma/ cosmetic formulations.

Integrating the extraction, storage, and retrieval of formulations with the skin model Revisiting the goal of formulation design variant generation; given a specific kind of *FormulationCategory*, we should be able to query the functionalities that category contains, and for each functionality, query all the ingredients associated with it. With the access to weight ranges of the ingredients, if we finalize the list of ingredients along with the ability to order the actions, then we can arrive at a set of complete formulation variants.

We propose the following way of testing a list of design variants thus obtained. In several engagements, the customers often already give a preferred list of critical ingredients, where the rest of the ingredients and the other details of a specific *FormulationCategory* need to be put together. We assume the availability of some ingredients in the testing process.

1. **Using the Digital Skin:** We attempt to understand the interaction/behaviour of ingredients at hand with skin model on following aspects: (a) free energy profiles (b) diffusion profiles and coefficient (c) permeation coefficient (d) order parameter and (e) mechanical properties. We expect that the testing of given ingredients using the in-silico skin model to provide hints towards the final goal of choosing relevant supporting ingredients for the formulated product. As an example, suppose the given ingredients after in-silico testing result in permeation coefficients below a required threshold, then we can choose some of the supporting/inactive ingredients for the sole purpose of enhancing the permeability of the given ingredients.

2. **Querying the Database of Formulations:** This step proceeds as described above and earlier in the section on NLP-ML-driven formulation design. This step helps in identifying probable candidates that can function as supporting ingredients along with the given ingredients.

3. **Testing with the Digital Skin Model:** We test the list of identified and finalized ingredients for their interactions with the in-silico skin model to make sure none of them either in isolation or in combination (especially with given ingredients) result in an effect detrimental for the functionality of the product. If we do find such situations, we intend to store them along the similar lines as the rest of the formulation details, so that in the next iteration, such knowledge already enables ruling out such combinations of ingredients.

In our opinion, such combination of generating and testing design variants will likely result in considerable cost and time-to-market reduction.

FROM FORMULATION TO A FORMULATED PRODUCT- A DIGITAL TWIN PERSPECTIVE

Although the *in-silico* design and testing of formulations as elucidated above is an exciting line of investigation, there is much more to it, from laboratory to commercialization.

Product design in the formulation industry is a complicated event involving multiple stakeholders across the organization. More often, different teams need to work closely to ensure the creation of profitable and sustainable products. The teams include sales and marketing, research and development, procurement, manufacturing and production, management and finance, and quality control teams. Every single piece of information shared by each of these teams is considered during the product development cycle and manifests itself in the final product.

Figure 14. Digital twin for formulation design

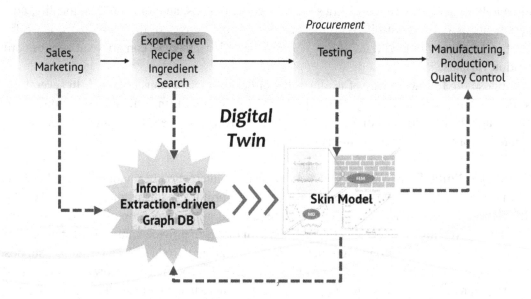

In usual practice, the sales and marketing team is responsible for gathering information (via interviews, surveys, consumer behaviour analysis) with regards product attributes (functional, engineering, sensorial, regulatory) thus defining a broad scope of the product for the R&D team. Formulation chemists in the R&D team tend to refer to previous formulations matching similar requirements by manually going through a plethora of reports, journal articles, conference proceedings, patents, followed by serendipity driven experimentation and testing to arrive at the desired concoction.

It's at this stage that our work described in detail in the previous sections would greatly aid the scientists by providing a digital infrastructure for in-silico design and testing of formulations, what we refer to as a *digital twin for formulation design*, as illustrated in Figure 14. The notion of the digital twin refers to a digital replica of actual and potential physical entities, processes, people, places, systems and devices used for various purposes. In our case, both the graph database and the skin model represent the digital twin of the "generate and test" aspects of the formulation design. As described in the previous section, it is also possible to enrich the database of formulations and their constituents by storing the observations from the skin model to the database. It is more than evident that a typical formulated product development cycle involves enormous information sharing across a diverse value chain and set of teams with varied expertise. Thus, it is imperative that key stakeholders at every stage, have access to the right amount of information in the correct form to ensure business continuity and expedite product launch.

Once we finalize the formulation constituents (ingredients/mixtures, their weight fractions, recipe, conditions) at lab-scale, it is taken up for scale-up. Scale-up is usually performed step by step from lab-pilot-commercial scale, eliminating areas of doubts and uncertainty while ensuring economic feasibility. The idea is to reduce time, effort and money spent in trial and error research, and to provide assistance to make informed decisions on the specific set of experiments needed to validate the findings. We assume that we get a new product design query with a set of product attributes such as smoothness for a cream (Zhang et al., 2017) or scratchproofness for a coating. We plan to use a model similar to (Bagajewicz, 2007) that integrates product functionality, price, manufacturing, and supply chain.

CONCLUDING REMARKS

The current research and literature in product design suggests how to incorporate ingredients under different constraints but lacks an extensible database with the ability to execute non-trivial queries. We have shown in this chapter how to create a database of various details of formulated products from both offline and online textual sources. We demonstrated how to constructs dictionaries of ingredients and discussed the notion of neighbourhoods. We also described the steps to follow to generate possible product design variants. We are currently working further on two steps, finalizing the set of ingredients, and then ordering the actions on the chosen ingredients with specific conditions. Once we can finalize the ingredients and order the actions to create a complete recipe, we showed that it is possible to test the generated product design variants with an in-silico model. Although several challenges as mentioned above and discussed earlier remain unaddressed, we believe that overall our approach comprising of the ability to search through an extensible database of product details, integration possibilities with in-silico models for testing, and reduced reliance on experts, leads to product design variant generation and testing that is faster, better, and cheaper respectively.

REFERENCES

Angles, R., & Gutierrez, C. (2008). Survey of graph database models. *ACM Computing Surveys*, *40*(1), 1–39. doi:10.1145/1322432.1322433

Arrieta-Escobar, J. A., Bernardo, F. P., Orjuela, A., Camargo, M., & Morel, L. (2019). Incorporation of heuristic knowledge in the optimal design of formulated products: Application to a cosmetic emulsion. *Computers & Chemical Engineering*, *122*, 265–274. doi:10.1016/j.compchemeng.2018.08.032

Badhe, Y., Gupta, R., & Rai, B. (2019). Structural and barrier properties of the skin ceramide lipid bilayer: A molecular dynamics simulation study. *Journal of Molecular Modeling*, *25*(5), 140. doi:10.100700894-019-4008-5 PMID:31041534

Bagajewicz, M. J. (2007). On the role of microeconomics, planning, and finances in product design. *AIChE Journal. American Institute of Chemical Engineers*, *53*(12), 3155–3170. doi:10.1002/aic.11332

Bernardo, F. P., & Saraiva, P. M. (2015). A conceptual model for chemical product design. *AIChE Journal. American Institute of Chemical Engineers*, *61*(3), 802–815. doi:10.1002/aic.14681

Chatterjee, P., & Alvi, M. M. (2014). Excipients and active pharmaceutical ingredients. In *Pediatric Formulations* (pp. 347–361). New York, NY: Springer. doi:10.1007/978-1-4899-8011-3_24

Conte, E., Gani, R., & Ng, K. M. (2011). Design of formulated products: A systematic methodology. *AIChE Journal. American Institute of Chemical Engineers*, *57*(9), 2431–2449. doi:10.1002/aic.12458

Dionisio, K. L., Phillips, K., Price, P. S., Grulke, C. M., Williams, A., Biryol, D., ... Isaacs, K. K. (2018). The Chemical and Products Database, a resource for exposure-relevant data on chemicals in consumer products. *Scientific Data*, *5*(1), 180125. doi:10.1038data.2018.125 PMID:29989593

Flick, E. W. (1989-2014). *Cosmetic and toiletry formulations* (Vol. 1-8). Elsevier.

Gajula, K., Gupta, R., Sridhar, D. B., & Rai, B. (2017). In-Silico skin model: A multiscale simulation study of drug transport. *Journal of Chemical Information and Modeling*, *57*(8), 2027–2034. doi:10.1021/acs.jcim.7b00224 PMID:28718641

Gani, R., & Ng, K. M. (2015). Product design–molecules, devices, functional products, and formulated products. *Computers & Chemical Engineering*, *81*, 70–79. doi:10.1016/j.compchemeng.2015.04.013

Gupta, R., Dwadasi, B. S., & Rai, B. (2017). *U.S. Patent Application No. 15/466,653*. Washington, DC: US Patent Office.

Gupta, R., Dwadasi, B. S., Rai, B., & Mitragotri, S. (2019). Effect of Chemical Permeation Enhancers on Skin Permeability: In silico screening using Molecular Dynamics simulations. *Scientific Reports*, *9*(1), 1456. doi:10.103841598-018-37900-0 PMID:30728438

Gupta, R., Gajula, K., Dwadasi, B., & Rai, B. (2018). *U.S. Patent Application No. 15/900,448*. Washington, DC: US Patent Office.

Gupta, R., Kashyap, N., & Rai, B. (2017). Transdermal cellular membrane penetration of proteins with gold nanoparticles: A molecular dynamics study. *Physical Chemistry Chemical Physics*, *19*(11), 7537–7545. doi:10.1039/C6CP08775B PMID:28252121

Gupta, R., & Rai, B. (2017). Effect of size and surface charge of gold nanoparticles on their skin permeability: A molecular dynamics study. *Scientific Reports*, *7*(1), 45292. doi:10.1038rep45292 PMID:28349970

Gupta, R., & Rai, B. (2018). Electroporation of Skin Stratum Corneum Lipid Bilayer and Molecular Mechanism of Drug Transport: A Molecular Dynamics Study. *Langmuir, 34*(20), 5860–5870. doi:10.1021/acs.langmuir.8b00423 PMID:29708340

Gupta, R., Sridhar, D. B., & Rai, B. (2016). Molecular dynamics simulation study of permeation of molecules through skin lipid bilayer. *The Journal of Physical Chemistry B, 120*(34), 8987–8996. doi:10.1021/acs.jpcb.6b05451 PMID:27518707

Harper, P. M., & Gani, R. (2000). A multi-step and multi-level approach for computer aided molecular design. *Computers & Chemical Engineering, 24*(2-7), 677–683. doi:10.1016/S0098-1354(00)00410-5

Hill, M. (2009). Chemical product engineering—The third paradigm. *Computers & Chemical Engineering, 33*(5), 947–953. doi:10.1016/j.compchemeng.2008.11.013

Isaacs, K. K., Goldsmith, M. R., Egeghy, P., Phillips, K., Brooks, R., Hong, T., & Wambaugh, J. F. (2016). Characterization and prediction of chemical functions and weight fractions in consumer products. *Toxicology Reports, 3*, 723–732. doi:10.1016/j.toxrep.2016.08.011 PMID:28959598

Isaacs, K. K., Phillips, K. A., Biryol, D., Dionisio, K. L., & Price, P. S. (2018). Consumer product chemical weight fractions from ingredient lists. *Journal of Exposure Science & Environmental Epidemiology, 28*(3), 216–222. doi:10.1038/jes.2017.29 PMID:29115287

Jayabal, H., Dingari, N. N., & Rai, B. (2019). A linear viscoelastic model to understand skin mechanical behaviour and for cosmetic formulation design. *International Journal of Cosmetic Science, 41*(3), 292–299. doi:10.1111/ics.12535 PMID:31032974

Kiddon, C., Ponnuraj, G. T., Zettlemoyer, L., & Choi, Y. (2015, September). Mise en place: Unsupervised interpretation of instructional recipes. In *Proceedings of the 2015 Conference on Empirical Methods in Natural Language Processing* (pp. 982-992). 10.18653/v1/D15-1114

Kim, S., Thiessen, P. A., Bolton, E. E., Chen, J., Fu, G., Gindulyte, A., ... Wang, J. (2015). PubChem substance and compound databases. *Nucleic Acids Research, 44*(D1), D1202–D1213. doi:10.1093/nar/gkv951 PMID:26400175

Lee, C. K. H., Choy, K. L., & Chan, Y. N. (2014). A knowledge-based ingredient formulation system for chemical product development in the personal care industry. *Computers & Chemical Engineering, 65*, 40–53. doi:10.1016/j.compchemeng.2014.03.004

Martín, M., & Martínez, A. (2013). A methodology for simultaneous process and product design in the formulated consumer products industry: The case study of the detergent business. *Chemical Engineering Research & Design, 91*(5), 795–809. doi:10.1016/j.cherd.2012.08.012

Michalun, M. V., & DiNardo, J. C. (2014). *Skin care and cosmetic ingredients dictionary*. Cengage Learning.

Mysore, S., Kim, E., Strubell, E., Liu, A., Chang, H. S., Kompella, S., ... Olivetti, E. (2017). *Automatically extracting action graphs from materials science synthesis procedures*. arXiv preprint arXiv:1711.06872

Robinson, I., Webber, J., & Eifrem, E. (2013). *Graph databases*. O'Reilly Media, Inc.

Wibowo, C., & Ng, K. M. (2001). Product-oriented process synthesis and development: Creams and pastes. *AIChE Journal. American Institute of Chemical Engineers*, *47*(12), 2746–2767. doi:10.1002/aic.690471214

Wibowo, C., & Ng, K. M. (2002). Product-centered processing: Manufacture of chemical-based consumer products. *AIChE Journal. American Institute of Chemical Engineers*, *48*(6), 1212–1230. doi:10.1002/aic.690480609

Zhang, L., Fung, K. Y., Wibowo, C., & Gani, R. (2018). Advances in chemical product design. *Reviews in Chemical Engineering*, *34*(3), 319–340. doi:10.1515/revce-2016-0067

Zhang, L., Fung, K. Y., Zhang, X., Fung, H. K., & Ng, K. M. (2017). An integrated framework for designing formulated products. *Computers & Chemical Engineering*, *107*, 61–76. doi:10.1016/j.compchemeng.2017.05.014

ENDNOTES

[1]   AceForm 4.0 Value Chains in Formulations Manufacturing: EU Horizon 2020 Research D3.3, D3.4 https://formulation-network.eu/perch/resources/admin/aceform-common-vision-and-roadmap-for-formulated-productsnov18.pdf

[2]   Apache PDFBox https://pdfbox.apache.org/

[3]   * indicates that there could be multiple objects, appearing as a comma-separated list or even as a list of objects joined by and(s).

[4]   Open IE https://demo.allennlp.org/open-information-extraction

[5]   Spacy Dependency Parser https://spacy.io/usage/linguistic-features/#dependency-parse

[6]   Cypher graph query language https://neo4j.com/developer/cypher-query-language/

[7]   EU CosIng https://ec.europa.eu/growth/sectors/cosmetics/cosing_en

[8]   For instance, a "cetyl alcohol" entry at Wikipedia https://en.wikipedia.org/wiki/Cetyl_alcohol

[9]   The "cetyl alcohol" entry at PubChem https://pubchem.ncbi.nlm.nih.gov/compound/1-Hexadecanol

[10]   The "cetyl alcohol" entry at Chebi https://www.ebi.ac.uk/chebi/searchId.do?chebiId=16125

[11]   The "cetyl alcohol" entry at ChemSpider http://www.chemspider.com/Chemical-Structure.2581.html

[12]   As we progress in the ongoing work, we are also trying to reduce redundancies in the formulation graph schema presented earlier. This is a problematic task esp. with regards the ingredients since we have to manage synonyms of ingredients as they partake in specific formulations.

[13]   Verbatim text from Triethanolamine entry on Wikipedia https://en.wikipedia.org/wiki/Triethanol-amine

[14]   And therefore, are not in the neighbourhood of those ingredients.

[15]   Both anatomically and physiologically, depending on the purpose they are intended to fulfil.

[16]   Top Five Reasons to Stop Animal Testing https://www.peta.org/blog/top-five-reasons-stop-animal-testing/

[17]   EU extends ban on animal-tested cosmetics https://www.euronews.com/2013/03/11/eu-extends-ban-on-animal-tested-cosmetics

APPENDIX

Examples of action graphs for recipes using open IE (with stacking) and dependency parsing (also with stacking).

Figure 15.

```
              ACID-PH OIL-IN-WATER CREAM - B

RAW MATERIALS                                          % By Weight

Oil Phase:
WITCONOL MST (Glyceryl Stearate)                          10.0
WITCONOL APM (PPG-3 Myristyl Ether)                        3.0
Perfecta Petrolatum                                        5.0
WITCONOL H-35A (PEG-8 Stearate)                            5.0
WITCAMIDE MAS (Stearamide MEA Stearate)                    3.0
EMPHOS D70-30C (Sodium Glyceryl Oleate Phosphate)          0.5
Cetyl Alcohol                                              2.0
Propylparaben                                              0.1

Water Phase:
EMCOL 4072 (Disodium Hydrogenated Cottonseed Glyceride
     Sulfosuccinate)                                       3.0
Glycerin USP                                               3.0
Methylparaben                                              0.15
Fragrance, Color                                           q.s.
Water                                          q.s. to 100

    Heat each phase to 70 to 75C and stir until uniform. Add the
Water Phase to the Oil Phase at 70 to 75C with moderate agita-
tion and maintain agitation and temperature for 15 minutes. Let
cool, with slow stirring; avoid air entrainment during cooling
cycle. Pour at or below 28C.
```

EXTRACTION USING OPEN INFORMATION EXTRACTION

Action	Mixture	Condition
Heat	Each phase	to 70 to 75c
Stir	Each phase	Until uniform
Add	water phase	To the oil phase at 70 to 75c
Maintain	Each phase + water phase + oil phase	Agitation and temperature For 15 minutes
Let	Each phase + water phase + oil phase	cool
Avoid	Each phase + water phase + oil phase	Air entrainment during cooling cycle
Cooling	Each phase + water phase + oil phase	cycle
Pour	Each phase + water phase + oil phase	At or below 28c

EXTRACTION USING STACKING AND DEPENDENCY PARSING

Action	Mixture	Condition
Heat	Each phase	to 70 to 75c
Stir	Each phase	Until Uniform
Add	Water phase + Oil phase	The water phase to the oil phase at 70 to 75C with moderate agitation and
Maintain	Each phase + Water phase + Oil phase	Agitation and temperature for 15 minutes
Let	Each phase + Water phase + Oil phase	Cool With slow stirring
Avoid	Each phase + Water phase + Oil phase	Air entrainment
Pour	Each phase + Water phase + Oil phase	At or below 28C

Figure 16.

<table>
<tr><td colspan="2" align="center">CAMOMILE HAND CREAM</td></tr>
<tr><td>RAW MATERIALS</td><td>% By Weight</td></tr>
<tr><td>A.</td><td></td></tr>
<tr><td>SOFTISAN 601</td><td>38.0</td></tr>
<tr><td>MIGLYOL 829</td><td>6.0</td></tr>
<tr><td>Hard paraffin</td><td>3.0</td></tr>
<tr><td>B.</td><td></td></tr>
<tr><td>Karion F</td><td>5.0</td></tr>
<tr><td>Propylene glycol</td><td>3.0</td></tr>
<tr><td>Preservative</td><td>q.s.</td></tr>
<tr><td>Water</td><td>ad 100.0</td></tr>
<tr><td>C.</td><td></td></tr>
<tr><td>Perfume oil</td><td>q.s.</td></tr>
<tr><td>Extrapon Camomile Special</td><td>2.0</td></tr>
</table>

Preparation:
A and B are heated separately to 75-80C and B is emulsified into A.
The perfume is added below 40C.

EXTRACTION USING OPEN IE

Action	Mixture	Condition
Heated	A+B	To 75-80c and B
Emulsified	A+B	Into A.
Added	A+B	Below 40c

EXTRACTION USING STACKING AND DEPENDENCY PARSING

Action	Mixture	Condition
Heated	A + B	Separately to 75-80c
Emulsified	A + B	Into
Added	perfume	Below 40c

Figure 17.

<table>
<tr><td colspan="2" align="center">ANTIPERSPIRANT CREAM</td></tr>
<tr><td>RAW MATERIALS</td><td>% By Weight</td></tr>
<tr><td>AMERLATE P</td><td>1.50</td></tr>
<tr><td>AMERCHOL L-101</td><td>2.50</td></tr>
<tr><td>SOLULAN 16</td><td>2.00</td></tr>
<tr><td>Glyceryl monostearate, neut.</td><td>7.50</td></tr>
<tr><td>Spermwax</td><td>3.00</td></tr>
<tr><td>Glycerine</td><td>2.00</td></tr>
<tr><td>Veegum HV</td><td>1.75</td></tr>
<tr><td>Water</td><td>41.75</td></tr>
<tr><td>Chlorhydrol, 50%</td><td>38.00</td></tr>
<tr><td>Perfume and Preservative</td><td>q.s.</td></tr>
</table>

White, light-textured o/w cream with quick rub-in

Procedure:
Disperse the Veegum in the water using high speed mixing. Add the water phase at 70C to the oil phase at 70C while mixing. Continue mixing and cool to 50C. Warm the Chlorhydrol to 50C and add it slowly to the batch. Continue mixing and cool to 35C. Homogenize.

EXTRACTION USING OPEN IE

Action	Mixture	Condition
Disperse	The veegum	In the water
Using	Water + veegum	High speed mixing
Add	Water + veegum	at 70c
Continue	Water + veegum	Mixing
Cool	Water + veegum	To 50C
Warm	chlorhydrol	To 35C

EXTRACTION USING STACKING AND DEPENDENCY PARSING

Action	Mixture	Condition
Disperse	Veegum + Water	Veegum in using high speed mixing
Add	Water phase + Oil phase	At 70c to oil phase while mixing
Continue	Veegum + Water + Water phase + Oil phase	Mixing cool to 50c
Warm	Chlorhydrol	Chlorhydrol to 50c
Add	Chlorhydrol + Veegum + Water phase + Oil phase	It slowly to batch
Continue	Chlorhydrol + Veegum + Water phase + Oil phase	Mixing
Cool	Chlorhydrol + Veegum + Water phase + Oil phase	To 35c
Homogenize	Chlorhydrol + Veegum + Water phase + Oil phase	

Chapter 11
Materials Design, Development, and Deployment in Manufacturing Industry:
A Digital Paradigm

B. P. Gautham

TCS Research, Tata Consultancy Services, India

Sreedhar Reddy

TCS Research, Tata Consultancy Services, India

ABSTRACT

The materials and manufacturing industry is undergoing transformation through adoption of various digital technologies. Though the adoption of digital platforms for operational needs is significant, their adoption for core design and development of products and their manufacturing are limited. While the use of physics and data-driven modeling-and-simulation tools is increasing, these are not systematically leveraged for larger benefit. Besides these tools, product design and development requires deep contextual knowledge necessitating systematic capture of data and knowledge. To achieve this, we need flexible digital platforms that enable integration of diverse design domains and tools through a common semantic basis and construction of engineering decision workflows leveraging various simulation tools and knowledge. This chapter builds these requirements through presenting three case studies from the materials manufacturing industry and presents requirements for a digital platform. Finally, one such platform, TCS PREMAP, being developed by the authors is described in some detail.

INTRODUCTION

Across the ages of civilization, materials played an important role as stepping stones for progress to the next era. The science and engineering of materials, their manufacture and utilizing them in products has evolved over many centuries making significant contributions to the strides of human development.

DOI: 10.4018/978-1-7998-0108-5.ch011

Our understanding of the underlying physics of materials has advanced tremendously in the recent past. Yet, despite these advances, materials engineering practice still remains somewhat traditional, heavily dependent on expertise and knowledge of individuals and trial and error driven experiments. For example, deploying a new aerospace material takes about 20 years from conceptualization to deployment in a flying aircraft (Pollock, et al., 2008). Even in less critical industries, it still require many years, up to a decade, for full-scale realization of new materials in products. This is not a desirable state to be in for the enterprises of the future.

The advent of computers has made significant contributions to the utilization of various forms of modeling and simulation of materials under diverse circumstances and this has led to significant acceleration of materials and manufacturing engineering, all the way from design and development to deployment. Mathematical modeling based on the physics of the material behavior, coupled with judicious empirical relationships laid the foundation for modeling and simulation in materials engineering. This along with advances in high performance computing and numerical methods such as finite element methods contributed to what can be seen as the "Materials 3.0" revolution (Jose & Ramakrishna, 2018). Yet, the materials engineering remains largely expertise and experimentation driven and the design of materials and their manufacture and deployment of products remains in silos to a large extent. Apart from the design and development of materials, production of materials and converting these materials in raw-forms to products in a manufacturing set-up requires simultaneous analysis of the material evolution and the corresponding manufacturing process. Modeling and simulation for manufacturing processes is utilized to varied degrees of success in the manufacturing industry and cannot be said to have made the same kind of inroads that it has for product design (McDowell, et al., 2010). There has also been considerable research on the use of expert systems to aid decision making in manufacturing processes and to some extent even exploited in the industry (Wong, Chong, & Park, 1994). Further, usage of digital technologies for continuous monitoring of the performance of a manufactured product in service and the related decision making is still in its infancy, at least from the perspective of materials engineering. The recent advances in integrated computational materials engineering (Pollock, et al., 2008) are allowing to break these silos and make "integrated engineering" a reality. In parallel, the advances in application of AI to mine the large amount of experimental and simulation data generated during the discovery and design of materials is attempting to reduce the serendipity involved in material discovery (Rodgers & Cebon, 2006), (OSTP, 2011), (Ramprasad, Batra, Pilania, Mannodi-Kanakkithodi, & Kim, 2017), (Agrawal, Deshpande, Cecen, Basavarsu, & Choudhary, 2014). The concepts of "Digital Thread" for tracking the life cycle of products in a circular economy and "Digital Twin" to enable analysis, diagnostics and prognostics of various outcomes of manufacturing processes and product performance in the field have been gaining widespread industrial acceptability (Lieder & Rashid, 2016).

In light of these rapid developments and adoption of newer paradigms and technologies, there is a significant need to re-look at the entire life cycle and transform the way materials are designed, manufactured and deployed into products, to make the next level of difference to the manufacturing and materials industry. The transformation is made feasible by new digital technologies, better sensors, availability of large amounts of data and deeper understanding of materials. Leveraging all this requires significant changes in the way engineering is carried out and this in turn requires powerful, versatile and flexible digital infrastructure.

This chapter focuses on the transformation coming from the key digital forces of computing, big data and artificial intelligence (AI) on core engineering activities involving material design & development, deployment of materials in products and manufacturing of materials and products and the authors views on the way forward. Section 2 provides some case studies from the industry based on the author's experience followed by a summary of current status of the use of digital technologies in Section 3. Section 4 discusses the author's proposition on enabling platforms for the digital transformation and summarizes the work being carried out at the author's organization. This chapter is intended to give a perspective on the opportunities, key needs of a digital platform for carrying out core engineering decisions involving materials design, development & deployment and aimed at leaders and technocrats developing digital technologies for this need.

CASE STUDIES FOR DIGITALIZATION DRIVEN TRANSFORMATION

While significant digitalization has been achieved in general with regards to business as well as manufacturing operations, core materials / product engineering and manufacturing engineering, which often form the heart of materials and manufacturing industrial sectors are less digitalized in view of their complexity, diversity of needs and dependence on experts. In this section, we discuss some industrial examples of the need for digitalization and digitalization enabled transformation for material and product development.

Design and Manufacture of Friction Pads: Leveraging Data and Knowledge

This is an example related to a supplier of automotive products based on friction materials. This organization has facilities for development and production of friction pads for automotive OEM needs and has locations across the world. Custom friction pads are developed for each model of the automobile for OEMs based on the requirements of the vehicle such as its weight, maximum speed, requirements of breaking distance, regulation related aspects based on geography, etc. Typically, an application engineer gets the details of these requirements, makes a decision on possible composition of material and cost of production and makes a quick estimate for the quotation purposes with some help from materials designers known as "formulators". This process often starts with finding the nearest past design and making intelligent guesses for the changes required for estimation of costs involved in development and production. This process will broadly lock up the profitability of the product independent of the actual final development process and the cost of production thereof.

One of the key challenges the application engineer and later the formulator face is excessive reliance on their memory to recollect products of similar requirement being developed in the past and further getting their hands on that information from the past. Most often the information is available in diverse forms of reports that contain aspects related to the requirements for which the design is being carried out, composition of the friction pad which typically consists of twenty or more materials of different types and the processing conditions. These reports also contain information regarding the extensive test performance of these products. The complexity increases as this information is available in multiple locations in multiple forms. A large amount of experimentation is done for each product but the associated knowledge gain is not recorded systematically. Further, the knowledge of influence of different classes of materials used and the choices of individual materials from each class is broadly based on heuristic understanding and is often shared in internal conferences or through interaction over emails in an informal fashion. As the final design decisions also depend on the availability and cost of raw materials that vary geographically and temporally, the decision making becomes complex. Though the larger development process is captured through use of PLM (Fairfull, Baker, Warde, & Cherns, 2019) platforms and some digital tools are used for some of the engineering decision purposes, majority of the work is done in spreadsheets leveraging tacit knowledge of the engineers. With this background, this company has embarked on development of a digital platform that enables:

1. Standardized and uniform methods for managing data at various stages of product development, right from requirements to customer feedback
2. Leverage past data and build tools that aid application engineers to address new requirements for better quotation purposes
3. Use state of the art AI/ML tools to construct prescriptive models from data to help application engineers as well as formulators
4. Mine the large amount of knowledge that is captured in the form of comments using text mining tools to develop rules that can be leveraged as a knowledge base
5. Seamless integration with PLM and MES tools with core design enabling tools
6. Integrated collaboration platforms for sharing tacit knowledge

Manufacturer of Steel Products: Use of State-of-the-Art Modeling and Simulation Tools for New Product Development

This example pertains to a steel industry where different stakeholders from research and development to production engineers need to leverage state of the art physics based simulation tools and data for various types of decision making. Here, the research and development department would be interested in:

1. Developing multi-scale physics driven simulation models that help design new grades of steels,
2. Augment the capabilities coming from physics driven modeling and simulation with data driven models,
3. Use these for developing new grades of steels,
4. Further use these tools and other process performance tools for process optimization,
5. Leverage these tools in developing proof of concepts for application of their products by customers and
6. Develop knowledge that can be used by their department as well as production departments.

The production department would be interested in use of the same for developing product variants based on customer requirements, process optimization and dealing with corrective measures when some of the upstream processes deviate from requirements. The profiles of the users in these divisions are different. While users from the research or product development departments may have expertise in modeling and simulation, users from the production department would largely be tool users and the tools have to be made usable by them in their decision making without the need for deep knowledge of modeling and simulation. In a similar fashion, application engineers who position the material products to customers also have to use these tools in proving the concepts of the usage and benefits of their material products to their end customer requirements and these engineers will have intermediate capabilities with regard to modeling and simulation.

The key common requirements of this organization are to:

1. Use state of the art multiscale simulation tools pertaining to diverse steps of production,

2. Tune these models to specific plant conditions and store these tuned models and bind them contextually to individual mills and production facilities,

3. Leverage a large amount of past data to construct data based models that aid physics based models, enable easy construction of such data based models,

4. Capture a large amount of tacit knowledge available across the organization, especially buried in many reports from the past,

5. Have the flexibility to configure and integrate tools and tacit knowledge on a need basis to serve specific needs of decision making and

6. Finally make these tools available for all stakeholders with diverse expertise

Manufacturer of a Specialty Particulate Product: Leveraging Tacit Knowledge, Data and Simulation for Process Decisions for Product Variants

This example pertains to a global manufacturing company of a specialty carbon based particulate products used in multiple industrial applications. The company has to produce variants of a class of products for multiple applications and customers. The manufacturing plants are distributed globally and the raw materials for these plants differ to some extent based on sourcing conditions. For example, some locations have stable raw material supply of similar quality whereas other locations encounter larger variation of quality as well as price fluctuations due to which the plant has to take calls on raw materials sourced frequently. Based on specific product requirements, the plant engineer makes decisions on the blend of raw materials as well as process conditions in terms of temperatures to be maintained at different parts of the process and locations at which different raw materials are to be fed along. However, most of these raw materials belong to a narrow range of material types. While different plants have slightly different manufacturing set-ups, the broader configuration of all these plants are similar. Despite the broader similarity of raw materials and manufacturing process setups, decisions are taken locally at the individual plant level based on knowledge of plant engineers and tools at their disposal. The knowledge exists in the form of standard operational practices (SOPs) and these are not fully documented at all plants. Further, different plants use different and diverse modeling and simulation tools developed either within the plant or by the corporate research and development teams. The usage of these tools is not uniform and also the tools for each plant are either developed independently or customized without a common change management practice with poor visibility to changes occurring in individual tools, making the availability and adoption of simulation models based decisions varied and limited. As there is no well-established method for continuous re-tuning of models for emerging conditions of the manufacturing equipment, maintaining these tools for emerging conditions is weak. Further, these models are not sufficiently integrated with the processes of operations engineers and do not enable easy leverage of knowledge (Thumb rules, SOP's etc.) for effective decision making. The management of this company is looking for digitalization and transformation of their product development and manufacturing as follows:

1. Digitization of knowledge capture (Standardization of terminology, thumb rules, SOP's, formal machine processible representation),

2. master models for each type of unit which are easily customizable for individual units along with tuning,

3. enable easy building of data based models and creation of new knowledge

4. global access to master models,

5. models connected with other plant digital systems such as ERP and MES for information related to the raw materials (availability and cost), plant conditions etc. which are required for models and knowledge base to guide decision making on raw material blend and process conditions

6. integrated workflows involving knowledge and models for decision making across process operations and product development,

7. seamless upgrade/update of models/workflow with changing capabilities/process conditions across plants with direct data connection to the plant, and

8. integrated models available to appropriate plant engineers to make decisions with easy to use interfaces

Unlike in some of the other manufacturing industries such as automotive industry, the materials manufacturing industry has considerably less adoption of digital platforms for their product (materials) and process development. Though these industries do use a number of enterprise digital platforms such as Enterprise Resource Planning (ERP) and manufacturing execution systems (MES) use of digital platforms for core engineering activities is limited. In view of highly experimental nature of materials development processes, some industries have well adapted Laboratory Information Management Systems (LIMS) for their experimental data and also have adapted some enterprise material data management tools for managing the generated material data. Some of the industries also use a number of computational tools for modeling and simulation and recently some ML/AI tools as well. However, most of these simulation and data tools are used in a disjoint fashion and not inter linked.

The next section discusses some aspects of the current state of use of digital platforms by the materials industry.

NEED AND CHALLENGES OF DIGITAL PLATFORMS FOR MATERIALS AND MANUFACTURING ENGINEERING

In all the cases discussed above, the stakeholders are in need of state-of-the-art digital platforms to enable better engineering decision making and knowledge retention utilizing state of the art in modeling and simulation – data based or physics driven. The general needs of the digital platforms for the materials development and manufacturing industry can be summarized as:

- Need to link various steps all the way from customer requirements gathering through product development, supply chain, manufacture and customer feedback to enhance industry's viability
- Need to store information of all kinds in a digital form that should be retrievable easily and contextually
- Ability to curate knowledge and make it formally available to all relevant users
- Seamless integration for product development between application engineering, product engineering, manufacturing and supply chain reducing silos of decision making
- Need to democratize use of modeling and simulation and data sciences by engineers in their day to day decision-making process

Proliferation of such a unified digital platform will be difficult due to many challenges involved. Some of the challenges are:

- Developing and deploying a digital platform flexible enough to cater to these diverse needs
- Getting people to accept a standard terminology
- Getting people to accept state-of-the-art tools
- Getting people to use the digital platforms away from their comfort zones

To be successful these challenges have to be addressed in a staged manner as shown in Figure 1 below.

Figure 1. Progressive transformation through digital platforms

DIGITAL PLATFORMS FOR MATERIALS & MANUFACTURING ENGINEERING

To enable the vision outlined in sections 2 & 3 we need a highly flexible and scalable digital platform. The platform should provide a standardized means to represent and integrate data and knowledge from multiple domains viz., materials, products and processes across multiple life-cycle stages (Gautham, Singh, Ghaisas, Reddy, & Mistree, 2013). It should provide a means to extract and integrate data and knowledge from multiple sources in multiple forms such as structured, semi-structured and un-structured knowledge. It should also allow for creation of workflows for specific needs such as material design, product design, manufacturing process design, etc. that leverage appropriate modeling and simulation tools, data sources and knowledge. It should provide for interfaces through which multiple users can work with simulation tools and data sources and construct workflows with seamless exchange of information. Engineers should be provided with context-appropriate knowledge both at the stage of creation of engineering workflows as well as while executing them in a manner that helps them make right decisions. The platform should also be able to continuously learn from the execution of these workflows to refine the knowledge and simulation models to help make better decisions in future. All this functionality should be available as a scalable and reusable framework upon which different applications can be built for varied domains and design goals.

Such a flexible platform should have the following capabilities (Gautham, Reddy, Das, & Malhotra, 2017):

- A common, flexible and scalable semantic basis (language) to represent and integrate diverse domains of interest (e.g. materials, products, processes, simulation models, etc.)
- Ability to capture design process workflows at an abstract level and use them for solving specific engineering problems
- Ability to integrate various simulation models, simulation tools, databases and decision-support systems. The simulation models could be physics-based models or surrogate models learnt from data.

- Ability to extract and integrate data and knowledge from various structured, unstructured and semi structured sources
- Ability to leverage knowledge in the design process in a context sensitive manner to enable informed decision making
- Ability to continuously learn and adapt using past design and operational data
- Ability to easily create purpose specific design applications

The industry already uses a number of diverse digital enabling platforms and tools for development of engineered products. At an enterprise level, product life-cycle management (PLM) platforms are widely used with well-established commercial platforms being available (Fairfull, Baker, Warde, & Cherns, 2019). While PLM platforms enable orchestration of engineering workflows and management at a higher level, their ability to deal with detailed simulations, laboratory experiments, design knowledge, etc. are limited. Material data management and intelligent platforms such as Granta MI (https://grantadesign.com/) provide solutions for management of materials information in engineering enterprises with ability to link with PLM platforms and simulation tools. Tools such as iSight (https://www.3ds.com) and ModeFrontier (https://www.esteco.com/) provide solutions for design and simulation process automation. Further, a number of platforms from universities such as AixViPMaP (Koschmieder, et al., 2019) provide capabilities for integrated computational materials engineering, providing horizontal and vertical integration of simulation.

While these platforms and solutions provide means to address a number of issues related to materials engineering, they lack some of the key issues highlighted earlier, such as scalable semantic basis, contextual knowledge delivery through digitally interpretable knowledge, integrated learning, design process capture at various abstract levels, easy reuse and extensibility etc. Authors have been developing a digital platform called TCS PREMAP (Platform for Realization of Engineered Materials and Products) at Tata Consultancy Services (TCS) to address the above needs and the details of this are presented in the next section.

TCS PREMAP Platform: An Overview

TCS PREMAP is designed to be a generic and extensible platform that can support a variety of purpose specific applications catering to a variety of usage scenarios across different materials, products and manufacturing processes (Gautham, Singh, Ghaisas, Reddy, & Mistree, 2013),. To do this, it has to be able to represent a variety of entities, enable end-to-end integration between entities of different domains, life-cycle stages, simulation models, tools, data sources, algorithms, etc. Figure 2 gives a conceptual overview of the PREMAP platform. A set of domain models provide the sematic foundation to represent and integrate data and knowledge pertaining to different design domains such as materials, products, processes, etc. These models then serve as the basis for defining workflows to solve specific design problems. A workflow specifies the steps in a design process, namely the activities to be performed, decisions to be made and the data, knowledge, simulation models and tools required to do this effectively and efficiently. At each stage in the workflow definition process, the platform's knowledge base can be consulted to select right processes, models, data sources, simulation models, etc., that are appropriate for the problem being solved. Once workflows for a given design process are set up, they can be executed to solve design problems. During workflow execution, based on the problem context, appropriate knowledge is accessed to guide design decisions and model-based simulations are carried out to explore the design space. A learning engine mines the data generated during workflow executions to extract knowledge that can be leveraged in future design processes.

In the following paragraphs we give a more detailed description of some of the key components of the architecture. A comprehensive description of the architecture can be found in (Gautham et al, 2017).

Figure 2. Conceptual overview of TCS PREMAP

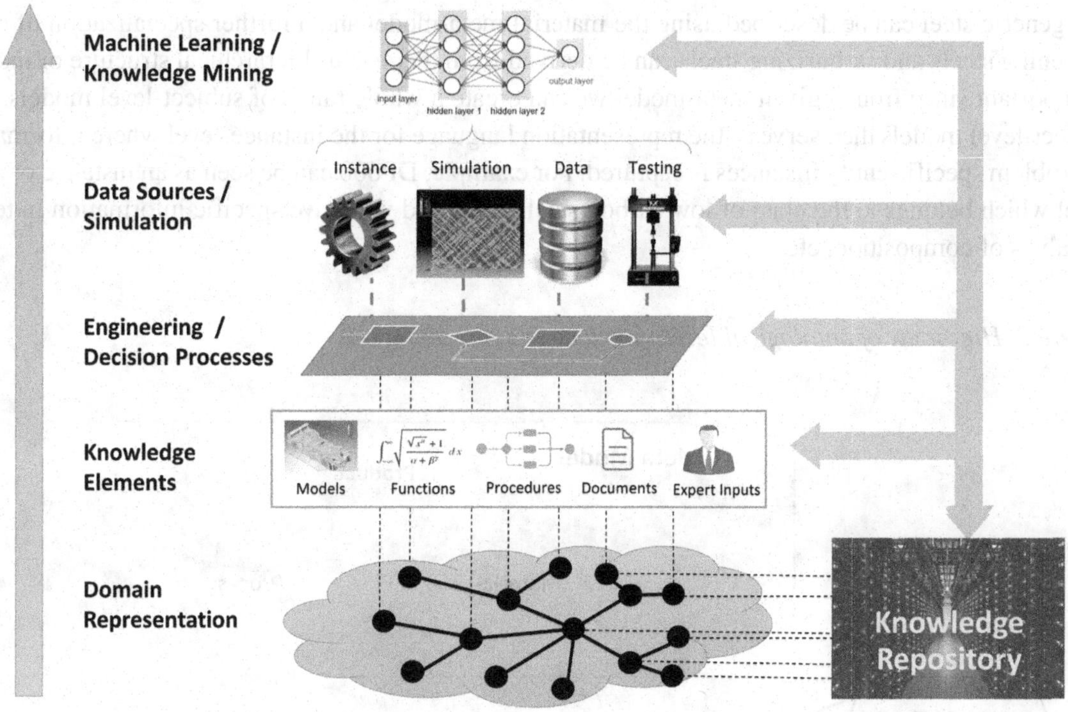

Domain Representation

The foundational aspect of the platform is the domain representation layer, which provides a common semantic basis (standardized language) for representing entities within the applicable domains and the relationships between them. This language has to be highly flexible and scalable and should be able to represent knowledge such that it can be seamlessly leveraged while answering questions related to the domain. To achieve this, we utilize the software engineering paradigm of model-based engineering (Kulkarni & Reddy, 2004), which is used to develop an ontological representation of the domain using meta-models as the abstract, primitive building blocks from which purpose specific subject models can be instantiated.

Figure 3 provides a high-level view of the domain representation structure of TCS PREMAP. It comprises of three ontological levels – the meta-level, the subject-level and the instance-level (ontology is a machine-interpretable language for representing information). A number of meta-level models describing high-level concepts of the areas of interest, such as materials, processes, products, simulation tools, computational mesh, etc. have been carefully designed after rigorous study and analysis to capture generic aspects of these areas. These meta models come pre-built with the platform and form the basis for developing subject-specific models at the subject-level. For example, a material meta-model facilitates representation of material composition, hierarchical microstructure, properties of the material, material classification as well as information such as the coordinate systems in which properties and microstructure are defined. The meta-models are connected to each other and form an integrated set. A subject-level model can be derived from the appropriate meta-model and within the subject-level model one can have a hierarchy with layers of progressive specialization. As can be seen from Figure 3, a generic steel can be described using the material meta-model and a further specialization of case-hardening steels and carburizing steels can be derived from there. This hierarchical structure of models is important since from a given meta-model we can create a whole range of subject-level models. The subject-level models then serve as the representation language for the instance-level where information of problem specific entity instances is captured. For example, DP600 can be seen as an instance of a DP Steel which belongs to the class of low carbon steels Steel and will have specific information in terms of values of composition, etc.

Figure 3. Hierarchy of ontological levels for domain representation

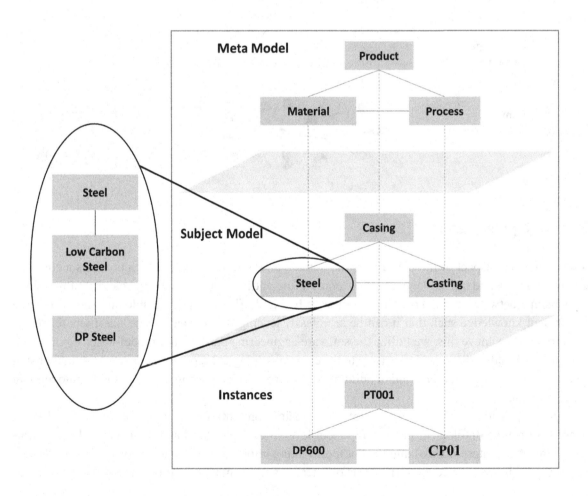

The meta-model definitions form the fundamental language of the platform while users can define their own domain by defining subject-level models. Instances can be created using these subject-level models by setting appropriate values to the elements of the model. With this, for every combination of subject-level models, numerous instances can be created for exploring the design space.

Knowledge Capture, Representation, Retrieval and Inclusion into the Design Process

The knowledge engineering framework in TCS PREMAP enables knowledge-guided decision making both during creation of workflows and during their execution by delivering context-appropriate knowledge to enable engineers to make right decisions. Figure 4 gives an overview of the architecture of the knowledge engineering framework. The knowledge repository stores knowledge of different kinds -- rules, models, procedures, documents, etc., all specified in terms of the domain ontology along with an associated reasoning engine. Since the domain ontology in our case is specified at multiple levels knowledge can also be captured at multiple levels. There is a context sensitive knowledge retrieval component which identifies a designer's intent in a design process, gathers context information from the design process and retrieves knowledge that is appropriate to the context and executes it. There is a knowledge mining component for mining knowledge from unstructured sources such as books, publications, reports, etc. There is a machine learning component for integrated learning from data generated within the design processes, simulations and experiments.

The platform uses a knowledge modeling approach for purposive, context aware knowledge management. The knowledge model has four parts -- domain ontology, knowledge element model, intent model and context model. Intent model specifies the intents for which knowledge needs to be acquired. An intent may be a goal one wants to achieve, a task one wants to perform, a decision one wants to make, etc. Knowledge element model provides a means to represent knowledge in different forms - rules, models, procedures, etc. Context model provides a means to specify the context in which a given knowledge element is applicable. A context is essentially a description of a situation. All these models are specified in terms of domain ontology. Knowledge engine uses the knowledge model to support context sensitive knowledge retrieval. At each stage in the design process, the engine identifies the designer's intent, collects context information relevant to the intent, reasons with it and constructs a query to find matching knowledge elements and executes them to provide context specific guidance.

Design Workflows

Design workflows enable systematic exploration of the design space. This happens at two levels. At the outer level domain knowledge guides a designer to select a subspace that is promising for the problem on hand. At the inner level, model based simulation helps carry out a detailed exploration within this subspace. At any stage if the design choices made so far do not lead to a satisfactory outcome, the workflow rolls back to an earlier decision point to explore a new path. Which decision point to rollback to can again be guided by knowledge. All the paths of exploration (both successful and unsuccessful) and the data generated by them are persisted in a database. A learning engine mines this database to extract knowledge that can be leveraged in future design processes.

Figure 4. TCS PREMAP knowledge engineering framework

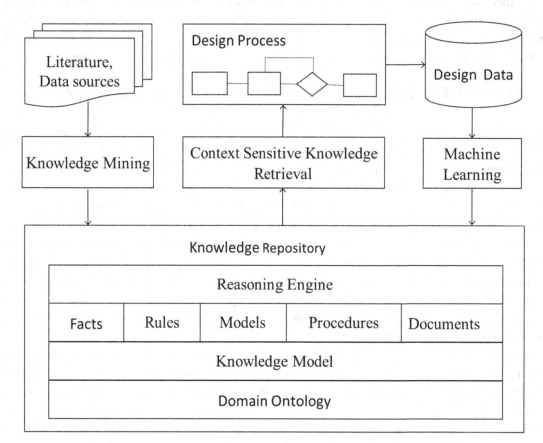

Learning From Past Design Runs

Over a time, engineers / designers would have performed a large number of executions of the instantiated design workflows and would have made a number of decisions within the workflows in terms of right parameters chosen, acceptance of outcomes of a step, etc. These executions with different design requirements would have resulted in different sets of design data. This would form a rich source which can be mined to extract insights. Learning from past designs and using these learnings for future design is an essential ingredient of a next generation engineering design platform. Figure 4 gives an overview of the machine learning framework used in TCS PREMAP.

The machine learning process has several stages such as data preparation (from data collected from past runs), feature extraction, model selection, experimentation, etc. All these are domain-knowledge dependent, and this knowledge is context dependent. The machine learning framework uses the aforementioned knowledge engine to retrieve knowledge for these actions based on the specific learning intent and context to make decisions. After models are learnt, they are stored back into the knowledge repository with applicability ranges under the same context and intent. These models can then be retrieved and used in the future while working on similar design problems.

Figure 5. Overview of the machine learning framework

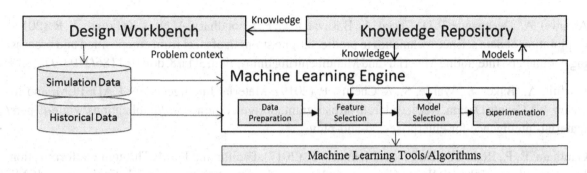

Putting it All Together

The heart of TCS PREMAP is its meta modeling based ontological framework. The meta models provide the semantic foundation to define, represent and integrate diverse design domains, simulation models, tools, databases and decision-support systems. Workflows can be defined for integrated engineering of materials, products and manufacturing processes cutting across life cycle stages. Knowledge guided decision making is at the heart of these workflows. TCS PREMAP provides a context aware knowledge management framework where context is central to how knowledge is captured and retrieved to enable intelligent decision making in engineering workflows. An integrated learning framework enables continuous learning from the problems solved on the platform.

As discussed in the previous section, while there are a number of tools addressing different aspects of the engineering space, the needs of the emerging digital era demand a next generation platform that provides a strong semantic foundation to address all these aspects together in an integrated manner with knowledge and AI at its core to drive the next level of transformation in the manufacturing industry and TCS PREMAP is one such attempt.

SUMMARY

This chapter discussed the digital transformation requirements of the materials and manufacturing industry. Unlike business processes and manufacturing operations, core product development and engineering activities have seen much less utilization of digital platforms. This arises out of the diversity of needs that simultaneously evolve at a higher pace and the involvement of specialist subject matter experts. We have discussed a few case studies from industry where the organization was in the journey of adopting digital platforms for their core engineering activities. The key requirements here are standardization of terminology, ability to integrate varieties of modeling and simulation tools and data in a decision supporting engineering workflow supported with contextual knowledge. We have discussed various aspects of how this can be achieved by describing a digital platform called TCS PREMAP being developed by the authors.

REFERENCES

Agrawal, A., Deshpande, P. D., Cecen, A., Basavarsu, G. P., Choudhary, A. N., & Kalidindi, S. R. (2014). Exploration of data science techniques to predict fatigue strength of steel from composition and processing parameters. Integrating Materials and Manufacturing Innovation, 3(1), 8. doi:10.1186/2193-9772-3-8

Fairfull, A., Baker, S., Warde, S., & Cherns, P. (2019). Material Intelligence for CAD, PLM, and Industry 4.0. Granta Design. Retrieved from https://grantadesign.com/industry/publications/white-papers/material-intelligence-for-enterprise-cad-and-plm/

Gautham, B. P., Reddy, S., Das, P., & Malhotra, C. (2017). Facilitating ICME Through Platformization. In PProceedings of the 4th World Congress on Integrated Computational Materials Engineering (ICME 2017) (pp. 93-102). Springer. doi:10.1007/978-3-319-57864-4_9

Gautham, B. P., Singh, A. K., Ghaisas, S. S., Reddy, S., & Mistree, F. (2013). Article. In A. Chakrabarti & R. V. Prakash (Eds.), *ICoRD'13, Lecture Notes in Mechanical Engineering* (p. 1301). Springer India.

Jose, R., & Ramakrishna, S. (2018). Materials 4.0: Materials big data enabled materials discovery. Applied Materials Today, 10, 127–132. doi:10.1016/j.apmt.2017.12.015

Koschmieder, L., Hojda, S., Apel, M., Altenfeld, R., Bami, Y., Haase, C., . . . Schmitz, G. (2019). AixViPMaP—An Operational Platform for Microstructure Modeling Workflows. Integrating Materials and Manufacturing Innovation, 8(2), 122–143. doi:10.1007/s40192-019-00138-3

Kulkarni, V., & Reddy, S. (2004). Model-driven development of enterprise applications. In *Proc. International Conference on the Unified Modeling Language* (pp. 118-128). Springer.

Lieder, M., & Rashid, A. (2016). Towards circular economy implementation: A comprehensive review in context of manufacturing industry. *Journal of Cleaner Production*, *115*, 36–51. doi:10.1016/j.jclepro.2015.12.042

McDowell, D., Panchal, J., Choi, H.-J., Seepersad, C., Allen, J., & Mistree, F. (2010). *Integrated Design of Multi-Scale, Multifunctional Materials and Products*. Elsevier Inc.

OSTP. (2011). Materials genome initiative for global competitiveness. National Science and Technology Council. Retrieved from https://www.whitehouse.gov/sites/default/files/microsites/ostp/materials_genome_initiative-final.pdf

Pollock, T., Allison, J. E., Backman, D., Boyce, M. C., Gersh, M., Holm, E., & Woodward, C. (2008). *Integrated computational materials engineering: a transformational discipline for improved competitiveness and national security*. National Academies Press.

Ramprasad, R., Batra, R., Pilania, G., Mannodi-Kanakkithodi, A., & Kim, C. (2017). Machine learning in materials informatics: Recent applications. *NPJ Computational Materials*, *3*. doi:10.103841524-017-0056-5

Rodgers, J., & Cebon, D. (2006). Materials Informatics. *MRS Bulletin*, *31*(12), 975–980. doi:10.1557/mrs2006.223

Wong, B. K., Chong, J. K., & Park, J. (1994). Utilization and Benefits of Expert Systems in Manufacturing. *International Journal of Operations & Production Management*, *14*(1), 38–49. doi:10.1108/01443579410049298

Chapter 12
Orchestrating the C3 Journey of the Digital Enterprise

Devadatta Madhukar Kulkarni
Tata Consultancy Services, USA

Ramakrishnan S. Srinivasan
Tata Consultancy Services, USA

Kyle S. Cooper
Tata Consultancy Services, USA

Rajeev Shorey
Tata Consultancy Services, USA

Jeffrey D. Tew
Tata Consultancy Services, USA

ABSTRACT

As businesses embrace digital technologies and drive business growth, this transformation demands a reimagination of their products, processes, and work beyond just "digitalization." The enterprise starts by capturing diverse sensor data and integrates just-in-time data to achieve "connected" stage. It further uses data along with contextual intelligence to drive integrated decisions in "collaborative" stage. It aspires to share decision making between machines and humans and evolves into "cognitive" stage. In this C3 journey—connected to collaborative, further to cognitive—enterprises need to take advantage of innovative technologies across machines, facilities, and operations in the ecosystem of products, processes, and partners. The authors highlight the nuances and opportunities across the C3 journey focusing on manufacturing value chains. Customers can orchestrate their C3 journey using innovative digital solutions outlined here for information sharing and interactive analytics that will deliver best business results with data-driven decisions.

DOI: 10.4018/978-1-7998-0108-5.ch012

INTRODUCTION: C3 JOURNEY IN DIGITAL TRANSFORMATION

Since the beginning of the 21st century, advances in information and communication technologies (ICT) have fueled a "digital transformation" of all different industry operations and all aspects of society. These digital technologies enable the business goals of most enterprises, such as accelerating production efficiency, product design, revenue growth and customer reach, delivering better competitive advantage. Further digitalizing products and processes can improve cost-effectiveness and provide a high-quality customer experience (Tata Consultancy Services [TCS], 2018). However, across the breadth of the enterprises, minimal collaboration among multiple partners (involved in producing and delivering a product or service to customers), aging automation infrastructure, lack of digital standards along with risk-averse concerns about data and intellectual property security are critical issues in the rate of adoption of digital technologies and the realization of sustained improvement in productivity, revenue or quality.

As businesses embrace digital technologies and address major roadblocks, they recognize that this transformation demands a reimagination of their products, processes and work beyond just digitalization, wherein current solutions are inadequate. In this journey, they need to take advantage of innovative technologies across machines, facilities and operations at various levels of their ecosystem of products, processes and partners. Most enterprises in their digital journey will be working with diverse partnering teams and systems that are possibly in different states of C3 evolution – Connected, Collaborative or Cognitive, each evolving to its next level (Figure 1). The most vibrant ecosystems continue to refine their links to get more relevant data, to refine and speed up contextual integration, and to further automate their execution of more complex environments. In the following paragraphs, we further detail the Connected, Collaborative, and Cognitive states.

Enterprises typically will collect and track data across multiple devices and systems, then integrate contextual insights and analyze their relations to manage performance metrics of the ecosystem. Such a business system achieves a "Connected" state, which enables real-time data, drives quick alerts and warnings to manage disruption or variation, and presents alternatives visible to the stakeholders.

Over time and across the locations in this connected network, multiple teams can further share and update necessary information, verify ongoing assumptions, and rebalance competing performance metrics using interactive scenario analytics. In such a "Collaborative" state, business teams can leverage easy-to-use platforms and interfaces to share and validate the single view of truth through challenging each other's intuition, confirming insights, and converging to the best business decisions.

As the partners in their digital journey of using connected data and converging to the best decisions, they can further share the load of decision making with the sensors and devices. The historical sensor data, events and decisions can guide opportunities for automated actions to address certain frequent but low risk issues while the learnings gained by the team along with manipulation of both physics-based and data-driven models can provide more intelligent ways to handle complex challenges. In this evolution of teams sharing decision making with sensors, a business system attains "Cognitive" state simplifying its daily work load and further leveraging self-healing fixes for anticipated issues.

Figure 1. States of C3 evolution

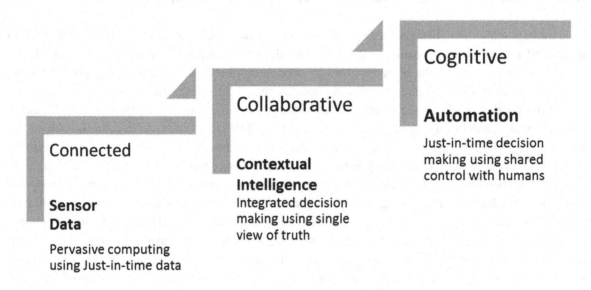

DIGITAL FORCES AND BUSINESS 4.0 VISION

Tata Consultancy Services (TCS) has invested in the "Digital Five Forces" - that are propelling this universal digital transformation: mobility and pervasive computing, social media, cloud computing, big data and analytics and artificial intelligence (AI) and robotics (Krishnan 2017).

Another key enabler of digital transformation is Internet of Things or IoT (Figure 2). The Internet of Things lays foundation to the continuous integration of information and communication technologies across linked ecosystem of sensors and systems in diverse processes and partners. The IoT glue empowers the journey with its emerging technologies, protocols and standards while addressing major challenges on bandwidth, speed and security. IoT is a composite force as it is combination of several of the digital five forces. Each of the digital forces is by itself quite potent, "but a combination of the forces can reimagine business models, products and services, customer segments, channels, business processes, and workplaces in any industry" (Krishnan, 2017). These digital technologies are also at the core of Industry 4.0 that includes three major principles around fusion of virtual and real world, production cyberphysical systems with plug and play integration of automation, and dynamic production network across flexible value chains incorporating operations management principles (Korves, 2015).

TCS's thought leadership model Business 4.0 harnesses the digital forces mentioned above as well as Industry 4.0 principles and empowers any customer's digital transformation journey. Business 4.0 uses digital technologies as foundational enablers and identifies the four business behaviors of driving mass personalization, creating exponential value, building a partnering ecosystem, and embracing risk, to derive maximum benefit from the business transformation (TCS, 2018, 2019). These business behaviors are built atop the pillars of Intelligent, Agile, Automated, and on the Cloud. Together, the pillars and behaviors of Business 4.0 enable companies to solve a business problem or create new business opportunities, using an amalgamation of digital technologies. The business enterprise can orchestrate its C3 journey utilizing the digital forces with just-in-time data and interactive analytics to drive business growth that is accelerated through the business behaviors laid out in Business 4.0.

Figure 2. The digital five-forces and IoT (Chandrasekaran, 2016)

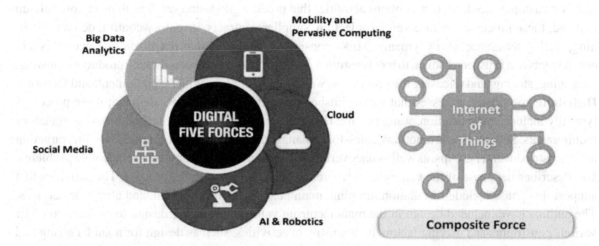

C3 Transformation for the Manufacturing Value Chain

The versatile C3 framework using the five digital forces is amply powerful to be applied to "digital transformation" in any industry. To highlight the nuances and opportunities across the C3 journey, the authors focus on applications across manufacturing value chain.

Over the past two centuries, manufacturing has progressed from expert craftsmen creating unique objects by hand to factories mass producing goods, utilizing a combination of machines and humans. This progress was fueled by innovations like steam power, assembly lines, and automation of manufacturing and continues to evolve, providing opportunities and posing challenges. This growth has been further accelerated by digital technologies across diverse manufacturing value chains for discrete processes like building automobiles or airplanes, or continuous processes producing chemicals or steel. The core "Make" process of manufacturing goods is sandwiched between an upstream supply chain that provides raw materials and services and a downstream sales chain that moves the manufactured products to end customers. This affords the manufacturing ecosystem with a complex mix of value chain partners including designers, suppliers, service providers and retailers. These collective entities and allied operations form a complex and extensive manufacturing value chain, as depicted in Figure 3. A brief description of each process in the manufacturing value chain is provided below.

Figure 3. Manufacturing value chain and related enterprise processes

Design includes all the activities that determine the function, form and structure of the product, to satisfy a customer need. **Source** contains activities that procure goods and services to meet downstream demand; these processes include vendor selection, supplier contracts, inventory control, delivery planning, quality assurance, and payments. **Make** consists of processes that transform raw materials and components to a finished product, to meet customer demand. These processes include production, testing, packaging, storing, and releasing the product, as well as managing machinery, equipment, and factories. **Distribute** comprises processes that move finished goods to meet customer demand; these processes typically include transportation, warehousing, fleet management, invoicing, and addressing regulatory requirements. **Sell** involves promotions, sales-force management, distribution channels, pricing, targeting appropriate consumer groups, as well as uncovering new customer needs, and solving customer problems. **Use** describes the phase of the value chain, where the customer is using the product. The activities that support this phase include installation, training, maintenance, repair, overhaul, and after-sale services. The authors have included design in the manufacturing value chain, as the design team must consider various constraints and driving factors in downstream activities, such as design for manufacturing and design for sustainability.

Potential Opportunities in Manufacturing

Continuously evolving value chains have built a vibrant manufacturing ecosystem. Given the spread and depth of economic activity across the manufacturing value chain, it has the highest multiplier effect of any economic sector, wherein each $1 spent results in a return of $ 3.60 to the economy (Meckstroth, 2016). Manufacturers face significant challenges in meeting rapidly changing customer demand, accelerating quality product with emerging technologies, and driving resilient operations across the ecosystem. They continue to drive the business opportunities through exploring reimagination of the core structures across products, processes and partners as they pursue innovative applications of digital technologies in their C3 journey.

Manufacturing has accumulated more data than any other industry but is lagging behind in extracting the benefits, and even trails other industries in digital adoption (Probst et al., 2018). Partly these challenges arise from the complexity in refreshing legacy infrastructure, the required increase in investment costs, and the lack of interoperability and security standards across layers of its own and partner networks. Of course, it also faces significant execution roadblocks across its partners especially in three areas – right mix of interdisciplinary talent, integration of dependable digital platforms, and culture of sharing data and information.

There are learnings from other industries that have driven cost or customer benefits from the digital transformation. The telecom industry moved from proprietary switching platforms in the early part of this century to off-the-shelf computing platforms running standards-based technologies, and the banking industry moved from siloed transaction systems to connected systems with enhanced availability and security. Others such as the oil and gas industry instrumented remote pipelines and rigs to obtain early warning signals and avoid costly failures (Fryer, 2017).

TCS is well positioned to take advantage of these learnings from other industries and use its systems integration and consulting expertise to partner with the manufacturing customers in much needed reimagination of visible business processes, resilient operations, and robust data integration across the ecosystem. As a customer embarks on the C3 journey, the innovative digital solutions for information sharing and interactive analytics will deliver best business results with data driven decisions (Ramanujan et al., 2017).

MANUFACTURING RESEARCH ECOSYSTEM OF SOLUTIONS FOR THE C3 JOURNEY

Over past three years, Manufacturing Research (MR) and TCS Cincinnati Innovation Lab team collaborated with Manufacturing, HiTech, Retail and CPG business units, individual customers during Innovation Days, along with Co-Innovation Network (COIN) partners to build several decision solutions with common data and information structures, innovative algorithms and analytics, and also had an opportunity to test them with initial Proofs of Concept. This set of solutions positions MR team to plan an ecosystem in key manufacturing decision areas such as Order Management, Pricing & Revenue Optimization, Sourcing Cost Optimization or Total Profit Optimization. The MR team has also successfully partnered with business and COIN teams to explore key questions around communication structures, energy optimization, and cybersecurity in IoT networks and automotive product & service networks. Its engagements in Innovation Research Interchange (IRI) and Industrial Internet Consortium (IIC) has further strengthened its benchmarking and competitive position in the key opportunity areas. The IIC partnership has been instrumental in the creation of the Testbed for Smart Manufacturing as well as its security standards across key layers gearing up further to the next Testbed on Facility Ops Security.

The MR ecosystem of solutions is architected based on the platform model, with an emphasis on reusable functional and analytics modules. Here functional modules are aimed at facilitating user interaction with the solution such as specifying the problem, providing and reviewing inputs, visualizing outputs and alternatives, and configuring scenarios, while analytics modules are focused on acquiring data, analyzing it with methods like optimization and simulation, and generating recommendations. These recommendations themselves can deliver immediate business decisions and their enhancements based upon learning algorithms can address evolutionary challenges for teams or the entire organization, continuously improving business results. We showcase the above features through five MR solutions in the following sections.

Showcase: Five MR Solutions for Digital Transformation

This section showcases the main MR solutions and supporting capabilities. Each solution addresses a critical business problem in the manufacturing value chain and contains functional and analytics modules that customers can use to make decisions to solve the problem.

Figure 4 shows a high-level view of representative solutions for accelerating customer's digital transformation in its C3 journey. Currently solutions are positioned to highlight at what stage of the C3 journey the customer can use them the best. However the customer can self-assess their maturity along the C3 journey and easily customize the solution based upon their needs and envisioned opportunity to accelerate it to the next C3 stage - say Connected to Collaborative using additional links with active business process and teams, and say from Collaborative to Cognitive using the team's learning cycles across the processes and scenarios to enable shared decisions using proper machine-man synergy. MR provides five core solutions which businesses may employ towards their C3 journey.

The following sections are overviews of the above five core solutions and their evolution: Real-time Facility Productivity Optimizer (RFPO), IoT Security Threat Manager (ISTM), Digital Collaboratory (DC), System Disruption Manager (SDM) and Product Order Generator Optimizer (POGO).

Figure 4. Representative MR core solutions for C3 journey

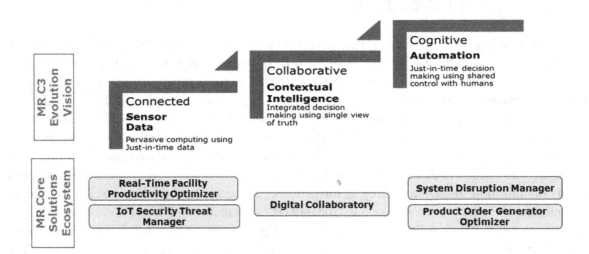

1. Real-Time/Assembly Facility Productivity Optimizer (RFPO)

In an industrial setting, manufacturers face challenges with assembly facility performance due to lack of coordination and analysis of diverse sensor data. Poor visibility of inventory, resources and workforce in the manufacturing environment has considerable negative impact on cost and on-time fulfillment of downstream demands. Improving Work-in-Progress (WIP) visibility is very costly and often impractical given the effort required to modify the tracking instrumentation on the factory floor and the processing of the tracking data once acquired. MR team has leveraged the Industrial Internet Consortium (IIC) testbed processes and partners with its evolving IIC reference architecture and security frameworks to build a Testbed for Smart Manufacturing addressing the WIP visibility problem to analyze productivity opportunity using sensor data.

MR team has mapped a three-step approach (Figure 5) in the use of IoT technologies for productivity improvement from the IIC Testbed process experience – Connect & Architect, Digitize & Analyze, and Deploy & Learn.

The first step is Connect and Architect: build a 3-tier architecture - as defined by the Industrial Internet Reference Architecture or IIRA (Industrial Internet Consortium [IIC], 2017a). This architecture melds Information Technology (IT) and Operational Technology (OT). IT is characterized by computer and communication systems, while OT is characterized by physical assets such machines and other hardware. As machines are IoT'ized, software applications are used to collect data from sensors and effect changes in the machines through actuators. The IIRA is shaped by four basic viewpoints, namely, business, usage, functional, and implementation, and can be extended to include additional viewpoints based on the context of a specific application. The four viewpoints address the concerns of multiple stakeholders such as business decision makers, system engineers, component architects, and system operators, thus resonating with the Collaborative state in the C3 model.

The three tiers of the testbed – as defined in IIRA - are Edge, Platform, and Enterprise. The Edge tier collects data from sensors and devices connected through a proximity network. The Platform tier plays an intermediary role; it is connected to the Edge tier through an access network and to the Enter-

Figure 5. The 3-step business improvement process using IoT

prise tier through a service network. The data collected in the Edge tier is aggregated and analyzed in the Platform tier which also forwards control commands from Enterprise to Edge. The Enterprise tier is used by decision-makers to visualize the tracked or analyzed data and to issue control commands to the Edge devices. Multiple capabilities of IIoT are combined in the 3-tier architecture including connectivity, sensing, control, data transformation, communication, management services, and business applications (Bhattacharjee, 2018). Example components of the testbed in each tier are: physical sensors on factory machines and RFID in the Edge tier; TCS Universal Connected Platform (TCUP) – TCS IOT middleware – and analytics modules in the Platform tier; and Enterprise Resource Planning (ERP) and visualization modules in the Enterprise tier.

It is to be noted that the end-to-end architecture needs to be secure. Security has been ensured by leveraging the Industrial Internet Security Framework (IISF). The IISF (IIC, 2016) is one of the first detailed documents on Industrial IoT (IIoT) security. The IISF leverages the overarching concept of "trustworthiness" in an IIoT system. The five key characteristics of trustworthiness are security, safety, reliability, resilience and privacy; these characteristics combine and balance elements of trust in both IT and OT domains. Security provides protection from unauthorized changes to a system, and has sub-elements of confidentiality, integrity, and availability. Safety ensures system operation without damaging people, property, or environment. Reliability is the ability of the system to function within specified performance limits and time period and is related to availability. Resilience is the property of a system to avoid or absorb the impact of disruptions and recover quickly from any decline in performance. Privacy provides rights to people to safeguard their information and decide who can access that information.

The second step is Digitize and Analyze: use virtual technologies to improve productivity. The integration of sensors and machines enables the collection of data which can be analyzed to optimize manufacturing processes. Such data can also be augmented by newer technologies such as creating a data-driven (coupled with physics-based) digital twin for the physical process. A digital twin is a software representation of machines and processes that is used to evaluate and optimize performance for better business outcomes. The combination of physical and synthesized data with advanced analytics drives productivity, improves quality, reduces costs, while creating business value and ensuring trustworthiness. Industrial analytics – "the use of analytics in IIoT systems" (IIC, 2017b) – are deployed in all three tiers of the IIRA and used to assess systems, optimize missions, detect event relations, discover patterns and predict outcomes. The analysis can take place in multiple time horizons such as: machine-time horizon for real-time detection and control, operation-time horizon for fault detection and maintenance, and planning-time horizon for business planning and insights. Another classification of industrial analytics that combines time scales with types of applications includes baseline analytics for health assessment and fault detection (milliseconds), diagnostic analytics for root cause analysis (minutes), and prognostic analytics for fault prediction including type and probability (hours).

The third step is Deliver and Learn: deploy initiative and drive to the next level. The architected solution is deployed considering different factors such as the scope, response time, and bandwidth. A number of different tools and solutions have to be integrated to achieve the business objectives. Since these tools typically originate from multiple vendors, the connectivity relationships and communication protocols must be synchronized. The IIoT systems are closely monitored; data on overall system state and traffic are collected and analyzed to detect anomalies or even potential threats, as well as a range of security actions to safeguard the system. To ensure the maximum benefit from the IIoT system, the fruits of data collection and analytics must be leveraged via learning. Techniques of machine learning foster a data-driven approach to build complex models inferred from input data and make predictions on the system. There are two major categories of learning methods and algorithms: unsupervised and supervised (IIC, 2017b). The data acquired from sensors must be blended with adequate domain expertise to uncover hidden patterns, detect potential attack scenarios, and guide future actions.

Smart Supply Chain Testbed - Manufacturing

The focus of the Smart Supply Chain testbed is on the manufacturing segment of Supply Chain Management. The market segment selected is HiTech manufacturing, specifically discrete manufacturing. The challenges for a manufacturing supply chain include poor visibility of inventory, resources and workforce in the manufacturing environment. These challenges have considerable negative impact on the cost and on-time fulfillment in the supply chain. However, improving visibility is very costly and often impractical given the effort required to modify the tracking instrumentation on the factory floor and the processing of that tracking data once acquired.

The testbed addresses these challenges by providing a facility for users to explore improving visibility by experimenting with various manufacturing tracking scenarios via simulation and experimenting with various stacks of Business Management Software at the Platform and Enterprise levels.

Working with partners, such as Cisco, Siemens, Oracle, Tego, and Infineon, the TCS MR team IoT'ized a TCS PCB factory with real time WIP tracking to enhance visibility across the machines in assembly lines for Phase 1. The key process steps in PCB manufacturing are PCB load, pick and place components, inspection, component insertion, wave soldering, and final testing. Lack of visibility created numerous problems such as: high levels of safety stock due to delay and quality issues in component supply, component stock-outs causing line stoppages, and line balancing issues due to less optimized resourcing decisions. The team created a digital twin using Siemens Tecnomatix that replicates the actual process digitally and simulates manufacturing activities (Figure 6). The insights gained from the digital twin were used to fine tune physical manufacturing.

The team targeted six production metrics to highlight the benefits of WIP process tracking. The metrics used and the impact observed are shown in Table 1. Some key learnings from implementing Phase 1 of the Smart Supply Chain Testbed include:

Figure 6. Digital Twin for simulating manufacturing process flow

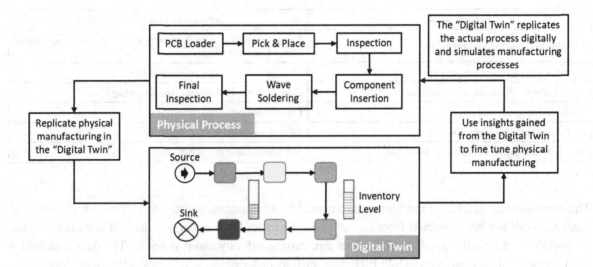

- Choice of IoT sensors, gateways, and network depends on ambient conditions – such as temperature and humidity - of a factory.
- Field trials and hardware testing for IoT projects are an expensive affair.
- The continual changes happening in sensors in terms of costs and capability of IoT hardware need to be considered while investing.
- Physical infrastructure layer has to be flexible and scalable to accommodate changes in equipment technology.
- Integration with enterprise applications such as ERP is vital to get real time analysis and actionable insights.
- Digital twin is vital for simulation, emulation, and scenario studies to cover risks and costs of on-field experimentation.
- Multiple process changes are required for implementation of this IoT solution, to create process automation and flexibility.

For Phase 2, the testbed validates learnings from Phase 1 using deployment in a real factory. TCS is using manufacturing operations within a cell of nine machines to validate the Phase 1 key learnings to improve machine tool productivity. The deployment of IoT in the Machinery & Equipment operations is architected to enhance productivity across the nine machines in a cell at Precision Component Manufacturing. A key goal is improving visibility of tool wear & reset to avoid human errors. This capability enables improvement of tool life and reduction of operator fatigue/errors. Phase 2 provides a physics-based model opportunity for using IoT data. A Digital Twin replicates the actual process digitally and simulates the manufacturing processes. The insights gained from the Digital Twin build right framework for necessary decision support to fine tune physical manufacturing and improve productivity.

Prior to implementing the IIoT system for tool wear monitoring, tool wear was identified by operator experience based on sound and spindle load (which varies from 4-6% to 20-30%). A few tools have shorter life and require either application of wear compensation or replacement during machining.

Table 1. Metrics used to measure improvement in factory operations

Production Aspects	Description and Impact on Metrics
Visibility to manufacturing operations	75% reduction in time lag in visibility and report refresh rate reduced from 1 hour to 15 minutes
Operation stoppage due to resource crunch	15% improvement in resource availability
Percent of rework/scrap due to routing error	Completely resolved the rework/scrap routing errors
Impact on production output	Capacity and throughput increased by 5%
Cost savings by using Digital Twin	5% cost impact in terms of productivity
Percent of time gap between target & production	10% improvement in schedule adherence

This scenario mandates each machine to be manned by an operator. In order to prepare for Phase 2, the plant network has been isolated from the internet to protect from cyber-attacks. IoT data is collected on spindle load, spindle speed, axial depth of cut, cutting velocity and part count. The data collected is used for performance analysis, while ERP data such as order number, order quantity, and shift details are used for measuring production status. Considering various aspects of tool geometry and machining practices, wear rate in terms of measurable value is given by the data captured online. Tool wear is estimated in a non-invasive way to eliminate operator errors. Further, Remaining Useful Life (RUL) of the tool is predicted using tool wear, thereby improving accuracy and reducing machine downtime. A comprehensive Smart Factory Solution is being jointly developed by TCS and a leading precision component manufacturer on MindSphere platform. The sensor data captured can drive many more valuable predictive analytics opportunities.

This architecture with specific Digital Twin Simulation and Productivity analytics tools constitutes the foundation of a platform-based solution for Real-time Facility Productivity Optimizer. With the focus on integration and analysis of the tracking sensor data to solve a business problem, RFPO is viewed as a "Connected" solution.

2. IoT Security Threat Manager (ISTM)

In the digital transformation journey, IoT has a wide range of applications including monitoring of products, premises, supply chain operations, and customer experiences (TCS, 2015). Key enablers of such applications are the collection of diverse data and the interconnectedness between physical systems and software systems for analysis and control. This increased intensity and connectivity is accompanied by a rise in vulnerability and risk across layers of the ecosystem, where the threat level can manifest through a remote, local or physical adversary. Threat refers to uncertainty in the information security context and is interpreted as any instance that impedes the normal operation of the IIoT systems. An attack surface describes all the system constituents that are exposed to attacks. Some examples of IoT attack surfaces in the context of an automobile are, for example, in-vehicular network components such as the communications gateway, the Electrical Control Units (ECUs), the Controller Area Network (CAN) bus, indirect physical systems such as the On Board Diagnostics (OBD-II) and USB ports, wireless links such as WiFi, Bluetooth and GPS, and Vehicle-to-Vehicle (V2V) and Vehicle-to-Infrastructure (V2I) communication links. Attack vectors refer to the types of attack, such as physical attack and attack on software. Each industry, each technology and each system has its own set of attack vectors.

Interest and investments in IoT have been on the rise, but they are accompanied by the awareness of security risks (TCS, 2015). The criticality of IoT security is underlined by advisories from U.S. government agencies. The National Intelligence Council (2008) warns, "**...** to the extent that everyday objects become information security risks, the IoT could distribute those risks far more widely than the Internet has to date." According to the National Security Telecommunications Advisory Committee (2014), "The strong growth in interconnected, potentially adaptive devices implies a larger cyber security attack surface with potentially cascading adverse effects in both the cyber and physical domains."

Security has become critical to manage adoption of digital technologies in manufacturing operations. This can be initially be viewed as a combination of securing both Information Technologies (IT) and Operational Technologies (OT) in the applications of IoT across the industrial context. However, the interfaces with products, machines, teams and customers increase the attack surface and take them into broader challenges in safety and privacy.

In order to manage security of IoT systems, the authors highlight the framework that can be detailed further based upon specific area and layer of the attack surface and initial assessment of severity and impact of an individual or combination of threats. Key capability required by a customer is to bring in a basic understanding of the detailed system architecture, along with potential attacks and available defense mechanisms across the network. ISTM framework can start with that basic understanding and allow its continuous enhancement using incident logs or learnings to establish the Attack and Defense database. Using the threat profile and architecture interfaces, the framework will start by predicting potential threat propagation paths across the network and simultaneously configuring sequence of mitigation steps using defense mechanisms. As the propagation analytics captures potential amount and spread of impact, the mitigation alternatives can be prioritized using Risk Sensitivity Analyzer to work across the attack surface.

ISTM's layered analytics structure (Figure 7) allows customization at required level of needed security for either managing threat incidents or business continuity. MR team is currently in the process of planning the next IIC testbed to test and validate the framework for Facility Operations Security.

Figure 7. Layered architecture of ISTM

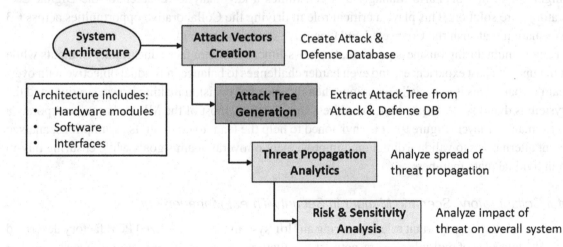

The IISF details security requirements for all modules and links within and across the three tiers – Edge, Platform, and Enterprise - of the IIoT systems (IIC, 2017a, Sabella et al., 2018). The ISTM solution developed by MR team exemplifies the "Connected" aspect of C3 and is aligned with the structure of IIoT Trustworthiness proposed by the Industrial Internet Consortium (IIC, 2016). Trustworthiness of IIoT systems is envisioned to build upon security as outlined in the IISF including four additional tenets: reliability, safety, privacy, and resilience.

3. Digital Collaboratory (DC)

In accelerating the digital transformation, multiple teams need to collaborate through sharing the latest information and developing a shared view of reality, across all phases of the manufacturing value chain to deliver best business results. The Digital Collaboratory (DC) is a "Collaborative" solution envisioned to integrate diverse data and provide relevant intuitive analytics for teams on their platforms of choice, using direct and natural interfaces.

As shown in Figure 8, DC combines the power of digital learning with teamwork in social collaboration to augment decision making. Business stakeholders use experience-based intuition and data-driven insights to drive team decisions. The team has to continuously interact to confirm assumptions, challenge intuition, and validate insights to develop a shared understanding of overall value of the team decision, closing the cognitive gap. The team arrives at an integrated decision while an individual objective may suffer. This section presents opportunities for applying this vision of digital collaboratory to achieve integrated decisions for typical cross-functional business processes like sourcing and warranty cost management. Just to give an example, DC will provide a foundation to the Collaborative solutions that would help sourcing ecosystem partners from Engineering, Purchasing, Supply Chain, and even Supplier teams to deliver lowest cost and best quality using interactive analytics tools to run scenarios and explore alternatives in part bundling, supplier selection, or negotiation strategies.

Scenario Manager

We highlight further Scenario Manager that constitutes a key analytics enabler for the Digital Collaboratory core solution. This plays a critical role in driving the Collaborative opportunities across C3 transformation that span the Connected and Cognitive states and beyond.

In any manufacturing business problem, the cross-functional team faces uncertainty in inputs while building upon its past experiences, and even harder challenges to balance individual objective with overall team's goals. This is especially daunting when the speed of decision making is accelerating, and the ecosystem is dynamically expanding. To address this question, most of the MR tools can incorporate a scenario manager layer (Figure 9). It is envisioned to help the team to confirm its assumptions, analyze different alternatives to validate directional improvement of overall team's goals while ensuring buy-in from individual team members.

Digital Collaboratory: Scenario Manger in Security Threat Management

Scenarios also play an important role in securing an IIoT system like the IoT'ized PCB factory described above. The interplay of multiple sensors, networks, actuators, and software systems introduces a number of vulnerabilities in the IIoT system. In connected solutions, the IIRA is conceptualized to accommodate

Figure 8. Digital Collaboratory: Augmenting business decisions

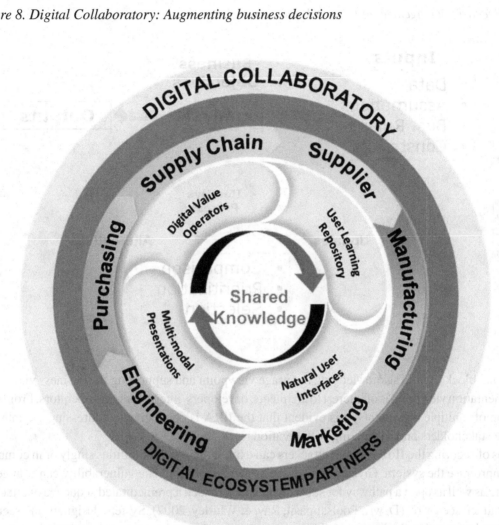

"Digital Collaboratory" = Digital Learning + Social Collaboration

multiple viewpoints across an enterprise - namely, business, usage, functional, and implementation viewpoints (IIC, 2017a).

The business viewpoint addresses the concerns of business decision makers, system engineers, and product managers, and deals with the business vision, values, objectives, and overall system requirements. The usage viewpoint covers how the system is used by operators, which is of interest to product managers, and system engineers and architects. The functional viewpoint outlines the main functional blocks along with their interdependencies and interfaces to external elements; this viewpoint caters to the concerns of developers, architects and integrators. The implementation viewpoint deals with the technologies, communication schemes, and lifecycle procedures of technologies required to implement

Figure 9. Scenario management to fast-track decision-making

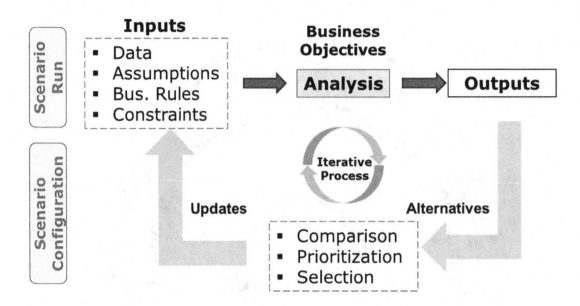

the functional blocks, while acknowledging the usage viewpoint and supporting the business viewpoint; the implementation viewpoint is of interest to architects, developers, integrators, and operators. From such an adoption of multiple viewpoints, it is evident that the IIRA is conducive to addressing the interests of multiple stakeholders and facilitating collaboration.

In terms of securing the IIoT systems, attackers can exploit these vulnerabilities singly or in combination to compromise the system. Given a state of the system, exploiting one vulnerability can change the system state as well as open a pathway for subsequent attacks. Such a premeditated sequence of attacks is called an "attack scenario" (Dewri, Poolsappasit, Ray, & Whitley, 2007). System designers and security managers are interested in the impact of different attack scenarios and corresponding defense measures.

The business objectives for security threat management in IIoT systems are minimizing the total security cost and the residual damage. Minimization of these dual objectives is formulated as a multi-objective optimization problem (Dewri et al., 2007). The inputs are the current state of the system, all known vulnerabilities, possible attacks, existing security controls, loss expectancies, and constraints (e.g., financial, policy). Starting with an IoT network, six possible attack scenarios are identified and represented as an attack tree. Each scenario is run through the optimization engine and the resulting costs and damage are compared and prioritized. The related security controls are assessed and implemented in a collaborative fashion.

A team consisting of five roles - Vulnerability Analyst, Defense Planner, Threat Analyst, Mitigation Planner and Security Supervisor is engaged in scenario threat management (Figure 10). Vulnerability Analyst tracks and refreshes the database consisting of attack vectors and potential defense mechanisms for a given IoT system. Defense Planner generates an attack tree for a given threat or series of threats, and maps defense mechanisms for them, Threat Analyst then maps the propagation of threats and assesses imminent spread of threat impact. Mitigation Planner selects and prioritizes defense mechanisms with analysis of estimated recovery effort. Security Supervisor coordinates the team activities, finalizes and executes mitigation plans at best cost and least impact for a threat instance. The Supervisor further captures learnings from the threat management experience and updates team processes or tools. This team clearly provides an example of Threat management ecosystem partners using the interactive analytics tools in layered architecture of Figure 7 for IoT Security Threat Manager.

Figure 10. IoT security threat manger: Team collaboration view

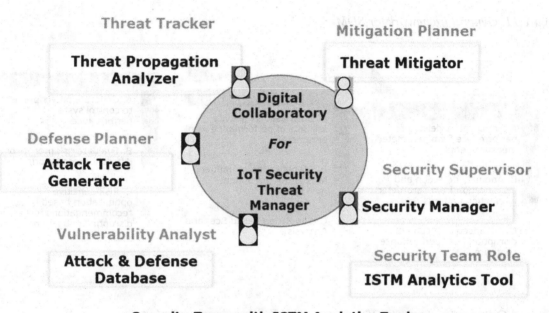

To navigate change, businesses need to adopt rapid decision making in terms of creating, comparing and analyzing alternatives with varying inputs and assumptions for all decisions. Digital Collaboratory offers qualitative and/or quantitative explorations of different alternatives taking into account inputs and assumptions from multiple stakeholders for a given decision. The digital technologies further accelerate them through rapid execution while validating evolving data and assumptions from diverse sources.

4. System Disruption Manager (SDM)

There is a huge data explosion taking place across the entire manufacturing value chain, fueled by IoT. The data generated from heterogeneous machines, products & workforce needs to be analyzed efficiently and in real-time. Manufacturing ecosystem will improve productivity and resilience using connected data and operations. This requires the systems to handle explosive growth in data and updates along with rapidly evolving user interfaces and platforms. Managing the global network of such systems smoothly through the digital evolution is a formidable challenge. Managing robust system performance requires the system management team to track right drivers for performance stability in a systematic fashion. System Disruption Manager solution provides predictive capability for potential performance failure or decay 24 hours in advance. This is further combined with the organizational objectives and practices to drive specific mitigation solutions using prescriptions to control or modify trends or related thresholds for a targeted set of drivers. This can be a critical enabler for managing business continuity for system management team for individual system, or further the network thereof. The general framework for SDM shown in Figure 11, embodies all stages of the C3 model. However, since the focus is on the prescriptions, SDM is viewed as a "Cognitive" solution.

Figure 11. General framework for SDM

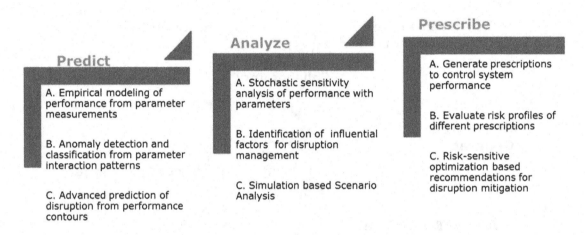

System Outage Predictor (SOP)

A specific solution under SDM is the System Outage Predictor (SOP), in the context of SAP system failures at a Tier 1 supplier. In 2014, five database crashes and app server outages caused severe losses in production order processing. The top three system failure modes were identified as: users not able to login, an overwhelmed business process, and slow system response.

A common metric – Dialog Response Time – is used for the above failure modes; an anomaly occurs if the Dialog Response takes longer than 1200 milliseconds. Of the causal factors affecting dialog response time, 29 were attributed to the app server, 12 to the operating system, and 9 to the database. Given this background, the problem statement is: Is it possible to predict potential system failure and associated control factors 24 hour in advance to initiate maintenance?

MR team established a "data-driven," time varying functional relationship between the causal factors and dialog response time. Forecasts for the input factors were derived using machine learning; with these input forecasts, the output dialog response time was forecast using the functional relationship. Tracking the forecasts vs. actuals, an accuracy of 85-90% was observed. Hence the SOP solution used adaptive fusion of machine learning algorithms for accurate forecasts 12 hours and 24 hours ahead of system outage.

Critical System Disruption Manager (CSDM)

The Critical System Disruption Manager (CSDM) builds on pure data-driven models to analyze interactions among system parameters and on their local sensitivity to recommend prescriptions. The goal of CSDM is to manage system disruptions using parameter specific prediction and risk-based recommendations for mitigation.

A specific application of CSDM is shown in management of the Enterprise Service Bus (ESB) in an auto OEM. A typical ESB connects to more than 300 interfaces, transfers 5 GB of data per day, and processes 0.5 million messages per day. This can play critical role in planning schedules. ESB is a business-critical system, as its performance decay causes production losses. The questions are: a) can data-driven performance analysis predict potential system disruption 24 hours in advance? b) can it further recommend actions to improve ESB performance? Using the CSDM framework, parameter specific machine learning models have been developed to predict ESB behavior 24 hours in advance. The models achieved more than 80% accuracy for 28 (of 32) parameters and above 90% for 18 parameters.

These two applications, namely the performance decay prediction for SAP and prescriptions to mitigate disruptions in ESB highlight the utility of SDM.

5. Product Order Generator Optimizer (POGO)

Manufacturers of configurable products such as automobiles and smart phones face an important problem of deciding on the right set of products (in terms of features) to offer in the market and their pricing so as to maximize the aggregate contribution margin- a surrogate metric for profit. Configurable products in general can be visualized to conform to a product hierarchy where Market, Brand, Product Family and a Product Model represent the levels of hierarchy. A configuration of this product model is composed by selecting one feature variant from a set of feature families. To highlight the example of a typical automotive product, feature families such as sunroofs or wheels have feature variants, like sunroof family has single, double or "retractable single sunroof", while wheels family has "18 inch steel", "20 inch steel" or "18 inch aluminum". In a future connected vehicle, the feature variants for vehicle steering could be envisioned to be "joystick" or "voice activated guidance" or "touch based steering". Given a product with the list of its all feature families and variants in them, a configuration is built by selecting at most one feature variant from each of the option families. Configuration build constraints dictate the feasibility of offering certain features or their combinations on a product, mostly driven by product performance. Similarly, marketing and supply chain teams can add the requirements on penetration rate or total volume of each option variant for a product. Further one can associate margin to each option variant resulting into margin of a configuration to be the sum of the margins of its constituent option variants. For a given product demand, finding the volume mix of its feasible configurations with total maximum margin satisfying upper and lower bounds on the penetration rate and total volume of each of its option variants is a complex combinatorial problem. POGO yields two types of solutions to this problem - a Minimal Set Solution which works towards finding the least number of feasible configurations required to satisfy the constraints and a Target Set Solution which finds a target number (as specified by the user) of feasible configurations. While minimal set provides the planners a parsimonious list of configurations as a base line to reduce complexity, the Target Set Solution allows them to enhance variety in the offerings through sensitivity analysis of margin with product volume or penetration rates and supply of selected option variants.

We will use the example of POGO to outline the evolution of a typical MR solution along its C3 journey. POGO can start with proper integration of "Connected" data across product structures in terms of allowed option families and its option variants, and combinations thereof, along with demand data from product sales or available capacity from supplier for each option variant (Figure 12). With a given volume allocation for projected demand, the cross-functional team can run scenarios on sensitivity of its mix or total margin using inputs, say rules from engineering, penetration rates from marketing, or supply volume from supply chain. This would clearly drive "Collaborative" decisions with a single view of truth. The scenarios on number of minimal or target solutions required to generate certain volume levels of a given product will estimate actionable thresholds to analyze and communicate right level of complexity and variety without losing demand – that will step POGO into its "Cognitive" stage. Similar to SDM, POGO spans all aspects of the C3 model, but is viewed mainly as a "Cognitive" solution.

Figure 12. POGO solution: System view

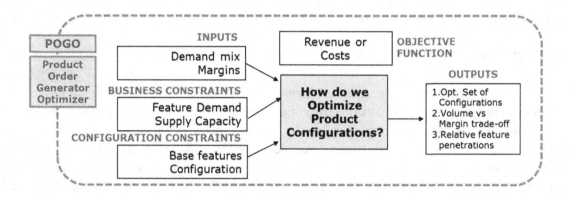

SUMMARY

Digital transformation offers a clear and present opportunity for businesses to increase efficiency and revenue, satisfy and grow customers, or reduce cost and risks. Rapidly advancing sensor, communication and computing technologies will accelerate and sustain the transformation through partners across supply, sales, production or technology opportunities. However, with the expanding scope and scale of the continuously emerging applications, this digital ecosystem faces crucial challenges in scaling, updating and securing information and operational interfaces across the devices and systems.

Businesses evolve along the digital transformation starting with Connected (linking and leveraging just-in-time data), to Collaborative (driving global team decisions through shared contextual and value understanding), and further to Cognitive (running rapid learning cycles to partner in decision making with devices) to deliver business value better and faster. The authors articulate this as C3 evolution of digital transformation ecosystem.

MR team has conceptualized core technology solutions that can be customized to solve customers' business problems in accordance with their position across the C3 journey - Connected to Collaborative to Cognitive – and their technology and business goals. The authors showcase five core solutions: RFPO and ISTM in the Connected state, DC in the Collaborative state, SDM and POGO in the Cognitive state. These core solutions and their extensions address key business challenges across the different processes in the manufacturing value chain.

The MR core solutions and their customized avatars complement each other and empower customers to exploit digital technologies in addressing critical problems across their C3 journey. The key highlight here is how these core solutions can link and leverage shared data and interactive analytics to manage end to end dependencies across manufacturing value chain processes. POGO enables configuring customer offerings to grow profits at lower complexity without losing demand. Digital Collaboratory helps the team balance product performance and quality expectations with security cost. SDM helps the operations team to plan and mitigate outages in system operations by taking cues from 24 hours in advance alerts, and ISTM manages IoT security using best mix of defenses against attacks progressing through the network.

While currently MR core solutions are demonstrated in reference to applications for manufacturing customers, they have resonated very well with customers across Consumer Products, Retail and HiTech industries as well. While the current MR solutions address value objectives for profitability, quality and resilience driving customer's competitive position, the ecosystem's capability to grow along the customer's C3 journey taking right data, information and decision capabilities to the next level will accelerate customer's digital transformation, leading to a position of sustained leadership.

REFERENCES

Bhattacharjee, S. (2018). *Practical Industrial Internet of Things Security: A practitioner's guide to securing connected industries*. Birmingham, UK: Packt Publishing Ltd.

Chandrasekaran, N. (2016). *Leadership in a Digital World* [PDF document]. Retrieved from https://www.tcs.com/content/dam/tcs/pdf/discover-tcs/investor-relations/key-events/TCS_Analyst_Day_2016_Leadership_in_Digital_World.pdf

Dewri, R., Poolsappasit, N., Ray, I., & Whitley, D. (2007). Optimal security hardening using multi-objective optimization on attack tree models of networks. In S. De Capitani di Vimercati, P. Syverson, & D. Evans (Eds.) *Proceedings of the 14th ACM conference on Computer and Communications Security* (pp. 204-213). Alexandria, VA: ACM. 10.1145/1315245.1315272

Fryer, J. (2017). The Road To IIoT: What Can We Learn From Other Industries? *Manufacturing.net*. Retrieved from https://www.manufacturing.net/article/2017/01/road-iiot-what-can-we-learn-other-industries

Industrial Internet Consortium. (2016). *The Industrial Internet of Things. Volume G4: Security Framework* (Report No. IIC:PUB:G4:V1.0:PB:20160919). Retrieved from https://www.iiconsortium.org/pdf/IIC_PUB_G4_V1.00_PB.pdf

Industrial Internet Consortium. (2017a) *The Industrial Internet of Things. Volume G1: Reference Architecture* (Report No. IIC:PUB:G1:V1.80:20170131). Retrieved from https://www.iiconsortium.org/IIC_PUB_G1_V1.80_2017-01-31.pdf

Industrial Internet Consortium. (2017b). *The Industrial Internet of Things. Volume T3: Analytics Framework* (Report No. IIC:PUB:T3:V1.00:PB:20171023). Retrieved from https://www.iiconsortium.org/pdf/IIC_Industrial_Analytics_Framework_Oct_2017.pdf

Korves, B. (2015). *The Future of Manufacturing – On the way to Industry 4.0* [PDF document]. *Siemens.* Retrieved from https://ec.europa.eu/information_society/newsroom/image/document/2015-44/14_korves_11951.pdf

Krishnan, K. A. (2017). Digitally Reimagining Mobility. In M. Tandon & P. Ghosh (Eds.), *Mobility Engineering* (pp. 59–68). Singapore: Springer. doi:10.1007/978-981-10-3099-4_8

Meckstroth, D. J. (2016). *The Manufacturing Value Chain Is Much Bigger Than You Think!* (Technical Report). Retrieved from Manufacturers Alliance for Productivity and Innovation Foundation website: https://mapifoundation.org/s/PA-165_web_0.pdf

National Intelligence Council. (2008). *Disruptive civil technologies: Six technologies with potential impacts on us interests out to 2025* (Technical Report). Retrieved from https://fas.org/irp/nic/disruptive.pdf

National Security Telecommunications Advisory Committee. (2014). *Final NSTAC Internet of Things Report.* Retrieved from https://www.cisa.gov/publication/2014-nstac-publications

Probst, L., Lefebvre, V., Martinez-Diaz, C., Bohn, N., Klitou, D., Conrads, J., & CARSA. (2018). *Digital Transformation Scoreboard 2018: EU businesses go digital: Opportunities, outcomes and uptake.* European Commission Report.

Ramanujan, D., Bernstein, W. Z., Chandrasegaran, S. K., & Ramani, K. (2017). Visual analytics tools for sustainable lifecycle design: Current status, challenges, and future opportunities. *Journal of Mechanical Design, 139*(11), 111415. doi:10.1115/1.4037479 PMID:29170612

Sabella, A., Irons-Mclean, R., & Yannuzzi, M. (2018). *Orchestrating and Automating Security for the Internet of Things: Delivering Advanced Security Capabilities from Edge to Cloud for IoT.* Indianapolis, IN: Cisco Press.

Tata Consultancy Services. (2015). *Internet of things: The complete re-imaginative force.* TCS Global Trend Study [PDF document]. Retrieved from https://sites.tcs.com/internet-of-things/

Tata Consultancy Services. (2018). *Business 4.0. The behaviors of digital transformation* [PDF document]. Retrieved from https://www.tcs.com/content/dam/tcs/pdf/discover-tcs/business/The%20Behaviors%20of%20Digital%20Transformation.pdf

Tata Consultancy Services. (2019). *Winning in a Business 4.0 World* [PDF document]. Retrieved from https://www.business4.tcs.com/

Chapter 13
The Digital Enterprise as an Emerging Landscape for Universities and Their Operation

Balbir S. Barn
Middlesex University, London, UK

ABSTRACT

This chapter presents a framing discussion around the notion of a digital enterprise in the context of higher education. The chapter makes the assumption that a university like a commercial enterprise can draw significant benefit from acting as a digital enterprise. The discussion indicates that some of a university's existing and historical activities are in line with notions of a digital enterprise. The chapter proposes a framework for assessing the readiness of a university with respect to its actions as a digital enterprise recognising the complexity of domains residing within the confines of a university environment. Critically, the chapter argues that such a future systems project should not only consider positive use cases but also recognise that a digital enterprise may have unplanned and unintentional consequences. Hence, this chapter argues that new forms of governance may also be required alongside the planned journey to a digital enterprise world.

INTRODUCTION

There is a case for arguing that we are in the throes of a paradigm shift as organizations adopt the practices of so-called Digital Enterprises. As in the case of the steam engine and electrification from the 18th Century onwards, the technologies underpinning the digital enterprise: mobility, big data, artificial intelligence, social media and cloud services are beginning to significantly transform the industrial and public sector landscape. The current shift is different from the earlier e-business cases where transactional systems or aspects of a business were technology enabled for the Internet. Now, a digital enterprise represents a wholesale change in the modus operandi of an organization through sensor based data collection and real time modification to core business processes as a response to changing business drivers.

DOI: 10.4018/978-1-7998-0108-5.ch013

Figure 1. Digital twin, key components and types

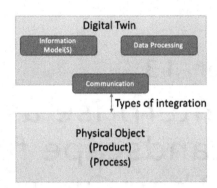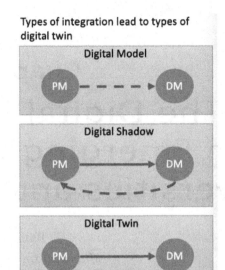

The notion of a digital enterprise is difficult to pin down and definitions are hard to come by. Academic literature is a particular lacuna with respect to a viable definition. Definitions that are generally available are sourced from commercial organisations and often present a platform specific notion of a digital enterprise. A typical definition found is: "A digital enterprise is an organization that uses technology as a competitive advantage in its internal and external operations." (Rouse, 2011). Other definitions follow a similar theme. "A true digital enterprise will integrate information, processes, work and people so that the entire organisation can collaborate more efficiently and effectively, and therefore produce more valuable products and services." (Rossi, 2015).

Digitalization is the dominant antecedent for large-scale and sweeping transformations across business. It is not simply a matter of IT investment, instead, operating models need to be re-thought, processes by which new talent is recruited are needed and if necessary new digital business models (that may require cannabilisation of existing products) are required (Matt et al. 2015). Georzig and Bauernhansl (2018) note transformation changes the paradigm of doing things and propose that digital transformation is a fundamental change process in enterprises initiated by new competitive advantages through the evolution of IT into an essential part of the value creation.

Part of the digitalization agenda is the role of *Digital Twins*. Such a technology, albeit guilty of being annotated as a silver bullet, is critical to the realisation of transformational change anticipated through digitalization. Digital twin technology enables a near real-time view of key products and processes in an organisation. However, like the digital enterprise, digital twins also suffer from a lack of precise definition. Two recent systematic reviews (Lu et al., 2019, Kritzinger et al., 2018) providing coverage of digital twins indicate some convergence to a definition:

Digital Twin refers to a description of a component, product, system or process by a set of well-aligned, descriptive and executable models:

- The Digital Twin is the semantically linked collection of the relevant digital artefacts including design and engineering data, operational data and behavioural descriptions.
- The Digital Twin evolves with the real system along the whole life cycle and integrates the currently available and commonly required data and knowledge.

Digital twins enable an effective configuration and change of a physical artefact or process where potential outcomes can be easily explored without recourse to physical intervention. Communication channels between the physical artifact and the digital twin also determine the type of integration. In fact, so called digital twins may simply be *digital models*, where the model is constructed through a manual communication step from the physical model to the digital model. Then there are *digital shadows* where the digital model is updated through an automated process, but the physical model is kept in synchronization by a manual process. Finally, there is the digital twin where both physical and digital models are completely in synch through automated protocols (see Figure 1). Elsewhere in this volume, further research on digital twins is presented.

To some extent, Universities have been embarking on limited efforts that touch upon notions of a digital enterprise. For example, there is significant use of data analytics through the use of dashboards (https://www.jisc.ac.uk/learning-analytics), mobile phone apps that support students on their learner journeys and reconfiguring of learning spaces utilizing full connectivity. Even student attendance through device recognition using proximity sensors is being implemented. The range of technologies being utilised demonstrates the journey to a digital enterprise. Critically, what is not visible are the strategic threads that bring together actions that demonstrate how internal and external operations are being changed, where data and processes are being truly integrated to generate additional value. For example, while a student's attendance of a course may be linked to performance, it may also be linked to how a course has been timetabled in terms of the rooms allocated and the time slot provided. Do these get changed in the next run of the course and data re-measured perhaps leading to improved attendance? Given the complexity of a higher education institution (HEI), the range of stakeholders, the products on offer, the locked value residing in latent relationships between sub-domains within a university organization, it is clear that there are significant opportunities and even competitive advantage to be had.

The question arises, why then, are universities not yet a digital enterprise? Given that universities are traditionally seen as centres of knowledge creation and innovation, it is paradoxical that universities are also seen to be slow in adopting new organizational management practices such as the notion of a digital enterprise. It is this paper's thesis that this reluctance or naivety is potentially due to the lack of an articulation of conceptual understanding of what a digital enterprise means in the context of higher education and where most value can be extracted. Hence, this paper sets out the landscape of higher education and its proclivity for enacting digital enterprise behaviours. A conceptual framework of key components of a HEI digital enterprise are presented. The paper also offers a more critical position in that it outlines specifically, a negative use case of one potentially unintended outcome – the increased opportunity of instrumentalisation of students and staff through digital enterprise technologies.

The remainder of the chapter is structured as follows: Section 1 provides an overview and background to the key technologies and interventions that could be broadly ascribed to the digital enterprise concept. Section 2 presents a framework for assessing aspirations and progress a university may demonstrate as it attempts to become a digital enterprise. Section 3 accounts for alternative use cases of digital enterprises and provides a more critical perspective of unintended consequences of digital enterprises. Section 4 provides some final concluding remarks.

BACKGROUND

The idea of a University as a Digital Enterprise is largely a future project; however, aspects of a digital enterprise are being enacted currently. First, let us consider some key components of a digital enterprise. While the earlier definition suffices for a broad understanding, it is useful to unpick some of the key technologies and how elements of these technologies are already being used. Diana et al. (2013) propose five critical areas of technology that are drivers of transformation:

1. **Big data** (De Mauro, A., Greco, M., & Grimaldi 2016): companies, customers, partners and machines are all generating more data than before. This data is both structured and un-structured where the latter increases in value if it can be assimilated.
2. **Social media** has enabled a shift in the balance of power from businesses to consumers, creating a powerful two-way communication mechanism (see Li et al, (2017) for an example), and is a key platform for building loyalty or crowdsourcing new innovations (Mount & Martinez, 2014).
3. **Mobility** afforded by advances in mobile telecommunications is pervading and transforming business through a variety of actions. For example, new products and services target customers based on location (Rajendran, 2017). Productivity increases as accessibility of corporate resources from mobile devices is made possible (Palvia et al. 2015) and business processes can also change to account for mobility (such as the re-routing of service calls).
4. **Cloud computing** offers scalability and economy by providing on-demand services through broad network access and resource pooling. A range of applications are delivered through a "software as a service" or even platforms and infrastructures as services (Mell & Grance, 2009). Individually, these technology elements have been utilized but it is the interplay between technologies that offer even greater innovation, although not without attendant risk. For example, a Pew report (Madden & Rainee, 2015) reported that the biggest issue to preventing widespread use of location services was privacy.
5. Finally, there is the use of **artificial intelligence**, or more specifically, the application of machine learning techniques to make sense of data to support decision-making and the general notion of the "intelligent enterprise" (World Economic Forum, 2016).

This section now outlines how some of these technologies have been used to-date. In the UK, the Joint Information Systems Committee (JISC) operating on behalf of all UK universities explored how UK universities could utilize shared services such as virtual learning environments and HR systems for economic and efficiency reasons (JISC, 2013), Although numerous case studies and examples were developed by JISC and subsequently reported, the success of shared services remains limited partly due to the differences between HEIs and their business processes (Barn et al, 2006) and some of the exposed risks through trying to share services around non-core activities (Clark, Ferrell & Hopkins, 2011). Widespread cloud service acceptance is in place for utility services such as email and document sharing (e.g. Microsoft Office 365). More recent examples of niche shared services include software as a service products for managing board and committee papers (https://www.jisc.ac.uk/board-and-committee-papers-framework) and a service to allow researchers and institutions to meet their policy requirements for the deposit and curation of research data (https://www.jisc.ac.uk/open-research-hub). The latter is also a good sub-domain example of an offering from IBM (2012) aimed at research management that is part of product suites targeting the notion of a *smart* university.

Since the 1990s, the core areas of the business of higher education, primarily teaching and learning, but also including research and knowledge transfer, has seen significant use of technology to enhance learning. A comprehensive systematic review conducted by Kirkwood and Price (2014) reported that much activity has centred on two aspects: Firstly, the replication of existing practice (rather like the move of bricks and mortar companies moving aspects of their transactional services online) and secondly, making resources available online. Less effort has been expended on structural changes to teaching practice and processes. The notion of enhancement also remains difficult to pin down. Related to this, the annual report from the New Media Consortium published in conjunction with EDUCAUSE notes that a key long-term challenge for which a solution remains elusive is how to address the achievement gap, the disparity between enrolment and achievement gap of student groups (Becker et al., 2017). Technology enhanced learning (TeL) often presents as value-neutral proposition aid to addressing this gap.

The increase in the uptake of mobile devices and the largest demographic of mobile device users being 18-29-year olds (Pew 2017), has meant that TeL has increasingly become mobile device oriented. A recent systematic review by Crompton and Burke (2018) reported on the impact of mobile devices on student achievement was the most explored research area, yet evidence of success of impact remains relatively un-systemised and if findings from a meta-analysis of the impact of technology on learning effectiveness were to be generalised, the impact of technology mobile devices only has a moderate mean effect (Sung, Chang, & Liu, 2016). Indirect use of TeL may be a better route.

TeL has also been executed through the use of social media technologies. Many reviews of the use of social media in higher education have been conducted. For example, reviews have mostly been framed around social media and teaching (Tess, 2013) or the use of social media by the student body (Davies et al, 2012). Only recently, Manca and Whitworth (2018) conducted a systematic review of social media and workplace practices. The broadening of the scope to include the idea of workplace is important as it provides greater input of the role of social media on the university as digital enterprise. Notably, findings from this review report on the use of social media for administrative interventions. Much of the reported activity is in the area of institutional marketing such as building ties with alumni, branding and general marketing. It is observable that there is an absence of studies of the use of social media in or influence over decision-making and management information practices within HE institutions. For example, such an omission points to a significant opportunity for immediate improvements in knowledge creation processes through improved information sharing.

More recent developments have seen the notion of a *smart university* take shape. This follows on naturally from developments in smart city discussions. The 2016 report on world population demographics by the United Nations indicates that through a rising economy and social transformation, increasing urbanization will result in 60% of the world population living in cities. When this is combined with environmental sustainability concerns and an increasingly ageing population (especially in the global north), then there will be increasing demands on cities to improve governance, safety, security and service delivery. Hence, there has been a debate on the use of new technology-based solutions to support new ways of urban planning and living. A potential solution to this debate is the notion of a smart city. While there is no clear consensus on a definition for smart cities (Neirotti et al. 2014). There is general agreement that characteristics of a smart city encompass ubiquitous sensing components and accompanying network infrastructure that offer real-time monitoring in various urban domains. Central to the concept of a smart city is the prioritization of big data collection (volume, heterogeneity, speed) coupled with machine learning in order to optimize service delivery in urban domains such as waste management, mobility, and power management. Given some of the technological characteristics, it is evident from this that there is similarity with the Digital Enterprise concept and there is a natural evolution to the idea of a smart university.

Uskov et al, (2017) have, following an extensive but not systematic literature review, developed a conceptual framework outlining the key characteristics of a smart university. One key property is the smartness level ranging from adaptation to inferring, self-learning and ultimately self-organization. However, the definitions presented are not sufficiently disambiguated. While many concepts are presented and enumerated through instances (such as stakeholders, pedagogy, classrooms etc.), a notable absence is the management and administrative functions such as marketing and registry processes). A digital enterprise would be expected to address such functional areas.

In summary, it is clear that elements of a digital enterprise are being enacted, but an integrated approach that generates value across all the technology drivers is not yet established. The use of machine learning in academic analytics is still relatively under-utilized. Further, as noted in the introduction, advances in the notion of a digital twin is also a necessary pre-condition and using such technology a part of a digital twin project remains largely unexplored. Notably though, some experimental activity in this area is emerging (Barat et al, 2019). One argument is that the complexity of the university domain from pedagogic practice, course design, quality assurance to transactional exchanges such as automated class registration means that the university as a digital enterprise remains a future project. The next section proposes a conceptual framework for understanding how university could operate as a digital enterprise. The structures proposed support an integrative approach and recognize the multi-dimensionality and complexity of a university environment.

COMPONENTS OF A UNIVERSITY AS A DIGITAL ENTERPRISE

As noted earlier, the most complex aspect of a university is the multiple domains that reside within the overarching structure of a university. Figure 1 provides an overview of the key sub-domains. These domains have resonance with typical dimensions of a smart city. For example, Giffenger et al. (2007) reported in Mattoni et al. (2016), propose six smart axes: Governance, People, Economy, Environment, Living and Mobility. Owoc & Marciniak (2013) propose knowledge management as a cornerstone of smart university. In this paper, it is suggested that knowledge management or the idea of a knowledge grid comprises four elements namely: knowledge creation through research, knowledge transfer outside of the university, learning of knowledge (done throughout the organisation) and the dissemination of teaching of knowledge. These actions happen independently and with freedom from interference or constraints. This is the traditional Humboldtian purpose of a university (Östling, 2018). It is of course, this intellectual freedom that can place a challenge on the operation of a university as a digital enterprise. The positioning of universities as teaching only institutions, especially following changes in the regulatory regime that has allowed the construction of several private teaching institutions with university status in the UK, could indicate that this traditional view of a university is being diluted.

This paper proposes that the universe of discourse comprises four broad areas, People, Governance, Knowledge Grid and Environment. Each high level domain and associated sub-domains represents areas where digital enterprise development can take place. The People domain represents the communities of different actors or stakeholders. While Student and Academic are self-explanatory, Non-Academic will include administrative officers, the executive, and also ancillary staff such as porters. Partners are all stakeholders engaged in some form of relationship with the university. Environment represents different spaces where digital innovation can take place. Environment, for example covers all types of space both within the university and external to it. While there will still be a requirement for specialist teaching spaces such as labs, shared community spaces such as hallways, lobbies, coffee areas are now also increasingly seen as places where learning happens (Broz, 2016). Closed Spaces, are meeting rooms and offices where there is normally restricted access for students. External Environment represents the wider setting of a university. The Governance domain is an area that is has been relatively neglected in the Smart University discourse but remains critical for a vision of a digital enterprise. Governance happens through external pressure enacted through public policy (c.f. the changes in the UK HE policy through the formulation of the Office of Students (https://www.officeforstudents.org.uk)). Governance is also enacted through the Executive, Registry (management of data concerning programmes and students) and services such as student welfare and IT services. The Knowledge Grid domain covers the essential purpose of the higher education: the creation of new knowledge and its transfer to external stakeholders and through acts of learning and teaching.

Figure 2. University domains of interest

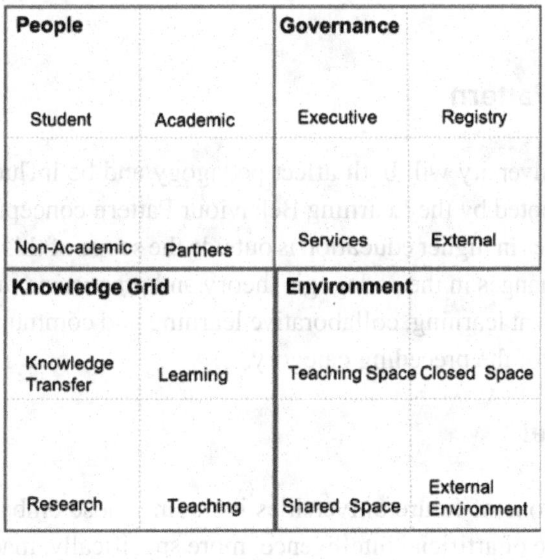

People		Governance	
Student	Academic	Executive	Registry
Non-Academic	Partners	Services	External
Knowledge Grid		**Environment**	
Knowledge Transfer	Learning	Teaching Space	Closed Space
Research	Teaching	Shared Space	External Environment

In this proposal, each domain or sub-domain (documented in Figure 2) can be elaborated further through properties assigned to one or several dimensions. Technology or Learning Behaviour Pattern dimension may not apply to a given domain (hence the 0..* cardinality). Figure 3 presents an overview of these dimensions and is described in further detail below.

Technology

The Technology dimension derives from the central premise of the underlying technologies that underpin a digital enterprise discussed in the introduction section. These include: Big data, mobility, social media, cloud services and artificial intelligence.

Figure 3. Domains and their dimensions

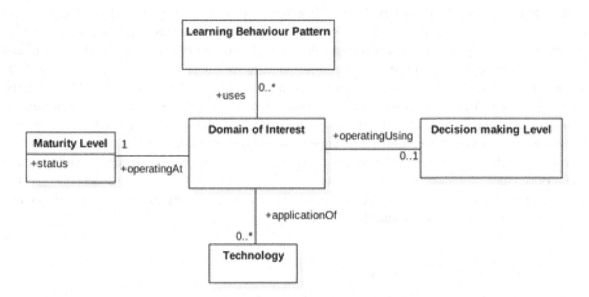

Learning Behaviour Pattern

A digital enterprise of a university will both affect pedagogy and be influenced by pedagogic norms. In Table 1, pedagogy is denoted by the Learning Behaviour Pattern concept. Detailed discussion of the changing pedagogic practices in higher education is outside the scope of this paper however it is possible summarise advances and changes in the pedagogic theory and practice nexus through the categories of: directed learning, independent learning, collaborative learning and community learning. Each category represents an advancement of the preceding category.

Decision Making Level

As noted earlier, a cornerstone of future universities including those embarked on a digital enterprise project, is the increasing use of artificial intelligence, more specifically, machine learning in day to day operational decision making across the domains. Van Otterlo (2013) defines machine learning as "any methodology and set of techniques that can employ data to come up with novel patterns and knowledge

Table 1. Learning behaviour pattern

Guided Learning	Traditional didactic, socratic method using lectures and tutorials.
Independent Learning	Student learns independently through found or supplied resources.
Collaborative Learning	Students learn through co-activity with others. Project based requiring extensive communication between co-learners.
Community Learning	Broadens collaborative learning to extend learning outside of the institution and into the community where participants may not be formally designated as learners (enrolled) at a university.

Table 2. Decision-making levels

Current	Data is used to inform decision making and changes executed by humans.
Adaptive	Data is used to automatically modify components such as teaching and learning methods, resources and presentation of resources during an execution of an activity
Anticipation	Data is used to automatically obtain or modify existing data, knowledge, or behavior for use as a planning strategy for later automated modification of components as a predicted response to different events or forces.

and generate models that can be used for effective predictions about the data". Machine learning has the capacity to define or modify decision-making rules autonomously. Within a broader intelligence requirement, machine learning may provide increasing levels of decision making capability as shown in Table 2. These levels are proposed as a more compact alternative to those described in Uskov et al. (2018).

Maturity Level

A domain can exhibit a maturity level reflecting how well it operates as a conjunction of technology, intelligence and learning approach. The idea of a maturity level is adopted from the Software process maturity model (Humphrey, 1988) and the same level definitions are applied here. Thus, a domain can operate at one of five levels, Initial, Repeatable, Defined, Managed and Optimised.

The central hypothesis is that a University or its sub-domains when operating as a Digital Enterprise will utilise: learning behaviour patterns; operate at a machine learning driven decision-making level; will have deployed a technology such as cloud services, social media, big data and mobility and across those components have demonstrated maturity at a stated level. However, to truly realise a university as a digital enterprise it also necessary to consider how a digital twin can be used a part of the solution. Only then is it possible to construct toolkits for measuring progress towards a digital enterprise. The (sub) domains, the dimensions and the maturity level has the potential for providing a conceptual roadmap for digital enterprise development.

EVALUATION SCENARIO

Consider the following scenario as an illustration adapted from (Androutsopoulos, 2015):

The University of Southern England runs the first year of an undergraduate BSc computer science programme that comprises 5 projects requiring student centred team working. On completion of all five projects students will have gained the necessary grounding in computer science at level 4. Students on teams complete projects and demonstrate specific student observable outcomes (SOBs) that equate to topics that students would be expected to learn as per the Quality Assurance Agency benchmark for the subject area (www.qaa.ac.uk/docs/qaa/subject-benchmark-statements/sbs-computing-16.pdf). A SOB is observed by teachers to have been completed at one of three levels of achievement (Threshold, Expected, Excellent). Observations are recorded using iPads and other mobile technology and students are able to get instant feedback on their work and if necessary adjustments can be made for example, a student may choose to use a different programming language to demonstrate a solution to a problem.

In the supporting system, a student logging in can easily see how they are progressing across all SOBs and note their position with respect to the overall class regarding completion of SOBs. Accesses to the system, and academic performance overall contribute to a University wide student dashboard where data from multiple sources is aggregated supporting simple predictive analytics. The approach has now been adopted in other curriculum areas.

In this example, several sub-domains within the University are in operation and each can have a different level of maturity. For the purposes of an initial evaluation of the validity of the underlying concepts, a simple subjective viewpoint is offered. The student sub-domain exhibits aspects of a digital enterprise in three dimensions. Along the Learning Behavior Pattern dimension, the project-based curriculum and required team-working suggest elements of collaborative learning pedagogic practice. For the Intelligence level dimension, the tool for collecting specific student observable behaviors supports data-centric analysis that currently does not exhibit any automated adaptation. However, teacher supported adaptation is possible using the data. The system and the tools ecology indicate a range of technologies are being used that lay the foundations of digital enterprise including devices supporting mobility, cloud-based services and the beginnings of big data. Although the core dimensions are at relatively early stage of digital enterprise representation, the adoption of the approach for other curriculum areas places this example at the Repeatable maturity level. Thus the conceptual structures provided in section 3 allow us to make a subjective assessment of a current position. To advance to a new position, we should envisage data collected through this SOB mechanism becoming available at an institutional level and being integrated with other data such as attendance data.

At a more foundational level, analysis from a digital twin perspective reveals that the assessment model is a *digital shadow* of an assessment. That is, data from the target model is extracted and digitally represented and then periodically the target model is updated.

CHALLENEGES TO A UNIVERSITY AS A DIGITAL ENTERPRISE

The University as a digital enterprise is presented as a positive use case. Opportunities are indeed significant and entailed in the paradigmatic shift. But now is also the time to review some of the negative use cases. Big data, storage in the cloud and subsequent ease of access, the use of machine learning for predictive analytics, as well as creating a perfect storm for new opportunities, also create the conditions for loss of informational privacy of stakeholders within the university system.

As the Humboldtian tradition gets diluted, in recent times, Universities have responded to external change through a willingness to engage with approaches taken from the private sector. Partly, this is because is because of an increasing managerialism within the higher education sector where this response has been broadly interpreted as a form of 'new public management' (Hood, 2005) and inculcated in higher education as 'new managerialism' (Deem & Brehoney, 2005). However, a key contributing factor is the rate of technological change impacting the sector. Thus, recent incarnations of new public management are the implementation of higher education policy and practice through tools that include: targets, measures, evaluations and comparisons and so promoting an ongoing culture of performativity similar to that seen in English schooling (Ball, 2003). By performativity, the definition from Clapham (Clapham, 2013) is adopted: as the "legitimization of that which contributes to maximal performance of a system". The emerging dominant model in HE is the use of data driven analytics whereby dashboards, aggregating data from a range of different sources are presented in a form that enables key stakeholders to make informed decisions. As the leaders at Nottingham Trent University assert: "…it has transformed the university culture into a data driven business approach". (Becker et al. 2017, p14). Simultaneously, the same dashboards raise ethical concerns such as knowingly keeping students enrolled when it is clear they are not ready for higher education. In 2016, predictive analytics data was used by Mount St Mary's University to encourage early drop out of students who were likely to fail in the future (Ezeugo & Palmer, 2018).

The digital enterprise creates conditions for continuous collection of data and so enabling "opportunities" such as improving performance – performativity to be presented. Where units of work, business processes and transactional data is collected through data surveillance, it is perhaps more straightforward to assume that a typical NPM goal of improved efficiency, optimization or simple cost cutting is the motivation. In this mode, the primary purpose is largely one of normalization and discipline. (One such example is the frequently common requirement to ensure that goals are given percentage targets so that audit spread sheets can show red, green and amber cells). However, given that a university is a complex, socio-technical environment with many different types of stakeholders, surveillance is a much more diffuse affair operating in multiple forms, levels, motivations and through different means.

The transactional unit of surveillance - data, itself is problematic. For example, a key assumption is that the data collected are objective, neutral measures of what is happening in a university. If computations are used to further process the data, then a further assumption is that the algorithms used to process the data are also value-free. Beyond NPM, data surveillance-based interventions are largely framed as benign, the use cases presented are invariably positive and valid concerns such as privacy are often presented as a trade-off against benefits of improved services. Collection of large volumes of data in a university environment results in both accidental and explicit surveillance of members of the institution. Kitchin (2014) suggests that the data collected may be:

- Targeted, where the gaze of a technology-based proxy authority is aimed at individuals or places;
- Automated, where data is generated as an inherent function of the ICT component, such as in sensors;
- Volunteered, where data is freely given by students or staff, such as through interactions on educational or proxy social media platforms.

All three forms of data collection offer modalities for surveillance in a university operating as a digital enterprise. Targeted surveillance can be mediated through the use of barcode scanning systems installed in classrooms (ostensibly to measure room usage but leading to information about an individual's attendance). Automated data collection through the use of under-desk sensors measure presence and hence room usage but provides a deep insight into an individuals' work patterns. Social media platforms such as Yammer (for corporate communications), or Slack for student projects provides quantified data about some notion of engagement. Prinsloo and Rowe outline similar concerns on ethical considerations in the collection of student data (Prinsloo and Rowe, 2015).

The use of digital technologies offers both a new scale and new theories of networked or distributed surveillance where both the human and the data double (the representation of a student or an academic as an informational representation) are surveilled. Moreover, the watchers also change. Large corporations, often the biggest drivers behind so-called academic analytics are looking for both technological lock-in and ways of monetizing surveilled data. A university may offer many data collection points, each such collection point offering what Latour refers to, in surveillance terms, as an oligopticon or partial vantage points (Latour, 1999). Only through data synthesis, pattern matching, and machine learning techniques are new analyses and conclusions available. The machinery of ICT infrastructure offered by corporations, such as sensors and cloud-based technology is ideal for the construction of so-called surveillance assemblages (Haggerty and Ericson, 2000) whereby disparate systems are integrated and function as a single system or dashboard.

Integrated data collection and the implicit surveillance suggests that current practices of governance will need adaptation and innovation in parallel to the technological innovation being deployed. Such governance changes will need to consider some key challenges:

- **Technocratic Governmentality - Leading to 'Fabricated' Narratives:** Continuous monitoring of student or academic activity, analysis and then decision-making presumes an instrumented rationality and then subsequent control. Danger exists where reasons may not be sought, instead, emergent, 'interesting' correlations are acted on that preclude moral reflection (see also value-sensitive algorithms). Moreover, data becomes political and is no longer objective. Technocratic governmentality may lead to 'fabricated' narratives which occlude or ignore information that cannot be measured easily. For example, workload models assume a notional total of working hours, academics may exceed this notional total but 'formal audit systems sidestep this 'messy' reality' (Craig, Amernic, and Tourish, 2014) and instead a fabricated narrative that is not representative of reality is created. The mechanism of surveillance to enforce this technocratic governmentality risks undermining the intrinsic motivations of academics.

- **Reification of Bio-Power:** In Foucault's conception of bio-power, ideas of power and knowledge that are fed to the human, leaves the human docile and able to be disciplined and thus reifying power differentials. In the health sector for example, health apps, tracking technology has the potential to be developed such that patients will be no longer be independently reliant on taking their medications. Google maps on the mobile phone creates a similar dependence. In higher education, the promise of mobile apps to accompany a student on their journey (NPM speak) through higher education promises greater autonomy, personalized information and a sense of belonging. The app, however can easily malfunction or be deliberately disabled leading to an asymmetrical power relation between those who manage the app and its services and the students availing of the services. Disabling an app may for example occur when fees have not been paid in a timely way. A further concern is around license acceptance and the likelihood that students will read the associated terms and conditions of the app.

- **Value-Sensitive Algorithms:** In the same manner that data is not apolitical, algorithms underpinning academic analytics and decision making are also not apolitical. Algorithms embed values of their designers and because of the inherent lack of transparency of the computation undertaken in the algorithm nor are the values easy to identify. In the context of technology artefacts, values are what Friedman refers to as: ownership and property; privacy, freedom from bias, universal usability, trust, autonomy, informed consent and identity. She defines values as: what a person or group of people consider important in life (Friedman, 1996). Further, reinforcement, or erosion of such values occurs through the use of software either through deliberate design or through accident. Algorithms also pose other issues such as: probable results (with inevitable uncertainty), unfair outcomes (inherent biases), and traceability concerns where data combinations are difficult to track back (Mittelstadt et al., 2016).

- **Corporate data colonialism:** The role of large corporations, through outsourcing by universities, is promoting a neoliberal political economy such that corporations are in a position to colonize data generated in public environments with a view to monetization of that data. There is recognition that there is some risk in adopting the term colonialism as a metaphor. In the historical sense, colonialism, the appropriation of land, resources and bodies by powerful countries, provided the preconditions for the emergence of industrial capitalism. Likewise, we can anticipate a new form of capitalism where data, combined with transformations and inferential techniques provide opportunities for creating surplus value (Couldry and Mejias, 2018). Dangers of technology lock-in must be carefully assessed through new methodologies and tools. One such mechanism is the recently introduced General Data Protection Regulation (GDPR). GDPR provides the rules for processing of personal data of natural persons, denotes sensitive data and sets out the rights of citizens and obligations of organizations that process personal data (Nicolaidou and Georgiades, 2017).

Whether a digital twin can truly represent products or processes of a university environment is an open research question. In a manufacturing context, processes, supply chains case studies are available. Similarly, in the structural health monitoring domain, digital twin case studies have also been documented. In a university context, the core product is a programme of study (e.g. BSc Computer Science). As a product, this could be subject to a digital representation from a health perspective (the quality assurance of the product). For this digital representation to evolve in line with the evolution of the programme, and for it to advance to a digital twin then queries to check and improve its health have to be done in line. E.g. student feedback received ad hoc to be automatically reflected in the programme as a product. Clearly, then issues of versioning are problematic and it may not be possible for a representation to be exhibited as true digital twin.

CONCLUSION

The university as a digital enterprise notion is essentially a concept within a future project framework, in that current developments should be viewed as an interim solution. It is clear that many activities that universities have been executing exhibit some of the properties of a digital enterprise. It is also evident that the complexity of the sub-domains residing within a university, together with the purpose of a university in a wider societal context, places additional challenges to gaining the benefits from acting as a digital enterprise. It is also reasonable to assume that some form of digital twin (whether it a digital model, digital shadow or a true digital twin) can be used to contribute to the university as digital enterprise. The proposed framework is an initial step to developing tools for assessing digital enterprise readiness in higher education. Perhaps most significantly, the paper also outlines some of the issues that a fully functioning digital enterprise may raise with respect to surveillance and privacy concerns. As institutions work towards increasing use of smart capabilities (automated data collection coupled with algorithmic processing for decision making), it makes sense to develop in parallel, appropriate governance models and frameworks that work to addressing some of the challenges / concerns described above. The framework proposed in this paper provides some initial thinking to support such governance concerns.

ACKNOWLEDGMENT

Thanks to Dr Simon Best, Middlesex University for providing some initial feedback and useful additional reading on an earlier draft of this paper.

REFERENCES

Anderson, T., & Dron, J. (2018). Integrating learning management and social networking systems. *Italian Journal of Educational Technology*, *25*(3), 5–19.

Androutsopoulos, K., Gorogiannis, N., Loomes, M., Margolis, M., Primiero, G., Raimondi, F., ... Zivanovic, A. (2014). A racket-based robot to teach first-year computer science. *7th European Lisp Symposium*, 54.

Ball, S. J. (2003). The teacher's soul and the terrors of performativity. *Journal of Education Policy*, *18*(2), 215–228. doi:10.1080/0268093022000043065

Barat, S., Kulkarni, V., Clark, T., & Barn, B. S. (2019). An actor based simulation driven digital twin for analyzing complex business systems. *Proceedings of the 2019 Winter Simulation Conference* 10.1109/WSC40007.2019.9004694

Barn, B., Dexter, H., Oussena, S., & Petch, J. (2006). A synthesis approach for deriving reference models for SOA frameworks. *IADIS International Journal on Computer Science and Information Systems*, *1*(2), 100–116.

Becker, S. A., Cummins, M., Davis, A., Freeman, A., Hall, C. G., & Ananthanarayanan, V. (2017). *NMC horizon report: 2017 higher education edition*. The New Media Consortium.

Bleiklie, I. (2018). New Public Management or Neoliberalism. *Higher Education*.

Boschert, S., Heinrich, C., & Rosen, R. (2018). Next generation digital Twin. *Proceedings of TMCE*.

Broz, D. (2016). *10 ideas for tomorrow's campus*. Retrieved from https://www.bdcnetwork.com/blog/10-ideas-tomorrow's-campus

Clapham, A. (2013). Performativity, fabrication and trust: Exploring computer-mediated moderation. *Ethnography and Education*, *8*(3), 371–387. doi:10.1080/17457823.2013.792676

Clark, M., Ferrell, G., & Hopkins, P. (2011). *Study of early adopters of shared services and cloud computing within Higher and Further Education*. Report produced by HE Associates for JISC. Available at https://docs.google.com/viewer?a=v&pid=explorer&chrome=true&srcid=0B6psyHRq0wqPYzY1OD QxYzEtYjNiMS00ZTBiLTg5ZDQtMmQzNGY1NGZhMjk3&hl=en_US

Couldry, N., & Mejias, U. (2018). Data colonialism: Rethinking big data's relation to the contemporary subject. *Television & New Media*.

Craig, R., Amernic, J., & Tourish, D. (2014). Perverse audit culture and accountability of the modern public university. *Financial Accountability & Management*, *30*(1), 1–24. doi:10.1111/faam.12025

Crompton, H., & Burke, D. (2018). The use of mobile learning in higher education: A systematic review. *Computers & Education, 123*, 53–64. doi:10.1016/j.compedu.2018.04.007

Davis, C. H. F., Del-Amen, R., Rios-Aguilar, C., & González Canché, M. S. (2012). *Social media in higher education: A literature review and research directions*. Center for the study of HE, report printed by the University Of Arizona and Claremont Graduate University. https://works.bepress.com/hfdavis/2/

De Mauro, A., Greco, M., & Grimaldi, M. (2016). A formal definition of Big Data based on its essential features. *Library Review, 65*(3), 122–135. doi:10.1108/LR-06-2015-0061

Deem, R., & Brehony, K. J. (2005). Management as ideology: The case of 'new managerialism' in higher education. *Oxford Review of Education, 31*(2), 217-235.

Diana, F., McKinney, T., & Mulcahy, K. (2013). The Digital Enterprise, A Framework for Transformation. *TCS Consulting Journal, 5*. Accessed: https://www.slideshare.net/stuartlamb/the-digitalenterprisevol-510131131121044548phpapp01

du Toit, J., & Verhoef, A. H. (2018). Embodied digital technology and transformation in higher education. *Transformation in Higher Education, 3*(1), 1–8.

Ezeugo, E., & Palmer, I. (2018). *Five Ways to Turn Data-Informed Student Nudging from Bad to Good*. Retrieved from https://www.edsurge.com/news/2018-03-13-five-dangers-of-data-informed-student-nudging

Friedman, B. (1996). Value-sensitive design. *Interactions, 3*(6), 16–23.

Giffinger, R., Fertner, C., Kramar, H., & Meijers, E. (2007). *City-ranking of European medium-sized cities*. Vienna, UT: Cent. Reg. Sci.

Goerzig, D., & Bauernhansl, T. (2018). Enterprise architectures for the digital transformation in small and medium-sized enterprises. *Procedia CIRP, 67*, 540–545. doi:10.1016/j.procir.2017.12.257

Haggerty, K. D., & Ericson, R. V. (2000). The surveillant assemblage. *The British Journal of Sociology, 51*(4), 605-622. PMID:11140886

Hood, C. (2000). Paradoxes of public-sector managerialism, old public management and public service bargains. *International Public Management Journal, 3*(1), 1–22. doi:10.1016/S1096-7494(00)00032-5

Humphrey, W. S. (1988). Characterizing the software process: A maturity framework. *IEEE Software, 5*(2), 73–79. doi:10.1109/52.2014

IBM. (2012). *Smarter education with IBM*. Retrieved from https://www-935.ibm.com/services/multimedia/Framework_-_Smarter_Education_With_IBM.pdf

JISC. (2013). Shared Services. *JISC*. Retrieved January from https://www.jisc.ac.uk/full-guide/shared-services

Kirkwood, A., & Price, L. (2014). Technology-enhanced learning and teaching in higher education: What is 'enhanced' and how do we know? A critical literature review. *Learning, Media and Technology, 39*(1), 6–36. doi:10.1080/17439884.2013.770404

Kitchin, R. (2014). The real-time city? Big data and smart urbanism. *GeoJournal, 79*(1), 1–14. doi:10.100710708-013-9516-8

Kritzinger, W., Karner, M., Traar, G., Henjes, J., & Sihn, W. (2018). Digital Twin in manufacturing: A categorical literature review and classification. *IFAC-PapersOnLine, 51*(11), 1016–1022. doi:10.1016/j.ifacol.2018.08.474

Latour, B. (1999). On recalling ANT. *The Sociological Review, 47*(S1), 15–25. doi:10.1111/j.1467-954X.1999.tb03480.x

Li, L. P., Juric, B., & Brodie, R. J. (2017). Dynamic multi-actor engagement in networks: The case of United Breaks Guitars. *Journal of Service Theory and Practice, 27*(4), 738–760. doi:10.1108/JSTP-04-2016-0066

Lu, Y., Liu, C., Kevin, I., Wang, K., Huang, H., & Xu, X. (2020). Digital Twin-driven smart manufacturing: Connotation, reference model, applications and research issues. *Robotics and Computer-integrated Manufacturing, 61*, 101837. doi:10.1016/j.rcim.2019.101837

Madden, M., & Rainie, L. (2015). *Americans' Attitudes About Privacy, Security and Surveillance*. Available at: https://www.pewinternet.org/2015/05/20/americans-attitudes-about-privacy-security-and-surveillance/

Manca, A., Lafferty, N., Fioratou, E., Smithies, A., & Hothersall, E. (2014, October). Integrating Twitter into an undergraduate medical curriculum: Lessons for the future. In *European Conference on e-Learning* (p. 330). Academic Conferences International Limited.

Manca, A., & Whitworth, A. (2018). Social Media and Workplace Practices in Higher Education Institutions: A Review. *The Journal of Social Media in Society, 7*(1), 151–183.

Matt, C., Hess, T., & Benlian, A. (2015). Digital Transformation Strategies. *Business & Information Systems Engineering, 57*(5), 339–343. doi:10.100712599-015-0401-5

Mattoni, B., Pagliaro, F., Corona, G., Ponzo, V., Bisegna, F., Gugliermetti, F., & Quintero-Núñez, M. (2016, June). A matrix approach to identify and choose efficient strategies to develop the Smart Campus. In *Environment and Electrical Engineering (EEEIC), 2016 IEEE 16th International Conference on* (pp. 1-6). IEEE. 10.1109/EEEIC.2016.7555571

Mell, P., & Grance, T. (2009). The NIST definition of cloud computing. *National Institute of Standards and Technology, 53*(6), 50.

Mittelstadt, Allo, Taddeo, Wachter, & Floridi. (2016). The ethics of algorithms: Mapping the debate. Big Data & Society, 3(2).

Mount, M., & Martinez, M. G. (2014). Social media: A tool for open innovation. *California Management Review, 56*(4), 124–143. doi:10.1525/cmr.2014.56.4.124

Neirotti, P., De Marco, A., Cagliano, A. C., Mangano, G., & Scorrano, F. (2014). Current trends in Smart City initiatives: Some stylised facts. *Cities (London, England), 38*, 25–36. doi:10.1016/j.cities.2013.12.010

Nicolaidou, I. L., & Georgiades, C. (2017). The GDPR: New Horizons. In *EU Internet Law*. Springer. doi:10.1007/978-3-319-64955-9_1

Östling, J. (2018). *Humboldt and the modern German university: An intellectual history*. Lund University Press.

Owoc, M., & Marciniak, K. (2013, September). Knowledge management as foundation of smart university. In *Computer Science and Information Systems (FedCSIS), 2013 Federated Conference on* (pp. 1267-1272). IEEE.

Palvia, P. C., Brown, W. S., Brown, W., & Palvia, P. (2015). Are Mobile Devices Threatening Your Work-Life Balance? *International Journal of Mobile Communications, 13*(3).

Perrotta, C., & Williamson, B. (2018). The social life of Learning Analytics: Cluster analysis and the 'performance'of algorithmic education. *Learning, Media and Technology, 43*(1), 3–16. doi:10.1080/1 7439884.2016.1182927

Pew. (2017). *Mobile fact sheet*. Retrieved January, 2017 from Pew Research Center https://www.pewinternet.org/fact-sheet/mobile/

Prinsloo & Rowe. (2015). *Ethical considerations in using student data in an era of big data*. http://repository.uwc.ac.za/handle/10566/2872

Rajendran, V. (2017). *Location Based Services: Expected Trends and Technological Advancements – Geo awesomeness*. Retrieved from https://geoawesomeness.com/expected-trends-technological-advancements-location-based-services/

Rossi, B. (2015). What is a true digital enterprise? *Information Age*. Retrieved January 2017 from https://www.information-age.com/what-true-digital-enterprise-123459026/

Rouse, M. (2011). *What is digital enterprise?* Retrieved January 2017 from https://searchcio.techtarget.com/definition/Digital-enterprise

Sun, G., Cui, T., Yong, J., Shen, J., & Chen, S. (2018). MLaaS: A cloud-based system for delivering adaptive micro learning in mobile MOOC learning. *IEEE Transactions on Services Computing, 11*(2), 292–305. doi:10.1109/TSC.2015.2473854

Sung, Y. T., Chang, K. E., & Liu, T. C. (2016). The effects of integrating mobile devices with teaching and learning on students' learning performance: A meta-analysis and research synthesis. *Computers & Education, 94*, 252–275. doi:10.1016/j.compedu.2015.11.008

Tess, P. A. (2013). The role of social media in higher education classes (real and virtual): A literature review. *Computers in Human Behavior, 29*(5), A60–A68. doi:10.1016/j.chb.2012.12.032

Uskov, V., Bakken, J. P., Aluri, L., Rachakonda, R., Rayala, N., & Uskova, M. (2018, March). Smart pedagogy: innovative teaching and learning strategies in engineering education. In *2018 IEEE World Engineering Education Conference (EDUNINE)* (pp. 1-6). IEEE. 10.1109/EDUNINE.2018.8450962

Uskov, V. L., Bakken, J. P., Karri, S., Uskov, A. V., Heinemann, C., & Rachakonda, R. (2017, June). Smart University: Conceptual Modeling and Systems' Design. In *International Conference on Smart Education and Smart E-Learning* (pp. 49-86). Springer.

Van Otterlo, M. (2013) A machine learning view on profiling. In *Privacy, Due Process and the Computational Turn-Philosophers of Law Meet Philosophers of Technology*. Abingdon: Routledge.

West, D., Huijser, H., & Heath, D. (2016). Putting an ethical lens on learning analytics. *Educational Technology Research and Development*, *64*(5), 903–922. doi:10.100711423-016-9464-3

World Economic Forum White Paper Digital Transformation of Industries in collaboration with Accenture. (2016). Retrieved from http://reports.weforum.org/digital-transformation/wp-content/blogs.dir/94/mp/files/pages/files/digital-enterprise-narrative-final-january-2016.pdf

Zhu, M., Sari, A., & Lee, M. M. (2018). A systematic review of research methods and topics of the empirical MOOC literature (2014–2016). *The Internet and Higher Education*, *37*, 31–39. doi:10.1016/j.iheduc.2018.01.002

KEY TERMS AND DEFINITIONS

Big Data: Evolving term that describes a large volume of structured, semi-structured and unstructured data that has the potential to be mined for information and used in machine learning projects and other advanced analytics applications.

Digital Enterprise: An organisation that integrates information, processes, work and people so that the entire organisation can collaborate more efficiently and effectively, and therefore produce more valuable products and services.

Digital Twin: A description of a component or system or process that comprises a range of executable models that are semantically linked and evolve with the real system.

Knowledge Grid: A unique offering of a university that comprises the four key elements of a university's function: research, knowledge transfer, learning and teaching.

Smart University: A university that provides innovative ways of working, learning and teaching in spaces that creatively integrate advanced hardware and software platforms that utilise big data, sensors, social media and machine learning.

Social Media: Collective of online communications channels dedicated to community-based input, interactions, content sharing and collaboration.

Chapter 14
Enterprise IT Operations:
Cognitive Automation and ignio™

Harrick Vin
Tata Consultancy Services, India

ABSTRACT

Over the past decade or so, for most enterprises, information technology (IT) has shifted from being a support function to be a synonym for business wellness. During the same period, though, the scale and complexity of IT for running business has grown significantly; today, performing any business function requires complex interplay of many, often invisible and dynamically changing, technology components. This is making design resilient and interruption-free IT a significant challenge. This chapter discusses limitations of traditional approaches for managing enterprise IT operations; introduces the concept of cognitive automation, a novel approach that blends intelligence with automation to transform enterprise IT operations; and describes the design of ignio™, a cognitive automation platform for enterprises. The author concludes by highlighting the challenges in driving cognitive transformation of enterprise operations and providing some suggestions for embarking upon this journey.

INTRODUCTION

Over the past several decades, information technology (IT) has become central to every industry and business. IT has been used extensively in every business for a variety of use-cases, including: (1) to enhance customer experience, (2) to accelerate business growth by introducing new products and services, or by expanding into new markets quickly, (3) to improve operational efficiency, and (4) to reduce operational risks. In fact, because of the significant impact of IT on business, most enterprises are rapidly becoming *"technology companies, with appropriate domain-knowledge and freedom-to-operate licenses in relevant jurisdictions"*. Further, the role of IT has shifted from being a *support function*, to be the synonym for *business wellness*.

While this is music to the ears of everyone working in the IT industry, the rapid rise of importance of IT has also increased significantly the expectations of business from IT (Weiser et al, 1993). Any glitch or failure of IT now has direct impact on business – leading to loss of revenue, loss of credibility with

DOI: 10.4018/978-1-7998-0108-5.ch014

customers, health and safety issues for employees, as well as regulatory and other compliance failures. Further, inability to take advantage of and adapt quickly to technological advances exposes businesses to technology-led disruptions; after all, proliferation of IT has greatly reduced the barrier of entry for newcomers into any business.

As they say, with great *power* comes great *responsibility*—the responsibility to make IT reliable, resilient to failures, easy to adapt, update and manage.

Unfortunately, enterprise IT teams are struggling to deal with this responsibility. Most enterprise IT systems today involve complex interplay of many different, often invisible, technology components. Further, with the emergence of software-defined technologies, fine-grain componentization (with microservices and APIs), among others, the technology components involved in supporting any business function change dynamically and rapidly, often without the knowledge of most stakeholders. This significantly increases the complexity of reasoning about reliability and security of systems. With continuous and accelerating pace of technology innovations, the complexity of enterprise IT systems is increasing, worsening the problem.

Industry best-practices for managing IT environments for enterprises were defined a decade or two ago, assuming that the technology components, involved in supporting business functions, and their inter-dependencies are well-documented and change infrequently. Most of these assumptions do not hold for modern and rapidly evolving enterprise IT systems, rendering most of the best practices inadequate to meet the demands of modern IT systems and IT-led businesses.

In this chapter, we first describe traditional approaches for managing enterprise IT operations along with their limitations. Then we introduce the concept of *cognitive automation*, a novel approach that blends intelligence with automation to transform enterprise IT operations. We describe the design of *ignio*™, a cognitive automation platform designed for enterprise IT operations. We conclude by highlighting the challenges in driving cognitive transformation of enterprise operations and provide some suggestions for embarking upon this journey.

STATE OF THE ART

Today, most enterprises rely upon a combination of the following *three* approaches to manage their IT environments, each with significant shortcomings (Berruti et al, 2017; Wang et al, 2009; Kephart et al, 2003; Weiser et al, 1993; Sterritt et al, 2003).

Approach #1: Reduce complexity through standardization.

Technology standardization is often used as a strategy by enterprise IT teams to limit diversity and thereby reduce complexity. This approach either involves post-facto *rationalization* by migrating non-standard technologies to chosen standard, or up-front *prevention* of introduction of non-standard technologies through architectural guidelines and processes.

Most enterprise technology rationalization projects take too long to implement (and are often difficult to justify financially). Further, in most enterprises, there is a constant struggle between the change-the-business and run-the business team. Change-the-business teams aspire to drive *growth* and strive to adopt emerging technologies rapidly (and thereby add greater technology diversity and complexity in the environment). Run-the-business teams, on the other hand, aspire to *optimize the existing* and strive to limit the diversity and complexity to ensure efficient operations. There is never any clarity on the *necessary* diversity required to meet these two diverging expectations.

Approach #2: Manage complexity using divide-and-conquer.

Enterprises today partition their IT environments either by technology or by functionality and assign the responsibility of managing these partitions to different teams. This approach limits the scope and complexity handled by each team. Further, it simplifies the process of training of people for day-to-day operational activities within each partition, thereby accelerating creation of specialist pools.

Unfortunately, this approach creates *knowledge silos*, making it difficult for any individual or team to construct an end-to-end view of the IT environment, isolate cause upon observing anomalous behavior, or assess impact of any change. This not only increases the reliance of enterprises on tacit knowledge and experience of individuals, but also limits the ability of the enterprise to adapt quickly to emergent conditions.

Approach #3: Reduce the cost of managing complexity through automation.

Automation is implemented in most enterprises either at the *task* or *activity* levels.

Task-level automation is often implemented using a set of disparate tools, one for each type of technology or operational function (e.g., technology provisioning, compliance checks, human-resource management, etc.). Unfortunately, each such tool needs to be configured with significant amount of enterprise context information to become effective. This not only requires significant effort, but also makes it difficult to maintain consistency of configurations across tools. In most enterprises, these islands of automation have delivered mostly tactical productivity benefits and relatively low return-on-investments.

Activities, as opposed to tasks, generally cut across multiple technology and functional silos. *Activity-level automation* in most enterprises is implemented using *robotic process automation (RPA)* tools. RPA involves converting procedures for performing an operational activity to a workflow or a program, and then executing it on-demand. This approach has its roots in manufacturing, where a factory (or an assembly line) produces the same product for an extended period of time. Not much changes on a daily basis. This, unfortunately, is not true for enterprise IT and operations. An enterprise IT environment is expected to accommodate constant changes in the functionality it offers, the business workload it supports, and even the versions of underlying technology it consumes. Such changes often require the standard operating procedures—and hence, RPA scripts—to be updated constantly. And this has proved to be difficult to do in most enterprise. Consequently, the RPA approach has proved to be difficult to sustain or scale in most enterprises.

The combination of importance of the problem and the inherent limitations of the conventional approaches necessitates a fresh approach—one that scales to the complexity and demands of an enterprise, enables an enterprise to prepare-for-tomorrow while efficiently managing-the-present, as well as adapts to changes gracefully. Next section describes *cognitive automation*, an approach to address these challenges.

COGNITIVE AUTOMATION

The concept and design of cognitive automation draws inspiration from how human beings deal with complex situations. To do so, humans blend the abilities to become context-aware, detect anomalies and anticipate future events, determine what to do in a context given an objective, operationalize the decision by selecting and performing a sequence of actions best-suited for the context, and learn and adapt continuously based on the experiences.

The goal of cognitive automation is to mimic precisely these human abilities, in stark contrast from robotic approaches that simply mimic human actions (McKinsey, 2019).

To realize this vision, cognitive automation must blend four distinct types of abilities or intelligence: (1) Recognition intelligence, (2) Reasoning intelligence, (3) Operative intelligence, and (4) Learning intelligence.

Recognition Intelligence

The objective of recognition intelligence is to construct contextual awareness, a *360-degree view*, by identifying the entities constituting an environment along with their structural and behavioral attributes.

Recognition intelligence blends three different levels of data assimilation and mining abilities:

- Mining of structured data, represented as a set of records containing numerical, categorical, date and time, among other, values.
- Mining of semi-structured data, collected as logs from different components of a system.
- Mining of unstructured data, including blobs of text, images, video, among others.

Reasoning Intelligence

The objective of reasoning intelligence is to draw inferences about the environment, including derivation of normal behavior profiles of entities and their attributes, detection of anomalies and deviations from expected behavior, anticipation of likely future events requiring attention, as well as determination of a set of response actions.

Reasoning intelligence involves four different levels of abilities:

- *Descriptive reasoning*: Insights about what has been happening;
- *Diagnostic reasoning*: Inferences about why something is happening;
- *Predictive reasoning*: Predictions about what is likely to happen in the future; and
- *Prescriptive reasoning*: Selections of specific actions that one should undertake in response to diagnosis or predictions.

Descriptive, diagnostic and predictive reasoning involve amalgamation of statistical data analysis, machine learning and artificial intelligence (AI) techniques. Domain knowledge is often used to augment these techniques to go beyond cooccurrences and correlations to causation, and thereby improve the accuracy of inferences. Prescriptive reasoning, on the other hand, blends AI techniques, for planning and action selection (e.g., what-if and if-what analysis), with domain knowledge.

Operative Intelligence

The objective of operative intelligence is to perform the set of actions suggested by reasoning intelligence to update the state of the system. Integrating operative intelligence with recognition and reasoning intelligence enables the construction of a closed-loop system, involving sense, think and act.

Operative intelligence involves three different levels of sophistication:

- Ability to execute atomic *tasks*, defined on individual components of a system;
- Ability to perform an *activity*, by executing a pre-defined sequence of tasks; and
- Ability to handle *situations*, by adapting the execution of tasks and activities on-the-fly based on the outcome of previous tasks and activities.

To execute tasks, one needs knowledge about the domain of the components (e.g., how to create and configure a server or a database). To perform an activity, one needs to understand the process of weaving tasks to achieve an objective. Handling situation is the most complex; it requires additional abilities to manage ambiguity, non-determinism, and choices gracefully.

Learning Intelligence

Learning enables a system to enhance its abilities progressively.

Learning can happen through explicit training or by leveraging experiences. Experiential learning can be further classified as unsupervised-, supervised- and reinforcement learning. Unsupervised learning involves a system learning purely based on past experiences, without any human involvement. Supervised learning involves a human-in-the-loop to classify each and every past experience. Reinforcement learning involves a human-in-the-loop to assess the decisions taken by a machine, which in turn can be used by the machine to learn.

Each of these learning techniques has its advantages and limitations; hence, an advanced learning system needs to blend judiciously all of these forms of learning and switch from one form to another based on the context.

While each of these concepts, individually, have been around for quite some time, over the past few years, the concept of cognitive automation has become realizable. This *perfect storm* is caused by the confluence of three trends:

- **Proliferation of Instrumentation.** With the advent of Internet of Things, soft sensing, etc., it is becoming feasible to instrument every aspect of a system to create deep and real-time visibility. This is providing the much-needed data foundation for cognitive automation.
- **Rise of Intelligent Machines:** Over the past decade, we have witnessed (1) significant improvements in AI/ML algorithms and the availability of algorithm libraries, and (2) availability of abundant computing capacity on-demand (through cloud platforms). These trends have simplified the development of intelligent machines.
- Software-defined everything. With everything becoming software-defined (with software APIs), it is becoming possible to perform actions onto any systems remotely, under software control. This is making it possible to design powerful, real-time closed-look systems.

IGNIO™

ignio™ is a *cognitive automation product* designed specifically for enterprise IT operations (Weiser et al, 1993) In particular, ignio™ combines recognition, reasoning, operative and learning intelligence with domain knowledge about enterprise IT.

Much like a human expert, ignio™ needs to be taught the domain of enterprise IT. In particular, ignio™ is configured with:

- The ontology of enterprise IT components (e.g., servers, storage, network, firewalls, operating systems, databases, application servers, etc.) as well as how software applications are assembled using these components;
- Structural relationships across enterprise IT components (e.g., a database is a software that runs on an operating system, which in turn runs on a server).
- Behavioral attributes (e.g., performance metrics such as response time latencies and request processing throughput) and the corresponding data sources for each component.
- Operative knowledge (e.g., actions required to perform tasks and activities) for each component.

Configured with this knowledge, ignio™ operates in four steps.

First, ignio™ constructs unified *blueprint* of enterprises' IT environment by assimilating and mining unstructured and semi-structured data sources, such as enterprise IT infrastructure monitoring tools, platform and application-level logs, IT service management tools and platforms, among others. ignio™ handles multiple overlapping data sources and versions; performs data integrity and completeness checks; as well as drives systematic and progressive improvement of the blueprint through guided addition of new data sources.

Second, ignio™ uses reasoning intelligence (a combination of statistical data analysis, machine learning and AI techniques) to self-learn enterprises' context and characterize normal behavior. ignio™ uses its context-awareness to predict future system behavior under expected and anomalous conditions. Together, these techniques allow ignio™ to produce actionable insights and recommendations.

Third, ignio™ combines self-learned contextual knowledge about the enterprises' IT estate along with pre-configured operative knowledge (about tasks and activities) to perform activities and handle situations autonomously.

Fourth, ignio™ supports two methods for continuous learning: Explicit training and experiential self-learning. ignio™ also defines a formal language to capture knowledge about any system. Enterprises can utilize the ignio™ Studio to populate knowledge about their systems.

By combining these steps, ignio™ replaces traditional manual and reactive IT operations activities involving complex workflows with a context-aware, intelligent, proactive and autonomous software. With ignio™, work simply gets done, it does not flow. ignio™ performs most of the activities autonomously and collaborates with people when it does not know how to perform a task. This changes the role of people from doers-of-work to trainers-of-ignio and handlers-of-exceptions.

In what follows, we describe two commonly-used and important use-cases of ignio™ (Wang et al, 2009).

Anticipate and Trigger Just the Right Actions at the Right Time

Enterprises today are drowning in deluge of data, generated by vast collections of systems and monitoring tools. Traditional solution — of building manually-operated command centers where people monitor data, events and alerts and determine appropriate actions — is falling short. Independently and manually configured monitoring and alert aggregation tools, with configurations not in tune with the current operational realities, yield large volumes of false and redundant alerts. Teams waste effort in handling false alerts while genuine alerts go unattended, putting enterprises at risk. Generating the right alert at the right time and triggering the right action, preferably proactively, is a distant dream for most enterprises.

To address this challenge, ignio™ first learns enterprise's context (referred to as the *blueprint*) by assimilating and mining unstructured and semi-structured data from monitoring tools and logs. It characterizes normal behavior for each system component, and the variation of the normal behavior over time. ignio™ then configures monitoring tools with the derived and dynamic normal behavior information to detect transient and persistent anomalies. By combining self-learning with automated configurations, ignio™ ensures consistent and accurate configurations of tools. This significantly reduces volume of false alerts.

In enterprise IT systems, a failure or anomalous condition at one component often propagates to and becomes visible as anomalies for many other attributes and at several other components. To eliminate these redundant alerts, ignio™ leverages the structural and behavioral model of enterprise IT systems and aggregates related alerts.

Finally, ignio™ leverages self-learned uni- and multi-variate forecasting models to predict future system behavior and impending anomalies.

Together, these techniques allow ignio™ to anticipate and trigger just the right actions at the right time. It leads to over 90% reduction in alert volumes; and, more importantly, prioritization of alerts based on business impact. This dramatically improves the effectiveness of alerts handling.

Rapid and First-Time-Right Diagnosis and Action Prescription

A high severity incident, causing business outage and impact, is the most dreaded event in the day-in-the-life of an enterprise IT executive. Yet, methods for handling incidents remain relatively primitive. The industry-best practice involves bringing relevant parties on an incident resolution bridge. Unfortunately, because of the structural layers and silos, no one on such an incident bridge has complete contextual knowledge, requiring the team to rely upon cumulative tacit knowledge and trial-and-error to triage an incident. This often takes too long.

ignio™ addresses these challenges by combining automated diagnosis, action prescription and automated execution of prescribed actions.

ignio™ first uses enterprise blueprint to understand the incident's IT systems context. It then uses a combination of rule-based, case-based or model-based reasoning to identify possible cause(s) leading to the observed incident. Whereas rule-based approach relies upon pre-configured expert knowledge, case-based approach used past incident history to postulate possible causes.

The model-based approach is the most accurate, albeit the most expensive and hardest to configure. In this approach, ignio™ uses the structural context of the incident to perform a real-time health check of all the components. ignio™ then leverages the self-learned normal behavior profiles to identify anomalies, if any, at each of these components. Finally, ignio™ identifies the most likely cause through a spatio-temporal analysis of all identifies anomalies.

Once a cause is identified, ignio™ then selects one of the known remedy actions to correct the cause, and thereby recover from the incident.

The combination allows ignio™ to achieve rapid, first-time right diagnosis and resolutions, while reducing the time to resolve the incident (and hence the total business pain minutes) by over 90%.

FUTURE OPPORTUNITIES

The concept of cognitive automation and its realization in ignio™ are quite powerful. Yet, realizing their full potential in an enterprise is far from easy, because of several challenges.

First, transforming an enterprise's operating model from *process-centric* to *data-driven* is essential for realizing the potential of cognitive automation. To become data-driven, an enterprise must first establish deep visibility into the structural and behavioral aspects enterprise IT, as well as ensure that the integrated blueprint constructed using the visibility remains relevant and current in the presence of continuous changes. This itself is a significant challenge.

Second, implementation of cognitive automation transforms the *nature of work* from *intuition-centric* and *manual* to *machine-augmented (evidence-based)* and *autonomous*. This improves the time, cost and quality of work. The business benefits, however, are dependent on the context. Thus, rolling out of cognitive automation requires careful planning, balancing speed and ease of implementation with significance of outcomes. In the absence of this careful planning, such large-scale transformation programs fail to deliver expected outcomes.

Finally, introduction of cognitive automation for managing enterprise IT environment changes the role of people from *doers-of-work* to *trainers-of-cognitive-machines* and *handlers-of-exception*. This requires significant changes in skills of people, and poses a significant organizational change management problem.

CONCLUSION

Over the past decade or so, for most enterprises, information technology (IT) has shifted from being a support function, to be a synonym for business wellness. During the same period, though, the scale and complexity of IT for running business has grown significantly; today, performing any business function requires complex interplay of many, often invisible and dynamically changing, technology components. This is making design resilient and interruption-free IT a significant challenge. This chapter discusses limitations of traditional approaches for managing enterprise IT operations; introduces the concept of cognitive automation, a novel approach that blends intelligence with automation to transform enterprise IT operations; and describes the design of ignio™, a cognitive automation platform for enterprises. The author concludes by highlighting the challenges in driving cognitive transformation of enterprise operations and provide some suggestions for embarking upon this journey.

REFERENCES

Berruti, Nixon, Taglioni, & Whiteman. (2017). *Intelligent Process Automation: The engine at the core of next-generation operating model.* https://www.mckinsey.com/business-functions/mckinsey-digital/our-insights/intelligent-process-automation-the-engine-at-the-core-of-the-next-generation-operating-model

Ganek & Corbi. (n.d.). The dawning of the autonomic computing era. IBM Systems Journal, 42(1), 5–18.

How to operationalize AI in your business. (n.d.). *IBM*. Retrieved from: https://www.ibm.com/watson

Kephart, J. O., & Chess, D. M. (2003). The vision of autonomic computing. *Computer, 36*(1), 41–50.

McKinsey. (2019). *Driving impact at scale from automation and AI.* Retrieved from: https://www.mckinsey.com/~/media/McKinsey/Business%20Functions/McKinsey%20Digital/Our%20Insights/Driving%20impact%20at%20scale%20from%20automation%20and%20AI/Driving-impact-at-scale-from-automation-and-AI.ashx

Sterritt, R., & Bustard, D. (2003). Towards an autonomic computing environment. *14th International Workshop on Database and Expert Systems Applications*, 694-698. 10.1109/DEXA.2003.1232103

Wang, Y. (2009). A cognitive informatics reference model for autonomous agent systems. *International Journal of Cognitive Informatics and Natural Intelligence, 3*(1), 1–16. doi:10.4018/jcini.2009010101

Weiser, M. (1993, July). Some Computer Science Problems in Ubiquitous Computing. *Communications of the ACM, 36*(7), 75–84. doi:10.1145/159544.159617

Compilation of References

Aalst, W. M. P. d. (2011). *Process Mining: Discovery, Conformance and Enhancement of Business Processes.* Heidelberg, Germany: Springer. doi:10.1007/978-3-642-19345-3

Abolhassan, F. (2017). *Cyber security. Simply. Make it happen.* Springer. doi:10.1007/978-3-319-46529-6

Abraham, S., & Nair, S. (2015). *A predictive framework for cyber security analytics using attack graphs.* arXiv preprint arXiv:1502.01240

Abraham, R. (2013). Enterprise Architecture Artifacts As Boundary Objects - A Framework Of Properties. *Proceedings of the 21st European Conference on Information Systems (ECIS 2013).*

Agha, G. (1986a). *Actors: A Model of Concurrent Computation in Distributed Systems.* Cambridge, MA: MIT Press.

Agha, G. (1986b). An Overview of Actor Languages. *SIGPLAN Notices, 21*(10), 58–67. doi:10.1145/323648.323743

Agrawal, A., Deshpande, P. D., Cecen, A., Basavarsu, G. P., Choudhary, A. N., & Kalidindi, S. R. (2014). Exploration of data science techniques to predict fatigue strength of steel from composition and processing parameters. Integrating Materials and Manufacturing Innovation, 3(1), 8. doi:10.1186/2193-9772-3-8

Aier, S., Kurpjuweit, S., Saat, J., & Winter, R. (2009). Enterprise Architecture Design As An Engineering Discipline. *Ais Transactions On Enterprise Systems, 1*(1), 36–43.

Allen, J. (2013). *Effective Akka.* O'Reilly Media, Inc.

Amado, R. (2018). *How Cybercriminals are using Blockchain DNS: From the Market to the Bazar.* Retrieved December 5, 2019, from https://www.digitalshadows.com/blog-and-research/how-cybercriminals-are-using-blockchain-dns-from-the-market-to-the-bazar/

Amir, E., Levi, S., & Livne, T. (2018). Do firms underreport information on cyber-attacks? Evidence from capital markets. *Review of Accounting Studies, 23*(3), 1177–1206. doi:10.100711142-018-9452-4

Anastasakis, K., Bordbar, B., Georg, G., & Ray, I. (2007, September). UML2Alloy: A challenging model transformation. In *International Conference on Model Driven Engineering Languages and Systems* (pp. 436-450). Springer. 10.1007/978-3-540-75209-7_30

Anderson, L. W. (2001). *A taxonomy for learning, teaching, and assessing: A revision of Bloom's taxonomy of educational objectives, abridged edition.* White Plains.

Anderson, P. (1999). Perspective: Complexity theory and organization science. *Organization Science, 10*(3), 216–232. doi:10.1287/orsc.10.3.216

Anderson, T., & Dron, J. (2018). Integrating learning management and social networking systems. *Italian Journal of Educational Technology*, *25*(3), 5–19.

Androutsopoulos, K., Gorogiannis, N., Loomes, M., Margolis, M., Primiero, G., Raimondi, F., ... Zivanovic, A. (2014). A racket-based robot to teach first-year computer science. *7th European Lisp Symposium*, 54.

Angles, R., & Gutierrez, C. (2008). Survey of graph database models. *ACM Computing Surveys*, *40*(1), 1–39. doi:10.1145/1322432.1322433

Antonakakis, M., April, T., Bailey, M., Bernhard, M., Bursztein, E., Cochran, J., ... Zhou, Y. (2017). Understanding the Mirai Botnet. In *26th USENIX Security Symposium (USENIX Security 17)* (pp. 1093-1110). USENIX.

Araujo, C. (2016, March). The Digital Enterprise Hype Cycle. *Institute for Digital Transformation*. Retrieved from https://www.institutefordigitaltransformation.org/defining-digital-enterprise/

Aravind. (2017). *Technology providing a helping hand to those fighting with mental health issues*. Retrieved from Technology providing a helping hand to those fighting with mental health issues: https://economictimes.indiatimes.com/industry/healthcare/biotech/healthcare/technology-providing-a-helping-hand-to-those-fighting-with-mental-health-issues/articleshow/61083373.cms

Armstrong, J. (1996). Erlang - a Survey of the Language and its Industrial Applications. *Proceedings of the symposium on industrial applications of Prolog (INAP)*, 8.

Arrieta-Escobar, J. A., Bernardo, F. P., Orjuela, A., Camargo, M., & Morel, L. (2019). Incorporation of heuristic knowledge in the optimal design of formulated products: Application to a cosmetic emulsion. *Computers & Chemical Engineering*, *122*, 265–274. doi:10.1016/j.compchemeng.2018.08.032

Ashby, W. R. (1981). *Mechanisms of Intelligence: Ashbys Writings on Cybernetics*. Eipiphiny Society.

Astrom, K. J., & Wittenmark, B. (2013). *Adaptive control*. Courier Corporation.

Atkinson, C., & Kühne, T. (2008). Reducing Accidental Complexity In Domain Models. *Software & Systems Modeling*, *7*(3), 345–359. doi:10.100710270-007-0061-0

Ausherman, N. (2018). *Dealing with Cyber Attacks - Steps You Need to Know*. NIST.

Axelrod, R., & Hamilton, W. (1981). The evolution of cooperation. *Science*, *211*(4489), 1390–1396. doi:10.1126cience.7466396 PMID:7466396

Azahar, W. (2017). *Is employee burnout affecting your workforce turnover rate?* Retrieved from Is employee burnout affecting your workforce turnover rate?: https://www.humanresourcesonline.net/employee-burnout-affecting-workforce-turnover-rate/

Badhe, Y., Gupta, R., & Rai, B. (2019). Structural and barrier properties of the skin ceramide lipid bilayer: A molecular dynamics simulation study. *Journal of Molecular Modeling*, *25*(5), 140. doi:10.100700894-019-4008-5 PMID:31041534

Bagajewicz, M. J. (2007). On the role of microeconomics, planning, and finances in product design. *AIChE Journal. American Institute of Chemical Engineers*, *53*(12), 3155–3170. doi:10.1002/aic.11332

Baig, M. Z., & Kavakli, M. (2019). A Survey on Psycho-Physiological Analysis & Measurement Methods in Multimodal Systems. In *Multimodal Technologies Interact* (pp. 3, 37). Academic Press.

Bailey, A. (2017, February 21). *Future Workforce: The network organization*. Retrieved from Accenture Website: https://www.accenture.com/gb-en/blogs/blogs-future-workforce-network-organisation

Bailey, A. (2017, March 10). *Future Workforce: Fragmentation.* Retrieved from Accenture Website: https://www.accenture.com/gb-en/blogs/blogs-future-workforce-fragmentation

Bailey, A. (2017, March 24). *Future workforce: Defining the digital enterprise leader.* Retrieved from Accenture Website: https://www.accenture.com/gb-en/blogs/blogs-defining-digital-enterprise-leader

Balan, R. K., Lee, Y., Wee, T. K., & Misra, A. (2014). The challenge of continuous mobile context sensing. *Sixth International Conference on Communication Systems and Networks (COMSNETS)*, 1-8. 10.1109/COMSNETS.2014.6734869

Balaraman, V., Hayatnagarkar, H., Singh, M., & Duggirala, M. (2016). *Towards better crisis management in support services organizations using fine grained agent based simulation.* Phuket, Thailand: PRIMA. doi:10.1007/978-3-319-44832-9_24

Ball, S. J. (2003). The teacher's soul and the terrors of performativity. *Journal of Education Policy, 18*(2), 215–228. doi:10.1080/0268093022000043065

Band, I., Ellefsen, T., Estrem, B., Iacob, M.-E., Jonkers, H., Lankhorst, M. M., ... Thorn, S. (2016). *ArchiMate 3.0 Specification.* The Open Group.

Banks, J. C. J. (1984). Discrete Event Simulation. Prentice Hall.

Barat, S., & Kulkarni, V. (2010). Developing configurable extensible code generators for model-driven development approach. In SEKE (pp. 577-582). Academic Press.

Barat, S., Khadilkar, H., Meisheri, H., Kulkarni, V., Baniwal, V., Kumar, P., & Gajrani, M. (2019). Actor Based Simulation for Closed Loop Control of Supply Chain using Reinforcement Learning. In *Proceedings of the 18th International Conference on Autonomous Agents and MultiAgent Systems* (pp. 1802-1804). International Foundation for Autonomous Agents and Multiagent Systems.

Barat, S., Khadilkar, H., Meisheri, H., Kulkarni, V., Baniwal, V., Kumar, P., & Gajrani, M. (2019, May). Actor Based Simulation for Closed Loop Control of Supply Chain using Reinforcement Learning. In *Proceedings of the 18th International Conference on Autonomous Agents and MultiAgent Systems* (pp. 1802-1804). International Foundation for Autonomous Agents and Multiagent Systems.

Barat, S., Kulkarni, V., Clark, T., & Barn, B. (2018). A Model Based Approach for Complex Dynamic Decision-Making. [Springer.]. *Communications in Computer and Information Science, 880*, 94–118. doi:10.1007/978-3-319-94764-8_5

Barat, S., Kulkarni, V., Clark, T., & Barn, B. S. (2019). An actor based simulation driven digital twin for analyzing complex business systems. *Proceedings of the 2019 Winter Simulation Conference* 10.1109/WSC40007.2019.9004694

Barat, S., Kumar, P., Gajrani, M., Meisheri, H., Baniwal, V., Khadilkar, H., & Kulkarni, V. (2019). Reinforcement learning of supply chain control policy using closed loop multi-agent simulation. *Multi-Agent Based Systems Workshop (AAMAS)*.

Barbero, M., Jouault, F., & Bézivin, J. (2008). Model driven management of complex systems: Implementing the macroscope's vision. In *15th Annual IEEE International Conference and Workshop on the Engineering of Computer Based Systems (ECBS 2008)*, (pp. 277-286). IEEE. 10.1109/ECBS.2008.42

Barjis, J. (2009). Collaborative, Participative and Interactive Enterprise Modeling. In *Enterprise Information Systems, 11th International Conference, ICEIS 2009, Milan, Italy, May 6-10, 2009. Proceedings*, volume 24 of *Lecture Notes in Business Information Processing*, (pp. 651-662). Springer.

Barn, B., Dexter, H., Oussena, S., & Petch, J. (2006). A synthesis approach for deriving reference models for SOA frameworks. *IADIS International Journal on Computer Science and Information Systems, 1*(2), 100–116.

Barret, T. (2019). *Blockchain, IoT and DNS*. Retrieved December 5, 2019, from https://ccnso.icann.org/sites/default/files/field-attached/presentation-blockchain-iot-dns-11mar19-en.pdf

Barrett, P. (2019). *Digital wellbeing: caring for employees in an 'always on' culture*. Retrieved from https://www.hrzone.com/lead/future/digital-wellbeing-caring-for-employees-in-an-always-on-culture

Barth, A., Jackson, C., Reis, C., Team, T., & Google Team. (2008). *The Security Architecture of the Chromium Browser*. Technical report. Stanford University.

Barto, A. G., & Mahadevan, S. (2003). Recent advances in hierarchical reinforcement learning. *Discrete Event Dynamic Systems*, *13*(1-2), 41–77. doi:10.1023/A:1022140919877

Bazzan, A. L., & Klugl, F. (2013). Introduction to intelligent systems in traffic and transportation. *Synthesis Lectures on Artificial Intelligence and Machine Learning*, *7*(3), 1–137. doi:10.2200/S00553ED1V01Y201312AIM025

Beautement, A., Angela, S., & Mike, W. (2009). The Compliance Budget: Managing Security Behaviour in Organisations. In *Proceedings of the 2008 Workshop on New Security Paradigms* (pp. 47–58). ACM.

Becker, J., Delfmann, P., Eggert, M., & Schwittay, S. (2012). Generalizability and applicability of model-based business process compliance-checking approaches—A state-of-the-art analysis and research roadmap. *Business Research*, *5*(2), 221–247. doi:10.1007/BF03342739

Becker, S. A., Cummins, M., Davis, A., Freeman, A., Hall, C. G., & Ananthanarayanan, V. (2017). *NMC horizon report: 2017 higher education edition*. The New Media Consortium.

Begum, S., Barua, S., & Ahmed, M. U. (2014, July 3). Physiological sensor signals classification for healthcare using sensor data fusion and case-based reasoning. *Sensors (Basel)*, *14*(7), 11770–11785. doi:10.3390140711770 PMID:24995374

Behaviour Change for Good Initiative. (n.d.). Retrieved from Wharton, University of Pennsylvania: https://bcfg.wharton.upenn.edu/

Bellifemine, F., Poggi, A., & Rimassa, G. (1999). JADE–A FIPA-compliant agent framework. *Proceedings of PAAM*, 99, 33.

Bellotti, F., Berta, R., & De Gloria, A. (2010). Designing Effective Serious Games: Opportunities and Challenges for Research. *International Journal of Emerging Technologies in Learning*, 22-35.

Bellotti, F., Kapralos, B., Lee, K., Moreno-Ger, P., & Berta, R. (2013). Assessment in and of Serious Games: An Overview. *Advances in Human-Computer Interaction*, *2013*, 1–11. doi:10.1155/2013/136864

Berger, T., Rublack, R., Nair, D., Atlee, J. M., Becker, M., Czarnecki, K., & Wąsowski, A. (2013, January). A survey of variability modeling in industrial practice. In *Proceedings of the Seventh International Workshop on Variability Modelling of Software-intensive Systems* (p. 7). ACM. 10.1145/2430502.2430513

Bernardo, F. P., & Saraiva, P. M. (2015). A conceptual model for chemical product design. *AIChE Journal. American Institute of Chemical Engineers*, *61*(3), 802–815. doi:10.1002/aic.14681

Berruti, Nixon, Taglioni, & Whiteman. (2017). *Intelligent Process Automation: The engine at the core of next-generation operating model*. https://www.mckinsey.com/business-functions/mckinsey-digital/our-insights/intelligent-process-automation-the-engine-at-the-core-of-the-next-generation-operating-model

Bertsekas, D. P. (2005). Dynamic programming and optimal control. Athena Scientific.

Bézivin, J. (2005). On the Unification Power of Models. *Software & Systems Modeling*, *4*(2), 171–188. doi:10.100710270-005-0079-0

Bhattacharjee, S. (2018). *Practical Industrial Internet of Things Security: A practitioner's guide to securing connected industries*. Birmingham, UK: Packt Publishing Ltd.

Bhattacharyya, R., & Vijayaraghavan, K. (2016). *Retrieved from 46% of workforce in firms in India suffer from some or the other form of stress: Data*. https://economictimes.indiatimes.com/jobs/46-of-workforce-in-firms-in-india-suffer-from-some-or-the-other-form-of-stress-data/articleshow/52696795.cms

Bianchi, D., & Tosun, O. K. (2019). *Cyber Attacks and Stock Market Activity*. Available at SSRN 3190454

Bianchi, R., Schonfeld, I., & Laurent, E. (2018). Burnout syndrome and depression. In Y. Kim (Ed.), Understanding depression: Volume 2. Clinical manifestations, diagnosis and treatment (pp. 187-202). Singapore: Springer. doi:10.1007/978-981-10-6577-4_14

Biggio, B., Nelson, B., & Laskov, P. (2012). *Poisoning Attacks Against Support Vector Machines.* arXiv preprint arXiv:1206.6389

Bird, J. (2016). *DevOpsSec: Securing Software Through Continuous Delivery*. Academic Press.

Bjeković, M., Proper, H. A., & Sottet, J.-S. (2012). Towards a coherent enterprise modelling landscape. In *Short Paper Proceedings of the 5th IFIP WG 8.1 Working Conference on the Practice of Enterprise Modeling, Rostock, Germany, November 7-8, 2012*, volume 933 of *CEUR Workshop Proceedings*. CEUR-WS.org.

Bjeković, M., Sottet, J.-S., Favre, J.-M., & Proper, H. A. (2013). A framework for natural enterprise modelling. In *IEEE 15th Conference on Business Informatics, CBI 2013, Vienna, Austria, July 15-18, 2013*, (pp. 79-84). IEEE Computer Society Press. 10.1109/CBI.2013.20

Bjeković, M., Proper, H. A., & Sottet, J.-S. (2014). Embracing pragmatics. In Conceptual Modeling - *33rd International Conference, ER 2014, Atlanta, GA, USA*, October 27-29, 2014. *Proceedings,* volume 8824 *of* Lecture Notes in Computer Science, (pp. 431-444). Springer.

Blair, G., Bencomo, N., & France, R. B. (2009). Models@ run.time. *Computer, 42*(10), 22–27. doi:10.1109/MC.2009.326

Blau, A. (2017, December). Better Cybersecurity Starts with Fixing Your Employees' Bad Habits. *Harvard Business Review*.

Bleiklie, I. (2018). New Public Management or Neoliberalism. *Higher Education.*

Blitz, M. J. (2018). Lies, Line Drawing, and Deep Fake News. *Oklahoma Law Review, 71*, 59.

Blockchain. (2019). *Wikipedia - Blockchain*. Retrieved December 5, 2019, from https://en.wikipedia.org/wiki/Blockchain

Bock, A. (2013). *A Conceptual Modeling Method For Managing Decision Processes In Enterprises* (Master Thesis). University Of Duisburg-Essen.

Bock, A. (2015). Beyond Narrow Decision Models: Toward Integrative Models Of Organizational Decision Processes. In D. Aveiro, U. Frank, K. J. Lin, & J. Tribolet (Eds.), *Proceedings Of The 17th IEEE Conference On Business Informatics (Cbi 2015)*. Lisbon: IEEE.

Bock, A., & Frank, U. (2016). Memo Goalml: A Context-Enriched Modeling Language To Support Reflective Organizational Goal Planning And Decision Processes. In I. Comyn-Wattiau, K. Tanaka, I.-Y. Song, S. Yamamoto, & M. Saeki (Eds.), *Conceptual Modeling: 35th International Conference, Er 2016* (Pp. 515–529). Cham: Springer. 10.1007/978-3-319-46397-1_40

Bommel, P. v., Hoppenbrouwers, S. J. B. A., Proper, H. A., & Weide, T. P. d. (2007). QoMo: A Modelling Process Quality Framework based on SEQUAL. Academic Press.

Borshchev, A. (2013). *The big book of simulation modeling: multimethod modeling with AnyLogic 6.* AnyLogic North America.

Boschert, S., Heinrich, C., & Rosen, R. (2018). Next generation digital Twin. *Proceedings of TMCE.*

Bose, A. (2017). *The illness India doesn't recognise: Why we cannot afford to ignore mental health.* Retrieved from The illness India doesn't recognise: Why we cannot afford to ignore mental health: https://www.moneycontrol.com/news/trends/health-trends/the-illness-that-india-doesnt-recognise-why-we-cannot-afford-to-ignore-mental-health-2384243.html

Bouabdallah, S., Noth, A., & Siegwart, R. (2004). PID vs LQ control techniques applied to an indoor micro quadrotor. *Proc. of The IEEE International Conference on Intelligent Robots and Systems (IROS)*, 2451-2456. 10.1109/IROS.2004.1389776

Boyd, S., & Sastry, S. (1986). Necessary and sufficient conditions for parameter convergence in adaptive control. *Automatica, 22*(6), 629–639. doi:10.1016/0005-1098(86)90002-6

Branson, C. (2018, Dec 20). *Employee Experience Designer: The New Role of HR.* Retrieved from HR Daily Advisor: https://hrdailyadvisor.blr.com/2018/03/22/new-role-hr-employee-experience-designer/

Brasser, F., Müller, U., Dmitrienko, A., Kostiainen, K., Capkun, S., & Sadeghi, A. R. (2017). Software Grand Exposure: SGX Cache Attacks are Practical. In *11th USENIX Workshop on Offensive Technologies.* USENIX.

Breaux, T. D., & Anton, A. I. (2005, June). Deriving semantic models from privacy policies. In *Sixth IEEE International Workshop on Policies for Distributed Systems and Networks (POLICY'05)* (pp. 67-76). IEEE. 10.1109/POLICY.2005.12

Bresciani, P., Perini, A., Giorgini, P., Giunchiglia, F., & Mylopoulos, J. (2004). Tropos: An agent-oriented software development methodology. *Autonomous Agents and Multi-Agent Systems, 8*(3), 203–236. doi:10.1023/B:AGNT.0000018806.20944.ef

Briggs, R. O., Kolfschoten, G. L., Vreede, G. J. d., & Dean, D. L. (2006). Defining Key Concepts for Collaboration Engineering. *Proceedings of 12th Americas Conference on Information Systems (AMCIS 2006).*

Brinkkemper, S. (1996). Method Engineering: Engineering Of Information Systems Development Methods And Tools. *Information and Software Technology, 38*(4), 275–280. doi:10.1016/0950-5849(95)01059-9

Broz, D. (2016). *10 ideas for tomorrow's campus.* Retrieved from https://www.bdcnetwork.com/blog/10-ideas-tomorrow's-campus

Bubna, R., Raveendran, J., Kumar, S., Duggirala, M., & Malik, M. (2018). A partially grounded agent based model on demonetization outcomes in India. *Summer Simulation Conference.*

Buckl, S., Matthes, F., Neubert, C., & Schweda, C. M. (2010). A Lightweight Approach to Enterprise Architecture Modeling and Documentation. In *CAiSE Forum*, volume 72 of *Lecture Notes in Business Information Processing*, (pp. 136-149). Springer.

Bulgurcu, B., Cavusoglu, H., & Benbasat, I. (2010). Information security policy compliance: An empirical study on rationality-based beliefs and information security awareness. *Management Information Systems Quarterly, 34*(3), 523–548. doi:10.2307/25750690

Busoniu, L., Babuska, R., & De Schutter, B. (2008). A comprehensive survey of multiagent reinforcement learning. *IEEE Transactions on Systems, Man and Cybernetics. Part C, Applications and Reviews, 38*(2), 2008. doi:10.1109/TSMCC.2007.913919

Butler, H., Hondred, G., & van Amerongen, J. (1992). *Model Reference Adaptive Control: Bridging the gap from theory to practice.* Academic Press.

Cabot, J., Claris, R., & Riera, D. (2008, April). Verification of UML/OCL class diagrams using constraint programming. In *2008 IEEE International Conference on Software Testing Verification and Validation Workshop* (pp. 73-80). IEEE. 10.1109/ICSTW.2008.54

Cacioppo, J., Tassinary, L., & Berntson, G. (2007). *Handbook of Psychophysiology*. Cambridge University Press.

Cadwalladr, C., & Graham-Harrison, E. (2018). Revealed: 50 Million Facebook Profiles Harvested for Cambridge Analytica in Major Data Breach. *Sat, 17*, 22–03.

Caire, P., Genon, N., Heymans, P., & Moody, D. L. (2013). Visual notation design 2.0: Towards user comprehensible requirements engineering notations. *21st IEEE International Requirements Engineering Conference (RE2013)*, 115-124. 10.1109/RE.2013.6636711

Camus, B., Bourjot, C., & Chevrier, V. (2015). Combining DEVS with multi-agent concepts to design and simulate multi-models of complex systems (WIP). *Proceedings of the Symposium on Theory of Modeling & Simulation: DEVS Integrative M&S Symposium*, 85–90.

Candes, E. J., & Tao, T. (2005). Decoding by linear programming. *IEEE Transactions on Information Theory, 51*(12), 4203–4215. doi:10.1109/TIT.2005.858979

Cao, C., & Hovakimyan, N. (2008). Design and analysis of a novel L_1 adaptive control architecture with guaranteed transient performance. *IEEE Transactions on Automatic Control, 53*(2), 586–591. doi:10.1109/TAC.2007.914282

Cashell, B., Jackson, W. D., Jickling, M., & Webel, B. (2004). The Economic Impact of Cyber-attacks. Congressional Research Service Documents, CRS RL32331.

Cassenti, D. (2009). *Performance Moderated Functions Server's (PMFserv) Military Utility: A Model and Discussion*. Army Research Laboratory.

Casti, J. (2000). BizSim - Business in a box. *Artificial Life and Robotics, 4*(3), 125–129. doi:10.1007/BF02481332

Casti, J. L. (1994). *Complexification explaining a paradoxical world through the science of surprise*. HarperPerennial - A Division of Harper Collins Publishers.

Cavoukian, A. (2010). Privacy by Design: The Definitive Workshop. A Foreword by Ann Cavoukian, ph.d. *Identity in the Information Society, 3*(2), 247–251. doi:10.100712394-010-0062-y

Cemex. (2019). *Smart Silo - How it works*. Retrieved from https://www.cemexusa.com/products-and-services/services/smart-silo

CERT National Insider Threat Center. (2018). Common Sense Guide to Mitigating Insider Threats. CERT, Carnegie Mellon University.

Chandrasekaran, N. (2016). *Leadership in a Digital World* [PDF document]. Retrieved from https://www.tcs.com/content/dam/tcs/pdf/discover-tcs/investor-relations/key-events/TCS_Analyst_Day_2016_Leadership_in_Digital_World.pdf

Chatterjee, P., & Alvi, M. M. (2014). Excipients and active pharmaceutical ingredients. In *Pediatric Formulations* (pp. 347–361). New York, NY: Springer. doi:10.1007/978-1-4899-8011-3_24

Chatterjee, S., Sarker, S., & Valacich, J. S. (2015). The Behavioral Roots of Information Systems Security: Exploring Key Factors Related to Unethical IT Use. *Journal of Management Information Systems, 31*(4), 49–87. doi:10.1080/07421222.2014.1001257

Chesley, J. A., & Wenger, M. S. (1999). Transforming an Organization: Using models to foster a strategic conversation. *California Management Review, 41*(3), 54–73. doi:10.2307/41165997

Chew, E. K. (2016). iSIM: An integrated design method for commercializing service innovation. *Information Systems Frontiers*, *18*(3), 457–478. doi:10.100710796-015-9605-y

Chin, W. W., Salisbury, W. D., Pearson, A. W., & Stollak, M. J. (1999). Perceived cohesion in small groups: Adapting and testing the perceived cohesion scale in a small-group setting. *Small Group Research*, *30*(6), 751–766. doi:10.1177/104649649903000605

Chiu, E. (2019). *Preparing Enterprises for the Quantum Computing Cybersecurity Threats*. Retrieved December 5, 2019, from https://cloudsecurityalliance.org/artifacts/preparing-enterprises-for-the-quantum-computing-cybersecurity-threats/

Choe, E. K., Lee, N. B., Lee, B., Pratt, W., & Kientz, J. A. (2014). Understanding quantified-selfers' practices in collecting and exploring personal data. In *Proceedings of the 32nd annual ACM conference on Human factors in computing systems (CHI '14)* (pp. 1143-1152). New York: ACM. 10.1145/2556288.2557372

Chris, R. (n.d.). *6 ways to develop a security culture from top to bottom*. Retrieved from https://techbeacon.com/security/6-ways-develop-security-culture-top-bottom

CJ, G., Pandit, S., Vaddepalli, S., Tupsamudre, H., Banahatti, V., & Lodha, S. (2018). Phishy - A Serious Game to Train Enterprise Users on Phishing Awareness. In *Proceedings of the 2018 annual symposium on computer-human interaction in play companion extended abstracts* (pp. 169-181). New York: ACM.

Clapham, A. (2013). Performativity, fabrication and trust: Exploring computer-mediated moderation. *Ethnography and Education*, *8*(3), 371–387. doi:10.1080/17457823.2013.792676

Clark, M., Ferrell, G., & Hopkins, P. (2011). *Study of early adopters of shared services and cloud computing within Higher and Further Education*. Report produced by HE Associates for JISC. Available at https://docs.google.com/viewer?a=v&pid=explorer&chrome=true&srcid=0B6psyHRq0wqPYzY1ODQxYzEtYjNiMS00ZTBiLTg5ZDQtMmQzNGY1NGZhMjk3&hl=en_US

Clark, T., Sammut, P., & Willans, J. (2008). *Applied Metamodelling: A Foundation For Language Driven Development* (2nd ed.). Ceteva. Retrieved From Http://Www.Eis.Mdx.Ac.Uk/Staffpages/Tonyclark/Papers/Applied%20metamodelling%20%28second%20edition%29.Pdf

Clark, T., Kulkarni, V., Barat, S., & Barn, B. (2017, June). ESL: an actor-based platform for developing emergent behaviour organisation simulations. In *International Conference on Practical Applications of Agents and Multi-Agent Systems* (pp. 311-315). Springer. 10.1007/978-3-319-59930-4_27

Clebsch, S. (2015). The pony programming language. *The Pony Developers*. https://www.ponylang.org/

Colbert, A., Yee, N., & George, G. (2016). The digital workforce and the workforce of the future. *Academy of Management Journal*, *59*(3), 731-739.

Conte, E., Gani, R., & Ng, K. M. (2011). Design of formulated products: A systematic methodology. *AIChE Journal. American Institute of Chemical Engineers*, *57*(9), 2431–2449. doi:10.1002/aic.12458

Couldry, N., & Mejias, U. (2018). Data colonialism: Rethinking big data's relation to the contemporary subject. *Television & New Media*.

Craig, R., Amernic, J., & Tourish, D. (2014). Perverse audit culture and accountability of the modern public university. *Financial Accountability & Management*, *30*(1), 1–24. doi:10.1111/faam.12025

Cram, A., Jeffrey, P., & D'Arcy, J. (2017). Seeing the forest and the trees: A meta-analysis of information security policy compliance literature. *Proceedings of the 50th Hawaii International Conference on System Sciences*. 10.24251/HICSS.2017.489

Crompton, H., & Burke, D. (2018). The use of mobile learning in higher education: A systematic review. *Computers & Education, 123*, 53–64. doi:10.1016/j.compedu.2018.04.007

Crossler, E., Johnston, A. C., Lowry, P. B., & Hud, Q. (2013). Future directions in information security resarch. *Computers & Security, 32*, 90–101. doi:10.1016/j.cose.2012.09.010

Cruse, A. (2000). *Meaning in Language, an Introduction to Semantics and Pragmatics*. Oxford, UK: Oxford University Press.

CSP. (2018). *Employee Burnout: Tackling One of the Biggest HR IssuesPosted October 8, 2018 | By csponline*. Retrieved from https://online.csp.edu/blog/human-resources/employee-burnout

Currall, S. C., & Towler, A. J. (2003). *Research methods in management and organizational research: Toward integration of qualitative and quantitative techniques*. Sage Publications.

Curtain, R. F., & Zwart, H. (2012). *An introduction to infinite-dimensional linear systems theory* (Vol. 21). Springer Science & Business Media.

Czarnecki, K., Østerbye, K., & Völter, M. (2002, June). Generative programming. In *European Conference on Object-Oriented Programming* (pp. 15-29). Springer.

Daft, R. (2007). *Understanding the Theory and Design of Organizations*. Mason, OH: Thomson South-Western.

Daft, R. (2012). *Organization theory and design*. Nelson Education.

Daft, R. L., & Lewin, A. Y. (1990). Can organization studies begin to break out of thenormal science straitjacket? An editorial essay. *Organization Science, 1*(1), 1–9. doi:10.1287/orsc.1.1.1

Dardenne, A., Van Lamsweerde, A., & Fickas, S. (1993). Goal-directed requirements acquisition. *Science of Computer Programming, 20*(1-2), 3–50. doi:10.1016/0167-6423(93)90021-G

Davenport, S., & Ford, R. (2014). SGX: the Good, the Bad and the Downright Ugly. *Virus Bulletin, 14*.

Davis, C. H. F., Del-Amen, R., Rios-Aguilar, C., & González Canché, M. S. (2012). *Social media in higher education: A literature review and research directions*. Center for the study of HE, report printed by the University Of Arizona and Claremont Graduate University. https://works.bepress.com/hfdavis/2/

Davis, J., & Magrath, S. (2013). *A survey of cyber ranges and testbeds (Tech. Rep.). Defence Science And Technology Organisation Edinburgh*. Cyber And Electronic Warfare Div.

De Mauro, A., Greco, M., & Grimaldi, M. (2016). A formal definition of Big Data based on its essential features. *Library Review, 65*(3), 122–135. doi:10.1108/LR-06-2015-0061

De Oliveira, L. B., & Camponogara, E. (2010). Multi-agent model predictive control of signaling split in urban traffic networks. *Transportation Research Part C, Emerging Technologies, 18*(1), 120–139. doi:10.1016/j.trc.2009.04.022

De Tommasi, M., & Corallo, A. (2006, October). SBEAVER: a tool for modeling business vocabularies and business rules. In *International Conference on Knowledge-Based and Intelligent Information and Engineering Systems* (pp. 1083-1091). Springer. 10.1007/11893011_137

Deem, R., & Brehony, K. J. (2005). Management as ideology: The case of 'new managerialism' in higher education. *Oxford Review of Education, 31*(2), 217-235.

Deloitte Insights. (2018). *Deloitte Insights, The Fourth Industrial Revolution is here—are you ready?* Deloitte Development LLC. Retrieved 2019 5, Feb, from https://www2.deloitte.com/content/dam/insights/us/articles/4364_Industry4-0_Are-you-ready/4364_Industry4-0_Are-you-ready_Report.pdf

Deloitte. (2018). *The rise of the social enterprise, 2018 Deloitte Human Capital Trends Report.* Deloitte. Retrieved from https://www2.deloitte.com/content/dam/insights/us/articles/HCTrends2018/2018-HCtrends_Rise-of-the-social-enterprise.pdf

Deloitte. (2018). *The Rise of the Social Enterprise.* Deloitte Consulting.

Denning, S. (2018). *How Stress Is The Business World's Silent Killer.* Retrieved from How Stress Is The Business World's Silent Killer: https://www.forbes.com/sites/stephaniedenning/2018/05/04/what-is-the-cost-of-stress-how-stress-is-the-business-worlds-silent-killer/#6cc30bb46e06

Dery, K. (2019, May 29). *How to future proof your workforce for the digital era.* Retrieved from The Enterprisers Project: https://enterprisersproject.com/article/2019/5/digital-transformation-how-future-proof-workforce

Dewri, R., Poolsappasit, N., Ray, I., & Whitley, D. (2007). Optimal security hardening using multi-objective optimization on attack tree models of networks. In S. De Capitani di Vimercati, P. Syverson, & D. Evans (Eds.) *Proceedings of the 14th ACM conference on Computer and Communications Security* (pp. 204-213). Alexandria, VA: ACM. 10.1145/1315245.1315272

Diana, F., McKinney, T., & Mulcahy, K. (2013). The Digital Enterprise, A Framework for Transformation. *TCS Consulting Journal, 5.* Accessed: https://www.slideshare.net/stuartlamb/the-digitalenterprisevol510131131121044548phpapp01

Dietterich, T. G. (2000). Hierarchical reinforcement learning with the maxq value function decomposition. *Journal of Artificial Intelligence Research, 13,* 227–303. doi:10.1613/jair.639

Dietz, J. L. G. & Hoogervorst, J. A. P. (2007). Enterprise Ontology and Enterprise Architecture - how to let them evolve into effective complementary notions. *GEAO Journal of Enterprise Architecture, 1.*

Dietz, J. L. G. (2006). *Enterprise Ontology - Theory and Methodology.* Heidelberg, Germany: Springer. doi:10.1007/3-540-33149-2

Dietz, J., Hoogervorst, J., Albani, A., Aveiro, D., Babkin, E., Barjis, J., ... Winter, R. (2013). The Discipline Of Enterprise Engineering. *International Journal Of Organisational Design And Engineering, 3*(1), 86–114. doi:10.1504/IJODE.2013.053669

Dionisio, K. L., Phillips, K., Price, P. S., Grulke, C. M., Williams, A., Biryol, D., ... Isaacs, K. K. (2018). The Chemical and Products Database, a resource for exposure-relevant data on chemicals in consumer products. *Scientific Data, 5*(1), 180125. doi:10.1038data.2018.125 PMID:29989593

Dobrokhodov, V., Kaminer, I., Kitsios, I., Xargay, E., Cao, C., Gregory, I., ... Valavani, L. (2011). Experimental validation of L1 adaptive control: The Rohrs counterexample in flight. *Journal of Guidance, Control, and Dynamics, 34*(5), 1311–1328. doi:10.2514/1.50683

Dodge, R., Daly, A. P., Huyton, J., & Sanders, L. D. (2012). The challenge of defining wellbeing. *International Journal of Wellbeing, 2*(3), 222–235. doi:10.5502/ijw.v2i3.4

Dorri, A., Kanhere, S. S., Jurdak, R., & Gauravaram, P. (2017). *Blockchain for IoT security and privacy: The case study of a smart home. In 2017 IEEE international conference on pervasive computing and communications workshops (PerCom workshops)* (pp. 618–623). IEEE. doi:10.1109/PERCOMW.2017.7917634

Doyle, J. C., Glover, K., Khargonekar, P. P., & Francis, B. A. (1989). Statespace solutions to standard H_2/H_∞ control problems. *IEEE Transactions on Automatic Control, 34*(8), 831–847. doi:10.1109/9.29425

Drazin, R., & Sandelands, L. (1992). Autogenesis: A perspective on the process of organizing. *Organization Science, 3*(2), 230–249. doi:10.1287/orsc.3.2.230

DSCI. (2019). *Cyber Insurance in India.* Retrieved October 3, 2019, from https://www.dsci.in/sites/default/files/documents/resourcecentre/Cyber%20Insurance%20In%20India.pdf

du Toit, J., & Verhoef, A. H. (2018). Embodied digital technology and transformation in higher education. *Transformation in Higher Education, 3*(1), 1–8.

Duan, Y., Andrychowicz, M., Stadie, B., Ho, J., Schneider, J., Sutskever, I., ... Zaremba, W. (2017). *One-shot imitation learning* (Vol. 31). NIPS.

Duggirala, M., Malik, M., Kumar, H. H., & Balaraman, V. (2017). Evolving a grounded approach to behavior composition. *Winter Simulation Conference.*

Dukes, E. (2019, Jan 8). *The Employee Experience: What It Is and Why It Matters.* Retrieved from Inc.: https://www.inc.com/elizabeth-dukes/the-employee-experience-what-it-is-and-why-it-matt.html

Dydek, Z., Annaswamy, A., & Lavretsky, E. (2010). Adaptive control and the NASA X-15-3 ight revisited. *IEEE Control Systems Magazine, 30*(3), 32-48.

E.T., A., Sticha, P. J., Brdiczka, O., & Shen, J. (2013). A Bayesian network model for predicting insider threats. *IEEE symposium on security and Privacy workshops.*

Eiter, T., Ianni, G., & Krennwallner, T. (2009, August). Answer set programming: A primer. In *Reasoning Web International Summer School* (pp. 40–110). Berlin: Springer.

El-Tantawy, S., Abdulhai, B., & Abdelgawad, H. (2013). Multiagent reinforcement learning for integrated network of adaptive traffic signal controllers (MARLINATSC). *IEEE Transactions on Intelligent Transportation Systems, 14*(3), 1140–1150. doi:10.1109/TITS.2013.2255286

Enterprisers Project. (2019). *What is digital transformation?* Retrieved from https://enterprisersproject.com/what-is-digital-transformation

Eskandari, S., Leoutsarakos, A., Mursch, T., & Clark, J. (2018). A First Look at Browser-Based Cryptojacking. In *2018 IEEE European Symposium on Security and Privacy Workshops (EuroS&PW)* (pp. 58-66). IEEE.

Esprit Consortium Amice. (1989). *Open System Architecture For Cim.* Berlin: Springer.

Etzioni, A. (1964). *Modern Organizations.* Prentice Hall.

Evans, M., Maglaras, L. A., He, Y., & Janicke, H. (2016). Human Behaviour as an Aspect of Cybersecurity Assurance. *Security and Communication Networks, 9*(17), 4667–4679. doi:10.1002ec.1657

Evtyushkin, D., Ponomarev, D., & Abu-Ghazaleh, N. (2016). Jump Over ASLR: Attacking Branch Predictors to Bypass ASLR. In *The 49th Annual IEEE/ACM International Symposium on Microarchitecture* (p. 40). IEEE.

Eykholt, K., Evtimov, I., Fernandes, E., Li, B., Rahmati, A., Xiao, C., . . . Song, D. (2017). *Robust Physical-World Attacks on Deep Learning Models.* arXiv preprint arXiv:1707.08945

Ezeugo, E., & Palmer, I. (2018). *Five Ways to Turn Data-Informed Student Nudging from Bad to Good.* Retrieved from https://www.edsurge.com/news/2018-03-13-five-dangers-of-data-informed-student-nudging

Fairfull, A., Baker, S., Warde, S., & Cherns, P. (2019). Material Intelligence for CAD, PLM, and Industry 4.0. Granta Design. Retrieved from https://grantadesign.com/industry/publications/white-papers/material-intelligence-for-enterprise-cad-and-plm/

Falkenberg, E. D., Verrijn-Stuart, A. A., Voss, K., Hesse, W., Lindgreen, P., Nilsson, B. E., . . . Stamper, R. K. (Eds.). (1998). A Framework of Information Systems Concepts. IFIP WG 8.1 Task Group FRISCO. IFIP.

FBI. (2018). *Internet crime report.* Retrieved September 20, 2019, from https://pdf.ic3.gov/2018IC3Report.pdf

Feja, S., & Fotsch, D. (2008). Model checking with graphical validation rules. In *Proceedings of 15th Annual IEEE International Conference and Workshop on the Engineering of Computer Based Systems ECBS 2008* (117-125). Belfast, UK: IEEE Computer Society.

Feltus, C., Proper, H. A., Metzger, A., Garcia Lopez, J. C., & Gonzalez Castineira, R. (2018). Value cocreation (VCC) language design in the frame of a smart airport network case study. In *32nd IEEE International Conference on Advanced Information Networking and Applications, AINA 2018, Krakow, Poland,* May 16-18, 2018, (pp. 858-865). IEEE Computer Society. 10.1109/AINA.2018.00127

Ferguson, B., Tall, A., & Olsen, D. (2014). National cyber range overview. In *Proceedings of the 2014 IEEE Military Communications Conference* (pp. 123-128). Washington, DC: IEEE. 10.1109/MILCOM.2014.27

Ferrara, E. (2019). The History of Digital Spam. *Communications of the ACM, 62*(8), 82–91. doi:10.1145/3299768

Ferstl, O. K., & Sinz, E. J. (1998). Modeling Of Business Systems Using The Semantic Object Model (Som): A Methodological Framework. In P. Bernus, K. Mertins, & G. Schmidt (Eds.), International Handbooks On Information Systems: Vol. 1. Handbook On Architectures Of Information Systems (Pp. 339–358). Berlin: Springer.

Fill, H.-G., & Karagiannis, D. (2013). On The Conceptualisation Of Modelling Methods Using The Adoxx Meta Modelling Platform. *Enterprise Modelling and Information Systems Architectures, 8*(1), 4–25. doi:10.1007/BF03345926

Finlay, L., & Payne, C. (2019). The Attribution Problem and Cyber Armed Attacks. *AJIL Unbound, 113,* 202–206. doi:10.1017/aju.2019.35

Fleischmann, A., Schmidt, W., Stary, C., Obermeier, S., & Börger, E. (2012). *Subject-oriented Business Process Management.* Heidelberg, Germany: Springer. doi:10.1007/978-3-642-32392-8

Fleurey, F., Steel, J., & Baudry, B. (2004, November). Validation in model-driven engineering: testing model transformations. In *Proceedings. 2004 First International Workshop on Model, Design and Validation,* 2004 (pp. 29-40). IEEE. 10.1109/MODEVA.2004.1425846

Flick, E. W. (1989-2014). *Cosmetic and toiletry formulations* (Vol. 1-8). Elsevier.

Foerster, J., Assael, I. A., de Freitas, N., & Whiteson, S. (2016). Learning to communicate with deep multi-agent reinforcement learning. Advances in Neural Information Processing Systems, 2137-2145.

Forbes. (2013). *Why Are So Many Employees Disengaged?* Retrieved from www.forbes.com: https://www.forbes.com/sites/victorlipman/2013/01/18/why-are-so-many-employees-disengaged/#2f5878ed1e22

Forrester, J. W. (1994). System dynamics, systems thinking, and soft OR. *System Dynamics Review, 10*(2-3), 245–256. doi:10.1002dr.4260100211

Frank, U. (1998). *Evaluating Modelling Languages: Relevant Issues, Epistemological Challenges and a Preliminary Research Framework.* Technical Report 15. University of Koblenz-Landau.

Frank, U. (2002). Multi-perspective Enterprise Modeling (MEMO) conceptual framework and modeling languages. In *System Sciences, 2002. HICSS. Proceedings of the 35th Annual Hawaii International Conference on*, (pp. 1258–1267). IEEE.

Frank, U. (2011). *The Memo Meta Modelling Language (Mml) And Language Architecture. 2nd Edition* (Icb Research Report No. 43). Retrieved From Icb University Of Duisburg-Essen, Campus Essen Website: Http://Www.Icb.Uni-Due. De/Fileadmin/Icb/Research/Research_Reports/Icb-Report_No43.Pdf

Frank, U. (2018). *The Flexible Modelling And Execution Language (Fmmlx) Version 2.0: Analysis Of Requirements And Technical Terminology*. ICB Research Report No. 66.

Frank, U. (2002). Multi-perspective Enterprise Modeling (MEMO) - Conceptual Framework and Modeling Languages. In *HICSS '02: Proceedings of the 35th Annual Hawaii International Conference on System Sciences (HICSS'02)* (vol. 3, p. 72). Washington, DC: IEEE Computer Society Press. 10.1109/HICSS.2002.993989

Frank, U. (2013). Domain-Specific Modeling Languages - Requirements Analysis And Design Guidelines. In I. Reinhartz-Berger, A. Sturm, T. Clark, Y. Wand, S. Cohen, & J. Bettin (Eds.), *Domain Engineering: Product Lines, Conceptual Models, And Languages* (pp. 133–157). Springer. doi:10.1007/978-3-642-36654-3_6

Frank, U. (2014). Multilevel Modeling: Toward A New Paradigm Of Conceptual Modeling And Information Systems Design. *Business & Information Systems Engineering, 6*(6), 319–337. doi:10.100712599-014-0350-4

Fredrikson, M., Jha, S., & Ristenpart, T. (2015). Model Inversion Attacks that Exploit Confidence Information and Basic Countermeasures. In *Proceedings of the 22nd ACM SIGSAC Conference on Computer and Communications Security* (pp. 1322-1333). ACM. 10.1145/2810103.2813677

Freund, J., & Rücker, B. (2012). *Real Life BPMN*. Camunda.

Friedenthal, S., Moore, A., & Steiner, R. (2014). *A practical guide to SysML: the systems modeling language*. Morgan Kaufmann.

Friedman, B. (1996). Value-sensitive design. *Interactions, 3*(6), 16–23.

Friedman, T. L. (2005). *The World is Flat: A Brief History of the Twenty-first Century*. New York: Farrar, Straus and Giroux.

Fryer, J. (2017). The Road To IIoT: What Can We Learn From Other Industries? *Manufacturing.net*. Retrieved from https://www.manufacturing.net/article/2017/01/road-iiot-what-can-we-learn-other-industries

Gajula, K., Gupta, R., Sridhar, D. B., & Rai, B. (2017). In-Silico skin model: A multiscale simulation study of drug transport. *Journal of Chemical Information and Modeling, 57*(8), 2027–2034. doi:10.1021/acs.jcim.7b00224 PMID:28718641

Ganek & Corbi. (n.d.). The dawning of the autonomic computing era. IBM Systems Journal, 42(1), 5–18.

Gani, R., & Ng, K. M. (2015). Product design–molecules, devices, functional products, and formulated products. *Computers & Chemical Engineering, 81*, 70–79. doi:10.1016/j.compchemeng.2015.04.013

Gardner, T., Griffin, C., Koehler, J., & Hauser, R. (2003, November). A review of OMG MOF 2.0 Query/Views/Transformations Submissions and Recommendations towards the final Standard. In *MetaModelling for MDA Workshop* (Vol. 13, p. 41). Academic Press.

Garton, E. (2017). Employee burnout is a problem with the company, not the person. *Harvard Business Review*.

Gaukstern, E., & Krishnan, S. (2018). Cybersecurity Threats Targeting Networked Critical. *Medical Devices (Auckland, N.Z.)*.

Gautham, B. P., Reddy, S., Das, P., & Malhotra, C. (2017). Facilitating ICME Through Platformization. In PProceedings of the 4th World Congress on Integrated Computational Materials Engineering (ICME 2017) (pp. 93-102). Springer. doi:10.1007/978-3-319-57864-4_9

Gautham, B. P., Singh, A. K., Ghaisas, S. S., Reddy, S., & Mistree, F. (2013). Article. In A. Chakrabarti & R. V. Prakash (Eds.), *ICoRD'13, Lecture Notes in Mechanical Engineering* (p. 1301). Springer India.

Gentry, C. (2009). *A Fully Homomorphic Encryption Scheme* (Unpublished Doctoral Dissertation). Stanford University. crypto.stanford.edu/craig

George, J. J., & Leidner, D. E. (2019). From Clicktivism to Hacktivism: Understanding Digital Activism. *Information and Organization, 29*(3), 100249. doi:10.1016/j.infoandorg.2019.04.001

Georgiou, T., & Smith, M. (1997). Robustness analysis of nonlinear feedback systems: An input-output approach. *IEEE Transactions on Automatic Control, 42*(9), 1200–1221. doi:10.1109/9.623082

Gharote, M., Phuke, N., Patil, R., & Lodha, S. (2019). Multi-objective Stable Matching and Distributional Constraints. *Soft Computing, 23*(9), 2995–3011. doi:10.100700500-019-03763-4

Gibbons, S. (2017, July 9). *Service Design 101*. Nielsen Norman Group.

Gibson, I. (2007). An approach to hospital planning and design using discrete event simulation. *Proceedings of the Winter Simulation Conference 2007*. 10.1109/WSC.2007.4419763

Giffinger, R., Fertner, C., Kramar, H., & Meijers, E. (2007). *City-ranking of European medium-sized cities*. Vienna, UT: Cent. Reg. Sci.

Giles, M. (2019). *Triton is the World's Most Murderous Malware, and it's Spreading. MIT Technology Review*.

Gils, B. v., & Proper, H. A. (2018). Enterprise modelling in the age of digital transformation. In *The Practice of Enterprise Modeling - 11th IFIP WG 8.1. Working Conference, PoEM 2018, Vienna, Austria, October 31 - November 2, 2018, Proceedings, volume 335 of Lecture Notes in Business Information Processing*, (pp. 257-273). Springer.

Glaessgen, E., & Stargel, D. (2012, April). The digital twin paradigm for future NASA and US Air Force vehicles. In *53rd AIAA/ASME/ASCE/AHS/ASC Structures, Structural Dynamics and Materials Conference 20th AIAA/ASME/AHS Adaptive Structures Conference 14th AIAA* (p. 1818). Academic Press.

Godfrey, G. A., & Powell, W. B. (2002). An adaptive dynamic programming algorithm for dynamic eet management, i: Single period travel times. *Transportation Science, 36*(1), 21–39. doi:10.1287/trsc.36.1.21.570

Goerzig, D., & Bauernhansl, T. (2018). Enterprise architectures for the digital transformation in small and medium-sized enterprises. *Procedia CIRP, 67*, 540–545. doi:10.1016/j.procir.2017.12.257

Gogolla, M., & Doan, K. H. (2017). Quality Improvement of Conceptual UML and OCL Schemata through Model Validation and Verification. In *Conceptual Modeling Perspectives* (pp. 155–168). Cham: Springer. doi:10.1007/978-3-319-67271-7_11

Golnaraghi, F., & Kuo, B. (2010). Automatic control systems. *Complex Variables, 2*, 1–1.

González, F., Yu, Y., Figueroa, A., López, C., & Aragon, C. (2019). *Global Reactions to the Cambridge Analytica Scandal: An Inter-Language Social Media Study*. Academic Press.

Goodwin, G., Ramadge, P., & Caines, P. (1980). Discrete-time multivariable adaptive control. *IEEE Transactions on Automatic Control, 25*(3), 449–456. doi:10.1109/TAC.1980.1102363

Gordijn, J., & Akkermans, H. (2003). Value based requirements engineering: Exploring innovative e-commerce ideas. *Requirements Engineering Journal*, *8*(2), 114–134. doi:10.100700766-003-0169-x

Grassi, P. A., Fenton, J. L., Newton, E. M., Perlner, R. A., Regenscheid, A. R., Burr, W. E., & Richer, J. P. (2019). Digital Identity Guidelines. *NIST Special Publication*, *800*, 63–3.

Greefhorst, D., & Proper, H. A. (2011). *Architecture Principles - The Cornerstones of Enterprise Architecture*. Heidelberg, Germany: Springer.

Grieves, M. (2014). *Digital twin: Manufacturing excellence through virtual factory replication*. White paper, pages 1–7.

Grieves, M. (2005). Product lifecycle management: The new paradigm for enterprises. *International Journal of Product Development*, *2*(1-2), 71–84. doi:10.1504/IJPD.2005.006669

Grieves, M. (2011). *Virtually perfect: Driving innovative and lean products through product lifecycle management*. Space Coast Press.

Grieves, M. (2012, July). Virtually Indistinguishable. In *IFIP International Conference on Product Lifecycle Management* (pp. 226-242). Springer.

Grieves, M. (2019). Virtually Intelligent Product Systems: Digital and Physical Twins. In S. Flumerfelt, K. G. Schwartz, D. Mavris, & S. Briceno (Eds.), *Complex Systems Engineering: Theory and Practice* (pp. 175–200). American Institute of Aeronautics and Astronautics. doi:10.2514/5.9781624105654.0175.0200

Grieves, M., & Vickers, J. (2017). Digital twin: Mitigating unpredictable, undesirable emergent behavior in complex systems. In *Transdisciplinary perspectives on complex systems* (pp. 85–113). Cham: Springer. doi:10.1007/978-3-319-38756-7_4

Grignard, A., Taillandier, P., Gaudou, B., Vo, D. A., Huynh, N. Q., & Drogoul, A. (2013). GAMA 1.6: Advancing the art of complex agent-based modeling and simulation. *International Conference on Principles and Practice of Multi-Agent Systems*, 117–131. 10.1007/978-3-642-44927-7_9

Grint, K. (2010). Wicked problems and clumsy solutions: The role of leadership. In The New public leadership challenge (pp. 169-186). Academic Press.

Grönroos, C., & Ravald, A. (2011). Service as Business Logic: Implications for Value Creation and Marketing. *Journal of Service Management*, *22*(1), 5–22. doi:10.1108/09564231111106893

Grover, L. K. (1996). *A fast quantum mechanical algorithm for database search*. arXiv preprint quant-ph/9605043

Gu, S., Holly, E., Lillicrap, T., & Levine, S. (2017). Deep reinforcement learning for robotic manipulation with asynchronous o_-policy updates. *Robotics and Automation (ICRA), 2017 IEEE International Conference on*, 3389-3396.

Gudka, K., Watson, R. N., Anderson, J., Chisnall, D., Davis, B., Laurie, B., ... Richardson, A. (2015). Clean Application Compartmentalization with SOAAP. In *Proceedings of the 22nd ACM SIGSAC Conference on Computer and Communications Security* (pp. 1016-1031). ACM.

Guizzardi, G. (2006). On Ontology, ontologies, Conceptualizations, Modeling Languages, and (Meta)Models. In *Databases and Information Systems IV - Selected Papers from the Seventh International Baltic Conference, DB&IS 2006, July 3-6, 2006, Vilnius, Lithuania, volume 155 of Frontiers in Artificial Intelligence and Applications*, (pp. 18-39). IOS Press.

Guo, H., Yuan, Y., Archer, N. P., & Connelly, C. E. (2011). Understanding Nonmalicious Security, Violations in the Workplace: A Composite Behavior Model. *Journal of Management Information Systems*, *28*(2), 203–236. doi:10.2753/MIS0742-1222280208

Gupta, R., Dwadasi, B. S., & Rai, B. (2017). *U.S. Patent Application No. 15/466,653.* Washington, DC: US Patent Office.

Gupta, R., Gajula, K., Dwadasi, B., & Rai, B. (2018). *U.S. Patent Application No. 15/900,448.* Washington, DC: US Patent Office.

Gupta, R., Dwadasi, B. S., Rai, B., & Mitragotri, S. (2019). Effect of Chemical Permeation Enhancers on Skin Permeability: In silico screening using Molecular Dynamics simulations. *Scientific Reports*, *9*(1), 1456. doi:10.103841598-018-37900-0 PMID:30728438

Gupta, R., Kashyap, N., & Rai, B. (2017). Transdermal cellular membrane penetration of proteins with gold nanoparticles: A molecular dynamics study. *Physical Chemistry Chemical Physics*, *19*(11), 7537–7545. doi:10.1039/C6CP08775B PMID:28252121

Gupta, R., & Rai, B. (2017). Effect of size and surface charge of gold nanoparticles on their skin permeability: A molecular dynamics study. *Scientific Reports*, *7*(1), 45292. doi:10.1038rep45292 PMID:28349970

Gupta, R., & Rai, B. (2018). Electroporation of Skin Stratum Corneum Lipid Bilayer and Molecular Mechanism of Drug Transport: A Molecular Dynamics Study. *Langmuir*, *34*(20), 5860–5870. doi:10.1021/acs.langmuir.8b00423 PMID:29708340

Gupta, R., Sridhar, D. B., & Rai, B. (2016). Molecular dynamics simulation study of permeation of molecules through skin lipid bilayer. *The Journal of Physical Chemistry B*, *120*(34), 8987–8996. doi:10.1021/acs.jpcb.6b05451 PMID:27518707

Guri, M., Zadov, B., & Elovici, Y. (2019). Odini: Escaping Sensitive Data from Faraday-Caged, Air-Gapped Computers via Magnetic Fields. *IEEE Transactions on Information Forensics and Security.*

Gürses, S., Troncoso, C., & Diaz, C. (2011). Engineering Privacy by Design. *Computers. Privacy & Data Protection*, *14*(3), 25.

Gutmann, P. (2007). The Commercial Malware Industry. *DEFCON Conference.*

Guyer, P. (Ed.). (1998). Critique Of Pure Reason. Cambridge: Cambridge Univ. Press.

Gwynne, P. (2018). *Practical quantum computers remain at least a decade away.* Retrieved December 5, 2019, from https://physicsworld.com/a/practical-quantum-computers-remain-at-least-a-decade-away/

Hackerone. (2019). *The Hacker Powered Security Report 2010.* Retrieved October 3, 2019, from https://www.hackerone.com/sites/default/files/2019-08/hacker-powered-security-report-2019.pdf

Haggerty, K. D., & Ericson, R. V. (2000). The surveillant assemblage. *The British Journal of Sociology*, *51*(4), 605-622. PMID:11140886

Haller, M., Brandl, P., Leithinger, D., Leitner, J., Seifried, T., & Billinghurst, M. (2006). *Shared Design Space: Sketching ideas using digital pens and a large augmented tabletop setup.* Advances in Artificial Reality and Tele-Existence. doi:10.1145/1179133.1179163

Haller, P., & Odersky, M. (2009). Scala actors: Unifying thread-based and event-based programming. *Theoretical Computer Science*, *410*(2), 202–220. doi:10.1016/j.tcs.2008.09.019

Halpin, T. (2007). Fact Oriented Modeling – Past, Present and Future. In J. Krogstie, A. L. Opdahl, & S. Brinkkemper (Eds.), *Conceptual Modelling in Information Systems Engineering* (pp. 19–38). Berlin: Springer-Verlag. doi:10.1007/978-3-540-72677-7_2

Hamers, R. (2017). *We want to be a tech company with a banking license.* Academic Press.

Hammer, M. (1990). Re-engineering work: Don't automate, obliterate. *Harvard Business Review*, *68*(4), 104–112.

Harmer, J., Gisslen, L., del Val, J., Holst, H., Bergdahl, J., Olsson, T., . . . Nordin, M. (2018). *Imitation learning with concurrent actions in 3D games.* arXiv preprint arXiv:1803.05402

Harmsen, A. F., Proper, H. A., & Kok, N. (2009). Informed governance of enterprise transformations. In *Advances in Enterprise Engineering II - First NAF Academy Working Conference on Practice-Driven Research on Enterprise Transformation, PRET 2009, held at CAiSE 2009, Amsterdam, The Netherlands, June 11, 2009. Proceedings, volume 28 of Lecture Notes in Business Information Processing*, (pp. 155-180). Amsterdam, The Netherlands: Springer. 10.1007/978-3-642-01859-6_9

Harper, P. M., & Gani, R. (2000). A multi-step and multi-level approach for computer aided molecular design. *Computers & Chemical Engineering*, *24*(2-7), 677–683. doi:10.1016/S0098-1354(00)00410-5

Harris, Z. (1968). *Mathematical structures of language. Interscience tracts in pure and applied mathematics.* Academic Press.

Haslam, C., Atkinson, S., Brown, S. S., & Haslam, R. A. (2005). Anxiety and depression in the workplace: Effects on the individual and organisation (a focus group investigation). *Journal of Affective Disorders*, *88*(2), 209–215. doi:10.1016/j.jad.2005.07.009 PMID:16122810

Hassan, W. U., Guo, S., Li, D., Chen, Z., Jee, K., Li, Z., & Bates, A. (2019). Nodoze: Combatting Threat Alert Fatigue with Automated Provenance Triage. NDSS.

Hayatnagarkar, H., Singh, M., Kumar, S., Duggirala, M., & Balaraman, V. (2016). Can a buffering strategy reduce workload related stress? Autumn Simulation Multi-conference.

Health and Safety Executive. (2018). *Work-related ill health and occupational disease in Great Britain.* Retrieved from Work-related ill health and occupational disease in Great Britain: https://www.hse.gov.uk/statistics/causdis/index.htm

Hebig, R., Seibel, A., & Giese, H. (2012). On the unification of megamodels. *Electronic Communications of the EASST*, 42.

Heineman, G. T., & Councill, W. T. (2001). *Component-based software engineering. Putting the pieces together.* Addison-Wesley.

Hemp, P. (2004). Presenteeism: At work-but out of it. *Harvard Business Review*, 49–58. PMID:15559575

Henderson, J. C., & Venkatraman, N. (1993). Strategic alignment: Leveraging information technology for transforming organizations. *IBM Systems Journal*, *32*(1), 4–16. doi:10.1147j.382.0472

Heumann, T., Keller, J., & Türpe, S. (2010). *Quantifying the Attack Surface of a Web Application. Sicherheit 2010.* Sicherheit, Schutz und Zuverlassigkeit.

Hewitt, C., & Smith, B. (1975). *A plasma primer. Draft.* Cambridge, MA: MIT Artificial Intelligence Laboratory.

Hidas, P. (2002). Modelling lane changing and merging in microscopic traffic simulation. *Transportation Research Part C, Emerging Technologies*, *10*(5), 351–371. doi:10.1016/S0968-090X(02)00026-8

Hiller, J. S. (2014). Civil cyberconflict: Microsoft, Cybercrime, and Botnets. *Santa Clara Computer and High-Technology Law Journal*, *31*, 163.

Hill, M. (2009). Chemical product engineering—The third paradigm. *Computers & Chemical Engineering*, *33*(5), 947–953. doi:10.1016/j.compchemeng.2008.11.013

Hillston, J. (2003). *Model Validation and Verification*. Retrieved from http://www.inf.ed.ac.uk/teaching/courses/pm/Note16.pdf

Hitchman, S. (2002). The Details of Conceptual Modelling Notations are Important - A Comparison of Relationship Normative Language. *Communications of the AIS, 9*(10).

Hitchman, S. (1995). Practitioner Perceptions On The Use Of Some Semantic Concepts In The Entity Relationship Model'. *European Journal of Information Systems, 4*(1), 31–40. doi:10.1057/ejis.1995.4

Holland, J. H. (2006). Studying complex adaptive systems. *Journal of Systems Science and Complexity, 19*(1), 1–8. doi:10.100711424-006-0001-z

Homoliak, I., Toffalini, F., Guarnizo, J., Elovici, Y., & Ochoa, M. (2019). Insight into Insiders and it: A Survey of Insider Threat Taxonomies, Analysis, Modeling, and Countermeasures. *ACM Computing Surveys, 52*(2), 30. doi:10.1145/3303771

Hong, J. (2012). *The Current State of Phishing Attacks*. Academic Press.

Hong, S., Frigo, P., Kaya, Y., Giuffrida, C., & Dumitras, T. (2019). *Terminal Brain Damage: Exposing the Graceless Degradation in Deep Neural Networks under Hardware Fault Attacks*. arXiv preprint arXiv:1906.01017

Hood, C. (2000). Paradoxes of public-sector managerialism, old public management and public service bargains. *International Public Management Journal, 3*(1), 1–22. doi:10.1016/S1096-7494(00)00032-5

Hoppenbrouwers, S. J. B. A., Proper, H. A., & Weide, T. P. d. (2005). A fundamental view on the process of conceptual modeling. In *Conceptual Modeling - ER 2005, 24th International Conference on Conceptual Modeling, Klagenfurt, Austria, October 24-28, 2005, Proceedings*, volume 3716 of Lecture Notes in Computer Science, (pp. 128-143). Springer. 10.1007/11568322_9

Horl, S. (2016). *Agent-based simulation of autonomous taxi services with dynamic demand responses*. Academic Press.

Hornecker, E., & Buur, J. (2006). Getting a grip on tangible interaction: a framework on physical space and social interaction. In *Proceedings of the SIGCHI conference on Human Factors in computing systems*, (pp. 437-446). ACM Press. 10.1145/1124772.1124838

How to operationalize AI in your business. (n.d.). *IBM*. Retrieved from: https://www.ibm.com/watson

Huisman, J. (2019). *Magic Quadrant for Security Awareness Computer-Based Training*. Retrieved October 3, 2019, from https://www.gartner.com/en/documents/3950454/magic-quadrant-for-security-awareness-computer-based-tra

Humphrey, W. S. (1988). Characterizing the software process: A maturity framework. *IEEE Software, 5*(2), 73–79. doi:10.1109/52.2014

Huppert, F. A., & Cooper, C. L. (2014). *Wellbeing: A Complete Reference Guide, Interventions and Policies to Enhance Wellbeing* (Vol. 6). John Wiley & Sons.

Iacob, M., Jonkers, D. H., Lankhorst, M., Proper, E., & Quartel, D. D. (2012). *ArchiMate 2.0 Specification: The Open Group*. Van Haren Publishing.

IBM. (2012). *Smarter education with IBM*. Retrieved from https://www-935.ibm.com/services/multimedia/Framework_-_Smarter_Education_With_IBM.pdf

Ifinedo, P. (2015). Effects of Organizational Citizenship Behavior and Social Cognitive Factors on Employees' NonMalicious Counterproductive Computer Security Behaviors: An Empirical Analysis. *International Conference on Information Resource Management, AIS2015*, 1-13.

Industrial Internet Consortium. (2016). *The Industrial Internet of Things. Volume G4: Security Framework* (Report No. IIC:PUB:G4:V1.0:PB:20160919). Retrieved from https://www.iiconsortium.org/pdf/IIC_PUB_G4_V1.00_PB.pdf

Industrial Internet Consortium. (2017a) *The Industrial Internet of Things. Volume G1: Reference Architecture* (Report No. IIC:PUB:G1:V1.80:20170131). Retrieved from https://www.iiconsortium.org/IIC_PUB_G1_V1.80_2017-01-31.pdf

Industrial Internet Consortium. (2017b). *The Industrial Internet of Things. Volume T3: Analytics Framework* (Report No. IIC:PUB:T3:V1.00:PB:20171023). Retrieved from https://www.iiconsortium.org/pdf/IIC_Industrial_Analytics_Framework_Oct_2017.pdf

Intelligence and National Security Alliance. (2017). *Assessing the mind of the malicious insider: Using behavioral model and data analytics to improve continuous evaluation.* Academic Press.

Internet Bug Bounty. (2019). *The Internet Bug Bounty.* Retrieved October 3, 2019, from https://internetbugbounty.org/

Ioannou, P. (1986). Decentralized adaptive control of interconnected systems. *IEEE Transactions on Automatic Control, 31*(4), 291–298. doi:10.1109/TAC.1986.1104282

Ioannou, P. A., & Sun, J. (1996). *Robust adaptive control* (Vol. 1). Prentice-Hall.

Ioannou, P., Annaswamy, A., Narendra, K., Jafari, S., Rudd, L., Ortega, R., & Boskovic, J. (2014). L_1-adaptive control: Stability, robustness, and interpretations. *IEEE Transactions on Automatic Control, 59*(11), 3075–3080. doi:10.1109/TAC.2014.2318871

Isaacs, K. K., Goldsmith, M. R., Egeghy, P., Phillips, K., Brooks, R., Hong, T., & Wambaugh, J. F. (2016). Characterization and prediction of chemical functions and weight fractions in consumer products. *Toxicology Reports, 3*, 723–732. doi:10.1016/j.toxrep.2016.08.011 PMID:28959598

Isaacs, K. K., Phillips, K. A., Biryol, D., Dionisio, K. L., & Price, P. S. (2018). Consumer product chemical weight fractions from ingredient lists. *Journal of Exposure Science & Environmental Epidemiology, 28*(3), 216–222. doi:10.1038/jes.2017.29 PMID:29115287

Isaak, J., & Hanna, M. J. (2018). User Data Privacy: Facebook, Cambridge Analytica, and Privacy Protection. *Computer, 51*(8), 56–59. doi:10.1109/MC.2018.3191268

Islam, R., Henderson, P., Gomrokchi, M., & Precup, D. (2017). *Reproducibility of benchmarked deep reinforcement learning tasks for continuous control.* arXiv preprint arXiv:1708.04133.

ISO. (2013). *ISO/IEC/IEEE 42010:2011 - systems and software engineering - architecture description. Standard.* Geneva, Switzerland: International Organization for Standardization.

IXIA. (2016). *Cyber Range: Improving Network Defense and Security Readiness.* Retrieved October 3, 2019, from https://www.testforce.com/testforce files/newsletter/Aug 2016/ixia.pdf

Jayabal, H., Dingari, N. N., & Rai, B. (2019). A linear viscoelastic model to understand skin mechanical behaviour and for cosmetic formulation design. *International Journal of Cosmetic Science, 41*(3), 292–299. doi:10.1111/ics.12535 PMID:31032974

Jin, G., Tu, M., Kim, T.-H., Heffron, J., & White, J. (2018). Game Based Cybersecurity Training for High School Students. In *Proceedings of the 49th ACM Technical Symposium on Computer Science Education* (pp. 68-73). New York, NY: ACM. 10.1145/3159450.3159591

JISC. (2013). Shared Services. *JISC.* Retrieved January from https://www.jisc.ac.uk/full-guide/shared-services

Jones, S., & Scott Evans, R. (2008). An Agent Based Simulation Tool for Scheduling Emergency Department Physicians. *AMIA Annual Symposium Proceedings*, 338-342.

Jose, R., & Ramakrishna, S. (2018). Materials 4.0: Materials big data enabled materials discovery. Applied Materials Today, 10, 127–132. doi:10.1016/j.apmt.2017.12.015

Judd, M., & Fritsch, J. (2018). *Comparing Security Controls and Paradigms in AWS, Google Cloud Platform and Microsoft Azure*. Retrieved October 3, 2019, from https://www.gartner.com/en/documents/3877942/comparing-security-controls-and-paradigms-in-aws-google-

Jung, R., & Reichert, M. (Eds.)., R., Niemietz, H., de Kinderen, S., and Aier, S. (2013). Can boundary objects mitigate communication defects in enterprise transformation? Findings from expert interviews. In *Proceedings of the 5th International Workshop on Enterprise Modelling and Information Systems Architectures, EMISA 2013, St. Gallen, Switzerland, September 5-6, 2013*, volume 222 of *Lecture Notes in Informatics*, (pp. 27-40). Gesellschaft für Informatik.

Kahneman, D., Lovallo, D., & Sibony, O. (2011, June). The Big Idea: Before You Make That Big Decision. *Harvard Business Review*.

Kang, K. C., Cohen, S. G., Hess, J. A., Novak, W. E., & Peterson, A. S. (1990). *Feature-oriented domain analysis (FODA) feasibility study (No. CMU/SEI-90-TR-21)*. Carnegie-Mellon Univ Pittsburgh Pa Software Engineering Inst. doi:10.21236/ADA235785

Kant, I. (1998). *Critique Of Pure Reason*. Cambridge: Cambridge Univ. Press. doi:10.1017/CBO9780511804649

Kaplan, M. J., Richter, W., & Ware, D. (2019, August 1). Retrieved December 2019, from https://www.securitymagazine.com/articles/90637-how-cybersecurity-can-best-support-the-digital-enterprise

Kates, A., & Galbraith, J. R. (2007). *Designing Your Organization: Using the STAR Model to Solve 5 Critical Design Challenges*. Jossey-Bass.

Kecheng, L., Clarke, R. J., Andersen, P. B., Stamper, R. K., & Abou-Zeid, E.-S. (Eds.). (2002). *IFIP TC8/WG8.1 Working Conference on Organizational Semiotics - Evolving a Science of Information Systems*. Kluwer.

Keeney, M., Kowalski, E., Cappelli, D., Moore, A., Shimeall, T., & Rogers, S. (2005). Insider Threat Study:Computer System Sabotage in Critical Infrastructure Sectors. SEI, Carnegie Mellon University.

Kefalidou, G. (2015). *Overview of the state of the art (SoA) requirements: Personalised Airport Systems for Seamless Mobility & Experience*. University of Nottingham.

Kephart, J. O., & Chess, D. M. (2003). The vision of autonomic computing. *Computer*, 36(1), 41–50.

Khadilkar, H. (2019). A scalable reinforcement learning algorithm for scheduling railway lines. *IEEE Transactions on Intelligent Transportation Systems*, 20(2), 727–736. doi:10.1109/TITS.2018.2829165

Khambete, P. (2011). *A pattern language for touch point ecosystem user experience: a proposal*. Bangalore: ACM. doi:10.1145/2407796.2407805

Kholkar, D., Sunkle, S., & Kulkarni, V. (2017). Semi-automated creation of regulation rule bases using generic template-driven rule extraction. ASAIL@ ICAIL.

Kiddon, C., Ponnuraj, G. T., Zettlemoyer, L., & Choi, Y. (2015, September). Mise en place: Unsupervised interpretation of instructional recipes. In *Proceedings of the 2015 Conference on Empirical Methods in Natural Language Processing* (pp. 982-992). 10.18653/v1/D15-1114

Kim Zetter. (2014). *Hacker Lexicon: What is an Air Gap?* Retrieved September 20, 2019, from https://www.wired.com/2014/12/hacker-lexicon-air-gap/

Kim, W. (1997). *ThAL: An actor system for efficient and scalable concurrent computing* (PhD thesis). University of Illinois at Urbana-Champaign.

Kim, S., Thiessen, P. A., Bolton, E. E., Chen, J., Fu, G., Gindulyte, A., ... Wang, J. (2015). PubChem substance and compound databases. *Nucleic Acids Research, 44*(D1), D1202–D1213. doi:10.1093/nar/gkv951 PMID:26400175

Kindervag, J. (2010). *Build Security Into Your Network's DNA: The Zero Trust Network Architecture*. Forrester Research Inc.

Kinman, G., & Jones, F. (2008). A life beyond work? Job demands, work-life balance, and wellbeing in UK academics. *Journal of Human Behavior in the Social Environment, 17*(1-2), 41–60. doi:10.1080/10911350802165478

Kirchner, L. (2005). Cost Oriented Modelling Of It-Landscapes: Generic Language Concepts Of A Domain Specific Language. In J. Desel & U. Frank (Eds.), *Lecture Notes In Informatics: P-75, Enterprise Modelling And Information Systems Architectures: Proceedings Of The Workshop In Klagenfurt, October 24-25, 2005* (Pp. 166–179). Bonn: Gesellschaft Für Informatik.

Kirkwood, A., & Price, L. (2014). Technology-enhanced learning and teaching in higher education: What is 'enhanced' and how do we know? A critical literature review. *Learning, Media and Technology, 39*(1), 6–36. doi:10.1080/17439884.2013.770404

Kish, D., & Carpenter, P. (2017). *Forecast Snapshot: Security Awareness Computer-based Training, Worldwide, 2017*. Retrieved October 3, 2019, from https://www.gartner.com/en/documents/3629840/forecast-snapshot-security-awareness-computer-based-trai

Kissel, R. (2011). *Glossary of key information security terms*. Diane Publishing. doi:10.6028/NIST.IR.7298r1

Kitchin, R. (2014). The real-time city? Big data and smart urbanism. *GeoJournal, 79*(1), 1–14. doi:10.100710708-013-9516-8

Kiyavitskaya, N., Zeni, N., Breaux, T. D., Antón, A. I., Cordy, J. R., Mich, L., & Mylopoulos, J. (2008, October). Automating the extraction of rights and obligations for regulatory compliance. In *International Conference on Conceptual Modeling* (pp. 154-168). Springer. 10.1007/978-3-540-87877-3_13

Klee, H., & Allen, R. (2016). *Simulation of dynamic systems with MATLAB and Simulink. Crc Press. Kothari, C. R. (2004). Research methodology: Methods and techniques.* New Age International.

Klemmer, S. R., Newman, M. W., Farrell, R., Bilezikjian, M., & Landay, J. A. (2001). The designers' outpost: a tangible interface for collaborative web site design. In *Proceedings of the 14th annual ACM symposium on User interface software and technology*, (pp. 1-10). ACM Press. 10.1145/502348.502350

Ko, L. L., Divakaran, M. D., Liau, Y. S., & Thing, S. (2017). Insider threat detection and its future directions. *International Journal of Security and Networks*, 168-187.

Kober, J., Bagnell, J. A., & Peters, J. (2013). Reinforcement learning in robotics: A survey. *The International Journal of Robotics Research, 32*(11), 1238-1274.

Kocher, P., Genkin, D., Gruss, D., Haas, W., Hamburg, M., Lipp, M., ... Yarom, Y. (2018). *Spectre Attacks: Exploiting Speculative Execution.* arXiv preprint arXiv:1801.01203

Kohl, N., & Stone, P. (2004). Policy gradient reinforcement learning for fast quadrupedal locomotion. *Robotics and Automation, 2004. Proceedings. ICRA'04. 2004 IEEE International Conference on, 3*, 2619-2624. 10.1109/ROBOT.2004.1307456

Kolbjørnsrud, V., Amico, R., & Thomas, R. (2016, November 2). How Artificial Intelligence will Redefine Management. *Harvard Business Review*, 2–6.

Konda, V. R., & Tsitsiklis, J. N. (2000). Actor-critic algorithms. Advances in neural information processing systems, 1008-1014.

Korves, B. (2015). *The Future of Manufacturing – On the way to Industry 4.0* [PDF document]. *Siemens*. Retrieved from https://ec.europa.eu/information_society/newsroom/image/document/2015-44/14_korves_11951.pdf

Koschmieder, L., Hojda, S., Apel, M., Altenfeld, R., Bami, Y., Haase, C., . . . Schmitz, G. (2019). AixViPMaP—An Operational Platform for Microstructure Modeling Workflows. Integrating Materials and Manufacturing Innovation, 8(2), 122–143. doi:10.1007/s40192-019-00138-3

Kowtha, S., Nolan, L. A., & Daley, R. A. (2012). Cyber Security Operations Center Characterization Model and Analysis. *IEEE Conference on Technologies for Homeland Security*, 470-475. 10.1109/THS.2012.6459894

Kraft, S. (2018). *Companies are facing an employee burnout crisis*. Retrieved from https://www.cnbc.com/2018/08/14/5-ways-workers-can-avoid-employee-burnout.html

Kreisselmeier, G., & Anderson, B. (1986). Robust model reference adaptive control. *IEEE Transactions on Automatic Control*, 31(2), 127–133. doi:10.1109/TAC.1986.1104217

Krishnan, K. A. (2017). Digitally Reimagining Mobility. In M. Tandon & P. Ghosh (Eds.), *Mobility Engineering* (pp. 59–68). Singapore: Springer. doi:10.1007/978-981-10-3099-4_8

Kritzinger, W., Karner, M., Traar, G., Henjes, J., & Sihn, W. (2018). Digital Twin in manufacturing: A categorical literature review and classification. *IFAC-PapersOnLine*, 51(11), 1016–1022. doi:10.1016/j.ifacol.2018.08.474

Krogmann, K., Schweda, C. M., Buckl, S., Kuperberg, M., Martens, A., & Matthes, F. (2009). Improved Feedback for Architectural Performance Prediction Using Software Cartography Visualizations. In Architectures for Adaptive Software Systems, volume 5581 of Lecture Notes in Computer Science, (pp. 52-69). Springer. doi:10.1007/978-3-642-02351-4_4

Krogstie, J., Lindland, O. I., & Sindre, G. (1995). Defining Quality Aspects for Conceptual Models. In *Information System Concepts: Towards a consolidation of views - Proceedings of the third IFIP WG8.1 conference (ISCO-3)*, (pp. 216-231). Marburg, Germany: Chapman & Hall/IFIP WG8.1. 10.1007/978-0-387-34870-4_22

Krogstie, J. (2002). A Semiotic Approach to Quality in Requirements Specifications. In *Proceedings of the IFIP TC8 / WG8.1 Working Conference on Organizational Semiotics: Evolving a Science of Information Systems*, (231-250). Deventer, The Netherlands: Kluwer. 10.1007/978-0-387-35611-2_14

Krogstie, J. (2008). Using EEML for combined goal and process oriented modeling: A case study. *CEUR Workshop Proceedings*, 337, 112–129.

Kula, R. G., German, D. M., Ouni, A., Ishio, T., & Inoue, K. (2018). Do developers update their library dependencies? *Empirical Software Engineering*, 23(1), 384–417. doi:10.100710664-017-9521-5

Kulkarni, R., & Rajamani, A. (2017). *Here's how you should customize learning*. Retrieved from People matters: https://www.peoplematters.in/article/create-the-future/heres-how-you-should-customize-learning-16898

Kulkarni, V. (2010, October). Raising family is a good practice. In *Proceedings of the 2nd International Workshop on Feature-Oriented Software Development* (pp. 72-79). ACM. 10.1145/1868688.1868699

Kulkarni, V. (2016, May). Model driven development of business applications: a practitioner's perspective. In *Proceedings of the 38th International Conference on Software Engineering Companion* (pp. 260-269). ACM. 10.1145/2889160.2889251

Kulkarni, V. (2019). Towards an Adaptive Enterprise. In *Proceedings of the 12th Innovations on Software Engineering Conference* (p. 31). ACM.

Kulkarni, V., Barat, S., Clark, T., & Barn, B. (2015a). Toward overcoming accidental complexity in organisational decision-making. In *Model Driven Engineering Languages and Systems* (pp. 368–377). MODELS.

Kulkarni, V., Barat, S., Clark, T., & Barn, B. (2015b). Using simulation to address intrinsic complexity in multi-modelling of enterprises for decision making. In *Proceedings of the Conference on Summer Computer Simulation*, (pp. 1–11). Society for Computer Simulation International.

Kulkarni, V., Barat, S., Clark, T., & Barn, B. (2017). Supporting Organisational Decision Making in Presence of Uncertainty. *The European Symposium on Modeling and Simulation (EMSS 2017)*, Barcelona, Spain.

Kulkarni, V., Barat, S., & Roychoudhury, S. (2012, September). Towards business application product lines. In *International Conference on Model Driven Engineering Languages and Systems* (pp. 285-301). Springer. 10.1007/978-3-642-33666-9_19

Kulkarni, V., & Reddy, S. (2003). Separation of concerns in model-driven development. *IEEE Software*, *20*(5), 64–69. doi:10.1109/MS.2003.1231154

Kulkarni, V., & Reddy, S. (2004). Model-driven development of enterprise applications. In *Proc. International Conference on the Unified Modeling Language* (pp. 118-128). Springer.

Kulkarni, V., & Reddy, S. (2004, October). Model-driven development of enterprise applications. In *International Conference on the Unified Modeling Language* (pp. 118-128). Springer.

Kumar, S., Duggirala, M., Hayatnagarkar, H., & Balaraman, V. (2017). Understanding impact of supervisory support on work outcomes using agent based simulation. *Modelling Symposium, ISEC*.

Langefors, B. (1966). *Theoretical Analysis of Information Systems*. Lund, Sweden: Studentlitteratur.

Langner, R. (2011). Stuxnet: Dissecting a cyberwarfare weapon. *IEEE Security and Privacy*, *9*(3), 49–51. doi:10.1109/MSP.2011.67

Lankhorst, M. M., Torre, L. d., Proper, H. A., Arbab, F., Boer, F. S. d., & Bonsangue, M. (2017b). Foundations. Academic Press.

Lankhorst, M. M., Hoppenbrouwers, S. J. B. A., Jonkers, H., Proper, H. A., Torre, L. d., Arbab, F., ... Wieringa, R. J. (2017a). *Enterprise Architecture at Work - Modelling, Communication and Analysis* (4th ed.). Heidelberg, Germany: Springer.

Lankhorst, M. M., Janssen, W. P. M., Proper, H. A., Steen, M. W. A., Zoet, M. M., Molnar, W. A., ... Linden, D. J. T. d. (2012). *Agile Service Development: Combining Adaptive Methods and Flexible Solutions*. Heidelberg, Germany: Springer. doi:10.1007/978-3-642-28188-4

Lankhorst, M. M., Torre, L. d., Proper, H. A., Arbab, F., & Steen, M. W. A. (2017c). *Viewpoints and visualisation*. doi:10.1007/978-3-662-53933-0_8

Laszka, A., Zhao, M., & Grossklags, J. (2016). *Banishing Misaligned Incentives for Validating Reports in Bugbounty Platforms*. Computer Security-ESORICS.

Latour, B. (1999). On recalling ANT. *The Sociological Review*, *47*(S1), 15–25. doi:10.1111/j.1467-954X.1999.tb03480.x

Lee, H. L., Padmanabhan, V., & Whang, S. (1997). Information distortion in a supply chain: The bullwhip effect. *Management Science*, *43*(4), 546-558.

Lee, C. K. H., Choy, K. L., & Chan, Y. N. (2014). A knowledge-based ingredient formulation system for chemical product development in the personal care industry. *Computers & Chemical Engineering*, *65*, 40–53. doi:10.1016/j. compchemeng.2014.03.004

Lee, I. (Ed.). (2017). *The Internet of Things in the Modern Business Environment*. IGI Global. doi:10.4018/978-1-5225-2104-4

Leon, A. D. (2015). *Impacts of Malicious Cyber Activities* (Unpublished Doctoral Dissertation). Johns Hopkins University.

Leone, N., Pfeifer, G., Faber, W., Eiter, T., Gottlob, G., Perri, S., & Scarcello, F. (2006). The DLV system for knowledge representation and reasoning. *ACM Transactions on Computational Logic*, *7*(3), 499–562. doi:10.1145/1149114.1149117

Levina, N., & Vaast, E. (2005). The Emergence of Boundary Spanning Competence in Practice: Implications for Implementation and Use of Information Systems. *Management Information Systems Quarterly*, *29*(2), 335–363. doi:10.2307/25148682

Levitt, B., & March, J. G. (1988). Organizational learning. *Annual Review of Sociology*, *14*(1), 319–338. doi:10.1146/annurev.so.14.080188.001535

Lévy, F., & Nazarenko, A. (2013, July). Formalization of natural language regulations through SBVR structured english. In *International Workshop on Rules and Rule Markup Languages for the Semantic Web* (pp. 19-33). Springer. 10.1007/978-3-642-39617-5_5

Lieberman, H. (1981). *A preview of ACT 1*. MIT Artificial Intelligence Laboratory, A.I. Memo No. 625.

Lieder, M., & Rashid, A. (2016). Towards circular economy implementation: A comprehensive review in context of manufacturing industry. *Journal of Cleaner Production*, *115*, 36–51. doi:10.1016/j.jclepro.2015.12.042

LifeDojo: Behaviour Change Solution. (n.d.). Retrieved from LifeDojo: https://www.lifedojo.com/programs

Lifschitz, V. (2008). What is answer set programming? In *Proceedings of the Twenty-Third AAAI Conference on Artificial Intelligence, AAAI 2008* (pp. 1594-1597). Chicago, IL: AAAI Press.

Li, I., Dey, A., & Forlizzi, J. (2010). *A stage-based model of personal informatics systems*. CHI. doi:10.1145/1753326.1753409

Li, L. P., Juric, B., & Brodie, R. J. (2017). Dynamic multi-actor engagement in networks: The case of United Breaks Guitars. *Journal of Service Theory and Practice*, *27*(4), 738–760. doi:10.1108/JSTP-04-2016-0066

Lillehagen, F., & Krogstie, J. (2010). *Active Knowledge Modeling of Enterprises*. Heidelberg, Germany: Springer.

Lillicrap, T. P., Hunt, J. J., Pritzel, A., Heess, N., Erez, T., Tassa, Y., Silver, D., and Wierstra, D. (2015). *Continuous control with deep reinforcement learning*. CoRR, abs/1509.02971.

Lim, S. J., Shanton, C., Sean, M., & Atif, A. (2009). *Exploring the Relationship between Organizational Culture and Information security culture. Australian Information Security Management*. Edith Cowan University.

Lindros, K., & Tittel, E. (2016). *What is Cyber Insurance and Why You Need It*. Retrieved October 3, 2019, from https://www.cio.com/article/3065655/what-is-cyber-insurance-and-why-you-need-it.html

Lipp, M., Schwarz, M., Gruss, D., Prescher, T., Haas, W., Mangard, S., . . . Hamburg, M. (2018). *Meltdown*. arXiv preprint arXiv:1801.01207

LitanA. (2018, April 5). Retrieved from https://blogs.gartner.com/avivah-litan/2018/04/05/insider-threat-detection-replaces-dying-dlp/

Littman, M. L. (1994). Markov games as a framework for multi-agent reinforcement learning. In *Machine learning proceedings 1994* (pp. 157–163). Elsevier. doi:10.1016/B978-1-55860-335-6.50027-1

Liu, Y., Slotine, J., & Barabasi, A. (2011). Controllability of complex networks. *Nature*, *473*(7346), 167–173. doi:10.1038/nature10011 PMID:21562557

Live Work Studio. (2013). *The Changing Nature of Service & Experience Design.* Retrieved from Live Work Studio: https://www.liveworkstudio.com/blog/the-changing-nature-of-service-experience-design/

Li, Y., McCune, J., Newsome, J., Perrig, A., Baker, B., & Drewry, W. (2014). Minibox: A Two-way Sandbox for x86 Native Code. *USENIX Annual Technical Conference*, 409-420.

Lobo, S., Sharma, S., Hirom, U., Mahamuni, R., & Khambete, P. (2019). *Extending Service Blueprint for New Age Services.* doi:10.1007/978-981-13-5977-4_68

Loh, C. S., Sheng, Y., & Ifenthaler, D. (2015). *Serious Games Analytics - Methodologies for Performance Measurement, Assessment, and Improvement.* doi:10.1007/978-3-319-05834-4

Loucopoulos, P., Stratigaki, C., Danesh, M. H., Bravos, G., Anagnostopoulos, D., & Dimitrakopoulos, G. (2015). Enterprise capability modeling: concepts, method, and application. In *Enterprise Systems (ES), 2015 International Conference on*, (pp. 66–77). IEEE. 10.1109/ES.2015.14

Lusch, R. F., & Nambisan, S. (2015). Service Innovation: A Service-Dominant Logic Perspective. *Management Information Systems Quarterly*, *39*(1), 155–175. doi:10.25300/MISQ/2015/39.1.07

Lusthaus, J. (2019). Beneath the Dark Web: Excavating the Layers of Cybercrime's Underground Economy. *IEEE European Symposium on Security and Privacy Workshops*, 474-480. 10.1109/EuroSPW.2019.00059

Lu, Y., Liu, C., Kevin, I., Wang, K., Huang, H., & Xu, X. (2020). Digital Twin-driven smart manufacturing: Connotation, reference model, applications and research issues. *Robotics and Computer-integrated Manufacturing*, *61*, 101837. doi:10.1016/j.rcim.2019.101837

Lyons, T. F. (1971). Role clarity, need for clarity, satisfaction, tension, and withdrawal. *Organizational Behavior and Human Performance*, *6*(1), 99–110. doi:10.1016/0030-5073(71)90007-9

Madden, M., & Rainie, L. (2015). *Americans' Attitudes About Privacy, Security and Surveillance.* Available at: https://www.pewinternet.org/2015/05/20/americans-attitudes-about-privacy-security-and-surveillance/

Magalhães, R., & Proper, H. A. (2017). Model-enabled Design and Engineering of Organisations. *Organisational Design and Enterprise Engineeering*, *1*(1), 1–12. doi:10.100741251-016-0005-9

Mahamuni, R. H., Khambete, P., & Mokashi-Punekar, R. (2019). *Behaviour Progression Framework for Designing Sustained Behaviour Change. In Research into Design for a Connected World* (pp. 39–50). Bangalore, India: Springer. doi:10.1007/978-981-13-5974-3_4

Mahr, B. (2011). On the epistemology of models. In G. Abel & J. Conant (Eds.), *Rethinking Epistemology* (pp. 1–301). De Gruyter. doi:10.1515/9783110253573.301

Maillart, T., Zhao, M., Grossklags, J., & Chuang, J. (2016). Given Enough Eyeballs, All Bugs are Shallow? Revisiting Eric Raymond with Bug Bounty Programs. *Journal of Cybersecurity*, *3*(2), 81–90. doi:10.1093/cybsec/tyx008

Malavolta, I., Lago, P., Muccini, H., Pelliccione, P., & Tang, A. (2012). What industry needs from architectural languages: A survey. *IEEE Transactions on Software Engineering*, *39*(6), 869–891. doi:10.1109/TSE.2012.74

Manca, A., Lafferty, N., Fioratou, E., Smithies, A., & Hothersall, E. (2014, October). Integrating Twitter into an undergraduate medical curriculum: Lessons for the future. In *European Conference on e-Learning* (p. 330). Academic Conferences International Limited.

Manca, A., & Whitworth, A. (2018). Social Media and Workplace Practices in Higher Education Institutions: A Review. *The Journal of Social Media in Society, 7*(1), 151–183.

Mann, I. (2017). *Hacking the Human: Social Engineering Techniques and Security Countermeasures.* Routledge. doi:10.4324/9781351156882

Maquil, V., Zephir, O., & Ras, E. (2012). Creating Metaphors for Tangible User Interfaces in Collaborative Urban Planning: Questions for Designers and Developers. *Proceedings of COOP* 2012. 10.1007/978-1-4471-4093-1_10

Marcus, B., & Heinz, S. (2004). Antecedents of Counterproductive Behavior at Work: A General Perspective. *The Journal of Applied Psychology, 89*(4), 647–660. doi:10.1037/0021-9010.89.4.647 PMID:15327351

Martín, M., & Martínez, A. (2013). A methodology for simultaneous process and product design in the formulated consumer products industry: The case study of the detergent business. *Chemical Engineering Research & Design, 91*(5), 795–809. doi:10.1016/j.cherd.2012.08.012

Maslach. (1982). *Burnout: The Cost of Caring.* Englewood Cliffs, NJ: Prentice-Hall.

Maslach, C., Schaufeli, W. B., & Leiter, M. P. (2001). ob burnout. *Annual Review of Psychology, 52*(1), 397–422. doi:10.1146/annurev.psych.52.1.397 PMID:11148311

Masri, K., Parker, D., & Gemino, A. (2008). Using Iconic Graphics in En- tity Relationship Diagrams: The Impact on Understanding. *Journal of Database Management, 19*(3), 22–41. doi:10.4018/jdm.2008070102

Matt, C., Hess, T., & Benlian, A. (2015). Digital Transformation Strategies. *Business & Information Systems Engineering, 57*(5), 339–343. doi:10.100712599-015-0401-5

Matthes, F., Neubert, C., & Steinhoff, A. (2011). Hybrid Wikis: Empowering Users to Collaboratively Structure Information. *6th International Conference on Software and Data Technologies (ICSOFT)*, 250-259.

Mattoni, B., Pagliaro, F., Corona, G., Ponzo, V., Bisegna, F., Gugliermetti, F., & Quintero-Núñez, M. (2016, June). A matrix approach to identify and choose efficient strategies to develop the Smart Campus. In *Environment and Electrical Engineering (EEEIC), 2016 IEEE 16th International Conference on* (pp. 1-6). IEEE. 10.1109/EEEIC.2016.7555571

Mayer, N., Barafort, B., Picard, M., & Cortina, S. (2015). An ISO Compliant and Integrated Model for IT GRC (Governance, Risk Management and Compliance). In Systems, Software and Services Process Improvement, volume 543 of Communications in Computer and Information Science, (pp. 87-99). Springer.

Mayne, D. Q., Rawlings, J. B., Rao, C. V., & Scokaert, P. O. (2000). Constrained model predictive control: Stability and optimality. *Automatica, 36*(6), 789–814. doi:10.1016/S0005-1098(99)00214-9

Ma, Z., Reynolds, J., Dickinson, J., Wang, K., Judd, T., Barnes, J. D., ... Bailey, M. (2019). The Impact of Secure Transport Protocols on Phishing Efficacy. *USENIX Workshop on Cyber Security Experimentation and Test.*

Mc Kinsey. (2018). *Insider threat: The human element of cyberrisk.* Retrieved December 2019, from https://www.mckinsey.com/business-functions/risk/our-insights/insider-threat-the-human-element-of-cyberrisk

McAfee. (2019). *Cloud-native: The Infrastructure-as-a-service Adoption and Risk.* Retrieved October 3, 2019, from https://cloudsecurity.mcafee.com/cloud/en-us/forms/white-papers/wp-cloud-adoption-risk-report-iaas.html

McDowell, D., Panchal, J., Choi, H.-J., Seepersad, C., Allen, J., & Mistree, F. (2010). *Integrated Design of Multi-Scale, Multifunctional Materials and Products.* Elsevier Inc.

McKinsey. (2019). *Driving impact at scale from automation and AI*. Retrieved from: https://www.mckinsey.com/~/media/McKinsey/Business%20Functions/McKinsey%20Digital/Our%20Insights/Driving%20impact%20at%20scale%20from%20automation%20and%20AI/Driving-impact-at-scale-from-automation-and-AI.ashx

Mcmillan, C. J. (1980). Qualitative models of organisational decision-making. *Journal of General Management, 5*(4), 22–39. doi:10.1177/030630708000500402

Meadows, D., & Wright, D. (2008). *Thinking in systems: A primer*. Chelsea Green Publishing.

Meadows, D. H., & Wright, D. (2008). *Thinking in systems: A primer*. Chelsea Green Publishing.

Meckstroth, D. J. (2016). *The Manufacturing Value Chain Is Much Bigger Than You Think!* (Technical Report). Retrieved from Manufacturers Alliance for Productivity and Innovation Foundation website: https://mapifoundation.org/s/PA-165_web_0.pdf

Meister, J. (2016). Consumerization Of HR: 10 Trends Companies Will Follow In 2016. *Forbes*. Retrieved from https://www.forbes.com/sites/jeannemeister/2016/01/07/consumerization-of-hr-10-trends-innovative-companies-will-follow-in-2016/#272dd7d06b5a

Meister, J. (2018, Jan 11). AI plus human intelligence is the future of work. *Forbes.com*. Retrieved from https://www.forbes.com/sites/jeannemeister/2018/01/11/ai-plus-human-intelligence-is-the-future-of-work/#3ccb9db62bba

Mell, P., & Grance, T. (2009). The NIST definition of cloud computing. *National Institute of Standards and Technology, 53*(6), 50.

Mendling, J. (2008). Event-driven process chains (epc). In *Metrics for process models* (pp. 17–57). Berlin: Springer. doi:10.1007/978-3-540-89224-3_2

Mendling, J., Weber, I., Aalst, W. M. P., Brocke, J., Cabanillas, C., Daniel, F., ... Zhu, L. (2018). Blockchains for Business Process Management - Challenges and Opportunities. *ACM Transactions on Management Information Systems, 9*(1), 1–16. doi:10.1145/3183367

Mental Health America. (2019). *Depression In The Workplace*. Retrieved from Depression In The Workplace: http://www.mentalhealthamerica.net/conditions/depression-workplace#i

Meriam-Webster. (2003). *Meriam-Webster Online*. Collegiate Dictionary.

Messerschmidt, J. E. (2013). Hackback: Permitting Retaliatory Hacking by Non-state Actors as Proportionate Countermeasures to Transboundary Cyberharm. *Colum. J. Transnat'l L., 52*, 275.

Michalski, R. S. (1993). Inferential theory of learning as a conceptual basis for multi strategy learning. *Machine Learning, 11*(2-3), 111–151. doi:10.1007/BF00993074

Michalun, M. V., & DiNardo, J. C. (2014). *Skin care and cosmetic ingredients dictionary*. Cengage Learning.

Miller, M. S., Tribble, E. D., & Shapiro, J. (2005). Concurrency among strangers. In *International Symposium on Trustworthy Global Computing*, (pp. 195–229). Springer. 10.1007/11580850_12

Mirkin, B. M., & Gutman, P. (2003). Decentralized output-feedback MRAC of linear state delay systems. *IEEE Transactions on Automatic Control, 48*(9), 1613–1619. doi:10.1109/TAC.2003.817000

Mittelstadt, Allo, Taddeo, Wachter, & Floridi. (2016). The ethics of algorithms: Mapping the debate. Big Data & Society, 3(2).

MLEVEL. (2019). *The training optimization platform*. Retrieved from MLEVEL: http://www.mlevel.com/platform/

Mnih, V., Kavukcuoglu, K., Silver, D., Rusu, A. A., Veness, J., Bellemare, M. G., & ... . (2015). Human-level control through deep RL. *Nature*, *518*(7540), 529. doi:10.1038/nature14236 PMID:25719670

Moody, D. L. (2009). The "Physics" of Notations: Toward a Scientific Basis for Constructing Visual Notations in Software Engineering. *IEEE Transactions on Software Engineering*, *35*(6), 756–779. doi:10.1109/TSE.2009.67

Moody, D., Sindre, G., Brasethvik, T., & Solvberg, A. (2003). Evaluating the quality of information models: empirical testing of a conceptual model quality framework. In *Proceedings of the 25th international conference on software engineering*, (pp. 295–305). IEEE Computer Society. 10.1109/ICSE.2003.1201209

Moore, A. P., Perl, S. J., Cowley, J., Collins, M. L., Cassidy, T. M., & VanHoudnos, N. (2016). *The Critical Role of Positive Incentives for Reducing Insider Threats*. Software Engineering Institute, Carnegie Mellon University.

Morris, C. (1946). *Signs, Language and Behaviour*. Englewood Cliffs, NJ: Prentice Hall.

Mount, M., & Martinez, M. G. (2014). Social media: A tool for open innovation. *California Management Review*, *56*(4), 124–143. doi:10.1525/cmr.2014.56.4.124

Myrbakken, H., & Colomo-Palacios, R. (2017). Devsecops: A Multivocal Literature Review. *International Conference on Software Process Improvement and Capability Determination*, 17-29. 10.1007/978-3-319-67383-7_2

Mysore, S., Kim, E., Strubell, E., Liu, A., Chang, H. S., Kompella, S., . . . Olivetti, E. (2017). *Automatically extracting action graphs from materials science synthesis procedures*. arXiv preprint arXiv:1711.06872

Myyry, L., Siponen, M., Pahnila, S., Vartiainen, T., & Vance, A. (2009). What levels of moral reasoning and values explain adherence to information security rules? An empirical study. *European Journal of Information Systems*, *18*(2), 126–139. doi:10.1057/ejis.2009.10

Nabukenya, J., Bommel, P. v., & Proper, H. A. (2009). A theory-driven design approach to collaborative policy making processes. In *42st Hawaii International International Conference on Systems Science (HICSS-42 2009), Proceedings (CD-ROM and online), 5-8 January 2009, Waikoloa, Big Island, HI, USA*, (pp. 1-10). IEEE Computer Society.

Nabukenya, J., Bommel, P., Proper, H. A., & Vreede, G. J. (2011). An Evaluation Instrument for Collaborative Processes: Application to Organizational Policy-Making. *Group Decision and Negotiation*, *20*(4), 465–488. doi:10.100710726-009-9177-7

Nagabandi, A., Kahn, G., Fearing, R. S., & Levine, S. (2018). Neural network dynamics for model-based deep RL with model-free fine-tuning. *Robotics and Automation (ICRA), 2018 International Conference on*, 7559-7566.

Nagel, K. S. (1997). *TRANSIMS traffic flow characteristics*. arXiv preprint adap-org/9710003

Nagel, K., Stretz, P., Pieck, M., Donnelly, R., Leckey, S., & Barrett, C. (1998). Transim Report Series: Transims traffic flow characteristics. Academic Press.

Nahorney, B. (2017). *ISTR Email Threats 2017*. An ISTR Special Report.

Nair, A., McGrew, B., Andrychowicz, M., Zaremba, W., & Abbeel, P. (2018). Overcoming exploration in reinforcement learning with demonstrations. *Robotics and Automation (ICRA), 2018 International Conference on*, 6292-6299. 10.1109/ICRA.2018.8463162

Nakakawa, A., Bommel, P., & Proper, H. A. (2011). Definition and validation of requirements for collaborative decision-making in enterprise architecture creation. *International Journal of Cooperative Information Systems*, *20*(1), 83–136. doi:10.1142/S021884301100216X

Nakakawa, A., Bommel, P., Proper, H. A., & Mulder, J. B. F. (2018). A situational method for creating shared understanding on requirements for an enterprise architecture. *International Journal of Cooperative Information Systems*, *27*(4), 1850010. doi:10.1142/S0218843018500107

Narendra, K., & Lin, Y. (1980). Stable discrete adaptive control. *IEEE Transactions on Automatic Control*, *25*(3), 456–461. doi:10.1109/TAC.1980.1102365

National Academies of Sciences. (2017). Foundational Cybersecurity Research: Improving Science, Engineering, and Institutions. Washington, DC: The National Academies Press.

National Intelligence Council. (2008). *Disruptive civil technologies: Six technologies with potential impacts on us interests out to 2025* (Technical Report). Retrieved from https://fas.org/irp/nic/disruptive.pdf

National Security Telecommunications Advisory Committee. (2014). *Final NSTAC Internet of Things Report*. Retrieved from https://www.cisa.gov/publication/2014-nstac-publications

Negroponte, N. (1996). *Being Digital*. New York: Vintage Books.

Neirotti, P., De Marco, A., Cagliano, A. C., Mangano, G., & Scorrano, F. (2014). Current trends in Smart City initiatives: Some stylised facts. *Cities (London, England)*, *38*, 25–36. doi:10.1016/j.cities.2013.12.010

Nelson, H. J., Poels, G., Genero, M., & Piattini, M. (2012). A conceptual modeling quality framework. *Software Quality Journal*, *20*(1), 201–228. doi:10.100711219-011-9136-9

Neumayr, B., Schrefl, M., & Thalheim, B. (2011). Modeling Techniques For Multi-Level Abstraction. In R. Kaschek & L. Delcambre (Eds.), Lecture Notes In Computer Science: Vol. 6520. *The Evolution Of Conceptual Modeling* (pp. 68–92). Springer. doi:10.1007/978-3-642-17505-3_4

Nicolaidou, I. L., & Georgiades, C. (2017). The GDPR: New Horizons. In *EU Internet Law*. Springer. doi:10.1007/978-3-319-64955-9_1

Nielsen, L. (2013). The Encyclopedia of Human-Computer Interaction (2nd ed.). Academic Press.

Nijssen, S. (2007). *SBVR: Semantics for business. Business Rules Journal*.

NIMHANS. (2016). *Summary-National Mental Health Survey-NIMHANS*. Retrieved from Summary-National Mental Health Survey-NIMHANS: http://indianmhs.nimhans.ac.in/Docs/Summary.pdf

NIST. (2018). *Cyber Ranges*. Retrieved October 3, 2019, from https://www.nist.gov/sites/default/files/documents/2018/02/13/cyber ranges.pdf

NIST. (2019). *Post-Quantum Cryptography – Project Overview*. Retrieved December 5, 2019, from https://csrc.nist.gov/projects/post-quantum-cryptography/

Nobles, C. (2018). Botching Human Factors in Cybersecurity in Business Organizations. *HOLISTICA-Journal of Business and Public Administration*, *9*(3), 71–88. doi:10.2478/hjbpa-2018-0024

Nordbotten, J. C., & Crosby, M. E. (1999). The effect of graphic style on data model interpretation. *Information Systems Journal*, *9*(2), 139–155. doi:10.1046/j.1365-2575.1999.00052.x

North, J., Macal, C., Aubin, J., Thimmapuram, P., Bragen, M., Hahn, J., ... Hampton, D. (2010). Multiscale Agent Based Consumer Market Modeling. *Complexity*, *15*(5), 37–47.

Nussbaum, R. (1983). Some remarks on a conjecture in parameter adaptive control. *Systems & Control Letters*, *3*(5), 243–246. doi:10.1016/0167-6911(83)90021-X

Object Management Group. (2006). *Meta Object Facility (Mof) Core Specification: Version 2.0*. Author.

Object Management Group. (2010). *Meta Object Facility 2.0*. Author.

Object Management Group. (2010). *Unified Modeling Language - Superstructure. Technical Report version 2.4.1*. OMG.

Object Management Group. (2015). *SBVR Specification V1.3*. Retrieved from https://www.omg.org/spec/SBVR/1.3

Ogata, K., & Yang, Y. (2002). *Modern control engineering* (Vol. 4). Prentice Hall.

Ogden, C. K., & Richards, I. A. (1923). *The Meaning of Meaning - A Study of the Influence of Language upon Thought and of the Science of Symbolism*. Oxford, UK: Magdalene College, University of Cambridge.

OMG. (2003). *MDA Guide v1.0.1. Technical Report omg/2003-06-01*. Needham, MA: Object Management Group.

Omidshafiei, S., Pazis, J., Amato, C., How, J. P., & Vian, J. (2017). Deep decentralized multi-task multi-agent reinforcement learning under partial observability. *Proceedings of the 34th International Conference on Machine Learning, 70*, 2681-2690.

Op 't Land, M., & Proper, H. A. (2007). Impact of principles on enterprise engineering. In *Proceedings of the Fifteenth European Conference on Information Systems, ECIS 2007, St. Gallen, Switzerland*, 2007, (pp. 1965-1976). University of St. Gallen.

Op 't Land, M., Proper, H. A., Waage, M., Cloo, J., & Steghuis, C. (2008). *Enterprise Architecture - Creating Value by Informed Governance*. Heidelberg, Germany: Springer.

Oppl, S., & Stary, C. (2009). Tabletop concept mapping. In *Proceedings of the 3rd International Conference on Tangible and Embedded Interaction*, (pp. 275-282). ACM.

Orcutt, M. (2018). *How secure is blockchain really?* Retrieved December 5, 2019, from https://www.technologyreview.com/s/610836/how-secure-is-blockchain-really/

Ornes, S. (2016). Core Concept: The Internet of Things and the Explosion of Interconnectivity. *National Academy of Sciences, 113*(40), 11059-11060.

Osterwalder, A., & Pigneur, Y. (2010). *Business Model Generation: A Handbook For Visionaries, Game Changers, And Challengers* [1 Sound Disc]. Willowbrook, IL: Audio-Tech Business Book Summaries.

Osterwalder, A., & Pigneur, Y. (2009). *Business Model Generation: A Handbook for Visionaries, Game Changers, and Challengers*. Amsterdam, The Netherlands: Self Published.

Osterwalder, A., Pigneur, Y., Bernarda, G., & Smith, A. (2015). *Value Proposition Design How to Create Products and Services Customers Want*. Hoboken, NJ: Wiley.

Östling, J. (2018). *Humboldt and the modern German university: An intellectual history*. Lund University Press.

OSTP. (2011). Materials genome initiative for global competitiveness. National Science and Technology Council. Retrieved from https://www.whitehouse.gov/sites/default/files/microsites/ostp/materials_genome_initiative-final.pdf

Overbeek, S., Frank, U., & Köhling, C. A. (2015). A Language For Multi-Perspective Goal Modelling: Challenges, Requirements And Solutions. *Computer Standards & Interfaces, 38*, 1–16. doi:10.1016/j.csi.2014.08.001

Owoc, M., & Marciniak, K. (2013, September). Knowledge management as foundation of smart university. In *Computer Science and Information Systems (FedCSIS), 2013 Federated Conference on* (pp. 1267-1272). IEEE.

Pahnila, S., Siponen, M., & Mahmood, A. (2007). Employees' Behavior Towards IS Security Policy Compliance. *40th Hawaii International Conference on System Sciences (HICSS 07)*. 10.1109/HICSS.2007.206

Palvia, P. C., Brown, W. S., Brown, W., & Palvia, P. (2015). Are Mobile Devices Threatening Your Work-Life Balance? *International Journal of Mobile Communications, 13*(3).

Paranjape, A. A., & Chung, S. (2018). Robust adaptive boundary control of semilinear PDE systems using a dyadic controller. *International Journal of Robust and Nonlinear Control, 28*(8), 3174–3188. doi:10.1002/rnc.4075

Paranjape, A., & Chung, S. (2016). Sub-optimal boundary control of semilinear PDEs using a dyadic perturbation observer. *Proc. 55th IEEE Conference on Decision and Control*, 1382-1387. 10.1109/CDC.2016.7798459

Park, H. I., Monnot, M. J., Jacob, A. C., & Wagner, S. H. (2011). Moderators of the relationship between person-job fit and subjective well-being among Asian employees. *International Journal of Stress Management, 67*.

Paschek, D., Luminosu, C., & Draghici, A. (2017). Automated business process management - In times of digital transformation using machine learning or artificial intelligence. *MATEC Web of Conferences, 121*.

Passera, S., Kärkkäinen, H., & Maila, R. (2012). *When, how, why prototyping? A practical framework for service development*. Academic Press.

Peirce, C. S. (1969). *Volumes I and II - Principles of Philosophy and Elements of Logic. Collected Papers of C. S. Peirce*. Harvard University Press.

Perrotta, C., & Williamson, B. (2018). The social life of Learning Analytics: Cluster analysis and the 'performance'of algorithmic education. *Learning, Media and Technology, 43*(1), 3–16. doi:10.1080/17439884.2016.1182927

Peter, M., Nina, G., Ronja, M., Melanie, V., & Vogt, J. (2017). Productivity vs security: Mitigating conflicting goals in organizations. *Information & Computer Security, 25*(2), 137–151. doi:10.1108/ICS-03-2017-0014

Pew. (2017). *Mobile fact sheet*. Retrieved January, 2017 from Pew Research Center https://www.pewinternet.org/fact-sheet/mobile/

Pohl, K., Böckle, G., & van Der Linden, F. J. (2005). *Software product line engineering: foundations, principles and techniques*. Springer Science & Business Media. doi:10.1007/3-540-28901-1

Pollock, T., Allison, J. E., Backman, D., Boyce, M. C., Gersh, M., Holm, E., & Woodward, C. (2008). *Integrated computational materials engineering: a transformational discipline for improved competitiveness and national security*. National Academies Press.

Ponemon Institute, IBM. (2019). *Cost of a data breach*. Ponemon Institute, IBM.

Porter, M. E. (2001). The Value Chain And Competitive Advantage. In D. Barnes (Ed.), *Understanding Business Behaviour. Understanding Business: Processes* (pp. 50–66). London: Routledge U.A.

Powell, W. B. (2007). *Approximate Dynamic Programming: Solving the curses of dimensionality* (Vol. 703). John Wiley & Sons. doi:10.1002/9780470182963

Powell, W. B. (2012). *AI, or and control theory: A rosetta stone for stochastic optimization*. Princeton University.

Preskill, J. (2018). Quantum Computing in the NISQ era and beyond. *Quantum, 2*, 79. doi:10.22331/q-2018-08-06-79

Price Waterhouse Coopers. (2018). Workforce of the future: The competing forces shaping 2030. *Price Waterhouse Coopers*. Retrieved from https://www.pwc.com/gx/en/services/people-organisation/publications/workforce-of-the-future.html

Prinsloo & Rowe. (2015). *Ethical considerations in using student data in an era of big data.* http://repository.uwc.ac.za/handle/10566/2872

Probst, L., Lefebvre, V., Martinez-Diaz, C., Bohn, N., Klitou, D., Conrads, J., & CARSA. (2018). *Digital Transformation Scoreboard 2018: EU businesses go digital: Opportunities, outcomes and uptake.* European Commission Report.

Proper, H. A. (2014). Enterprise architecture: Informed steering of enterprises in motion. In *Enterprise Information Systems - 15th International Conference, ICEIS 2013, Angers, France, July 4-7, 2013, Revised Selected Papers, volume 190 of Lecture Notes in Business Information Processing,* (pp. 16-34). Springer.

Proper, H. A., & Op 't Land, M. (2010). Lines in the Water - The Line of Reasoning in an Enterprise Engineering Case Study from the Public Sector. In *Practice-Driven Research on Enterprise Transformation - Second Working Conference, PRET 2010, Delft, The Netherlands, November 11, 2010. Proceedings, volume 69 of Lecture Notes in Business Information Processing,* (pp. 193-216). Delft, The Netherlands: Springer.

Proper, H. A., Halpin, T. A., & Krogstie, J. (Eds.). (2007). *Proceedings of the 12th Workshop on Exploring Modeling Methods for Systems Analysis and Design (EMMSAD 2007), held in conjunction with the 19th Conference on Advanced Information Systems (CAiSE 2007), Trondheim, Norway.* CEUR-WS.org.

Proper, H. A., Bjeković, M., Gils, B. v., & de Kinderen, S. (2018a). Enterprise architecture modelling - purpose, requirements and language. In *Proceedings of the 13th Workshop on Trends in Enterprise Architecture (TEAR 2018).* IEEE. 10.1109/EDOCW.2018.00031

Proper, H. A., Hoppenbrouwers, S. J. B. A., & Veldhuijzen van Zanten, G. E. (2017). *Communication of enterprise architectures.* doi:10.1007/978-3-662-53933-0_4

Proper, H. A., & Lankhorst, M. M. (2014). Enterprise architecture - towards essential sensemaking. *Enterprise Modelling and Information Systems Architectures, 9*(1), 5–21. doi:10.100740786-014-0002-7

Proper, H. A., Winter, R., Aier, S., & de Kinderen, S. (Eds.). (2018b). *Architectural Coordination of Enterprise Transformation.* Heidelberg, Germany: Springer.

Prosser, W., P, J., Emanuelle, A., Brown, S., Matsinhe, G., Dekoun, M., & Lee, B. (2017). System redesign of the immunization supply chain: Experiences from Benin and Mozambique. *Vaccine, 35*(17), 2162-2166.

Purchase, H. C., Carrington, D., & Allder, J.-A. (2002). Empirical Evaluation of Aesthetics-based Graph Layout. *Empirical Software Engineering, 7*(3), 233–255. doi:10.1023/A:1016344215610

PWC. (2016). *Industry 4.0: Building the digital enterprise.* PWC. Retrieved Feb 04, 2019, from https://www.pwc.com/gx/en/industries/industries-4.0/landing-page/industry-4.0-building-your-digital-enterprise-april-2016.pdf

PWC. (2019). *Insurance 2020 & Beyond: Reaping the Dividends of Cyber Resilience.* Retrieved October 3, 2019, from https://www.pwc.com/gx/en/industries/financial-services/publications/insurance-2020-cyber.html

Qualtrics. (2019). *Employee Experience.* Retrieved from www.qualtrics.com: https://www.qualtrics.com/blog/employee-experience-stats/

Quantified Self. (n.d.). Retrieved from http://quantifiedself.com

Racz, N., Weippl, E., & Bonazzi, R. (2011, July). IT governance, risk & compliance (GRC) status quo and integration: an explorative industry case study. In *2011 IEEE World Congress on Services* (pp. 429-436). IEEE. 10.1109/SERVICES.2011.78

Rajendran, V. (2017). *Location Based Services: Expected Trends and Technological Advancements – Geo awesomeness*. Retrieved from https://geoawesomeness.com/expected-trends-technological-advancements-location-based-services/

Ralyté, J., Brinkkemper, S., & Henderson-Sellers, B. (2007). Situational Method Engineering: Fundamentals And Experiences. In *Proceedings Of The Ifip Wg 8.1 Working Conference, 12-14 September 2007, Geneva, Switzerland. Ifip - The International Federation For Information Processing* (Vol. 244). New York: Springer.

Ramanujan, D., Bernstein, W. Z., Chandrasegaran, S. K., & Ramani, K. (2017). Visual analytics tools for sustainable lifecycle design: Current status, challenges, and future opportunities. *Journal of Mechanical Design*, *139*(11), 111415. doi:10.1115/1.4037479 PMID:29170612

Ramprasad, R., Batra, R., Pilania, G., Mannodi-Kanakkithodi, A., & Kim, C. (2017). Machine learning in materials informatics: Recent applications. *NPJ Computational Materials*, *3*. doi:10.103841524-017-0056-5

Ramzan, Z. (2010). Phishing Attacks and Countermeasures. In Handbook of Information and Communication Security (pp. 433-448). Academic Press.

Rangoni, Y., Maquil, V., Tobias, E., & Ras, E. (2014). Implementing widgets using sifteo cubes for visual modelling on tangible user interfaces. In *Proceedings of the 2014 ACM SIGCHI symposium on Engineering interactive computing systems*, (pp. 205-210). ACM. 10.1145/2607023.2610271

Rao, A. S., & Georgeff, M. P. (1995). BDI agents: from theory to practice. ICMAS, 95, 312–319.

Ras, E., Maquil, V., Foulonneau, M., & Latour, T. (2012). Using tangible user interfaces for technology-based assessment - Advantages and challenges. In CAA 2012 *International Conference*. University of Southampton.

Razo-Zapata, I. S., Chew, E., & Proper, H. A. (2018). VIVA: A visual language to design value co-creation. In *20th IEEE Conference on Business Informatics, CBI 2018, Vienna, Austria, July 11-14, 2018*, Volume 1 - *Research Papers*, (pp. 20-29). IEEE Computer Society. 10.1109/CBI.2018.00012

Reddy, S. (2010). A Model Driven Approach to Enterprise Data Integration. In COMAD (p. 202). Academic Press.

Reisman, R. J. (2019). *Air Traffic Management Blockchain Infrastructure for Security*. Authentication, and Privacy.

Remis, N. (2016). *A Guide to Service Blueprinting*. San Francisco: Capital One.

Renee Baptiste, N. (2008). Tightening the link between employee wellbeing at work and performance: A new dimension for HRM. *Management Decision*, *46*(2), 284–309. doi:10.1108/00251740810854168

Riemer, K., & Schellhammer, S. (2018). Collaboration in the Digital Age: Diverse, Relevant and Challenging. In Collaboration in the Digital Age (pp. 1-12). Springer Link.

Robinson, I., Webber, J., & Eifrem, E. (2013). *Graph databases*. O'Reilly Media, Inc.

Robinson, S. (2008). Conceptual modelling for simulation Part I: Definition and requirements. *The Journal of the Operational Research Society*, *59*(3), 278–290. doi:10.1057/palgrave.jors.2602368

Rodgers, J., & Cebon, D. (2006). Materials Informatics. *MRS Bulletin*, *31*(12), 975–980. doi:10.1557/mrs2006.223

Rohrs, C., Valavani, L., Athans, M., & Stein, G. (1982). Robustness of adaptive control algorithms in the presence of unmodeled dynamics. *Proc. IEEE Conference on Decision and Control*, 3-11. 10.1109/CDC.1982.268392

Romanou, A. (2018). The Necessity of the Implementation of Privacy by Design in Sectors where Data Protection Concerns Arise. *Computer Law & Security Review*, *34*(1), 99–110. doi:10.1016/j.clsr.2017.05.021

Rosencrance, L. (2002, March 14). *Dow Corning launches business unit, Xiameter.* Retrieved from https://www.computerworld.com/article/2587477/dow-corning-launches-business-unit--xiameter.html

Rossi, B. (2015). What is a true digital enterprise? *Information Age.* Retrieved January 2017 from https://www.information-age.com/what-true-digital-enterprise-123459026/

Ross, J. W., Weill, P., & Robertson, D. C. (2006). *Enterprise architecture as strategy: creating a foundation for business execution.* Boston: Harvard Business School Press.

Ross, S., & Bagnell, J. A. (2010). Efficient reductions for imitation learning. *Proc. of The International Conference Artificial Intelligence and Statistics.*

Rothenberger, D. (2017). Physician burnout and well-being: A systematic review and framework for action. *Diseases of the Colon and Rectum, 60*(6), 567–576. doi:10.1097/DCR.0000000000000844 PMID:28481850

Rothenberg, J. (1989). The Nature of Modeling. In *Artificial intelligence, simulation & modeling* (pp. 75–92). New York: John Wiley & Sons.

Rouse, M. (2011). *What is digital enterprise?* Retrieved January 2017 from https://searchcio.techtarget.com/definition/Digital-enterprise

Roychoudhury, S., Sunkle, S., Choudhary, N., Kholkar, D., & Kulkarni, V. (2018). A Case Study on Modeling and Validating Financial Regulations Using (Semi-) *Automated Compliance Framework. In IFIP Working Conference on The Practice of Enterprise Modeling* (pp. 288-302). Springer.

Roychoudhury, S., Sunkle, S., Kholkar, D., & Kulkarni, V. (2017). A domain-specific controlled english language for automated regulatory compliance (Industrial Paper). In *Proceedings of the 10th ACM SIGPLAN International Conference on Software Language Engineering* (pp. 175-181). ACM. 10.1145/3136014.3136018

Rubinstein, I. S., & Good, N. (2013). Privacy by Design: A Counterfactual Analysis of Google and Facebook Privacy Incidents. *Berkeley Technology Law Journal, 28,* 1333.

Sabella, A., Irons-Mclean, R., & Yannuzzi, M. (2018). *Orchestrating and Automating Security for the Internet of Things: Delivering Advanced Security Capabilities from Edge to Cloud for IoT.* Indianapolis, IN: Cisco Press.

Sabri, E. H., & Beamon, B. M. (2000). A multi-objective approach to simultaneous strategic and operational planning in supply chain design. *Omega, 28*(5), 581–598. doi:10.1016/S0305-0483(99)00080-8

Safa, N. S., Solms, R. V., & Furnel, S. (2016). Information security policy compliance model in organizations. *Computers & Security, 56,* 1–13.

Sandkuhl, K., Stirna, J., Persson, A., & Wißotzki, M. (2014). Enterprise Modeling: Tackling Business Challenges With The 4em Method. The Enterprise Engineering Series. Berlin: Springer.

Sandkuhl, K., Fill, H.-G., Hoppenbrouwers, S. J. B. A., Krogstie, J., Matthes, F., Opdahl, A. L., ... Winter, R. (2018). From Expert Discipline to Common Practice: A Vision and Research Agenda for Extending the Reach of Enterprise Modeling. *Business & Information Systems Engineering, 60*(1), 69–80. doi:10.100712599-017-0516-y

Sandkuhl, K., Fill, H.-G., Hoppenbrouwers, S., Krogstie, J., Leue, A., Matthes, F., ... Winter, R. (2016). Enterprise modelling for the masses – from elitist discipline to common practice. In *IFIP Working Conference on The Practice of Enterprise Modeling,* (pp. 225–240). Springer. 10.1007/978-3-319-48393-1_16

Sandkuhl, K., Stirna, J., Persson, A., & Wißotzki, M. (2014). *Enterprise Modeling: Tackling Business Challenges with the 4EM Method.* Heidelberg, Germany: Springer.

SandleT. (2018, January 27). http://www.digitaljournal.com/business/how-businesses-can-protect-their-organizations-from-within/article/513278

Sargent, R. G. (2005). Verification and validation of simulation models. *Proceedings of the 37th conference on Winter simulation*, 130–143.

Sastry, S. (1984). Model-Reference Adaptive Control: Stability, Parameter Convergence, and Robustness. *IMA Journal of Mathematical Control and Information*, *1*(1), 27–66. doi:10.1093/imamci/1.1.27

Schaul, T., Quan, J., Antonoglou, I., & Silver, D. (2015). *Prioritized experience replay*. arXiv preprint arXiv:1511.05952.

Scheer, A.-W. (1992). *Architecture Of Integrated Information Systems: Foundations Of Enterprise Modelling*. Berlin: Springer. doi:10.1007/978-3-642-97389-5

Schelling, T. (1969). Models of Segregation. *The American Economic Review*, 488–493.

Scherer, M. (2017). *Performance and Scalability of Blockchain Networks and Smart Contracts* (Dissertation). Retrieved from http://urn.kb.se/resolve?urn=urn:nbn:se:umu:diva-136470

Schleich, B., Anwer, N., Mathieu, L., & Wartzack, S. (2017). Shaping the digital twin for design and production engineering. *CIRP Annals*, *66*(1), 141–144. doi:10.1016/j.cirp.2017.04.040

Schmidt, D. C. (2006). Model-driven engineering. *Computer-IEEE Computer Society*, *39*(2), 25–31. doi:10.1109/MC.2006.58

Schrijver, A. (1998). *Theory of linear and integer programming*. John Wiley & Sons.

Schulman, J., Wolski, F., Dhariwal, P., Radford, A., & Klimov, O. (2017). *Proximal policy optimization algorithms*. arXiv preprint arXiv:1707.06347.

Schulman, J., Levine, S., Abbeel, P., Jordan, M., & Moritz, P. (2015). Trust region policy optimization. *International Conference on Machine Learning*, 1889-1897.

Schwarz, M., Weiser, S., & Gruss, D. (2019). Practical Enclave Malware with Intel SGX. In *International Conference on Detection of Intrusions and Malware, and Vulnerability Assessment* (pp. 177-196). 10.1007/978-3-030-22038-9_9

Schwarz, M., Weiser, S., Gruss, D., Maurice, C., & Mangard, S. (2017). Malware Guard Extension: Using SGX to Conceal Cache Attacks. In *International Conference on Detection of Intrusions and Malware, and Vulnerability Assessment* (pp. 3-24). 10.1007/978-3-319-60876-1_1

Searle, J. R. (1979). A Taxonomy of Illocutionary Acts. In *Expression and Meaning: Studies in the Theory of Speech Acts*. Cambridge, UK: Cambridge University Press. doi:10.1017/CBO9780511609213.003

Selic, B. (2003). The pragmatics of model-driven development. *IEEE Software*, *20*(5), 19–25. doi:10.1109/MS.2003.1231146

Servia-Rodríguez, S., Rachuri, K. K., Mascolo, C., Rentfrow, P. J., Lathia, N., & Sandstrom, G. M. (2017). Mobile Sensing at the Service of Mental Well-being: a Large-scale Longitudinal Study. *International World Wide Web Conference Committee*.

Shao, S., Tunc, C., Satam, P., & Hariri, S. (2017). Real-time IRC Threat Detection Framework. In IEEE 2nd International Workshops on Foundations and Applications of Self Systems (pp. 318-323). IEEE.

Shaw, E. D., & Stock, H. V. (2011). *Behavioral risk indicators of malicious insider theft of intellectual property: Misreading the writing on the wall*. Symantec.

Shoham, Y., Powers, R., & Grenager, T. (2007). If multi-agent learning is the answer, what is the question? *Artificial Intelligence, 171*(7), 365–377. doi:10.1016/j.artint.2006.02.006

Shor, P. W. (1994, November). Algorithms for quantum computation: Discrete logarithms and factoring. In *Proceedings 35th annual symposium on foundations of computer science* (pp. 124-134). IEEE. 10.1109/SFCS.1994.365700

Shostack, G. L. (1984). Designing services that deliver. *Harvard Business Review*, 133–139.

Shukla, M., Manjunath, S., Saxena, R., Mondal, S., & Lodha, S. (2015). Poster: Winover Enterprise Dark Data. In *Proceedings of the 22nd ACM SIGSAC Conference on Computer and Communications Security* (pp. 1674-1676). ACM.

Shukla, M., Mondal, S., & Lodha, S. (2016). Poster: Locally Virtualized Environment for Mitigating Ransomware Threat. In *Proceedings of the 2016 ACM SIGSAC Conference on Computer and Communications Security* (pp. 1784-1786). 10.1145/2976749.2989051

Shu, R., Wang, P., Gorski, S. A. III, Andow, B., Nadkarni, A., Deshotels, L., ... Gu, X. (2016). A Study of Security Isolation Techniques. *ACM Computing Surveys, 49*(3), 50. doi:10.1145/2988545

Si, J., Barto, A. G., Powell, W. B., & Wunsch, D. (2004). *Handbook of learning and approximate dynamic programming* (Vol. 2). John Wiley & Sons. doi:10.1109/9780470544785

Silva, N., Gonçalves, P., Leite, I., Sousa, P., & da Silva, M. M. (2019). Lm2f: a life-cycle model maintenance framework for co-evolving enterprise architecture meta-models and models. *27th European Conference on Information Systems - Information Systems for a Sharing Society, ECIS 2019*.

Silverman, B. (2004). *Towards realism in human performance simulation*. University of Pennsylvania, ESE.

Simon, H. A. (1991). The architecture of complexity. In *Facets of systems science* (pp. 457–476). Springer. doi:10.1007/978-1-4899-0718-9_31

Simon, H. A. (1996). *The sciences of the artificial*. MIT Press.

Singh, M. e. (2018). KNADIA: Enterprise KNowledge Assisted DIAlogue Systems using Deep Learning. *IEEE International Conference on Data Engineering*. 10.1109/ICDE.2018.00161

Singh, M., Duggirala, M., Hayatnagarkar, H., Patel, S., & Balaraman, V. (2016). Towards fine grained human behavior simulation models. *Winter Simulation Conference*.

Sipp, C. M., & Elias, C. (2012). *Real Options and Strategic Technology Venturing: A New Paradigm in Decision Making* (Vol. 31). Springer Science & Business Media.

Sirjani, M., Movaghar, A., Shali, A., & De Boer, F. S. (2004). Modeling and verification of reactive systems using Rebeca. *Fundamenta Informaticae, 63*(4), 385–410.

Smith, K. T., Jones, A., Johnson, L., & Smith, L. M. (2019). Examination of Cybercrime and its Effects on Corporate Stock Value. *Journal of Information. Communication and Ethics in Society, 17*(1), 42–60.

Snoeck, M. (2014). *Enterprise Information Systems Engineering - The MERODE Approach*. Springer.

Sottet, J.-S. & Biri, N. (2016). Jsmf: a javascript flexible modelling framework. *FlexMDE@ MoDELS, 1694*, 42-51.

Souter, G. (2019). *Cyber Insurance Market Set to Grow Despite Challenges: Panel*. Retrieved October 3, 2019, from https://www.businessinsurance.com/article/20190924/NEWS06/912330822/Cyber-insurance-market-set-to-grow-despite-challenges-Panel

Spooner, J. T., & Passino, K. M. (1996). Adaptive control of a class of decentralized nonlinear systems. *IEEE Transactions on Automatic Control, 41*(2), 280–284. doi:10.1109/9.481548

Srinivasan, S., & Mycroft, A. (2008). Kilim: Isolation-typed actors for java. In *European Conference on Object-Oriented Programming*, (pp. 104–128). Springer.

Ssebuggwawo, D., Hoppenbrouwers, S. J. B. A., & Proper, H. A. (2009). Interactions, goals and rules in a collaborative modelling session. In *The Practice of Enterprise Modeling, Second IFIP WG 8.1 Working Conference, PoEM 2009, Stockholm, Sweden, November 18-19, 2009. Proceedings, volume 39 of Lecture Notes in Business Information Processing*, (pp. 54-68). Springer. 10.1007/978-3-642-05352-8_6

Stachowiak, H. (1973). *Allgemeine Modelltheorie*. Heidelberg, Germany: Springer. doi:10.1007/978-3-7091-8327-4

Stamper, R. K. (1996). Signs, norms, and information systems. In Signs at Work, (pp. 349-397). Walter de Gruyter. doi:10.1515/9783110819014-013

Star, S. L., & Griesemer, J. R. (1989). Institutional Ecology, 'Translations' and Boundary Objects: Amateurs and Professionals in Berkeley's Museum of Vertebrate Zoology 1907-39. *Social Studies of Science, 19*(4), 387–420. doi:10.1177/030631289019003001

Steffens, M., Rossow, C., Johns, M., & Stock, B. (2019). Don't Trust the Locals: Investigating the Prevalence of Persistent Client-side Cross-site Scripting in the Wild. *Network and Distributed System Security Symposium*. 10.14722/ndss.2019.23009

Sterritt, R., & Bustard, D. (2003). Towards an autonomic computing environment. *14th International Workshop on Database and Expert Systems Applications*, 694-698. 10.1109/DEXA.2003.1232103

Stirna, J., & Persson, A. (2007). Ten Years Plus with EKD: Reflections from Using an Enterprise Modeling Method in Practice. Academic Press.

Subramanian, J., Mahajan, A., & Paranjape, A. (2018). On controllability of leader-follower dynamics over a directed graph. *Proc. IEEE Conference on Decision and Control*, 2048-2055. 10.1109/CDC.2018.8619474

Šukys, A., Ablonskis, L., Nemuraitė, L., & Paradauskas, B. (2016). A Grammar for ADVANCED SBVR Editor. *Information Technology and Control, 45*(1), 27–41. doi:10.5755/j01.itc.45.1.9219

Sun, G., Cui, T., Yong, J., Shen, J., & Chen, S. (2018). MLaaS: A cloud-based system for delivering adaptive micro learning in mobile MOOC learning. *IEEE Transactions on Services Computing, 11*(2), 292–305. doi:10.1109/TSC.2015.2473854

Sung, Y. T., Chang, K. E., & Liu, T. C. (2016). The effects of integrating mobile devices with teaching and learning on students' learning performance: A meta-analysis and research synthesis. *Computers & Education, 94*, 252–275. doi:10.1016/j.compedu.2015.11.008

Sunkle, S., Kholkar, D., & Kulkarni, V. (2015a). Toward better mapping between regulations and operations of enterprises using vocabularies and semantic similarity. *Complex Systems Informatics and Modeling Quarterly*, (5), 39-60.

Sunkle, S., Kholkar, D., & Kulkarni, V. (2015b). Model-driven regulatory compliance: A case study of "Know Your Customer" regulations. In *2015 ACM/IEEE 18th International Conference on Model Driven Engineering Languages and Systems (MODELS)* (pp. 436-445). IEEE.

Sunkle, S., Kholkar, D., & Kulkarni, V. (2016). Comparison and synergy between fact-orientation and relation extraction for domain model generation in regulatory compliance. In *International Conference on Conceptual Modeling* (pp. 381-395). Springer. 10.1007/978-3-319-46397-1_29

Sutton, R. & Barto, A. (2012). *Reinforcement learning: An introduction*. MIT Press.

Sutton, R. S., & Barto, A. G. (1998). Introduction to reinforcement learning: Vol. 2. *No. 4*. Cambridge: MIT Press.

Tapscott, D., Ticoll, D., & A., L. (2000). *Digital Capital: Harnessing the Power of Business Webs*. Harvard Business Press.

Tapscott, D. (1996). *Digital Economy - Promise and peril in the age of networked intelligence*. New York: McGraw-Hill.

Tapscott, D., & Caston, A. (1993). *Paradigm Shift - The New Promise of Information Technology*. New York: McGraw-Hill.

Tata Consultancy Services Limited. (2019, Feb 4). *Digital transformation to business 4.0*. Retrieved from https://sites.tcs.com/bts/digital-transformation-to-business-4-0-pov/

Tata Consultancy Services. (2015). *Internet of things: The complete re-imaginative force*. TCS Global Trend Study [PDF document]. Retrieved from https://sites.tcs.com/internet-of-things/

Tata Consultancy Services. (2016). *A Personalized Humane Customer Experience – Delivered to you by Bots*. Retrieved from TCS: https://www.tcs.com/blogs/a-personalized-humane-customer-experience-delivered-to-you-by-bots

Tata Consultancy Services. (2018). *Business 4.0. The behaviors of digital transformation* [PDF document]. Retrieved from https://www.tcs.com/content/dam/tcs/pdf/discover-tcs/business/The%20Behaviors%20of%20Digital%20Transformation.pdf

Tata Consultancy Services. (2019). *Winning in a Business 4.0 World* [PDF document]. Retrieved from https://www.business4.tcs.com/

Tavares, F. (2019). *Google and NASA Achieve Quantum Supremacy*. Retrieved December 5, 2019, from https://www.nasa.gov/feature/ames/quantum-supremacy/

Taylor, J. R., Cooren, F., Giroux, N., & Robichaud, D. (1996). The Communicational Basis of Organization: Between the Conversation and the Text. *Communication Theory*, *6*(1), 1–39. doi:10.1111/j.1468-2885.1996.tb00118.x

Tess, P. A. (2013). The role of social media in higher education classes (real and virtual): A literature review. *Computers in Human Behavior*, *29*(5), A60–A68. doi:10.1016/j.chb.2012.12.032

Thalheim, B. (2013). The Conception of the Model. In *Business Information Systems - 16th International Conference, BIS 2013, Poznań Poland, June 19-21, 2013. Proceedings, volume 157 of Lecture Notes in Business Information Processing*, (pp. 113-124). Springer. 10.1007/978-3-642-38366-3_10

Thalheim, B. (2011). The Theory of Conceptual Models, the Theory of Conceptual Modelling and Foundations of Conceptual Modelling. In *Handbook of Conceptual Modeling* (pp. 543–577). Heidelberg, Germany: Springer. doi:10.1007/978-3-642-15865-0_17

The American Institute of Stress. (n.d.). Retrieved from https://www.stress.org/workplace-stress

The Open Group. (2009). *The Open Group Architecture Framework (Togaf) - Version 9*. Retrieved From Http://Www.Opengroup.Org/Togaf/

The Open Group. (2011). *TOGAF Version 9.1* (10th ed.). Zaltbommel, The Netherlands: Van Haren Publishing.

Theodorou, E., Buchli, J., & Schaal, S. (2010). Reinforcement learning of motor skills in high dimensions: A path integral approach. *Robotics and Automation (ICRA), 2010 International Conference on*, 2397-2403.

Thomas, M., & McGarry, F. (1994). Top-down vs. bottom-up process improvement. *IEEE Software*, *11*(4), 12–13. doi:10.1109/52.300121

Tisue, S., & Wilensky, U. (2004). Netlogo: A simple environment for modeling complexity. *International conference on complex systems*, 21, 16–21.

Tolk, A., Heath, B. L., Ihrig, M., Padilla, J. J., Page, E. H., Suarez, E. D., ... Yilmaz, L. (2013). Epistemology of modeling and simulation. In *Proceedings of the 2013 Winter Simulation Conference: Simulation: Making Decisions in a Complex World*, (pp. 1152–1166). IEEE Press. 10.1109/WSC.2013.6721504

Topaloglu, H., & Powell, W. (2006). Dynamic-programming approximations for stochastic time-staged integer multi-commodity-ow problems. *INFORMS Journal on Computing*, *18*(1), 31–42. doi:10.1287/ijoc.1040.0079

Torres, A. (2015). *Building a World-Class Security Operations Center: A Roadmap*. SANS Institute.

Travis, A., & Arthur, C. (2014). EU Court Backs 'Right to be Forgotten': Google Must Amend Results on Request. *The Guardian*. Retrieved October 3, 2019, from https://www.theguardian.com/technology/2014/may/13/right-to-be-forgotten-eu-court-google-search-results

Tribolet, J., Sousa, P., & Caetano, A. (2014). The Role of Enterprise Governance and Cartography in Enterprise Engineering. *Enterprise Modelling and Information Systems Architectures*, *9*(1), 38–49. doi:10.100740786-014-0004-5

Tupsamudre, H., Wasnik, R., Biswas, S., Pandit, S., Vaddepalli, S., Shinde, A., ... Lodha, S. (2018). GAP: A Game for Improving Awareness about Passwords. In *Joint Conference on Serious games* (pp. 66-78). 10.1007/978-3-030-02762-9_8

Turel, O., Xu, Z., & Guo, K. (2017). Organizational Citizenship Behavior Regarding Security: Leadership Approach Perspective. *Journal of Computer Information Systems*, 1–15. doi:10.1080/08874417.2017.1400928

Ullmann, S. (1967). *Semantics: An Introduction to the Science of Meaning*. Oxford, UK: Basil Blackwell.

Umar, A. (2005). IT infrastructure to enable next generation enterprises. *Information Systems Frontiers*, *7*(3), 217–256. doi:10.100710796-005-2768-1

Uskov, V. L., Bakken, J. P., Karri, S., Uskov, A. V., Heinemann, C., & Rachakonda, R. (2017, June). Smart University: Conceptual Modeling and Systems' Design. In *International Conference on Smart Education and Smart E-Learning* (pp. 49-86). Springer.

Uskov, V., Bakken, J. P., Aluri, L., Rachakonda, R., Rayala, N., & Uskova, M. (2018, March). Smart pedagogy: innovative teaching and learning strategies in engineering education. In *2018 IEEE World Engineering Education Conference (EDUNINE)* (pp. 1-6). IEEE. 10.1109/EDUNINE.2018.8450962

Utkin, V., Guldner, J., & Shi, J. (2009). *Sliding mode control in electromechanical systems*. CRC Press. doi:10.1201/9781420065619

Vacca, J. R. (2019). *Online Terrorist Propaganda, Recruitment, and Radicalization*. CRC Press. doi:10.1201/9781315170251

Van der Laan, E., & Salomon, M. (1997). Production planning and inventory control with remanufacturing and disposal. *European Journal of Operational Research*, *102*(2), 264–278. doi:10.1016/S0377-2217(97)00108-2

van der Linden, D. J. T., & Hadar, I. (2015). Cognitive Effectiveness of Conceptual Modeling Languages: Examining Professional Modelers. *Proceedings of the 5th IEEE International Workshop on Empirical Requirements Engineering (EmpiRE)*. 10.1109/EmpiRE.2015.7431300

van Engers, T. M., van Gog, R., & Sayah, K. (2004). A case study on automated norm extraction. Legal Knowledge and Information Systems. *Jurix*, 49-58.

Van Otterlo, M. (2013) A machine learning view on profiling. In *Privacy, Due Process and the Computational Turn-Philosophers of Law Meet Philosophers of Technology*. Abingdon: Routledge.

van Rest, J., Boonstra, D., Everts, M., van Rijn, M., & van Paassen, R. (2012). Designing Privacy-by-design. In *Annual Privacy Forum* (pp. 55-72). Academic Press.

Varela, C., & Agha, G. (2001). Programming dynamically reconfigurable open systems with SALSA. *ACM SIGPLAN Notices, 36*(12), 20–34. doi:10.1145/583960.583964

Varghese, B., & Buyya, R. (2018). Next Generation Cloud Computing: New Trends and Research Directions. *Future Generation Computer Systems, 79,* 849–861. doi:10.1016/j.future.2017.09.020

Vargo, S. L., & Lusch, R. F. (2008). Service-dominant logic: Continuing the evolution. *Journal of the Academy of Marketing Science, 36*(1), 1–10. doi:10.100711747-007-0069-6

Vargo, S. L., & Lusch, R. F. (2016). Institutions and axioms: An extension and update of service-dominant logic. *Journal of the Academy of Marketing Science, 44*(1), 5–23. doi:10.100711747-015-0456-3

Verizon. (2019). *Data Breach Investigations Report.* Retrieved September 20, 2019, from https://enterprise.verizon.com/resources/reports/dbir/

Verma, R., Saikia, S., Khadilkar, H., Agarwal, P., & Shroff, G. (2019). A reinforcement learning solution for the container selection and sequencing problem in ports. *Autonomous Agents and Multiagent Systems (AAMAS), 2019 International Conference on.*

Vogel, T., Seibel, A., & Giese, H. (2011). The role of models and megamodels at runtime. In J. Dingel & A. Solberg (Eds.), *Models in Software Engineering* (pp. 224–238). Berlin: Springer Berlin Heidelberg. doi:10.1007/978-3-642-21210-9_22

Volini, E., Occean, P., Stephan, M., & Walsh, B. (2017). *Digital HR: Platforms, people, and work, 2017 Global Human Capital Trends.* Retrieved from https://www2.deloitte.com/insights/us/en/focus/human-capital-trends/2017/digital-transformation-in-hr.html

Von Bertalanffy, L. (1968). General system theory. New York: Academic Press.

Vreede, G. J., Kolfschoten, G. L., & Briggs, R. O. (2006). Thinklets: A collaboration engineering pattern language. *International Journal of Computer Applications in Technology, 25*(2/3), 140–154. doi:10.1504/IJCAT.2006.009064

Wang, A., Liang, R., Liu, X., Zhang, Y., Chen, K., & Li, J. (2017). An Inside Look at IOT Malware. In *International Conference on Industrial IOT Technologies and Applications* (pp. 176-186). 10.1007/978-3-319-60753-5_19

Wang, Y. (2009). A cognitive informatics reference model for autonomous agent systems. *International Journal of Cognitive Informatics and Natural Intelligence, 3*(1), 1–16. doi:10.4018/jcini.2009010101

Watkins, B. (2014). *The Impact of Cyber Attacks on the Private Sector. Briefing Paper.* Association for International Affair.

Weick, K. E. (1995). *Sensemaking in Organizations.* Beverly Hills, CA: Sage.

Weiser, M. (1993, July). Some Computer Science Problems in Ubiquitous Computing. *Communications of the ACM, 36*(7), 75–84. doi:10.1145/159544.159617

West, D., Huijser, H., & Heath, D. (2016). Putting an ethical lens on learning analytics. *Educational Technology Research and Development, 64*(5), 903–922. doi:10.100711423-016-9464-3

White, S. A. (2004). Introduction to BPMN. *IBM Cooperation, 2*(0), 0.

White, S. A. (2008). *BPMN modeling and reference guide: understanding and using BPMN.* Future Strategies Inc.

Wibowo, C., & Ng, K. M. (2001). Product-oriented process synthesis and development: Creams and pastes. *AIChE Journal. American Institute of Chemical Engineers, 47*(12), 2746–2767. doi:10.1002/aic.690471214

Wibowo, C., & Ng, K. M. (2002). Product-centered processing: Manufacture of chemical-based consumer products. *AIChE Journal. American Institute of Chemical Engineers*, *48*(6), 1212–1230. doi:10.1002/aic.690480609

Willison, R., & Warkentin, M. (2009). Motivations for employee computer crime: Understanding and addressing. *IFIP TC 8 International Workshop on Information Systems Security Research*, 127 - 144.

Wilson, M., & Hash, J. (2003). Building an Information Technology Security Awareness and Training Program. *NIST Special Publication*, *800*(50), 1–39. doi:10.6028/NIST.SP.800-50

Wired Inc. (2018, April). *AI and the future of work.* Retrieved from https://www.wired.com/wiredinsider/2018/04/ai-future-work/

WittkopJ. (2017, December 21). Retrieved from https://www.intelisecure.com/blog/future-information-security/

Woelfle, M., Olliaro, P., & Todd, M. H. (2011). Open science is a research accelerator. *Nature Chemistry*, *3*(10), 745–748. doi:10.1038/nchem.1149 PMID:21941234

Wong, B. K., Chong, J. K., & Park, J. (1994). Utilization and Benefits of Expert Systems in Manufacturing. *International Journal of Operations & Production Management*, *14*(1), 38–49. doi:10.1108/01443579410049298

World Economic Forum White Paper Digital Transformation of Industries in collaboration with Accenture. (2016). Retrieved from http://reports.weforum.org/digital-transformation/wp-content/blogs.dir/94/mp/files/pages/files/digital-enterprise-narrative-final-january-2016.pdf

World Economic Forum. (2011). *The Global Economic Burden of Non-communicable diseases.* World Economic Forum, Harvard School of Public Health.

World Economic Forum. (2019). *The Global Risks Report 2019.* Retrieved September 20, 2019, from https://www.weforum.org/reports/the-global-risks-report-2019

World Health Organization. (2019). *Mental health in India.* Retrieved from Mental health in India: http://www.searo.who.int/india/topics/mental_health/about_mentalhealth/en/

Wouters, L. (2013). Towards the notation-driven development of dsmls. In *International Conference on Model Driven Engineering Languages and Systems*, (pp. 522-537). Springer. 10.1007/978-3-642-41533-3_32

Wout, J. v., Waage, M., Hartman, H., Stahlecker, M., & Hofman, A. (2010). *The Integrated Architecture Framework Explained.* Heidelberg, Germany: Springer. doi:10.1007/978-3-642-11518-9

Wyner, A. Z., & Peters, W. (2011, December). On Rule Extraction from Regulations. JURIX, 11, 113-122.

Yan, C., Xu, W., & Liu, J. (2016). *Can You Trust Autonomous Vehicles: Contactless Attacks against Sensors of Self-driving Vehicle.* DEFCON.

Yellowlees, P., & Chan, S. (2015). Mobile mental health care-An opportunity for India. *The Indian Journal of Medical Research*, *142*(4), 359. doi:10.4103/0971-5916.169185 PMID:26609025

Yonge, J. d. (2019). *For CEOs, Are the Days of Sidelining Global Challenges Numbered?* Retrieved September 20, 2019, from https://www.ey.com/en gl/growth/ceo-imperative-global-challenges

Yu, E., Strohmaier, M., & Deng, X. (2006, October). Exploring intentional modeling and analysis for enterprise architecture. In *2006 10th IEEE International Enterprise Distributed Object Computing Conference Workshops (EDOCW'06)* (pp. 32-32). IEEE. 10.1109/EDOCW.2006.36

Yuan, X., He, P., Zhu, Q., & Li, X. (2019). Adversarial Examples: Attacks and Defenses for Deep Learning. *IEEE Transactions on Neural Networks and Learning Systems, 30*(9), 2805–2824. doi:10.1109/TNNLS.2018.2886017 PMID:30640631

Zachman, J. A. (1987). A Framework For Information Systems Architecture. *IBM Systems Journal, 26*(3), 276–292. doi:10.1147j.263.0276

Zarwin, Z., Bjeković, M., Favre, J.-M., Sottet, J.-S., & Proper, H. A. (2014). Natural modelling. *Journal of Object Technology, 13*(3), 1-36.

Zeike, S., Bradbury, K., Lindert, L., & Pfaf, H. (2019). Digital Leadership Skills and Associations with Psychological Well-Being. *International Journal of Environmental Research and Public Health, 16*(14), 2628–2640. doi:10.3390/ijerph16142628 PMID:31340579

Zeni, N., Kiyavitskaya, N., Mich, L., Cordy, J. R., & Mylopoulos, J. (2015). GaiusT: Supporting the extraction of rights and obligations for regulatory compliance. *Requirements Engineering, 20*(1), 1–22. doi:10.100700766-013-0181-8

Zhang, L., Fung, K. Y., Wibowo, C., & Gani, R. (2018). Advances in chemical product design. *Reviews in Chemical Engineering, 34*(3), 319–340. doi:10.1515/revce-2016-0067

Zhang, L., Fung, K. Y., Zhang, X., Fung, H. K., & Ng, K. M. (2017). An integrated framework for designing formulated products. *Computers & Chemical Engineering, 107*, 61–76. doi:10.1016/j.compchemeng.2017.05.014

Zhu, M., Sari, A., & Lee, M. M. (2018). A systematic review of research methods and topics of the empirical MOOC literature (2014–2016). *The Internet and Higher Education, 37*, 31–39. doi:10.1016/j.iheduc.2018.01.002

About the Contributors

Vinay Kulkarni is a Chief Scientist of Tata Research Development and Design Centre (TRDDC) at Tata Consultancy Services (TCS). He is a member of the TCS Corporate Technology Council that oversees all R&D and innovation activities at TCS. His research interests include model-driven software engineering, self-adaptive systems, and enterprise modeling. His work in model-driven software engineering has led to a toolset that has been used to deliver several large business-critical systems over the past 15 years. Much of this work has found way into OMG standards, three of which Vinay contributed to in a leadership role. Vinay has several patents to his credit, and has authored several papers in scholastic journals and conferences worldwide. He has served as the conference and program chairperson for the premier ACM and IEEE international conferences in the area of software engineering; and served as a technical program committee member for many international conferences. Vinay also serves as Visiting Professor at Middlesex University, London.

Sreedhar Reddy is a Chief Scientist at Tata Research Development Design Centre of Tata Consultancy Services (TCS). His research interests include model-driven software engineering and database systems. His work in model-driven software engineering has led to a toolset that has been used to deliver several large business-critical systems over the past 20 years. Sreedhar is an alumnus of Indian Institute of Technology Kharagpur.

Balbir Barn is a Professor of Software Engineering at Middlesex University, UK. Balbir has over 15 years commercial research experience working in research labs at Texas Instruments and Sterling Software, where he was involved in the research and design of leading software products such as the IEF™. Balbir's research is focused on model driven software engineering where the goal is to use models as abstractions and execution environments to support enterprise architecture and application integration using complex events. He has led numerous externally funded projects which apply model driven principles to business processes, learning theories, and more recently, the theory building aspects to model driven engineering.

* * *

Vivek Balaraman heads the Behavior Business and Social Sciences Research Area in Tata Consultancy Services R & D. Vivek's current research focus is on approaches to derive fine grained grounded models of human behavior.

Souvik Barat is a senior scientist at Tata Consultancy Services Research (TCSR). He holds a PhD in Software Engineering from Middlesex University London. His research interests include Digital Twin, Enterprise modeling, System modelling and simulation, Model driven Engineering and Software Engineering.

Alexander C. Bock is currently a member of the Research Group for Information Systems and Enterprise Modeling at the University of Duisburg-Essen, Essen, Germany. He holds a M.Sc. and B.Sc. in Business Information Systems from the Institute for Computer Science and Business Information Systems (ICB) at the University of Duisburg-Essen. His main research interests are human decision making, problem solving, and the use of conceptual models to facilitate complex decision and problem solving processes. He also works on enterprise modeling, computerized decision support, and the philosophy of mind.

Rinu Chacko is a researcher in the Physical Sciences Research Area at Tata Research Development and Design Centre (TRDDC). Her current research focuses on the application of machine learning techniques in the field of cheminformatics. She completed her M.Tech. in Chemical Engineering from Indian Institute of Technology Madras and B.Tech. from National Institute of Technology Calicut. Prior to coming to TRDDC, she worked at the Vadodara Manufacturing Division of Reliance Industries Limited.

Kyle Cooper is a researcher for the Tata Consultancy Services' Manufacturing Research Innovation Lab in Cincinnati, Ohio where he builds solutions and conducts research to improve supply chain networks, sustainability, and manufacturing process visibility. Kyle is especially interested in solutions that employ simulation and optimization. He was awarded his Ph.D., Industrial Engineering in 2019 from Purdue University.

Mayuri Duggirala heads the Wellbeing research effort in the Behavior Business and Social Sciences Research Area within Tata Consultancy Services R&D.

Ulrich Frank holds the chair of Information Systems and Enterprise Modelling at the Institute of Computer Science and Business Information Systems at the University of Duisburg-Essen. His main research topic is enterprise modelling, i.e. the development and evaluation of modelling languages, methods and corresponding tools. In recent years, he focused especially on multi-level domain-specific modelling languages and corresponding tools. Further areas of research include method engineering, models at run time, methods for IT management and research methods. Together with Tony Clark from Sheffield University, he conducts the project "Language Engineering for Multi-level Modeling" (LE4MM). The project aims at further developing an integrated meta-modeling and meta-programming environment and, based on that, at the development of new self-referential enterprise systems that integrate enterprise software with conceptual models of themselves and the context they operate in at run time. Ulrich Frank is on the editorial board of the journals "Enterprise Modelling and Information Systems Architectures", "Business & Information Systems Engineering", "Software and Systems Modeling", "Information Systems and E-Business Management", and the "Journal of Information System Modeling and Design". He worked as a research fellow at the IBM Almaden Research Center in San Jose and had assignments as visiting researcher/professor at universities in various countries. Ulrich Frank served as the spokesman of the German Business Informatics Community within the German Informatics Society.

He is the German representative of the IFIP Technical Committee TC8 and a review board member of the Deutsche Forschungsgemeinschaft (German National Science Foundation).

B. P. Gautham is a principal scientist at TCS Research and heads a research and innovation program òn Integrated Computational Materials Engineering and development of TCS PREMAP platform. Gautham's primary interests include application of modeling and simulation – both physics based and data based – for engineering analysis with emphasis on materials engineering and manufacturing processes. He worked closely with various industries in trouble shooting, enhancing and optimizing manufacturing process with targets on quality, productivity and energy. His current interests extend to utilization of state-of-the-art machine learning and knowledge engineering frameworks for materials and mechanical engineering. Gautham has published over 80 papers in journals & conference proceedings encompassing areas of application of FEA, CFD, Data Sciences, Optimization and Robust Design applied to materials, manufacturing and product engineering. He has been on many international conference organizing committees and also reviewer for a number of journals. He obtained his BTech in Mechanical Engineering and PhD in Applied Mechanics from Indian Institute of Technology- Madras, Chennai. Gautham has been with TCS Research since 1994.

Wided Guédria is a researcher in the IT for Innovative Services (ITIS) department / Trusted Service Systems (TSS) unit, at the Luxembourg Institute of Science and Technology (LIST). She is part of the iSEE research group focusing on modelling and improvement of service intensive systems. Her main research topics concern Interoperability, systemic modelling, enterprise architec- ture, Informed Design and informed decision making. Dr Guédria received her PhD. in production engineering, Automatic and Signal Processing, from the University of Bordeaux 1, France, in 2012. She is scientific leader and Coordinator of the TG1 e-Health in Interop/vlab and member of the scientific advisory and management board of the INTEROP- Grande Région, France.

Deepak Jain works with the Physical Sciences research area at TCS Research, Pune where he is leading research in the materials informatics domain. He completed his M.Tech in Mechanical Engineering from Indian Institute of Technology Bombay, India in 2015 and has since been an active member of the Physical Sciences team. Deepak's research interests include cheminformatics, applied machine learning and deep learning in the domain of material science.

Harshad Khadilkar holds a BTech (2009) from IIT Bombay, followed by an MS (2011) and PhD (2013) from the Massachusetts Institute of Technology. He has worked on the development of optimal control algorithms for networked systems in multiple domains, including transportation, logistics, energy, and supply chain. In the last few years, his research has focussed on the use of machine learning approaches for solving large-scale, real-world control problems.

Deepali Kholkar is a senior researcher in TCS with 20+ years experience in model-driven development and verification and validation of models.

Devadatta M. Kulkarni is a Principal Scientist for Manufacturing Research and the TCS Innovation Lab in Cincinnati, Ohio. Dr. Kulkarni is working on TCS's Supply Chain Research and Digital Manufacturing and Operations Innovation globally. He is a well-known professional consultant and expert in Commodity Sourcing, Supply Chain Management, IoT Analytics and Security, along with decision models in Manufacturing Value Chains. He has worked on both innovation and finance sides of a major automotive OEM business and brings in unique experience of architecting and implementing technology frameworks for enterprise transformation. Dr. Kulkarni has successfully extended his accomplished academic career into productive industrial researcher role with sustained publications including six U.S. patents, over 50 internal GM reports, and over 30 external, archival publications in leading professional journals. Dr. Kulkarni was awarded his B.S., Mathematics in 1979 at Pune University, his M.S., Mathematics in 1982, and his Ph.D., in 1985, both from Purdue University.

Sachin Lodha is part of TCS's Corporate Technology Office. He leads Cybersecurity and Privacy Research and Innovation efforts within TCS. In particular, Dr Lodha has a special interest in privacy and related topics. His efforts on that front have led to multiple research papers, patents, and award winning innovations that are now available as commercial TCS products. Dr Lodha graduated with a B.Tech. in Computer Science and Engineering from the Indian Institute of Technology, Bombay, in 1996 and received his Ph.D. in Computer Science from Rutgers University, USA, in 2002.

Ravi Mahamuni is a senior scientist and heads the Service Design Research effort in the Behavior Business and Social Sciences Research Area in Tata Consultancy Services R&D. He is a service design researcher and practitioner, and pursuing his PhD in Service Design from Indian Institute of Technology Guwahati, India. He is a Bachelor of Electronics Engineering (1995), Postgraduate Diploma in Advanced Computing (1997) and MBA (2012). He is an author of 18 plus research papers and lead inventor of 10 plus patents. His research interest is the aspects that inform design for behaviour change and how service designers can facilitate the behaviour change that people and communities desire. He is a lead service designer for various in-house service design initiatives like employee onboarding, employee integration and employee referral services. He has developed ten plus technology products and anchored several service design projects.

Aditya A. Paranjape is a scientist in the Software Systems and Services Research Area at TCS Research in Pune, India. He holds a PhD in Aerospace Engineering from the University of Illinois at Urbana-Champaign. He specializes in control theory, flight dynamics and mobile robotics. His research interests include optimal adaptive control, infinite dimensional systems, flight mechanics and multi-agent systems.

Sachin Patel is a senior scientist at Tata Consultancy Services, Research and works with the Behavioural, Business and Social Sciences Research group. He holds a Bachelor's degree in Computer Science and his research interests include behaviour sensing, affective computing, quantified self systems, model-driven software engineering and model-based testing. He has led multiple innovation projects from ideation to deployment, and currently heads the making of a Human behaviour sensing and interventions platform. In his previous stint as a software professional he has acquired extensive experience in managing and delivering large enterprise software projects.

Ashwini Patil is working at Tata Research Development and Design Centre as a Research Engineer. She has received her Master's degree with the Award of Excellence in Computer Science and Engineering from Visvesvaraya National Institute Of Technology, Nagpur, India, in 2018. Her research interests include Machine Learning and Natural Language Processing.

Henderik A. Proper, Erik to friends, is an FNR PEARL Laureate, and Head of Academic Affairs of at the Luxembourg Institute of Science and Technology (LIST) in Luxembourg, and senior research manager within its IT for Innovative Services (ITIS) department. He also holds an adjunct chair in Computer Science at the University of Luxembourg. Erik has a mixed background, covering a variety of roles in both academia and industry. His professional passion is the further development of the field of enterprise engineering, and enterprise modelling in particular. His long experience in teaching and coaching a wide variety of people enables him to involve and engage others in this development. He has co-authored several journal papers, conference publications and books. His main research interests include enterprise engineering and enterprise modelling, which includes enterprise architecture, systems theory, business/IT alignment and conceptual modelling Erik received his Master's degree from the University of Nijmegen, The Netherlands in May 1990, and received his PhD (with distinction) from the same University in April 1994. In his Doctoral thesis he developed a theory for conceptual modelling of evolving application domains, yielding a formal specification of evolving information systems. After receiving his PhD, Erik became a senior research fellow at the Computer Science Department of the University of Queensland, Brisbane, Australia. During that period he also conducted research in the Asymetrix Research Lab at that University for Asymetrix Corp, Seattle, Washington. In 1995 he became a lecturer at the School of Information Systems from the Queensland University of Technology, Brisbane, Australia. During this period he was also seconded as a senior researcher to the Distributed Systems Technology Centre (DSTC), a Cooperative Research Centres funded by the Australian government. From 1997 to 2001, Erik worked in industry. First as a consultant at Origin, Amsterdam, The Netherlands, and later as a research consultant and principal scientist at the Ordina Institute for Research and Innovation, Gouda, The Netherlands. In June 2001, Erik returned to academia, where he became an adjunct Professor at the Radboud University Nijmegen. In September 2002, Erik obtained a full-time Professorship position at the Radboud University Nijmegen. In Januari of 2008, he went back to combining industry and academia, by combining his Professorship with consulting and innovation at Capgemini, with the aim of more tightly combining his theoretical and practical work. Finally, in May 2010 Erik moved to the Luxembourg Institute of Science and Technology as a PEARL chair, while also continuing his chair at the Radboud University Nijmegen in the Netherlands. As of June 2017, Erik holds an adjunct chair at the University of Luxembourg.

Asha Rajbhoj is a Senior Scientist at Tata Consultancy Services. Her research interests include model-driven software engineering, artificial intelligence, and enterprise modeling. An alumnus of College of Engineering Pune, India.

Jayasree Raveendran is a Senior Scientist in the Behavior Business and Social Sciences Research Area in TCS R&D. She has a Ph.D. in Management Studies from Indian Institute of Technology Madras with specialization in Behavioral Finance. Her research interests include the fields of Behavioral Economics, Decision Sciences, Behavior Change and Investor Behavior. Jayasree heads the Norms Compliance research effort in BBS where current research focus is on detecting and mitigating insider threat in various contexts including information security.

Suman Roychoudhury is a PhD from university of Alabama, Birmingham. He has been working with TCS for 9+ years and has publications in several top tier conferences on energy efficient computation, model-driven engineering, cost estimations, language engineering, and domain-specific languages.

Krati Saxena is working as a Researcher at Tata Research Development and Design Centre, Pune. She has completed Masters of Engineering from Kyushu Institute of Technology, Japan and Bachelors of Technology from Indian Institute of Technology Jodhpur. Her research areas and previous publications mainly focus on Natural Language Processing, Machine Learning, Image processing, and Deep Learning.

Rajeev Shorey is a Principal Scientist with TCS Research and Innovation. He received his Ph.D and MS (Engg) in Electrical Communication Engineering from the Indian Institute of Science (IISc), Bangalore, India in 1997 and 1991 respectively. He received his B.E degree in Computer Science and Engineering from IISc in 1987. Dr. Shorey has to his credit 60 publications in international journals and conferences and 12 US patents. His areas of interest are Wireless & Wired Networks, IoT, Automotive Cyber Security, 5G Networks and Smart Manufacturing. Dr. Shorey is a Fellow of the Indian National Academy of Engineering and a Distinguished Scientist of ACM.

Manish Shukla is a scientist in Tata Research Development and Design Centre. His current area of interest includes: cybersecurity analytics, system security, malware analytics, data privacy. He has more than 10 granted patents and more than 16 filed patents in the field of cybersecurity in various geographies.

Jean-Sébastien Sottet is a researcher at Luxembourg Institute of Sciences and Technologies since 2011. His research work mainly stands on model-engineering. He notably applied modelling approaches and technologies to different fields such as user interface generation, software product-lines, reverse engineering and, more recently, enterprise architecture. He is now focusing on modeling and model management dedicated to regulatory compliance and regulatory risk management.

Ramakrishnan Srinivasan is a Principal Scientist in the Cincinnati Innovation Lab at Tata Consultancy Services, where he conducts applied research in the supply chain domain, with a focus on risk management. He has over 25 years of industrial experience with a rich background in applied research supply chain application software, mechanical design, manufacturing, and industrial engineering. Dr. Srinivasan has about 25 publications including conference papers, journal articles, book chapters, and a book. He was awarded his Ph.D., Mechanical Engineering in 1994 from the University of Texas at Austin.

Sagar Sunkle is a PhD from UNI Magdeburg, Germany. He has been working with TCS for 7+ years. He has several publications in top tier conferences on model-driven engineering, enterprise architecture, and using natural language processing and machine learning for ontology generation and information extraction.

Jeffrey D. Tew is the Chief Scientist for the Manufacturing Research and TCS Innovation Lab in Cincinnati, Ohio whose focus is leading and developing TCS's Supply Chain Research and Manufacturing Systems and Innovation activities globally. Dr. Tew is an internationally known professional consultant and expert in Manufacturing, Transportation and Supply Chain Management (SCM), along with other related business disciplines. Dr. Tew has a long history of effective interactions with several of the leading research universities in the world. Dr. Tew also has maintained a strong publication record throughout his career, including filing 19 U.S. Patents with 11 awarded to date, over 80 internal GM R&D publications and reports and over 35 external, archival publications in leading professional journals. Dr. Tew was awarded his B.S, Mathematics in 1979, his M.S., Applied Statistics in 1981, and his Ph.D., in 1986, all from Purdue University.

Harshal Tupsamudre has done his B.Tech. from COEP and M.Tech from IIT Kharagpur with specialization in Cryptography. He has been with TCS Research for more than 5 years. He is the key contributor in many research patents, publications and projects; in the area of Information Security and Usable Security. His areas of interests are Algorithms, combinatorial optimization and evolutionary algorithms.

Index

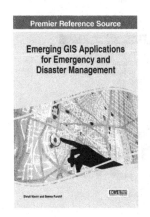 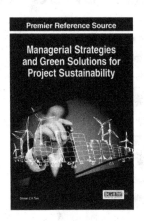  

Printed in the United States
By Bookmasters